ACCLAIM FOR H.W. BRANDS'S

Andrew Jackson

"Altogether splendid. . . . Scrupulous in its scholarship, it is aimed at the general reader and it is very good to read. It is also deeply informative, without being in the least hagiographic, about its remarkable subject and the world he lived in and changed so greatly."
—*The New York Sun*

"Engaging. . . . A definitive work."   —*Pittsburgh Post-Gazette*

"He covers a complex life with extraordinary ease. . . . Brands has mined the archives and produced a creditable, highly readable and definitely worthwhile study."   —*Chicago Tribune*

"Gives readers a great sense of the man and the rugged Western life that molded him. . . . It offers insight into how one American leader gained his fame."   —*San Francisco Chronicle*

"Wonderfully told. . . . His life story is the stuff of legends."
—*The Seattle Times*

"Vivid. . . . Breaks the bonds of academic writing with pace, detail and a sense of the sweep of history."   —*San Antonio Express-News*

"[Brands] writes with a measured glide that catches the reader's interest. He is talented, brilliant in description, and easy in tone; in short, Brands is fun to read."   —*The News-Observer*

H.W. BRANDS

Andrew Jackson

H. W. Brands is the Dickson Allen Anderson Professor of History at the University of Texas at Austin. The author of *Lone Star Nation* and *The Age of Gold*, he was a finalist for the Pulitzer Prize for Biography for *The First American: The Life and Times of Benjamin Franklin*. He lives with his family in Austin, Texas.

ALSO BY H.W. BRANDS

Lone Star Nation: The Epic Story of the Battle for Texas Independence

The Age of Gold: The California Gold Rush and the New American Dream

The Strange Death of American Liberalism

The First American: The Life and Times of Benjamin Franklin

The Selected Letters of Theodore Roosevelt (editor)

Critical Reflections on the Cold War:
Linking Rhetoric and History (editor, with Martin J. Medhurst)

The Use of Force after the Cold War (editor)

Beyond Vietnam: The Foreign Policies of Lyndon Johnson (editor)

Masters of Enterprise: Giants of American Business from John Jacob Astor and
J. P. Morgan to Bill Gates and Oprah Winfrey

What America Owes the World: The Struggle for the Soul of Foreign Policy

T.R.: The Last Romantic

Since Vietnam: The United States in World Affairs, 1973–1995

The Wages of Globalism: Lyndon Johnson and the Limits of American Power

The Reckless Decade: America in the 1890s

The United States in the World: A History of American Foreign Policy

Into the Labyrinth: The United States and the Middle East, 1945–1993

The Devil We Knew: Americans and the Cold War

Bound to Empire: The United States and the Philippines

Inside the Cold War:
Loy Henderson and the Rise of the American Empire, 1918–1961

India and the United States: The Cold Peace

The Specter of Neutralism:
The United States and the Emergence of the Third World, 1947–1960

Cold Warriors: Eisenhower's Generation and American Foreign Policy

Andrew Jackson

HIS LIFE and TIMES

H.W. BRANDS

ANCHOR BOOKS

A DIVISION OF RANDOM HOUSE, INC.

NEW YORK

FIRST ANCHOR BOOKS EDITION, OCTOBER 2006

Copyright © 2005 by H.W. Brands

All rights reserved. Published in the United States by Anchor Books, a division of Random House, Inc., New York, and in Canada by Random House of Canada Limited, Toronto. Originally published in hardcover in the United States by Doubleday, a division of Random House, Inc., New York, in 2005.

Anchor Books and colophon are registered trademarks of Random House, Inc.

The Library of Congress has cataloged the Doubleday edition as follows:
Andrew Jackson, his life and times / H.W. Brands. —1st ed.
p. cm.
Includes bibliographical references and index.
1. Jackson, Andrew, 1767–1845. 2. Presidents—United States—Biography. 3. United States—Politics and government—1829–1837. I. Title.
E382.B83 2005
973.5'6'092—dc22
[B]
2005042178

Anchor ISBN-10: 1-4000-3072-2
Anchor ISBN-13: 978-1-4000-3072-9

Author photograph © Barton Wilder Custom Images
Book design by Terry Karydes
Maps by Mike Regan

www.anchorbooks.com

Printed in the United States of America
10 9 8 7 6 5 4 3 2 1

CONTENTS

Prologue vii

Map: Jackson's Battlefields xii

CHILD OF THE REVOLUTION (1767–1805)
1 *The Prize* 3
2 *I Could Have Shot Him* 19
3 *Alone* 29
4 *Away West* 42
5 *Shadowed Love* 56
6 *Republicans and Revolutionaries* 66
7 *Fighting Words* 83
8 *Rendering Judgment* 96

SON OF THE WEST (1805–1814)
9 *Conspiracy* 113
10 *Affair of Honor* 129
11 *All Must Feel the Injuries* 139
12 *Master and Slaves* 147
13 *Nor Infamy upon Us* 154
14 *Native Genius* 164
15 *Old Hickory* 174
16 *Sharp Knife* 188
17 *The River of Blood* 205

AMERICAN HERO (1814–1821)
18 *Peace Giver* 225
19 *The Spanish Front* 236
20 *Pirates and Patriots* 249

21   *Day of Deliverance*   263

22   *The Second Washington*   284

23   *East by Southwest*   300

24   *Party and Politics*   312

25   *Judge and Executioner*   322

26   *The Eye of the Storm*   332

27   *Conquistador*   342

THE PEOPLE'S PRESIDENT (1821–1837)

28   *Cincinnatus*   363

29   *The Death Rattle of the Old Regime*   376

30   *Democracy Triumphant*   389

31   *Democracy Rampant*   406

32   *Spoils of Victory*   414

33   *Tools of Wickedness*   421

34   *Jacksonian Theory*   431

35   *False Colors*   439

36   *Attack and Counterattack*   455

37   *Or Die with the Union*   472

38   *Justice Marshall for the Defense*   483

39   *Wealth versus Commonwealth*   494

40   *An Old Friend and a New Frontier*   506

PATRIARCH OF DEMOCRACY (1837–1845)

41   *The Home Front*   529

42   *To the Ramparts Once More*   541

43   *The Soul of the Republic*   553

Sources   561

Annotated Bibliography   597

Acknowledgments   608

Index   609

John Quincy Adams had seen this day coming for years.

His only consolation was that he had helped postpone it till now.

The son of the man he considered most responsible for American

independence, Adams felt a peculiar responsibility for the outcome of the

republican experiment. And these last few years the experiment hadn't

been turning out well at all. His father, John Adams, and most of the

other Founders had feared that republicanism would degenerate into

democracy: that government *of* the people would become government *by*

the people. Nothing in history disposed them to look hopefully on such a

development, for never in history had ordinary people run their own

affairs without very quickly running them into the ground. The elder

Adams linked arms after the Revolution with those who sought to curb the popular excesses of the revolutionary era; at Philadelphia in 1787 a convention of skeptics wrote a constitution that took power from the states and conferred it on the central government, and in doing so diminished the influence of the people in politics generally. As vice president and then president, John Adams continued to work to keep power out of the hands of the unlettered and incompetent, and in the hands of those best suited by education and experience to exercise it responsibly.

But it was a losing cause. A first setback occurred when Thomas Jefferson defeated John Adams for president. Jefferson was more the aristocrat than Adams, as anyone who compared Monticello, where Jefferson's slaves worked their master's plantation, with the Adams home in Massachusetts, where Adams himself tilled his modest garden, could see at once. But Jefferson cast himself as the tribune of the people, and he carried the day. James Madison was hardly less elegant than Jefferson, but he, too, posed as the defender of the many against the few. By the end of Madison's presidency the formula had been perfected, and James Monroe, yet another Virginia planter, entered the executive mansion almost unopposed.

John Quincy Adams watched and learned. He noted, among other things, that being secretary of state gave a man a large head start toward the presidency. Jefferson had been secretary of state before becoming president; so also Madison and Monroe. Consequently when Monroe offered to make Adams his secretary of state, the offer included a presumption of the presidency thereafter, and Adams gladly accepted.

Yet even while he did his time as a diplomat, the political climate continued to shift. Like an autumn storm that rose in the West and gathered strength as it approached the Atlantic, the wind of democracy began to blow in the valleys of the Ohio and Mississippi and gained force on its way east. New states entered the Union with few restrictions on the vote, and their example caused the old states to change their own rules. Equally alarming to those—like Adams—who counted on the restraining effect of representation, the states began to allow voters, rather than the state legislatures, to choose presidential electors. Campaigns for president became popularity contests. The highest office in the land went to the favorite of the lower classes.

Adams escaped the early gusts, winning the presidency in 1824 by luck and political art. But during his four years as president he often wished he hadn't won, so abusive was his treatment at the hands of those who claimed to speak for the people. And now—on the morning of March 4, 1829—he prepared to deliver the presidency to the man the people, in all their ignorant majesty, had chosen.

The morning of Adams's defeat should have been the morning of Andrew Jackson's greatest triumph. And in some ways it was. Everything Adams deplored about the direction of American politics, Jackson applauded. To Jackson, the current contest in America was simply the latest stage of the historic struggle against privilege that ran back to the Magna Carta and included the Protestant Reformation of the sixteenth century, the English Revolution of the seventeenth, and the American Revolution of the eighteenth. At each stage the people seized more of what by right belonged to them, from those who intended that power remain the monopoly of the few. Finally, for the first time in American history, and for one of the very few times in human history, the people had chosen one of their own to govern them. And now they were to install him in the highest office in the land. A man would have been dead to noble emotion not to feel the power and meaning of the moment.

Jackson felt it all—and much besides. The thousands of farmers, mechanics, and crossroads merchants who had come to Washington City to inaugurate him, and the hundreds of thousands of their brethren who had voted for him, could almost taste the fruits of their hero's triumph, but Jackson alone knew what the victory had cost him. He had been fighting for the people's right to direct their own affairs since the Revolutionary War, when, as a mere boy, he took up arms against Britain. A gash to the head from a British sword left him with a permanent crease in his skull and an abiding hostility to all things British; smallpox contracted in a British prison marked the beginning of a lifetime of compromised health. The war also cost him his mother and brothers (his father had died before his birth), throwing him orphaned upon a turbulent, threatening world.

As a young man he entered politics in Tennessee. He battled the antidemocratic forces in the state and the nation, going so far as to challenge George Washington when the father of his country adopted what Jackson took to be excessive airs. His audacity on behalf of the people earned him enemies who slandered him and defamed even his wife, Rachel. He dueled in her defense and his own, suffering grievous wounds that left him with bullet fragments lodged about his body.

When the British again threatened American autonomy, by provoking Indian attacks in the West and seizing ships and sailors on the Atlantic, Jackson joined his voice to those of others demanding war in defense of American security and rights. When the war came, he led an offensive against the Indians and, upon its success, took charge of the defense of the Mississippi against Britain's attempt to sever the United States along the line of the great river. At New Orleans in 1815 he threw the redcoats back, to their astonishment and that of most of his compatriots. The victory won him the adulation of the American people, who hailed him as a second Washington, but the campaign added to the ranks of his political enemies, who carped at his boldness and his impatience with the forms of military command.

The second war against Britain made clear to many Americans something Jackson had sensed from the first: that the struggle for American popular rights was of a piece with the struggle for North America itself. The opponents of popular rights had filled the ranks of the Loyalists during the first war against Britain; the same opponents, or their heirs, had been conspicuously apathetic, in some cases seditious, during the second British war. Jackson's victory at New Orleans didn't end the British threat; the British still held Canada, and their ally Spain occupied Florida and Mexico. As long as these foes hovered about America's borders, the American experiment in self-government remained in peril. And while it did, Jackson couldn't rest.

Not that he would have rested anyway. His entire life, Jackson had known only struggle. He struggled against poverty as a child, against authority as a youth, against the British and Spanish and Indians as a soldier, against the enemies of popular rule as an elected official. His struggles defined him.

They also defined his era in American history, which was how he came to symbolize it. Much later, after America became a world power, it could be difficult to remember a time when the success of the American experiment in self-government did not seem assured. But it never seemed assured to Jackson and most of his generation. He and they fought two wars against Britain, an undeclared naval war against France, and countless battles against Indians. They struggled for independence, for security, for the land that provided the opportunity to pursue the happiness of which their Declaration of Independence spoke. They also fought among themselves: over the meaning of the American Revolution, over the Constitution, over republicanism and democracy, over slavery and expansion. Perhaps Jackson exaggerated the degree of danger his country and his conception of government faced. But if he did, he wasn't alone, and it was all those who shared his perception of the precariousness of their world who had made him their president.

And so he came to Washington. Yet even this greatest of his public triumphs was marred by the cruelest personal blow he had ever suffered. Just before he was to leave the Hermitage, his home near Nashville, for Washington, Rachel died. The proximate cause was physical, a failing heart. But the deeper cause was the strain his race for the presidency had placed on her mind and soul. In their desperation to cling to power, the partisans of John Quincy Adams had recirculated and embellished the earlier libels against Rachel's character. Jackson blamed the Adams men for her death, but he couldn't help asking himself whether he had been complicit. It was, after all, his ambition for the presidency that had provoked the latest attacks against her. If he had retired to the Hermitage, as she wished, rather than continue his struggle against the foes of popular rule, she would still be alive. The knowledge was a burden, the heaviest he had ever borne.

But as he rose from the ground beside her grave, the very weight of her death confirmed his resolve to carry the struggle forward. He couldn't bring her back, yet he could fight on, to ensure that those who killed her not benefit from their crime. Like most other great warriors, Jackson had always conflated the personal with the public; his own enemies became the enemies of his cause. So they did now, more than ever.

And on the morning of March 4, 1829, with the memory of Rachel in his heart and the cause of the people in his mind, he set off from his hotel to the Capitol to take his oath of office.

Jackson's
Battlefields

Mississippi   Territory

Louisiana

MOBILE ○

FORT · MIMS

Lake
Pontchartrain

NEW · ORLEANS

Lake Borgne

Mobile Bay

FORT · BOYER

ENGLISH · TURN

MISSISSIPPI RIVER

Gulf of Mexico

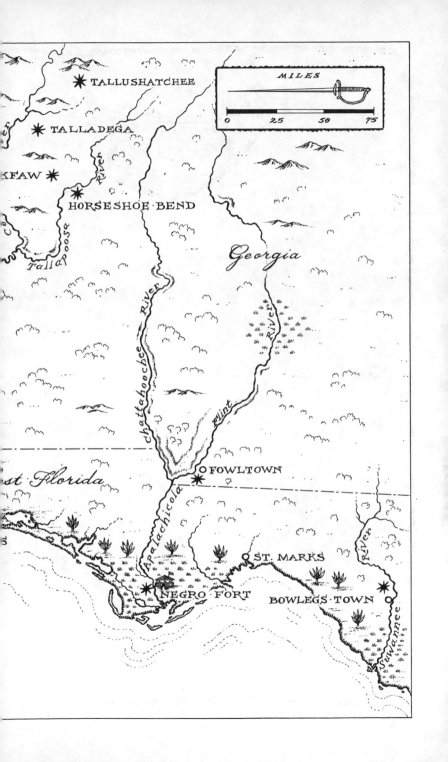

Andrew Jackson
HIS LIFE AND TIMES

Child

of the

Revolution

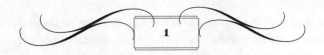

THE PRIZE

The struggle for North America began long before Andrew Jackson

was born. Like similar struggles on all the inhabited continents, it ran

back millennia, perhaps to the moment humans first found their way

across the Arctic plain from Asia. Oral tradition and archaeological

evidence indicate that conflict was a regular feature of life among the

North Americans. They fought for forests where the game was most

abundant, for rivers where the fish were thickest, for bottomlands

where their corn and beans and squashes grew most readily. Great

warriors were the heroes of their tribes, emulated by other men,

sought by women, hallowed in memory. Strong tribes expanded

their territories, driving the weak to less-favored regions and

sometimes to extinction. Diplomacy complemented military force:

the Iroquois confederation made that alliance a terror to its neighbors.

The arrival of the Europeans added new elements to the competition. These far-easterners possessed weapons the aboriginals hadn't seen: steel knives, swords, and axes; muskets and rifles; cannon. But their most potent agents of conquest were ones neither they nor their victims understood: the pathogens to which long exposure had inured the Europeans but that devastated the native Americans. In many instances the novel diseases raced ahead of European settlers, who arrived to discover human deserts and concluded that the Christian God in his wisdom and power had prepared the way for their colonies.

But the diseases didn't kill all the Indians. Those who survived often welcomed the interlopers, at least at first. Especially after smallpox and the other epidemics killed as many as three-fourths of the members of the afflicted tribes, there seemed room enough for all. And the newcomers' traders brought goods the natives quickly learned to value: iron pots, which bested clay for durability; steel blades, which held an edge longer than flint or obsidian; rifles, which felled game at distances arrows couldn't reach and gave their possessors an advantage in battle over tribes that lacked them. Some purists among the Indians rejected everything European, but most of the natives adapted happily to the improved lifestyle the new technology brought.

In time, however, the palefaces got pushy. Their farmers followed the traders and expropriated Indian land. This was when the real struggle started. In New England in the 1670s a coalition led by a chief the English called King Philip contested the advancing settlement by destroying several towns and killing the inhabitants. The English fought back, with the help of Indians holding a grudge against Philip's group, and eventually won. Philip was beheaded and his captured followers enslaved.

The Indians' resistance grew more sophisticated. They discovered that the Europeans belonged to more than one tribe, with the French as hostile to the English as either were to any of the Indians. Some Indians sided with the French, others with the English, and when the French and English went to war—as they did once a generation—the various Indian tribes exploited the opportunities to their own advantage. The largest of the conflicts (called the French and Indian War by the English in America) began in 1754 and inspired the Delawares and Shawnees, allies of France, to try to drive the English away from the frontier. To this end they launched a campaign of terror against British settlements in the Ohio Valley. The terror began successfully and over three years threatened to throw the English all the way back to the coast. But British victories in Canada and elsewhere weakened the French and emboldened Britain's own allies, including the Iroquois, and when the war ended in 1763 the French surrendered all their North American territories.

This was good news for Britain's American subjects but bad news for nearly all the Indians of the frontier, including Britain's allies. As long as the British and French had vied for control in America, each had to bid for the support of the Indians, who learned to play the Europeans against one another. With the French departure the bidding ended and the Indians were left to confront British power alone.

The Ottawa chief Pontiac was among the first to appreciate the new state of affairs. The Ottawas had long been rivals of the Iroquois and were recently allies of the French. For both reasons they fought against the British in the French and Indian War. When that war ended in French defeat, Pontiac saw disaster looming for the Ottawas—and for Indians generally. A tall, powerful warrior with a striking mien, he was also a charismatic political leader and an adroit diplomat. The fighting between Britain and France had hardly ceased before he welded together a coalition of tribes dedicated to expelling the British from the interior of the continent. Pontiac's forces besieged Fort Detroit above Lake Erie during the spring of 1763. From there the offensive spread north and east along the Great Lakes and south into the Ohio Valley. One British garrison after another was surrounded and destroyed. As this was a psychological offensive as much as a military one, the methods of destruction often included the most gruesome treatment of those soldiers, traders, and dependents who fell into the attackers' hands.

The assault on a British fort at Mackinac showed the swiftness with which the Indians commenced their attacks and the brutality with which they completed them. Pontiac's campaign was spreading faster than the news of it, and the troops and traders at Mackinac knew of no reason to fear the large group of Ojibwas who approached the fort in amicable fashion and commenced a game of lacrosse immediately beneath the walls. The British came out to watch, as they did on such occasions. The intensity of the game mounted, until one of the players threw the ball close to the gate. The laughing, cheering spectators took no alarm when both teams tore after it. But then the players dropped their lacrosse sticks, snatched war axes from under the robes of their women, and rushed through the unguarded gate. The surprise was total and the carnage almost equally so. A trader named Alexander Henry, who managed to hide in a storage closet, left a chilling account:

> Through an aperture, which afforded me a view of the area of the fort, I beheld, in shapes the foulest and most terrible, the ferocious triumphs of barbarian conquerors. The dead were scalped and mangled; the dying were writhing and shrieking under the unsatiated knife and tomahawk; and from the bodies of some, ripped open, their butchers were drinking the blood, scooped up in the hollow of joined hands, and quaffed amid shouts of rage and victory.

The story was much the same all along the frontier. The offensive continued to outrace reports of it, and in many cases the first intimation the English settlers and soldiers had of trouble was the arrival of war parties. One by one the garrisons fell, until Pontiac and his allies controlled the entire region west of Fort Pitt, at the forks of the Ohio. Isolated frontier settlements were even more vulnerable and the destruction was commensurately greater. Some two thousand settlers were killed, and about four hundred soldiers. Many others were taken hostage. Those who survived the attacks and evaded capture fled east, bearing tales of calamity and horror.

The British commander in North America, Jeffrey Amherst, a large man with a big nose and a deeply held conviction that his talents were being wasted in the colonies, received the news of the western disaster at his headquarters in New York. Although the reports shocked him, he wasn't surprised at the behavior of the Indians, whom he considered savages beneath regard by civilized men. This attitude was common among the British, and it had helped trigger the current uprising. (By contrast, the French, whose imperial policy relied less on displacing the Indians than on trading with them, developed a more sophisticated view of the indigenes.) Amherst terminated the practice of sending gifts to Britain's Indian allies, and he curtailed the trade in guns and ammunition. He judged that though the Indians had been useful against the French, now that the French were vanquished it was time to make the Indians understand who the true rulers of North America were.

While Amherst had to respect the fighting ability of the Indians, he blamed incompetence among his subordinates for the success of Pontiac's offensive. Upon receiving a report of a massacre of the British garrison at Presque Isle, which followed the fort's surrender by its commanding officer, he could hardly contain his anger. "It is amazing that an officer could put so much faith in the promises of the Indians as to capitulate with them, when there are so many recent instances of their never failing to massacre the people whom they can persuade to put themselves in their power," he wrote in his journal. "The officer and garrison would have had a much better chance for their lives if they had defended themselves to the last, and if not relieved, they had confided to a retreat through the woods or got off in a boat in the night. These people are undoubtedly murdered unless the Indians may have feared to do it lest we may retaliate. There is absolutely nothing but fear of us that can hinder them from committing all the cruelties in their power."

Amherst determined to answer the terror of the Indians with terror of his own. Knowing that the Indians rightly feared the white men's diseases more than anything else about the Europeans, he directed Henry Bouquet, the commander of the western district, to launch a campaign of biological warfare. "Could it not be contrived to send the smallpox among the disaffected tribes of Indians?" Amherst inquired. "We must on this occasion use every stratagem in our power to reduce them."

Bouquet responded at once. Some of his own troops were suffering from smallpox; he proposed to take blankets from the sick men and distribute them among the Indians. "I will try to inoculate the ———— with some blankets that may fall in their hands, and take care not to get the disease myself," he told Amherst. (Whether discretion caused him not to identify the targets or he hadn't decided which Indians to infect is unclear.)

Amherst approved the plan. "You will do well to try to inoculate the Indians by means of blankets, as well as to try every other method that can serve to extirpate this execrable race," he said.

Bouquet distributed the blankets. By the time he did, they may have proved redundant, as the smallpox had already jumped from the whites in the area to the Indians. Yet the outcome was certainly what Bouquet and Amherst desired. "The smallpox has been very general and raging among the Indians since last spring," an observer wrote several months later. A subordinate of Bouquet—who, unlike his commander, wasn't beyond pity—

reported from the front, "The poor rascals are dying very fast with the smallpox; they can make but little resistance and when routed from their settlements must perish in great numbers by the disorders."

Aided by the epidemic, the British managed to roll back the Indian advances. Bouquet battered an Indian army at Bushy Run near Fort Pitt, and he sent his troops to burn Indian villages and drive off their inhabitants, many of whom then perished of hunger and disease. The villages were always the weak spot of Indians, for although Indian warriors were masters at raiding garrisons and terrorizing settlers, they lacked the numbers and firepower to defend their own women and children against British counterattack. In the face of Bouquet's scorched-earth strategy, Pontiac's allies fell away band by band and tribe by tribe, to make peace with the British.

Yet the outcome was far from an undiluted victory for British arms. To entice Pontiac's allies to the peace table, the British government recalled Amherst and repealed most of the measures the Indians resented. As a result, it wasn't hard for many of the Indians to conclude that, in dealing with the Europeans, war worked. (For Pontiac personally, the failure to drive the British from the Ohio marked a defeat from which he never recovered. His fellow Ottawas turned to others for leadership, and the younger warriors derided the old man as a relic of the past. In 1769 he was fatally stabbed by a Peoria Indian at a trading post on the Mississippi River. None of the Ottawas, not even his own sons, lifted a finger to avenge him.)

The lesson American colonists drew from Pontiac's War was similar in content to that drawn by the Indians but altogether different in tone. The uprising had sent shudders all along the American backcountry, from New York to Georgia. In every community that lived within sight or consciousness of the great forest that stretched away to the west, the reports of the Indian atrocities—with the torture of prisoners and the mutilation and cannibalism of the murdered recounted in excruciating detail—caused hearts to clutch and eyes to examine every grove of trees for signs of the enemy's approach. The flood of refugees from the war provided additional evidence of the scope and meaning of the Indian uprising. An inhabitant of Frederick, Maryland, noted, "Every day, for some time past, has offered the melancholy scene of poor distressed families driving downwards through this town with their effects, who have deserted their plantations for fear of falling into the cruel hands of our savage enemies, now daily seen in the woods." A witness in Winchester, Virginia, explained, "Near 500 families have run away within this week. I assure you it was a most melancholy sight to see such numbers of poor people, who had abandoned their settlements in such consternation and hurry that they had hardly anything with them but their children. And what is still worse, I dare say there is not money enough amongst the whole families to maintain a fifth part of them till the fall; and none of the poor creatures can get a hovel to shelter them from the weather, but lie about scattered in the woods."

For the refugees, and for the many more who held on to their homes but watched their cold, hungry compatriots stream by, the outcome of Pontiac's War was decidedly unsatisfactory. Except for the traders, who required the Indians as customers, nearly all the Americans who lived anywhere near the frontier considered the Indians an existential danger. Few would have mourned had every one of the natives fallen victim to British arms or European disease. And when the post-Pontiac settlement essentially restored the status quo, the Americans once more saw the tomahawk hanging over their heads.

*A*mong those who fought against Pontiac were members of a peculiar tribe with origins in the foggy North Atlantic. During the first decade of the seventeenth century—at the same time as the founding in America of English Jamestown and French Quebec—King James of England and Scotland planted a colony of English and Scots in the north of Ireland. The purpose of the Ulster plantation was to subdue the unruly Irish, who were considered by the English to be fully as savage as the Indian tribes of North America. So refractory were they that few Englishmen accepted James's invitation to emigrate to Ulster, leaving it to the Scots to claim the Irish territory James opened to them. Nor were these just any Scots, but bands of Lowlanders who had fought for centuries against rival tribesman—or clansmen—of the Scottish Highlands. The centuries of battle had forged a character equal to almost any challenge requiring courage and determination. As one Scotsman explained, "When I do consider with myself what things are necessary for a plantation, I cannot but be confident that my own countrymen are as fit for such a purpose as any men in the world, having daring minds that upon any probable appearance do despise danger, and bodies able to endure as much as the height of their minds can undertake." Another Scotsman, perhaps more candid, characterized those who accepted James's offer rather differently: "Albeit amongst these Divine Providence sent over some worthy persons for birth, education and parts, yet the most part were such as either poverty, scandalous lives, or, at the best, adventurous seeking of better accommodation, set forward that way."

The emigrants found plenty of adventure and call for bravery on arrival in Ireland, for the Irish yielded ground most grudgingly to the newcomers, who had to fight for every acre they occupied. Nor did the struggle ease with passing time. The Irish continued to resent the intrusion, and with each generation that was born, the fight began anew. In time—after three hundred years—the Irish would succeed in reclaiming most of their island from the British. But they never succeeded in dislodging the stubborn Ulstermen.

Yet life in Ireland wasn't all the Scots had hoped. Their new lands weren't markedly more fertile than those they had left behind, and the linen trade, in which many found supplementary employment, was subject to periodic depression. When their beloved Presbyterianism came under attack from some of James's successors, many decided to decamp to other British plantations, across the Atlantic. The voyage west was often an ordeal. Unlike many other early emigrants, who pooled resources and traveled in companies, the fiercely individualistic Scotch-Irish (as they were called by the time they reached America) typically traveled individually or in single families. Hunger was a frequent companion on the crossing. Starvation wasn't unknown, nor cannibalism. Pirates robbed the emigrants and sometimes murdered them. Those who made it to America felt they could survive anything fate might throw their way. One observer described a particular Scotch-Irishman in terms that could have applied to any number of them: "His looks spoke out that he would not fear the devil should he meet him face to face."

As religious dissenters, many of the Scotch-Irish were drawn to Pennsylvania, the haven for unorthodoxy established by Quaker William Penn. As men and women of modest means, most, after disembarking at Philadelphia or another of the Delaware River ports, headed for the backcountry beyond Lancaster. During the mid-eighteenth century—when famine gripped large parts of Ireland, including the north—as many as ten thousand

Scotch-Irish left Ulster each year for America. The route from Belfast to Philadelphia and thence to the Pennsylvania frontier became a regular Scotch-Irish highway.

The topography of the western land, in particular the valleys between the ridges that ran from northeast to southwest, channeled the later arrivals among the newcomers to the Shenandoah Valley of Virginia and eventually to the uplands of the Carolina frontier. Wherever they settled, they gained a reputation for practical piety and aggressive independence. A saying among their neighbors held that the Scotch-Irish kept the Sabbath and anything else they could lay hands on.

𝒜mong the Ulster immigrants were a man named Andrew Jackson and his wife, Elizabeth. Andrew was one of four sons of a linen draper named Hugh Jackson, whose luck at the linen craft wasn't sufficient to entice any of the boys to follow in his footsteps. Instead they went into farming. But they never acquired the capital to purchase land and had to content themselves with renting plots from the better-to-do. One son, his father's namesake, went off to the army, with whom he fought against the French and Indians in America, in the uplands of the Carolinas. On returning home he told Andrew and the others what a lovely country that was and how a man who might never hope to own property in Ulster could easily become a freeholder in the Carolinas. There was the small matter of those Indians, who remained unreconciled to the presence of large numbers of immigrants, but the Ulster Scots had been fighting their neighbors for centuries, and the Indians couldn't be any tougher than the Highlanders or the Irish.

Elizabeth Jackson heard similar stories, included in letters from four sisters who had emigrated to the same vicinity her brother-in-law extolled. She and Andrew had two young sons, Hugh and Robert. Looking to their future, she saw little reason to expect better than their father had done if the family stayed in Ulster. And daunting though the uprooting and the voyage over the ocean seemed in prospect to one who had never been far from home or aboard a ship, with so many other neighbors leaving for the New World the decision to go lost some of its recklessness.

Andrew and Elizabeth and the boys set sail from Carrickfergus, just down the lough from Belfast, in the spring of 1765. The details of the voyage have been lost, as has the identity of the port of American landing. But Philadelphia seems likeliest, or perhaps some dock on the Delaware below Philadelphia. Their goal was a region called the Waxhaw, in the piedmont on the border between North Carolina and South Carolina, in the valley of the Catawba River. Elizabeth's sisters lived in the Waxhaw; besides making the new place feel more familiar, their presence would help Andrew and Elizabeth settle in and would afford a measure of security in the event of trouble.

Getting from the Delaware River to the Catawba required five hundred miles of overland travel across Pennsylvania, Maryland, Virginia, and North Carolina. That country was no longer exactly wild, and the travelers didn't have to worry much about Indian attack, but great stretches of the road were lonely, the entire trek was wearying, and before they reached their destination Andrew and Elizabeth almost certainly asked themselves what every emigrant asked, at one time or another: why they had ever left home.

The Catawba River was named for the Catawba Indians, whose history summarized much of the experience of Indians in America since the arrival of the Europeans. The Catawbas were a young tribe, an amalgam of peoples of the Carolina piedmont whose ancestral tribes had been shattered by disease, decimated by warfare against the English and other Indians, especially the Five Nations of the Iroquois confederacy, and demoralized by enslavement, again both by the English and other tribes. The remnants of these ancestral tribes banded together for self-defense, calling themselves Catawbas. With arms from traders operating out of Virginia and the Carolinas, the Catawbas counterattacked against the Iroquois and such Iroquois allies as the Tuscaroras. By the 1760s they had managed to hold their own. In part because of their dependence on the arms trade, they were considered fairly docile with respect to whites and hence suitable neighbors for settlers who accepted that vigilance was the price of survival anywhere near the frontier.

The Jacksons were welcomed to the Waxhaw by Elizabeth's sisters, who were delighted to have more of their kin among them and who were proud to show how well they were doing in the new land. One sister, Jane, was married to James Crawford, the owner of a large farm in the fertile bottomlands of Waxhaw Creek, a tributary of the Catawba River. From their comfortable house overlooking the post road the Crawfords watched gangs of African slaves till their fields. Another sister, Margaret, was married to George McCamie, who had a farm just down the road from the Crawfords and a house with an imposing stone chimney (in a place where most made do with chimneys of wood and mud). Two other sisters were married to brothers named Leslie. Though less far along the road to prosperity, these also had made a fair start.

A start was all Andrew and Elizabeth Jackson could hope for upon arrival. The journey from Ulster had nearly exhausted their modest resources, leaving Andrew little with which to purchase land. The most fertile fields, in the flood plains of the river and creeks, were already taken and could be purchased only at a premium. Andrew might have crossed the divide into the next valley, but that would have placed him and Elizabeth and the boys farther from her sisters. So he settled for, and settled on, a rather unpromising red-clay tract in the pines above Twelve Mile Creek, about a three-hour walk from the Presbyterian meeting house that formed the center of community life in the Waxhaw.

Establishing ownership of land in the backcountry was often a problem, and had been for decades. The problem originated in the difference between Indian and European conceptions of property ownership. To the extent most Indian tribes "owned" land, they did so communally. Communal ownership of land wasn't historically unknown in Europe, and it still served as the basis for "commons" and other general-use zones. But in European societies where the cultivation of crops provided the principal sustenance of the people—rather than merely supplementing hunting and gathering, as among most Indians—individual ownership of specified pieces of ground had long since become the norm. When Europeans, with their individualistic ideas of land ownership, entered Indian lands unclaimed by any individual Indians, it was tempting for the Europeans to assume that no one owned the land and that it was available for the taking.

Even when the Europeans acknowledged Indian ownership, problems arose from differences between their notions of governance and those of the Indians. Not surprisingly, given the importance the Europeans placed on land titles, governments in Europe considered the control of land a central responsibility. Entire bodies of law, and the institutions of government that supported them, had grown up around the establishment and transfer of titles to land. The Indians had their own forms of government, which dealt with matters of war and peace but rarely with issues relating to land ownership. Consequently, on those occasions when European officials sought to purchase land from the Indians, it was by no means always clear which Indians had the authority to sell it. Sometimes the Europeans, acting in good faith, paid certain members of a tribe for what they thought was title to land, only to have other members dispute the deal. At least equally often the Europeans acted in bad faith, essentially bribing complaisant tribesmen to sell land both parties knew the sellers had no right to alienate.

Nor were the difficulties of ownership confined to official relations between the indigenes and the immigrants. Settlers from the colonies often headed toward the frontier and simply started farming on lands that appeared unoccupied and unclaimed. These "squatters" typically acted as though the labor of clearing and planting a piece of ground gave them title to it, and they could be as jealous of trespassers—Indian or white—as any legally sanctioned landowners. They were the bane of the colonial governments, for though they refused to recognize restrictions on their squatting activities, they demanded protection from those governments when their squatting provoked resistance from the Indians, as it often did.

In a different, though not necessarily less troublesome, category than the squatters were the speculators. Unlike the squatters, the speculators intended not to make homes on the frontier but merely to make money. Their strategy was to acquire title to large tracts of land, either directly from the Indians or, after that practice was outlawed (because of the abuses it invited), from the colonial governments or from the British Crown. They then sent out surveyors, who mapped their holdings and wrote up legal descriptions. Finally they sold the lands, ideally at a handsome profit, to settlers. Temptations to corruption and manipulation arose at every step of the process. Indians could be coerced into selling. Colonial assemblies could be bribed. The British Crown could be lobbied. And honest complications often occurred in the surveying, from sloppiness or lack of funds to do the job right. Moreover, because the speculators were commonly resented as profiteers, squatters were hardly more respectful of their titles than of Indians' titles. And because years could pass between the grant of titles to the speculators and the development of the properties covered by the titles, squatters could build homes and raise families on the properties before anyone objected or even noticed.

*W*hether Andrew Jackson simply squatted on the property on Twelve Mile Creek or made some prior arrangement with the man who claimed title to the tract is unclear. The only document that survives regarding the conveyance of title from Thomas Ewing, the legal owner, is dated three years after Andrew started clearing and planting the property. And this document reveals the casual approach to surveying that vexed land titles in the backcountry for many years. The property was described as "200 acres . . . beginning at a White Oak south side of the Creek by a small Branch & runs thence N 10 E 180 poles"—a pole was a rod, or sixteen and a half feet—"to a Red Oak by a small Branch hence N 80 Wst. 180 poles to a R.O. then S 10 W 180 poles to a Red Oak thence to the beginning."

Whether or not he legally owned the land, Andrew acted as though he did or soon would. Especially in the early years of transforming a wilderness tract into a productive property, frontier farming was interminably laborious. From spring to autumn, the normal round of plowing, planting, weeding, and harvesting kept a man busy every daylight moment. But it was after the crops were in that the really hard work began, for there was always more of the forest to be cleared and prepared for the plow. The pines that grew from the red soil of the Waxhaw weren't especially large or unkind to the ax, but they were many and had to be felled one by one.

Andrew's incentives to labor increased during the family's second year in America. Hugh was three years old and Robert one when Elizabeth informed her husband that she was pregnant again. During the winter of 1766–67, through cold rains and intermittent snows, Andrew attacked the forest with redoubled energy. The baby would arrive before spring; he wanted to have several more acres ready for the plow by then.

His desire exceeded his strength. He injured himself while working—family tradition said he was trying to lift a log heavier than one man could handle—and he was forced to bed. Something else must have been involved, perhaps including general exhaustion from extended overwork, for he fell ill and died.

Not all in the Waxhaw were working as hard that winter as Andrew Jackson. With snow covering the ground and ice coating the roads, time passed slowly for many of his neighbors. In part for this reason they were happy to give poor Andrew the full honors of a wake and a proper funeral procession, both of which required libations of the sort that could fortify a man against the cold of the season and the chill thoughts of his own mortality. So well fortified were the members of the procession that, according to local story, Andrew's coffin fell from the wagon on the way to the graveyard and wasn't missed till the procession reached the burial ground. With some embarrassment and more whiskey, the pallbearers retraced their steps and recovered the body, which was belatedly committed to the red clay. Andrew Jackson, who had crossed the ocean to claim his share of Adam's bequest and broken his body to make a few hundred acres his own, now slept in an eight-foot plot that would be his forever.

𝒫erhaps Elizabeth was comforted by this thought. She needed the comforting, for she faced the daunting prospect of bringing a third child, suddenly fatherless, into a world where the protection and support of a man were almost essential to the survival of his wife and children. Fortunately, she could turn to her sisters and their husbands (demonstrating her and Andrew's prudence in planting themselves near kin). After the funeral, and as the day of her delivery drew near, she and the boys moved in with Jane and James Crawford. There, on the morning of March 15, 1767, Elizabeth gave birth to a son she named for her late husband. (The Crawford house was located just across the border in South Carolina. In later years, after the younger Andrew Jackson became famous, North Carolinians eager to adopt him articulated a version of the nativity story that had Elizabeth stopping at the home of a second sister, in North Carolina, en route to the Crawfords, and there giving birth. The subject of the story himself never credited it, always claiming South Carolinian birth, even after South Carolina sided with his enemies.)

The Crawford home became the Jackson home. By an arrangement that almost certainly was never formalized but simply evolved, Elizabeth assumed the role of housekeeper and second mother to the eight Crawford children, in exchange for her and her own three boys' maintenance. The responsibilities of her role, and perhaps the emotional burden of living upon her relations, seem to have reinforced a sober, Calvinist streak; from dawn to dusk she rarely let a minute slip unfilled by some useful task.

Sundays, of course, were the exception. The sabbath was devoted to the worship of the Lord, in the Presbyterian church where the elder Andrew had been eulogized and the younger Andrew baptized. Elizabeth's devotion was such that for a time she believed her third son should be a minister. As he learned to talk and otherwise express himself, he showed every sign of being the brightest of her three and the most likely to master the literary arts required of a man of the cloth. To prepare young Andrew for his vocation, Elizabeth sent him to an academy operated by Dr. William Humphries. (Hugh and Robert made shift at the local common school.) Besides the usual letters and numbers, Andrew was introduced to Latin and Greek. He and they never became good friends, but enough of the acquaintance lasted to let him appreciate the classical tags that adorned the rhetoric and writing of the era and affix a few of his own.

Despite Andrew's academic aptitude, it didn't take Elizabeth long to realize that her youngest wasn't meant for the ministry. He was a wild child, with an almost unmanageable will and a defiant temper. How much of this he inherited is impossible to know. Certainly it fit the mold of the Ulsterman. Yet the circumstances of his upbringing contributed their share to the formation of his character. He had no father, and his mother was so busy running the Crawford household that she couldn't readily monitor his behavior. Nor did James or Jane Crawford, with so many children of their own, pay much attention to their nephews. As a result, Andrew was reared as much by the children of the neighborhood as by any adults.

In time the neighbors from his childhood would tell stories about him. Most of the stories reflected the feisty, stubborn streak of a skinny boy who felt he had to fight for anything of value. A heavier contemporary recalled that when they would wrestle, Andrew would be the one thrown to the ground three times out of four. "But he would never *stay throwed*. He was dead game, even then, and never would give up." Another story told how some pranksters loaded a rifle with powder to the muzzle and got Andrew, unaware, to fire it. The recoil knocked him down and nearly unconscious, but he retained sufficient presence of mind to threaten the humorists: "By God, if one of you laughs, I'll kill him."

In adulthood, Andrew Jackson's enemies would ridicule his inability to write a sentence without misspellings and would cite it as evidence of an incurable ignorance. Jackson indeed lacked much of what his better-schooled contemporaries took for granted, starting with a decent formal education. How long he stayed in school is uncertain, but his unfamiliarity with the conventions of orthography suggests it wasn't long. (Conceivably he suffered from dyslexia or other learning disability, but bad spelling aside, there is nothing to indicate this.) Other famous men, including Benjamin Franklin and Abraham Lincoln, have lacked much formal education but become masters of the English language. Jackson didn't fit that pattern, although even his critics acknowledged that he spoke and wrote with power and vividness. He eventually became an enthusiastic reader, albeit of practical works, including newspapers, rather than of philosophy or literature. Yet in youth, even had he shown an interest in reading, he would have found little opportunity to indulge it in the backcountry community where he grew up. The Bible was available, of course, and from the evidence of his later life, Jackson read it from cover to cover. But beyond the good book were very few other books.

Jackson's early biographers, who included some of his staunchest political supporters, liked to assert that what his education lacked in book learning, it made up for in experience of the world. To some degree this was true: the bright boy couldn't help picking up life lessons wherever they arose. It would be a mistake, though, to place much weight on this essentially democratic-romantic notion. By most objective measures, Andrew Jackson's was a deprived upbringing: deprived of educational opportunity, deprived of parental supervision, deprived of more than the most modest standard of living, deprived of much chance to develop self-esteem. His mother doubtless loved him, and he revered her memory all his life. Yet her love aside, Andrew Jackson had a bleak boyhood, better forgotten.

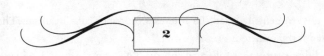

I COULD HAVE SHOT HIM

By Jackson's tenth birthday the struggle for North America had taken a new turn. The wars for the West—first against France, then against Pontiac—had been expensive, and British taxpayers complained of the debt. As part of a general retrenchment, the British government determined to pull troops back from the frontier. But it couldn't easily do so if the settlers persisted in getting into trouble with the Indians.

Therefore, to keep the settlers and Indians apart, the government in 1763 banned new settlements beyond the mountains.

The ban annoyed the settlers, who had hoped for just the opposite result upon the end of the French and Indian War. The expulsion of the French opened the way to additional settlements—or should have, if the

British government had had the interests of Americans in mind. The ban suggested it did not.

So did measures that followed shortly. The Stamp Act of 1765 taxed the Americans as they had never been taxed before. Strong American opposition—amounting to riots in several colonies—forced the repeal of the act, but the Townshend duties of 1767 imposed new taxes in other forms. Americans again resisted, with boycotts of British products. The boycotts didn't produce repeal but they did foster fellow thinking among the Americans, who increasingly viewed the British—or at least the British government—as hostile. When British troops fired on a crowd in Boston in 1770, the incident was quickly dubbed a "massacre." When another Boston crowd in 1773 protested a London-imposed monopoly on tea by dumping a cargo of leaves into the harbor, and the British government responded by closing the harbor and passing other punitive measures, the Americans convened a "continental congress" to coordinate the defense of American rights against British encroachment. When fighting between British regulars and American militiamen broke out at Lexington and Concord in 1775, the Continental Congress raised an army, and in 1776 it declared the American colonies to be free and independent states.

*J*acksonian mythology later asserted that young Andrew was chosen to read the Declaration of Independence when a copy of that document first reached the Waxhaw in the summer of 1776. Perhaps he was, but it seems odd that such an important task should be assigned to a boy not yet ten. On the other hand, considering the division of opinion in the Carolinas regarding independence, Jackson's seniors may have been happy to let him do the honors. If the independence project turned out badly, the British would be less likely to punish a child.

For years after the fighting began, a bad outcome appeared entirely possible. The problem wasn't simply the inexperience and poor provisioning of the Continental Army, although that didn't help matters. The deeper problem was that for all the brave words and unanimous declarations of the Continental Congress, the Americans were far from united in their desire to separate from Britain. Wherever British troops landed, they were greeted by grateful Tories, or Loyalists. When they occupied New York, they found many Tories eager to supply them. After they drove to Philadelphia and settled into what had been the American capital till their approach scattered the Continental Congress, they spent a pleasant winter among friends (while General George Washington and the Continental Army shivered and starved at Valley Forge). Before 1780 the rebels won only a single major battle—at Saratoga in the autumn of 1777—and though this earned them an alliance with France, it hardly guaranteed them victory.

Yet Washington enjoyed the advantage of time. He didn't so much have to win the war as avoid losing. For the rebels, the struggle against Britain was an essential affair, a battle for their homeland. For the British government, it was a discretionary matter. America was but a part of the British empire, and if that part became too expensive to maintain and defend, the imperial government could cut its losses and withdraw.

British commanders understood the situation and in 1780 determined to bring the war to a swift conclusion. Their strategy was to exploit the divisions among the Americans: to make the revolutionary war a civil war. Against a united America the British knew they stood no chance. Their troops were too far from home, too far from safe harbor and reprovision. But against a divided America their prospects were good. A divided America might be worn down, won over, and wooed back village by village, county by county, province by province. The ringleaders of the rebellion would flee or be captured, and the populace would accept what everyone in England accepted: that the Crown and Parliament were supreme. No doubt political adjustments would be made: the Americans could be granted seats in Parliament, dulling their complaint about being taxed without being represented. But the empire would stand secure.

The strategy would begin in the South. Tory sentiments were strongest there, especially among the planters of the tidewater districts, whose ties of family, finance, and sentiment to the mother country were broad and deep. The royal navy would deliver an army to the Carolinas, where Lord Cornwallis, the army's commander, would launch a dual offensive: with regular British troops against fixed positions and with American Tory regiments against the rebels in the field.

༄ ༄ ༄

*L*ieutenant Colonel Banastre Tarleton cut a figure that made men envious and women swoon. "A picture of a man he was!" remarked one (male) admirer among many. "Rather below the middle height, and with a face almost femininely beautiful, Tarleton possessed a form that was a perfect model of manly strength and vigor. Without a particle of superfluous flesh, his rounded limbs and full broad chest seemed molded from iron, yet, at the same time, displaying all the elasticity which usually accompanies elegance of proportion." Tarleton appreciated his physical gifts and took pains to show them off. His cavalry jacket was tailored smartly and his white riding breeches clutched his thighs. He wore the plumed helmet of the king's dragoons, and his saber danced jauntily as he rode.

His temperament matched his appearance and military calling. He was dashingly brave; a fellow officer described him as "full of enterprise and spirit, and anxious of every opportunity of distinguishing himself." And he was still very young: twenty-three when he received command of the British Legion, a regiment of Tories known for their green jackets (which distinguished them from the red-coated regulars and helped them blend into the forest), their familiarity with the local terrain and folkways, and their fierce opposition to the rebels, who threatened the way of life they had learned to cherish.

But none of the legionnaires was as fierce as their commander. Tarleton's very name became a curse among the rebels, and a caution even among the Tories, on account of his utter ruthlessness in prosecuting the war. In theory, the rebels were all traitors to the Crown and liable to summary execution. In practice, most British commanders treated men under American arms as soldiers subject to the practices of civilized warfare. Tarleton preferred theory to practice. To some degree his ruthlessness reflected arrogance. With other British officers, he considered the Americans—even his own—beneath him. They were crude, unlettered, and indifferent to most of what made life fine for a man of the imperial metropolis. But to a greater degree his ruthlessness was calculated. He and his Tories would sow terror among the rebels and thereby compel them to abandon their cause. In the war behind the war—in the struggle for the allegiance of the American people—terror was Tarleton's weapon of choice.

In the spring of 1780, while British regulars under General Henry Clinton besieged Charleston, Lieutenant Colonel Tarleton launched a series of raids inland. Moving stealthily, marching all night, the green-clad Legion surprised a rebel force at Monck's Corner and won a stunning victory. In their defeat the rebels discovered what kind of man they were dealing with. Several members of the British Legion assaulted a group of American women who had taken shelter in a nearby plantation house. Whether the assailants understood that the women were in fact Tories—that is, on their own side—is unclear; what registered on all who heard of the incident was that Tarleton's men were brutes with no sense of decency, shame, or even simple humanity. Nor did the green-jackets recognize any rules on the field of combat itself. Attacking with swords and bayonets, they continued hacking and thrusting even after the rebels indicated a will to surrender. A Frenchman fighting on the rebel side saw he was surrounded and asked quarter. Tarleton's men kept hacking until the French officer was "mangled in the most shocking manner," in the words of an eyewitness. He lingered in agony for several hours before dying. Until the end the Legionnaires taunted him and laughed at his pain.

In May Clinton captured Charleston, and Tarleton drove deeper inland. Chasing a rebel force that was retreating toward North Carolina, Tarleton caught the rebels on the border between North and South Carolina, in the Waxhaw district. Tarleton was badly outnumbered, and his men were staggering from having marched a hundred miles without pause, but he prepared to attack at once. He offered the rebels the chance to surrender and warned of the consequences if they didn't. "If any persons attempt to fly after this flag is received," he said, "rest assured that their rank shall not protect them, if taken, from rigorous treatment."

The rebel commander, Abraham Buford, refused to surrender to the much smaller force, and Tarleton ordered a charge. He threw one column of his dragoons against the rebel left and another against their center, while he personally led a third column against the right. Buford, apparently unable to believe that Tarleton could move so decisively, ordered his men to hold their fire till the Tories were almost upon the rebel lines. Such patience might have worked against infantry or even cavalry showing the ordinary effects of fifty hours on the march, but it failed against Tarleton's dragoons, who easily absorbed the shock of the single volley the rebels were able to get off before being overwhelmed by the charging horses and their saber-swinging riders.

The confusion among the rebels turned to rout. Some tried to surrender, others to flee; a few fought desperately on. Tarleton's dragoons treated all alike: with unbridled ferocity. Their sabers and bayonets slashed and stabbed long after the outcome of the battle had been decided. Tarleton, who personally cut down the rebel standard bearer even as his own horse was being shot from under him, allowed the killing to continue unabated. A rebel surgeon, after treating the victims of the massacre, remarked, "Not a man was spared; and it was the concurrent testimony of all the survivors that for fifteen minutes after every man was prostrate they"—Tarleton's dragoons—"went over the ground plunging their bayonets into everyone that exhibited any signs of life, and in some instances, where several had fallen over the other, these monsters were seen to throw off on the point of the bayonet the uppermost, to come at those beneath." Tarleton himself, reporting the victory to his British superiors, declared laconically, "I have cut 170 officers and men to pieces."

*A*ndrew Jackson was thirteen years old that brutal summer, at home in the Waxhaw district with his widowed mother and his two older brothers. Elizabeth was an ardent rebel, and Hugh rode with the rebel militia. Robert and Andrew were too young for military service, but they weren't too young to look after Elizabeth as Tarleton's dragoons approached the Waxhaw. The Tories slowed to burn barns and crops and houses throughout the predominantly rebel district, allowing the Jacksons to escape. After the raiders moved on, Elizabeth and the boys returned to their ravaged neighborhood—only to have to flee once more when the Tories came back. For several months the Waxhaw was in constant turmoil.

Several months is a long time in the life of a thirteen-year-old, and when those months include the stern lessons of war, a boy grows up quickly. Andrew ached to join the rebel militia and avenge the losses his family suffered. When word arrived that Hugh had died on campaign, not even Elizabeth's fears for her youngest could keep him out of the contest. The militia leaders judged him still too young to fight, but they let him serve as scout and courier, galloping the back roads of the Waxhaw with dispatches and the latest news of armed action. He observed a rebel assault on British forces at

Hanging Rock, an attack that started promisingly and might have finished so but for the heat of the day and the attackers' thirst, which they assuaged with captured rum. As their thirst diminished, so did their interest in fighting, and what might have been a decisive victory turned out to be merely a morale booster.

The following fortnight brought word of a calamitous rebel defeat at Camden, south of the Waxhaw, where Cornwallis routed Horatio Gates, the rebel hero of Saratoga. Gates's defeat left the backcountry helpless, and as Cornwallis and his redcoats pushed north, the Waxhaw once more emptied. Elizabeth had kin near Charlotte, some forty miles over the border in North Carolina. To Charlotte she and Robert and Andrew fled. Through the end of 1780 they remained in the north, while Cornwallis and the British had their way in the Waxhaw, destroying what little remained of the property of the rebels, seizing what cattle and horses hadn't already been eaten or driven off, and installing Tories in positions of prominence and power.

The Tory presence didn't prevent the return of most of the refugees, including Elizabeth Jackson and her surviving sons. But it did prevent the return of peace, and for several months the ugliest kind of partisan warfare raged throughout the Waxhaw. Neighbor hunted neighbor; friends by day became foes by night. Beyond the patent horrors of the fratricidal campaign, the guerrilla character of the fighting strained the nerves of all and broke the spirit of some. One man, without warning, began striking murderously at those around him, killing everyone within reach until the madness passed and he discovered, to his own shock as much as anyone else's, some twenty corpses in various states of dismemberment. Others, more courageous than crazy, yet still self-destructive, burned their homesteads rather than let them fall into the hands of the enemy.

Andrew Jackson rode with the rebels, now as an irregular soldier. One night he and Robert, who had also enlisted, were assigned with several others to guard the house of a well-known rebel, which came under attack from a large group of Tories. The attackers fired into the house, and fourteen-year-old Andrew and the other defenders returned the fire. One young man, Andrew's cousin, was killed at his side. The position of the defenders grew increasingly grim, until a bugle calling the cavalry charge pierced the darkness. The Tory attackers, assuming the gunfire had attracted rebel reinforcements, abandoned the assault and fled into the night. Shortly after they left, a lone, unmounted rebel, with bugle in hand, appeared from the trees, chuckling to himself at the gullibility of the Tories.

Not every encounter ended so happily. Disturbed at the revival of rebel activity in the Waxhaw, the British dispatched a troop of dragoons to sweep the area. Jackson and about forty others rode out to meet them. The British gained the advantage, capturing several of the rebels and scattering the rest. Jackson and his cousin Thomas Crawford galloped away across the fields with the dragoons close behind. Crawford's horse mired in a muddy patch, and before Jackson could turn to help him, a dragoon cut Crawford with his sword and took him prisoner. Jackson fled, eventually reaching safety in a thicket.

There he met Robert, who had survived a similar close scrape. The brothers spent the rest of that day and all the following night in the woods, hiding. Andrew was rail-thin already, and Robert wasn't much stouter, and after thirty-six hours without food they were on the verge of fainting. They crept to the home of their captured cousin, hoping to get a meal from their aunt. But some area Tories, either guessing that the Jackson boys would visit their cousin's house or simply spotting their horses, alerted the dragoons, who surrounded the house and captured the boys before they could put up a fight.

The British soldiers thereupon began systematically destroying the household belongings of Mrs. Crawford, before her eyes and those of her children. Furniture was broken, bedding was torn, dishes were smashed: the modest accumulation of a family's lifetime was ruined in minutes. Jackson, helpless at sword point, must have been mortified at what he had brought upon his aunt. ("I'll warrant Andy thought of it at New Orleans," a cousin declared decades later.) A British officer, perhaps intending to complete the lad's humiliation, ordered him to clean his—the officer's—muddy boots. At this point Jackson's mortification flashed to anger, and he indignantly refused. The officer, determined to chastise the cheeky rebel, drew his sword and aimed a blow at the boy's head. Jackson raised his left hand and deflected the blow but received a severe gash on his hand and another on his head. With blood pouring down his face and from his hand, he defiantly stood his ground and dared the officer to strike again.

The officer must have been tempted to kill Jackson on the spot, but he decided to put him to better use. The dragoons didn't know the country, and the officer rightly guessed that Jackson did. The officer had orders to find a particularly troublesome rebel named Thompson. He insisted that Jackson show the way to Thompson's house and threatened to execute him if he led them awry. Jackson acceded to the demand but simultaneously frustrated it. There were two roads to Thompson's house, one that went there directly, the other that circled within sight of the place a half mile before actually arriving. Jackson chose the latter, assuming that Thompson would be watching the road and that a half-mile head start was all he would need. Jackson's assumption proved out, and he had the silent pleasure of watching Thompson ride away ahead of the dragoons, who were none the wiser for their failure.

Andrew, Robert, Thomas Crawford, and several other prisoners were then forcibly taken to Camden, where the British were collecting captured rebels. Jackson's wound had stopped bleeding, but the pain was excruciating and the loss of blood produced a searing thirst. The prisoners' guards, however, allowed them no water—or food either—on the journey, and when Jackson and the others tried to scoop water in their hands from the creeks they forded en route, their captors made them stop.

The prison camp was an abomination. More than two hundred inmates were crowded into a narrow annex to the county jail. They lacked beds, clothing, food, water, medicine—everything essential to prevent the outbreak of disease, which naturally occurred. Before long smallpox was raging through the camp, and the prisoners provided textbook illustrations of the progress of the disease, as the recently infected mingled with those farther gone, who in turn lay elbow to knee with the dying and the unburied dead. "I frequently heard them groaning in the agonies of death," Jackson recalled years later.

For many days Jackson somehow managed to avoid infection. Prospects of rescue appeared to rise upon the approach of a rebel army under Nathanael Greene. From the distraction of the guards, the bustle about the camp, and the boasts of the British soldiers that they would do to Greene what their fellows had done to Horatio Gates—boasts that were accompanied by threats to hang all the prisoners—Jackson and the other prisoners divined the day the British were to commence the battle. To gain a view of the contest that might well decide their fate, Jackson borrowed an older prisoner's razor and with great effort whittled a hole in one of the boards that had been nailed over the jailhouse windows.

From his peephole he reported to his fellow prisoners how the rebels, making effective use of artillery and small arms, initially forced the British to retreat. The news lifted the prisoners' spirits. But then the British regrouped and counterattacked, and the rebel lines bent and broke. Greene was lucky to escape with his army intact.

Jackson and the other prisoners couldn't help despairing. They saw nothing ahead but indefinite detention, broken only perhaps by death from the epidemic that continued to rage among them. The cause for which they had fought appeared equally endangered, raising the prospect that they would die in vain.

With time to reflect, Jackson must have thought of his mother, his dead brother, the father he had never known. And at the mercy of the British, he doubtless recalled a moment when he might have materially changed the course of recent events. Early in the Waxhaw fighting, not long after the massacre that made Banastre Tarleton infamous, the British colonel had ridden unknowingly past a place where Jackson had taken refuge. The boy could hear the horses snorting and almost make out what the Tory raiders were saying as they marched by. "Tarleton passed within a hundred yards," Jackson remembered many years later. Still vexed at himself for his missed opportunity, he added, "I could have shot him."

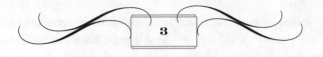

ALONE

*W*hat Andrew Jackson inherited from his father is hard to say,
due to the elder man's early death. What he inherited from his mother is
easier to identify, starting with an iron determination that allowed no
obstacle to stand in the way of necessary action. Elizabeth's determination
had kept her fatherless brood together till the war split them up, and
now it kept her from resting till she reclaimed her surviving sons from
their disease-ravaged prison. After she learned of the capture of Robert
and Andrew, she traced their path the forty miles to Camden, refusing to
allow Tories, Indians, or outlaws to stand between a mother and her
children. In Camden she hid her rebel sentiments sufficiently to persuade
the British to exchange Andrew and Robert for some British prisoners
their American captors couldn't afford to keep.

The journey north to home was as arduous as the march south had been. Robert was gravely ill and in considerable pain. Elizabeth was exhausted from her efforts to find the boys and effect their release. Andrew was in the best condition of the three, and because they had only two horses among them, he walked while they rode. Yet even he was sorely fatigued and badly malnourished. It didn't help his condition that the British had confiscated his shoes and jacket, compelling him to walk barefoot, cold, and wet through the upcountry spring.

Robert survived the journey only to expire on his second day home. Andrew was ill by then himself, having, as now became apparent, contracted smallpox in prison and incubated the disease on the way back. He grew feverish and delirious, and soon the characteristic pustules were slowly exploding across his skin. Elizabeth could do nothing but mop his brow with a cool cloth, keep him covered against the recurrent chills, and pray that he was one of those fortunates for whom the disease proved less than fatal.

In fact it did, as Andrew demonstrated a constitutional toughness that would characterize all his days. But his illness was a serious one and his recovery slow. Not for months was he fully himself again. As it happened, those months marked a lull in the fighting in the Waxhaw, and he was granted the rest he needed.

But there was no rest for Elizabeth. With Andrew safe—and Hugh and Robert dead—her thoughts turned to her nephews, whom she had raised almost as sons. William and James Crawford were prisoners at Charleston, where conditions were said to be as bad as those at Camden. She made the difficult journey there—160 miles, over country ravaged by the war—in hopes of bringing William and James home. But though her courage and determination remained as great as ever, her body now failed her. The months of flight, deprivation, and worry had reduced her resistance, and she contracted cholera. Within days she was dead.

Andrew got the sad news in the form of a bundle of her clothes. He had lost his father to overwork, and now his two brothers and his mother to war. At fourteen he faced the world alone.

⌒ ⌒ ⌒

*O*rphans were less rare in the eighteenth century than they would be later. Maternal death in childbirth left many infants without mothers. Accident and disease claimed numerous fathers, as well as some of those mothers who survived their children's delivery. For young children, the loss of both parents was as difficult then as it would ever be, depriving them of both economic and emotional sustenance. For a child of Andrew Jackson's age, the economic shock of orphanhood was mitigated by the fact that he was nearly an adult by contemporary standards.

Yet the emotional shock was still severe. In later years he liked to talk about the parting advice his mother gave him. As she left for Charleston to tend the prisoners there, she said:

> Andrew, if I should not see you again I wish you to remember and treasure up some things I have already said to you: In this world you will have to make your own way. To do that you must have friends. You can make friends by being honest, and you can keep them by being steadfast. You must keep in mind that friends worth having will in the long run expect as much from you as they give to you. To forget an obligation or be ungrateful for a kindness is a base crime—not merely a fault or a sin, but an actual crime. Men guilty of it sooner or later must suffer the penalty. In personal conduct be polite, but never obsequious. No one will respect you more than you esteem yourself. Avoid quarrels as long as you can without yielding to imposition. But sustain your manhood always. Never bring a suit at law for assault and battery or for defamation. The law affords no remedy for such outrages that can satisfy the feelings of a true man. Never wound the feelings of others. Never brook wanton outrage upon your own feelings. If you ever have to vindicate your feelings or defend your honor, do it calmly. If angry at first, wait till your wrath cools before you proceed.

Thus Jackson remembered his mother. Perhaps she really said everything he ascribed to her. Perhaps he conflated what she did say with what he thought or wished she had said. The important thing is that his memory of his mother—whether accurate or embellished—became his guiding star. "Gentlemen," he explained to the group hearing this recollection, "her last words have been the law of my life." And they were almost his only inheritance. "I might about as well have been penniless, as I already was homeless and friendless. The memory of my mother and her teachings were after all the only capital I had to start in life, and on that capital I have made my way."

It took Jackson time to discover the wisdom in his mother's advice about avoiding quarrels. While still recuperating from smallpox, he lived with his uncle Thomas Crawford, who also hosted a Captain Galbraith of the American army commissary. The captain possessed, by Jackson's later account, "a very proud and haughty disposition," which didn't sit well with the boy. "He had a habit of telling anecdotes in which he always figured as the hero. He had a way of telling them that was ludicrous, and I could mimic him so closely that anyone in the next room would think Galbraith himself was talking. He was a Highland Scotchman, one of the few Whig"—that is, rebel—"Highlanders, and he had a broad Caithness brogue, which I could imitate perfectly. Finally, one day he happened to overhear me at this amusement, and took me to task for, as he put it, insulting a man so much older and so much superior; a man—or 'mon,' as he called it—who had so often risked his life for the country. Upon this I remarked that commissaries were not famous for risking their lives, and probably all the killing he had ever done was beef-critters and sheep to feed the real fighting men of the army."

This enraged Galbraith, who threatened to horsewhip the boy. Jackson had defended his honor against a British combat officer—and bore the scars to prove it—and he refused to be chastised by an American mess master. "I immediately answered that I had arrived at the age to know my rights, and although weak and feeble from disease, I had courage to defend them, and if he attempted anything of that kind I would most assuredly send him to the other world."

In later years, when Jackson acquired a reputation for dueling, his enemies exaggerated this affair into an attempted assassination, of an American army officer no less. Jackson dismissed such tales as ludicrous. "It was too foolish to talk about, merely a difficulty between a pompous man and a sassy boy." Yet Jackson's Uncle Thomas didn't want any fights among the house-guests, and he made Jackson apologize for poking fun at the elder man. Jackson grudgingly complied. "But I never liked him and avoided him after that."

*J*ackson left the Crawford house a short while later. The mature Jackson economized on truth when he said that his mother's memory was his only starting capital in life. Not long after her death he learned that his paternal grandfather had died in Scotland and left him "three hundred or four hundred pounds sterling," by Jackson's recollection. This was no huge fortune—being equivalent to perhaps forty thousand dollars in the early twenty-first century—but it was far more than Jackson had ever seen or expected to call his own.

To claim the windfall he had to travel to Charleston. The British still occupied the city but rather less confidently than before, as the fighting had taken an unexpected turn. Cornwallis followed his successful campaign in the South with a foray into Virginia, where he hoped to corner Washington and end the war. But it was Washington—and his French allies—who did the cornering, pinning Cornwallis against the Chesapeake at Yorktown and compelling the surrender of his army. This hardly decided the overall contest between the United States and Britain; separate British forces still controlled New York, Charleston, and other parts of America, with reserves in Canada and the West Indies. But the Yorktown debacle caused the ministry in London to recalculate the balance between cost and benefit in continuing the war, and before long British diplomats were meeting in Paris with American envoys to negotiate terms of peace.

In December 1782, while the negotiations continued, the British evacuated Charleston. Jackson joined the small flood of refugees who returned to their homes upon the British departure. The city showed the effects of the occupation, yet even in its tattered condition it was the most exciting place Jackson had ever visited. Its taverns welcomed a man with ready money, and its sporting community introduced the country boy to gambling: on cards, on horses, on dice. The result was predictable; within weeks Jackson's money was gone.

Significantly, though, the one gambling story that survives from this period has Jackson winning. According to this tale, he had already frittered away his cash and fallen in debt to his landlord when he ventured into an establishment where the dice were rolling. One player, admiring Jackson's fine horse (horses being another indulgence from this period, and one from which Jackson never recovered), offered to bet two hundred dollars against the animal, on one roll of the dice. Jackson couldn't resist. Shaking the bones, he cast them across the felt—and won. "I had new spirits infused into me," he declared many years later. Jackson was president at the time of the telling, and as the country's chief magistrate he wished to avoid giving a bad impression, so he quickly added, "From that moment to the present time I have never thrown dice for a wager."

Having run through his money, the young man—he was not yet sixteen years old—returned to the Waxhaw. He reentered school briefly before deciding—to the later hilarity of those who considered him the epitome of ignorance—to *teach* school. His time at the front of the class made no lastingly apparent mark, for good or ill, on his pupils, and it afforded Jackson neither the psychic nor the financial rewards to inspire him to continue in that line.

He might have turned to farming, having inherited the two hundred acres his father had killed himself clearing. (Elizabeth had perfected the title after her husband's death.) Perhaps the circumstances of his father's demise were enough to put Jackson off husbandry. Perhaps his taste of the high life of Charleston spoiled him for the plodding career of a farmer. Perhaps he simply felt the stirrings of the ambition that would characterize his whole adult life—the desire, in part, of the unfavored child to win the esteem of others. From whatever combination of reasons, he chose to become a lawyer.

𝒯he war was finally over by now. In September 1783 the British and American diplomats at Paris signed a treaty by which Britain formally acknowledged American independence and ceded title to a domain stretching from the Atlantic to the Mississippi and from Canada to Florida.

With the Paris treaty the struggle for North America entered a new phase. The British were by no means eliminated from the contest; they still controlled Canada and were allied with Spain, which held title to Florida and Louisiana. But the Americans now entered the struggle as independent actors, with a nation and a government of their own. Their hold on the Atlantic slope, where the vast majority of their three and a half million people lived, on farms and in villages and in a handful of cities, was secure.

Yet beyond the mountains, where the forests ran down nearly unbroken to the Mississippi, their hold was tenuous to nonexistent. Some of the Indians noticed the withdrawal of the British and sensed in it the same sort of trouble that had followed the withdrawal of the French. As the Americans, freed from the restrictions on western settlement that had helped provoke the war, prepared to push into the great valley, the Indians prepared to resist.

The legal profession, in the 1780s as later, was to American society what the clergy and the military were to certain other countries and cultures: an avenue of advancement for those with talent and ambition but with neither wealth nor connections. Protestant America had no church hierarchy to speak of, precluding the priestly route to success, and it had no standing army, making a military career unappealing. Yet every society requires means for the humble able to get ahead, lest their frustrated ambitions destabilize the status quo. In America, the law long served that purpose.

In the 1780s the law was almost as much a frontier as the western reaches of the national domain. The Revolution had displaced the principal lawyers of the country, who tended to be Tories and now attempted to construct new practices in Canada or England. It also created an entirely new set of laws, with each state writing a constitution (some states more than one), and the nation as a whole doing the same. Although the English common law still formed the basis for much of the day-to-day work of lawyers, that body of precedents had to be reinterpreted in light of the utterly un-English, un-common-law notion that the basic laws of the land (of the states and the nation) could be drafted de novo and superimposed on centuries of case law like a legal deus ex machina. What did all this mean? How would the new system work? This was for the lawyers to argue and the judges—lawyers themselves, in nearly all cases—to decide.

If law was a frontier, law *on* the frontier was doubly so. In the cities the standards of legal training were well understood and were enforced—as law or guild practice—by persons and institutions attached to the status quo. In the towns and villages of the interior, the standards were more haphazard, more like the standards that had allowed Andrew Jackson to become a teacher. A young man would apprentice with an attorney, who might or might not pay attention to what the young man was learning. When the apprentice thought he could talk his way past a board of examiners, who might or might not examine his expertise closely, he struck out on his own.

The arrangement suited Jackson. In the late winter of 1785, shortly before his eighteenth birthday, he apprenticed himself to Spruce Macay, a lawyer in Salisbury, North Carolina, two days' ride from the Waxhaw. Macay's primary qualification for pedagogy was his modest library of law books, a prerequisite for anyone wishing to take on apprentices, of whom he maintained a small but steady supply. Jackson and his fellow attorneys-in-training, including an ambitious fellow named John McNairy, lived in the village tavern, which doubled as a rooming house for long-term visitors on low budgets. Jackson and the others spent days in Macay's crowded office, filing papers, finding precedents, tracing statutes, running errands, and doing whatever else was needed to keep the practice running. If Macay devoted much time to instructing his charges in the law, he did so unobtrusively. Osmosis was his educational philosophy.

By nights Jackson and the others acted like the unattached, irresponsible young men they were. They drank, gambled (perhaps at dice, Jackson's later denial notwithstanding, but certainly at cards, horses, and cocks), and played practical jokes, in the poor taste typical of practical jokes. Jackson invited two prostitutes to a Christmas ball the local dancing school put on. His humorous intention, such as it was, got lost in the cloud of scandal that arose when the two scarlet women—a mother and daughter—accepted the invitation and appeared at the event. The proper ladies of the town were shocked, the mother and daughter were embarrassed, and Jackson was compelled to explain himself. To the respectables he said he meant no harm, that he didn't think the strumpets would actually *attend*. What he said to the mother and daughter went unrecorded.

Around Salisbury Jackson acquired a reputation as a wild thing going quickly wrong. Years after he left, the townsfolk remembered an evening when Jackson and his friends toasted their mutual health and then, lest the glasses be used for less noble purposes, hurled them into the fire. With the logic of apprentice lawyers, they reasoned that the same argument compelled them to hurl the chairs they sat on into the fire. And then the table. And then the drapes, and everything else in the room that wasn't nailed down. The building survived the pyrotechnics, but barely. Decades later an acquaintance from that period asserted that the people of Salisbury were fairly certain that Andrew Jackson would come to no good in life. "None of them believed he would ever settle down. Most of them thought he would get himself killed before he was many years older." An elderly matron of the village, upon hearing that Jackson was running for president, demanded, "What? Jackson for president? *Jackson? Andrew* Jackson? The Jackson that used to live in Salisbury? Why, when he was here he was such a rake that my husband would not bring him into the house. . . . If Andrew Jackson can be president, anybody can!"

At the beginning of 1787, several weeks before his twentieth birthday, Jackson decided that he had learned all Spruce Macay could teach him. He determined to complete his legal education under the guidance of Colonel John Stokes, a Revolutionary War veteran who had lost a hand in the fighting. For prosthesis Stokes employed a silver knob, with which he tapped his desk while reading and hammered the jury box when arguing cases in court. Stokes was a capable lawyer, one of North Carolina's best, which may have been why Jackson sought him out. Or it may have been his reputation for bravery under fire, which Jackson considered no less important. What Jackson learned from Stokes is also problematic. Perhaps the old soldier simply taught Jackson to believe in himself, for just six months later Jackson stood before a two-judge board of the North Carolina Superior Court of Law and Equity to be examined for fitness to practice law. Noting that Jackson "is sufficiently recommended to us as a person of unblemished moral character"—quite likely Stokes was the recommender—"and upon examination had before us, appears to possess a competent degree of knowledge in the Law," the board admitted Jackson "to plead and practice as an Attorney."

*O*ne young man who entered the legal profession in the western districts during the early years of the American republic announced his practice with a statement of principles:

1. I will practice law because it affords me opportunities of being a more useful member of society.

2. I will turn a deaf ear to no man because his purse is empty.

3. I will advise no man beyond my comprehension of his cause.

4. I will bring none into law who my conscience tells me should be kept out.

5. I will never be unmindful of the cause of humanity; and this comprehends the widows, fatherless, and those in bondage.

6. I will be faithful to my client, but never so unfaithful to myself as to become a party in his crime.

7. In criminal cases I will not underrate my own abilities, for if any client proves a rascal, his money is better in my hands, and if not, I hold the option.

8. I will never acknowledge the omnipotence of the Legislature, or consider their acts to be law beyond the spirit of the Constitution.

9. No man's greatness shall elevate him above the justice due to my client.

10. I will not consent to a compromise where I conceive a verdict essential to my client's future reputation or protection, for of this he can not be a complete judge.

11. I will advise the turbulent with candor, and if they will go to law against my advice, they must pardon me for volunteering it against them.

12. I will acknowledge every man's right to manage his own cause if he pleases.

Andrew Jackson might not have phrased his view of the legal profession just so, but the combination of idealism and practicality, of collective and personal advancement, that the notice conveyed did in fact inform his approach to the law—and to much of his life. Like very many men in the young nation, Jackson believed that what served the public good served him, and often vice versa. A lawyer could make a mark, and a living.

But the lawyer needed clients. As one of the first he chose himself. The "unblemished moral character" to which the examining judges referred soon seemed a figure of speech, for within two months of being licensed to practice in the courts of North Carolina, Jackson found himself haled into court to answer a charge of trespass and destruction of property. The details of the case are murky. The fact that Jackson had four codefendants suggests the kind of bacchanalian wrecking that had led him to sacrifice the tavern furniture as a burnt offering. The five young men were released on their own recognizance and the case never went to trial, indicating an out-of-court settlement. Jackson certainly sighed in relief, knowing that conviction could have led to his disbarment before he fairly commenced his legal career.

But business was slow. Jackson traveled many miles across the piedmont searching for clients. He hired himself out to Randolph County when it required the indictment of one Samuel Graves. Jackson described how Graves "did with force and arms affecting to act under the authority of an execution seize into his possession and expose to sale one brown mare & saddle of the price of five pounds." What came of the indictment is unclear, but apparently the county liked the way Jackson worked, for it retained him in at least one other case. In Richmond, in Surry County, he took the other side of a criminal case, defending a man charged with theft. The accused and his lawyer were about equally hard up, and Jackson consented to take the case for a contingency: he would be paid only if he got an acquittal. He lost the case. He lived for a time in Martinsville, where some friends operated a general store, and he probably helped out there for a small wage.

But his income fell short of his expenses. He departed an inn owned by a man named John Lister, having not paid his bill. Lister halfheartedly tried to collect but then gave up—only to be reminded of the debt and the debtor after Jackson became famous fighting the British. Local tradition indicates that Lister retrieved the old bill and wrote across it: "Paid at the battle of New Orleans."

𝒯hough he was slow to make his mark as a lawyer, Jackson made an impression as a young man. "I often met him at parties, balls and other social occasions," Anne Jarret Rutherford recalled many years later. Annie Jarret was a proper young lady of Salisbury during Jackson's residence there and in fact saw him on the day he received his law license. "We all knew that he was wild among his own sex, that he gambled and was by no means a Christian young man." But he was far from the worst in the neighborhood. "He had no very bad habits; he was never known to be drunk or boisterous or rude even among his own associates." The frequency of his quarrels was overstated. "But this I must say—when he did have a quarrel it was apt to be a serious matter."

Jackson's appearance stuck in Annie Jarret's memory.

He always dressed neat and tidy and carried himself as if he was a rich man's son. The day he was licensed he had on a new suit, with broadcloth coat, ruffled shirt and other garments in the best of fashion. The style of powdering the hair was still in vogue then; but he had his abundant suit of dark red hair combed carefully back from his forehead and temples and, I suspect, made to lay down smooth with bear's oil. He was full six feet tall and very slender, but yet of such straightness of form and such proud and graceful carriage as to make him look well-proportioned.

In feature he was by no means good-looking. His face was long and narrow, his features sharp and angular and his complexion yellow and freckled. But his eyes *were* handsome. They were very large, a kind of steel-blue, and when he talked to you he always looked straight into your own eyes. I have talked with him a great many times and never saw him to avert his eyes from me for an instant. It was the same way with men. He always looked them straight in the eye, as much as to say, "I have nothing to be ashamed of and I hope you haven't." This and the gentle manner he had made you forget the plainness of his features.

When he was calm he talked slowly and with very good selected language. But if animated by anything, then he would talk fast and with a very marked North-Irish brogue, which he got from his mother and the Crawfords who raised him—all of whom grew to maturity in the old country. But either calm or animated, there was always something about him I cannot describe except to say that it was a *presence*, or a kind of majesty I never saw in any other young man.

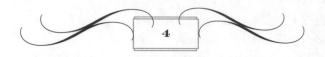

4

AWAY WEST

Every culture has its founding myth, its tale of how it came to be. For those peoples who fancy themselves forever in place, this often includes an account of the creation of the world. For others it involves how they got to where they are. The journeys entail hardship and loss; not everyone reaches the promised land. But those who do get there live on in the collective consciousness.

The founding myth of middle Tennessee was the story of an epic boat trip down the Holston and Tennessee rivers and then up the Ohio and Cumberland. The leader of the journey was John Donelson, a Virginian with a wife, eleven children, and a fervent belief that fortune awaited him if he only knew where to look. In 1779 Donelson guided a boat he called the *Adventure* and some thirty or forty other craft carrying perhaps sixty families, including his own, to a valley in the heart of the trans-Appalachian wilderness, hundreds of miles from anything that passed for civilization. Donelson had visited the Cumberland Valley and decided that the soil in the river bend near the Big Salt Lick was as fine as any in North America. He arranged with James Robertson, another Virginian, to establish a colony there. Robertson would take a small party overland to ready the way for the larger group, which Donelson would direct, with all their worldly possessions, by water.

The river journey began at Fort Patrick Henry, on the western slope of the Blue Ridge. The demands of the harvest had kept these farm families working till late autumn, and preparations for the journey delayed them further, so that they got off only three days before Christmas 1779, when the cold weather had already set in. "Took our departure from the fort," Donelson wrote in his journal of the voyage, "and fell down the river to the mouth of Reedy creek, where we were stopped by the fall of water and most excessive hard frost."

For two months the emigrant fleet struggled with the cold and the winter's low water. Rain eventually raised the river but created problems of its own. "Rain about half the day," Donelson recorded on March 2, 1780. "About twelve o'clock Mr. Henry's boat, being driven on the point of an island by the force of the current, was sunk, the whole cargo much damaged, and the crew's lives much endangered, which occasioned the whole fleet to put on shore and go to their assistance." Vessel, crew, and cargo were rescued with difficulty. And amid the excitement one member of the expedition, a young man, wandered off and didn't return, "though many guns were fired to fetch him in." For three days the young man stayed missing— "to the great grief of his parents"—till Donelson felt obliged to order the flotilla on. Luckily the lad, realizing he was lost, headed downstream and caught the last boats before they disappeared into the west. Two days later the bitter cold returned, claiming the life of one of the Negro slaves. The day after that, a woman of the expedition bore a child.

Indians were a constant danger. They threatened the main body of the fleet and preyed on those who became separated. Donelson described the "tragical misfortune of poor Stuart, his family and friends, to the number of twenty-eight persons." A member of the Stuart group had come down with smallpox, whereupon Donelson decreed that they should follow the main body at a distance, keeping a kind of floating quarantine. This turned out to be their death sentence. "The Indians, . . . observing his helpless situation, singled him off from the rest of the fleet, intercepted him, killed and took prisoners the whole crew." Others in the expedition shuddered in helpless horror. "Their cries were distinctly heard by the boats in the rear."

In mid-March the expedition reached the Muscle Shoals of the Tennessee River, an infamous stretch of rapids. "The water being high made a terrible roaring, which could be heard at some distance among the driftwood heaped frightfully upon the points of the island, the current running in every possible direction. Here we did not know how soon we should be dashed to pieces, and all our troubles ended at once. Our boats frequently dragged on the bottom, and appeared constantly in danger of striking; they warped as much as in a rough sea." When, to the amazement of all, the expedition passed this trial without loss of life, Donelson thanked "the hand of Providence."

They reached the Ohio in late March. "Our situation here is truly disagreeable," Donelson wrote from the banks of the larger river. "The river is very high, and the current rapid, our boats not constructed for the purpose of stemming a rapid stream, our provision exhausted, the crews almost worn down with hunger and fatigue." Donelson's plan was to ascend the Ohio to the mouth of the Cumberland, and the Cumberland to the Big Salt Lick. But some of those who had traveled downstream so many weeks couldn't bear the thought of pushing their way up, against the Ohio's spring torrent, and so chose to continue down the Ohio to the Mississippi. Donelson stuck to the original plan. "I am determined to pursue my course, come what will."

The distance to the Cumberland's mouth was only fifteen miles, but it consumed four hard days of rowing, poling, and picking their way through the eddies close to the Ohio's shore. When they reached the Cumberland, some in the group thought it looked too small to be that river. Donelson couldn't be certain. "But I never heard of any river running in between the Cumberland and Tennessee," and so he ordered the fleet to enter the stream. Within a day it broadened, suggesting that they were indeed on the right river. They assuaged their hunger by shooting buffalo that came down to the stream to drink. The beasts had had a hard winter; their flesh was edible but poor. By contrast a swan, having wintered in the south, "was very delicious." Yet the swan meat didn't go far, and the food situation grew more dire. "We are without bread, and are compelled to hunt the buffalo to preserve life. Worn out with fatigue, our progress at present is slow."

Progress continued to be slow for three more agonizing weeks. The travelers supplemented their buffalo diet with greens they called "Shawnee salad." Several of the travelers decided they could go no farther and dropped out along the river. But on April 24, after four months on the water, the resolute core of the expedition reached its goal. "This day we arrived at our journey's end at the Big Salt Lick, where we have the pleasure of finding Captain Robertson and his company. It is a source of satisfaction to us to be enabled to restore to him and others their families and friends, who were entrusted to our care and who, some time since perhaps, despaired of ever meeting again. Though our prospects at present are dreary, we have found a few log cabins which have been built on a cedar bluff above the lick by Capt. Robertson and his company."

$\mathcal{T}$he remarkable thing about the Donelson voyage was not the hardship the emigrants survived, which, though daunting, differed in degree rather than kind from the trials men and women in the West endured every day. Rather, the remarkable thing was the little distance the voyagers netted for all their time and effort. Their river miles amounted to nearly a thousand, but they ended up barely a fifth that far from the place they started. A crow might have completed the journey in a day, humans walking on a decent road in a week. But there was no such road, making the roundabout trip by water the only feasible way to transport families and their belongings.

Transportation wasn't a problem for the people of the frontier alone. During the 1780s the difficulty of distance was a rock on which the Union nearly broke—although whether it was more dangerous than other submerged boulders was a matter of interpretation. In the aftermath of the Revolutionary War, the United States were decidedly plural, having united for the purpose of fending off the British, a purpose that vanished upon the peace. The Articles of Confederation continued to link them, but because the articles had been drafted deliberately weak, the links bound no state to do much it didn't want to do. The national government could requisition operating funds from each state but couldn't compel payment, which meant that it often didn't get paid. It could preach amity and cooperation to the states but couldn't prevent their waging economic war on one another. It could urge the states to keep their defenses strong but couldn't support a decent army or conscript anyone to fight.

The weaknesses of the Confederation caused many Americans to worry that their republican experiment was coming undone. When domestic unrest broke out in Massachusetts, led by Revolutionary War veteran Daniel Shays, the worries mounted. When the British refused to relinquish control of forts in the Ohio Valley, which they had promised in the Paris treaty to do, the weakness at the center became a source of national embarrassment. Those most worried and embarrassed mobilized in favor of a stronger central government. James Madison and Alexander Hamilton organized a convention at Annapolis in 1786. When the turnout proved disappointing, they rescheduled for Philadelphia the following summer.

The Philadelphia convention initially confronted what seemed an insurmountable barrier: the requirement under the Articles of Confederation that amendments receive the unanimous endorsement of the states. But what Madison, Hamilton, and the others couldn't climb over they skirted, proposing not to amend the Articles but to write an entirely new constitution. It was a bold gambit, one that risked angry disavowal by those who had sent the delegates to Philadelphia. Yet it was a move they considered necessary in view of the current crisis. The delegates aimed to craft a stronger union, one with the energy and power to accomplish the purposes of a proud and growing nation. They worked through the hot Pennsylvania summer, meeting in closed session in the same hall where the Continental Congress had approved independence eleven years earlier. In September they revealed their blueprint to the world, asking the states to ratify the new charter and put the old, weak government out of its—and their—misery.

The Philadelphia charter was elegant in places, workmanlike in others, downright clunky in yet others. Like all works of committee it embodied compromise. One obvious compromise regarded representation in the new Congress. States with few inhabitants had wanted to maintain the Confederation principle of one vote per state. Heavily peopled states desired representation by population. The result was a hybrid legislature, with the Senate embodying the small-state position and the House of Representatives the big-state view. Another compromise determined the selection of the president: not by the Congress or by the states directly but by an electoral college created anew every quadrennium. Who would the president represent, then? It was a fair question. Some in the convention sought to ban slavery, deeming it antithetical to the basic principles of liberty and self-government. Yet the slave-thick southern states stood together, defending their peculiar institution as necessary to their economic development. The most the anti-slavery delegates could win was a delayed (and only implicit) ban on the overseas slave trade, by common consent the worst aspect of the slave system.

But the truly fateful compromise, the one that made the others—especially the slavery finesse—potentially lethal was the waffling on where sovereignty in the new government lay. Were the states supreme, or the national government? Many of the delegates were lawyers, and their lawyerly skill was never more evident than in their ability to cloud this central issue. Readers weren't nine words into the preamble before they were scratching their heads. "We the people of the United States of America"—how was this to be construed? An emphasis on "people" suggested national primacy. A stress on "States" pointed to the states, as did the facts that the delegates to the convention voted by states and that the proposed constitution was referred to the states for ratification, with equal weight given to every one.

The waffle didn't fool opponents of the new constitution, who spied a centralist plot in the Philadelphia proceedings. Many of the old revolutionaries turned away, complaining that the proposed government would deprive them of liberties hard won by war. To replace the grasping authority of Britain, they declared, with that of a central American government would be ironic, tragic, and stupid.

But the supporters of the constitution were clever. They contended that the new government would be strictly limited to the powers expressly granted it. Where the charter was silent, they said, the states would take precedence. Even as they winked to assure themselves and their friends that the new government would be a signal improvement over the Confederation, they cooed to skeptics that nothing much, really, had changed.

The compromises contained in the constitution—especially on slavery and sovereignty—would vex America for decades. Andrew Jackson as president would find himself tripping over the loose ends the drafters left lying across the American frame of government. But in the autumn of 1787 another aspect of the constitutional debate drew almost as much attention. For decades political theorists had contended that republics could sustain themselves only in compact geographical areas. Pointing to the city-states of Greece and to preimperial Rome, they argued that compactness created a sense of common purpose and allowed citizens and rulers to know one another well, and that these advantages diminished dangerously over distance. What republic had ever survived being extended over a large geographical area? None the drafters of the constitution could cite. As this reasoning pertained to the American situation, it supported the antifederalists, who contended that New Hampshire could never know Georgia, nor the hamlets on the frontier the cities of the seaboard. Single states stretched the republican principle already; a centralized government would snap it. More prosaically, the long distances in America made centralized government unworkable. If the citizens of Massachusetts or South Carolina had to travel to Philadelphia (or New York or wherever the national capital turned out to be) every time they needed to conduct their government business, they would have no time for more productive activities. One reason America broke away from Britain was that getting decisions out of London took so long.

The federalists countered this complaint in various ways, but none more ingenious than that devised by James Madison. In the tenth article of the collection that became known as the *Federalist Papers*, Madison turned the received reasoning about the size of republics on its head. Extensive republics, he asserted, were actually *more* stable than small ones. In a small republic, one or two factions could easily conspire against the general interest, engineer a majority, and subvert the liberties of the rest. In a large republic, the factions would be more dispersed, rendering conspiracy and subversion more difficult and rare. "Extend the sphere," Madison said, "and you take in a greater variety of parties and interests; you make it less probable that a majority of the whole will have a common motive to invade the rights of other citizens; or, if such a common motive exists, it will be more difficult for all who feel it to discover their own strength and to act in unison with each other." What others considered a weakness of large republics—the dispersion of their people and the diversity of their interests—Madison touted as a strength.

Whether Madison's argument convinced anyone was hard to tell. At times he himself didn't appear to believe it. But it definitely didn't persuade the residents of the backcountry villages and farms, who cherished their independence and didn't look kindly on ceding any of it to a distant government they neither knew nor trusted. Frontier antifederalists in the Carolinas damned the constitution as the death of liberty and held a funeral. "The people had a coffin painted black, which, borne in funeral procession, was solemnly buried, as an emblem of the dissolution and interment of public liberty," an eyewitness recorded. "They feel that they are the very men who, as mere militia, half-armed and half-clothed, have fought and defeated the British regulars in sundry encounters. They think that after having disputed and gained the laurel under the banners of liberty, now, that they are likely to be robbed both of the honour and the fruits of it."

But not for decades would the voice of the West mean much in American politics. Despite the complaints of the frontiersmen, the constitution was ratified, and the country embarked on its great experiment in federalism.

$\mathcal{T}$he alienation of the West from the East would give Andrew Jackson his opportunity in national politics; for now it contributed to one of the great—failed—experiments in American history. At the time John Donelson had reached the Big Salt Lick, the valley of the Cumberland was part of North Carolina. Yet during the next half decade, the government of North Carolina decided that its western region was too much trouble to govern, and it ceded the district to the United States. The Confederation Congress, amid its own troubles, was slow to respond, with the result that the territory that would become Tennessee hung in legal limbo, lacking a government of any kind.

Nearly all the inhabitants had emigrated from states that had recently written constitutions to replace their colonial charters, and to these emigrants it came naturally to write another constitution, for a state of their own. They named their state Franklin, after the Founding Father with the greatest interest in the West. For decades before the American Revolution, Benjamin Franklin had argued that the West held the key to America's future. At the end of the Revolutionary War he directed the negotiations that ensured that the United States owned the territory all the way to the Mississippi River. Though Franklin had never been anywhere near the Mississippi—being a city boy his entire life—he instinctively appreciated the importance of the great river for the future of the West. When Spain demanded control of the Mississippi as a condition for assisting the United States against Britain, he rejected the idea out of hand. "A neighbor might as well ask me to sell my street door," he said.

The founders of the state of Franklin agreed with the famous doctor on the importance of the West and the Mississippi, and in August 1784 they sent delegates to Jonesboro, on the Nolichucky River, to discuss their grievances against North Carolina and the United States. The delegates voted unanimously to establish a state government. Four months later a constitutional convention drafted a charter for Franklin.

But then the republican spirit ran into the capitalist spirit. Among the Franklinites were a substantial number of speculators, who sought a state government primarily to secure titles to land. When the speculators began fighting among themselves, Franklin's progress toward statehood stalled. It didn't help matters that the Franklinites received no encouragement from Congress, which would ultimately have to ratify their handiwork. For a few years Franklin operated a land office and conducted diplomacy with Indian tribes, but neither its land titles nor its Indian treaties carried weight with anyone besides those directly involved. When Congress, following adoption of the federal Constitution, created the Southwest Territory in 1790, the state of Franklin vanished into the mists of the Smoky Mountains.

$\mathcal{Y}$et the sentiments that gave rise to Franklin weren't so easily dispelled. Since the voyage of the Donelson party, the inhabitants of the western region had wondered whether geography didn't dictate that their future lay with whatever country controlled the Mississippi. And when John Jay, in defiance of Benjamin Franklin's dictum about front doors, proposed a treaty with Spain that would have ceded control of the Mississippi to the Spanish, the westerners were outraged. Some tried to block the treaty; others discussed joining the enemy. The latter group commenced clandestine talks with Spanish officials, offering to lead a secession movement that would take the West out of the Union and into the Spanish empire.

James Wilkinson was the most active of the pro-Spanish conspirators. In 1787 he loaded two flatboats with farm produce and floated to New Orleans, where he sold his cargo for a hefty profit. This aspect of his journey drew the notice of all upstream, who had wondered how their goods would be received at the Spanish port. But commerce was Wilkinson's cover for a deeper game. While in New Orleans he secretly renounced his American citizenship and swore fealty to the king of Spain, and he proposed a scheme for detaching the trans-Appalachian districts from the United States and attaching them to Spain's dominions. America's westerners, he said, were desperate for access to the Mississippi and New Orleans. They would seek the protection of whatever government could guarantee them this. "The leading characters of Kentucky . . . ," he told Estevan Miró and Martín Navarro, respectively the Spanish governor and commandant at New Orleans, "urged and entreated my voyage hither in order to develop if possible the disposition of Spain towards their country and to discover, if practicable, whether she would be willing to open a negotiation for our admission to her protections as subjects." Wilkinson dissembled here; the separation scheme was his idea. Nor did he want it shared, even with—or especially with—those leading characters of Kentucky until it was a fait accompli. "Gentlemen," he concluded to Miró and Navarro, "I have committed secrets of an important nature, such was would, if they were divulged, destroy my fame and fortune forever. . . . If the plan should eventually be rejected by the Court, I must rely on the candor and high honor of a dignified minister to bury these communications in eternal oblivion."

Miró and Navarro passed Wilkinson's proposal to the viceroy of New Spain, who in turn forwarded it to the Spanish government. The council of state considered the plan with interest but decided not to press the matter "until the Kentuckians attain the independence from the United States to which they aspire." Meanwhile, though, the separatists should be encouraged in commerce and other activities that fostered separation. And Wilkinson should be given a "hope of remuneration" to keep him interested.

These matters took many months, and by the time Wilkinson got the reply to his first proposal, the United States had a new constitution and a more assertive government. Though neither was popular west of the mountains, each possessed sufficient novelty to make many Kentuckians want to wait and see what became of them. This complicated Wilkinson's plan. He judged it politic to push independence for the West rather than attachment to Spain. The latter might draw Spain into war with the United States or Britain or both, and in such a war Spain could never defend its new acquisition. Western independence, on the other hand, would be less provocative and almost equally to Spain's purpose. "That section of the country," Wilkinson said, in a second memorial to the Spanish government, "bound by its own interests, would still continue to serve as a barrier for Louisiana and Mexico as fully as if it were under the jurisdiction of Spain." To facilitate the separation, Spain should make covert payments to influential individuals; Wilkinson helpfully supplied a list of recipients and appropriate amounts, ranging from five hundred to two thousand dollars. For himself he asked seven thousand dollars. He again stressed the need for discretion, lest discovery of his plan "expose me to great embarrassment."

Miró and the Spanish could keep secrets. Not for decades would Wilkinson's Spanish connection cause him the embarrassment he feared, and then because Andrew Jackson made a point of calling him on it. Meanwhile Wilkinson secretly collected a pension from the Spanish government and openly encouraged the settlers of the Cumberland to name their neighborhood the Mero District, in misspelled honor of the Spanish governor.

*I*t was to the Mero District that Andrew Jackson relocated about the time the Spanish court answered Wilkinson's first proposal. The open agitation for the state of Franklin and the veiled discussions with Spain caused North Carolina to reconsider its cession of its western lands, and after talks with some of the inhabitants of the interior it reasserted its jurisdiction and established institutions of governance. Foremost of these institutions was a court, with power to punish crime, compel payment of debts, and otherwise bring order to the frontier. The court required a judge, and the judge a solicitor, or prosecutor. Neither post was a plum. Each appealed chiefly to lawyers lacking profitable practice in the East. Jackson perhaps hoped for the judgeship, but it went to his Salisbury roommate John McNairy, who had better political connections. Yet McNairy tapped Jackson for the solicitor's job. In the summer of 1788 the judge and the prosecutor prepared to travel to

Nashville, the town that had grown up near the Big Salt Lick and that served as capital of the Mero District.

Conditions of travel had improved in the eight years since the Donelson party's voyage but not by much. Though the Cumberland had been settled, the two hundred miles of wilderness that separated it from Jonesboro remained almost as howling as ever. Wild animals roamed freely, and Indians attacked those intruders for whom they had no use. McNairy and Jackson reached Jonesboro without incident, but they waited there for reinforcements before pushing farther west.

Perhaps his impatience to be at his new post made Jackson touchy. Perhaps he felt that a prosecutor needed to establish a reputation for brooking no slights. Perhaps the sensitivity of the skinny, fatherless child who had to battle for everything in life simply pushed to the surface. Whatever the reason, Jackson in Jonesboro precipitated his first duel. Waightstill Avery was a graduate of the College of New Jersey (later Princeton), a distinguished veteran of the Revolutionary War, and one of the most respected attorneys in North Carolina. In fact, Jackson had applied to apprentice with Avery but been turned down. At Jonesboro the two men—the dean of the North Carolina bar and the rank novice—took opposite sides in a civil suit. Unsurprisingly, Jackson found himself overmatched. "The cause was going against him, and he became irritable," Avery's son recalled later. "My father rather exultingly ridiculed some legal position taken by Jackson, using, as he afterwards admitted, language more sarcastic than was called for. It stung Jackson, who snatched up a pen, and on the blank leaf of a law book wrote a peremptory challenge, which he delivered there and then."

Avery didn't take the courtroom challenge seriously, so Jackson reiterated it the next day. "When a man's feelings and character are injured he ought to seek a speedy redress," he wrote Avery. "You received a few lines from me yesterday, and undoubtedly you understand me. My character you have injured, and further you have insulted me in the presence of a court and a large audience. I therefore call upon you as a gentleman to give me satisfaction." Lest he be brushed off again, Jackson specified the time and place: "This evening after court adjourned."

"My father was no duelist," Avery's son said. "In fact, he was opposed to the principle, but with his antecedents, in that age and country, to have declined would have been to have lost caste." Avery said nothing to Jackson in court about the challenge, yet as soon as the trial went to the jury, he sought a man to act as his second. This fellow arranged the details with a man Jackson had engaged for the same purpose. The parties met in a low-lying area north of Jonesboro after sunset. By now Jackson's anger had cooled, and he apparently acceded to the advice of the seconds that honor would be assuaged even if no blood flowed. At any rate, after Jackson and Avery stepped off the agreed-upon distance, they fired and both deliberately missed. "General Jackson acknowledged himself satisfied," Avery's son concluded. "They shook hands, and were friendly ever after."

*B*y early October 1788 enough emigrants had gathered at Jonesboro to risk the journey west. The state of North Carolina, hoping to demonstrate its concern for the Mero District (and thereby neutralize some of the secessionist sentiment), had enlisted a special squadron of armed guards to travel with the emigrants through the most dangerous stretches of the wilderness. The guards had particular instructions to ensure the safe arrival at Nashville of Judge McNairy and Solicitor Jackson. To lose the court's charter officers to Indians would have been very bad for civic morale.

Sixty families made the trek. The road was too narrow and stump-strewn to accommodate four-wheeled vehicles, and even the two-wheeled oxcarts a few of the emigrants drove had a difficult time. Most of the travelers' goods were packed on horses, mules, or the travelers themselves. "I had my saddlehorse—a fine young stallion—and a stout pack-mare carrying my personal effects," Jackson recalled. "These were my spare clothes, blankets, etc., half a dozen books, with small quantities of ammunition, tea, tobacco, liquor, and salt." For arms he carried a pair of pistols in saddle holsters, a pistol worn on his belt, and a new rifle.

Jackson almost had occasion to use his guns. On guard one night he heard owls in the forest beyond the halo of light cast by the campfire. He listened carefully, for he had heard owls before, but none quite like these. Suddenly he decided they weren't owls at all, but Indians preparing to attack. He awoke some members of the party who had local knowledge, and they agreed that the birds sounded suspicious. Quietly but quickly the party broke camp and took to the road. Later Jackson and the others learned that a group of hunters had occupied their camp shortly after Jackson's party left, and been attacked by Indians, with fatal results.

At the end of October 1788, Jackson's train reached the bend in the Cumberland where Donelson had ordered his boats ashore. Nashville by this time boasted a handful of stores and taverns, a distillery, and an eclectic array of log cabins, horse sheds, and chicken coops. Jackson didn't record his first impressions. Possibly he compared it with the towns farther east and wondered what he had got himself into. Perhaps, on the other hand, he detected opportunity in the very rawness of the place. He had turned twenty-one the previous spring, and he was commencing his majority with no advantages but his native intelligence and his ambition. Nashville was half his age, but it too relied on wit and drive, in this case of its few hundred inhabitants. The young man and the younger community made a likely couple.

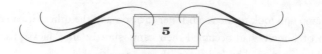

5

SHADOWED LOVE

John Donelson was dead by the time Andrew Jackson reached

Nashville, but no one could say quite how he had died. He had planted his

family on a Cumberland farm they called Clover Bottom for the lush

meadow that sprang from the black, flood-deposited earth. Yet Donelson

and his boys had only just got their first corn crop in the ground when the

river made another deposit, burying the crop and forcing the family to

higher elevation. Subsequent Indian troubles discouraged a return to

Clover Bottom, and the Donelsons beat a temporary retreat into Kentucky.

They were back on the Cumberland by 1785, when Donelson installed his

wife and the children who hadn't yet left home in a log house ten miles

from Nashville. He farmed during the summer and took odd jobs during

the winter. Among those jobs was surveying for speculators hoping to turn a profit on western lands. He was surveying in the woods not far from Nashville when he met a violent death. As Indians were still very active in the area, they initially appeared the likely culprits. Yet examination of the corpse revealed that it retained its scalp but not its wallet, and suspicion fell on white highwaymen. They were never found, though, and the mystery was never solved.

During the next few years the Donelson children continued to scatter. But one returned to the nest. Rachel Donelson was described by a contemporary as possessing a "beautifully molded form, lustrous black eyes, dark glossy hair, full red lips, brunette complexion, though of brilliant coloring, a sweet oval face rippling with smiles and dimples." She must have been alluring, for she had no trouble attracting admirers, starting with Lewis Robards. Rachel and Robards (apparently pronounced "Roberts," to judge by the frequent misspellings to that effect) met during the Donelsons' sojourn in Kentucky. They married not long after her seventeenth birthday and stayed behind when John and Mrs. Donelson took the other children back to the Cumberland. For a time the young couple got on well, living with Robards's widowed mother, who grew attached to her daughter-in-law. But when the widow Robards took in a boarder named Peyton Short, trouble developed. Short found Rachel attractive, and she appreciated his gallantries. Probably these were mere flirtations, but Robards became jealous. He accused Rachel of unfaithfulness and Short of cuckolding him. Rachel protested her innocence, and Robards's mother told him to calm down. But he refused to be mollified. He cast his wife from his—or rather his mother's—house and sent her packing for the Cumberland.

Rachel reached Nashville about the same time Andrew Jackson did. The new solicitor required housing and upon inquiry learned that Mrs. Donelson would be happy for a lodger. She could use the money, but, more important, she wanted the protection a male would provide. In Indian country every gun helped.

Jackson bunked in a small cabin a short distance from the main house on the Donelson property. Before long he acquired a roommate, John Overton. Like Jackson, Overton was a lawyer; he would go on to a distinguished career at the Tennessee bar. He had been a boarder at the widow Robards's house in Kentucky when Rachel and Lewis Robards were living there. He saw the rift develop between husband and wife, and after Rachel returned to her mother's home, he watched Robards grow lonely and remorseful. The widow Robards, upset at the loss of her daughter-in-law and convinced that her son had seen his error, asked Overton to intercede. "The old lady told me he regretted what had taken place, and wished to be reconciled to his wife," Overton recalled. Overton insisted on hearing it from Robards. "He assured me of his regret respecting what had passed; that he was convinced his suspicions were unfounded; that he wished to live with his wife, and requested that I would use my exertions to restore harmony." Overton then set out for Nashville and reached the Donelson place a few weeks after Jackson moved in.

His mediation worked. Rachel was almost as unhappy at the separation as Robards was. She may have still loved him, but in addition she confronted a dismal future as an abandoned wife. Divorce was difficult to obtain in those days, requiring a special act of the legislature, which in turn required having, or cultivating, influential friends. As her wedding had taken place in Kentucky, which was still a part of Virginia, freedom from Robards necessitated traveling across the mountains to Richmond or hiring someone to make the trip. At a minimum the process would consume years and more money than Rachel could easily spare. As events would prove, Rachel didn't know all the details of obtaining a divorce. But she knew it wouldn't be easy, and it might well be impossible, especially if Robards fought it. So when he related, through Overton, that he wanted a reconciliation, she consented. He traveled from Kentucky to join her.

Robards owned a piece of land on the south bank of the Cumberland, several miles from the Donelson home. He intended that he and Rachel should make their home there, but in the meantime he lived with Rachel in Mrs. Donelson's house. He came to know Andrew Jackson, as Jackson and Overton took their meals with Robards, Rachel, and Mrs. Donelson.

But Robards's old suspicions resurfaced. "Not many months elapsed before Robards became jealous of Jackson," Overton remembered. Overton thought the jealousy reflected the fevered state of Robards's mind rather than anything objective—and objectionable—between Jackson and Rachel. Overton wasn't unbiased between Robards and Jackson; at the time he told his story he and Jackson had been friends for almost forty years. But their friendship was grounded in his assessment of Jackson's character, which Overton knew as well as anyone, starting with their time at Mrs. Donelson's, where they "lived in the cabin room and slept in the same bed," as Overton put it. "As young men of the same pursuits and profession, with but few others in the county with whom to associate, besides sharing, as we frequently did, common dangers, such an intimacy ensued as might reasonably be expected."

At first Jackson was unaware of Robards's suspicions. But before long they became unmistakable. Overton suggested that he and Jackson find other lodgings. Jackson assented yet didn't wish to leave with his integrity impugned. He went to talk to Robards.

This compounded the trouble. Tact would never be Jackson's strong suit; he almost always spoke from the heart and to the point. He did so to Robards. Just what he said is unknown, but it doubtless began with a defense of his own character and probably escalated to aspersions on Robards's. Robards grew livid. He hurled insults at Jackson and threatened to beat him.

When Jackson was mildly angry, it typically showed in his face and voice. But when something really provoked him, his manner calmed. It did so now. He quietly challenged Robards to a duel.

Robards refused. Instead he damned Jackson and Rachel in the same breath and vowed to have nothing more to do with either. He returned to Kentucky, leaving his wife with her mother. Jackson carried out his intention of departing the Donelson home and found lodgings elsewhere.

I had the pleasure of seeing Capt. Fargo yesterday, who put me under obligations of seeing you this day," Jackson wrote in February 1789 to Daniel Smith, the brigadier general of the militia of the Mero District. "But as the weather seems dull and heavy it prevents my coming up." Consequently Jackson committed to a letter what he would have told Smith in person, starting with an account of his conversation with this most intriguing visitor.

Anthony Fagot (not "Fargo") was a merchant operating out of St. Louis who, like many in that neighborhood, traced his roots to France, which had owned the Louisiana territory till it passed to Spanish control at the end of the French and Indian War. And like other traders along the Mississippi, he was trying to negotiate his way among the various claimants to the region:

the Spanish, who claimed all of the west bank of the river and parts of the east; the Americans, who claimed most of the east bank; and the Indians, who claimed both banks. At the time he met Jackson, Fagot was attempting to open a regular trade between the Americans on the Cumberland and the Spanish at New Orleans. James Wilkinson had shown that such trade was possible; Fagot wanted to make it profitable. Commerce required the cooperation of the Spanish at New Orleans, who consistently taxed produce sent down the river from the American settlements and occasionally banned it. It also required the cooperation, or at least the acquiescence, of the Indians, who often harried traders crossing their lands and not infrequently killed them.

Fagot was as subtle as Wilkinson and others of that generation of schemers. He played a Spanish game in New Orleans, an American game in the Cumberland, and an Indian game between. Talking to Jackson, he told of his esteem for the United States. "He expresses a great friendship for the welfare and harmony of this country," Jackson told General Smith. "He wishes to become a citizen." He also wished to promote friendship between the United States and Spain. This would benefit trade both directly, by encouraging Americans to send their produce south and the Spanish to receive it, and indirectly, by facilitating joint action against the Indians. Jackson was developing an interest in trade, and with everyone else in the Cumberland he was painfully aware of the Indian threat. Fagot wanted to speak with Smith. Jackson urged Smith to see the Frenchman and listen to his plan. "I think it the only immediate way to obtain a peace with the savage."

Jackson was in deeper water here than he knew. Smith took Jackson's advice and received Fagot. Smith expressed innocuous amity, which Fagot subsequently represented to Governor Miró as a desire for the Mero District to secede from the United States in favor of Spain. Some in the district did feel such a desire, but not Smith and not Jackson. Before long Jackson would embrace exactly the opposite idea: that what Spain owned should become American. At that point he would regret having had anything to do with Fagot.

⌒ ⌒ ⌒

The Fagot affair revealed something besides Jackson's innocence of frontier diplomacy. It showed Jackson's understanding that the militia commander—currently Daniel Smith—was the most important man in the district. This simple fact would explain much of Jackson's career during the next thirty years, as he gravitated toward military command rather than civilian office. In the meantime it reflected the remarkably tenuous hold the inhabitants of the Cumberland settlements had on life in their new home.

A chronicler of early Tennessee tallied settlers killed by Indians, noting that during the first decade and a half of its existence, the Cumberland lost a man, woman, or child about every ten days, sometimes in the most ghastly fashion. The early summer of 1791 was especially cruel.

June 2d, 1791, the Indians killed John Thompson in his own cornfield within five miles of Nashville. June 14th, they killed John Gibson and wounded McCoon in Gibson's field, eight miles from Nashville. They killed Benjamin Kirdendall in his own house in Summer county, and plundered his house of every thing the Indians could use. In June, 1791, three travelers from Natchez to Nashville were found dead on the trace near the mouth of the Duck river; there were eight in company, and only two came in. On the 3d of July, 1791, Thomas Fletcher and two other men were killed on the north side of the Cumberland; their heads were entirely skinned. In the same month a man was killed within a hundred and fifty yards of Major Wilson's, on the public road, as he was riding up to his house. On the 12th, Thomas White was killed in the Cumberland mountains.

The violence colored every aspect of life for the settlers. No man traveled unarmed, even from cabin to fields. Rifles rested across plow handles throughout the valley. Children didn't fetch water or pick berries without an escort. Widows competed for lodgers or second husbands: anyone handy with weapons. When the attacks grew especially intense, fields went unplowed and crops unharvested. Later generations of Americans, without knowing why, would discover rest for the soul in parklike vistas where open spaces separated trees with branches pruned well above the ground. The westerners of Jackson's generation—like people of a thousand generations before them—knew perfectly well why such parks appealed to them: they allowed the hunted to see where the hunters weren't. But until the settlers cleared the fields, every canebrake (with reeds towering to twenty feet, their stalks impenetrably close together), every oak copse (with trunks thicker than a man's body and branches intertwined), every riverbank (with walls of sedges and curtains of willows) put them on guard. They lived in a state of siege and acted like a people under assault.

Their heroes were the men who could protect them. Every able-bodied male was expected to serve in the militia, whose members chose their own leaders. This made the election of militia officers the closest thing to democracy that existed in the West (or any other part of the country, outside the townships of New England). To be chosen commander of the militia was a great honor. The militia general was the beau ideal of the men, the protector in chief of the women and children. Most important, his position owed to merit and ability, not to wealth or connections. Westerners could tolerate incompetence in judges, prosecutors, and other officials, without jeopardizing their very existence, but incompetence in militia officers meant that lives—perhaps many lives, and farms and even whole communities—would be lost. For this reason, the westerners chose their officers very carefully.

$\mathcal{B}$y the time Jackson left the home of Mrs. Donelson, upon Lewis Robards's second abandonment of his wife, he seems to have developed romantic feelings for Rachel. They might well have been latent from the start, given her obvious attractiveness. Doubtless the misbehavior of Robards toward Rachel aroused a certain protectiveness in Jackson. And the fact that Robards accused him of unacceptable intimacies could have made him feel that if he were going to be condemned anyway, he might as well be condemned for cause.

However it happened, Jackson found himself in the grip of the same emotion that has deranged young persons, and more than a few older ones, since humans acquired wits to lose. Sometime during 1789 Jackson determined to have Rachel for his own. She was still legally bound to Robards, but the moral tie—the bond of trust and affection that makes any marriage real—had been broken by Robards's mistreatment of her, which by now included infidelities Robards scarcely bothered to deny. And sometime during this same period, Rachel decided to have Jackson for her own.

A divorce appeared no closer than it had been, so the two lovers acted without it. Just what they did and, more to the point, when they did it have been the source of controversy ever since. John Overton and Jackson's defenders later asserted that Mrs. Donelson, on hearing that Robards intended to return from Kentucky to claim his wife again, laid plans to escape with Rachel to Natchez, in Spanish-administered (though American-claimed) territory on the east bank of the Mississippi, where she had friends. But the journey itself, across hundreds of miles of Indian territory, would be dangerous, and Mrs. Donelson could find only one male escort. This man, a Colonel Stark, asked Jackson to join them. He agreed.

The journey required several weeks during the winter of 1790–91, by the Overton account. Jackson saw Rachel and her mother safely installed with their friends, and he returned to Nashville in time to conduct the business of the prosecutor's office in April 1791. He had been back but a short while when he learned that Robards had obtained an act from the Virginia legislature authorizing him to sue for divorce from Rachel. The grounds for the divorce suit were "that the defendant hath deserted the plaintiff, and that she hath lived in adultery with another man since such desertion." Rachel's alleged lover wasn't named, but Robards certainly had Jackson in mind. Overton and the Jackson partisans asserted that the charge of adultery was unfounded, the product of the same fevered imagination that had plagued Robards's marriage from the start. Jackson had become Rachel's protector but nothing more.

In fact, the adultery charge was almost certainly true. Overton's chronology, by design or forgetfulness, was off by a year on certain crucial points. Spanish and other records reveal that the Donelson-Jackson journey to Natchez occurred in the winter of 1789–90. Nor was Jackson a late addition to the traveling party. Jackson had been in Natchez earlier in the year exploring opportunities to trade. At that time he had sworn the oath of allegiance to Spain required of all Americans intending to do business or reside in the area. Quite conceivably the journey to Natchez was Jackson's idea. If Jackson and Rachel were to be together, it couldn't be in Nashville, at least not yet. Too many people knew that Rachel was still married to Robards. But Natchez was far away, beyond the reach of Robards should he really be intent on returning, beyond the gaze of censorious neighbors, and beyond the effective power of American law. In Natchez Jackson and Rachel could live as husband and wife, and no one would bother them. If Robards heard of the elopement, he might well divorce Rachel, which would be all the better.

Jackson's partisans afterward asserted that their man, upon learning that Robards had indeed initiated divorce proceedings, returned to Natchez, where he and Rachel were wed. Together they traveled back to Nashville in the autumn of 1791 and presented themselves to the community as husband and wife.

Again the timing is off. Documents relating to the estate of John Donelson and drafted in January 1791 list Rachel as "Rachel Jackson." And various evidence demonstrates that the couple were back in Nashville by that spring. The assertion that they were married in Natchez is also open to dispute, as no record of a ceremony has been found nor witness to the event.

The most likely explanation is that Jackson and Rachel, impatient at the legal impediment to their love, eloped to Natchez and simply began to cohabit. What were their long-term plans? They themselves probably didn't know. Like many other young lovers, they couldn't see past the moment of their infatuation. One thing is certain: Jackson didn't know he would one day become a candidate for president and have to explain his actions to the world. He was twenty-two, had no particular prospects, and was in love. Rachel was the best thing in his life, and he would risk everything else—which wasn't much, at this point—to be with her.

They probably guessed that any controversy would die down. Robards would divorce Rachel. If they returned to Nashville the neighbors would find other things to gossip about. Life would go on.

And so it did. Whether they arrived in Nashville in the spring or the autumn of 1791—in either case, after the news of Robards's divorce action—they did so as husband and wife. No one asked to see a divorce decree or a marriage license. The Donelson clan closed around Rachel and her new husband, judging him a great improvement over the old one.

The union, however irregularly accomplished, provided Jackson an emotional security he had never experienced. Fatherless since birth, motherless since his early teens, with neither surviving siblings nor close cousins, Jackson made Rachel the emotional center of his universe. "My Dearest Heart," he wrote her on one occasion when his job took him away, "It is with the greatest pleasure I sit down to write you. Though I am absent my heart rests with you. With what pleasing hopes I view the future period when I shall be restored to your arms, there to spend my days in domestic sweetness with you, the Dear Companion of my life." Rachel became the one unchallengeable truth in Jackson's fractious and often violent world. His many enemies leveled all manner of allegations against him in his long career in public life, but no one ever questioned his utter faithfulness and devotion to Rachel.

Consequently he was embarrassed and angered when he discovered, on a working visit to Jonesboro in late 1793, that Robards's divorce from Rachel had only just been granted. Robards had started the process more than two years earlier but not finished it till now. This discomfiting news, besides reviving the troublesome questions of Jackson and Rachel's elopement, revealed that even their purported marriage was illegal. Overton suggested a quiet wedding ceremony to settle the matter. "To this suggestion he replied that he had long since been married," Overton recalled.

Yet Overton pointed out that whatever Jackson and Rachel might think, the courts had their own logic. Jackson reluctantly succumbed to Overton's reasoning, and in January 1794 he and Rachel exchanged vows before a Nashville justice of the peace. And there the matter rested for several years, till Jackson and Rachel almost forgot it had ever been an issue.

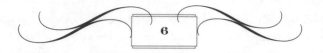

6

REPUBLICANS AND

REVOLUTIONARIES

The most important accomplishment of the first Congress elected under the 1787 Constitution was approval of the ten amendments that became known, after ratification by the states, as the Bill of Rights. Antifederalists had demanded these as their price for accepting the Constitution, and the federalists couldn't figure out how to say no. A more modest feat of the first legislature was putting Andrew Jackson briefly out of work. When Congress created the Southwest Territory— bordered on the east by the states of Virginia, North Carolina, and Georgia; on the north by the Ohio River; on the west by the Mississippi; and on the south by Spanish Florida—it deprived North Carolina of its western half and Jackson of his job as North Carolina's western solicitor.

Yet the work had to be done, whether by an employee of North Carolina or of the federal government. Jackson pointed this out to William Blount, the governor of the new federal territory, who thereupon named him attorney for the Mero District of the Southwest Territory.

Blount was Jackson's first political patron. A more promising mentor would have been hard to imagine, at least at first. Blount was the oldest of his father's thirteen children (who confusingly included, besides William, a son named Willie, pronounced, perhaps even more confusingly, "Wylie"). William fought in the American Revolution under Horatio Gates, before and after which he served in the North Carolina legislature. He represented North Carolina in the Confederation Congress and at the Philadelphia constitutional convention. Blount's ardent federalism, in a state full of antifederalists, made him an obvious candidate for governor of the new Southwest Territory when the federal government got around to creating it.

Blount's interest in the southwest was more than political, however. Since the mid-1780s he had speculated heavily in lands along the Tennessee River, and he hoped to employ his political power to make those speculations pay. This was nothing unusual in an era when speculation was America's national pastime and when many supporters of the federal Constitution didn't bother to deny that ratification would greatly increase the value of their speculative interests. At first Blount confined his political fiddling to negotiations with the Cherokees and other Indians, who were enticed and coerced into ceding territory to white settlers. As long as the Indians were the only victims of his legerdemain, he continued to be popular.

Some of his popularity rubbed off on Jackson. Within months of appointment as district attorney, Jackson was honored by being named a trustee of Davidson Academy, the first educational establishment in the Cumberland and the forerunner of the University of Nashville.

Jackson's chores as attorney for the state, and as trustee of the academy, didn't come close to filling his time. He took on other clients, who often lacked money to pay counsel and so offered land deeds instead. Cash was a chronic problem on the frontier, and other items circulated in its place. Corn, cattle, and horses filled in for money, but nothing was so ubiquitous as paper representing land. In time prices for goods and services came to be quoted in acres, with "six-forty" representing a square mile, or 640 acres, "three-twenty" half a square mile, and so on. Jackson afterward remarked that during this period he accepted enough land in fees "to make a county, if all in one tract."

His work took him from one end of the Mero District to the other. Conceivably he envisioned himself entering elective politics one day, but whether he did or didn't his exposure to all aspects of western life was perfect training for a future candidate. He encountered people at their best, when he won his clients' cases, and at their worst, when he didn't. He learned to handle himself in difficult situations, which not infrequently involved physical combat. Years later he offered advice to a young man who carried a stick for self-defense:

> If any one attacks you, I know how you'll fight with that big black stick of yours. You'll aim right for his head. Well, sir, ten chances to one he'll ward it off; and if you *do* hit him, you won't bring him down. No, sir, you take the stick *so* [grasping the stick to demonstrate], and punch him in the stomach, and you'll drop him.
>
> I'll tell you how I found that out. When I was a young man practicing law in Tennessee, there was a big bullying fellow that wanted to pick a quarrel with me, and so trod on my toes. Supposing it accidental, I said nothing. Soon after, he did it again, and I began to suspect his object. In a few minutes he came by a third time, pushing against me violently, and evidently meaning *fight*. He was a man of immense size, one of the very biggest men I ever saw. As quick as a flash, I snatched a small rail from the top of a fence, and gave him the point of it full in his stomach. Sir, it doubled him up. He fell at my feet, and I stamped on him. Soon he got up *savage*, and was about to fly at me like a tiger. The bystanders made as though they would interfere. Says I, "Gentlemen, stand back, give me room, that's all I ask, and *I'll* manage him." With that I stood ready with the rail pointed. He gave me one look, and turned away a whipped man.

*B*eyond the courtroom battles and the street fights, Jackson moonlighted as a merchant and speculator. The circumstances and extent of his trade are hard to discern, but fragmentary records show him trafficking in a wide variety of goods. In the summer of 1795 he and a partner paid $644.80 for "contingent expences arising on the preparation, carriage, boating &c. of a cargo of merchandize" purchased in Philadelphia and delivered to Nashville. These goods were sold at a Nashville store Jackson operated with his brother-in-law Samuel Donelson. Its inventory included butcher knives, sharpening files, stirrup irons, silk hose, ladies' hats, pocket handkerchiefs, calico, linen, coffee, tea, sugar, raisins, and wine.

But Jackson's trading instincts revealed themselves most plainly in his numerous transactions involving land. During his first few years in Nashville, he seems to have made little overt effort to purchase land; most of his acquisitions were in payment for services rendered. But on May 12, 1794, he entered into a partnership with John Overton to buy and sell much larger quantities of land. According to their agreement, the partners were "to bear an equal proportion of all purchases, losses, and expenses, and to receive an equal part of all profits, advantages, and emoluments arising from the lands so purchased." Two days later the Jackson-Overton partnership contracted to purchase 15,000 acres for 500 pounds. (To ease their chronic money shortage, westerners traded in three currencies: American dollars, British pounds, and Spanish pesos.) The day after that, Jackson and Overton acquired another 10,000 acres for 400 pounds, and in July 30,000 acres for 1,000 pounds. In May 1795 they picked up another 25,000 acres in two separate transactions that were part of a larger, more complicated scheme (as indicated by the nominal purchase price of 10 shillings).

The complications increased. Overton and Jackson transferred land between themselves. Jackson entered into partnership with others besides Overton. But the worst complications arose from the fact that title to much of the land wasn't at all clear. Only a minor portion of the Mero District had been legally acquired from the Indians by treaty—mainly the 1791 Treaty of Holston with the Cherokees. The rest was up for grabs (as indicated by a 1783 North Carolina law commonly called the Land Grab Act, authorizing settlers to claim western land still owned by Indians). Much of the land Jackson and Overton acquired fell outside the area of authorized settlement. In the spring of 1795 Jackson traveled to Philadelphia to purchase goods for his store and dispose of some of his and Overton's tracts. Overton advised him to be "candid and unreserved with the purchasers with respect to the situation and quality of the lands and particularly inform them that they are situated without the Treaty of Holston." But then Overton had second thoughts, concluding that candor might impede a profitable sale. He wrote in the margin beside his earlier advice: "This clause to your own discretion; perhaps it would be best to raise as few difficulties [as possible]."

Jackson encountered difficulties enough without raising any of his own. Jackson and Overton paid very little cash for the land they acquired; the great majority of their purchases were on credit, which meant that they had to sell land at a profit in order to finance further speculation. But the market for western land rose and fell on the state of relations with the Indians and with the British in Canada and the Spanish in Louisiana, on the vagaries in the money supply, and on the intangibles that affect every speculation. In the spring of 1795 supply outstripped demand, and Jackson had trouble locating a buyer in Philadelphia. "To my sad experience I found nothing doing, no purchaser but Mr. Allison," Jackson wrote Overton on the way home. David Allison was a merchant and speculator who had lived in Nashville but now worked out of Philadelphia. More savvy than Jackson, he let the visitor stew through what Jackson called "difficulties such as I never experienced," before Jackson gave in and accepted Allison's price for 50,000 acres. More than that, Jackson accepted Allison's note in payment for the land. Believing Allison's credit good, Jackson endorsed the note and used it to pay for the trade merchandise he required for his store. This made him liable for Allison's willingness and capacity to pay. In the meantime it cast a pall over the trip and an uncharacteristic discouragement over Jackson. "I am very much fatigued, even almost unto death," he told Overton.

His troubles didn't end on his reaching home. Samuel Donelson, who traveled to Louisville to check on the goods Jackson had shipped from Philadelphia, wrote to say there had been a delay. The wagons from Philadelphia to Fort Pitt (Pittsburgh) were slow arriving, and the first boat heading down the Ohio to the Cumberland was full. So Jackson's goods were placed on another boat, manned by an associate of the shippers. The transfer produced further delays. "They have not the smallest expectation that his boat will arrive here before theirs starts for the mouth of the Cumberland," Donelson said. He added that he had been haranguing the shippers to get things moving and would continue to do so. "I shall use all industry I possibly can to forward the boat on." But Jackson had better consider alternative plans.

Worse news arrived from Jackson's suppliers in Philadelphia. "We are sorry so soon after your departure to follow you with the advice that any notes or acceptances of David Allison's now falling due are not generally or regularly paid, and that there is little reason to expect he will be more punctual hereafter." They added, "We shall have to get our money from you." But Jackson didn't have the money, and he wouldn't get it till he sold his goods.

The dunning continued. Jackson received a notice from another Philadelphia firm to which he had signed over an Allison note. Allison's liquidity had not revived. "His note therefore that we received from you for goods which is due on the 13th of next month in all probability will not be paid by him. We therefore request you will make provision for the same."

Jackson was stuck. He couldn't pay his suppliers till his customers paid him, and he wouldn't have enough customers to do so till the rest of his goods arrived. In Jackson's day debt was a serious matter. People went to prison for debt. Jackson couldn't know that Allison would be imprisoned for the debts that now entangled Jackson or that Allison would die in prison after a degrading year there. But he knew others who ended up behind bars when the money ran short, and he took the intended lesson from their experience.

The result was that he abandoned his mercantile business. He sold the store—literally lock, stock, and barrel—to Elijah Robertson, the brother of Nashville cofounder James Robertson. With the proceeds he paid his Philadelphia creditors, and he walked away congratulating himself that the fiasco hadn't been worse.

A small but not insignificant aspect of Jackson's business during this early period was commerce in slaves. The great debate over slavery, which would grow in strength and virulence during the rest of Jackson's life, was just beginning. The republican premise of the American Revolution, and in particular the ringing egalitarianism of the Declaration of Independence, with its unqualified assertion that "all men are created equal," prodded consciences in several northern states to abolish slavery. Vermont and Massachusetts did so at once; Pennsylvania and some other states mandated gradual abolition. Yet these were relatively painless gestures, as slavery had never figured centrally in the northern economies. The decision by Congress in 1787 to bar slavery from the Northwest Territory fell into the same pro forma category—symbolically important but practically of little immediate effect.

In the southern states and the Southwest Territory, slavery played a much larger role than in the North. Slaves formed the backbone of plantation labor in the Carolinas and Georgia and a lesser though still substantial portion of the workforce elsewhere. Whether southern consciences were more calloused than their northern counterparts during this period is open to question; certainly the cost of abolition would have been higher to the South than it was to the North. In any event, the South held on to its slaves.

If Jackson ever reflected on the underlying moral issues involved in slavery, he kept such thoughts to himself. Did he think slavery was a good thing? No, or at least he never said he did—unlike numerous apologists for the peculiar institution, especially toward the end of Jackson's life. But many things on earth weren't good, including war, famine, and disease. Jackson didn't second-guess the Creator regarding those existential evils, and he didn't second-guess the Creator—who, on Jackson's reading of the Bible, allowed bound labor—regarding slavery.

Jackson's involvement with slavery began almost inadvertently. He acquired what appears to have been his first slave—a young woman named Nancy, in 1788—not by purchase but in exchange for legal services rendered to a client who ran short of cash. Two years later he and Rachel received two more slaves, named George and Molly, as part of the settlement of John Donelson's estate.

Gradually Jackson began buying and selling slaves outright. In July 1791 he purchased a slave named Tom, "about seven and twenty years old," according to the bill of sale, for 60 pounds. In December of that year, he bought six-year-old Aaron for 100 pounds. He acquired Peg, "about twenty-six years old," in January 1793 for services rendered, and Roele in November for 150 dollars. In 1794 he purchased Hannah and her child Bet for 80 pounds, another Betty and her children Hannah and Tom for 125 pounds, and Mary for 233 dollars. In 1795 he bought an unnamed (in the surviving record) slave for 175 dollars. In 1796 he bought two slave boys, named Sawney and Charles, for an unspecified sum. In 1797 he sold and then bought back a teenage slave named Suck, in each transaction for 290 dollars.

These almost certainly were not the sum of Jackson's dealings in slaves, but their relatively modest number indicates that he was a slaveholder rather than a slave trader. The lands he acquired included farms that had to be plowed and sown and weeded and harvested. His slaves worked those properties. In 1796 he purchased—for seven hundred dollars—a square mile of land he called Hunter's Hill. There, on the south bank of the Cumberland above Nashville, he built a home for Rachel and himself. (Ironically or otherwise, the original white claimant to the property was Lewis Robards.) Several of Jackson's slaves lived and worked at Hunter's Hill, in the fields and around the house.

By the mid-1790s, despite his failure as a merchant, Jackson had established the basis for his future material success. He was wealthy in land, which wasn't worth much in anything else yet but someday would be. The formula for western wealth was simple (and was the same as it had been for generations and would be for generations more): get there early, acquire land cheap, wait for more settlers to arrive, and sell at a profit. It was how a man grew up with the country, and it was what Jackson intended to do.

*I*n the summer of 1789, while Jackson was settling into Nashville, while George Washington and the federal Congress settled into New York, and while the state of Franklin settled into the sea of history and myth, a very unsettling series of events began unfolding in Europe. The people of Paris revolted against King Louis XVI with a force that surprised even them and astonished most onlookers. Americans initially embraced the French assertion of popular rights, as an extension of the cause they had set in motion more than a decade earlier. "The convulsions in France are attended with some disagreeable circumstances," Benjamin Franklin observed, "but if by the struggle she obtains and secures for the nation its future liberty and a good constitution, a few years' enjoyment of those blessings will amply repair all the damages their acquisition may have occasioned. God grant that not only the love of liberty but a thorough knowledge of the rights of man may pervade all the nations of the earth, so that a philosopher may set his foot anywhere on its surface and say, 'This is my country.' "

Such was easier for Franklin to say than for some of his compatriots, in that Franklin died before the French Revolution was a year old, before the disagreeable circumstances to which he referred turned really bloody. The revolution became a civil war as the aristocracy struggled desperately to preserve their privileges and then their lives, and ultimately an international war as Britain and France's other neighbors tried to prevent the spread of the revolutionary infection. At this point Americans began to take sides— not officially, as President Washington responded to the outbreak of war in Europe by declaring American neutrality, but emotionally, as Americans reacted to the events in strikingly divergent ways. Thomas Jefferson, the author of the Declaration of Independence and at this point Washington's secretary of state, cheered for France. The "liberty of the whole earth," Jefferson said, depended on the ability of republican France to fend off the attacks by its reactionary rivals. Appealing to the alliance with France by which the United States had won its independence, Jefferson argued that American honor and necessity required a tilt toward Paris. Alexander Hamilton, Washington's secretary of the Treasury and closest confidant, took the opposite view. Whatever the initial merits of the French Revolution, Hamilton judged, they had been washed away in the blood of the Terror. Real liberty required restraining France and restoring order in Europe. Britain was trying to do just that and therefore deserved American support.

The argument over the French Revolution was about more than the affairs of Europe. It ran to the heart of the arguers' views of government and the people. In holding for France, Jefferson and his followers—many of whom had opposed ratification of the Constitution—signaled their continuing confidence in the people as against government, their preference for the principles of 1776 over those of 1787. They believed the people were naturally good and required only opportunity and encouragement to manifest their goodness. Less government was better than more, and the state governments were better than the central government. By contrast, Hamilton and his followers distrusted human nature and relied on government to keep it in check. They had supported the Constitution of 1787, which they conceived as a corrective to the libertarian excesses of 1776. They continued to try to strengthen government against the people, and the federal government against the states.

The split between Jefferson's crowd, who called themselves Republicans, and Hamilton's, the Federalists, acquired economic and regional overtones. The Federalists were strong among the merchant and monied classes, especially in the Northeast. The Republicans looked to the landed folk, particularly the planters and farmers of the South and West. Each difference tended to reinforce the others, so that by the mid-1790s Republicans and Federalists glared at each other across a widening gulf of ideology, economics, and section.

The glaring got ugly during Washington's last years as president. Washington professed to be above partisan politics, but his administration drifted toward Hamilton's conservative, pro-British Federalism, causing Jefferson to quit in disgust. This freed Washington to drift further toward the Federalists. In 1795 he sent John Jay, Hamilton's coauthor (along with James Madison) on the *Federalist Papers* and currently chief justice of the Supreme Court, to London to negotiate a treaty of friendship and commerce with Britain. American merchants sought an end to British seizures of American ships—the result of Britain's blockade of France—and greater access to British markets. They and their sailors additionally wanted the British to stop kidnapping—"impressing"—American seamen alleged to have deserted from the British navy. Finally, Washington hoped to persuade the British to complete their evacuation of the Ohio Valley. Jay succeeded in opening the British East Indies to American commerce, and he obtained a paper promise that the British would evacuate forts in the Northwest. But the other issue—in particular, the seizure of American ships and sailors—went unresolved.

Hamilton and the Federalists, and Washington, were willing to accept this half loaf, and the president laid Jay's treaty before the Senate for ratification. But Jefferson and the Republicans condemned it as a sellout of everything the United States ought to stand for. They were especially incensed by the secrecy surrounding the negotiation of the treaty, as it smacked of the aristocracy they thought they had overthrown. Jay was hanged in effigy by angry Republicans, who also hurled rocks at the head of the real Hamilton. The treaty cleared the Senate but by the slimmest of margins. The Republicans tried to block the treaty in the House of Representatives, stalling an essential appropriations bill. Yet this failed, too, leaving the Republicans to gnash their teeth in frustration.

*J*ackson encountered the partisan warfare on his visit to Philadelphia, again the nation's capital. "What an alarming situation," he wrote in October 1795 to Nathaniel Macon, a congressman from North Carolina. "Will it end in a civil war, or will our country be relieved from its present ignominy by the firmness of our representatives in Congress?" Jackson wasn't a party man, but all his instincts were with the Republicans. He despised Britain as much as ever, and he distrusted those who favored the wealthy and wanted to transfer power from the states to the central government. He joined the Republicans in decrying the Jay treaty. He urged Macon to oppose the treaty and thereby "have the insulting, cringing, and ignominious child of aristocratic secrecy removed, erased, and obliterated from the archives of the grand republic of the United States." Jackson followed certain Republicans in declaring the treaty unconstitutional. "I say unconstitutional because the Constitution says that the president by and with the advice and consent of the Senate is authorized to make treaties; but in the present treaty the advice of the Senate was not required by the president prior to the formation of the treaty, nor the outlines of said treaty made known to the Senate until after made." Jackson cited Emmerich von Vattel, the distinguished scholar of the law of nations, to the effect that sovereigns are merely agents of the nations they represent and ought not to go beyond what they have reason to believe the people of their nations desire. "The president (from the remonstrance from all parts of the Union) had reason to presume that the nation of America would not have ratified the treaty, notwithstanding the 20 aristocratic nabobs of the Senate had consented to it."

Jackson's anger at the Jay treaty might have passed without issue but for a political coincidence. A 1795 census of the Southwest Territory revealed that the region contained 67,000 free persons (not including Indians) and 11,000 slaves. As the threshold for forming a state was sixty thousand ("counting the whole of the free persons . . . adding three-fifths of all other persons," in the slavery-obfuscating language of the day), the territory's political classes set to work writing a constitution and otherwise preparing for admission to the Union. A constitutional convention gathered at Knoxville in January 1796. Jackson joined James Robertson and three other delegates representing Davidson County.

Jackson's decision to attend the convention marked a crucial turn in his career path, although it didn't seem so at the time. Persons trained in the law were comparatively rare on the frontier, and Jackson would have seemed a shirker had he resisted selection to the Davidson delegation. Perhaps he sensed that a good showing at Knoxville would lead to greater things. More likely he went because his friends and colleagues urged him to, and he had nothing to keep him away.

As matters developed, he made his presence felt from the start. The records of the convention are incomplete, leaving Jackson's precise role uncertain. But the memories of his colleagues there indicated that he took an active, if sometimes indirect, part in the convention's work. "Jackson, though exerting a paramount influence in its deliberations, made few important motions himself," Francis Blair asserted. "His method was to have someone who agreed with him—always some earlier settler than himself—make the desired motion. Then he would second it and speak at once powerfully in its support." Blair wasn't at the convention and apparently had this from someone who was. Yet he spoke from his own personal observation of Jackson when he described the style that long characterized Jackson's speech.

He was not then or ever afterward what is commonly termed an orator. But he was a fluent, forceful and convincing speaker. When he addressed a body of men, whether jury, convention or political mass meeting, he talked to them. He did not orate. He had none of the arts of oratory, so-called. His voice, though strong and penetrating, was untrained. He had no idea of modulation, but let his inflections follow his feelings, naturally, as he went along. His gesticulation was even less trained and artful than his voice. About the only gestures he knew were the raising of both hands above his head to indicate reverence or veneration; the spreading of both arms wide out to indicate deprecation; and the fierce pointing of his long, gaunt forefinger straight forward, like a pistol, to indicate decision, dogmatism or defiance. And candor compels me to say that he used that forefinger more than any other limb or member in his gesticulation.

His vocabulary was copious and he never stood at a loss for a word to express his sense. When perfectly calm or not roused by anything that appealed to his feelings rather than to his judgment, he spoke slowly, carefully and in well-selected phrase. But when excited or angry he would pour forth a torrent of rugged sentences more remarkable for their intent to beat down opposition than for their strict attention to the rules of rhetoric or even syntax.

But in all situations and mental conditions his diction was clear and his purpose unmistakable. No one ever listened to a speech or a talk from Andrew Jackson who, when he was done, had the least doubt as to what he was driving at.

At the constitutional convention Jackson argued against an early proposal for a unicameral state legislature. Whether from an honest admiration of Congress or from a calculated judgment that flattery would help the state constitution receive the required federal approval, he contended that what suited the national government ought to suit a new state. The convention swung to his side and approved a dual legislature.

By at least one account, Jackson played a pivotal role in selecting the name of the new state. Several delegates from the region around Knoxville wanted to revive the name Franklin. Other delegates wished to honor Washington. Jackson thought too many states already had been named for individuals (Virginia, Maryland, the Carolinas, and Georgia for English monarchs; New York, Pennsylvania, and Delaware for the favorites of monarchs). Four years earlier Kentucky had graced itself with an Indian name, and Jackson thought Tennessee should follow the example, keeping the name of the river that had made the first settlements possible. Years later, a Jackson partisan (who wasn't at Knoxville) said Jackson had praised the melodiousness of "Tennessee" as a word that had "as sweet a flavor on the tongue as hot corn-cakes and honey." Perhaps he did note the euphony, but simile wasn't Jackson's natural mode. Whatever his precise argument, after he seconded James Robertson's motion that the state be called Tennessee, the motion carried by a large majority.

The convention concluded its work in early February 1796 and sent the draft constitution east. Thomas Jefferson called it "the least imperfect and most republican of any of the American States'," which was precisely why the same Federalists in Congress who supported the Jay treaty objected to it. The presidential election of 1796 was approaching, and unlike the uncontested coronations of George Washington, this one would be fought out. Tennessee leaned strongly Republican, which boded ill for the Federalist candidate, John Adams, and well for his Republican rival, Jefferson. The theory of self-government counted too heavily to keep a new state out of the Union indefinitely, but some Federalists hoped to keep it out till after the balloting for president. As things happened, the Republicans and republicanism got the better of the Federalists, and after some minor delay Tennessee was admitted. But in the bargain the Federalists limited Tennessee's representation in the House of Representatives to a single congressman until after the census of 1800.

That single congressman was Andrew Jackson. The Knoxville convention had afforded the first opportunity for the politically ambitious of Tennessee to gather in a single place and size one another up, and they were sufficiently impressed by the young lawyer from Nashville to conclude that he ought to represent the new state at Philadelphia. Jackson later claimed that he could have been chosen senator had he wished but that he declined because he did not want to make a career in politics or be gone from Nashville for the length of a senator's term. Perhaps he could have been chosen, but until March 15, 1797, he couldn't have been seated in the Senate, as he lacked the required thirty years of age. In any event, his name was put forward for congressman, and in October 1796 he was elected, essentially without opposition.

For the second time in a little over a year, he set out on the long ride to Philadelphia. He was forty-two days on the road and wore out two horses before entering Philadelphia on a third horse (which he kept for many years). He arrived in early December as Congress was convening for what in those days was its short term. He heard Washington's farewell address, in which the departing president warned his compatriots against the poison of partisanship and the insidiousness of entanglements in the affairs of other nations. " 'Tis our true policy to steer clear of permanent alliances with any portion of the foreign world," Washington declared.

Jackson endorsed these sentiments but took the highly unusual step of protesting the address. During Washington's two terms till now, Congress had responded to the president's annual message with an innocuous message of its own, passed by a pro forma voice vote. But the partisanship of the campaign for Washington's successor inspired Republicans in Congress to make a fight over the gesture. Jackson joined eleven other members of the House in voting against accepting Washington's speech. Jackson took issue with Washington on some substance. "From the president's speech it would seem that the British were doing us no injury, committing no depredations, that all the depredations on our commerce was done by the French nation, when on the contrary from the best calculations that can be made the British capture twenty to one," he wrote a friend. But his principal complaint was against the whole idea of the president's speech, which aped, he thought, the English king's speeches to Parliament. And the response by Congress simply ratified the practice, besides sounding too much like Parliament's answer to the king. "In my mind, this address of Congress to the President was a servile imitation of that custom," he said later. "My vote was not against the address as such, but against the custom, or the servile imitation of a kingly custom that it grew out of."

Jackson's objection would resonate once the Republicans claimed the presidency, and Jefferson would abandon the practice of delivering the president's annual message in person before Congress. (The practice would not be revived until the twentieth century, by Woodrow Wilson.) Meanwhile the freshman congressman from Tennessee made his presence felt on another subject. In 1793 John Sevier and the Tennessee militia had conducted a reprisal expedition against Cherokees who had attacked settlements in eastern Tennessee. The campaign had been successful but expensive, and Sevier and the others hoped for compensation from the federal government. Jackson sponsored a resolution authorizing payment.

The War Department objected, claiming that Sevier and the militiamen had overstepped the bounds of frontier defense and conducted an unauthorized campaign of aggression. Jackson disagreed most vigorously. The measures taken against the Cherokees were "just and necessary," he said. "When it was seen that war was waged upon the state, that the knife and the tomahawk were held over the heads of women and children, that peaceable citizens were murdered, it was time to make resistance. . . . I trust it will not be assuming too much if I say that, being an inhabitant of the country, I have some knowledge of this business. From June to the end of October"—in 1793—"the militia acted entirely on the defensive, when twelve hundred Indians came upon them, carried their station and threatened to attack the seat of government itself"—Knoxville. Jackson went on to say that even if the campaign had been unwarranted, the men who stood to lose should payment be denied were the rank and file of the militia, who put down plows and tools and risked their lives on behalf of their families and neighbors. "As the troops were called out by a superior officer, they had no right to doubt his authority. Were a contrary doctrine admitted, it would strike at the very root of subordination. You might as well say to the soldiers, 'Before you obey the commands of your superior officer, you have a right to inquire as to the legality of the service upon which you are about to be employed, and until you are satisfied you may refuse to take the field.' " No army could operate on such a principle, and neither could a militia.

Several senior members of the House, including James Madison of Virginia and Albert Gallatin of Pennsylvania, found Jackson's case compelling, and with their support the measure passed. Congress appropriated $22,816 to reimburse the members of the Sevier expedition.

As members of Congress have always known, taking care of their constituents is the surest route to reelection. And when Jackson returned to Tennessee in March 1797, following the adjournment of Congress, with nearly twenty-three thousand dollars for his constituents, they felt well taken care of.

The only question was whether he ought to be promoted to the Senate. On the road home he celebrated his thirtieth birthday, qualifying him by age for the upper house. Shortly thereafter the Senate career of Jackson's former sponsor, William Blount, was cut unexpectedly short. Blount's political intrigues had gone beyond defrauding Cherokees to a sin the government of the United States was forced to take seriously: private diplomacy. With others in Tennessee, Blount considered Spanish control of the Mississippi intolerable. (The Tennessee constitutional convention had taken upon itself to insert an affirmation of freedom of the great river into the state's bill of rights. "That an equal participation in the free navigation of the Mississippi River is one of the inherent rights of the citizens of this State," the Tennessee charter declared, "it cannot, therefore, be conceded to any prince, potentate, power, person or persons whatever.") Blount allegedly plotted an attack against the Spanish in Louisiana and Florida, in order that those territories be transferred to Britain, which presumably would look kindlier on American navigational needs.

The evidence adduced against Blount consisted primarily of a letter he wrote in April 1797 to James Carey, a federal agent to the Cherokees. In this letter Blount spoke vaguely about a "plan"—vaguely enough that the Senate committee investigating the matter was forced to concede that "the plan hinted at . . . is so capable of different constructions and conjectures that your Committee at present forbear giving any decided opinion respecting it." But the very vagueness, and Blount's unwillingness, when questioned, to enlighten the committee, made it appear all the more sinister. At a moment when war with either Britain or France appeared imminent, the administration of John Adams didn't want Blount or anyone else embroiling the United States in troubles with Spain. Prodded by the president, the Senate voted to expel Blount. To ensure that he not return, the House moved to impeach him, but the Senate decided it would be silly to hold a trial in which the penalty upon conviction would be removal from the Senate of someone already removed.

Expulsion from the Senate on grounds of defending the right of Tennesseans to navigate the Mississippi made Blount a hero in his home state. On his return from Philadelphia he was at once elected to the state senate and named its speaker. Jackson had defended Blount against his accusers, partly out of loyalty and partly because he agreed that Spain's choke hold on the Mississippi must be broken. Blount appreciated the support and helped engineer Jackson's election by the state legislature to the federal Senate.

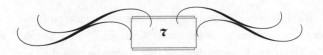

FIGHTING WORDS

Where the Cherokees came from is a difficult question. One strain of Cherokee myth made them one of those tribes that didn't come from anywhere: they had always lived in the southern Appalachian region, which the Great Spirit gave them at the creation of the earth. Another version related a migration from some forgotten former home. Linguistic and archaeological evidence points to the vicinity of the Great Lakes, as does a tradition among the Delaware Indians of having defeated the Cherokees there and driven them south.

However they reached the highlands of what would become the western Carolinas and eastern Tennessee, they were firmly entrenched in that neighborhood when Hernando de Soto marched north from Florida in the spring of 1540. De Soto had helped Francisco Pizarro conquer Peru several years earlier, and he hoped to achieve a similar success in North America. De Soto picked up the name Chilakee ("other people") for the Cherokees, apparently from their neighbors, but neither the name nor the people it signified helped him find what he was really looking for—gold— and so he marched off. The Spanish forgot the region and its inhabitants for more than a century, and no other Europeans followed them there.

During this period the Cherokees perfected their mastery of their mountain home. They were the most aggressive people of the region, deeming war the sublime human endeavor. "War is their principal study, and their greatest ambition is to distinguish themselves by military actions," observed an Englishman who encountered them in the eighteenth century. "Their young men are not regarded till they kill an enemy or take a prisoner." The old men of the tribe, though long past fighting age themselves, "use every method to stir up a martial ardor in the youth." More effective—youth being youth—were the urgings of the fair sex. "The women (who as among whites know how to persuade by praises or ridicule the young men to what they please) employ their art to make them warlike." Every family vied for distinction on the warpath. "Those houses in which there's the greatest number of scalps are most honored. A scalp is as great a trophy among them as a pair of colours among us." The Cherokees themselves avowed their devotion to war. When whites attempted to arrange a peace settlement between the Cherokees and the Tuscaroras, the Cherokee leaders objected: "We cannot live without war. Should we make peace with the Tuscaroras, we must immediately look out for some others with whom we can be engaged in our beloved occupation."

The Cherokees' penchant for war survived their first exposure to smallpox. In the 1730s the disease swept through the southern Appalachians, killing as many as half the Cherokees. This had predictably disruptive effects on the social life of the tribe, but the face the Cherokees presented to the world was nearly as formidable as ever. The French and British vied for their allegiance, causing the Cherokees to send diplomats to the European settlements and even to England itself. In London a Cherokee delegation arranged an alliance with the British Crown in exchange for firearms and ammunition. A young colonel in Virginia, charged with defending that colony against the French and France's Indian allies, was delighted at the news. "They are more serviceable than twice their number of white men,"

George Washington declared. "Their cunning and craft cannot be equaled. Indians are the only match for Indians." On second thought revising his estimate upward, Washington added, "It is certain that five hundred Indians have it in their power to more annoy the inhabitants than ten times their number of white men."

The Cherokees helped the British against the French, but they also helped themselves against the British. They allowed the British to build a fort—Fort Loudon—in eastern Tennessee, in exchange for more weapons, but when the British reneged on their end of the bargain and then insulted several members of the tribe, the Cherokees attacked the fort, killed many of its defenders, and drove off the rest.

The assault triggered a war between the British and the Cherokees, which outlasted the French and Indian War. The British drove deep into Cherokee territory, against the Cherokee villages. The destruction the British wreaked caused even some of their own soldiers to wince. Lieutenant Francis Marion (soon to become famous for his exploits against the British) recorded:

> We proceeded, by Colonel Grant's orders, to burn the Indian cabins. Some of the men seemed to enjoy this cruel work, laughing heartily at the curling flames, but to me it appeared a shocking sight. Poor creatures, thought I, we surely need not grudge you such miserable habitations. But when we came, according to orders, to cut down the fields of corn, I could scarcely refrain from tears. Who, without grief, could see the stately stalks with broad green leaves and tasseled shocks, the staff of life, sink under our swords with all their precious load, to wither and rot untasted in their mourning fields?
>
> I saw everywhere around, the footsteps of the little Indian children, where they had lately played under the shade of their rustling corn. When we are gone, thought I, they will return, and peeping through the weeds with tearful eyes, will mark the ghastly ruin where they had so often played. "Who did this?" they will ask their mothers. And the reply will be, "The white people did it—the Christians did it!"

The campaign achieved its brutal objective. Though killing few Indians directly, it drove thousands of Cherokee women and children into the mountains, where they faced starvation during the coming winter. The Cherokee warriors sued for peace, deciding the British made better allies than enemies.

The Cherokees remained allies of Britain as troubles developed between the British and the Americans. And as the troubles escalated into war and the British became enemies of the Americans, so did the Cherokees. They were joined in their enmity by several other tribes who considered the nearby Americans more threatening than the distant British. In May 1776 a grand war council convened at Chota, a Cherokee town on the Little Tennessee River. War chiefs of the Cherokees, Delawares, Ottawas, Mohawks, and other tribes listened to Cornstalk, the most powerful warrior of the Shawnees, describe his own tribe's affliction in terms they all felt equally.

In a few years the Shawnees, from being a great nation, have been reduced to a handful. They once possessed land almost to the seashore, but now have hardly enough ground to stand upon. The lands where the Shawnees have but lately hunted are covered with forts and armed men. When a fort appears, you may depend upon it that there will soon be towns and settlements of white men. It is plain that the white people intend to extirpate the Indians. It is better for the red men to die like warriors than to diminish away by inches. The cause of the red men is just, and I hope that the Great Spirit who governs everything will favor us.

Cornstalk offered encouragement to those who would join him. "Now is the time to begin. No time should be lost. If we fight like men, we may hope to enlarge our bounds." He offered warning to those who held back. "If any nation shall refuse to join us now, we shall hereafter consider them the common enemy of all red men. When affairs with the white people are settled, we shall then fall upon such nations and destroy them."

All looked to Dragging Canoe, the war chief of the Cherokees. For a generation the Shawnees and Cherokees had been bitter enemies, with each tribe raiding and murdering the other at every opportunity. But when Cornstalk brought out a large and elaborate war belt and poured vermilion over it, to represent the blood of the settlers, and offered it to Dragging Canoe, the Cherokee leader accepted the present and sealed the alliance.

Ꮬ   Ꮬ   Ꮬ

John Sevier had much in common with the Cherokees, starting with his talent for war. Till Jackson stole his mantle, Sevier was widely acclaimed as the greatest Indian fighter in the American West. More than thirty times he mounted campaigns against the Cherokees and their neighbors, and every time he came home the victor.

The Seviers had originated in France, where the family name was Xavier. John's grandfather was a Huguenot—a French Protestant—who fled to London to escape religious persecution. John's father found London too English for his tastes, and his own father too French, and so he emigrated to America, far from both. He took a wife in Maryland and carried her to Virginia, where John was born in 1745. The boy grew up quickly, assisting in a store his father established for trade with the Indians and himself taking a wife at the age of sixteen. John became a trader on his own and wandered west across the mountains in pursuit of the Indians' business. In 1773 he guided his family to the Holston River on the western slope of the Smokies and constructed a trading post there.

From trading in tools, weapons, and provisions to trading in land was a small step but one fraught with the largest consequences. Sevier headed a group of speculators who signed a 1775 treaty with several Cherokee leaders entailing the transfer of a substantial tract on the Watauga and Holston rivers to the whites in exchange for two thousand pounds sterling. The sale split the Cherokee nation, with Dragging Canoe denouncing his father, Little Carpenter, for signing away the Cherokee birthright. To Sevier and the other whites he declared, "You have bought a fair land, but there is a cloud hanging over it. You will find its settlement dark and bloody."

The outbreak of the American Revolution gave Dragging Canoe and the other Cherokee irredentists an opportunity to make good on his threat. The tribes of the Chota alliance envisioned pinning the settlers between themselves on the west and the British on the east, with the result being the interlopers' destruction. For a time the alliance did wreak terror and mayhem on the American settlements. But Sevier discovered his gift for war and his fellow frontiersmen a stubbornness born of desperation, and they clung fiercely to their outposts. In July 1776, at the moment the Continental Congress was approving independence for the United States, Sevier joined the defense of Fort Watauga against Indian attackers. At the height of the siege the defenders watched in astonishment as a previously captured white girl broke away from the Indian lines, raced toward the fort, scaled the wall, and leaped down inside. The quick-thinking Sevier aided the last phase of her escape, catching the plucky lass as she plummeted toward the ground. He was impressed by her courage, and she by his strength; some years later, after the death of Sevier's first wife, they married.

The settlers soon shifted from defense to attack. Sevier led a series of campaigns against the Cherokees, burning their villages, fields, and livestock and killing as many of their warriors as he could. Midway through the so-called Chota Expedition, Sevier and his fellow commander, Arthur Campbell of Virginia, delivered an ultimatum to those Cherokees still in the field: "You know you began the war by listening to the bad counsels of the King of England and the falsehoods told you by his agents. We are now satisfied with what is done, as it may convince your nation that we can distress you much at any time when you are so foolish as to engage in war against us. If you desire peace . . . we, out of pity to your women and children, are disposed to treat with you on that subject." Sevier and Campbell told the Cherokees to dispatch six of their head men to receive the terms of peace. "If we receive no answer . . . we will then be compelled to send another strong force into your country that will be prepared to remain in it, to take possession of it as a conquered country, without making you any compensation for it."

Some of the Cherokees did sue for peace, but others remained at war, prompting Sevier to launch an offensive that became legendary along the Smokies. He hurled his force of one hundred and fifty men against the Cherokees' thousand, tracking them over the steepest summits, through the narrowest canyons, and into the remotest recesses of the mountains. With fire and sword he broke the back of the Indian resistance and became a hero in the process.

Meanwhile he found time to lead his mountaineer militia against the British and their Tory allies. As part of Cornwallis's Carolina offensive, Major Patrick Ferguson prepared to cross the divide into the region of the western waters. He issued a warning that if the rebels of that district didn't lay down their weapons at once he would seek them out and destroy them. Sevier and Colonel Isaac Shelby decided not to await Ferguson's approach but to take the battle to him. Joining forces with William Campbell, they crossed the Smokies and then the Blue Ridge, adding to their numbers as they went. In early October 1780 they caught Ferguson at King's Mountain, a flattened ridgetop where the British had dug in. If the mountaineers had attacked with bayonet, as the British expected, they would have been cut to ribbons. But they lacked bayonets and any desire to use them, relying instead on their rifles. Firing alternately from opposite sides of the plateau, they raked the British and Tory forces unmercifully. The slaughter took a bit more than an hour. Some 230 were killed (including Ferguson) and some 700 taken prisoner. After the battle several captured Tories were hanged for particularly heinous crimes. The rebels lost 28 killed and about 60 wounded.

King's Mountain was one of the great rebel victories in the Revolutionary War. Theodore Roosevelt, writing a century later, made it the centerpiece of his six-volume paean to the courage and fortitude of the American frontiersmen, *The Winning of the West*. "At a crisis in the great struggle for liberty, at one of the darkest hours for the patriot cause," Roosevelt wrote, "it was given to a band of western men to come to the relief of their brethren of the seaboard and to strike a telling and decisive blow for all America. When the three southern provinces lay crushed and helpless at the feet of Cornwallis, the Holston backwoodsmen suddenly gathered to assail the triumphant conqueror. Crossing the mountains that divided them from the beaten and despairing people of the tidewater region, they killed the ablest lieutenant of the British commander, and at a single stroke undid all that he had done."

John Sevier, as the leader of the Holston men, covered himself in glory that day and on the strength of his military reputation became the leading figure of the western district. He headed those westerners who founded the state of Franklin, and he served as its first (and only) governor. As governor he was arrested by the authorities of North Carolina, on charges of treason against that state. This simply made him more popular west of the mountains. "Had the destroying angel passed through the land and destroyed the first born in every section; had the chiefs and warriors of the whole Cherokee nation fallen upon and butchered the defenseless settlers, the feelings of retaliation and revenge would not have been more deeply awakened in their bosoms," wrote one of those westerners, more literary than most. "They had suffered with him; they had fought under him; with them he had shared the dangers and privations of a frontier life and a savage warfare; and they were not the spirits to remain inactive when their friend was in danger." Springing to action, Sevier's fellows rallied to his aid and by dire threat compelled his release. After Franklin's government folded, Sevier's neighbors elected him to the North Carolina senate. Upon North Carolina's ratification of the federal Constitution, he was elected to the new Congress as the first member from west of the mountains. He served only several months, though, till North Carolina (again) ceded its western territory to the United States, depriving Sevier of his congressional district.

Yet he soon received an appointment from President Washington as brigadier general of the Tennessee militia. He was active in the politics of the Southwest Territory and took a leading part in the territorial legislature. He continued to speculate in land and formed a business and political alliance with James Blount. The alliance paid off when, upon the admission of Tennessee to the Union, Blount went to the Senate and Sevier was elected governor.

𝓘t was as governor of Tennessee that Sevier crossed swords with Andrew Jackson. Appropriately, perhaps, the issue was swords: the swords of command in the Tennessee militia. In the autumn of 1796, as the officers of the militia prepared to choose their local commanders, Sevier strove to ensure the victory of a friend and political ally in the Mero District. His method was the premature commissioning of some recently elected junior officers thought to favor his candidate.

Or at least Jackson considered the commissioning premature. And when he discovered what was afoot, he tried to stop it. He was at the Mero election in Nashville when Sevier crony Joel Lewis read a letter from Sevier defending the commissioning. Jackson professed to be stunned. "Viewing, sir, with horror," he wrote Sevier, "a private letter from the executive of the state, produced to influence the officers to do that which, in my opinion, was an unconstitutional act, and which would establish a precedent dangerous to the rights of the people, I proceeded to reply to Mr. Lewis with some warmth."

Perhaps Jackson was genuinely horrified by what he considered the dangerous unconstitutionality of Sevier's action. But there was more to the dispute. Jackson had his eye on the militia command for himself, and he recognized that a victory for Sevier in the district elections would make his own campaign harder at the state level. It is unclear whether Sevier knew of Jackson's intent to make the race for major general, but he would have been blind not to see Jackson's ambition and naive not to guess that Jackson could be a dangerous rival. Sevier was neither blind nor naive, and he attempted to cut Jackson's legs from under him. To friends he wrote that Jackson's objections at Nashville were "the scurrilous expressions of a poor pitiful petty fogging lawyer," which ought to be "treated with contempt." Apparently this language circulated fairly widely, for Jackson heard what Sevier's supporters were saying, and he even managed to acquire a copy of Sevier's letter.

Jackson may or may not have been surprised at Sevier's campaign of sabotage, but he certainly was angry. He wrote the governor demanding to know why he had been attacked behind the veil of confidence (imperfect though it proved to be). "Why those private letters? . . . Why not (if you thought I had injured you), a letter directly to me, calling upon me for an explanation?" Jackson said he had thought he and Sevier were friends, as they had communicated cordially when Jackson was in Congress. To learn that the governor had been slandering him behind his back came as a shock. "This conduct requires an explanation and the injury done my private character and feelings requires redress."

These were fighting words, or so Jackson intended them. He had been held up to ridicule by the most powerful man in Tennessee, and neither his self-esteem nor his ambition could let the slight pass. That Sevier was also the most popular man in Tennessee, the ever-victorious Indian fighter, didn't deter Jackson from calling him out. If anything, it made Sevier a more tempting target.

But Sevier refused to fight Jackson. He had nothing to gain from a duel with the younger, less distinguished man and much to lose, including his life. So far Jackson's demand for satisfaction was a private matter, but even if it became public Sevier's reputation for courage would allow him to shrug it off. The governor couldn't be dueling every hothead who took offense at something he said or did. "The voice of calumny has more than once been busied in trying to effect my political destruction," he wrote Jackson. He went on to try to calm Jackson down. There had been a misunderstanding, he said. Jackson's words had been misrepresented. "I have had too many attacks upon my own character to be desirous of attacking that of any other citizen. Rest assured then, sir, any observations I made in the letters you have quoted were not bottomed on malice; they were the language of a man who thought himself highly injured, and if it betrayed a little imprudence, I will here add that like yourself, when passion agitates my breast I cannot view things in the calm light of mild philosophy."

Jackson accepted Sevier's explanation—for the time being. "Facts may be misstated, and it is not improbable they were," he replied. Yet tension persisted. "I feel the sweetness and necessity of protecting my feelings and reputation whenever they are maliciously injured, as sensibly as yourself or any other person." Perhaps Jackson intended this as a warning. Perhaps he was simply sharing his philosophy of life. Either way, it was something Sevier should keep in mind.

Jackson and Sevier maintained civil relations during the Senate term that commenced in the autumn of 1797. A principal issue for Tennesseans was control of the public lands in the state. The federal government contended that those public lands belonged to the United States, not to Tennessee. And in the interest of peace between whites and Indians, it sought to enforce with some rigor the treaties that preserved Indian lands to the Indians. The Tennessee government claimed the lands for itself and its citizens, and it sided with whites who had settled on the Indian lands without full clearance to do so. By favoring the Indians, Sevier said, the federal government encouraged the natives to prey upon the citizens of Tennessee. "It is painful to hear the cries of the people of this state against a partial conduct in favor of a savage tribe that can only be noticed or favoured for their atrocious murders, robberies, and a dissolute wantonness to commit every diabolical crime that could possibly suggest itself to savage imagination," he wrote Jackson. The situation had gotten so bad, Sevier said, that Tennesseans were looking to Spain for help. "A great number of people are determined to descend the Mississippi. . . . I fear one half our citizens will flock over into another government; indeed they are now doing it daily." The purpose of the federal government was to assist the states, not harm them; in this it was failing miserably. "Instead of our state in its infancy being encouraged, fostered, and matured, it appears that measures are calculating to check and destroy its happiness, if not its existence."

What Sevier advocated, and what most Tennesseans wanted, was the right to settle all the way south to the great bend of the Tennessee River. The region around Muscle Shoals was especially strategic, as it was a short portage from the Tennessee to the Tombigbee River, which connected to the Gulf of Mexico via Mobile Bay. The importance of this link was obvious to anyone in Tennessee, for it saved several hundred river miles en route to the outside world and it mooted questions about Spanish control of the Mississippi. Of course it raised new questions about Spanish control of Mobile Bay, as part of Florida, but more than a few westerners judged that Florida wouldn't stay Spanish for long. In any event, access to Muscle Shoals was a crucial first step on the way to the Gulf and to freedom and happiness for the West. "The prevention of a settlement at or near the Muscle Shoals is a manifest injury done the whole western country," Sevier told Jackson. "And as long as it is the case, we shall be debarred from the navigation which leads by the way of Mobile, perhaps an outlet to commerce equal if not superior to any in the United States."

Jackson shared Sevier's view and represented it in Philadelphia. He and the other members of the Tennessee delegation met with President Adams, and they laid before Congress a remonstrance from the Tennessee legislature asking for authorization to take control of the public lands in the state.

But neither the administration nor Congress was willing to sign over hundreds of thousands of acres simply because the Tennesseans wanted them. Tennessee wasn't the only state where the issue of public lands arose, and policy had to take account of larger questions. Besides, neither the Federalist administration nor the Federalists in Congress had any desire to encourage emigration to Tennessee, where something in the air made otherwise sensible men turn incorrigibly Republican. Adams agreed in principle to new negotiations with the Cherokees regarding the line of permitted settlement, but a fresh treaty remained far off and a resolution of the land issue even farther.

Across the Atlantic the affairs of Europe took a spectacular and ominous turn. The excesses of the French Revolution had precipitated a powerful royalist reaction, which the desperate republicans countered by appealing to a young artillery officer who had shown a gift for command in the Italian theater of the continuing and now almost continent-wide war. Napoleon Bonaparte rose to the occasion and rescued the republic. And he continued rising, like one of the rockets his artillerymen used to illuminate targets at night, till he held the fate of France in his hands. And because France figured so centrally in the affairs of Europe, he seemed to have much of the continent at his fingertips.

Andrew Jackson never met Napoleon, but in early 1798 he cheered him from afar. Many Republicans looked on the general as the savior of the French Revolution, but none embraced him more enthusiastically than Jackson—in large part because, in addition to saving the revolution, Napoleon appeared poised to spread it to England. "Bonaparte with 150,000 troops inured to conquer is ordered on the coast," Jackson wrote excitedly to James Robertson. "Do not then be surprised if my next letter should announce a revolution in England. Should Bonaparte make a landing on the English shore, tyranny will be humbled, a throne crushed, and a republic will spring from the wreck—and millions of distressed people restored to the rights of man by the conquering arm of Bonaparte."

Jackson's enthusiasm for Napoleon and France was accompanied by a disdain for John Adams and the Federalists. Though Adams showed less zeal for Britain than such arch-Federalists as Alexander Hamilton (whom Adams despised, and vice versa), he still leaned toward Britain in the war between those countries. And when the French commissioned privateers to prey on British-bound American shipping, he was inclined to treat their sins as mortal and those of Britain, which was still seizing French-bound American ships, as venial. He sent a high-level commission to Paris to register America's upset and demand satisfaction.

The diplomacy went slowly. "No news that can be relied on from our commissioners at Paris," Jackson wrote to his brother-in-law John Donelson in late January 1798. "But it is reported, and I believe on good authority, that France will not declare war on us." Yet that didn't mean the crisis was over. "There are a number in Congress, and to their strength I may add the Heads of Departments, that have a wish to declare war against that nation, or, in other words, do such acts as would in their consequences be similar to a declaration of war." The Adams administration made no attempt to be fair-minded between Britain and France, Jackson complained. "The partiality for Britain has too evidently appeared." Moreover, the Anglophiles in the administration were purging those with dissenting views. "They have fallen on a plan to remove from office every man who professes Republican principles, and fill those offices with men who will bend to the nod of the Executive. This is not mere conjecture, but is openly avowed by some of the Heads of Departments to be the rule lately established by the Executive, and this day openly avowed on the floor of Congress." Virtue, talent, and experience no longer counted, only loyalty to the administration. Jackson was deeply alarmed. "If a man cannot be led to believe as the President believes in politics (and God forbid that a majority should), he is not to fill an office in the United States. This, sir, I view as more dangerous than the establishment of religion, for it is truly an attempt to establish politics and to take away the right of thinking."

Jackson's disdain for the policies of the Adams administration was matched by his disgust at the manners of the Federalists and other easterners. To Willie Blount, the stepbrother of William Blount, Jackson wrote a description of how folks in Philadelphia settled their quarrels. "Sticks and spittle are substituted by the Eastern representatives in place of pistols. Two engagements of this kind have lately taken place on the floor of the representative branch, the first with spittle or tobacco juice, the second with a club and tongues." The result? "The expense of sixteen days spent in debating the subject in the House of Representatives. In their disgrace and expense of the Union, twelve thousand dollars. This will serve for a specimen of Eastern quarrels."

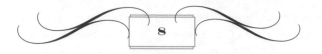

RENDERING JUDGMENT

*I*n the spring of 1798 Jackson abruptly quit the Senate. He packed the few items he had taken to Philadelphia and, with little explanation to anyone, mounted his horse and headed home. *H*e afterward remarked vaguely that the man most likely to succeed him—Daniel Smith, who did indeed take his place—could serve Tennessee in the Senate better than he could. This may have been true, but it hardly tells the full story. Jackson didn't lack confidence in his abilities. There were few things worth doing that he didn't think he could do as well as the next man.

*T*he crux of the issue was whether his work in the Senate was worth doing. Jackson gravely doubted it. So far as he could tell, the members spent their sessions in windy debates about matters of small consequence, casting ayes and nays for obscure amendments to minor bills, preening for the galleries, and treating the public business with derision. Had the senators been serious men, they wouldn't have limited themselves to "sticks and spittle" in their disputes but would have settled their differences in the honorable fashion, with pistols. Jackson took himself too seriously to waste his time on such inanities.

There was another way of putting it, less uncharitable to his fellow legislators. After three months in the House and another three in the Senate, Jackson discovered he wasn't cut out for politics, at least not legislative politics. His was an executive temperament. He could make decisions far more easily than he could make compromises. He had much greater confidence in his own judgment than in that of others. Action came naturally, patience harder. He believed a single honest man more likely to find truth than any committee. He was a born leader who couldn't make himself into a follower.

His impatience at the antics of Congress was evident to the president of the Senate, the vice president of the United States. Thomas Jefferson first encountered Andrew Jackson in Philadelphia. Years later Jefferson reportedly told Daniel Webster that Jackson was the prisoner of overpowering emotions. "His passions are terrible. When I was President of the Senate, he was Senator, and he could never speak from the rashness of his feelings. I have seen him attempt it repeatedly, and as often choke with rage."

There is reason to question the strict accuracy of these secondhand remarks. Jefferson was speaking a quarter century after the fact, amid a bitter contest for president between Jackson and John Quincy Adams. Webster, an Adams man, was trying to get the former president to disqualify Jackson, which Jefferson obligingly did. "I feel much alarmed at the prospect of seeing General Jackson President," Jefferson asserted. "He is one of the most unfit men I know of for such a place. He has very little respect for law or constitutions. . . . He is a dangerous man."

Jefferson may indeed have recalled Jackson choking with passion in the Senate, but if he did it probably had less to do with any inherently ungovernable anger in Jackson than with Jackson's vexation at how much time of the members and expense to the public were being consumed with such little effect. Perhaps other men could put up with such nonsense, but Jackson couldn't.

ᑫ   ᑫ   ᑫ

*A*nother cause drew him back from Philadelphia. Jackson missed Rachel, and he knew that she missed him. In those days of slow and tedious travel, few members of Congress brought their wives with them to the capital. The eight hundred horseback miles from Nashville to Philadelphia were particularly difficult, and Jackson didn't even consider inflicting them on Rachel. As a result, in contemplating a career in Congress he forecast many long months away from her. He didn't think he could ask that of her, and he didn't want to ask it of himself. Little of the correspondence between Jackson and Rachel survives, most having been destroyed in a fire in 1834. But what does survive reveals a husband devoted to his wife, longing to be reunited with her, and determined to make their separations fewer and shorter. As early as 1796, when personal business took him to Knoxville, Jackson wrote home: "I mean to retire from the business of public life, and spend my time with you alone in sweet retirement, which is my only ambition and ultimate wish." He remarked that it was late at night, and he'd had a long day. But he couldn't go to bed without writing to let her know he was thinking of her.

> May it give you pleasure to receive it. May it add to your contentment until I return. May you be blessed with health. May the goddess of slumber every evening light on your eyebrows and gently lull you to sleep, and conduct you through the night with pleasing thoughts and pleasant dreams. Could I only know you were contented and enjoyed peace of mind, what satisfaction it would afford me whilst travelling the lonely and tiresome road. It would relieve my anxious breast and shorten the way. May the great "I am" bless you and protect you until that happy and wished for moment arrives when I am restored to your sweet embrace, which is the nightly prayer of your affectionate husband.

Perhaps more than some other wives, Rachel missed her husband when he was gone. She worried at his travels across long stretches of wilderness, knowing of many travelers who hadn't come home. His departure for

Philadelphia to take his Senate seat apparently tested her sorely. From Knoxville, Jackson wrote Robert Hays, the husband of Rachel's sister, requesting that he look after Rachel. "I must now beg of you to try to amuse Mrs. Jackson and prevent her from fretting. The situation in which I left her (bathed in tears) fills me with woe. Indeed, sir, it has given me more pain than any event of my life."

Rachel's sorrow and fear evidently evoked physical illness, which aggravated her emotional state. Jackson inquired with every letter to friends in Nashville how she was doing, and he grew impatient when the news was scanty or absent. "It is such a neglect that I feel it sensibly," he wrote. When the news did come through, and especially when it indicated improvement, he was gratefully pleased. "I hold myself much indebted to him for his letter," he wrote of a message from one of their friends.

Nearly all husbands feel protective toward their wives, but Jackson had special reason for feeling he needed to guard Rachel and shield her from a trying world. From the start of their relationship he had been her protector, her rescuer from an abusive and vengeful spouse. Yet the very rescue—their elopement—had created other problems, initially of law and persistently of social perception, which magnified his desire to protect her. And of course, though Nashville was more civilized and secure than it had been on his arrival a decade earlier, Indians still posed a threat. Rachel was nervous for him when he traveled; he was nervous for her when he was gone.

Had Jackson felt he was doing important work in Philadelphia, he might have pushed his worries about Rachel aside. In all probability nothing would happen to her, and she'd get over her sadness and worry at his departing. But when the politicians in Philadelphia spent their time—and his—bickering over trivia and bloviating over matters of merely personal concern, he decided he could do more good for Rachel back home than for Tennessee in Philadelphia. Let the politicians handle politics; an honest man had real work to do.

Jackson's work in Nashville included much that was familiar. He resumed his land dealing and the farm operations his land acquisitions entailed. And he tried his luck at commerce again, not least because his farm operations required him to buy supplies and sell his crops, both in a market short of cash. A letter from Jackson to a Philadelphia merchant explained a typical barter arrangement: "I have come to a conclusion to purchase your merchandise, if they are assorted in such a manner as will suit the market of this country. . . . I would give four or five tracts of land of 640 acres each . . . the balance of the merchandise payable in cotton."

He also undertook something new. A few months after arriving back in Nashville Jackson received a note from John Sevier. "It has been communicated to me by several respectable characters," the governor said, "that was you appointed by the Executive one of the judges of the Superior Court of Law and Equity, they had reasons to believe you would accept the said appointment. This information is truly satisfactory to the Executive. . . . Please consider yourself as already appointed."

Why Sevier offered Jackson the judgeship is unclear. The governor already recognized in Jackson a rival; perhaps he hoped that by putting him on the state's supreme court he could divert Jackson's ambition into harmless channels.

Why Jackson accepted the job is easier to explain. His dealings in land, farming, and commerce were going well enough that he and Rachel could live on a judge's modest salary, but not so well as to entice him away from public life. Jackson hoped to achieve a certain level of material comfort, but what he really craved was respect. A seat on the state's highest court was quite an accomplishment for the poor boy with no parents.

What Sevier offered, and Jackson accepted, was an interim appointment. But three months later the Tennessee legislature made the appointment permanent.

*Y*et if Jackson wasn't cut out for writing laws, his talent for interpreting them was only marginally more obvious. His legal training had just sufficed to get him admitted to the bar, and since commencing his profession he had had neither the opportunity nor the inclination to delve more deeply into jurisprudence. Moreover, his temperament was all wrong. An impartial dispensing of justice would seem to require a dispassionate personality, but Jackson's was just the opposite. His sense of right and wrong anchored his whole outlook on life; if justice pointed one way and the law another, the law would surely lose.

On the other hand, although Jackson's personality didn't fit the judge's traditional mold, it suited his time and place. Most westerners had little patience for law per se, which often struck them as pettifoggery. Like Jackson they believed justice was something any honest man could discern. And they appreciated Jackson's decisiveness. The duties of a superior court judge included riding a circuit of several towns and villages. A story was told how one day Jackson was dispensing justice at a crossroads when the proceedings were interrupted by a local rowdy. This man, either drunk or belligerent by nature, brandished a pistol and a sheath knife and threatened homicide against Judge Jackson, against the jury, and against everyone else associated with that morning's dispensation of justice. Jackson ordered the sheriff to arrest the rowdy for contempt of court. The sheriff tried but failed. The man was too violent to be apprehended, he said. Jackson then ordered the sheriff to summon a posse. The sheriff did so but had no better luck. The bully intimidated the posse and remained at large.

Jackson by now was thoroughly irked at both the bully's bad manners and the paralysis of local law enforcement. He ordered the sheriff to summon him—Jackson—as a member of the posse. The sheriff was skeptical, but Jackson insisted and was duly enlisted to bring the bad man in.

Jackson declared a ten-minute recess in the trial. He doffed his judicial robe, took up his pistol, and strode out the door. The rowdy was ranting amid a crowd of people not far from the courtroom door. Jackson parted the crowd and approached the man, who had worked himself into a full lather. Jackson showed his gun and said, "Surrender, you infernal villain, this very instant, or I'll blow you through."

Everyone gasped, wondering how the bully would respond. To general amazement he meekly handed over his weapons and allowed himself to be led away. When the onlookers recovered their breath, one inquired why the ruffian had surrendered to a single man after holding an entire posse at bay.

"Why, when he came up, I looked him in the eye," the prisoner said, "and I saw shoot. There wasn't shoot in nary other eye in the crowd. So I says to myself, says I: Hoss, it's about time to sing small, and so I did."

Maybe things happened this way. Likely the story grew better with the telling. Whatever its strict accuracy, it captured an impression of Jackson that spread around Tennessee. Here was a man to watch, and respect.

*T*he judgeship was Jackson's for life, if he wanted it. His commission said he held the post "during good behavior," which meant he could be removed only by impeachment. But though he valued the respect that came with the position, in other ways the job was less than ideal. He had underestimated the cost of the travel the job required. "I am in possession of a very independent office," he wrote a friend, "but I sink money—the salary is too low. . . . The judiciary scarcely bears my expence." And though he himself was no Blackstone, his partners on the court were even shorter on legal training. "I cannot expect much beneficial aid from the talents of Judge [David] Campbell, although an agreeable companion." A seat was coming open. Jackson hoped it would be filled by someone who knew the law. "Should one be appointed whose legal abilities were not superior to ours, the responsibility on me would be too great."

The saving grace of the judgeship was that it didn't monopolize his time. He continued to pursue his speculative and mercantile ventures, albeit with partners who conducted most of the day-to-day operations. Even so, he regularly considered retiring from the bench. But as often as he did, his friends and supporters urged him to think again, declaring that he was more qualified than anyone else available. James Robertson recounted traveling about Tennessee and hearing the people express their "general wish and opinion" that Jackson remain on the court. Robertson added, "It is likewise the hearty wish of your friend and humble servant"—Robertson himself. Almost the entire Tennessee house of representatives and several state senators sent Jackson a statement registering their "peculiar concern" at rumors that Jackson might step down. "Talents like yours were given for public good," the petitioners asserted. "We hope at this momentous crisis, when party is raging in a most extraordinary manner"—actually, party was raging in a rather ordinary manner—"you will not retire from the service of your country and leave them to struggle with the loss."

Jackson acceded to the popular will. "Retirement to private life has been, for some time, to me a very desirable event," he explained in a public response to the appeal from the legislators. "But you have said my further services as a judge would be useful. When my services are thus called for, they belong to my country, and your voice is obeyed."

*H*e did add a condition: "if health will permit me." This wasn't a rhetorical flourish. Though generally hale so far in his life, Jackson encountered the same afflictions nearly everyone else did in that medical stone age. The causes of infectious disease still stumped the experts; smallpox, typhoid fever, cholera, and yellow fever ravaged the populated districts of the United States with disheartening frequency. A yellow fever epidemic decimated Philadelphia in 1793 and another did nearly as much damage in 1797. Disease disrupted traffic on the Mississippi almost every summer, as crews heard of people dying in New Orleans and refused to drop down the river to that infamous zone of infection.

The lesser density of population on the frontier attenuated some of the epidemics, but the frontier posed its own set of challenges to personal health. Long journeys on horseback overworked the spine; Jackson periodically complained of what he identified as rheumatism. In the winter of 1798 he slipped on an icy road and wrenched his knee, which "confined me for some days." Once a stable caught fire at Jonesboro, causing Jackson to leap out of bed to help save the horses. "During this distressing scene I was a great deal exposed, having nothing on but my shirt," he told Rachel. "I have caught a very bad cold which has settled on my lungs, occasioned a bad cough and pain in my breast." The worrisome thing about colds in those days was that no one knew if they were simply colds or the harbingers of something more serious. Pneumonia threatened travelers especially, who could be caught far from shelter by snow or, what was worse, soaking and chilling rain. Tuberculosis—"consumption"—carried away men and women otherwise in their prime and could be transmitted easily in the close quarters of carriages and roadside inns.

Life expectancies in Jackson's day were much lower than they would be two centuries later. To a considerable degree this reflected higher infant and childhood mortality: the first five years were the most lethal. Anyone tough enough to survive that stretch had a fair expectation of reasonable tenure on earth. But accidents did happen, and epidemics did occur. And even healthy people were infested by parasites of one sort or another. Malaria was endemic in much of the United States. In America the malaria parasite didn't often kill, but the "ague and fever," as the disease was called, was as unremarkable as the common cold. Intestinal parasites came and went. Lice and bedbugs were the travelers' bane, causing the fastidious to carry their own bedding and use it, even when they paid for a bed at an inn. The sexually adventurous risked venereal disease. If the disease was treated, with mercury typically, the cure might be as dangerous as the disease. If untreated, certain forms—syphilis, notoriously—could seem to subside only to return with harrowing symptoms later.

Given that his father and mother had died relatively young, and his brothers even younger, Andrew Jackson at thirty-five had reason to watch his health. His wrenched knee in fact got better, though it tended to stiffen in cold weather, and the cough he incurred rescuing the horses eventually subsided. But good health was a gift, not a guarantee.

Though Jackson agreed to remain a judge, the troubles that made him want to quit persisted. The travel kept him away from Rachel, and the expense caused them both to wonder how long their finances could bear the drain. Jackson's philosophy of serving the will of the people would become his guiding star, but for now it threatened to bankrupt him. On his rides around the circuit he pondered how to escape his predicament.

He discovered an exit in early 1802, when the command of the Tennessee militia came open. To one like Jackson, valuing respect above all, the position was the true prize of Tennessee politics. No one, not even the governor, was held in higher esteem than the major general of the militia. The pay was higher than that of a judge, a welcome point but not crucial, as, by Jackson's reading of the Tennessee constitution, he could keep his judgeship even while serving as militia commander. A judge couldn't become governor or a member of the state legislature without violating the separation of powers, but the militia was different. Or so Jackson, who had helped write the state constitution, contended. And no one effectively contradicted him.

Which was not to say no one challenged him. John Sevier did, albeit at the polls rather than in court. Sevier completed three consecutive terms as Tennessee governor in 1801 and was constitutionally required to sit out a term before running again. When Major General George Conway died and an election to succeed him was slated for February 1802, Sevier sought to parlay his reputation as an Indian fighter into gainful employment at the head of the Tennessee militia.

The simultaneous decisions of the two men to seek the militia command shattered the truce that had existed between them. In the election the field officers of each of the militia districts caucused and cast their ballots. Jackson won the votes of the officers from the Cumberland and vicinity. Sevier carried his home districts in the eastern part of the state. The result was a tie. Sevier then proposed a second ballot. Jackson refused, asserting that nothing in the constitution or any statute authorized such a revote. Instead the decision must go to the governor.

As it happened, Jackson and the new governor, Archibald Roane, had been friends since they received their licenses to practice law in Washington County, North Carolina, on the same day. Roane repaid the friendship by casting the tiebreaking vote for Jackson, who on April 1, 1802, became major general of the Tennessee militia.

*I*n many regards, the command of the militia was the best office Jackson ever held. The people of Tennessee addressed him as general and considered him the first warrior of the state. He held the post—like his judgeship—during "good behavior," which meant that he was answerable only to his conscience and the requirements of Tennessee defense. In theory he reported to the governor, but in practice he often dealt directly with the War Department in Washington.

Not surprisingly, what to Jackson were the advantages of the office were to Sevier cause for bitterness at having lost it so narrowly. By battlefield experience Sevier should have won the election easily. He had beaten the British at King's Mountain and the Indians in dozens of engagements before and since. What had Jackson done besides being captured after a skirmish and wounded resisting a shoe shine?

Sevier's annoyance at Jackson only increased when Sevier launched a campaign to reclaim the governor's house and Jackson, predictably, endorsed Roane. Sevier attacked Roane's integrity, causing Jackson to rally to his friend's defense with a counterattack in which he revived the charges of fraud against Sevier in the land deals of the previous decade. "To do this is not my wish," Jackson disclaimed, unconvincingly, in a letter to the *Tennessee Gazette*. "My only object is to exonerate Mr. Roane from the imputations maliciously circulated against him, and to prevent a character, charged with crimes of a deep dye from ascending to the executive chair, an event which would wound the character of the state and reflect disgrace upon every good citizen in it." Jackson asserted that Sevier had conspired in the destruction of the original records of land ownership and the replacement of the bona fide entries with forged claims. He alleged further that Sevier had resorted to bribery to keep the replacement quiet. Jackson reproduced letters and affidavits supporting his allegations, including a suspicious offer by Sevier of three parcels of land to a North Carolina official in exchange for altering records.

The voters of Tennessee took a more tolerant view of fraud than Jackson did, and they retired Roane in favor of Sevier. This merely moved the Jackson-Sevier feud to another level, pitting the chief executive of Tennessee against the state's highest military officer, who was also a justice of the state's superior court. Jackson's court work regularly carried him to Knoxville, then the state capital, where Sevier resided. Knoxville being a small town, the antagonists could hardly avoid each other. One day they met outside the courthouse and exchanged words. Their voices rose as their emotions engaged, and onlookers gathered around. After heated words, Sevier apparently challenged Jackson to draw arms. But since Jackson carried only a cane, against Sevier's sword, he declined. The hot language continued. Evidently Sevier alluded to Jackson's lack of military experience before becoming major general, for Jackson defended his services to the state and the nation.

"Services?" Sevier riposted. "I know of no great service you rendered the country, except taking a trip to Natchez with another man's wife."

Silence enveloped the courthouse square. Everyone realized that Sevier had crossed a fateful line. The clouded origins of Jackson's marriage to Rachel were no secret, but respect for her if not for him kept the common knowledge quiet. Now that Sevier had broken that quiet, another quiet— perhaps deadly—took its place. All strained to hear Jackson's response.

"Great God!" he said. "Do you mention *her* sacred name?"

Jackson would have had it out with Sevier at once had he been better armed. Even so, collateral shooting did erupt briefly. "One man was grazed by a bullet," eyewitness Isaac Avery said. "Many were scared, but luckily no one was hurt." Avery added, "Jackson's exclamation, 'Great God!' became a by-word among the young men at Knoxville."

By the next day Jackson's passion had subsided sufficiently that he was able to write Sevier a letter. But even after twenty-four hours his pen still scorched the page.

> The ungentlemanly expressions and gasconading conduct of yours relative to me on yesterday was in true character of yourself, and unmasks you to the world, and plainly shows that they were the ebullitions of a base mind goaded with stubborn proofs of fraud and flowing from a source devoid of every refined sentiment or delicate sensation. . . . The voice of the people has made you a governor. This alone makes you worthy of my notice or the notice of any gentleman. To the office I bear respect. . . . As such I only deign to notice you, and call upon you for that satisfaction and explanation that your ungentlemanly conduct and expressions require. For this purpose I request an interview ["interview" being the term for a duel]. . . . My friend who will hand you this will point out the time and place when and where I shall expect to see you with your friend and no other person. My friend and myself will be armed with pistols. You cannot mistake me or my meaning.

Sevier didn't want to duel Jackson. He considered the younger man an upstart against whom he had no need to defend his reputation. Besides, he was governor of Tennessee, and Tennessee law as of the previous year forbade dueling. Yet he didn't feel he could ignore the challenge. Even a hero of the Indian wars had to answer such a direct affront. So he fired back a note that matched Jackson's insult for insult—in places, word for word: "Your ungentlemanly and gasconading conduct of yesterday, and indeed at all other times heretofore, have unmasked yourself to me and to the world. The voice of the Assembly has made you a judge, and this alone has made you worthy of my notice or any other gentleman's. To the office I have respect." Sevier went on to say, in a nod to the law, "I shall wait on you with pleasure at any time and place not within the State of Tennessee, attended by my friend with pistols, presuming you know nothing about the use of any other arms. Georgia, Virginia, and North Carolina are all within our vicinity." He closed by quoting Jackson: "You cannot mistake me and my meaning."

Jackson wouldn't accept Sevier's condition. "This, sir, I view as a mere subterfuge," he replied. "Your attack was in the town of Knoxville. In the town of Knoxville did you take the name of a lady into your polluted lips. In the town of Knoxville did you challenge me to draw, when you were armed with a cutlass and I with a cane. And now, sir, in the town of Knoxville you shall atone for it or I will publish you as a coward and a poltroon." Sevier's offer to fight in a neighboring state, Jackson insisted, was "a proposition made by you to evade the thing entirely." Jackson nonetheless made a counterproposal: "If it will obviate your squeamish fears, I will set out immediately to the nearest part of the Indian boundary line." On Indian soil they could legally settle their differences. "I shall expect an answer in the space of one hour."

"I am happy to find you so accommodating," Sevier responded. "My friend will agree upon the time and place of rendezvous." But Sevier was still in no hurry to fight Jackson. He instructed his friend to tell Jackson that their meeting could take place no sooner than five days hence. Jackson would have to wait.

Jackson was outraged. He published his threatened condemnation of the governor. "To all who shall see these presents greeting—Know ye that I, Andrew Jackson, do pronounce, publish, and declare to the world that his Excellency John Sevier, Esqr., Governor, Captain General and commander in chief of the land and naval forces of the State of Tennessee, is a base coward and poltroon. He will basely insult, but has not the courage to repair the wound."

Sevier had to answer. "I am again perplexed with your scurrilous and poltroon language," he wrote. "I have constantly informed you that I would cheerfully wait on you in any other quarter"—than Tennessee—"and that you had nothing to do but name the place and you should be accommodated. I am now constrained to tell you that your conduct, during the whole of your pretended bravery, shows you to be a pitiful poltroon and coward." Yet Jackson might still retrieve his reputation. "If you wish the interview, accept the proposal I have made you, and let us prepare for the campaign."

They agreed to meet at Southwest Point, Virginia, a day's ride from Knoxville. Jackson went ahead, with Sevier to follow. But the business of government—and his continuing reluctance to be tested by this young hothead—held Sevier in Knoxville forty-eight hours. Jackson waited, and waited, and finally decided that Sevier really was the coward and poltroon he had been stating him to be.

He started to return to Knoxville, riding in company with Thomas Vandyke, a surgeon's assistant with the U.S. Army at Fort Southwest Point. Not far from Kingston, Tennessee, they saw Sevier and his son James approaching. Jackson dismounted, drew pistols, and walked toward Sevier, who also dismounted and readied his guns. Jackson called Sevier an assortment of names and demanded that the two settle their dispute on the spot. "Sevier replied that he would not fire, and that he did not wish to be assassinated," Vandyke recounted shortly afterward. Vandyke assured Sevier that this was no assassination. "I then requested that the gentlemen should both deliver me their pistols, and meet in a proper manner on the field of honor. General Jackson agreed to the proposition. General Sevier positively refused." After more swearing between the two, Vandyke urged them to holster their pistols and remount their horses. They did so, with ill grace. "Scurrility ensued. General Jackson observed that there had been too much low abuse made use of, and that he would correct him. General Jackson then drew his sword cane and pistol, and rode up to General Sevier. General Sevier drew his sword, dismounted, and let his horse loose. General Jackson pursued him around us, as we"—Vandyke and two other riders who happened along—"sat upon our horses, several times. Young Mr. Sevier drew his pistol on General Jackson, on which I immediately drew mine and observed that I should protect Mr. Jackson." A second eyewitness told this part of the story slightly differently. "Judge Jackson swore that he would cane him . . . and as Jackson advanced toward him, the Governor drew his sword, which frightened his horse and he ran away with the Governor's pistols. . . . Judge Jackson immediately drew his pistol and advanced again, on which the Governor went behind a tree and damned Jackson. Did he want to fire on a naked man? On which the Governor's son drew his pistol and advanced toward his father. . . . Doctor Vandyke immediately drew his pistol and advanced toward the Governor's son."

By both accounts the two disputants retrieved their horses and rode off, each cursing the other for cowardice, poltroonry, and conduct unbecoming any kind of gentleman. In Knoxville each told his version of the story to friends and followers, who amplified the competing versions in the area newspapers. "Let us ask," wrote one Sevier partisan, "how many hundreds of respectable characters are in this and several other states who have been eyewitnesses of the governor's courage? . . . Is he not the man whose exertions have taken from the numerous hordes the savage wilds and placed on them a rising, growing, and respectable republic?" The governor had no need to prove his courage. As for Jackson: "The judge, shark-like, intending to grasp the prey into his voracious jaws, has unfortunately darted himself out of the water flat on his own back, upon a dirty beach, from where it will be impossible for him, with all his serpentile windings, to make his retreat with credit."

A Jackson advocate answered that the blame all lay with Sevier, for "vulgar and ungentlemanly expressions" drawn from "the most secret recesses of his infernal disposition." The governor had claimed his greater age as reason not to fight Jackson. "If you had saw the ease with which his Excellency dismounted, and the good use he made of his heels after he had dismounted, you would have thought him a youth of not more than eighteen."

The affair afforded entertainment for months afterward, as each side spent the autumn and winter recounting the insults and outrages committed and suffered by their champions. Few minds, apparently, were changed by all the words and ink.

Yet for those paying close attention to Jackson, the spat with Sevier revealed something significant. Sevier never took Jackson's challenge seriously because he considered it politically motivated, which it was in part. And for Sevier, politics was politics, a game that didn't lack importance but hardly rose to the level of putting one's life in jeopardy.

Jackson didn't play games, at least not with politics. He took politics very seriously, for politics involved honor, reputation, and principle. These meant more to Jackson than life itself. He would have fought Sevier over politics even if he had expected to die in the duel.

And he certainly didn't play games with Rachel's reputation. When Sevier, having affronted Jackson politically, compounded his sin by slandering Rachel, there was no chance Jackson would forgive him. And he never did.

1805–1814

Son of the West

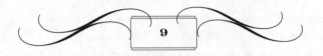

9

CONSPIRACY

In radical youth Thomas Jefferson sometimes uttered sentiments he learned to regret. Of the executions of the early French Revolution, he asserted, "My own affections have been deeply wounded by some of the martyrs of this cause, but rather than it should have failed I would have seen half the earth desolated; were there but an Adam and an Eve left in every country, and left free, it would be better than as it now is." Later, watching settlers spread beyond the mountains into the valleys of the Ohio and Mississippi rivers, he remarked, "If they see their interests in separation, why should we take sides with our Atlantic rather than our Mississippi descendants? God bless them both, and keep them in union, if it be for their good; but separate them, if it be better."

The Reign of Terror and Napoleon Bonaparte took the edge off Jefferson's enthusiasm for revolution; the Louisiana Purchase and Aaron

Burr compelled him to reconsider trans-Appalachian separatism. Jefferson's election as president in 1800 marked a shift in the tone and direction of American politics. John Adams's single term had divided the country deeply; Jackson's complaints against the Federalists for their egregious Anglophilia were echoed and amplified by Republicans across the South and West, who soon found cause for additional complaints. After the confrontations on the Atlantic between French and American vessels escalated to an undeclared naval war, the Federalist Congress approved the Alien and Sedition Acts, which exploited the troubles with France to outlaw much domestic dissent. Jefferson, Adams's vice president under the awkward original scheme for choosing the chief executive, secretly penned a resolution for the Kentucky legislature asserting the right of states to judge the constitutionality of federal laws and to nullify—prevent the enforcement of—those measures that failed the test. James Madison drafted a similar resolution for Virginia. Three decades later, the Kentucky and Virginia resolutions would be thrown defiantly at Andrew Jackson; for the time being they fueled a campaign for president, between Adams and Jefferson, that set scurrility standards not approached till Jackson ran against Adams's son. Jefferson won a bruising victory that his Republican supporters lauded as a triumph for the people and his Federalist rivals damned as a harbinger of anarchy.

Jefferson proposed a truce in his inaugural address. "We are all republicans; we are all federalists," he said. No one really believed him, but the gesture indicated a desire to restore civility to American political life. It helped Jefferson's purposes that the Federalists were too busy sniping at one another to maintain their attacks upon the Republicans. (This sniping was partly responsible for Jefferson's election; in the 1800 campaign the most virulent criticism of Adams came not from the Republicans but from Alexander Hamilton's wing of the Federalists.)

At the level of substance, although Jefferson's victory didn't commence an age of popular rule, it did install the party more sympathetic to that notion. Hamilton and the high Federalists hardly disguised their disdain for the masses; Jefferson embraced the masses philosophically even if his own life of leisure and erudition often seemed removed from their workaday sphere. "It is rare that the public sentiment decides immorally or unwisely, and the individual who differs from it ought to distrust and examine his own opinion," Jefferson declared, in words Hamilton would have choked on before uttering. Jefferson's policies reflected his concern for the common folks. He worked to reduce government spending and to shift the tax burden from consumers to businesses; where a choice existed between action by the federal government and action by the states, he generally deferred to the states, as being closer to the people.

In one area, though, Jefferson materially increased the scope of federal power. The decennial census of 1800 showed an American population of 5.3 million, including one million slaves. This total was a third larger than that of ten years earlier, reflecting what most Americans were happy to deem a healthy rate of growth. But the rapid growth, combined with another statistic from the census—that almost nineteen Americans out of twenty lived on or near farms—occasioned worry in the more prescient. The national domain in 1800 was no larger than it had been in 1783, when the population was little more than half its current size. All those farmers, and certainly their children and grandchildren, would need more land lest they crowd upon one another and suffer the social and political ills Americans associated with densely populated Europe.

The problem was especially acute for Jefferson. As the leader of the party of the more rural regions, the president felt a special responsibility to ensure that America's farmers had room into which to expand. The West— meaning, at the time of Jefferson's election, the states of Kentucky and Tennessee, the western part of Georgia, and the territories of Ohio, Indiana, and Mississippi—was by no means full. But one didn't have to be a mathematician to realize that at America's current rate of growth, the West would be as populated in a few generations as the East was now.

Consequently, when the opportunity arose to purchase the Louisiana territory—the western half of the Mississippi Valley—Jefferson couldn't resist. Napoleon had lately dreamed of reviving France's American empire; to this end he extorted Louisiana back from Spain. But a rebellion persisted in the French sugar colony of Haiti, and yellow fever decimated the expeditionary force Napoleon sent to suppress it, forcing a change of the Bonaparte mind. Jefferson meanwhile dispatched James Monroe to join Robert Livingston in Paris and try to purchase New Orleans. "There is on the globe one single spot, the possessor of which is our natural and habitual enemy,"

Jefferson explained. "It is New Orleans." To the astonishment of Livingston and Monroe, Napoleon countered their offer to purchase New Orleans with an offer to sell all of Louisiana.

The offer was too tempting to refuse, but Jefferson first had to quiet his conscience. Nothing in the Constitution explicitly authorized the acquisition of new territory, and Jefferson had always insisted that what the Constitution didn't explicitly authorize couldn't legitimately be done. He briefly considered an amendment to the Constitution but decided that the mercurial Bonaparte might change his mind again. The Federalists gloated at Jefferson's discomfiture, and some complained that the last thing the country needed was more western farmers. But neither he nor they could bring themselves to let political consistency, political advantage, or anything else block the bargain of their lifetimes. Jefferson accepted Napoleon's offer, the Senate ratified it, and the House joined the Senate in funding the $15 million deal.

This was where Aaron Burr entered the picture, and not far from where Andrew Jackson's political career almost ended three decades prematurely. Burr was a handsome fellow with persuasive gifts he might have inherited from his grandfather Jonathan Edwards, the Congregationalist minister whose terrifyingly vivid sermons sometimes drove listeners to suicide. But not everyone was persuaded; as a young lieutenant in the Revolutionary War, Burr incautiously intimated that he knew more about military strategy than General Washington did. Washington rid himself of this pesky boy, and Burr learned his lesson, at least for a time. He served gallantly and effectively during the American retreat from Long Island, at Valley Forge, and during the New Jersey campaign of 1778.

But the war wasn't moving fast enough for him, and when ill health afforded an excuse for a furlough he extended it to retirement. He shocked his erstwhile comrades by marrying an English officer's widow, whose money helped him launch a lucrative postwar practice at the New York City bar. His clients and friends landed him appointment as New York state's attorney general and then, after the adoption of the 1787 Constitution, election by the state legislature to the United States Senate. In this election he defeated the father-in-law of Alexander Hamilton. Whether or not this contributed to Hamilton's ill feeling toward Burr, the two became bitter rivals, with Hamilton heading New York's Federalists and Burr the state's Republicans.

Burr joined Jefferson on the losing Republican ticket in 1796, and again on the Republican ticket in 1800. When the electoral votes—under the rules giving each elector two votes, with the first-place finisher becoming president and the second-place candidate vice president—were tallied, Jefferson and Burr each had seventy-three votes. This hadn't been the plan, or at least it hadn't been the plan of Jefferson and nearly all those who voted for the Virginian. That it might have been Burr's plan occurred to some observers when Burr declined to step aside in favor of Jefferson. The House of Representatives required dozens of ballots to make Jefferson president, with the impasse ending only after Hamilton, choosing what seemed to him the lesser of evils, urged his Federalist followers to vote for Jefferson. "He is by far not so dangerous a man and he has pretensions to character," Hamilton said of Jefferson. "As to *Burr*, there is nothing in his favour. His private character is not defended by his most partial friends. He is bankrupt beyond redemption except by the plunder of his country. . . . If he can, he will certainly disturb our institutions to secure himself *permanent power* and with it *wealth*."

Burr's behavior as president of the Senate (the sole chore constitutionally assigned the vice president) was above reproach. But between Jefferson's understandable suspicions and Hamilton's continuing animus, Burr's future seemed dim. He reasonably anticipated his exclusion from the ticket for another Jefferson term and so ran for governor of New York in the spring of 1804. His loss owed much to the opposition of Hamilton, who continued to deprecate his character and motives to all who would listen and read.

Burr thereupon challenged Hamilton to a duel, demanding satisfaction for the damage done his honor and career. Hamilton accepted the challenge, albeit with ambivalence. He had lost his eldest son in a duel, and if he himself died he would leave his wife and children deeply in debt. But he couldn't discover an alternative acceptable to his notions of honor. The two New Yorkers crossed the Hudson to evade New York's ban on dueling, and at sunrise below Weehawken confronted each other at ten paces. Hamilton had spoken to friends of wasting his shot: of firing into the air. Whether Burr heard of this is impossible to know. He certainly couldn't count on it. Besides, at the critical moment Hamilton gave every indication of shooting to kill, and at ten paces he had an excellent chance of succeeding. The witnesses disputed who fired first, but there was no disputing the mortal wound Hamilton suffered. He lingered, in pain and intermittent delirium, till the following day, when he finally succumbed.

Burr emerged from the encounter physically unscathed but politically ruined. A New York grand jury, ignoring that the duel had taken place in New Jersey, indicted him for murder. The Federalists were livid and vengeful toward the slayer of their founder, while most Republicans considered Burr an embarrassment and a liability.

In his predicament Burr did what generations of Americans before and after him did: he looked to the West for a new start. He had gifts many prospective emigrants lacked. He was handsome in a way that attracted both the elegant and the rough, and men as much as women. He elevated plausibility to an art form, spinning the daydreams of his listeners into castles in their minds' eyes. He could prevaricate effortlessly and was just clever enough to stay a step ahead of his own contradictions.

He traveled to New Orleans, the entrepôt to the inland empire just acquired from France. Returning east he stopped in Tennessee, where he was feted as a celebrity and a minor hero. No one in Nashville held his killing of Hamilton against him. Honor was honor, and, besides, to most Tennesseans, the fewer Federalists the better.

Andrew Jackson and the other leading men of Nashville held a dinner for Burr, after which Jackson brought Burr home for a several-day visit. The two men discovered common interests, starting with horses. Burr loaned Jackson his best horseman, a slave named Sam. "He understands as well as any man living how to drive a carriage and manage horses and the care of horses, carriage and harness," Burr told Jackson. "He knows nothing else and during thirteen years service his honesty has never incurred a suspicion. He will, I hope, in some way make himself useful to you."

Jackson and Burr also discovered a shared desire to answer the question that arose in nearly every conversation regarding America's southwestern frontier: how long would the government at Washington suffer foreigners to threaten free use of the Mississippi? Too long already, Jackson and Burr agreed. The United States had purchased Louisiana from France, yet the Spanish held Florida and Texas. Jefferson was said to be negotiating for the purchase of Florida. "But notwithstanding the pacific temper of our government, there is great reason to expect hostility," Burr told Jackson. He considered this a positive sign, though. He explained that an anti-Spanish band of South Americans at New York were outfitting an expedition to sail against their homeland. Burr supposed Spain would protest the use of American soil for this filibustering and might even seize American vessels. France, Spain's ally, might take action as well. "It would not surprise me if on a knowledge of these facts at Paris and Madrid our vessels in the ports of those kingdoms should be seized and measures taken for the reduction of Orleans," Burr said. He hoped for such a provocation, as it would give Americans a chance to settle the issue once and for all. He counted on Tennessee to do its part. "Your country is full of fine materials for an army and I have often said that a brigade could be raised in West Tennessee which would drive double their number of Frenchmen off the earth." He urged Jackson, as commander of the Tennessee militia, to gird for war. "I take the liberty of recommending to you to make out a list of officers from colonel down to ensign for one or two regiments, composed of fellows fit for business and with whom you would trust your life and your honor."

Jackson compiled the list and sent it on. And he kept in touch with Burr, who spent the spring and summer of 1806 in constant motion, traveling to New Orleans again and all across the West. In October Burr was back in Nashville, plying Jackson with stories of Spanish perfidy and the ease with which the Spanish lands might be taken. Jefferson's attempt to purchase Florida, for a reported two million dollars, had failed. But neither Burr nor Jackson lamented the failure. "The certain consequence is war," Jackson declared. "And no doubt but less than two millions can conquer not only the Floridas but all Spanish North America."

Jackson thrilled at the prospect. "At least two thousand volunteers can be led into the field at a short notice," he told James Winchester, one of his brigade commanders. "That number, led by firm officers and men of enterprise, I think could look into Santa Fe and Mexico, give freedom and commerce to those provinces and establish peace and a permanent barrier against the inroads and attacks of foreign powers on our interior, which will be the case so long as Spain holds that large country on our borders. Should there be a war, this will be a handsome theater for our enterprising young men and a certain source of acquiring fame."

Jackson directed his brigadier generals to mobilize their troops. Relaying intelligence from Burr and others close to the frontier, he described threatening acts by a Spanish force operating along the Red River. "This armed force, under the sanction of their government, have imprisoned and transported five of the good citizens of the United States to the dominion of Spain. They have cut down and carried off the flag of the United States, which was erected in the Caddo nation of Indians and within the limits of the United States. They have compelled by force men in the employ of government when exploring the Red River to desist and come home, and they have taken an unjustifiable and insulting position on the east side of the river Sabine and within the Territory of New Orleans!!!" These affronts, Jackson declared, "make it necessary that the militia under my command should be in complete order and at a moment's warning ready to march."

Jackson also wrote to Jefferson. Bypassing both Governor Sevier and the federal secretary of war, Jackson told the president that Tennessee stood eager to defend American honor. "The public sentiment and feeling of the citizens within this state, and particularly within my division, are of such a nature and of such a kind that I take the liberty of tendering their services. . . . At one moment's warning after your signification that this tender is acceptable, my orders shall be given conformably."

Just days later, Jackson received the shock of his life. A young army captain named John Fort arrived in Nashville bearing reports of treasonous activity in the far Southwest. Adventurers, he asserted, were plotting against the United States. "Their intention was to divide the Union," Jackson recalled Fort saying. He asked Fort how they would do this.

He replied, by seizing New Orleans and the bank [of the Mississippi], shutting the port, conquering Mexico, and uniting the western part of the Union to the conquered territory.

I, perhaps with warmth, asked him how this was to be effected.

He replied, by the aid of the Federal troops, and the General

[James Wilkinson, governor of (Upper) Louisiana Territory] at their head.

I asked if he had this from the General.

He said he had not.

I asked him if Colonel Burr was in to the scheme.

He answered he did not know nor was he informed that he was: that he barely knew Colonel Burr but never had had any conversation.

I asked him how he knew this and from whom he got his information.

He said from Colonel Swartout in New York.

It was at this point that Jackson's shock occurred.

Knowing that Colonel Burr was well acquainted with Swartout, it rushed into my mind like lightning that Burr was at the head.

Jackson now realized that Burr's trips to New Orleans had involved more than sizing up the Spanish. He was estimating western sentiment in favor of secession from the Union. The former vice president apparently planned to become president—or king, or emperor—of his own new country, carved from the southwestern United States and northeastern Mexico and centered on the lower Mississippi and New Orleans. There was geographic logic to the audacious plan. The Mississippi was an obvious organizing principle for a political entity. Even Nashville felt its pull, which in turn reflected nothing more complicated than the gravity that drew the Cumberland to the Mississippi and the Mississippi to New Orleans and the Gulf of Mexico.

But geography couldn't disguise that any such scheme was treason, pure and simple. Jackson sought what served Tennessee, but his first loyalty was to the Union. If what Jackson suddenly suspected of Burr was true, the man was a traitor.

And Jackson was an accomplice, if an unwitting one. As his mind reeled from the lightning bolt of recognition of Burr's nefarious plan, he understood that he had compromised himself. He frantically dredged his memories for the encouraging words he had offered Burr, the letters he had written, the actions he had undertaken in support of Burr's scheme. Jackson blamed himself not for moral failure; he had done nothing that pained his conscience. But he cursed himself for stupidity, for not seeing what Burr was up to. He knew that a clear conscience might not protect him if Burr's perfidy became manifest. Jackson was lawyer enough to know that ignorance was nearly impossible to prove, and politician enough to realize that ignorance could be as damning in its own way as witting culpability.

Angry at Burr and angrier at himself, he sounded the alarm. "There is something rotten in the state of Denmark," he wrote to William Claiborne, governor of Orleans Territory, at New Orleans. "You have enemies within your own city that may try to subvert your government and try to separate it from the Union. . . . Be upon the alert." Jackson didn't retreat from his desire for war against Spain, but it mustn't be at hazard to the United States. "I hate the Dons. I would delight to see Mexico reduced, but I will die in the last ditch before I would yield a part to the Dons or see the Union disunited." To Tennessee senator Daniel Smith at Washington, Jackson delineated how the conspiracy must have been designed to unfold.

A difference exists between our government and Spain. Their minister at open war with our executive, a designing man forms an intrigue with him to regain the purchased Territory [Louisiana]. . . . The Spanish forces under pretext of defending their frontier (where there has been no encroachment) marches a formidable force within two hundred miles of New Orleans. Your governor of New Orleans [Claiborne] organizes the militia to help defend your Territory, but your general [Wilkinson] orders him home at the very moment that he is advancing to take possession of a position on the right bank of the Sabine. The two armies are near enough to make arrangement and to form plans of cooperation. At this moment a descent is made [by Burr and accomplices] from the Ohio and upper Louisiana on New Orleans, which is in a defenceless situation, two thirds of its inhabitants in to the plan. The town falls an easy prey to its assailants, and the two armies protect the conquerors with the aid of Spain, shut the port against the exportation of the West, and hold out allurements to all the western world to join and they shall enjoy free trade and profitable commerce.

Jackson granted that he was conjecturing details. But he didn't doubt that something akin to this was afoot. "I as much believe that such a plan is in operation as I believe there is a god. And if I am not mistaken, there are in the plan many high characters from New York to New Orleans." He urged Smith to inform Jefferson—but not others in the administration, who might be conspirators themselves.

$\mathcal{J}$efferson didn't need Jackson to warn him about Burr or about the western conspiracy. People had been telling him about both for months, which was precisely the president's problem. Hardly had Burr shot Hamilton before Federalists, some Republicans, and persons who preferred to keep their identities secret began raining rumor and innuendo on the White House. "He is meditating the overthrow of your Administration," one anonymous writer told Jefferson of Burr in December 1805. "His aberrations through the Western states *had no other object*. A foreign agent, now at Washington, knows since February last his plans and has seconded them." A few weeks later Joseph Hamilton Daveiss, the federal district attorney for Kentucky, wrote Jefferson, "Spanish intrigues have been carried on among our people. We have traitors among us. A separation of the union in favor of Spain is the object finally." Daveiss named Burr and Wilkinson as the arch-conspirators on the American side.

If Jefferson hadn't been distracted by other events, he might have paid more attention to the stories about Burr. His resounding reelection in 1804 nearly swept the Federalists from the field of American politics, promising decades of Republican rule, but the international troubles that had vexed America since the early 1790s broadened and intensified. The conflict between Britain and France allowed pirates operating out of North Africa to prey on American merchant ships, seizing the vessels and their cargoes and taking their crews hostage. Jefferson responded by ordering raids against the Barbary states, as the pirate-hosting princedoms were called. In the autumn of 1805, the British navy smashed the French fleet at Trafalgar, raising British hopes that Napoleon could be crushed and prompting London to order a blockade of France. Shortly the British blockaders began capturing

American ships by the dozen. The pacific Jefferson protested diplomatically; his more belligerent supporters demanded war.

For such reasons the Burr conspiracy took time to bubble to the surface of Jefferson's agenda. Yet by the summer of 1806 the president had to pay attention. In August Jefferson received a letter from Thomas Truxton, a navy veteran of the Barbary conflict, explaining that Burr had approached him about joining the conspiracy. In September George Morgan, a Jefferson loyalist, informed the president that Burr had laid out his separatist scheme during a recent dinner at Morgan's home near Pittsburgh. In October William Eaton, another Barbary veteran, added his voice to the conspiracy chorus, asserting what Andrew Jackson was concluding at about the same time: that Burr and Wilkinson were aiming to carve the West away from the United States and attach it to a part of Mexico similarly severed from Spanish control.

Burr wasn't oblivious to the leaking, but, on the principle that he hadn't broken any laws yet, he proceeded unfazed. The first serious wrinkle in his plans occurred when federal prosecutor Daveiss attempted to indict him for making preparations in Kentucky for war against Mexico. Burr hired Henry Clay, an ambitious young attorney, and fended off the indictment. But he decided not to tarry in Kentucky and went south to Tennessee.

In Nashville he encountered Jackson again. The meeting was strained yet more cordial than it might have been. After hearing from John Fort and inferring Burr's design, Jackson had written to Burr insisting on an explanation. Burr's reply has been lost, but Jackson paraphrased it in another letter, saying that Burr gave "an express pledge of honor that he had never had any ideas hostile to the Union or its interest." The subsequent refusal of the Kentucky grand jury to indict him lent weight to Burr's disclaimer. And Burr in person was as plausible as ever. He assured Jackson of his loyalty to the Union. His intentions, he said, had never gone beyond those of Jackson himself: to smite Spain and expand the realm of American liberty.

Jackson didn't know what to conclude. He had to admit that the evidence against Burr was indirect and largely partisan. And whatever Burr might have been *thinking*, he hadn't *done* anything illegal. And if he *had* dreamed of a southwestern empire, surely the recent hue and cry had put him off that. He might still be useful in a war against Spain, which Jackson continued to believe necessary and just.

Jackson may have been willfully fooling himself. If Burr wasn't guilty, then Jackson wasn't as stupid as he feared he had been, and his good name and future weren't in such jeopardy. Maybe he had overreacted. Maybe Burr was as innocent as he claimed. In any event, Jackson didn't have authority to arrest Burr or otherwise stand in his way. So he held his breath and hoped for the best. The two men parted on apparently friendly terms.

Yet Jackson determined to keep an eye on Burr. And he would be ready to move against him at an instant's notice. "Should danger threaten you," he told Governor Claiborne at New Orleans, "write me, and under your notification, on the wings of patriotism I will hasten to the point of danger, to support the Union of our country, the prop of freedom, with the arm of vengeance that shall burst on treason and on treasoners' heads."

$\mathcal{T}$hings didn't come to that. The conspiracy unraveled before Burr got anywhere near New Orleans. James Wilkinson, whose loyalty was, if anything, less certain than Burr's—Wilkinson was still on the Spanish payroll—decided to betray his partner to save himself. He wrote to Jackson asserting that treason was afoot. He said he had intercepted a letter to "Burr's chief agent here . . . which letter is evincive of his being a party to the conspiracy which agitates your country"—Tennessee—"and is intended to destroy the American nation." Should Burr's plans develop as intended, Wilkinson said, "this country"—Louisiana—"will be ruined." Wilkinson was aware that certain persons had linked his name to Burr's in the conspiracy. Wilkinson denied the charge as an utter calumny and demanded an opportunity to dispel "the delusions and villainies by which I have been misrepresented, persecuted and defamed." He declared that he "would steel through my father to defend the integrity of the Union. . . . I have no secrets except when necessary to the national interests."

Wilkinson also wrote to Jefferson, less straightforwardly. He sent the president a document describing "a numerous and powerful association extending from New York through the western states to territories bordering on the Mississippi." This association hoped to raise "eight or ten thousand men in New Orleans at a very near period." The ostensible aim of the irregular army was to attack Spanish Mexico at Vera Cruz, to which end its leaders had arranged the cooperation of the British navy. But Wilkinson was certain that more was involved. In a letter accompanying the document he told Jefferson, "I have no doubt the revolt of this Territory"—Louisiana— "will be made an auxiliary step" in the attack on Mexico. Wilkinson didn't identify Burr by name, but he knew he didn't have to, given everything that had been rumored of the former vice president.

Several weeks later Wilkinson forwarded to Washington what was intended to be the most damning evidence yet of Burr's perfidy. Burr had written Wilkinson a ciphered letter asserting that the plans were rapidly taking shape. "Everything internal and external favor our view," Burr wrote, in code. "Naval protection of England is secured. . . . Final orders are given to my friends and followers. It will be a host of choice spirits. . . . Our project, my dear friend, is brought to the point so long desired. I guarantee the result with my life and honor, with the lives, the honor and the fortune of hundreds, the best blood of our country. . . . The gods invite us to glory and fortune." Wilkinson sent this letter on to Jefferson, decoded but edited in a way that removed signs that Wilkinson was involved.

The mere fact of the ciphering, as much as the letter's contents, made it politically explosive. "Burr's enterprise is the most extraordinary since the days of Don Quixote," the president declared. "It is so extravagant that those who know his understanding would not believe it if the proofs admitted doubt. He has meant to place himself on the throne of Montezuma, and extend his empire to the Allegheny, seizing on New Orleans as the instrument of compulsion for our Western states."

The encrypted letter finally drove Jefferson to action. Stories about Burr were rifer and more lurid than ever in Washington, and the president's enemies taxed him for tolerating treason. Jefferson's Republican allies fretted that all their party's gains might be lost if Burr weren't brought to justice.

But catching Burr wasn't easy. Wilkinson had guessed it wouldn't be. "He might be hid in a greatcoat pocket," the general said, referring to Burr's slipperiness as well as his small stature. A manhunt began and encompassed much of the West. After several leads failed, the searchers tracked their quarry to Mississippi Territory, where Burr was run to ground and forced to surrender. But he lulled his captors into complacency and escaped. The hunt resumed, with a large bounty offered for the capture of the fugitive. In February 1807, Burr was retaken. He was transported east under armed guard. In South Carolina he again attempted escape but failed. He and his guards arrived at Richmond in late March.

The treason trial of Aaron Burr was the sensation of the summer of 1807. Jefferson weighed in heavily, bringing to bear all the power of the executive branch to ensure conviction. The prosecution, led by the United States attorney for the Virginia District, George Hay, compiled a list of 140 witnesses to testify against Burr. To encourage useful testimony, Jefferson sent Hay a sheaf of blank pardons for those who turned state's evidence.

Jefferson had reason to believe he'd need help, for the judge in the trial was John Marshall, the chief justice of the Supreme Court, who had been appointed by John Adams and had crossed swords with Jefferson more than once. Supreme Court justices in those days rode the circuit, and Marshall's circuit included Richmond, his hometown. Marshall was no friend to traitors, but he was only marginally more friendly to Jefferson and had no intention of letting the courts be coerced by a chagrined and vindictive president. Marshall's life goal was to establish the independence of the judiciary and its coequality with the executive and legislative branches. The Burr trial became an early battlefield in that struggle.

Jackson played a bit part in the Jefferson-Marshall fight. Summoned from Tennessee to testify before the grand jury, he explained that Burr had visited Nashville a number of times, inquiring about speculative opportunities in the West and talking of the likelihood of war with Spain. Jackson said he had told Burr that before he—Jackson—would ready the militia to march, he needed orders from the federal secretary of war. "Burr said surely he would produce the orders of the secretary," Jackson told the grand jury. Jackson recounted his interview with John Fort and explained that the army captain had implicated not Burr alone but Wilkinson too.

To Jackson's annoyance, the prosecution—which was to say, the president—heeded only part of his testimony. Jefferson spared neither effort nor expense to convict Burr yet ignored what seemed to Jackson the equal guilt of Wilkinson. In fact, the more Jackson considered the matter, the more he came to believe that Wilkinson, not Burr, was the one who needed to be punished and that the president was engaged in a vendetta that had nothing to do with national defense. "I am more convinced than I ever was before that *treason* was never intended by Burr," he wrote a friend. "If it ever was, you know my wish is, and always has been, that he be hung." But if Burr was guilty, so was Wilkinson. "Whatever may have been the projects of Burr, General Wilkinson has and did go hand in hand with him." Politics— between Republicans and Federalists, between Jefferson and Marshall—had fatally intruded on the sphere of justice. "I never deemed it just, nor never shall, to make the sacrifice of any individual as a *peace offering* to policy, and especially when others are permitted of equal guilt to pass with impunity."

Against inclination, Jackson found himself agreeing with the Federalist Marshall against the Republican Jefferson. And it was Marshall who triumphed in this test of will and savvy. Marshall so sifted the evidence and so instructed the jury as to render conviction impossible. He ruled that intent to commit treason—if in fact Burr had so intended—wasn't the same as treason itself. And he held the prosecution to the strict constitutional standard of two eyewitnesses to the treasonable act. After the prosecution failed to produce the witnesses, the jury deliberated less than half an hour before acquitting Burr.

The result was a signal victory for Marshall and the courts and a stinging defeat for Jefferson and the presidency. It was also an education for Jackson. Jackson muttered against Jefferson the whole way back to Nashville. The Republican president, the man who was supposed to represent the people, had shown himself to be no better than other politicians. In some respects he was worse, for the prosecution he perverted to politics touched the most sacred responsibility of any president: to preserve the Union. In obsessing about Burr, Jefferson disregarded Wilkinson, the greater threat. This wasn't how presidents were supposed to act.

10

AFFAIR OF HONOR

Jackson devoted his public life to battling birth and breeding
as requisites for personal advancement. But in a critical realm of
his private life he placed as much store in bloodlines and pedigree
as the haughtiest émigré from Bourbon France.

Jackson began racing horses long before he could afford to purchase

thoroughbreds. As a boy in the Waxhaw he tested himself and his mounts

against other boys and horses, and the distinction he earned was what led

to his selection as a courier for the patriot forces in the Revolutionary War.

At sixteen he was an authorized appraiser of horseflesh. The earliest

surviving document bearing Jackson's signature is a 1783 appraisal of "one

bay horse, brands unknown to the appraisers, value £150." Charleston

racehorses galloped away with his inheritance after the war and turned his face back toward the West. As an apprentice lawyer and then a novice practitioner he lacked the funds to purchase horses or even wager much on their speed, but no one in Nashville could ignore the races. And as Jackson acquired capital and standing in the community, he became a pillar of what even rabid democrats didn't blush at calling the "sport of kings."

In fact, though, the democrats were taking control of the sport. Organized horse racing in America had begun in the Northeast, particularly on Long Island, where a seventeenth-century British colonel indulged his passion for racing by building a track patterned after and named for the famous Newmarket course in England. Gradually the epicenter of equine activity shifted south, to Maryland and Virginia, with their milder winters and lusher pastures. Wealthy planters became the patrons of the sport, which knit the upper classes of America to those of the mother country by threads of affinity and selective (horse) breeding. The Revolution severed the threads, and though after the war turfmen on both sides of the water strove to restore them, they were never the same. Meanwhile the opening of Kentucky and Tennessee to settlement brought new and cheaper pastures to the sport. In time Kentucky would claim preeminence with its shimmering bluegrass, but in Jackson's day Tennessee, particularly the Cumberland, was where the serious racers and breeders took their animals and their business.

Until the first decade of the nineteenth century, racing in Tennessee was conducted on a casual, though hardly nonserious, basis. Proud owners matched their steeds against those of others equally prideful, and they and the spectators who gathered for the races laid bets on the outcome. But in 1804 the racing community staged its first organized trial, at Gallatin, an easy ride from Nashville. Jackson took part, entering his mare Indian Queen. The horse didn't win, yet the loss whetted Jackson's appetite for racing, as did the appearance that season of one of the most famous horses in America. Truxton (apparently named for the navy captain, whose swift ship *Constellation* was called the "Yankee Race Horse") had been sired by an English champion, Diomed, that upon crossing the Atlantic became the most important and valuable stud in American history. Truxton's owner in 1804, John Verell, brought the horse to Tennessee for the races, only to discover that he couldn't take the horse back out of the state due to a lien levied against him for an old debt. Jackson solved Verell's financial problem by assuming Verell's debt in exchange for Truxton. The debt was fifteen hundred dollars; Jackson threw in three geldings and promised two more if Truxton performed well in the next round of races.

Until this point Jackson had been one horseman among many, but with the purchase of Truxton he became the leading force in the Nashville racing community. He acquired another champion, Greyhound, and an interest in a racetrack at Clover Bottom. He organized races, with Truxton the favorite and principal attraction. And he looked forward to a long career for Truxton at stud, which would make his owner the foremost breeder in Tennessee.

Truxton's reputation naturally attracted the fastest and strongest challengers. To defeat Jackson's stallion would heighten any horseman's stature—and increase the value of his animals. Joseph Erwin judged his Ploughboy the equal of Truxton and was willing to back his judgment with money, or what substituted for money in the cash-short West. He scheduled a race with Jackson for November 1805. The wager was two thousand dollars, but side bets would multiply that amount several times. As warrant of his seriousness he posted an appearance bond: eight hundred dollars, payable to Jackson in the event Ploughboy failed to make the starting line. Several promissory notes covered the bond and the wager.

As race day approached, Erwin grew nervous. Ploughboy's training runs were slower than he had hoped and weren't getting faster. At the last moment Erwin decided to forfeit the eight hundred dollars rather than risk the entire two thousand. He informed Jackson, who matter-of-factly required delivery of the promissories.

What happened next occasioned dispute. Erwin wanted to substitute different notes for the promissories Jackson had inspected and approved at the time of the original agreement. Because promissories ranged drastically in their reliability and liquidity, such a switch could amount to reneging on the debt. By the testimony of the principals—Jackson and Erwin—the matter was settled to the satisfaction of both. But rumors circulated that Jackson had impugned the integrity of Erwin and his partner and son-in-law, Charles Dickinson, whose name was on some of the notes. Thomas Swann, a young man new in Nashville and trying to make an impression, insinuated himself into the dispute. Swann told Erwin and Dickinson that Jackson had accused against them of double-dealing. Jackson responded by declaring that anyone who said such a thing was "a damned liar."

Swann seems to have been setting Jackson up, for he immediately wrote Jackson a letter claiming injury and demanding satisfaction. "The harshness of this expression has deeply wounded my feelings," Swann said. "It is language to which I am a stranger, which no man acquainted with my character would venture to apply to me, and which . . . I shall be under the necessity of taking proper notice of."

Jackson knew about picking fights to advance his reputation, having done just that against John Sevier. But now, within weeks of his fortieth birthday, he was the one the young bucks challenged. He had no intention of letting them make their reputations at his expense. He swatted away Swann with a homily about truth and tale bearing.

> Let me, sir, observe one thing: that I never wantonly sport with the feelings of innocence, nor am I ever awed into measures. If incautiously I inflict a wound, I always hasten to remove it. If offence is taken where none is offered or intended, it gives me no pain. If a tale is listened to many days after the discourse should have taken place when all parties are under the same roof, I always leave the person to judge of the motives that induced the information, draw their own conclusions, and act accordingly. There are certain traits that always accompany the gentleman and man of truth. The moment he hears harsh expressions applied to a friend, he will immediately communicate it, that an open explanation may take place.

For reasons unclear, Jackson inferred that Dickinson was behind Swann's challenge. Some who knew Jackson asserted afterward that Dickinson had committed that most mortal of sins: aspersing the honor of Rachel. Though no surviving contemporary evidence supports this explanation, it fits the tragic denouement. After lecturing Swann on the gentlemanly way of treating misunderstanding, Jackson proceeded to identify its opposite. "*The base, poltroon and cowardly tale-bearer will always act in the background.*" Specifically naming Charles Dickinson, Jackson added, "I write it for his eye. . . . When the conversation dropped between Mr. Dickinson and myself, I thought it was at an end. As he wishes to blow the coal I am ready to light it to a blaze that it may be consumed at once and finally extinguished. . . . At all times be assured I hold myself answerable for any of my conduct, and should any thing herein contained give Mr. Dickinson the spleen, I will furnish him with an anodyne."

Perhaps Dickinson hadn't mentioned Rachel, or perhaps he preferred to answer Jackson's charge on the relatively higher ground of the horse race. In any event, when Swann relayed Jackson's insult to Dickinson, the latter retraced the issues of who said what to whom regarding the stakes and the notes. But he ended his letter in the same tone Jackson used toward him. "As to the word *coward*, I think it as applicable to yourself as anyone I know and I shall be very glad when an opportunity serves to know in what manner you give your anodynes and hope you will take in payment one of my most moderate cathartics."

Swann, for his part, didn't appreciate being elbowed out of what was becoming a most noteworthy quarrel. "Think not that I am intimidated by your threats," he wrote Jackson. "No power terrestrial shall prevent the settled purpose of my soul. . . . Your menaces I set at defiance, and now demand of you that reparation which one gentleman is entitled to receive of another."

Jackson paid no more attention to this than to Swann's earlier challenge. He declined to recognize Swann as a gentleman and threatened to thrash him rather than trade pistol fire. Swann confronted Jackson at a Nashville tavern, where Jackson began beating him with a cane. Onlookers broke up the fight, and Jackson strode off. Swann ran to the papers and published letters from references asserting that he was in fact a gentleman.

*M*any Nashville residents deemed the triangular feud an entertaining diversion from winter's gloom. Yet some city elders found the affair dismaying and anachronistic. James Robertson urged Jackson to calm himself and "not suffer passion to get the upper hand of your good sense." Robertson thought the whole business of dueling had gone on too long. "No honor can be attached either to the conquered or the conqueror, and certainly the consequences ought to be taken in view. Should you fall, your talents are lost to your country, besides the irreparable loss your family and friends must sustain. . . . On the other hand, were you to risk your life and in defending it take the life of your fellow mortal, might this not make you miserable so long as you lived?" Robertson pointed to Aaron Burr. "I suppose if dueling could be justifiable, it must have been in his case." But the victory had ruined his career and probably his conscience. "It is believed that he has not had ease in mind since the fatal hour he killed Hamilton." Robertson implored Jackson to listen to age. "Will you pardon me, my friend, when I tell you that I have been longer in the world than you have and . . . have heard the opinions of people more than you have, and do hear the false honor of dueling ridiculed by most thinking persons." He assured Jackson that no one in Nashville questioned his bravery. Now was the time to demonstrate other gifts. "You will have more than ten to one which will applaud your prudence in avoiding a duel."

Robertson's counsel slowed the momentum toward a reckoning, but not as much as Dickinson's departure from Nashville on business. In February Jackson published a defense of his conduct, which almost certainly convinced no one not previously inclined toward his view of the affair. He insulted some of Swann's and Dickinson's friends, one of whom, Nathaniel McNairy, challenged Jackson to back his words with weapons. Jackson evidently accepted, although perhaps for form's sake. The principals and seconds met on the field but the latter arranged a settlement that suited the former without the exchange of fire. Or maybe McNairy wasn't wholly satisfied, for he shortly fought a duel with one of Jackson's supporters, who was wounded.

A side effect of the assorted imbroglios was heightened interest in the contest that had started the whole affair. The Nashville *Impartial Review* of March 15 carried a notice:

> On Thursday the 3rd of April next will be run the greatest and most interesting match race ever run in the Western country, between General Jackson's horse Truxton, 6 years old, carrying 124 lbs., and Captain Joseph Erwin's horse Ploughboy, 8 years old, carrying 130 lbs. Those horses will run the two mile heats for the sum of 3000

dollars. . . . All persons are requested not to bring their dogs to the field, as they will be shot.

Race day arrived, attracting what Jackson called "the largest concourse of people I ever saw, unless in an army." Truxton had suffered a thigh injury in training, causing the leg to swell visibly. But after everything that had happened regarding the race, Jackson refused to withdraw him. The injury, however, suppressed some of the betting. "This was unfortunate, or Carthage would have been destroyed," Jackson said. As it was, Carthage was badly damaged. The race consisted of two heats, each of two miles. In a driving rain Truxton showed great heart, beating Ploughboy both times. "There was about 10,000 dollars won," Jackson recorded, "and if it had not been for the accident there would have been at least 20,000. Thus ends the fate of Ploughboy."

*J*ackson was still counting his money when Dickinson returned from New Orleans. The younger man's anger hadn't subsided in his absence. If anything his wounded honor had festered on the long journey south and back. He read Jackson's published version of the affair only to dismiss it as beneath reply, except to elaborate his earlier opinion of Jackson. "I declare him (notwithstanding he is a major general of the militia of Mero District) to be a worthless scoundrel, a paltroon and a coward," Dickinson wrote in the *Impartial Review*.

Quite possibly Jackson had been willing to let the matter blow over. James Robertson's views on dueling carried weight in Nashville and perhaps with Jackson himself. But against this latest affront he felt he had to respond. "Your conduct and expressions relative to me of late have been of such a nature and so insulting that it requires, and shall have, my notice," he informed Dickinson. "Insults may be given by men of such a kind that they must be noticed." Jackson said he would have taken action in reply to Dickinson's earlier letter but the author had left town. Now he was back and publishing pieces "more replete with blackguard abuse than any of your other productions." With mocking irony Jackson declared, "I hope, sir, your courage will be an ample security to me that I will obtain speedily that satisfaction due me for the insults offered, and in the way my friend, who hands you this, will point out."

With the gage undeniably down, planning for the duel proceeded. Dickinson's second, Hanson Catlet, suggested the morning of Friday, May 30, a week hence. Jackson's second, Thomas Overton, reflecting his principal's impatience to settle the matter, asked why they had to wait so long. "If you can not obtain pistols," Overton said half seriously, half scornfully, "we pledge ourselves to give you choice of ours." When Catlet hadn't answered this offer twenty-four hours later, Overton followed up angrily: "For God's sake, let the business be brought to issue immediately." But Catlet, with no other explanation than that an earlier date would "not now be convenient," stood firm for the 30th. Other details fell into place.

It is agreed that the distance shall be 24 feet, the parties to stand facing each other with their pistols down perpendicularly. When they are ready, the single word fire to be given, at which they are to fire as soon as they please. Should either fire before the word given, we pledge ourselves to shoot him down instantly. The person to give the word to be determined by lot, as also the choice of position.

The dueling ground was in Kentucky, in keeping with that state's more tolerant attitude toward affairs of honor. Near Harrison's Mill, on the bank of the Red River, was an open space in the hardwood forest sufficiently large to accommodate the antagonists and their retinues yet private enough to exclude the uninvolved. Jackson and Overton rode north from Nashville on Thursday, May 29, and spent the night at a tavern owned by a man named Miller. Dickinson, Catlet, and several of the younger man's friends made the same ride and stayed at the house of William Harrison a short distance down the river.

Dickinson was said to be in high spirits, which may have been a mask for his true feelings. Or they may have been real. He had reason to be hopeful. He was a marksman, reputedly able to place four balls within the space of a dollar coin at twenty-four feet. In a test of skill with pistols, he certainly expected to defeat Jackson, whose aim was no better than adequate.

But a duel was more than a test of marksmanship. It was at least as much a test of will. Rarely did duelists race to get off the first shot (unlike the gunfighters in the Wild West shootouts into which dueling would eventually evolve). Pistol fire was seldom instantly fatal, and so a wounded man might expect to shoot back. Strategy, therefore, required deciding whether to fire the first shot, in hopes of spoiling the opponent's aim, or to absorb the first shot in order to aim and fire more deliberately. Even with practiced marksmen, it wasn't unusual for the first shot to miss. Shooting for one's life was a different matter than shooting for amusement. A second shooter might then aim and fire at leisure.

Jackson determined to adopt the deliberate route. He lacked sufficient confidence in his aim to think he could debilitate Dickinson with a single quick shot. But he had supreme confidence in his will—in his capacity to get off a shot even with a pistol round in his own body. He later said, "I should have hit him, if he had shot me through the brain." That probably would have been beyond even Jackson, but if Dickinson missed Jackson's brain and his heart, he would indeed return fire. And it would be better to take the hit deliberately. Pistol bullets in those days were small, lacking the mass to knock a man down by their momentum. But the blow from a bullet could spoil a man's aim in the act of shooting. Wiser to take the blow, recover one's balance, and return a careful shot.

In late May the Kentucky sun rose well before seven. Yet the same trees that sheltered the dueling ground from the gaze of passersby prevented the sun from shining directly upon the duelists. Neither would be shooting into the sun or into sun-dappled shadow. The flat light yielded no favors or disadvantages. The two parties arrived separately a few minutes before seven. Dickinson's mood was as sober now as Jackson's had been all along. Both sides got quickly to business. Overton and Catlet drew straws. Catlet won the choice of position, Overton the fire command. The twenty-four feet—eight paces—were measured off. Jackson and Dickinson took their positions, pistols in hand at their sides.

Overton inquired if the two were ready. They nodded. He gave the command: "Fire!" Dickinson raised his pistol and pulled the trigger in a smooth, experienced motion. The crack of the discharge was lost in the surrounding trees as the smoke wafted away. Dickinson stared in amazement as Jackson stood his ground, apparently unhit. Jackson, his face grim as death, raised his own pistol, looked implacably into Dickinson's stricken eyes, and pulled the trigger. Nothing happened. Jackson examined his pistol and saw that the hammer had been but half-cocked. He completed the cock, aimed again, and fired. The bullet penetrated Dickinson's abdomen below the ribs. Dickinson slumped over and fell to the ground. Catlet and his other friends hurried to his side.

Only after Dickinson was beyond seeing him did Jackson move, and as he did, Overton discovered that he had been hit by Dickinson's bullet. Dickinson's aim had been true, but Jackson's loose coat, over his angular body, disguised the location of his heart. Dickinson's bullet missed Jackson's heart by little more than an inch. The bullet shattered itself against Jackson's breastbone and rib cage, inflicting a painful and bloody but not life-threatening wound—assuming infection didn't set in. Jackson mounted his horse and rode with Overton back to Miller's tavern.

Dickinson declined rapidly. In shock, he bled internally, and his friends could do nothing to stop the flow. They carried him to Harrison's house, where he lingered for several hours. A rider was dispatched to Nashville to fetch his young wife, who hurried north in horror. She arrived too late. Dickinson died with the dusk.

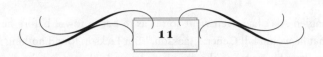

11

ALL MUST FEEL

THE INJURIES

*J*ackson may have been surprised to discover that James Robertson

was right about a duel's damaging a man's reputation. Not that he would

have altered his course: for Jackson a duel was about personal honor more

than about public opinion. Even so, he didn't anticipate the strongly

negative reaction to the news that he had killed Dickinson. Seventy-two

members of the Nashville community, including most of its mainstays

and guiding lights, petitioned the city's two papers—the *Tennessee*

Gazette and the *Impartial Review*—to drape their pages in

mourning for Dickinson, which the papers did.

*S*ome of Jackson's friends tried to laugh off the reaction. "There is

a few long faces in town," John Overton, Thomas Overton's brother,

asserted two days after the duel, "though but a few, for it seems this new-fangled Ajax had even went so far as to bet in town, before he went over, that he would kill General Jackson." But Jackson found nothing funny in the matter. He wrote to the papers and angrily demanded the names of the petitioners. "The thing is so novel," he told the *Review*, "that the names ought to appear, that the public might judge whether the true motives of the signers 'were a tribute of respect for the deceased' "—as the paper had represented—"or something else that at first sight does not appear." Preferring to avoid the wrath of one still hot from the dueling ground, twenty-six of the petition's signers removed themselves from the list, but the other forty-six allowed their names to be printed.

Armed with the names, Jackson went after the man he took to be the instigator of the petition. Thomas Watkins was a Nashville doctor who didn't like Jackson and especially didn't like dueling. Which dislike took precedence in his petition campaign is unclear to history, although it didn't seem unclear to Jackson at the time. "To dupe the citizens you held out to them that the thing was only intended to console the widow's tears, when from your late conduct it plainly appears that under the hypocritical garb of being moved by the widow's sorrow you were preparing in the background to give my reputation a stab, with the hidden shaft that none but base minds and cowardly assassins use."

Before Jackson printed this letter he sent Donelson Caffery, one of Rachel's many nephews, to Watkins's office with a copy. Caffery had collected statements from other petition signers explaining their motives, and he asked Watkins to reveal his thinking similarly. Watkins read Jackson's letter and indignantly refused. As Caffery recounted, "He observed that he was not bound to explain his motives to any man. . . . If Jesus Christ had called on him he should not consider himself bound to give his motives."

Briefly it appeared that another duel—perhaps more than one—might take place. Jackson's critics seized on the failure of his pistol to fire at first pull of the trigger and claimed that his second try was unethical. Misfires in duels generally counted as shots. The question in the current case was whether the miscock counted as a misfire. Jackson thought it didn't. His second, Thomas Overton, concurred, as did Dickinson's second, Catlet. Catlet went so far as to sign a statement certifying that "every circumstance in the affair which lately took place between General Jackson and Mr. Dickinson was agreeable to the impressions that Mr. Dickinson and myself were under."

Yet the criticism of Jackson persisted, publicly and privately, till Jackson's friends wondered where it all would end. John Overton, then in Jonesboro, heard disturbing rumors from the Cumberland. "A report arrived here that you and Swann"—who was trying to get back into the quarrel—"had fought, that both fell, Swann shot through the heart, of which he died in six minutes, and you through the head, from which instant death ensued." Had Overton fully credited the report he wouldn't have been writing Jackson. But he feared that enough was true to warrant reiterating the advice of James Robertson (with whom Overton may well have been in communication). "You have several warm friends here, and if you knew the uneasiness they suffered, and their impressions, I'm sure it would have some effect." To duel Swann would permanently damage Jackson's reputation. "It would be said that you delighted in human blood." Enough was enough. "No man, not even your worst enemies, doubts your personal courage. . . . You would gain much more by not noticing anything these people may say than otherwise. Be assured that their slander can do you no harm among your friends." Moreover, in dueling, Jackson jeopardized greater things. "Besides the mortification to your friends, you might in this way deprive yourself of that life which ought to be preserved for better purposes."

One of those better purposes hove into view at just this time. The conflict between Britain and France for mastery of Europe had become a death struggle, with the British controlling the waves and the French dominating the land. Napoleon tried to offset Britain's naval advantage by closing most of the continent to British shipping and to any neutral ships that visited British ports. Violators, including Americans, were subject to seizure by those French warships that had escaped the British sweep. This policy predictably encouraged American captains to sail directly for France. But the British blockade targeted just such ships, putting American captains and shipowners in a vise that squeezed tighter than ever before.

Yet the law of supply and demand was inexorable, and one notable effect of the French closure and the British blockade was to drive up prices for those cargoes that did get through. Even as merchants and shipowners complained to the American government about the violation by Britain and France of American neutral rights, many of them sent vessels east in hopes of capturing fat profits. Most Americans not directly involved had difficulty getting indignant.

Impressment was a different matter. As the Anglo-French war grew more desperate, the British adopted sterner measures for supplementing the ranks of their sailors. Every captain had orders to augment crews by almost any means, including kidnapping. Naval "press gangs" were notorious for sweeping the slums of London and Liverpool and trawling up anything with two legs that couldn't run fast enough to get away and two arms that couldn't hold tightly to whatever bedpost or street lamp that provided the last terrestrial anchor for the unfortunate soul. A century later Winston Churchill, then first lord of the admiralty, described the unholy trinity of British naval life as "rum, buggery, and the lash." The conditions predated Churchill by several generations of seamen.

Not surprisingly, Britain's reluctant sailors abandoned ship at most opportunities, of which American ports provided many. So long as the United States remained neutral between Britain and France, American ports were open to British and French naval vessels, which stopped in to refit and reprovision. The merchants of the ports were glad for the business, even if the refitting and reprovisioning enabled the British (and to a lesser degree the French) to continue their depredations against American shipping. British sailors were even happier for the port visits, which allowed the most desperate of them to stretch shore leave into expatriation.

The deserters weren't always welcome in their new country. Had they been upstanding types they probably wouldn't have found themselves in the British navy to begin with. But American shipmasters, who had their own manpower problems, were happy to hire experienced seamen, and the deserters frequently shipped out again, under the American flag.

This practice caused the most acute problem with Britain. Those same British captains who went to all the trouble to recruit sailors didn't stand idly by as their sailors deserted. They sent marines ashore to find the deserters and retrieve them, by force if necessary. The incursions wounded American pride, besides being bad for business along the waterfront. When the deserters found their way to American ships, British captains demanded the right to search the ships and haul off the deserters. This wounded American pride even more deeply, as it affronted not merely questionable waterfront neighborhoods but the American flag.

Impressment rankled Americans for years before becoming a casus belli—in the judgment of Andrew Jackson and many others—in early 1807. The incident that turned annoyance into outrage involved an American frigate, the *Chesapeake*, and the British frigate *Leopard*. The crew of the *Chesapeake* included several sailors who had deserted from the British navy. Some of these were British nationals but a few were native-born Americans previously impressed into British service. They weren't deserting so much as escaping to home. The commander of the *Cheseapeake*, James Barron, accordingly believed that the British had no moral right to come after them. As for legal right, because the *Chesapeake* was a vessel of the United States Navy and the United States was not at war with Britain, the British had no right to stop or search her.

But the British commander ignored such niceties and insisted on a search. When Barron refused, the *Leopard* opened fire. Her cannon rounds battered the hull of the *Chesapeake* and blasted her masts, killing three Americans and wounding eighteen others. Barron struck the colors of his crippled ship and submitted to a British search, which resulted in the carrying off of four men, three of them American citizens.

Had all this happened in the mid-Atlantic the shock to American pride would have been grievous. That it happened off Hampton Roads, within sight and sound of the Virginia coast, made it even more infuriating. What completed the affront was that the *Leopard* nonchalantly returned to American waters, anchoring at the mouth of Chesapeake Bay, presumably to await its next victim.

As news of the affair spread, so did the American anger. "British Outrage," shouted the Washington *National Intelligencer* into the Republican administration's ear. From Richmond a friend of the president wrote Jefferson regarding a public meeting just held. "All appeared zealously to vie who should be foremost in manifesting a patriotic indignation at the insult offered, and an invincible determination to avenge the wrong done to the government and to the people of our country." An observer at Baltimore described a rally in that city. "There appeared but one opinion—War—in case that satisfaction is not given." Jefferson himself acknowledged that the public mind was "made up for war." The British had gone too far. "They have often enough, god knows, given us cause of war before," the president said. "But it has been on points which would not have united the nation. But now they have touched a chord which vibrates in every heart." Jefferson added, "Now, then, is the time to settle the old and the new."

Jackson certainly believed the moment had come to settle affairs with the British. Those inveterate enemies of American freedom had left patriots no choice. "The degradation offered to our government by the British in the attack of our armed vessel the *Chesapeake* by the British ship *Leopard* within our waters . . . has roused every feeling of the American heart," he declared. Jackson shuddered for his country at "this humiliating blow against our independence and sovereignty." Britain must be chastised. The silver lining of the current ignominy was that the American people were finally alert to this fact. "War with that nation is inevitable."

Inevitable perhaps, but not swift. Jefferson's nature was more phlegmatic than Jackson's; Jefferson also had a keener sense of the limits of American power. Better than Jackson, he realized that America wasn't ready for war. Its navy was no match for Britain's, and its army was undermanned and underfunded. Its people might be brave, but they were scattered over half a continent and were often more loyal to state and section than to the country as a whole. Jefferson also had a greater respect than Jackson for the separation of powers in the American federal government. For all his embrace of loose construction in the Louisiana Purchase, Jefferson understood that only Congress could declare war. Congress wasn't in session and wouldn't return till the fall unless he brought the lawmakers back to the capital. But even that would take time, during which the iron of American anger would probably cool.

So instead of war he attempted diplomacy. He shut American waters to British warships and demanded an apology and reparations from the British government. He got the apology—London disowned the actions of the *Leopard*'s commander—and a promise of reparations. The British needed sailors but they didn't want a war with the United States at a critical moment of the struggle against Napoleon. Yet London conspicuously refused to alter the stated policies of seizure and impressment that had given rise to the Anglo-American troubles in the first place. On the contrary, it tightened the noose around Europe and thereby increased the number of American ships stopped and cargoes seized.

Jefferson still declined to resort to war. Hoping to turn the economic weapon against the British—and the French—he persuaded the Republican Congress, now back in session, to embargo American trade with Europe. At a minimum the embargo would remove American ships from harm's way. With better luck it would force one or both of the belligerents to back down, in the interest of restoring the valuable American trade.

The embargo exploded in Jefferson's face. New England merchants and shipowners hated it as impinging on their commercial freedom. They responded by smuggling, by voting for Federalists, whose number in the House of Representatives doubled at the next election, and by talking of seceding from a country so dominated by Virginia planters. Nor was the rest of the country spared. Farmers in the West and South watched in alarm and then anger as their crops piled up on wharves awaiting ships forbidden to sail. Those regions that didn't produce for export felt the embargo's effects in falling prices from the overall glut the embargo created.

Jackson was already irked at Jefferson over the Burr-Wilkinson affair, and he grew more exasperated upon the failure of the president to confront the British and demand satisfaction for their crimes against American honor and interest. After the *Chesapeake* shelling he led a protest in Nashville against British arrogance and in support of a vigorous American response. Many at the rally were ready to march to war right then, declaration or no declaration. Jackson would have been happy to lead them.

The embargo brought the British challenge closer to home. The depression it produced aggravated the chronic money problems of the frontier, triggering numerous foreclosures and lawsuits for payment of debt. Jackson had to defend himself in several cases, including one involving a farm owned by his brother-in-law John Caffery, who had borrowed two thousand dollars from John McNairy and listed the farm as collateral. When Caffery found himself short of cash, Jackson bailed him out by purchasing the farm and letting Caffery and his family stay on it. McNairy sued Jackson on grounds that he—McNairy—should have had first option on purchasing the farm. Jackson sought to shame McNairy for trying to take advantage of Caffery's difficulties, which, like those of everyone else caught in the eddies of the embargo and the vicissitudes of American finance, weren't entirely his fault. "Is it possible under these circumstances that you in your exalted station . . . will endeavour to deprive a numerous and worthy family of a habitation or sustenance?" Jackson demanded. "Impossible—the whole world (when the thing would be known) would execrate the act, and the gods would frown on it with indignation." McNairy, illiquid himself, refused to be shamed. He pressed the case, which dragged on for months till the courts compelled Jackson and Caffery to pay him $999 to clear the debt.

By then the defaults and foreclosures had become a blizzard. In Tennessee and across the West debtors demanded protection from creditors, asserting that they shouldn't have to shoulder the burden of a decision made by the president and Congress for the presumed benefit of the country as a whole. Most asked for a period of grace, enforced by stay laws to prevent the collection of debts. Had all the creditors been the greedy bankers of the debtors' rhetoric, the stay laws would have passed easily. But most of the creditors were themselves debtors who, if they couldn't collect the debts owed them, risked defaulting on debts of their own. Where was the justice in that? they demanded.

Jackson was among the latter class, at once owed and owing. He recognized, not least because he felt in himself, the strains the embargo was inflicting. For this reason he urged his fellow citizens to concentrate on the real cause of their common distress: Britain. At a rowdy Nashville meeting of debtors and creditors, where the former demanded stay laws and the latter denounced the very idea, Jackson turned the debate outward. "Our enemies have long calculated on our divisions," he said. New Englanders seemed bent on making those enemies right, but Tennesseans—united—must show them wrong. "All must feel the injuries we have received, all must be determined to resist them." From Nashville the message would echo to the Atlantic and beyond. "Let the event of this day's meeting prove to the world that no matter what privations we suffer, or inconveniences we feel, we are willing to expend the last cent of our treasure and the last drop of our blood in giving effect to any measures that may be taken in support of our liberty and independence."

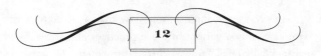

12

MASTER AND SLAVES

During the early nineteenth century, American practices and attitudes involving slavery continued to change. Additional northern states mandated an end to the institution, although most allowed owners to keep current slaves for years or decades. Congress outlawed the importation of slaves in 1808, a move that assuaged American consciences but posed little hardship on slaveholders, as American slaves reproduced fast enough to meet the needs of the domestic market. (In the West Indies and Brazil, by contrast, the far higher death rate necessitated regular replenishment of slave ranks to sustain the institution.) In fact the ban actually made slave owners wealthier, at least on paper, by restricting supply and driving up the prices of the slaves they owned. And the domestic trade—the buying and selling of slaves within and between states—continued.

Yet even this was acquiring an odor. Slave owners liked to portray their labor system as merely a variant of labor practices elsewhere. Slaves were called "servants," "hands," "boys," "girls," "my men." Masters thought of themselves as heads of large families that included slaves, albeit in a different category than the masters' own flesh and blood. (The categories overlapped when, as happened with unacknowledged frequency, slaves *were* the flesh and blood of the masters.) The slave trade, even the domestic version, intruded on this peaceful picture. It tore mothers and fathers from children, husbands from wives, and generally ripped the mask from the idyllic model. Though necessary to support the business of slavery, it was often relegated to agents from whom the genteel classes tried to distance themselves.

Andrew Jackson wasn't what most of his neighbors would have called genteel, but by the end of the first decade of the nineteenth century his rough edges were beginning to rub smooth. He was one of the best-known men in Tennessee, an important figure in state politics. He didn't lack rivals or critics, but even they had to respect his ability and concede that he had come a long way from inauspicious beginnings.

His home was the Hermitage, a property he acquired in 1804. Jackson bought the property from Nathaniel Hays, a neighbor next door to Jackson and Rachel at Hunter's Hill. Hays had staked his claim to the square mile in 1780, at the beginning of white settlement of the Cumberland, but like many others he had been forced to retreat in the face of Indian resistance. Eventually he returned, bringing his wife, three children, and a couple of slaves. He and the slaves built a house of logs—more than a cabin but no mansion—near a gravel-bottomed spring on the tract. He and they cut the mature hardwood trees that covered most of the property, and planted cotton in the black soil deposited during the previous several millennia—and renewed each spring—by the Cumberland and Stones rivers. Hays traded his cotton for merchandise at a store Jackson owned on the Hunter's Hill property. On those visits and others, he and Jackson talked politics and militia affairs. Rachel got to know Elizabeth Hays and her daughters. As nearest neighbors they became friends.

Thus it was with some regret that the Jacksons learned in 1804 that the

Hayses would be moving. Nathaniel was as restless as many other western-ers, and he decided the future looked brighter in Bedford County, south of Nashville. When he told Jackson he intended to sell, Jackson did some quick calculating. His business activities had left him holding thousands of dollars of debt he couldn't collect. He needed to raise cash lest he lose even more money and perhaps lose the Hunter's Hill farm. As that farm was worth much more than the Hays property, if he purchased the Hays place and sold Hunter's Hill he could pay his debts and still live in the neighborhood, which suited him and Rachel quite well.

Negotiating the switch required some ingenuity, but during the summer of 1804 Jackson accomplished it. He sold Hunter's Hill for $10,000 in July and purchased Hays's farm for $3,400 in August. The swap eased his debt burden substantially, although it damaged his cash flow, as the new place, which he and Rachel soon began calling the Hermitage, produced crops of considerably less value than Hunter's Hill's. The log house, moreover, was rustic compared with the home he and Rachel had been living in. But he hired a carpenter and paperhanger to spruce up the interior and added a new kitchen outbuilding a short while later. Meanwhile he set crews to work felling trees, cutting brush, erecting fences, repairing barns, and doing the hundred other chores required to make the Hermitage a profitable farm.

The heavy work on the Hermitage was done by slaves. Jackson owned fewer than a dozen field hands during the early years at the new place, but as the operations expanded he purchased more. By 1820 he held four dozen slaves, including his cook and house servants. During the next several years he continued to purchase slaves, so that by 1829 he held perhaps a hundred. This left him well short of the largest slaveholders in America—the big planters of the Carolinas and the Gulf coast, who owned several hundred slaves—but it made him one of the larger slave owners in Tennessee.

Jackson treated slavery as a business matter but one not devoid of hu-manity. He bought and sold slaves as his business required. He bargained for the highest prices when he was selling and the lowest when he was buying. He tried to avoid selling young children away from their mothers, in part be-cause it was bad for business—being hard on the mothers and children—but also because it offended his sympathies. Jackson could see both the logic and the feeling in a comment by a business associate regarding a decision to rescind the sale of a young boy apart from his mother: "They are family

Negroes. . . . The sale I had made and the distance would create great affliction among their relations."

Jackson could be a hard man, as the many who ran afoul of him during
his life discovered. Yet toward Rachel he was tender to a fault, as he was
toward children and horses. His feelings toward slaves fell between his feelings for children and for horses. The slaves were under his authority and
therefore must obey him. When they didn't, he could be brutally severe.
"Fifty Dollars Reward," he advertised after one slave ran away. "All reasonable expenses paid—and ten dollars extra, for every hundred lashes any person will give him, to the amount of three hundred." But if the slaves did
obey him, he treated them as humanely as his need to profit by their labor
allowed. He housed them decently, by the standards of the time, and he fed
them fairly well. He purchased medicine for them when they became ill. His
account books list "1 bottle castor oil . . . for negro woman" and "2 ozs.
unguent basilic for negro man's leg" among the prescriptions for his family
and his horses.

As the operations at the Hermitage expanded, and especially as he spent
more time away from home, he came to rely on overseers to manage the
slaves. The overseers were a source of chronic concern to Jackson, as they
frequently failed to strike what he considered the appropriate balance between authority and kindness. Cruelty was as out of place as excessive le-
nience. Both were bad for the slaves and bad for business. They were also
bad for the reputation of a public man.

𝒥t was Jackson's concern for his reputation that prompted his withdrawal
from the traffic in slaves. The exit wasn't easy or uncomplicated. In 1810 he
formed a partnership with Joseph Coleman and Horace Green, the former
of Nashville and the latter of Natchez. Like most of Jackson's many partnerships, this one served multiple purposes and traded in various commodities, including cotton, tobacco, and slaves. In 1811 Green led some two
dozen slaves, recently purchased from Richard Apperson, from Nashville to
Natchez, where he hoped to sell them for a higher price than they could
fetch on the Cumberland. But the market for slaves on the Mississippi was
saturated that season, and Green found no satisfactory buyer. Apparently

his tolerance for disappointment was low, for he quit the partnership suddenly, leaving the slaves with John Hutchings, an erstwhile Jackson partner.

Jackson learned of the situation several weeks later, and he traveled to the Mississippi to reclaim his property. The market for slaves hadn't improved by the time he got there, so he brought them back to Nashville. The route crossed the lands of the Choctaws, whose agent insisted that Jackson show a passport. Jackson had no passport and moreover was already annoyed at having to travel a thousand miles to remedy another business venture gone bad. He defied the agent and pressed past him to Nashville. Upon his arrival he made a point of denouncing the man to Governor Blount and in doing so didn't disguise the reason for his journey. Nor had he disguised it to anyone along the way. "It was well known that my business to that country was to bring away a number of negroes which had been sent to that country for sale, and from the fall of the market and scarcity of cash remained unsold," he told Blount.

Yet seventeen years later, when Jackson was running for president, he attempted to hide his slave-trading past. His rivals had heard of the Natchez trip and now publicized it to show that Jackson dealt in human flesh. A friendly newspaper responded by publishing a document dated May 18, 1811—about the time Horace Green acquired the slaves he took to Natchez—asserting that "the said Andrew Jackson has no interest in the purchase . . . of the negroes. . . . He only holds a lien on them for the payment of the purchase money." The wording of the affidavit is unusual. Business documents generally state matters positively rather than negatively. Equally curious, and perhaps more significant, is that the original document, if any, has disappeared.

Other documents from the period strongly suggest that Jackson *did* have an interest in the slaves. An entry in his account book for the Bank of Nashville reads: "A. Jackson amount of proportion of cash for negroes bought of Richard Epperson: $929." Jackson's ownership is also indicated by promissory notes from Jackson to Apperson and by an affidavit submitted by Jackson to an arbitrator sorting out the tangled affairs of the failed partnership.

Almost certainly Jackson was part owner of the slaves in question. Even more certain is that by the 1820s a personal history of slave trading had become a political liability for a national candidate. Jackson's supporters, with or without his knowledge, likely planted the dubious disclaimer. If Jackson was aware of the cover-up, he probably excused it on grounds that it treated a minor matter from long ago. No one ever asserted that slave trading was a major part of his business or denied that it declined for him with passing years. Perhaps the trouble the Apperson slaves caused him made him swear off the practice forever. The one thing that can be said with complete confidence is that times and attitudes were changing. Slaveholding wasn't a disqualification for national office, but slave trading might be. And Jackson knew it.

At the end of 1808 Rachel and Andrew Jackson became parents. By then they had been married nearly fifteen years (by the state of Tennessee's reckoning; more by their own). No offspring had blessed their union, for reasons unclear. Almost certainly they wanted children. In those days before state-sponsored pensions nearly every parent did, if only for assistance in old age. Jackson's bout with smallpox during the Revolutionary War may have rendered him sterile. Or the infertility may have originated with Rachel, who had lived with Lewis Robards long enough to have borne children had she been able. (Robards went on to father several children by a second wife.)

Rachel probably felt the lack of children more severely than Jackson did. Especially in those days, when fewer outlets existed for the creative energies of women, the average wife placed great store in having children. One imagines Rachel wondering, as the years passed, whether she would ever have a child to hold, to put to bed at night, to nurse when sick, to admire growing up. She doubtless shared her sorrows and frustrations with Jackson, although perhaps not all of them, for fear of seeming weak.

In December 1808, Elizabeth Donelson, the wife of Rachel's brother Severn, bore twin boys. Someone suggested that Rachel and Jackson rear one of the boys as their own. Twins always place an extra strain on families of newborns. Perhaps Elizabeth didn't feel strong enough to care for two babies. Perhaps two new mouths to feed were one more than Severn thought he could handle. Rachel may have asked, or Elizabeth may have offered, but somehow the women decided that Rachel would take one of the babies for her own. The men were consulted, of course, but almost certainly the initiative came from the women.

Jackson later contended that he and Rachel formally adopted Andrew Jackson Jr. a few weeks after his birth. Corroborating evidence is scanty. In that era Tennessee had no regular procedure for adoptions, relying rather on extended families to take care of their children without state intervention. Jackson said he petitioned the legislature for a special bill. But no bill, or even any petition, appears in the state records.

Jackson may have misremembered things. More likely he misrepresented them—from the best of intentions. Given the cloud surrounding the start of his and Rachel's marriage, he didn't want Andrew Jr. living under a similar shadow. It was Tennessee's fault, not the boy's, that the state made adoption difficult.

Whether formally adopted or not, Andrew Jr. received all the love any child could ask for. By the standards of the time, he was a child of his parents' old age. Jackson and Rachel were forty-one, and many of their contemporaries were grandparents. Doubtless partly for this reason they spoiled Andrew, as grandparents—or merely late parents—often do. He wanted for nothing money could buy, servants deliver, or parental attention bestow. Though named for his father, he couldn't have spent a childhood more different from Jackson's straitened youth, and this was just as Jackson wanted it.

A visitor to the Hermitage caught its master in a domestic pose. "I arrived at his house one wet chilly evening, in February, and came upon him in the twilight, sitting alone before the fire, a lamb and a child between his knees. He started a little, called a servant to remove the two innocents to another room, and explained to me how it was. The child had cried because the lamb was out in the cold, and begged him to bring it in." The visitor knew Jackson as a man of ferocious reputation. Seeing him with young Andrew and the lamb made him think the reputation wrong, or at least incomplete. "The ferocious man does not do that."

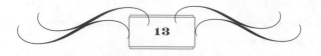

13

NOR INFAMY UPON US

*A*ndrew's arrival helped distract his father from business troubles. Besides the chronic shortage of money, entrepreneurs in the West faced the intractable problem of distance. The principal market for Nashville's produce was Natchez, five hundred miles away, leaving Nashville's merchants at the mercy of agents on long and tenuous tethers. Horace Green was only one of several unreliable characters whom Jackson was compelled to work with and who cost him thousands of dollars over the years. Distance created other difficulties. A dispute arose between Jackson and an ironmonger at Abingdon. "I cannot make out a statement . . . ," Jackson explained, "for want of the original contract, it being locked up and Mr. John Hutchings now at Natchez having the key." Perhaps Jackson was simply putting off his creditor. Jackson owed money but lacked cash.

He offered a horse—"a good draft horse and gentle in gear, and not a bad riding horse," he said—as payment for the debt. He added, "Send me a pair of boots of the manufactory of Abingdon . . . and close the accounts." Whether Jackson got the boots is unclear, but whatever he got didn't repay him for his headaches. "I always have the blue devils about me when old accounts are mentioned."

At times he thought of starting anew. Several friends had heard promising things about Madison County, to the west of Nashville. They were moving there and wanted Jackson to join them. They said he might be appointed judge of the county. Jackson was tempted. His business interests in Nashville weren't thriving and his enemies were, and the combination kept his blue devils alive. "I find it impossible to divest myself of those habits of gloomy and peevish reflection that the wanton and flagatious conduct and unmerited reflections of base calumny heaped upon me has given rise to," he told a friend and possible sponsor for the judgeship. He said he was willing "to try the experiment how far new scenes might relieve me from this unpleasant tone of thought." But an acceptable offer never came through, leaving him stuck where he was.

Still he dreamed of other places and new opportunities. His nephew Donelson Caffery traveled south to Spanish Florida and reported handsome prospects. "There is no business in this country like farming. An industrious man with a few negroes may soon make a fortune." The land was Spanish merely in name. "The Spanish authority here is suspended by a feeble thread. There is only a mere shadow of a government. The commandant of this place may be bribed to any thing. He will grant a decree for the recovery of money, and by the debtor's slipping a few dollars in his hand will suspend that decree during his pleasure." A few weeks later Caffery wrote again, declaring Florida ripe for the plucking. "The people in this country appear to be on the eve of shaking off the Spanish authority. A few popular men with spirit and sense enough to conduct an enterprise of the kind could at any moment revolutionize the province." Another informant, a son of Jackson's close friend (and second) Thomas Overton, was equally encouraging. "If you have never visited this country, I think, sir, it would be well worth your while, as it is much the finest I have ever seen. This, sir, is the place for making fortunes. I have persuaded my father much to remove here, but he pays no attention to my entreaties. I think were you to see this country, you would move the whole neighbor-hood."

*T*he allure of Florida—what soldier or American patriot wouldn't want to conquer such a country?—and the trials of business at home made Jackson wish more than ever that the war against Britain would begin. Spain was Britain's ally, and a war against the latter might easily involve the former. But everything pointed the opposite way. In the letter offering himself for judge of Madison County, Jackson explained that his interest in the job reflected his discouragement with respect to the big issue confronting the West and America generally. "I am well aware that no act of insult, degradation or contumely offered to our government will arouse them from their present lethargy and temporising conduct until my name sake"—the British minister in Washington happened to be named Jackson—"sets fire to some of our seaport towns. . . . Then perhaps the spirit of '76 may again arise."

Jackson's frustration over the war issue caused him to break with Jefferson regarding the president's successor. Jefferson had been grooming James Madison, and such was his control over the Republicans that the party's congressional caucus fell obediently into line in support of the secretary of state, despite the uproar over the *Chesapeake* shelling and the embargo. Jackson refused to follow the administration's line. Instead he joined an insurgent wing of the party in putting forward James Monroe, who as minister to Britain had argued forcefully against impressment. Jackson stumped around Tennessee for Monroe, with modest effect. And even that effect often wore off as soon as he left. "The only two converts you made while here have retrograded," an acquaintance in Carthage told Jackson. "They say that they only supported Monroe out of politeness to you. . . . I can assure you, sir, without you or some other friend of Monroe's return to this quarter, he will have but few friends."

Monroe's candidacy stalled long before the general election, in which Madison easily defeated Federalist Charles Pinckney. Yet Madison's victory, despite dealing a blow to Jackson and the insurgents, in fact left the discontented in a stronger position than previously. Jefferson was a giant of the revolutionary era, Madison a mere mortal. Jefferson could resist the complaints of his pro-war critics, Madison maybe not.

Jefferson did Madison the lame-duck favor of allowing repeal of the disastrous embargo, but he covered his retreat with a face-saving measure called the Nonintercourse Act, which maintained the embargo against Britain and France yet opened American trade to other countries. The law invited evasion, for once American vessels left port, ostensibly for Brazil or Russia or some other nonbanned country, they might head for whatever destination they chose. And it tied American policy in knots. French commanders captured American ships near Britain, claiming that they must actually be British since American ships weren't allowed to trade with the British. (In fact British merchant vessels were known to fly the American flag to disguise their nationality.) Forced to acknowledge the failure of the nonintercourse policy, Madison substituted an even more convoluted piece of legislation called Macon's Bill Number Two. This opened American trade with Britain and France but empowered the president to reimpose the embargo against either country should the other act decently toward the United States.

Madison's problem was the same one every president since George Washington had faced. Britain and France were each more powerful than the United States, and each considered its war with the other more important than good relations with America. If strangling France required trampling on America's rights, Britain would trample away. If repelling Britain necessitated treating American vessels as British, France would do so. America's European troubles might not end when the European war ended, but they certainly wouldn't end before that.

*E*specially in the early days of the American republic, the president didn't make foreign policy by himself. Congress was the equal of the executive on most aspects of the subject, and it insisted on its prerogatives. Madison understood the situation, which contributed to his hesitance regarding war.

Jackson understood the situation, too, and he initially blamed Congress for the government's failure to act against Britain. "The present Congress will not act with energy," he declared several months into the Madison presidency. "Some of our old Republican friends have either lost their usual good judgment or their political principle. From all which I conclude that as a military man I shall have no amusement or business."

The elections of 1810, however, brightened the outlook by infusing Congress with new blood. Henry Clay would become Jackson's archrival, but when he first entered the political arena they had much in common. Clay was self-educated, ambitious, and a westerner who saw the legal profession as a springboard to public life. His successful defense of Aaron Burr in the celebrated treason trial won him a national reputation and inspired his Kentucky compatriots to send him to Washington as their congressman. Seniority in those days meant less than ability, and Clay's ability was so obvious that his fellow congressmen made him their speaker within weeks of his arrival. The subject on which Clay spoke most loudly and consistently was the need for war against Britain, to vindicate the nation's honor, safeguard its frontiers, and secure its future.

"No man in the nation desires peace more than I," Clay asserted, unconvincingly. "But I prefer the troubled ocean of war, demanded by the honor and independence of the country, with all its calamities and desolations, to the tranquil, putrescent pool of ignominious peace." Clay noted that both Britain and France had violated American rights. And he said that if America could accommodate only one of the European powers, he wished it were Britain. But honor prevented that, leaving the country no choice. "I am for war with Britain, because I believe her prior in aggression. . . . Britain stands preeminent in her outrage on us." Skeptics asked how America could wage a war against such a mighty empire. America lacked the money, they said. Clay sneered. "Are we to be governed by the low, groveling parsimony of the counting room, and to cast up the actual pence in the drawer before we assert our inestimable rights?" Besides, the war would pay for itself. "The conquest of Canada is in your power. I trust I shall not be deemed presumptuous when I state, what I verily believe, that the militia of Kentucky are alone competent to place Montreal and Upper Canada at your feet."

John C. Calhoun entered the House a year after Clay, in part because the South Carolinian detoured north to attend Yale College and then the law school at Litchfield, Connecticut, directed by Tapping Reeve. But by 1807, when he was twenty-five, Calhoun had had enough of northern ways and northern winters, and he returned to South Carolina to start a legal practice and a political career. The two went forward simultaneously, both assisted by a marriage that won him allies among the planter class around Charleston. These allies sent him off to Washington in 1811, where he made friends with Henry Clay and won appointment to the influential committee on foreign affairs.

Calhoun's committee seat afforded a pulpit for decrying the perfidy of Britain and the folly of thinking the perfidy would cease without the chastisement of war. Speaking for the committee, Calhoun declared a war against Britain nothing less than a second war for American independence.

> Your Committee, believing that the freeborn sons of America are worthy to enjoy the liberty which their Fathers purchased at the price of so much blood and treasure, and seeing in the measures adopted by Great Britain a course commenced and persisted in which must lead to a loss of national character and independence, feel no hesitation in advising resistance by force. . . . Americans of the present day will prove to the enemy that we have not only inherited that liberty which our Fathers gave us, but also the will and power to maintain it. Relying on the patriotism of the Nation, and confidently trusting that the Lord of Hosts will go with us to battle in a righteous cause and crown our efforts with success, your Committee recommend an immediate appeal to arms.

While the "war hawks"—as their opponents called Clay, Calhoun, and the other advocates of armed resistance to Britain—demanded a declaration from Congress, Jackson prepared his troops. The Tennessee militia had been reorganized since Jackson's election as major general. Population growth, combined with hostility toward Jackson among friends of John Sevier, caused the legislature to split the state into two divisions for militia purposes. Jackson received command of the western district. He might have been more upset at the partition had he not realized—with everyone else who pondered the matter—that the western division, the one abutting the frontier, was the more important of the two and the more likely to see action. Anyway, Jackson knew that when action came the initiative would go to whoever seized it.

He commenced the seizure right after the *Chesapeake* incident. Sevier was again governor of Tennessee and therefore Jackson's superior. But Sevier moved too slowly for Jackson, who complained that he had waited "with anxious expectation for many weeks" to receive the governor's order to ready the militia, and it had never come. So he was obliged to give the order himself. "Place your brigades in the best possible state to perfect the quota that may be requested from you," he told his brigade commanders. "When there is a call to arms, there will be but one voice: Defend the liberties and independence of our country or die nobly in the cause."

Jackson's audacity forced Sevier to give the mobilization order. But by the time it arrived, Jackson had moved even farther toward war, and now he criticized the governor's order as insufficient regarding troop numbers and supplies. "If he knows his duty as a military man he never performs it," Jackson complained to James Winchester, one of his brigade generals.

Sevier retired shortly thereafter, to Jackson's relief. The new governor was Willie Blount, whom Jackson at once began to educate as to the needs of the state and the nation. "Our independence and liberty was not obtained without expense," he told Blount. "It was dearly bought both with blood and treasure. It must be preserved." Jackson sent the governor an ambitious plan for strengthening the militia. The able-bodied men of the state would be placed into two classes, one comprising those aged eighteen to twenty-eight, the other twenty-nine to forty. The former would be the first called to duty; the latter would constitute the reserves. Every three years a new classification would be made. "This will always keep ready for duty the young and healthy part of our citizens who will be able to undergo any hardship or fatigue and keep our militia in a proper state of discipline. . . . Our state in a very few years could furnish an army sufficient to face any enemy that could be introduced by an invading foe."

*W*hile Jackson girded for war, the Cumberland experienced another outbreak of the quotidian violence that made western life so uncertain. Patton Anderson was the brother of Jackson's militia aide William Anderson. In

October he was gunned down in the courthouse square in Shelbyville. Numerous witnesses identified the shooter as David Magness, who was arrested at once. The questions before the court that heard the case were the degree of his culpability—murder or manslaughter?—and the involvement of his father and brother—conspirators or merely supportive kin? The Andersons and Magnesses had long been enemies, and the trial attracted considerable attention. The Magnesses hired a phalanx of lawyers and summoned scores of witnesses to testify to their upstanding character and the extenuating circumstances of the shooting.

William Anderson was understandably upset at the death of his brother and the extraordinary efforts of the defense to secure acquittal. "If the trumpet of hell had been sounded and a general jubilee pervaded the whole infernal regions," he told Jackson, "such a lot of murderers, thieves and scoundrels could not have appeared as the Magnesses have to swear for them."

Jackson testified for the prosecution. He knew the events of the fatal hour only from hearsay but the deceased from personal experience. "My friend, Patton Anderson, was the natural enemy of scoundrels," he asserted, leaving the jury to draw the appropriate inference regarding the Magnesses.

The jury convicted David Magness of manslaughter and ordered him imprisoned for eleven months and branded with the letter *M*—for manslaughter—on his hand. The other Magnesses were acquitted but charged court costs. When they couldn't pay these or their attorneys' fees they were jailed as deadbeats. It was a mark of contemporary American jurisprudence, or at least its Tennessee variant, that the deadbeats spent longer behind bars than the killer.

A small consequence of the Magness trial that grew into something larger was a meeting between Jackson and Thomas Hart Benton. Benton had seen Jackson once before, at a superior court trial over which Jackson presided. Benton was seventeen at the time and found Jackson most impressive. "He was then a remarkable man, and had the ascendant over all who approached him, not the effect of his high judicial station, nor of the senatorial rank which he had held and resigned; nor of military exploits, for he had not then been to war; but the effect of his personal qualities: cordial and graceful manners, hospitable temper, elevation of mind, undaunted spirit, generosity, and perfect integrity." Benton first spoke to Jackson some years later. The younger man was beginning his legal career; the elder was major general of the Tennessee militia. Their paths crossed in a small town on the state's southern frontier. "He smiled, and we began a conversation in which he very quickly revealed a leading trait of his character: that of encouraging young men in their laudable pursuits. Getting my name and parentage, and learning my intended profession, he manifested a regard for me, said he had received hospitality at my father's house in North Carolina, gave me kind invitations to visit him, and expressed a belief that I would do well at the bar—generous words which had the effect of promoting what they undertook to foretell." At the Magness trial they met again. Benton was a junior member of the prosecution and nervously opened the case for the state. Jackson again provided encouragement. "He found my effort to be better than it was. He complimented me greatly, and from that time our intimacy began."

Benton shared Jackson's belief in the necessity for war against Britain, and as the conflict drew near he offered his services in the patriotic cause. "I have always been resolved to quit the gown for the sword whenever the sword was to be used," he told Jackson. He wanted to be an aide to the general, despite lacking obvious qualifications. "The truth is, I know of nothing that could recommend me to such a place. But the natural inclination which all young men feel, or ought to feel, to advance themselves in the world has induced me to say that if you should lack an officer of this kind, and should be able to find none better than myself, that I should deem myself honored by your approbation." Jackson, encouraging Benton yet again, gave the young man the job.

𝒯he clouds of war appear to be hovering around us," Jackson declared in May 1811, and they lowered with each passing month. The war hawks in Washington clamored more vigorously than ever for a declaration of belligerency, and some detected progress. "The Rubicon is passed," Tennessee senator Felix Grundy told Jackson regarding the mood of the Senate foreign relations committee. To smooth the road to war, the committee recommended filling out the ranks of the army and mobilizing the militia in the states. Madison continued to resist a war declaration, yet he acknowledged the need to prepare and in early 1812 issued a call for fifty thousand volunteers.

Jackson wished Madison had gone all the way to war, but he accepted mobilization as the next best thing. "Citizens!" he declared in a summons to the militia of western Tennessee.

> Your government has at last yielded to the impulse of the nation. Your impatience is no longer restrained. The hour of vengeance is now at hand. The eternal enemies of American prosperity are again to be taught to respect your rights. . . . War is on the point of breaking out between the United States and the King of Great Britain, and the martial hosts of America are summoned to the tented fields!

The other war hawks spoke of the struggle with Britain as a second war of independence; Jackson, who still bore scars from the first war of independence, held that view with special conviction. The approaching conflict was about violations of American rights, but it was also about vindication of American identity.

> Who are we? And for what are we going to fight? . . . We are the free born sons of America, the citizens of the only republic now existing in the world, and the only people on Earth who possess rights, liberties, and property which they dare to call their own. . . . We are going to fight for the reestablishment of our national character, misunderstood and vilified at home and abroad. . . . Will the people shrink from the support of their government—or, rather, will they shrink from the support of themselves? Will they abandon their great imprescriptable rights, and tamely surrender that illustrious national character which was purchased with so much blood in the war of the Revolution? No. Such infamy shall not fall upon us. The advocates of kingly power shall not enjoy the triumph of seeing a free people desert themselves and crouch before the slaves of a foreign tyrant.

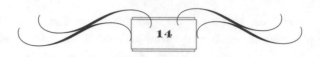

14

NATIVE GENIUS

In August 1811 William Henry Harrison encountered the most remarkable man he had ever met. Others were equally impressed, as Harrison observed.

The implicit obedience and respect which the followers of Tecumseh pay to him is really astonishing and more than any other circumstance bespeaks him one of those uncommon geniuses, which spring up occasionally to produce revolutions and overturn the established order of things. If it were not for the vicinity of the United States, he would perhaps be the founder of an Empire that would rival in glory that of Mexico or Peru. No difficulties deter him. His activity and industry supply the want of letters. For four years he has been in constant motion. You see him today on the Wabash and in a short time you hear of him on the shores of Lake Erie or Michigan, or on the banks of the Mississippi, and wherever he goes he makes an impression favorable to his purposes.

Harrison wasn't indulging idle curiosity in describing the Shawnee leader. He went on to say: "There can be no doubt but his object is to excite the Southern Indians to war against us."

Harrison was in his twelfth year as governor of Indiana Territory, following a decade of military and civilian service on the Ohio frontier. No one knew the Indians of the West better than Harrison, and no western Indian worried him more than Tecumseh. Until recently Tecumseh had labored in the shadow of his brother, the strangely charismatic figure whites called the Prophet. An injury in youth had taken the Prophet's right eye, which had the paradoxical effect of causing those who met him to sense that he saw things they didn't. There was nothing wrong with his tongue, which spoke fluently of things seen and unseen, past and future. The past and future ran together in the Prophet's mind's eye, which perceived an America without white men, where Indians lived as they had lived since before the eldest elders could recall, at peace with nature and enjoying its bounty. His vision was that of the Great Spirit, or so he said and his followers believed. They also believed that the Great Spirit spoke through him. And the Great Spirit said:

> My children, you complain that the animals of the forest are few and scattered. How shall it be otherwise? You destroy them yourselves for the skins only, and leave their bodies to rot or give the best pieces to the whites. I am displeased when I see this, and take them back to the earth that they may not come to you again. You must kill no more animals than are necessary to feed and clothe you. . . . I made all the trees of the forest for your use, but the maple I love the best because it yields sugar for your little ones. You must make it only for them, but sell none to the whites. . . . If you take more than is necessary for your own use, you shall die.

It was easy at first for whites to underestimate the Prophet and the appeal of his message to the western tribes. Thomas Jefferson did. "I concluded . . . that he was a visionary, enveloped in the clouds of their antiquities, and vainly endeavoring to lead back his brethren to the fancied beatitudes of their golden age," Jefferson said. "I thought there was little danger of his making many proselytes from the habits and comforts they had learned from the whites, to the hardships and privations of savagism, and no great harm if he did. We let him go on, therefore, unmolested."

Tecumseh was harder to ignore, being much of what his brother was not. Tecumseh was tall and athletically handsome, with arresting demeanor and gaze. "One of the finest looking men I ever saw," an American army captain wrote after meeting Tecumseh. "About six feet high, straight, with large, fine features, and altogether a daring bold-looking fellow." Tecumseh's eloquence was practical rather than mystical, his energy attuned to what might be achieved rather than what might be believed. While the Prophet spoke of a spiritual union of Indians against whites, Tecumseh traveled from village to village and nation to nation, forging a military alliance of Indians against whites. In one respect his task was easy, for by the beginning of the nineteenth century scarcely a tribe of the Ohio Valley hadn't been cheated out of land by the whites or by Indians corrupted by white promises and white liquor. In another respect, though, the very cheating made his job harder, for the Indians who signed away the land had cast their lot with the whites and weren't prepared to abandon their sponsors. Some of their resistance to Tecumseh's message revealed simple self-interest, the reluctance of the comfortable to risk what they had. But some of it reflected a reasoned judgment that the actual alternative to accommodation of whites wasn't removal of the whites but destruction of the Indians. Tecumseh might preach revival, they said, but he courted disaster.

Those Indians who opposed Tecumseh informed the whites, including Governor Harrison, of his movements and activities. Harrison grew especially nervous when he learned that Tecumseh had approached the British in Canada about weapons and supplies. Till now the trump card of American officials in Ohio and throughout the West had been their monopoly of the trade goods and provisions the Indians had come to depend on. The Prophet's message of Indian self-sufficiency threatened this monopoly but not seriously, in the judgment of Jefferson and other American officials who concluded that most Indians were addicted to the conveniences contact with whites had brought them. Tecumseh's challenge was more threatening because it was more realistic. He didn't eschew civilization but aimed to acquire it, or at least its accoutrements, from the British. "You, Father, have nourished us, and raised us up from childhood," he addressed the British commander at Fort Malden, on the Canadian side of the Detroit River, in the ceremonial language of Indian diplomacy. "We are now men, and think ourselves capable of defending our country, in which you have given us active assistance and always advice. We are now determined to defend it ourselves . . . and leave you behind, but expecting you will push forward towards us what may be necessary to supply our wants."

Harrison warned Tecumseh and his followers that they were inviting trouble. "Do not think that the red coats can protect you," he declared, referring to the British. "They are not able to protect themselves. They do not think of going to war with us. If they did, in a few moons you would see our flags wave on all the forts of Canada." Harrison asked Tecumseh and the Prophet to consider what they were up against. "I know your warriors are brave. . . . But what can a few brave warriors do against the innumerable warriors of the Seventeen Fires [the United States]? Our blue coats are more numerous than you can count, and our hunting shirts [militia] are like the leaves of the forest or the grains of sand on the Wabash."

How much Tecumseh knew of American politics at this time is unclear. If he had been listening to the war hawks, he must have questioned Harrison's assertion that there would be no war between the blue coats and the red coats. He might also have guessed that his own actions and those of his Indian allies could be instrumental in determining whether the Americans and British went to war. One thing he knew for certain: the Indians were losing the peace. Year after year the Americans seized more land, sometimes cloaking the seizure in the language of treaties, often not bothering. Tecumseh wasn't eager to fight. He didn't dispute Harrison's reckoning of the disparity between the numbers of Indians and of whites. But he saw little choice.

He confronted Harrison at a council that became famous throughout the West. In August 1810 Tecumseh and several dozen Indians from various tribes met the governor at Vincennes, the capital of Indiana Territory. By now it was plain to Harrison that Tecumseh was "the great man of the party," as the governor reported to the secretary of war at Washington. Harrison accordingly listened closely while Tecumseh presented the Indian case. The Shawnee leader recounted relations between the Indians of the Ohio Valley and the various interlopers. The French had come first. "They gave us many presents and treated us well. They asked for a small piece of country to live on" and were satisfied with that. The British followed and fought with the French. At first they too treated the Indians well. But then they fought with the Americans, and their fight became the Indians' fight. "They never troubled us for our lands, but they have done worse by inducing us to go to war." Several tribes suffered in the conflict between the British and the Americans, and nearly all suffered in the aftermath of the American victory. The Americans murdered Indians, even those bearing flags of peace, and stole their land. The Americans set one tribe against its neighbors and provoked them all to war.

> You try to force the red people to do some injury. It is you that is pushing them on to do mischief. You endeavour to make destructions. You wish to prevent the Indians to do as we wish—to unite and let them consider their land as the common property of the whole. You take tribes aside and advise them not to come into this measure. . . . You want by your distinctions of Indian tribes in allotting to each a particular track of land to make them to war with each other. . . . You are continually driving the red people. . . . At last you will drive them into the great lake.

Tecumseh didn't disguise his contempt for the accommodationists among the Indians or his strategy for dealing with them. He said he intended "to destroy village chiefs by whom all mischief is done. It is they who sell our land to the Americans. Our object is to let all our affairs be transacted by warriors." The warriors were taking matters into their own hands. "We shall have a great council at which all the tribes shall be present, when we will show to those who sold that they have no right to sell. . . . We will know what will be done with those chiefs that did sell the land to you. I am not alone in this determination. It is the determination of all the warriors and red people that listen to me." Harrison should take heed and act accordingly. "I now wish you to listen to me. If you do not it will appear as if you wished me to kill all the chiefs that sold you this land. I tell you this because I am authorized by all the tribes to do so. I am at the head of them all. . . . If you do not restore the land you will have a hand in killing them."

Harrison started to answer Tecumseh's charges. The governor said the United States had treated the Indians with fairness and justice. But he hadn't got far when Tecumseh suddenly stood up, as did his bodyguard of several young warriors with clubs. By Harrison's account, Tecumseh spoke "with great vehemence and anger" and, by the account of Harrison's interpreter, called the governor a liar. Harrison's own bodyguard leaped to the governor's side, and for a moment it looked as though the looming war would commence then and there. Yet restraint prevailed, even if it couldn't save this council session, which ended abruptly.

Harrison and Tecumseh met the next day, after tempers had cooled, but to no more positive effect. Harrison said he would relay Tecumseh's comments to the Great Chief—the American president. It would take time, though, as the American capital was far away.

Tecumseh said he would wait for an answer. "As the Great Chief is to determine the matter, I hope the Great Spirit will put some sense into his head to induce him to direct you to give up this land. It is true; he is so far off. He will not be injured by the war. He may still sit in his town and drink his wine, while you and I will have to fight it out."

Jackson knew Tecumseh and the Prophet only by reputation. Yet he understood what their movement meant for life all along the frontier. Indian attacks had continued to diminish during the first decade of the nineteenth century, but only a fool would have attributed the decline to any broad conversion of the natives to white manners and practices. Rather it reflected a fatalistic feeling that resistance was futile. This feeling might change in a moment, should an able and persuasive leader—Tecumseh, for example— begin preaching unity in strength. And if that leader had access to British weapons—as Tecumseh apparently did—there might be bloody hell to pay.

Jackson had long been nervous about British meddling. As the one responsible for the security of western Tennessee, he couldn't afford to be otherwise. In 1808 a man named William Meadows reported a harrowing escape from a large band of Creek warriors who had massacred three families and several other persons near the Tennessee River. Significantly, Meadows added that twelve white men were traveling with the war party that attacked him and the deceased. Jackson would have judged such an attack by Indians alone sufficient grounds for mounting a reprisal, but the presence of the whites among the Creeks struck him as especially alarming. "There can remain no doubt but the twelve whites with them must be agents of a foreign nation exciting the Creeks to hostilities against the United States," Jackson wrote President Jefferson. "These horrid scenes bring fresh to our recollection the influence during the Revolutionary War that raised the scalping knife and tomahawk against our defenseless women and children. I have but little doubt the present savage cruelty is excited from the same source. The blood of our innocent citizens must not flow with impunity. Justice forbids it, and the present relative situation of our country with foreign nations requires speedy redress and a final check of these hostile murdering Creeks." Jackson explained that he had put his militia units on the alert. Officers and men were ready to march. But the hard times had left them short of the weapons they required. Jackson hoped the president could help. "Without arms, although brave we cannot fight."

Three weeks later Jackson discovered, to his enormous embarrassment, that William Meadows was a spinner of tales. Exaggerated atrocity stories were a staple of frontier life. Often the exaggeration was the understandable result of trauma, of survivors overestimating the ordeals they had gone through. Sometimes it was deliberate, the work of persons who hoped to clear Indians from desirable land. Meadows's motives were unknown, but Jackson's investigation showed his report to be greatly embellished or wholly fabricated. "In all probability," Jackson admitted to Jefferson, "William Meadows is a base man and devoid of truth." Yet Jackson didn't retreat entirely from the argument his earlier letter had made. "I am still apprehensive that part of the Creeks are not friendly disposed towards the United States, and it is still probable that there are agents from some foreign power instigating them to mischief." This being the case, the militia continued to require increased support. Jackson said he had been paying certain militia expenses out of his own pocket. He was happy to do so, but his pockets had bottoms. And any policy that relied on the militia to support themselves was doomed to failure. They simply didn't have the resources.

Jackson shared with Jefferson a lesson he had learned in the Revolutionary War, one that would inform his military policy—and in fact his whole political philosophy—for the rest of his life. "The poor always make the best soldiers," he said. The rich were unreliable. "In the day of danger the wealthy enjoy too much ease to court danger." The poor knew hardship and danger from their daily lives. When the nation called, they were the first to answer. A republic that relied on the poor would survive, a republic that depended on the rich perhaps not.

*W*illie Blount had his own reasons for fanning fear of the Indians. When Blount succeeded John Sevier as governor of Tennessee in 1809, he initially hoped for peace with the Indians, but he insisted that it be peace on white—or, more precisely, Blount's—terms. Blount was Jackson's age and had lived in Tennessee nearly as long. He witnessed the chronic conflict between settlers and Indians, and by the time he became governor he concluded that the only solution was for the Indians to move across the Mississippi. "I am willing to act justly towards them," Blount wrote Jackson not long after entering the governor's house. But justice had to be tempered with realism. And, realistically, the Indians would never have peace so long as they were "surrounded by states thickly populated by people who have different interests." Blount proposed an exchange of real estate with the Cherokees and the Chickasaws: their current tribal lands for new lands west of the Mississippi. Tennessee didn't actually own any land over the river, but the United States owned the entire Louisiana Territory, and as one of the states Tennessee had a fair claim to part of that. A portion of Tennessee's claim could be transferred to the Cherokees and Chickasaws. "It would be promotive of their interest as nations to settle over the Mississippi," Blount told Jackson. "Game is there very abundant, the climate friendly to their constitutions, and much of the country is inhabited by people (Indians) whose manners and customs are more assimilated to theirs than those of the people where they now live." If they stayed where they were, they would lose their national character, if they survived at all. Beyond the river they could remain a cohesive people.

It went without saying that the emigration of the two tribes would benefit Tennessee. The state would gain land and eliminate the source of the friction that had vexed the people since the first white settlements. Blount thought his plan would serve the broader American interest as well. The residence of the Cherokees and Chickasaws—two relatively "civilized" tribes, and favorably disposed, at this point, toward the United States—would have a calming influence on their new neighbors. "Their intercourse with the neighboring Indians could by precept and example civilize them faster and make more favorable impressions on them of the friendship of the United States towards Indians in general than could be effected in any other way with ten-fold the expense."

*J*ackson would come to agree with Blount on the merits of putting distance between the whites and the Indians, but for now he needed the Cherokees, if not the Chickasaws, just where they were. As Tecumseh's message took hold, attacks against white settlements increased. In the spring of 1812 a band of Creeks killed six settlers in Humphreys County and carried off another, Martha Crowley, the wife of a riverboat man. Jackson was traveling when the first reports reached Nashville. By the time he got back the reports had been confirmed. "My heart bleeds within me on the receipt of the news of the horrid cruelty and murders committed by a party of Creeks on our innocent wives and little babes since I left home," he told Governor Blount. "*They must be punished.*" Jackson believed—correctly, as it turned out—that the British were behind the Creek rising. This made swift retribution all the more essential. "The sooner they can be attacked, the less will be their resistance and the fewer the nations or tribes that we will have to war with. It is therefore necessary for the protection of the frontier that we march into the Creek nation and demand the perpetrators at the point of the bayonet. If refused, that we make reprisals and lay their towns in ashes." Striking hard and fast would yield the additional benefit of forcing the hand of wavering Indians. "The Cherokees will join us if we show an immediate spirit of revenge." So critical was swiftness that the governor need provide only part of the expense of the campaign. "Give me the power to procure provisions and munitions of war by your orders, and I will pledge myself for the balance."

When Blount was slow to respond, Jackson took matters into his own hands. "I shall wait no longer than the 20th or 25th," he informed the governor in early July. "With such arms and supplies as I can obtain I shall penetrate the Creek towns until the captive, with her captors, are delivered up, and think myself justifiable in laying waste their villages, burning their houses, killing their warriors, and leading into captivity their wives and children until I do obtain a surrender of the captive and the captors."

To rally support for his insubordination, Jackson published an article in the Nashville *Democratic Clarion* entitled "The Massacre at the Mouth of Duck River." "It is now nearly two months since this cruel outrage, this act of war against the peaceful inhabitants of our country," Jackson wrote. "No vengeance has yet been taken; no atonement has yet been made." Jackson still hoped the government would shake off its criminal lethargy. But if it didn't, the people of Tennessee must act on their own. "It is impossible for them to permit the assassins of women and children to escape with impunity and with triumph. They cannot submit to the prospect of an Indian war, protracted through several years and kept alive by the murder of peaceful families in the dead hour of the night." The people had elected him to military command, and now he called on them. "Citizens! Hold yourselves in readiness. It may be but a short time before the question is put to you: *Are you ready to follow your general to the heart of the Creek nation?*"

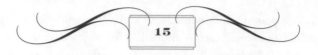

15

OLD HICKORY

Though Jackson didn't know it as he prepared to lead the Tennessee militia into battle, war had already been declared. In June 1812 Madison finally yielded to the demands of the war hawks and laid a bill of particulars against Britain before Congress. "British cruisers have been in the continued practice of violating the American flag on the great high way of nations, and of seizing and carrying off persons sailing under it," the president said. "Our commerce has been plundered in every sea; the great staples of our country have been cut off from their legitimate markets." British agents in the West consorted with Indians engaged in "a warfare which is known to spare neither age nor sex, and to be distinguished by features peculiarly shocking to humanity." Diplomacy had been tried to the limits of American patience and honor. War was the sole remaining resort.

Congress agreed with the president and on June 18 declared war. Yet the vote wasn't nearly unanimous: 79 to 49 for war in the House, 19 to 13 in the Senate. The 62 nays were mostly Federalists but included 22 Republicans, and they were predominantly—49 of the 62—from the Northeast. The war hawks had won in Congress, but their victory was tentative. If American armies stumbled in the field, recriminations would surely follow.

Jackson was overjoyed at Madison's action, belated though he judged it. Yet he wondered if the president really understood the danger America faced. Madison had mentioned the Indian threat almost as an afterthought to the main theme of his war message. This made sense in terms of national politics. All Americans could rally against Britain, but what did Pennsylvania or New Jersey care for the troubles of Tennessee? Yet to Jackson and most westerners, the Indian threat lay at the heart of the reason for war. Tecumseh had accomplished something no Indian leader since Pontiac had achieved: an alliance of several tribes against the whites. Memories of Pontiac's War—of the terror unleashed against men, women, and children; of refugees fleeing farms and villages for their lives—remained an active part of the western consciousness. The old folks told their children, who told *their* children, who shivered in their beds at the thought. Now the scourge had returned. The tomahawk and scalping knife were sharpened and raised. By all evidence, Tecumseh was even more adroit and persuasive than Pontiac had been. This new alliance was broader, stretching from the Great Lakes to the lower Mississippi. And it had the backing of the British, who had never scrupled to employ the natives against enemies of the Crown.

Jackson wanted to fight the British, but the Indians came first. "Before we march," he told his officers and men, "we must have an assurance that our wives and children are to be safe in our absence; and that assurance can only be derived from the surrender and punishment of the assassins who have taken refuge with the Creeks, or by marching an army into their country and laying it waste with fire and sword." Every able-bodied Tennessean must rally to the cause. "Woe to the man who is unwilling to do so! . . . The wretch who can view the massacre at the mouth of Duck river, and feel not his spirit kindle within him and burn for revenge, deserves not the name of a *man*; and the mother who bore him should point with the finger of scorn, and say, *"He is not my son."*

𝒯ecumseh was even happier than Jackson at the commencement of hostilities between the Americans and the British. The race war Tecumseh had been preaching—of Indians against whites—had already started, and it wasn't going well. After his confrontation with William Henry Harrison at Vincennes in 1810, Tecumseh had continued to travel and to stir up anger against the whites. Harrison couldn't track Tecumseh's movements in detail, but he knew what the Shawnee chief intended and how he aimed to achieve it. And in the autumn of 1811, when he learned that Tecumseh was away in the South, the Indiana governor determined to preempt the resistance Tecumseh was raising.

Harrison led a force of army regulars and militiamen up the Wabash River from Vincennes toward Prophetstown, a village at the mouth of the Tippecanoe River where Tecumseh's brother had gathered a large band of warriors. Harrison cited Indian attacks on white settlements as justification for invading what he conceded to be Indian land, but his own words and subsequent events revealed that he was seeking an excuse for battle, which he expected to win easily. "I have no reason to doubt the issue of a contest with the savages," he boasted to the secretary of war.

Tecumseh knew his alliance wasn't ready to take on the blue coats, which was why he had urged the Prophet to avoid a confrontation with the Americans at least until he returned from the South. Harrison knew this, too, which was why *he* was pressing ahead just now. As things developed, important factions of several nearby tribes chose to sit out the approaching battle, and some—notably the Delawares—provided Harrison intelligence about the Prophet's force.

Upon the Americans' approach, the Prophet assumed a brave posture. Perhaps he sincerely believed in the magic he promised his fighters. Perhaps he was simply trying to boost morale. Either way, he announced that the Great Spirit would strengthen their arms and shield them from the white men's bullets. And when the Americans, who outnumbered the Indians by two to one, encamped a mile from Prophetstown, he ordered a daring night-time attack.

Though the Americans had slept on their arms, the stealth and swiftness of the Indian attack staggered them. The regulars formed a defensive line but the militia scattered among the trees, the wagons, and anything else that afforded shelter from the Indian musket fire. The Americans had built bon-fires against the autumn cold and rain; these now served to silhouette them and assist the Indians' aim. The Indians, for their part, kept to the woods around the American camp and were all but impossible to see. During the first hour of the fighting, the American position was in constant danger of being overrun.

Yet the defenders held on, aided by their greater numbers and by the In-dians' short supply of ammunition. And as the eastern sky slowly bright-ened, the balance of the battle began to tip. Finally the Americans could see their attackers, had a chance of hitting them, and could consider a counter-attack. Harrison had been individually targeted by the Indians but been spared by fate as another officer, who had mounted Harrison's easily recog-nizable horse, was killed instead. When Harrison ordered the counterattack, his men, desperate to escape the positions where they had been pinned down, surged forward. They drove the Indians from the camp and thanked heaven for having survived.

The Americans got the worst of the fighting in terms of casualties. "Our killed and wounded amounted to 179," Harrison reported the next day. "Of these 42 are now dead and seven or eight more will certainly die." The Indian losses were considerably fewer, though harder to gauge. Yet the end of the battle left the Americans in command of the field.

Decades later Harrison's supporters would treat the Battle of Tippeca-noe as the turning point in the struggle for the Northwest. At the time, the battle itself was overshadowed by Harrison's obliteration of Prophetstown, which was left undefended upon the Indians' retreat. Even this accomplish-ment was less important than the destruction of the Indians' store of food for winter. As always, the weakest link in the chain of Indian defense was the need of their women and children to eat.

The unintended consequence of the American victory was to throw Tecumseh more to the side of the British than ever. The Prophetstown battle showed that the Americans could crush the Indians and that Harrison wouldn't hesitate to do so. But British backing might level the field.

This prospect explained why Tecumseh was so relieved when he learned that war between the British and the Americans had begun, and why he moved at once to exploit the opportunity it afforded. Not long after the American declaration, the government at Washington appointed William Hull, an ailing veteran of the Revolutionary War with healthy political connections, to lead an attack on Canada opposite Detroit. But Tecumseh forged a coalition of Indians from several tribes and inflicted a sudden sharp blow against an American advance party. The ambush frightened Hull, who knew every Indian atrocity story and sweated nights wondering what Tecumseh's red demons would do next. Hull's sleep was additionally disrupted when he learned that the American post at Mackinaw, on the strait linking Lakes Michigan and Huron, had surrendered to a large enemy force. This "opened the northern hive of Indians," Hull said afterward, "and they were swarming down in every direction." In a panic, he aborted the campaign against Canada and prepared to retreat to Ohio, only to be trapped by the arrival of a fresh regiment of British troops and enemy Indians. Its commander, Isaac Brock, knew of Hull's obsession with Indians and used it against him. Brock forged and let slip to the American general a document describing an Indian army approaching Detroit; in offering to let Hull surrender, Brock explained, "It is far from my inclination to join in a war of extermination, but you must be aware that the numerous body of Indians who have attached themselves to my troops will be beyond control the moment the contest commences." Hull's first response was horror at the fate that might befall the civilians in the fort. "My God!" he told an aide. "What shall I do with these women and children?" His second response was to accept Brock's terms and capitulate.

A worse disaster completed the northern debacle. While surrendering Detroit, Hull ordered the evacuation of Fort Dearborn, on the western shore of Lake Michigan at the mouth of the Chicago River. Most of the garrison preferred their chances behind the fort's walls to their prospects on the prairies outside, but the commander followed Hull's orders. He arranged an escort of Potawatomi Indians who pledged to see the whites to safety. But once in the open the Indians turned on the whites, killing most of them and, according to an eyewitness, beheading one officer and eating his heart.

The news stunned Nashville. The Anglo-Indian victories in the North couldn't but encourage the tribes throughout the West and heighten the danger everywhere. Jackson, busy trying to enlist militiamen, recognized the blow to public morale and fought back. "The disaster of the northwestern army should rouse from his apathy every man who has yet slumbered over the public welfare," he told potential recruits. "These are the times which distinguish the real friend of his country from the town-meeting bawler and the sunshine patriot. While *these* are covering their conduct with the thinnest disguises and multiplying excuses to keep them at home, the former steps forth and proclaims his readiness to march."

Jackson's words produced the desired effect. Nearly three thousand volunteers enlisted (giving Tennessee grounds for the nickname it would employ ever after: "the Volunteer State"). Confusingly, they didn't all enlist under the same conditions or for the same term of service. Some signed on for twelve months, some for six, some for three, some for as little as two. The short termers weren't necessarily less patriotic than the longer termers; often they were simply more skeptical about the possibility of actual battle or more committed to family or business affairs. In the enthusiasm of the muster, the discrepancy appeared hardly worth bothering about.

Shortly Jackson received his marching orders. The War Department had determined that the Tennessee militia should descend the Cumberland and the Mississippi to New Orleans, there to defend against a seaborne British assault.

Jackson still thought Tecumseh the greater immediate danger, but he wouldn't complain of a chance to fight the British, who were what made Tecumseh such a threat. "Every man of the western country turns his eyes intuitively upon the mouth of the Mississippi," he told his troops. "At the approach of an enemy in that quarter, the whole western world"—the American West, he meant—"should pour forth its sons to meet the invader and drive him back into the sea." Jackson said he was counting on his friends and neighbors. "Let us demonstrate to our brethren in all parts of the Union that the people of Tennessee are worthy of being called to the defence of the Republic."

Preparing for the journey south was a job in itself. Most of his men had never fought before; some had hardly been away from home. They required instruction on how to prepare for the campaign and what to bring. As this was a militia rather than a regular army, the men would supply most of their needs themselves. Jackson ordered the cavalry to report with sabers and pistols, the infantry with rifles. The noncommissioned officers and men must come with blankets. All would furnish their own uniforms. As winter was approaching, these should be supplemented by foul-weather gear.

The men responded enthusiastically, but one thing after another kept the expedition from departing. Many of the recruits simply lacked weapons; Jackson wrote to Washington pleading for "500 swords and 250 cases of pistols." The War Department issued notes to pay the men, but the Nashville economy lacked the money—and confidence in the government scrip—to convert the notes into cash. The problem wasn't merely a matter of accounting; the men needed real money to purchase supplies for the campaign and to provide for their families in their absence.

Jackson fretted the more with each delay. "The success of military men depends on celerity of movement and ought to be like lightning," he grumbled. He solved the money problem, or rather deferred it, by shaming a local banker into advancing a portion of the troops' pay in hard currency. And he decided to march without the swords and pistols, hoping they would catch him en route.

*J*ust before leaving he bade Rachel good-bye. She had observed the approach of war with an ambivalence born at once of her personal experience on the frontier, which inclined her to endorse whatever measures were necessary to end the Indian threat, and her love for the man who would lead the Tennessee troops into battle, which made her wish the war might never come. When it did arrive, she took greater charge of affairs at the Hermitage, freeing Jackson to concentrate on raising the militia. And as he prepared to head south, she gave him a miniature of herself for a keepsake.

"I shall wear it near my bosom," he promised. But the gesture, though deeply appreciated, was unnecessary. "My recollection never fails me of your likeness." Jackson wasn't especially religious at this stage of his life, but Rachel was, and he knew it eased her fears when he spoke in religious terms. "We part but for a few days, for a few fleeting weeks, when the protecting hand of Providence, if it is his will, will restore us to each other's arms. In storms, in battles, amidst the raging billows, recollect his protecting hand. . . . Let us not repine; his will be done." To the extent he considered the matter, Jackson believed that heaven smiled on America's cause; for this reason Rachel need not worry. "The god of battle and justice will protect us. Hence then dispel any gloomy ideas that our separation may occasion. Bear it with Christian cheerfulness."

And say good-bye to young Andrew. "Kiss him for his papa."

𝒜t the beginning of 1813—the calendar had turned before Jackson's army finally got away—the motive force of choice for travelers from Tennessee to the "lower country" along the Mississippi remained what it had been for travelers since the Stone Age: gravity. Jackson and his men piled into thirty boats at Nashville and headed down the Cumberland. The weather tested the novices among the troops. "We had an extreme hard frost last night, and many of us who were not accustomed to being exposed slept badly," wrote one of the expeditioners on the second day out. Ice clogged the Cumberland and closed some of its tributaries. But even winter occasionally smiled. "The morning burst forth in all the radiance of a clear sun, shining on the white frosted trees, which bended over the stream of the Cumberland. It was cold, but the sun suffused his warmth." Mishaps weren't many yet startled those to whom they occurred. One boat developed a leak and sank beneath its cargo of men, who crowded into another boat. At a Sunday service held aboard a third boat, the superstructure collapsed under the weight of the congregation.

Where the Cumberland met the Ohio, the ice delayed the fleet for four days. After the ice cleared and the boats set off again, the weather closed in. "It rained, hailed, and snowed all this day and night," the chronicler of the voyage recorded on January 25. The men—or at least their diarist—got a thrill at the Mississippi. "Who can withhold his emotions while viewing the beauties of this august river, this Father of Waters? It is the grand reservoir of the streamlets from a thousand hills! . . . The productions of every climate are destined to float on its bosom!" To see the great river was to know why it must be defended, why it must remain American.

Passage on the Mississippi was swift but dangerous. Snags lurked just below the surface. A boat hit a "sawyer," which ripped its hull and started it filling with water. For a horrifying moment all on board appeared doomed. "But Providence held the destiny of those men by a hair, and made Captain Martin the instrument of their salvation. . . . He was propelled as it were by instinct. His men rowed with Herculean strength." They reached the shore with seconds to spare.

A south wind warmed the men but increased their labors, for now all put oars to water to maintain their pace. On February 16 they reached their goal. "On our landing at Natchez the strand was crowded with spectators welcoming the largest army that ever appeared in view of Natchez." The next day the army made its grand entrance into the town. "We excited very general attention of the inhabitants, by whom we were treated with distinguished politeness, and also by all the officers both civil and military whom we met with."

*M*ost wars are fought by fits and starts; "hurry up and wait" has been the soldier's motto for centuries. America's War of 1812 fit the pattern, especially in the West. Jackson had been out of touch during the month of the voyage, but on reaching Natchez he received a letter from James Wilkinson, who commanded American forces in the West from headquarters in New Orleans. Jackson still distrusted Wilkinson; if Burr's accomplice had been in cahoots with the Spanish, why not with the British? Jackson's doubts disposed him to read Wilkinson's letter with close skepticism, especially once he caught its gist. Wilkinson ordered Jackson to remain at Natchez till further notice. The British hadn't arrived on the coast, Wilkinson explained, and so the services of the Tennessee volunteers weren't required there. Moreover, positive reasons existed for keeping the soldiers' distance from the lower river, starting with the hazard to their health as the warm season neared and the possibility that their services would be required in Florida, to which approach was easier from Natchez than from New Orleans. Wilkinson's tone was reasonable and respectful. He gave no hint of having heard all the nasty things Jackson had said about him regarding the Burr conspiracy. "If it is in my power to add to the comfort and accommodation of the band of patriots under your orders, it is only necessary to point out the mode to me," he told Jackson.

Jackson doubtless scanned this letter several times for evidence of ulterior motives. If Wilkinson possessed them, they weren't to be found here, and Jackson had no choice but to acquiesce in the army general's directive. He did point out that it contradicted previous orders from Washington, "the substance of which is to proceed to New Orleans and there await the orders of Government." But he would accept Wilkinson's judgment and do as told. "In the meantime I will be happy to communicate with you on the public safety and defence of the lower country, and will move my troops to any point best calculated for this object." He hoped they wouldn't have to wait long for new orders. "My wish is to keep them employed in active service, as indolence creates disquiet."

Jackson occupied his troops as best he could. They drilled, cleaned their weapons, practiced their shooting, and packed and repacked their kits to be able to march at a moment's notice. Meanwhile Jackson wondered what Wilkinson was up to and whether the War Department was deliberately slighting the militia in favor of its own soldiers. Since the Revolutionary War, Americans had gone to battle in two columns: the regulars and the militia. The former considered themselves superior in training and discipline, the latter in courage and initiative. There was something to each stereotype yet more to the fact that the regulars were raised by the national government while the militia were mustered by the states. In wartime the national government claimed command of all forces, which was why Jackson took orders from Wilkinson. But the tension never disappeared, and the abiding constitutional struggle over sovereignty—were the states supreme or the nation?—played itself out in the ranks of the military.

Jackson's suspicions of the army intensified dramatically upon receipt of a letter from John Armstrong, the recently appointed secretary of war. There was something wrong with the letter, as Jackson could tell from the start. It was dated January 5, although Jackson knew that Armstrong hadn't been sworn in until February. This might have been a simple misdating. But the substance of the letter was what was truly bizarre. "The causes for embodying and marching to New Orleans the corps under your command having ceased to exist, you will on receipt of this letter consider it as dismissed from public service," Armstrong said. There was no further explanation, only a directive to deliver to General Wilkinson any equipment or other property acquired at public expense. And a single line that hardly counted as gratitude: "You will accept for yourself and the corps the thanks of the President of the United States."

Jackson must have read this letter a dozen times. It made no sense. At great effort, substantial cost, and no little peril, he had led two thousand men several hundred miles from home in the dead of winter to defend their country. Now the secretary of war was telling them it was all for nothing. They must turn around and go home. And they must do so at their own expense.

For most of the next decade Jackson would battle the War Department more often and almost as bitterly as he fought the avowed enemies of the United States. The struggle began in Jackson's camp on the banks of the Mississippi in that late winter of 1813. He couldn't decide whether Armstrong's disbanding order was a case of economizing run amok, with the Madison administration trying to trim costs to avoid angering the war's opponents further; whether it was part of some nefarious plot between Armstrong and Wilkinson to weaken western defenses and deliver New Orleans to the British or the Spanish; or whether it was a way for the army to discredit the militia, perhaps compelling Jackson's men to continue to New Orleans individually, there to enlist in the regulars under Wilkinson.

Jackson didn't air all his suspicions in his response to Armstrong, but he did register his vigorous objections. Did the secretary, or anyone else in the administration at Washington, appreciate what disbanding in Natchez entailed?

> Those that could escape from the insalubrious climate are to be de-
> prived of the necessary support and meet death by famine. The re-
> maining few to be deprived of their arms pass through the savage
> land where our women, children, and defenceless citizens are daily
> murdered. Yet through that barbarous clime must our band of citi-
> zen soldiers wander and fall a sacrifice to the tomahawk and scalp-
> ing knife of the wilderness, our sick left naked in the open field
> and remain without supplies, without nourishment or an earthly
> comfort.

The government had called on its people to rally to the nation's defense, and Tennessee had answered. Was this how her volunteers were to be repaid?

The order was simply unacceptable, and Jackson refused to accept it. "I animated those brave men to take the field," he told Armstrong. And he would see them home. "I mean to commence my march to Nashville in a few days, at which place I expect the troops to be paid and the necessary supplies furnished by the agents of Government."

Jackson's pen was still smoking when he wrote to Felix Grundy, Tennessee's war-hawk congressman. Armstrong's order was so wickedly wrongheaded, Jackson declared, that he "must have been drunk when he wrote it or so proud of his appointment as to have lost all feelings of humanity and duty." Whether drunk or sober, unwitting or aware, Armstrong was furthering the army's design to destroy the militia. The design included institutional aggrandizement, but it went much deeper than that, to the very meaning of American self-government. Destroy the militia, Jackson argued, and nothing would stand between the people's rights and those who would take them away. "The path is plain. The militia not being competent to defend the country on a sudden war, it is necessary that a standing army in time of peace should be kept up. . . . This once done (and I have very little doubt of the intentions of some), the liberties of the country are gone forever."

But such would not occur while Andrew Jackson had strength to oppose it. He would preserve his portion of the militia and tend to his citizen-soldiers. "As long as I have friends or credit, I will stick by them."

*H*e broke the news to the troops the next day. He praised them for their alacrity in answering their country's call, for their steadfastness during the journey south, for their focus on learning the arts of the soldier. All this entitled them to the thanks of their compatriots and the esteem of their commander. "He knows that if you had met an enemy, from your pride, your patriotism, and attention to discipline you would have gained laurels for yourself and honor for the country from which you come." But for causes vouchsafed only to the government, the campaign was over. "We are now to turn our faces to the north."

Jackson declined to reveal that he was defying orders in leading his men home. What he did say was that they had a long and arduous march ahead of them. They would be passing through a "savage country," inhabited by hostile tribes. "It is necessary for the safety of the detachment that we march in good order, and that the whole detachment continue together until we arrive at Nashville." They could count on their commander. "He will not leave one of the sick nor one of the detachment behind. . . . The sick, as far as he has the power and means, shall be made comfortable. They shall all be taken along. Not one shall be left unless those that die, and in that event we will pay to them the last tribute of respect; they shall be buried with all the honors of war."

Even as Jackson wrote these words, he had no idea how he would carry them out. The return would be much harder than the journey south. Men had fallen ill and needed to be carried. More to the point, the march would be a *march* rather than a boat-drift downstream. The detachment's stores weren't exhausted but were dwindling. And the army refused to send or authorize more. "I dare not incur the responsibility of the expense which must attend the march of the corps of your command back to Tennessee," James Wilkinson wrote, politely but maddeningly. Jackson had no money with him, but he did have credit with Nashville merchants and bankers, which he was more than willing to employ though it threatened him with bankruptcy. He scornfully answered Wilkinson that what the government wouldn't furnish the soldiers who rallied to its banner, their own general would. He would "provide the means for their support out of my private funds." Should these fail, officers and men would eat their horses.

Jackson's defiance of authority—word got out that he was bucking orders—and his pledge of his personal resources on behalf of his men won him their love and admiration as nothing else could have. He might be cashiered, might lose his home and farm, but he would get them home safely. Jackson had never been much to look at. Next to the hale young men who composed his army, he appeared almost puny. But now they saw in him a toughness, a resilience on which they could rely. Someone compared him to a hickory branch: thin but impossible to break. The image caught on, and before long, when he rode down the line of march, his men pointed to him and said there goes Old Hickory.

The journey home was less momentous than the decision to make it.

Jackson signed a note for a thousand dollars to purchase provisions, which fed the men and spared the horses. The five hundred miles from Natchez to Nashville went more rapidly than even he could have hoped. The soldiers averaged almost twenty miles a day, their steps lightened by the knowledge that each mile and day brought them closer to home. The sick began to revive en route, buoyed by the same knowledge. The news of their approach preceded them, and when the column arrived at Nashville, the city turned out in force. "Long will the General live in the memory of the volunteers of West Tennessee for his benevolent, humane, and fatherly treatment to his soldiers," the *Nashville Whig* declared, capturing the common sentiment. "If gratitude and love can reward him, General Jackson has them."

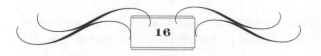

16

SHARP KNIFE

*E*ven Tennesseans, hardened as they were to personal feuds and affairs of honor, found it difficult to explain the fight that nearly killed Andrew Jackson, almost cost him his chance for military glory, and left him debilitated for months and in chronic pain for the rest of his life. The fight should never have happened and probably wouldn't have if Jackson had taken his role as father of his troops either more or less seriously than he did.

*T*wo roads led to the steps of the City Hotel in Nashville where the confrontation occurred. One was an offshoot of the Natchez Trace, the path trod by the Tennessee volunteers on their way home in the spring of 1813. Thomas Hart Benton, Jackson's protégé and aide-de-camp, later colonel of infantry, was among several junior officers who distrusted

James Wilkinson almost as much as Jackson did, and didn't want to be placed under his command. Yet apparently Benton agreed with Jackson that discretion dictated acquiescence, lest the bona fides of the Tennesseans come into question. At the time, neither man raised any question regarding the conduct of the other with respect to Wilkinson. Subsequently, though, Benton heeded rumors that Jackson had blamed him for fomenting unrest against Wilkinson. The rumors were absurd; Jackson far more likely would have praised criticism of Wilkinson than blamed it. But Benton indignantly demanded that Jackson set the record straight.

The second road to the City Hotel originated in a quarrel between Jesse Benton, Thomas Benton's brother, and William Carroll, one of Jackson's brigade majors. This quarrel, like so many others in that day and place, started trivially but accreted principle as it persisted, till finally it brooked no compromise. Jesse Benton challenged Carroll to a duel. Carroll accepted and asked Jackson to second him. Jackson seems to have declined at first, claiming advanced age and station. Whether he tried to talk Carroll out of the duel is less clear. But Carroll appealed to Jackson as to the father of his troops, and Jackson assented. The duel was even more ludicrous than most. Both men took bullets, Carroll in the hand and Benton in the buttocks. Duelists sometimes dodged or ducked to avoid being hit, but they weren't supposed to. A wound to the rear was at least as mortifying as it was painful.

Thomas Benton was away when the duel took place, but he shared his brother's embarrassment and blamed Jackson for his role in the affair. "You conducted it in a savage, unequal, unfair, and base manner," Benton said. "*Savage* because the young men were made to fight at ten feet distance, contrary to your own mode, to what is usual among gentlemen. . . . *Unequal* because the parties were made to wheel, an evolution which Mr. Carroll perfectly understood but which my brother knew nothing about. . . . *Unfair* because you concealed the mode of fighting from my brother. . . . *Base* because you avowed yourself to be the friend of my brother while giving to his adversary all these advantages over him." A man of Jackson's eminence should have restrained rather than encouraged dueling. "From your known influence over Mr. Carroll you might have managed the affair as you pleased; if not you were at least a free man and might have quit him if you did not approve his course."

Benton didn't quite challenge Jackson to a duel. But neither did he keep his complaints to himself. Before long all Nashville knew that the Bentons considered Jackson a dishonorable rogue. Jackson replied in writing to Thomas Benton's allegations, but the answer satisfied neither Thomas nor Jesse, and their complaining continued. Finally Jackson decided that one or both deserved a thrashing. He learned in early September that the two were staying at the City Hotel in Nashville. He rode to town from the Hermitage and took a room at the Nashville Inn nearby. Accompanied by John Coffee, another of his colonels, he strode past the City Hotel to the post office, to check his mail but also to check out the Bentons, who watched him walk by. On the way back he turned from the sidewalk to the door of the City Hotel and raised his riding whip against Thomas Benton, standing in the entrance.

At this point the story becomes confused, as often occurs in such cases. Jackson's partisans said Benton reached for a pistol, causing Jackson to draw his own gun. Benton's supporters asserted that Jackson drew first. All agreed that Jesse Benton, standing to the side, actually fired the first shots, at Jackson. One bullet caught Jackson squarely in the left shoulder, shattering bone and severing an artery. A second bullet hit his left arm. A third barely missed him. Jackson managed to squeeze off one shot before going down. Thomas Benton blasted away, as did John Coffee. Then the daggers came out. Stockley Hays, a nephew of Rachel Jackson, was passing by and heard the shooting. Seeing his uncle in danger, he dove upon Jesse and slashed him several times. Jesse pressed a pistol against Hays's heart and pulled the trigger, but the gun misfired. Alexander Donelson, another Jackson in-law, waded into the melee and nicked Thomas Benton, who had escaped the bullets by accidentally falling down a flight of stairs.

Finally, lest the fracas unduly alarm the guests, the management and the neighbors compelled the combatants to cease fire and drop dirks. (By an odd coincidence, three of those guests were Charles Fremon, his wife, Anne, and their infant son, John Charles, who would grow up to add an accent and a letter to his last name and, as John C. Frémont, wed Thomas Benton's daughter Jessie and carry Jackson's expansionist ideas to the Pacific Coast.) The only one seriously wounded was Jackson, who lay on the floor in a widening pool of his blood. Coffee and others carried him back to the Nashville Inn, where he ruined two mattresses with his hemorrhaging. Doctors were summoned and delivered their opinion that the left arm had to be sacrificed to save the patient. Jackson, barely conscious and fading, refused permission to amputate, and none of the physicians cared to cross him, even in his weakened condition. The medicine men applied slippery elm and other natural poultices, knowing they had nothing better than these Indian remedies.

The bleeding finally stopped on its own. The doctors knew Jackson was out of immediate danger, although there remained the problem of infection or gangrene, which could carry him off more slowly. For weeks he could scarcely stir.

Meanwhile the Bentons were marked men. "I am literally in hell here," Thomas Benton wrote just after the fight. "The meanest wretches under heaven to contend with: liars, affidavit-makers, and shameless cowards. All the puppies of Jackson are at work on me. . . . The scalping knife of Tecumseh is mercy compared to the affidavits of these villains. I am in the middle of hell here, and see no alternative but to kill or be killed." Benton grew convinced that Jackson's partisans were goading him to a duel for having wounded their hero. "My life is in danger."

The outnumbered Bentons left town. Thomas tossed his version of the affray over his shoulder as he went, accepted a commission in the regular army, and relocated to Missouri, where he commenced a political career. A decade elapsed before he met Jackson again, in Washington. The two were then senators, and they decided that the danger to the republic from John Quincy Adams dictated burying old differences. Jesse Benton was better at holding a grudge. He went to his grave damning Jackson for a scoundrel and a poltroon.

Tennessee shook its head over the Jackson-Benton scrape. Feuds and duels had lost their cachet from the early, rough years of Cumberland settlement, and though Jackson's friends loyally backed him, the larger community wondered what a man of his age and reputation was doing brawling with youngsters like the Bentons. Two decades previous, Jackson's injury might have been a badge of honor. Now it seemed a mark of stupidity. Before the fight he had been the darling of the state, the father-protector of her volunteers. Now he lay in a hotel bed, clinging to life and overhearing, through the fog of his pain, the puzzled criticism of those who had lately applauded him.

His reputation would have fallen further had the murmuring about him not been silenced by shocking news from the southern frontier. Tecumseh had been at work among the Creeks, Choctaws, and Seminoles, preaching union and defiance. By now he had honed his delivery and made his message almost irresistible. An eyewitness to a war council of Tecumseh and the Creeks remembered the Shawnee leader's effect on the Creek soldiers. "I have heard many great orators, but I never saw one with the vocal powers of Tecumseh," this observer said. "A thousand tomahawks were brandished in the air. Even the Big Warrior, who had been true to the whites, and remained faithful during the war, was, for the moment, visibly affected, and more than once I saw his huge hand clutch, spasmodically, the handle of his knife." Tecumseh told of his exploits in the north: "In defiance of the white warriors of Ohio and Kentucky, I have traveled through their settlements, once our favorite hunting grounds. No war whoop was sounded, but there is blood on our knives. The palefaces felt the blow, and knew not whence it came." He preached his race war more passionately than ever.

Accursed be the race that has seized our country and made women of our warriors. Our fathers, from their tombs, reproach us as slaves and cowards. I hear them now in the wailing winds. The Muscogee [another name for the Creek tribe] was once a mighty people. The Georgians trembled at your war whoop, and the maidens of my tribe, on the distant lakes, sung the prowess of your warriors and sighed for their embraces. Now your blood is white; your tomahawks have no edge; your bows and arrows were buried with your fathers. Oh, Muscogees, brush from your eyelids the sleep of slavery. Once more strike for vengeance, once more for your country. The spirits of the mighty dead complain. The tears drop from the weeping skies. Let the white race perish.

They seize your lands. They corrupt your women. They trample on the ashes of your dead. Back, whence they came, upon a trail of blood they must be driven. Back! Back! Ay, into the great water whose accursed waves brought them to our shores! Burn their dwellings! Destroy their stock! Slay their wives and children! The Red Man owns the country. War now! War forever! War upon the living! War upon the dead! Dig their very corpses from the grave. Our country must give no rest to a white man's bones!

This is the will of the Great Spirit, revealed to my brother, his familiar, the Prophet of the Lakes. He sends me to you. All the tribes of the north are dancing the war dance. Two mighty warriors across the seas [Britain and Spain] will send us arms.

Tecumseh will soon return to his country. My prophets shall tarry with you. They will stand between you and the bullets of your enemies. When the white men approach you, the yawning earth shall swallow them up. Soon shall you see my arm of fire stretch athwart the sky. I will stamp my foot at Tippecanoe, and the very earth shall shake.

Tecumseh did indeed return north, but his message stuck with a faction of Creeks who called themselves Red Sticks and followed a chief named William Weatherford. In the complex cultural history of the frontier, few men so puzzled white Americans as Weatherford. He was more white than Indian (his father was Scot, his mother half Scot and a quarter French), yet he was more devoted to Indian independence than most full-bloods. His devotion inspired him to join Tecumseh's race war, which triggered a civil war among the Creeks, between Weatherford's Red Sticks and the more assimilated members of the tribe.

The war among the Creeks produced terror and chaos on the southern frontier. White settlers fled their farms for the safety of forts and blockhouses erected along the Alabama and other rivers. Fort Mims was one such outpost, having grown up around the trading establishment of Samuel Mims, a day's ride northeast of Mobile and slightly farther northwest of Pensacola. Mims's fort was a ramshackle affair, with several buildings linked by an afterthought stockade. In the late summer of 1813 it sheltered, besides Mims and his family and the regular clerks and clientele, hundreds of settler families from the Alabama Valley. The Creek war had frightened them, and in their fright they took refuge within the nearest wooden walls, flimsy though Mims's were. They also implored Governor Claiborne of neighboring Orleans Territory to send soldiers to protect them. Claiborne consented, dispatching two hundred untested troops under the command of Major Daniel Beasley.

For a few weeks in August nothing happened, leaving Beasley to grumble at being sent to this hardship post. His troops spent lazy days avoiding the summer sun and watching the children frolic in the yard of the fort. The residents and guests wandered in and out through the open gate, stretching their legs, tending livestock, and slowly losing their fear of imminent attack. On August 29, two slaves ventured a few miles from the fort, only to run back claiming they had seen painted Indians. So complacent had Beasley become that he thought they were lying, stirring mischief for reasons only they knew. He ordered them flogged.

But that night and till dawn the next morning, the painted Indians the slaves had seen, and hundreds of others similarly made up, crept toward the fort. As the sun rose they flattened themselves to the earth in a swale a quarter mile from the stockade. For hours they lay silently, waiting for the noontime dinner drum that Weatherford had made the signal for the attack. They sweated; the sun rose higher. Finally the drum began to beat, calling the soldiers in to the mess hall and the children in from their games.

The Red Sticks rose silently from their hiding place. No one saw them until they surged across the open area ringing the fort and raised a soulrending war cry. Now Beasley, finally believing what he couldn't deny, ran to the gate of the stockade to close it before the attackers got there. He might have succeeded had it not stuck in soil washed down by recent rain. During the moment he needed to get it free, the fastest of the Red Sticks reached the opening. Beasley fell beneath their tomahawks and clubs, and they trampled over him into the fort.

Their very appearance appalled the defenders of the fort. "Every Indian was provided with a gun, war club, and a bow and arrows pointed with iron spikes," a survivor named Thomas Holmes recalled. "With few exceptions they were naked; around the waist was drawn a girdle from which was tied a cow's tail running down the back and almost dragging the ground. It is impossible to imagine people so horribly painted. Some were painted half red and half black. Some were adorned with feathers. Their faces were painted so as to show their terrible contortions."

The soldiers and residents mounted what resistance they could. The attackers hesitated when five of their prophets, who had declared that the white men's bullets would split in two and pass around their bodies, fell dead from undivided rounds. But their numbers—at least a thousand—were overwhelming. The Red Sticks slaughtered every white person they could reach, and when some of the whites took refuge in the buildings of the fort, Weatherford's men set the buildings on fire and murdered them as they streamed out. By certain accounts, Weatherford tried to stem the massacre, but the attackers' blood was up and they threatened to kill him if he stood in their way. Women and children died by the score and then the hundred, often dispatched in the most brutal fashion. Friendly Indians and black slaves were swept up in the carnage. The sole survivors were a dozen soldiers who cut a hole in the stockade and fled into the woods and some black slaves whom the Red Sticks appropriated for their own use. "The destruction of the fort is horrible to tell," Thomas Holmes wrote. "There were 553 citizens and soldiers and among the number about 453 women and children. . . . Only 13 escaped. The way that many of the unfortunate women were mangled and cut to pieces is shocking to humanity, for very many of the women who were pregnant had their unborn infants cut from the womb and lay by their bleeding mothers. They were stripped of every article of apparel; not satisfied with this, they inhumanly scalped every solitary one." An army major who later led a squadron to bury the dead gagged at what he found. "Indians, negroes, white men, women and children lay in one promiscuous ruin. All were scalped, and the females of every age were butchered in a manner which neither decency nor language will permit me to describe. The main building was burned to ashes, which were filled with bones. The plains and woods around were covered with dead bodies."

The Fort Mims massacre signaled a terrifying escalation of violence along the frontier. Inhabitants and onlookers were accustomed to spontaneous raids that killed isolated settlers by the handful. This attack was entirely different. It was premeditated, it targeted a garrisoned fort, and it produced hundreds of deaths. Everyone knew what Tecumseh had been preaching. The Fort Mims attack showed that the sermon was being taken to heart. One didn't have to be an alarmist to fear that the aboriginal war against all the whites had begun.

James Madison, hardly an alarmist on the Indian issue, recalled the Tennessee volunteers lately released from service. Governor Blount relayed the summons to Jackson, by now returned to the Hermitage but still in pain from his bullet wounds. The rush of adrenaline from the prospect of combat supplied a natural analgesic. "Brave Tennesseans!" Jackson declared. "Your frontier is threatened with invasion by the savage foe. Already they advance towards your frontier with their scalping knives unsheathed, to butcher your wives, your children, and your helpless babes. Time is not to be lost." Jackson ordered the troops to rendezvous at Fayetteville, in Lincoln County some eighty miles south of Nashville, in early October. As they had all heard of his injury, he felt obliged to assure them that he was ready to return to the field. "The health of your General is restored. He will command in person."

In fact his health was far from restored. Jackson had escaped infection largely because the doctors who treated him left the bullet in his shoulder in place. Physicians in those days didn't know what caused infection, but they did know that digging around in human flesh made it more likely. Yet their decision meant that his shoulder would never fully heal, which they also knew. In the short term his left arm was unusable. But he could get around, if not easily, and he could ride a horse, if not comfortably. And he *was* improving. "My health is good and my arm mending fast," he wrote Rachel, only a bit too reassuringly, from the mustering camp in mid-October.

By this time Jackson's worst fears about the Fort Mims massacre—that it signaled a unified Indian campaign all along the frontier—were subsiding. Intelligence from the southern districts reported that the Red Sticks were a minority among the Creeks and that most of the neighboring Cherokees wanted nothing to do with them. Jackson urged his lieutenants to cultivate the friendly Indians. "I wish you to receive and to treat with great kindness all such spies from the Creek nation as may offer you any communication," he told John Coffee, his best cavalry commander. And he approved a simple scheme for keeping friends and foes straight. "Our friends shall wear white plumes in their hair, or deer's tails."

Jackson and his men set off at a blistering pace, to catch and punish the

Red Sticks responsible for the Fort Mims atrocity before they could repeat the performance or disperse. His army covered thirty miles to Huntsville in eight hours the first day and kept pushing hard after that. Jackson's cavalry, under Coffee, moved even faster. But the enemy was elusive. Coffee conducted an armed reconnaissance into Creek territory, burning villages and capturing supplies but finding neither Weatherford nor his warriors. Jackson's Indian allies didn't initially do any better. "I have spies out constantly," a Cherokee leader named Pathkiller reported to Jackson from Turkey Town. "The day before yesterday our spies returned and they only discovered eleven fires about fifteen miles from this place. . . . They were not warring [parties] because women were seen about the fires."

Yet hints and rumors placed the Red Sticks in the vicinity of the Ten Islands of the Coosa River, and Jackson marched in that direction. "We are now within twenty miles of the Ten Islands and it is said within sixteen of the enemy," Jackson informed Governor Blount in late October. Jackson's spies said the Red Sticks numbered a thousand, but he had his doubts. "Any force they may have so near us, I cannot believe to be very great."

Jackson worried less about the Indians than about hunger. His army wasn't large but it went through wagons of food—when it could get them. Lately it hadn't seen any wagons and was living off the land, which in late autumn wasn't yielding much. Jackson's raiders scrounged from the Indian villages they burned. "I yesterday sent out Lieutenant Colonel Dyer with two hundred of the cavalry to attack a town called Littefutchee about twenty miles distant. This morning about four o'clock they returned, bringing with them about thirty prisoners: men, women, and children. The village they burnt. What is very agreeable, they state they found in the fields near the village a considerable quantity of corn, and in the country roundabout many beeves." Unfortunately Dyer's company lacked the means to transport all the food, and in any event foraging was no substitute for regular provisions. "We have been very wretchedly supplied," Jackson told Blount. "Scarcely two rations in succession have been drawn." The men's spirits remained good for the time being. "Whilst we can procure an ear of corn apiece, or anything that will serve as a substitute for it, we shall continue our exertions to accomplish the objects for which we were sent out. The cheerfulness with which my men submit to privations and are ready to encounter danger does honor to the government." But moods changed on empty bellies. "What I dread . . . infinitely more than the fact of the enemy is the want of supplies."

*J*ackson continued the search for Weatherford and the Red Sticks. He ordered Coffee's cavalry brigade to reduce the Creek town of Tallushatchee. "He has executed this order in elegant style," Jackson reported to Rachel a few days later, "leaving dead on the field one hundred and seventy-six, and taking eighty prisoners. Forty prisoners was left on the ground, many of them wounded, others to take care of them." Most of the prisoners were being transported to the nearest white settlement. But one—not exactly a prisoner, since he was an infant—was receiving special treatment. "I send on a little Indian boy for Andrew," Jackson told Rachel. "All his family is destroyed. He is about the age of Theodore."

Rarely did the two sides of Jackson—the fierce and the tender—appear so starkly counterpoised. The same letter that began with approval for an "elegant" raid that drenched an Indian town in blood ended with the news that Jackson and Rachel were adopting an Indian child orphaned by the action. This wasn't their first Indian adoption. The young boy named Theodore had come to live at the Hermitage earlier, under circumstances lost to history. Although Jackson didn't comment on the fact, he must have noticed the symmetry between his own behavior and that of Indian war chiefs, who could direct the most brutal attacks against adults and then take the orphans into their own lodges. Pity certainly moved the Indians in such cases, but at the same time the adopters sought to swell the ranks of their bands and tribes. In Jackson's case, he pitied the Creek child—named Lyncoya—but he also wanted to provide Rachel another child and Andrew (and Theodore) a brother. Before the Creek campaign ended, the southern tribes would call Jackson "Sharp Knife" and deem him a fearsome war chief. At the beginning he was already acting like a chief.

*T*he Creek War had begun as a conflict among the Creeks, and it retained that internecine aspect after the intervention of Jackson's forces. In early

November a band of Creeks friendly to the Americans found itself besieged at Talladega by a much larger contingent of Red Sticks. The friendlies, low on supplies and especially water, managed to get a message to Jackson at Ten Islands, thirty miles away. Jackson perceived a double opportunity in the situation: to strike the Red Sticks while they were preoccupied with their Creek enemies and to demonstrate that friendship with the Americans meant something tangible.

Immediately upon receiving the message, Jackson ordered his troops to set out. Swiftness was essential, for in heading to Talladega he necessarily left his camp at Ten Islands, which included the customary complement of sick soldiers and some lately wounded, undefended. Crossing the Coosa took his two thousand troops—twelve hundred infantry, eight hundred cavalry—several hours. Marching most of the way to Talladega filled the short November day and much of the ensuing night. He let his men catch their breath just short of the reach and awareness of the Red Sticks, but two hours before dawn they were on the trail again, moving forward slowly now, careful to give no sign of their approach.

"At sunrise we came within half a mile of them," Jackson explained in his after-action report. "Having formed my men, I moved on in battle order. The infantry were in three lines—the militia on the left, and the volunteers on the right. The cavalry formed the two extreme wings, and were ordered to advance in a curve, keeping their rear connected with the advance of their infantry lines, and enclose the enemy in a circle." Jackson had no solid idea how many the Red Sticks were, nor they how many the Tennesseans were. But he hoped to lure them away from their siege and into battle against his forces. With luck the friendly Creeks would then attack the Red Sticks from the rear. Even if they didn't, he hoped to encircle the Red Sticks and destroy them.

The battle commenced as planned. Jackson's forward guard poured several rifle volleys into the Red Sticks and then fell back to the main body of Tennessee troops. The Red Sticks, overcoming their surprise at being attacked from the rear, chased the Tennesseans. The center of Jackson's infantry line was supposed to step forward and meet the charge, but some of the men, through a combination of misunderstanding and momentary failure of nerve, began to retreat. Briefly the battle plan appeared to unravel. Jackson ordered a corps of cavalry to dismount and fill the gap in the lines.

"This order was executed with a great deal of promptitude and effect," he explained afterward. "The militia, seeing this, speedily rallied, and the fire became general along the front line." Now the enemy began to retreat, and the Tennesseans to pursue. "The right wing chased them with a most destructive fire to the mountains, a distance of about three miles." Jackson judged that if he hadn't been obliged to dismount his cavalry, the horsemen would have annihilated the enemy. As it was, the triumph was overwhelming: three hundred hostiles killed, against seventeen Tennesseans. Jackson couldn't have been prouder of his men. "All the officers acted with the utmost bravery, and so did all the privates, except that part of the militia who retreated at the commencement of the battle, and they hastened to atone for their error. Taking the whole together, they have realized the high expectations I had formed of them."

*A*s gratifying as the victory at Talladega was, it did nothing for Jackson's growing problem of supply. He had hoped some food might arrive at Ten Islands while his strike force was gone; none did. "We were out of provisions and half starved for many days, and to heighten my mortification when we returned here last evening had not one mouthful to give the wounded or well," he wrote Rachel. What kind of commander offered nothing better to his brave soldiers? "My mind for the want of provision is harassed. My feelings excoriated with the complaints of the men."

The complaints increased as the food supply diminished. "It is with extreme pain I inform you that a turbulent and mutinous disposition has manifested itself in my camp," Jackson wrote Governor Blount in mid-November. "Petition on petition has been handed from the officers of the different brigades containing statements of their privations and sufferings and requesting me to return into the settlements." Jackson couldn't blame the men for feeling ill-used. They had risked their lives and were now being left to starve. He tried to talk patience into them, arguing that provisions were on the way and must arrive soon. He bought a little time by having the brigade generals poll their officers. One brigade gave Jackson four days: if supplies didn't arrive in that time, they were leaving. Another brigade wanted to depart at once. Only Coffee and his cavalry brigade resolved to stay regardless.

*T*ecumseh's troubles were of a different sort. After the defeat of the Shawnees and their allies at Prophetstown in the autumn of 1811, he had returned north lest Harrison draw the Indians into other premature battles. Tecumseh knew the Americans could crush the Indians if the Indians stood alone, and he placed less faith than his brother in the intervention of the Great Spirit. Tecumseh looked not to heaven but to London, believing that the struggle between the British and the Americans would give the Indians their—only—opportunity to reclaim what they had lost during the previous several generations. The Indians must organize, but they must also be patient, waiting for the struggle between the red coats and the blue to develop.

Tecumseh's counsel gained credibility from an utterly unexpected source, one so strange as to beggar the imagination of nearly everyone who encountered it. Starting in December 1811 and lasting for several weeks, a series of enormous earthquakes shook the heartland of North America as no one living could recall it ever having been shaken. The quakes centered just south of the confluence of the Ohio and Mississippi rivers, but their rumbling was felt several hundred miles away. The heaving rerouted the Mississippi, creating channels where none had existed, lakes where there had been river, and islands where the land had been attached to the shore.

The region's prescientific peoples—of all races—naturally detected supernatural significance in the rare and frightening event, and they tried to fathom what that significance was. No credible evidence indicates that Tecumseh literally predicted the earthquakes, but he was clever enough not to deny claims that he had. He had been near the epicenter, and several versions of the story had him saying he would stamp his foot and shake the earth, bringing destruction to those who denied his message. Even those minimalists who doubted that he had actually predicted the quakes found it easy to see them as a sign of a new era, perhaps the one Tecumseh and his brother had forecast.

The outbreak of formal war between the British and the Americans rewarded Tecumseh's patience, and the early Anglo-Indian victories in the northwest made him more credible than ever. The rising of the Red Sticks in the Creek country suggested that his southern diplomacy hadn't been in vain. In early 1813 it was possible for Tecumseh—and Indian irredentists generally—to be more hopeful than they had been in decades that they might again be masters of the lands of their fathers.

But then the British began to lose their nerve. They didn't exploit their northwestern victories and drive deep into Ohio, as Tecumseh wished. And after Americans under Oliver Hazard Perry won a battle of the "big canoes" on Lake Erie, the British commander at Detroit, Henry Proctor, decided to retreat down the Thames River.

Tecumseh felt betrayed, and he told Proctor as much.

> Summer before last, when I came forward with my red brethren, and was ready to take up the hatchet in favor of our British father, we were told not to be in a hurry, that he had not yet determined to fight the Americans. . . . When war was declared, our father stood up and gave us the tomahawk, and told us that he was then ready to strike the Americans; that he wanted our assistance and that he would certainly get us our lands back, which the Americans had taken from us. . . . You always told us that you would never draw your foot off British ground; but now, father, we see you are drawing back. . . . We are sorry to see our father doing so without seeing the enemy. We must compare our father's conduct to a fat animal that carries its tail upon its back but when affrighted, he drops it between his legs and runs off.

When it became apparent that Tecumseh's scorn wouldn't change Proctor's mind, the Shawnee leader asked simply to be given the means to stand and fight the Americans.

> You have got the arms and ammunition which our great father sent for his red children. If you have an idea of going away, give them to us. . . . Our lives are in the hands of the Great Spirit. We are determined to defend our lands, and if it be his will, we wish to leave our bones upon them.

Proctor wouldn't do even this. He took his troops and weapons and headed north, leaving Tecumseh to decide whether to stand and fight or to follow. Complicating the issue, as always, was the question of Indian women and children. The British had promised to defend them, and Tecumseh had brought them forward to the British lines. But now the British were leaving them behind. Tecumseh knew he couldn't shield the women and children, without Proctor's help, from the Americans' wrath. It didn't take him more than a few bitter moments to realize he had to follow the redcoats down the river.

Proctor wasn't quite as faithless as Tecumseh feared. The British general retreated to a position he considered more defensible, and there he turned to meet the Americans. Tecumseh caught up with Proctor and walked among the British ranks in the moments before battle. "He was dressed in his usual deer skin dress, which admirably displayed his light yet sinewy figure," John Richardson, one of the British soldiers, recalled. "In his handkerchief, rolled as a turban over his brow, was placed a handsome ostrich feather. . . . He pressed the hand of each officer as he passed, made some remark in Shawnee appropriate to the occasion, which was sufficiently understood by the expressive signs accompanying them, and then passed away forever from our view." To Proctor, Tecumseh said, "Father, tell your young men to be firm, and all will be well."

Tecumseh must have known that more than firmness in the ranks was required. Proctor wasn't a coward, but neither was he much of a soldier. "His inferior officers say that his conduct has been a continued series of blunders," William Henry Harrison remarked after interviewing those officers, who became his prisoners in the battle for which Tecumseh was preparing the troops. "The contest was not for a moment doubtful." Proctor possessed the advantage of terrain, having chosen a battlefield that restricted Harrison's movements, and perhaps of numbers, although this was hard to tell, given the substantial portion of Indian irregulars on his side. (Harrison's force also included Indians of various tribes, but many fewer than Proctor's.) Yet the fighting style of the Americans, especially Harrison's Kentucky militia, suited the forest in which much of the fighting took place. "The American backwoodsmen ride better in the woods than any other people," Harrison explained. "A musket or rifle is no impediment to them, being accustomed to carry them on horseback from their earliest youth."

Harrison's mounted troops shattered the British lines at the start of the battle, leaving Tecumseh's Indian force to carry the weight of the contest. They fought gallantly, and none more gallantly than their leader. Tecumseh placed himself in the thickest of the struggle. He urged his comrades forward, shouting defiance and showing the way. In his exposed position he was an irresistible target for the American rifles. One bullet hit him in the arm. He paused just long enough to bind the wound before taking up weapons again. He drew more bullets and went down.

His fall demoralized his warriors, and the battle degenerated into a rout. Proctor fled the field, leaving several hundred of his troops to surrender. The casualties were surprisingly light, given the lopsidedness of the outcome. Harrison counted twelve British dead and twenty-two wounded, against twelve American dead and seventeen wounded. "The Indians suffered most," he added, "thirty-three of them having been found upon the ground besides those killed in the retreat."

The Indian dead included Tecumseh. "I saw him with my own eyes," Thomas Rowland, a major under Harrison, explained. "It was the first time I had seen this celebrated chief. There was something so majestic, so dignified, and yet so mild in his countenance, as he lay stretched on the ground where a few moments before he had rallied his men to the fight, that while gazing on him with admiration and pity, I forgot he was a savage. . . . He had such a countenance as I shall never forget."

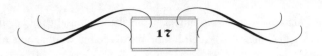

17

THE RIVER OF BLOOD

Tecumseh's death killed his hopes of rolling back the tide of white settlement. Indian resistance would continue, but the unity he preached and imperfectly accomplished couldn't survive without its apostle and ablest practitioner. Neither whites nor Indians had ever seen his like or would see it again.

Jackson applauded the death of the Shawnee leader and would have appreciated it more had he not been utterly occupied trying to hold his own army together. The men were constantly hungry. Provisions never arrived on time, and when they did arrive they fell far short of the need. Clothing wore thin and then out. Hundreds of miles of marching had put holes in shoes and boots, finally leaving the worst-shod unshod entirely. The weather turned cold, and the men shivered in the rain. The one

thing that kept many of the volunteers from abandoning the field dishonorably was the knowledge that their honorable discharge would come in early
December.

Or so they interpreted their terms of enlistment. Much of Jackson's force
had accompanied him to Natchez the previous winter, and these men counted
their twelve-month enlistment as starting with their muster in December
1812. They considered themselves no less brave or patriotic than anyone else
in Jackson's army—or than Jackson himself, for that matter—but they had
made plans based on service only till December 1813. Jackson hadn't helped
matters by his haste in recalling them to avenge the Fort Mims massacre. The
men had leaped to obey, but their very alacrity meant that many had had no
time to prepare either themselves or their families for a long absence. They
came without winter clothes and without having left means for their families
to survive till spring. Farmwork needed doing; mortgages had to be paid. "If
they do not get home soon, there are many of them who will be literally ruined," Colonel William Martin told Jackson on December 4.

Martin commanded the most restive regiment, and he found himself
caught between the understandable desire of his men to get home and Jackson's insistence that they stay. To encourage participation in the Creek campaign, Martin and his fellow officers had emphasized that the men wouldn't
be asked to serve beyond December 10. "This was one of our strongest arguments to get the men out," he told Jackson. Without it, many of them
wouldn't have come. For their discharge to be delayed would provoke great
distress and anger. Martin realized this wasn't what Jackson wanted to hear,
and so it was with trepidation that he made his men's case to the general.

It would be desirable for those men who have served with honor to
be honorably discharged, and that they should return to their families and friends without even the semblance of disgrace. . . . It is
with their General, whom they love, to place them in that situation.
They say, and with truth, that with him they have suffered, have
fought and have conquered. They feel a pride of having fought under his command. . . . But having devoted considerable portion of
their time to the service of their country, by which their domestic
concerns are much deranged, they wish to return and attend to their
own affairs. Above all things they wish to part with their General

with that cordiality with which they have served together. . . . This is the language and those are the feelings of these noble hearted soldiers.

Jackson was beginning to have doubts about the noble hearts of Martin's soldiers, but he was absolutely sure the colonel wasn't doing anything to enhance their nobility. Martin should be appealing to the patriotism of the men, Jackson judged, not pandering to their homesickness. Yet Jackson managed to hold his temper while he composed his response, which took the same high ground Martin trod. "It is well known that the 10th of December 1812 was the proudest day of my life," Jackson said. "It was the proudest day for West Tennessee. . . . We braved the snowy blasts and the dangers of the icy sea"—river, that is—"without murmur, did our duty and established a fame by our proper conduct." Officers and men had stood together against the "fatal order" of dismissal from service, and had returned to Tennessee together. They must stand together now. The men had enlisted for twelve months' service but had given barely four. Their term would expire not on December 10 but the following June. This should have been clear to the officers, who should have made it clear to the men.

Jackson closed with an appeal and a warning. "The honor of the volunteers has been the constant care, theme, and pride of life. It is so still, and I have a pleasing hope that they will nobly die before they will do an act that will disgrace them. I still have a pleasing hope, when they reflect upon the rules and articles of war, they never will attempt an act of mutiny." But they must know that if they did, he would act accordingly. "I will quell mutiny and punish desertion when and wheresoever it may be attempted. I shall always do my duty."

As a showdown loomed, a group of Jackson's officers tried to avert it. "Our men have come out with patriotic motives but were advised not to bring their clothing necessary for the present and approaching season," they said. The men's horses were worn out and required replacing. "If permitted to return only the shortest time to their homes," the officers promised, the troops "would get fresh horses and bring clothing, prepared to go with you through the winter season or until the end of the campaign." The men were not mutinous, merely hungry and cold. "We find this only one sentiment pervades the whole of our men, and hope you will modify your order."

Jackson didn't relish a showdown, either. He tried to prevent it by haranguing his superiors and provisioners to deliver the food and clothing his men so desperately needed. "In the name of God, what is McGee doing?" he demanded regarding one jobber who had taken the government's money but not delivered the bread he had promised. "It is wholly unaccountable that not a pound of it has ever arrived." And he explained to his men that even if he wanted to discharge them, he lacked the authority to do so. Only the governor could discharge the militia.

This last argument was correct but disingenuous. Jackson had never allowed lack of authority to prevent him from doing what he thought duty required, and he wouldn't have allowed lack of authority to prevent him from discharging the troops. Yet he employed the argument to give himself more time. He conspicuously applied to the governor for permission to discharge, knowing that the application and any response would consume two weeks or more and hoping that supplies would arrive in the meantime. He guessed that full bellies would change everything.

The tension escalated as December 10 approached. "What may be attempted tomorrow I cannot tell," Jackson wrote Coffee on the ninth. But Jackson was ready, and he wanted Coffee, who controlled the road home, to be ready as well. "Should they attempt to march off in mass, I shall do my duty. Should the mutineers be too strong, and you should meet any officers or men returning without my written authority, you will arrest and bring them back. . . . If they attempt to disobey your order, you will immediately fire on them and continue the fire until they are subdued."

That evening the crisis came to a head. One of Jackson's lieutenants arrived breathless at his tent with word that his brigade of volunteers was preparing to march north at daybreak. Jackson scribbled an order to the whole army: "The commanding general being informed that an actual mutiny exists in his camp, all officers and soldiers are commanded to put it down." The offending brigade was ordered to assemble in formation. Jackson directed that his artillery be placed in front of and behind the volunteer brigade, with cannons at the ready. Loyal militia units were stationed on the route north.

John Reid, who witnessed the confrontation at close firsthand, recorded the moment of truth.

The general rode along the line, which had been formed agreeably to his orders, and addressed them by companies, in a strain of impassioned eloquence. He feelingly expatiated on their former good conduct, and the esteem and applause it had secured them; and pointed to the disgrace which they must heap upon themselves, their families, and country, by persisting, even if they could succeed, in the present mutiny. But he told them they should not succeed but by passing over his body; that even in opposing their mutinous spirit he should perish honorably, by perishing at his post and in the discharge of his duty.

"Reinforcements," he continued, "are preparing to hasten to my assistance; it cannot be long before they will arrive. I am, too, in daily expectation of receiving information whether you may be discharged or not. Until then, you must not, and shall not, retire. I have done with entreaty; it has been used long enough. I will attempt it no more. You must now determine whether you will go, or peaceably remain. If you persist in your determination to move forcibly off, the point between us shall soon be decided."

At first they hesitated. He demanded an explicit and positive answer. They still hesitated, and he commanded the artillerist to prepare the match, he himself remaining in front of the volunteers and within the line of fire, which he intended soon to order.

Alarmed at his apparent determination, and dreading the consequences involved in such a contest, "let us return" was presently lisped along the line, and was soon after determined upon. The officers now came forward and pledged themselves for their men, who either nodded assent or openly expressed a willingness to retire to their quarters and remain without further tumult until information were had or the expected aid arrived.

Thus passed away a moment of the greatest peril, pregnant with the most important consequences.

None present ever forgot the performance. For many years Tennesseans told of Jackson threatening to blow his own men, and himself, to pieces to make his patriotic point. Participants disputed the details, including whether the threat to march had actually reached the point of mutiny. But none disputed Jackson's resolve.

*I*n Jackson's army that season was a young man named David Crockett. Born on the banks of the Nolichucky River in eastern Tennessee to a family plagued by bad luck, Crockett left home at twelve to seek his fortune. He never found much fortune but did discover a gift for hunting and a knack for telling stories. He moved west with the tide of settlement and in 1813 was living in Franklin County, just north of the Mississippi Territory border, when the shocking news of the Fort Mims massacre set all Tennessee on edge. Crockett was old enough to have family recollections of Indian massacres—"By the Creeks my grandfather and grandmother Crockett were both murdered in their own house," he said—and young enough (twenty-seven in 1813) not to have fought the Indians himself. "There had been no war among us for so long that but few who were not too old to bear arms knew any thing about the business. I, for one, had often thought about war, and had often heard it described." The stories inevitably evoked questions as to whether the younger generation could match the courage of their elders. The Mims massacre provided a chance to see. "When I heard of the mischief which was done at the fort, I instantly felt like going."

Crockett's dependents felt differently, as dependents of prospective heroes often do. "My wife, who had heard me say I meant to go to the war, began to beg me not to turn out. She said she was a stranger in the parts where we lived, had no connexions living near her, and that she and our little children would be left in a lonesome and unhappy situation if I went away." Crockett conceded the weight of her arguments. "But my countrymen had been murdered, and I knew that the next thing would be that the Indians would be scalping the women and children all about there if we didn't put a stop to it. I reasoned the case with her as well as I could, and told her that if every man would wait till his wife got willing for him to go to war, there would be no fighting done, until we would all be killed in our own houses." She wasn't convinced, but she realized she couldn't stop him. "Seeing I was bent on it, all she did was to cry a little and turn about to her work. The truth is, my dander was up, and nothing but war could bring it right again."

Crockett served as a scout for the cavalry regiment Jackson sent south ahead of the main body of troops. Asked to choose a partner, he selected a teenager named George Russell. Crockett's commander said Russell was too young, lacking even a beard. "I was a little nettled at this," Crockett recalled. "I know'd George Russell, and I know'd there was no mistake in him; and I didn't think courage ought to be measured by the beard, for fear a goat would have the preference over a man." Crockett carried the point, and the two ranged far ahead of Jackson's advancing force. They took part in the Battle of Tallushatchee, the one for which Jackson praised Coffee's "elegant style." In Crockett's telling the fight was more savage than elegant. Coffee's men, including Crockett, and their Indian allies, encircled the town and closed in on its inhabitants. Some of the women pleaded to be taken prisoner, and the Tennesseans began to oblige. But a group of nearly four dozen warriors barricaded themselves in a house, and when Crockett's company started to assault the building, a woman whom the Tennesseans apparently thought was surrendering fired an arrow that killed one of Crockett's comrades. "His death so enraged us all that she was fired on, and had at least twenty balls blown through her. . . . We now shot them like dogs; and then set the house on fire, and burned it up with the forty-six warriors in it."

Crockett and his comrades had shared the privations of Jackson's army before the battle, and their collective hunger now contributed to an especially gruesome aspect of the denouement of the Tallushatchee fight. Returning to their own camp and finding no rations there, they retraced their steps to the Indian town in hope of discovering some stores they had overlooked. "Many of the carcasses of the Indians were still to be seen. They looked very awful, for the burning had not entirely consumed them, but given them a very terrible appearance, at least what remained of them. It was, somehow or other, found out that the house had a potato cellar under it, and an immediate examination was made, for we were all as hungry as wolves. We found a fine chance of potatoes in it, and hunger compelled us to eat them, though I had a little rather not, if I could have helped it, for the oil of the Indians we had burned up on the day before had run down on them and they looked like they had been stewed with fat meat."

Crockett fought directly under Jackson at Talladega, and he marched with Jackson back to Ten Islands, where the general had hoped to receive the sorely needed provisions. "We were all likely to perish," Crockett said.

"The weather also began to get very cold; and our clothes were nearly worn out, and horses getting feeble and very poor." Crockett's colonel was among those officers who suggested to Jackson that the men be allowed to return home to fetch winter clothes and fresh horses.

And in the end Jackson was compelled to accede. The general could threaten to blow mutineers to kingdom come, but neither his threats nor his cannons could put food in the men's mouths or clothes on their backs. In the weeks after the showdown he quietly discharged the most malcontented, judging their departure good riddance, and he allowed others, including Crockett, to take a few weeks to refresh, restock, and get ready for the final offensive against the Red Sticks.

As Crockett was leaving Jackson's camp another young man, six years Crockett's junior, was arriving. Sam Houston had left home at about the same age Crockett did, although in Houston's case it was to run away and live with the Cherokees, his neighbors in the mountains of East Tennessee. Houston was a romantic by temperament. He had read Pope's translation of the *Iliad* so often he had it nearly by heart. And the plodding life of a farmer repelled him. His five brothers tracked him to an island in the Tennessee River where he had joined the family of Chief Oolooteka. The brothers demanded that he return with them to civilization and the plow. He refused, declaring (as he explained later, in the third person grandiloquent), that "the wild liberty of the red man suited his nature far better than the restraints of the white settlements." The brothers departed, thinking the novelty of Indian life would fade and he would come home. But it didn't, and he remained with the Cherokees. He adopted Cherokee speech, Cherokee dress, Cherokee tastes, and a Cherokee name: Colonneh, or Raven. "Nearly five years of experience in this mode of living initiated him into all the secrets of Indian life," he recounted of himself, "and gave him a knowledge of the savage character that made him a complete master over the Indian mind, as his intercourse with the red man in after years proved."

By the time Houston returned to white society, the War of 1812 had begun. He learned that the U.S. Army was paying cash bonuses to volunteers for service on the western frontier against the British and their Indian allies.

As these latter didn't include the Cherokees, who were siding with the Americans, he tendered his services. Tall, broad-shouldered, and physically self-confident, he made a distinct impression on his superiors, who included Jackson's former aide and current enemy, Thomas Hart Benton. Benton helped Houston obtain promotion from ensign to lieutenant, which office he held when the War Department in early 1814 finally heeded Jackson's call for reinforcements. Houston's Thirty-ninth Regiment marched south to meet Jackson's army at Fort Strother, not far from Ten Islands.

Nearly every young man who served under Jackson came to view the general as a second father, but for none did the paternal element matter more than for Houston. Houston had lost his actual father at an early age and spent much of his life looking for a substitute. Chief Oolooteka served for a time, and for this Houston was ever grateful. But a white boy couldn't plausibly model himself after an Indian chief—at least not a white boy whose ambition burned the way Houston's did, for reasons he couldn't entirely explain. Andrew Jackson, on the other hand—now *there* was a model for any lad. He was as fearless as Houston hoped he himself would be, as principled, as devoted to cause and country. From the moment they were introduced, during that difficult winter of the campaign against the Creeks, the young lieutenant sought to attract the general's attention and win his favor.

John Wood wanted less attention from Jackson, rather than more. Wood hadn't turned eighteen when he joined his older brother in one of Jackson's militia companies. He may or may not have known that this particular company had been among the most mutiny-minded in Jackson's army, held in camp at one stage only by the drawn weapons of Jackson loyalists. The episode angered the general and caused him to expect the worst of the company's members.

Jackson was still angry and distrustful when Wood retired early from picket duty one cold morning in February 1814. The boy had been out all night with neither food nor proper clothing, and the officer of the watch told him to get some breakfast. He was still eating when a second officer encountered him and demanded to know why he wasn't on duty. Wood answered in the tone of many of the militia, intensified in his case by hunger, weariness, and a certain innate emotionalism. His impertinent retort provoked the officer, who at once ordered him back to the perimeter. Wood refused, more disrespectfully. The altercation escalated, with the officer ordering Wood's arrest and Wood waving his rifle toward those who would have carried out the order.

When Jackson heard that someone from the mutinous company was again defying orders, he flew into a rage. "Which is the damned rascal?" he thundered. "Shoot him! Shoot him! Blow ten balls through the damned villain's body!"

Wood's comrades were considerably more frightened of Jackson than of the boy, and, braving Wood's brandished weapon, they persuaded him to put it down. He was taken into custody and placed under guard.

Nearly all hoped and apparently most expected that when Jackson's temper cooled, the boy would be released and his indiscretion forgotten. He was, after all, a youngster, new to soldiering. Whether Jackson realized how green Wood was became a matter of intense debate after Jackson entered national politics. He claimed to believe that Wood had been part of the earlier mutiny and that this new violation constituted a second capital offense. Jackson's enemies insisted that Jackson knew better and was looking for someone to make an example of.

In all likelihood Jackson was honestly mistaken. He cared deeply for his men, as he had showed many times and would show again. He typically forgave first offenders, as he had forgiven most of those in Wood's company.

But honest or otherwise, Jackson's mistake cost Wood dearly. Jackson convened a court martial and held it to a strict interpretation of the military code. The court found Wood guilty and ordered his execution. The whole army held its breath as Jackson let the lesson sink in. Nearly all expected to exhale as he suspended the sentence, as he surely must.

He didn't. Convinced that the survival of the army depended on the restoration of discipline—and believing Wood a recidivist—he ordered the execution to proceed. "The offenses of which you have been found guilty are such as cannot be permitted to pass unpunished in an army but at the hazard of its ruin," Jackson wrote to Wood in a letter read at the execution. "An army cannot exist where order and subordination are wholly disregarded. . . . The disobedience of orders and the contempt of officers speedily lead to a state of disorganization and ruin and mutiny." Speaking to the other troops more than to Wood, Jackson continued, "This is an important crisis in which if we all act as becomes us, every thing is to be hoped for towards the accomplishment of the objects of our government; if otherwise, every thing to be feared. How it becomes us to act, we all know, and what our punishment shall be if we act otherwise, must be known also."

Jackson never wrote a memoir of the Creek campaign (or of any other part of his life), but an account begun by John Reid, his chief aide, and completed under Jackson's supervision after Reid's sudden death, provided a close substitute. That work concluded its brief account of the Wood case with what certainly was Jackson's view of the execution and its denouement: "Painful as it was to the feelings of the general, he viewed it as a sacrifice essential to the preservation of good order. . . . The execution was productive of the happiest effects; order was produced, and that opinion, so long indulged, that a militia-man was for no offence to suffer death was, for the moment, abandoned. . . . A strict obedience afterwards characterized the army."

*O*bedience was essential in what followed. Jackson's scouts informed him that William Weatherford and the main body of Red Sticks had built a fortress near the confluence of the Tallapoosa and Coosa rivers, where the Tallapoosa looped back on itself in a horseshoe bend, forming a narrow-necked peninsula comprising between eighty and one hundred acres. A village occupied the end of the peninsula, while a forbidding breastwork of earth and logs crossed the three-hundred-yard neck and secured the village from frontal attack. In March 1814 some thousand warriors gathered there, along with a few hundred women and children. "It is impossible to conceive a situation more eligible for defense than the one they had chosen," Jackson recalled. "And the skill which they manifested in their breast-work was really astonishing. It extended across the point in such a direction as that a force approaching would be exposed to a double fire while they lay entirely safe behind it."

Jackson nonetheless determined to take the battle to the enemy. For months he had chased the Red Sticks, and now that they stood to fight, he wouldn't let his chance slip. He called on the men to show the courage of which he knew them capable. "An opportunity is at length offered you of manifesting your zeal to your country and avenging the cruelties committed upon our defenceless fellow citizens." The men had suffered to reach this day and place; now was the time to redeem their suffering. They had chafed at his insistence on discipline; now they would discover what discipline was for. "In the hour of battle you must be cool and collected. When your officer orders you to fire, you must execute the command with deliberateness and aim. *Let every shot tell.*" Jackson promised his men he would never order a retreat, and he felt confident they would never choose to retreat on their own. But just in case, he stated his policy clearly: "Any officer or soldier who flies before the enemy without being compelled to do so by superior force and actual necessity shall suffer death."

Jackson's battle plan reflected his overall strategy for the campaign. The objective was not the Red Stick village but the destruction of the enemy. For this reason it was essential to prevent escape. The village touched the river on three sides, and the Red Sticks had readied canoes for flight. Jackson deployed Coffee's cavalry and the friendly Cherokees and Creeks along the outside of the river bend, to cover the stream with gunfire in the event the enemy tried to cross. For the frontal assault against the breastwork, he relied on his Tennesseans. They had never stormed a stronghold, and he couldn't say how well they would perform such a harrowing maneuver. But he thought it only prudent to reserve this most dangerous part of the assault to the men who had been with him the longest.

The combined force of Tennesseans and friendly Indians camped six miles from the Horseshoe Bend on the night of March 26, and early the next morning they moved out. Coffee's cavalry and the Indians crossed the river and got behind the Red Stick village, while Jackson's infantry approached the breastwork from the front. Two small cannons accompanied the foot soldiers. Jackson positioned these on a high point only eighty yards from the closest part of the wall. At half past ten the cannons opened fire. Their three- and six-pound balls did little damage at first, and in fact the exposed artillerymen were in greater danger from the muskets of the Red Sticks behind the wall than the latter were from the cannon rounds.

But the cannon fire kept the defenders distracted while Jackson's Cherokee and Creek allies attacked from the rear. Apparently this attack was more than Coffee or Jackson had counted on. "I had ordered the Indians on our approach to the bend of the river to advance secretly and take positions on the bank of the river and prevent the enemy from crossing," Coffee explained to Jackson afterward. "Then within a quarter of a mile of the river, the firing of your cannon commenced when the Indians with me rushed forward with great impetuosity to the river banks. . . . While some kept up a fire across the river (which is about 120 yards wide) to prevent the enemy's approach to the bank, others plunged in the water and swam over the river for canoes that lay on the other shore in considerable numbers and brought them across, in which craft a number of these embarked and landed on the bank with the enemy." Between 150 and 200 Cherokees crossed the river, accompanied by a smaller number of Coffee's Tennesseans. "They advanced into the village and very shortly drove the enemy up the bank of the river to the fortified works from which they were fighting you."

Jackson gave the order for the frontal assault. A drum roll announced the charge, and the men gave a joyous war whoop as they surged forward. Jackson's aide John Reid described the moment in a letter to his wife. "I never had such emotions as while the long roll was beating, and the troops in motion," Reid said. "It was not fear, it was not anxiety or concern of the fate of those who were so soon to fall, but it was a kind of enthusiasm that thrilled through every nerve and animated me with the belief that the day was ours without adverting to what it must cost us."

The army volunteers and the militia together tore across the open space before the breastwork, absorbing heavy fire from the portholes in the wooden wall. At the wall itself they were in less immediate danger, but they once more exposed themselves by jamming their own muskets into the portholes and returning the Red Stick fire at point-blank range. "A terrible conflict ensued," John Reid told his father. It was man against man, lead against lead. The weapons, let alone the men, could hardly stand the heat. "In many instances the balls of the enemy were found welded to the muzzles of our guns."

The Tennesseans scrambled up the breastwork. The leaders of the assault inevitably faced the greatest danger. Lemuel Montgomery was first atop the wall and the first killed, by a bullet through the forehead. Others followed. "At length we mounted the walls and took possession of the other side," John Reid said. The fighting only intensified. "Now it was that the contest was not so much for victory as for life. On every side were heard the groans of the dying and the shouts of the victors."

Sam Houston was one of the first inside the battlements. His large frame, almost as tall as the wall itself, made an easy target as he went over the top. An Indian arrow impaled him in the upper thigh, but he continued forward, half falling inside the fort. Inspired by his example, other troops went over, driving the enemy back and away from the ramparts. The Tennesseans opened the gates and still more of their fellows poured through.

"The event could no longer be doubtful," Jackson wrote. "The enemy, although many of them fought to the last with that kind of bravery which desperation inspires, were at length entirely routed and cut to pieces. The whole margin of the river which surrounded the peninsula was strewed with the slain." But even after the outcome became apparent, the Red Sticks fought on. One band of diehards took refuge in a narrow defile covered by fallen logs. Jackson asked for volunteers to root them out. Houston had paused long enough to have a comrade extract the arrow from his thigh. The amateur surgeon tugged gently at first, but the barbed arrow refused to yield. He hesitated to pull harder, fearing Houston couldn't stand the pain and damage. Houston threatened to shoot the fellow if he didn't yank for all he was worth. He grimly did so, extracting a ghastly chunk of Houston's flesh along with the arrow and leaving Houston bleeding badly. Jackson rode by at just this time, commended Houston for gallantry, and told him to sit out the rest of the battle. But when Jackson called for the volunteers against the enemy redoubt, Houston once more stepped—or, in this case, hobbled—to the front. Shouting encouragement to the others, he charged the redoubt, only to be hit again, by a bullet to the shoulder and another to the arm. He slumped to the ground semiconscious.

The fighting continued, albeit with diminishing intensity, for hours. The surviving Red Sticks dug in beneath the river bank and behind rocks, holding their attackers at bay until finally overpowered. Darkness brought a halt, but the fighting resumed the next morning.

When the killing finally ceased, even Jackson was shocked by its extent. "The *carnage* was *dreadful*," he wrote Rachel. "Exclusive of those buried in their watery grave, who were killed in the river and who after being wounded plunged into it, there were counted five hundred and fifty seven." John Coffee estimated the dead in the river at 250 to 300. Many had tried to cross, Coffee said. "But not one escaped; very few ever reached the bank, and those were killed the instant they landed." The slaughter in the river was confirmed in substance if not detail by William Bradford, an infantry officer who remarked succinctly, "The river ran red with blood." Alexander Mc-Culloch noticed the same phenomenon. "The Tallapoosa might truly be called the river of blood," McCulloch said, "for the water was so stained that at ten o'clock at night it was very perceptibly bloody, so much so that it could not be used."

I think it is the most complete victory that has been obtained over the Indians in America," William Carroll wrote three days later. Carroll, in camp with Jackson and nursing a wound suffered in the battle, couldn't know that Horseshoe Bend not only was the most complete—that is, bloodiest—single victory of whites over Indians in American history to that date but would forever retain that dubious distinction. It was also the decisive victory in the climactic struggle for what was then the American Southwest. The Creek War represented the last, best hope of the counteroffensive preached by Tecumseh and the final phase of the contest for the dark and bloody ground of the old Southwest. In the bend of the Tallapoosa River, in the spring of 1814, Andrew Jackson seized the prize for which six generations of Euro-Americans and Native Americans had been fighting.

All this would become apparent in time, but in the immediate aftermath of the battle Jackson couldn't say just what he had won. He wasn't even sure he had defeated the Red Sticks. As he tallied the carnage he remarked to Rachel, "What effect this will produce on those infatuated and deluded people, I cannot yet say." For all the hostile Creeks killed at Horseshoe Bend, others remained at large, stubbornly refusing to lay down their arms. Jackson had no choice but to steel his troops for more fighting. He congratulated them on what they had accomplished. "The fiends of the Tallapoosa will no longer murder our women and children. . . . They have disappeared from the face of the earth." But he added, "Our enemy are not sufficiently humbled since they do not sue for peace. A collection of their forces again await our approach and remain to be dispersed." To Rachel he predicted one more battle. "I will give them, with the permission of heaven, the final stroke."

But the final stroke never fell—or, rather, it had already fallen. After Horseshoe Bend, Jackson's forces mounted raids on several Red Stick villages along the lower Tallapoosa. Yet the villages were all deserted. One of Coffee's men recalled an empty council house that contained grim evidence of the cause of the current campaign. "High up on the central pole inside were numerous arrows sticking straight out, on which hung the scalps of the men, women and children massacred at Fort Mims. These were taken down and decently buried." Further reconnaissance met no more resistance. The surviving Red Sticks had vanished, some apparently south to Spanish Florida, others into the general population of Creeks.

The hostile whose escape most vexed Jackson was William Weatherford. By chance Weatherford had been absent from Horseshoe Bend on the morning of the Tennesseans' attack, and it was Jackson's discovery that Weatherford wasn't among the killed that most caused him to think the war would continue. By this time Weatherford had a reputation among whites for bravery and elusiveness that made him seem the very soul of the Creek resistance. During one battle, when he was surrounded and apparently cut off from all escape, he seized a horse and galloped to the edge of a cliff that stood some eighty feet above the Alabama River. Without breaking the horse's stride he leaped the animal far out over the water while his pursuers watched in stupefaction. Horse and rider fell and fell and finally landed in the river with a tremendous splash. The frantic horse surfaced, its eyes rolling with terror, and kicked toward the opposite shore. The still-astonished Tennesseans saw Weatherford come up, clinging to the animal's mane with one hand, his rifle in the other. With a powerful kick of his own legs and a pull on the mane, he hoisted himself onto the horse's back. A few of the Tennesseans recovered sufficiently to fire a few rounds, but the Red Stick leader was out of range and soon gone.

If the war had been only about warriors, Weatherford probably would have remained a fugitive and continued fighting. But in the days and then weeks after Horseshoe Bend, he realized that further resistance would destroy not only his warriors—most of whom were dead already—but their dependents. As always, the women and children suffered the most. They hid in the forest from Jackson and his Indian allies, but in the forest they couldn't find enough food. They weakened, sickened, and began to die, forcing Weatherford to sue for peace. On the same horse that survived the leap into the Alabama, he rode to Fort Jackson, as the Tennesseans proudly called a structure built below the Horseshoe. Friendly Indians were coming and going, and no one much noticed Weatherford, even after he asked some of the soldiers where he might find their commander.

Jackson had never met Weatherford and didn't recognize him till the Creek leader identified himself. But he quickly appreciated the man's presence and gifts of leadership. William Carroll described the meeting. "He was a little scant of six feet tall, rather slender in build but sinewy and graceful," Carroll said of Weatherford. "His dress was part white and part Indian, like himself. His features were clean-cut and sharp, his nose like a hawk's beak and his complexion almost white. He spoke very slowly and deliberately in pretty fair English, but often hesitated for a word as if not much practiced in speaking that language. When he spoke the Muscogee tongue, though, he talked fast and apparently—to judge from the effect of his talk upon the Indians who could understand him—with great force. . . . He was one of nature's great men." On this occasion Weatherford was understandably subdued. "He was solemn in manner and seemed greatly depressed by the forlorn condition of his people, though he did not seem to care for his own fate, whatever it might be."

Jackson was surprised at seeing Weatherford and initially disconcerted. "I had directed that you should be brought to me confined," Jackson said. "Had you appeared in this way, I should have known how to have treated you."

"I am in your power," Weatherford responded.

Do with me as you please. I have done the white people all the harm I could. I have fought them, and I have fought them bravely. If I had an army I would yet fight and contend to the last. But I have none. My people are all gone. I can now do no more than to weep over the misfortunes of my nation. Once I could animate my warriors to battle, but I can not animate the dead. . . .

I have not surrendered myself thoughtlessly. Whilst there was a chance of success I never left my post nor supplicated peace. But now I ask it for my nation and not for myself. On the miseries and misfortunes brought upon my country, I look back with deepest sorrow and wish to avert still greater calamities. . . . You are a brave man and I rely upon your generosity. You will exact no terms of a conquered people but such as they can accede to. Whatever they may be, it would be madness and folly to oppose.

Jackson's answer to this speech went unrecorded by witnesses. Fanciful reconstructions by others had him sharing a brandy with his defeated foe, the two commanders meeting in mutual respect at battle's end. This would have been entirely unlike Jackson, for whom war wasn't a game but a deadly serious business. Weatherford might be brave, but he was, in Jackson's eyes, a murderer of innocents. More plausible is a version related by one who knew Weatherford and apparently got it from him. "General Jackson said to Weatherford that he was astonished at a man of his good sense, and almost a white man, taking sides with an ignorant set of savages, and being led astray by men who professed to be prophets and gifted with a supernatural influence. And more than all, he had led the Indians and was one of the prime movers of the massacre at Fort Mims." Weatherford, by this account, denied that he himself had believed in the prophets and asserted that much of what had happened at Fort Mims had been beyond his control. He asked Jackson to consider what would have been the reaction among whites had he—Weatherford—joined them against his red brothers. "It would have been attributed to cowardice and not thanked." He wished Jackson to know, although he didn't expect Jackson to believe, that he had been a restraining force among the Red Sticks. "Now, sir, I have told the truth," he closed. "If you think I deserve death, do as you please. I shall only beg for the protection of a starving parcel of women and children, and those ignorant men who have been led into the war by their chiefs."

Something in Weatherford's manner struck a chord in Jackson. Though he might have executed the Red Stick leader for his role in the Fort Mims murders, he didn't. In fact he held Weatherford only briefly. He chose to trust his sincerity, and on Weatherford's promise to try to persuade the remaining Red Sticks to surrender, Jackson let him go.

1814–1821

American

Hero

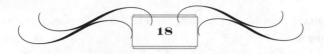

18

PEACE GIVER

𝒜 visitor to the nation's capital the month before the declaration of war against Britain was struck by the partisan divide between Republicans and Federalists. "The opposite parties live separate from each other, and have but little intercourse except on business," he wrote. "I once asked Mr. Potter [Elisha Potter, a Federalist congressman from Rhode Island] if it would not be better for the members of different parties to live more together and become more sociable with each other. He said they could not live in peace together, and that, after the contentions which they continually had in the hall"—Congress—"they required some rest and quiet when they got home. He said also that some of the Democrats"—Republicans—"are men of such unruly minds that it is extremely difficult to be upon good terms with them. 'There is that Willis Alston [Republican congressman from North Carolina],' said he. 'Why he is as clear a brute as ever wore a tail.' "

Wars often draw parties and factions together, as peacetime rivals rally against the common foe. The War of 1812 had the opposite effect in America, driving the parties apart. Federalists blamed the Republicans for the war, which disrupted their commerce and the ties to Britain they had reconstructed since the Revolutionary War. They criticized the administration and at every step tried to block all but the most narrowly defensive measures. Republicans responded by lashing the Federalists as Tories and traitors. "When war is declared," asserted a Republican paper in Baltimore, "there are but two parties: *Citizen Soldiers* and *Enemies—Americans* and *Tories*." Republicans in Baltimore took this maxim to the street, rioting against Federalists to tunes from the Revolutionary War ("We'll feather and tar every damned British Tory / And that is the way for American glory"). One man was killed in the riot, and nearly a dozen were injured, some quite badly.

Had the war been successful and short, the opposition wouldn't have mattered. But the war was neither, and even those who had been hottest for the conflict soon had to admit that things weren't going as they had anticipated. "I have intended, my dear Rodney, twenty times to write you," Henry Clay explained to an old friend during the first winter of the war, after the string of defeats in the Northwest. "But, really, such have been the mortifying incidents of the last campaign on that theater where all our strength was supposed to lay that I have not had the courage to portray my feelings to you." America's problems, Clay contended, started at the top. "It is vain to conceal the fact—at least I will not attempt to disguise with you— Mr. Madison is wholly unfit for the storms of war. Nature has cast him in too benevolent a mould. Admirably adapted to the tranquil scenes of peace, blending all the mild and amiable virtues, he is not fit for the rough and rude blasts which the conflicts of nations generate." Madison's advisers were no better, and the president failed to call them to account. "He is so hesitating, so tardy, so far behind the national sentiment, in his proceedings toward his war ministers, that he will lose whatever credit he might otherwise acquire by the introduction of suitable characters in their places."

The good news of the next several months was that the bad news wasn't worse. Spirits rose with Perry's victory on Lake Erie and Harrison's on the Thames, and then with Jackson's on the Tallapoosa. But hard upon these last good tidings from across the Appalachians came grim word from across the Atlantic. During the spring of 1814, during the very hours when Jackson was crushing the Creeks, British and allied European forces were defeating the French. The Napoleonic tide had crested at Moscow in 1812, where the Russians saved their country by burning their holy city. Deprived of shelter and sustenance, Napoleon was compelled to retreat before the Russian winter, which decimated his army and, more important, destroyed the sense of inevitability that had long been his principal asset. The Russians chased him west and were joined by the Prussians and the Austrians. The Spanish and Dutch revolted against their Bonapartist rulers and gave aid to the British. Napoleon parried the allied thrusts with his customary brilliance but with diminishing resources, and in the last days of March 1814—while Jackson's men were taking Horseshoe Bend—the allies took Paris. Like William Weatherford, Napoleon evaded his enemies awhile longer, but he too finally gave himself up.

Napoleon's defeat augured badly for America. "You are sufficiently aware of the total change in our affairs produced by the late revolution and by the restoration of universal peace in the European world, from which we are alone excluded," Albert Gallatin, Madison's Treasury secretary, wrote Henry Clay. "A well organised and large army is at once liberated from any European employment, and ready, together with a superabundant naval force, to act immediately against us. How ill prepared we are to meet it in a proper manner, no one knows better than yourself, but above all our own divisions and the hostile attitude of the eastern states give room to apprehend that a continuance of the war might prove vitally fatal to the United States."

The fatal blow began to fall during the summer of 1814. A British fleet penetrated the Chesapeake and landed troops on the Maryland shore. The redcoats proceeded west toward the American capital. "Having advanced within sixteen miles of Washington," British general Robert Ross reported, "and ascertained the force of the enemy to be such as might authorize an attempt at carrying his capital, I determined to make it. . . . A corps of about 1200 men appeared to oppose us, but retired after firing a few shots." Nor was the closer defense of the capital more effective. Ross threw his light cavalry and then his infantry against the enemy. "His first line, giving way, was driven on the second, which, yielding to the irresistible attack of the bayonet and the well-directed discharge of rockets, got into confusion and fled."

Nothing now stood between the British and the seat of American self-government. "I determined to march upon Washington, and reached that city at eight o'clock that night," Ross explained. The British lacked the numbers to occupy the capital for any length of time, but Ross intended to retaliate for an American raid on York, the capital of Upper Canada, in which various government buildings had been burned. "Judging it of consequence to complete the destruction of the public buildings with the least possible delay . . . the following buildings were set fire to and consumed: the capitol, including the Senate-house and the House of Representatives, the arsenal, the dockyard, Treasury, War Office, President's Palace, rope-walk, and the great bridge across the Potomac." A British veteran of the Napoleonic wars remembered the moment with soldierly satisfaction. "It would be difficult to conceive a finer spectacle," George Gleig wrote. "The sky was brilliantly illumined by the different conflagrations, and a dark red light was thrown upon the road, sufficient to permit each man to view distinctly his comrade's face. Except the burning of St. Sebastian's"—taken by Wellington's army in northern Spain in 1813—"I do not recollect to have witnessed at any period of my life a scene more striking or more sublime."

The experience was humiliating to every patriotic American. A country that couldn't protect its capital from enemy assault would quickly become a laughingstock among nations. Small comfort followed the repulse of the same British force when it attacked Baltimore two weeks later. The victory gave Americans an anthem to sing after Francis Scott Key, observing the defense of Fort McHenry, put American words to a British drinking song, but it provided little in the way of confidence or lasting security.

Republicans and a few Federalists tried to mask their mortification with anger at the behavior of the British. On learning that General Ross had been killed by an American sniper at Baltimore, *Niles' Register* recommended derisively that a monument be erected to "THE LEADER OF A HOST OF BARBARIANS who destroyed the capitol." Many Americans joined Henry Clay in lamenting Madison's ineptitude. One graffitist marked the sooty walls of the Capitol with a damning comparison: "George Washington founded this city after a seven years' war with England; James Madison lost it after a two years' war."

𝓕ederalists in New England took the burning of Washington as an opportunity to weaken the hold of the Republicans on the national government, and perhaps of the national government on New England. Gathering at Hartford, Connecticut, they vented their grievances against the war, against the Republicans, and against most of what had happened in American politics since John Adams left the presidency. Some spoke of secession, others of amendments to the Constitution. Just what they said was impossible for outsiders to know, for they barred the door of their meeting hall against ordinary citizens and published neither transcripts nor summary of the debates. After three weeks they produced a report recommending several constitutional amendments designed to make embargoes, war declarations, and the admission of new states more difficult; to reduce the representation in Congress of the South (by negating the three-fifths clause of the Constitution and thereby eliminating slaves altogether from the seat-determining totals); and to limit presidents to one term and prevent a single state—they were obviously thinking of Virginia—from having two presidents in succession.

Radicals among the Federalists complained that the recommendations didn't go far enough. Few admitted publicly to feeling closer to Britain than to Virginia, but their constant carping against Madison and the war made clear where their loyalties lay. The canny among the separatists counseled tactical patience. "No sensible man ought to expect that the *first* New England convention would do as much as the *last* out of several congresses of the patriots of the revolution," a Boston paper observed knowingly.

𝓦hen Jackson heard of the Hartford convention he was outraged. The country was at war, the very principle of self-government was in peril, and the Federalists were flirting with Britain. Jackson's nationalism had always been of a piece with his devotion to popular government; since the Revolutionary War, when he had fought simultaneously against British regulars and American Tories, he had understood the Union to be the best guarantee of popular rule, and vice versa. The Federalists were twice wrong and hence doubly dangerous. "These kind of men, although called Federalist, are really monarchist, and traitors to the constituted Government," he declared. By the time Jackson got the news the Hartford delegates had dispersed, but he left no doubt what he would have done if given the chance. "Had I commanded the military department where the Hartford convention met, if it had been the last act of my life I should have hung up the three principal leaders of the party." As an afterthought to his imagined execution, he added, "I am sure an independent court martial would have condemned them."

The Hartford Federalists didn't have to fear Jackson, as a thousand miles separated him from them, but they did have to notice the Tennessee general. Jackson's victory at Horseshoe Bend was a rare bright spot in the miserable war, and in its aftermath Americans from all across the country noticed its author. Newspapers in every city recounted the triumph. Millions of Americans who had never heard of Andrew Jackson now praised his bravery, determination, and skill, which contrasted so favorably with the timidity, fecklessness, and incompetence of nearly everyone else associated with the war.

The Madison administration embraced the general as tightly as it could. The War Department published Jackson's reports from the front. War Secretary Armstrong recommended a promotion. "Something ought to be done for General Jackson," he told Madison. The obvious thing, from the administration's standpoint, was to bring Jackson into the regular army, where his light would reflect up the chain of command to Washington, rather than back to Tennessee. A hitch arose on account of the current recess of Congress. "All therefore that can be done at present," Armstrong informed Jackson, "in reward for your able and gallant conduct during the campaign and in testimony of the public respect these have obtained is to make you a Brigadier of the line, with the brevet of Major General, and to invest you with the command of the Seventh Military District." But the difficulty disappeared when William Henry Harrison, in a dispute with the War Department, resigned his commission as major general, freeing up that rank for Jackson.

Jackson thought twice about the appointment. For all his embrace of the Union as an ideal, he retained the westerner's distrust of many of the agents and agencies of the national government. The War Department had done little good for Tennessee or, till now, for him. He recognized the motives of the Madison administration in putting him forward.

But he couldn't say no. When the nation called, the patriot answered. And the honor was very great. The orphan boy from the Revolutionary War was becoming one of the highest-ranking officers in the country. To be a major general of the Tennessee militia was a fine thing, but to be a major general in the army of the United States was something else again.

*W*ith the surrender of William Weatherford, Jackson could confidently declare the Creek campaign over. "Accept the expression of your general's thanks, and of his admiration," he told his men. "Within a *few weeks* you have annihilated the power of a nation that had for *twenty years* been the disturber of our peace. . . . Wherever these infatuated allies of our archenemy"—Britain—"assembled their forces for battle, you have seen them overthrown; wherever they fled, you have pursued them and dispersed them. The rapidity of your movements and the brilliancy of your achievements have corresponded with the valor by which you were animated." Forgetting, or at least ignoring in the moment of victory, the failures and lapses of the mutinous few, Jackson recounted the triumphs of the faithful many: how they had endured hunger and fatigue, how they had marched over mountains and forded swollen rivers, how they had found and defeated the enemy in his woodland fortress. Now the time had come to return home, and their general would gladly lead them there. "In performing this last act of duty I shall experience a satisfaction not to be expressed."

Jackson had just reached Nashville when his appointment to command the Seventh District came through from Washington. The Seventh District comprised Tennessee, Mississippi Territory, and Louisiana, and its command made Jackson responsible for negotiating the peace settlement with the Creeks. Accordingly he had time only to kiss Rachel hello before he had to kiss her good-bye and head south again.

He knew what he wanted from a treaty. The long marches to and from the lower country had given him plenty of time to think about the future of the Southwest. Despite having accepted the services of some of the Creeks against the others, he saw less to distinguish the friendlies from the hostiles than many of his compatriots did. Defeated hostiles could turn friendly, but irritated friendlies could turn hostile. Jackson may have been harder-hearted than some of his contemporaries, or perhaps he was simply more realistic, yet whatever the cause, he didn't believe that whites and Indians could live in peaceful proximity. At least they couldn't so long as the Indians clung to their tribal ways, which included the ability to make war against one another and against the whites. This wasn't wholly the fault of the Indians. White settlers were endlessly pushy, and foreign whites—British and Spanish— were always eager to provoke the Indians against Americans. Jackson couldn't do anything about the pushiness of the settlers, which came with human nature. But he could do something about the foreigners and about the Indians' ability to respond to provocations with a renewal of war.

The "grand policy of the government," he explained to Tennessee senator John Williams, ought to be to link the white settlements in Georgia with those of Tennessee and Mississippi Territory. The connected settlements would form a "bulwark against foreign invasion" and prevent the "introduction of foreign influence to corrupt the minds of the Indians." The settlements would also split the Creek nation, diminishing the capacity of irreconcilables among them to start another war. Perhaps surprisingly for the one who had led the fighting against them, Jackson thought the hostile Creeks ought not to be stripped of lands. Politics in the states that had contributed soldiers to the fighting required seizing some of the land to pay the costs of the campaign; Jackson couldn't prevent that. But even the hostile Creeks had to live. "Humanity dictates that the conquered part of the nation should be allotted sufficient space for agricultural purposes." Yet that space needn't be their traditional territory. Some might come from the lands of the friendly Creeks, who would simply have to make room.

The friendly Creeks wouldn't like Jackson's plan, and neither would their northern neighbors. Jackson believed that the collapse of Tecumseh's alliance and the current moment of American victory provided a chance to solve some long-standing problems. Cherokee and Chickasaw lands might be appropriated in the name of national defense. To the Chickasaws in particular, the American government might truthfully say, "You have proved to us that you cannot protect the whites on the roads through your country. The enemy you have permitted to pass through your nation, kill and plunder our nation, and carry off our women and children captives." Jackson didn't advocate simply seizing the land; the Indians must receive fair compensation for surrendering their rights. But the transfer was necessary. "Our national security requires it, and *their* security requires it. . . . It must be done."

And so it was. When the Creeks gathered at Fort Jackson, the leaders of the friendly bands predictably expected a reward for their loyalty. They discovered to their shock that Jackson proposed to punish them: for failing to keep order within the Creek nation and for thereby allowing the Red Sticks to commit their depredations against the whites. "The truth is," Jackson told a delegation of the Creek leaders, "the great body of the Creek chiefs and warriors did not respect the power of the United States. They thought we were an insignificant nation, that we would be overpowered by the British." How did Jackson know this? By the Creeks' response to Tecumseh. "If they had not thought so, Tecumseh would have had no influence. He would have been sent back to the British, or delivered to the United States as a prisoner, or shot. If my enemy goes to the house of my friend, and tells my friend he means to kill me, my friend becomes my enemy if he does not at least tell me I am to be killed." Jackson expressed sorrow that the Creeks had not heeded the words of their wise chiefs who had counseled continued attachment to the United States. "Had you listened to them, you would yet have been a rich, powerful, and happy people. Your woods would yet have been filled with flocks, and herds of cattle; your fields with corn. Your towns and villages would not have been burned, nor your women and children wandering in the woods, exposed to starvation and cold. But you listened to prophets and bad men; your warriors have been slain, your nation is defenceless—you are reduced to such want as to receive food from your father the President of the United States."

The Creek delegation protested Jackson's patent disingenuousness. He had been happy to exploit the division among the Creeks while the battle raged, they pointed out, but now he claimed that no such division existed.

Big Warrior, speaking for his fellows, didn't deny that the Red Sticks had warred upon the whites. But many other Creeks had refused to join them, and the result had been the war within the Creek nation. "The spilling blood of white people, and giving satisfaction for it, was the cause of war amongst us, and nothing else." How could Jackson say the friendly Creeks had done nothing to restrain the wrongdoers? What more could they have done? Big Warrior appealed to the memory of the first of the Great Fathers, General Washington, who had held out the arm of friendship to the Creeks and signed the initial treaty with them. "To that arm of friendship I hold fast." Beyond the claims of friendship and justice, Big Warrior reminded Jackson that not all the Creeks were reconciled to peace with the Americans and that the British were still bent on trouble. A punitive peace, by destroying the credibility of the friendly Creeks, would make the task of the British easier.

Jackson didn't need reminding of the British threat. In fact it was his fear of the British, more than his feelings about the Creeks, that motivated his peace plan. "The war is not over," he told Big Warrior and the others, regarding the conflict with Britain. And until that war was over the Americans had to look first to their security. Jackson pointed out that under the treaty with General Washington that Big Warrior cited, the Creeks were obliged to hand over enemies of the United States, including the likes of Tecumseh. They hadn't. "The United States would have been justified by the Great Spirit had they taken all the lands of the nation merely for keeping it a secret that her enemies were in the nation." The United States was not taking all the lands of the Creeks. They were left with more than enough to support themselves. But the American government insisted on separating the Creek lands from Spanish Florida, lest British agents or their Spanish accomplices continue to foment rebellion among the Creeks—a rebellion that would end only in the utter destruction of the Creeks. "We will run a line between our friends and our enemies. We wish to save our friends, protect them, support them. *We will do all these things*. We will destroy our enemies because we love our friends and ourselves. The safety of the United States and your nation requires that enemies must be separated from friends. We wish to know them from each other. We wish to be able to say to our soldiers: Here is one, there is the other. . . . *Therefore we will run the line*."

Jackson wouldn't force the Creek leaders to sign the treaty. "Our friends will sign the treaty," he said. And they would receive food, clothing, and the protection of the United States. Those who didn't sign the treaty would be considered enemies. But they would be allowed to go, with Jackson's help. "They shall have provisions to carry them away. We do not want them. We wish them to join their friends that all may be destroyed together."

Here Jackson wasn't being disingenuous, merely blunt. He knew that Big Warrior and the other chiefs had little alternative to signing the treaty. "The whole Creek nation is in a most wretched state," he wrote the War Department. Two seasons of war—and his own scorched-earth policy—had driven it to the brink of starvation. "Could you only see the misery and wretchedness of those creatures perishing from want of food and picking up the grains of corn scattered from the mouths of the horses and trodden in the earth," he told Rachel, "I know your humanity would feel for them." Jackson's humanity felt for them, too, but so did his strategic sense. After Big Warrior and the other chiefs signed the treaty, as Jackson guessed they would, he wrote to the War Department, "They *must* be *fed* and *clothed* or necessity will compel them to embrace the proferred friendship of the British."

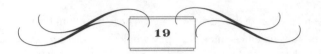

19

THE SPANISH FRONT

The Fort Jackson treaty was a gamble: that the Creeks would be more influenced by American threats than by British promises. The gamble paid off with most of the Creeks, who bitterly but nonviolently acquiesced to Jackson's dictation. Yet a minority did just the opposite, with the encouragement of the British. "The Creeks were depressed in spirit beyond all example," Jackson learned from an informant on the lower Mobile River. "They were about to give themselves up, when a runner came from the Apalachicola"—in Florida—"to Pensacola to inform them of the arrival of supplies from the British. They then became in a moment as insolent as they had been before submissive. Instead of surrendering, a party of twenty-five started out to collect cattle in the settlements east of Mobile river and bay."

Jackson took this challenge as an opportunity. He relayed the intelligence to the War Department in Washington, with a request for permission to clear up the problem. "Will the government say to me: Require a few hundred militia (which can be had for the campaign at one day's notice) and with such of my disposable force of regulars proceed to —— and reduce it. If so, I promise the war in the South has a speedy termination and British influence forever cut off from the Indians in that quarter."

The government wasn't ready to give Jackson such carte blanche or to fill in the blank with a specific reference. Washington was used to alarmist tales from the West, and officials of the Madison administration suspected similar embroidery here. Moreover, Jackson was talking about invading Spanish territory, and Madison, having trouble enough with Britain, had no desire to double his enemies. He ordered Jackson to gather additional intelligence and keep his powder dry but to stay clear of Spanish soil.

*W*hat constituted Spanish soil in the vicinity of Florida was a debated issue in 1814. The United States government in 1810 had unilaterally enforced its interpretation of the Louisiana Purchase—that Louisiana included the left bank of the Mississippi to the mouth of the river and stretched east almost to Pensacola—by occupying that district, including Mobile. The Spanish government accepted neither the interpretation nor the occupation but, lacking the troops to prevent the latter, was compelled to suffer the former. Spain did, however, garrison Pensacola, about sixty miles east of Mobile.

Jackson had his own interpretation of who ought to govern Florida, and it didn't include Spain. Without explicitly violating Madison's orders—yet—he launched a psychological offensive against the Spanish force at Pensacola. He traveled to Mobile and from there addressed a stream of messages to the commandant of the Pensacola garrison, Mateo González Manrique, that were at first direct, then presumptuous, and finally belligerent. "I am informed that the enemies of the United States, who have been murdering our unoffending women and children, have sought and obtained asylum from justice within the territory of Spain," Jackson said, regarding some Creek warriors still at large. "Information has also been received that permission was given to our open enemy, an officer commanding his Britannic majesty's frigate the *Orpheus*, to land within the territory of Spain 25,000 stand of arms with 300 barrels of ammunition, for the avowed purpose of enabling the vanquished Creeks to renew a sanguinary war with the United States." Jackson said he hoped these reports were unfounded. But he wanted González to know that he was monitoring the situation and would expect Spanish cooperation in tracking down the hostile Indians and preventing the British from violating Spain's neutrality.

González responded as Jackson doubtless expected and desired. He called the letter "impertinent" and "an insult." Jackson's courier, John Gordon, reported that González said "the Spaniards would die before they would comply with such a demand." Gordon added that rumors were circulating in Pensacola that Spain was about to declare war on the United States. Whether González had inspired the rumors, Gordon couldn't tell.

Jackson would have been happy for war against Spain, but he doubted things would come to that. "Whatever may be the wishes of the Spanish government," he remarked to a fellow American officer, "her weak and exhausted situation at present will prevent her from making war upon us. . . . She is too sensible of her own situation not to know that a declaration of war would deprive her of all her territory in North and South America as far as the isthmus of Darien. . . . The rumor of a declaration of war against us is unfounded."

James Madison wasn't so sure, which was why the War Department tried to calm Jackson down. James Monroe, who assumed direction of the department upon the retirement of John Armstrong, delivered a direct order to Jackson: "Take no measures which would involve this Government in a contest with Spain." Monroe didn't want to offend Jackson, so he assured him that President Madison approved the "manly tone" with which the general had asserted America's rights in Florida. But assertions were as far as things must go. "Very important interests are committed to you, and great confidence is entertained that you will meet the expectations of the Government in the discharge of your duties."

Conveniently for Jackson, orders from Washington required a month or more to reach Mobile. In the interim he felt free to conduct policy on his own, in particular to harass Commandant González. Spain, he told the Spanish officer, while professedly neutral in the conflict between the United States and Britain, had opened its arms to a "murderous, barbarous, rebellious banditti" who had massacred innocent American women and children. Spain's monarch called himself "his Catholic majesty," prompting Jackson to sneer that "*our* Christianity would blush" at harboring such criminals as Florida sheltered. If Spain wished to be treated as a neutral, it must act accordingly. "She must assume the neutral character she is bound to the United States for, and restrain the tomahawk and scalping knife, or the head which excites their use shall feel the sharpness of their edge." Should the United States have to chastise the renegades in Florida, González could expect no mercy. "An eye for an eye, tooth for tooth, scalp for scalp."

Jackson ensured that a copy of his letter reached Washington. When Madison read it, he doubtless wondered why he ever put this intemperate man in charge of the southern border. Jackson seemed bent on starting a war with Spain, in apparent disregard of the fact that the British threat was greater than ever. Madison must have asked himself who was more dangerous: the British or Jackson.

Yet Jackson knew what he was about. He insisted on provoking the Spanish—and the administration—precisely because he appreciated the British threat. "I received this evening at 5 o'clock from Pensacola the following information . . . ," he wrote to his adjutant, Robert Butler, "that his British Majesty's ships *Hermes, Carron*, and *Sophie* has arrived at Pensacola on the 5th instant, with 200 land forces and large supplies of arms, ordnance, and ordnance stores. . . . The *Orpheus* is expected in a few days with 14 sail of the line and many transports with 10,000 troops. It is further added that 14 sail of the line and transports has arrived at Bermuda, with 25,000 of Lord Wellington's army, etc., etc. Before one month the British and Spanish forces expect to be in possession of Mobile and all the surrounding country."

Jackson may have known that this report was exaggerated and premature. Butler was in Tennessee (trying mutiny cases from the Creek campaign), and Jackson hoped to scare Governor Blount into sending as many troops as possible south. But the British threat was real and grave.

Jackson showed his characteristic energy in preparing to meet it. "There will be bloody noses before this happens," he told Butler regarding a British attempt on Mobile. Jackson said he had ordered Indian agents to enlist every warrior willing to take the field on the American side, and put them on the army's payroll. He had called out every militiaman he was authorized to summon. The danger justified these actions and more. "We have to defend not only our territory but our liberties. . . . The whole combined coalition"—of British, Spanish, and hostile Indians—"are engaged in a league to subjugate America." Jackson would counter the threat, even if he had to exceed orders from Washington. "I mean to make a desperate struggle."

The struggle would start in Florida. Jackson understood that the prize of the Southwest was New Orleans, with its control of the Mississippi. He intended to fall back to that city, but before he did, he needed to secure Florida, lest the British gain a foothold from which they could launch a flanking maneuver against the Louisiana capital. Securing Florida was the aim of his psychological offensive against González. Jackson was fairly certain the Spanish wouldn't risk a war with the United States over Florida. Spain had far larger problems in the Americas; during the last few years nationalist movements in several colonies had raised the banner of revolt against Spanish authority. If the Spanish *were* foolish enough to add the United States to their enemies, Jackson was prepared to trounce them in Florida.

So he pressured González to the point where the Spanish commandant wouldn't resist an American incursion into Florida. He berated González for arming Indians unfriendly to the United States. "I shall arm my Indians," he said, by way of reply. He added that this new provocation, following Spain's previous sins, justified America's taking the Florida matter into its own hands. "You have thrown the gauntlet, and I will take it up."

In September 1814 the British made a prophet of Jackson by landing a squadron of marines and allied Indians below Mobile. They attacked Fort Bowyer, which controlled the entrance to Mobile Bay, and were soon poised to overrun the post. But luckily for the small American garrison, the wind turned, preventing the British ships in the pass from bringing their guns to bear on the fort. The Americans counterattacked and eventually compelled the British to withdraw.

Jackson recognized a close call when he saw it. Though he lauded, in a letter to James Monroe, "the gallant efforts of our brave soldiers in resisting and repulsing a combined British naval and land force," he understood that absent the most strenuous preventive measures, the outcome of a future British attack might not be so favorable.

The very next day Jackson received additional cause for alarm. A letter from New Orleans, from that city's "committee of safety," bewailed the parlous condition of security along the lower Mississippi. "This country is strong by nature but extremely weak from the nature of its population," the committee explained. The weakness resulted primarily from the large proportion of blacks, the committee said, noting that blacks outnumbered whites in Louisiana's plantation districts by as many as twenty-five to one. "The maintenance of domestic tranquility in this part of the state obviously forbids a call on any of the white inhabitants to the defense of the frontier." Indeed, additional white forces were required simply to keep the blacks in line, as the enemy had been trying to foment a slave insurrection. The local militia was poorly trained and badly armed, and the heterogeneous population of the city—which included many French and Spanish nationals, besides the blacks—rendered the militia unreliable. Only Jackson could save New Orleans and Louisiana. "We look to the forces under your command altogether for external defence and in a great measure for domestic tranquility." If the general would honor the city with a visit, this alone would go far toward improving the situation. "The good people of this state would be encouraged by your presence, the emissaries of the enemy and the partisans of foreign powers would dread the scrutiny of your intelligence, and the reputation which your talents have so justly acquired would inspire all with that confidence which we individually feel."

Jackson didn't like the tone of this letter one bit. He would defend New Orleans, but he needed the help of the inhabitants. The committee members were telling him to do it all himself. He told *them* a few things in reply, starting with some stern advice to start thinking of their black neighbors as allies rather than enemies. He summoned the "free coloured inhabitants of Louisiana" to rally to the cause of American liberty. "Through a mistaken policy, my brave fellow citizens, you have hitherto been deprived of a participation in the glorious struggle for national rights in which our country is engaged. This shall no longer exist; as sons of freedom you are now called upon to defend our most estimable blessing." He asked for black volunteers and offered inducements. "There will be paid the same bounty in money and lands now received by the white soldiers of the United States, viz. $124.00 in cash and 160 acres of land. The non-commissioned officers and privates will also be entitled to the same monthly pay." The black troops would select their own noncommissioned officers. "Due regard will be paid to the feelings of freemen and soldiers. You will not, by being associated with other men in the same corps, be exposed to improper comparisons or unjust sarcasm. As a distinct, independent battalion or regiment, pursuing the path of glory, you will undivided receive the applause, reward, and gratitude of your countrymen."

From the white response to Jackson's call for black troops, a naive observer might have thought he had advocated revolution. The planters who dominated Louisiana politics were aghast at the very thought of giving weapons to blacks. "They think that in putting arms into the hands of men of colour, we only add to the force of the enemy," Governor Claiborne told Jackson, explaining why he had declined to publish Jackson's call for black volunteers. Claiborne stressed to Jackson that he himself didn't share these retrograde ideas. He agreed that free blacks might be necessary to the defense of the state. But the suspicions and fears among the whites were real and had to be taken into account. Claiborne said he had spoken just the day before with two members of the committee of safety and had pointed out that the black troops would be under federal control and might at some point be transferred out of state. "They, however, seemed to think that the measure was only advisable provided there could be a guaranty against the return of the regiment. But if, at the close of the war, the individuals were to settle in Louisiana, with a knowledge of the use of arms and *that pride of distinction* which a soldier's pursuits so naturally inspires, they would prove dangerous."

If he hadn't realized it already, this exchange alerted Jackson that defending New Orleans would be a complicated business. And it spurred him to solve his Florida problem at once. After the British withdrew from Mobile Bay, they retired to Pensacola to repair their damaged ships and plan their next action. This made a mockery of Florida's neutrality. "It is in every sense an enemy's port," Jackson told Claiborne. He intended to treat it as such. He awaited only the arrival of reinforcements under John Coffee. "I trust shortly that I will be able to drive the lion from his den, and give thereby permanent security to this section of the lower country," he wrote Rachel. Slow-traveling news had just reached Mobile of the British destruction of Washington. The very thought made Jackson livid. It was a "disgrace to the nation," he said. But the anger he was sure his countrymen shared could be put to use. "It will give impulse and energy to our cause."

*W*hen Coffee reached Mobile, Jackson set out for Pensacola. He did so on his own responsibility and in direct violation of the administration's policy of not antagonizing the Spanish. He realized that the least he could do was explain himself. "As I act without the orders of government, I deem it proper to state my reasons for it," he wrote Monroe.

> I trust, sir, that the necessity of this act to the safety of this section of the Union; the hostility of the governor of Pensacola, resigning his forts to the British commander, thus assuming the character of a British territory; his permitting them to remain there to fit out one expedition against the United States, return there and refit, now to be preparing another; added to his having acknowledged that he has armed the Indians, sent them into our territory, capturing our citizens and destroying their property, and this too under a British officer; will be a sufficient justification in the eyes of my government for having undertaken this expedition. Should it not, I shall have one consolation: a consciousness of having done the only thing which can, under present circumstances, give security to this section and put down an Indian war. And the salvation of my country will be a sufficient reward for the loss of my commission.

It was entirely like Jackson to assume he knew better than the president and secretary of war what the defense of the nation, or at least his district, required, and to risk his career on that assumption. In any event, he appreciated the opportunity distance afforded an audacious commander. His assault on Pensacola would be a fait accompli long before Madison and Monroe even heard of it. By then he would be a hero or an insubordinate fool.

The march to Pensacola took five days. Jackson's invasion force included army regulars, Tennessee and Mississippi militia, and a large band of

Choctaws. Approaching the town on the evening of November 6, Jackson dispatched a messenger with an ultimatum for Commandant González. He listed Spain's violations of neutrality at Pensacola and declared that these violations had prompted his incursion into Florida. "I come not as the enemy of Spain, but I come with a force sufficient to prevent the repetition of those acts so injurious to the United States and so inconsistent with the neutral character of Spain. To effect this object is my determination." Jackson demanded possession of the fortifications of the town, with their arms. If these were handed over peaceably, he would sign a receipt his government would honor. "But if they are not delivered peaceably, let the blood of your subjects be upon your own head." Adding an element of emotional extortion, Jackson continued: "I will not hold myself responsible for the conduct of my enraged soldiers and Indian warriors." Jackson's letter gave González an hour to think the matter over and reply.

By accident or design, Spanish guns fired on Jackson's messenger, forcing him to retreat. "I am at a loss, sir, to know whether this conduct has been with an intention to insult the flag of my government, contrary to the usages of war in like cases," Jackson wrote González in a second letter, sent with a Spanish prisoner captured on Jackson's march to Pensacola. This time the message got through, only to be rebuffed by González himself. The Spanish commander professed puzzlement at Jackson's reference to "usages of war." The United States and Spain, he pointed out, were not at war. He denied Jackson's allegations of unneutrality. He conceded that the British had operated out of the Pensacola district, but he said they did so without his permission. And he rejected Jackson's demand to surrender the town and fortifications. "My duty does not permit me."

Jackson took this rejection as his signal for action. He feinted an assault against the west side of the town, under the guns of both the Spanish in their fort there and the British ships in the bay, before throwing the mass of his troops against the relatively undefended east side. The maneuver caught González quite by surprise. Jackson's troops stormed the Spanish position in the town and captured it with light losses. An American lieutenant hauled down the Spanish colors.

At this point González decided he'd had enough. By Jackson's telling he "begged for mercy." Whatever his words, González surrendered the town and the fort. The subordinate commanding the fort, however, which lay some distance from the town proper, had other notions. He rejected a surrender order from González and continued fighting.

Jackson thereupon directed that captured Spanish cannons in the town be turned on the fort. The fort's commander, observing the preparations for a bombardment, changed his mind and offered to join the surrender. But he haggled over details and dragged the process out till dark. Jackson grew impatient during the night and determined to force the issue at daybreak. He was giving the orders for the attack to begin when a terrific noise from the fort stopped him in midsentence. "A tremendous explosion was heard, and a column of smoke seen to ascend in that direction," he told Monroe. "Repetitions of the explosions soon convinced me that the British and Spanish were blowing up the works."

This spared Jackson the trouble of blowing up the fort himself. He had never intended to hold the town or the fort. He lacked the troops, which were in any event needed at New Orleans. His objective had been twofold: to drive the British from Pensacola and to impress on the Spanish and the Indians that the United States, not Britain, was the country to respect and fear in Florida. He was pleased to report to Monroe that his mission had been accomplished. "I had the satisfaction to see the whole British force leave the port, and their friends at our mercy."

*P*eople who knew the Adams men had theories about what made them so irascible. Some thought it was the Puritan streak that ran through the family, others the effect of those Braintree winters, which equaled nearby Boston's for bone-chilling cold but lacked the insulating effects of the city's social life. Benjamin Franklin thought John Adams simply daft, at least in stretches. "He means well for his country," Franklin said, "is always an honest man, often a wise one, but sometimes, and in some things, absolutely out of his senses." Thomas Jefferson marveled at Adams's "dislike of all parties and all men." John Quincy Adams inherited his father's distemper, although he may have gotten some as well from his mother, Abigail, who tolerated human imperfection no better than her husband did. The younger Adams abstained from pleasures as resolutely as from vices. He rose hours before the sun to read the Bible—in Greek, German, French, or occasionally English. He walked for exercise and knew exactly how far he traveled, having measured his stride to the toenail's breadth (two feet six and "eighty-eight one hundreds of an inch"). When weather allowed he swam, combining bath and constitutional in whatever pond, river, gulf, or ocean lay nearby. He preferred his own company to that of most other humans, and he wasn't especially fond of himself. He distrusted the political judgment of the common people as much as his father did. When the elder Adams lost to Jefferson in the 1800 presidential contest, Quincy blamed the defeat on Jefferson's "pimping to the popular passions."

Yet for all his prickliness, Quincy Adams had the makings of a brilliant diplomat. He had accompanied his father to France when *père* joined Franklin on the commission that negotiated peace with Britain after the Battle of Yorktown. The facility in French he acquired there served him well in an era when French was the lingua franca of diplomacy. At fourteen he escorted an American envoy to the Russian court at St. Petersburg, interpreting for the French-less fellow. He was appointed minister in his own right to the Netherlands by President Washington, and then to Prussia by his president father. When the passions of the people retired John Adams to Massachusetts, Quincy followed him there. But the state legislature soon sent him to Washington as a senator. He languished as a Federalist under Jefferson's Republican administrations, yet after the Federalists' obstructionism began veering toward separatism, he left his father's party for the party of his father's foe. Massachusetts dumped him on account of the apostasy, but James Madison retrieved him and made him minister to Russia. From that distance he supported the war against Britain, albeit less warmly and more diplomatically than Henry Clay or John Calhoun. When Madison required someone to negotiate peace terms with Britain, he could think of no one better qualified than Quincy Adams.

Yet politics prevented Madison from delivering plenipotentiary powers to Adams alone. Just as John Adams (and John Jay) had been sent to Paris to keep an eye on Franklin at the end of the first war of American independence, so Clay and Albert Gallatin (and Jonathan Russell and James Bayard) were sent to Ghent, in what would become Belgium when that country acquired independence, to keep an eye on Quincy Adams as the second war of independence wound down. Clay was included as a war hawk and ardent nationalist. Having helped get America into the war, he seemed just the man to help get America out. Treasury Secretary Gallatin presumably would guard America's economic interests.

He would also, Madison hoped, keep Clay and Adams from blows. The setting for the negotiations was pleasant, to a point. "Ghent looks clean and cheerful," wrote James Gallatin, Albert's seventeen-year-old son and secretary and an occasional note taker for the American commission. "The inhabitants speak only Flemish. All seem employed in commerce. . . . They call private residences *hôtels* in this country. The house is large and all the delegates are to lodge here. . . . The women are so ugly. . . . They always entertain here on Sunday—how different from London!" (The Gallatins had come through England, and James had been patriotically unimpressed.) "It is the gayest day. The working people have a cheerful holiday; in London they show joy by getting drunk."

The distractions of the city did little for relations between Adams and Clay. The two worked as poorly in harness as Franklin and the elder Adams had. Clay was expansive in temperament and fluent in speech but occasionally imprecise, while Adams was just the opposite. When Clay criticized one of their British counterparts as a "man of much irritation," Adams riposted, "*Irritability* . . . is the word, Mr. Clay, irritability." He added, with an arch look at Clay, "Like somebody else that I know." Clay countered, "That we do; all know him, and none better than yourself." Adams complained in his diary of the personal habits of Clay and the other commissioners. "They sit after dinner and drink bad wine and smoke cigars, which neither suits my habits nor my health, and absorbs time which I cannot spare." More than once Adams passed Clay in the hours before dawn, the former rising while the latter was just going to bed.

The other members of the commission observed the behavior of the two, sometimes with bemusement, often with irritation of their own. "Mr. Adams is in a very bad temper. Mr. Clay annoys him. Father pours oil on the troubled waters," James Gallatin wrote. On another day: "Clay uses strong language to Adams, and Adams returns the compliment. Father looks calmly on with a twinkle in his eye." Again: "Both Mr. Adams and Mr. Clay object to everything except what they suggest themselves. Father remains calm but firm and does all he can to keep peace."

On at least one thing all agreed, however: that the terms the British offered in the negotiations that began in August 1814 were intolerable. The

British proposed to let each side retain territory occupied during the war, to establish a sovereign Indian state carved from American territory in the West, and to allow their own vessels free navigation of the Mississippi. The first and second proposals would have alienated American land, the second would have blocked American expansion, and the third would have granted British warships free entry to the heart of America.

The Americans inferred from the British position that the government in London wasn't serious about peace. "Our negotiations may be considered at an end," Albert Gallatin wrote in a private message for James Monroe barely a week after the talks began. "Great Britain wants war in order to cripple us; she wants aggrandizement at our expense." The Americans rejected the British terms and countered with demands of their own: a reversion to the territorial status quo ante bellum, an end to impressment, an indemnity for damages done by British troops, and an agreement by both sides not to employ Indians in any future conflict between Britain and the United States.

The negotiations didn't exactly end, but neither did they move forward. It became apparent that London was counting on the current offensives in America to soften the diplomatic resistance in Ghent. Adams, Clay, and the other Americans hoped for the best but braced for worse. They groaned on the news of the burning of Washington and shared worried glances when they learned that the British were preparing an attack against New Orleans and the Mississippi. They had heard of Jackson's victory at Horseshoe Bend, but with everyone else they assumed that Wellington's invincibles were of a different and more formidable character than William Weatherford's Red Sticks. Nervously they settled in for the winter, expecting nothing to happen in the negotiations till the arrival of news of the battle for the great river of the American heartland.

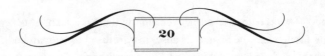

20

PIRATES AND PATRIOTS

ouisiana is a delightful country, and though the climate too often proves fatal to a foreigner, yet generally we ascribe to the climate what is the effect of our imprudence. I have been severely attacked this summer, and had nearly died, but at length I am acclimated."

he author of these words was John Windship, a Bostonian who migrated to Louisiana not long after his graduation from Harvard in 1809. He was still trying to make sense of his new home—of the climate and its effect on prudence and health, of the politics of the state (admitted to the Union in 1812), and of its assorted ethnic and racial groups—when the war with Britain broke out. The conflict was greeted with disdain in Louisiana. "The War of the U.S. is very unpopular with us," he wrote. "It was with difficulty that the requisition of General Flournoy"—for volunteers—"was complied with, even among the Americans. At New Orleans the French and the Spaniards absolutely refused to be marched. They declared themselves liege subjects of Spain or France. The Governor is a mere nullity. The government is an aristocratic democracy." Windship didn't explain what he meant by an aristocratic democracy, but the effects of the hybrid were no recommendation. "Great tumult exists in the city, and the prospect is very gloomy to the friends of peace and order. If the English should attack us, there is no force competent to repel them."

The antipathy toward war reflected the distinctive politics of Louisiana.

> Our political parties differ entirely from those of New England. Federalist and Democrat mean almost the same thing. The *American Party* differ as to the policy of the war. The *French Party* as to the right of our government to the country. The *Spanish Party* curse everything. The *Creoles* discontented. The *Negroes* insolent. The *Indians* sulky. What political chemist will ever unite us? Among the French it is a favorite opinion, and perhaps an ardent wish, that we should be reunited to the French empire. Among a large portion of the inhabitants—English, Scotch, Irish, Dutch, American, &c.—it is a matter of indifference to what power we fall provided cotton will sell at $20 per hundredweight.

The anarchic politics of Louisiana revealed—to the Federalist-bred Windship at least—the limits of local self-government. "The most enlightened men of this country consider the admission of Louisiana into the Union, as an independent state, as an impolitic and unfortunate measure. . . . There probably never was a people happier or more prosperous than the Louisianians before the late adoption. The expences of the government were defrayed from the treasury of the United States. . . . Our taxes were low and proportioned to the resources of the country; our people were quiet, and demagogues bawled in vain for influence and office." The current condition of the state was altogether different. "We have the noisy and ignorant satellites of a democracy to rule us. Party spirit rages among us. Taxation has become oppressive. The Creole population have become jealous of the Americans." Democrats—that is, Republicans—outnumbered Federalists, but the deeper divide was ethnic. "We are either French or Americans.

There can be no doubt but that the French are declining in power, and the Americans are not sufficiently prudent to hide it from them. We have all the advantages that superior education and enterprise will afford, while they on the other hand, are devoted to European prejudices and politics. . . . The purchase of this country by the Americans is mortifying to their vanity. They are sometimes told not to interfere with government, as that is a subject peculiar to ourselves. They have even been told that in purchasing the country we purchased them also, at no higher price than 50 cents per head."

The Spanish were just as unhappy. "They fondly recur to the despotism of Cadiz and commandants, and look with anxious hope to the progress of European conquest. They hate our laws and customs; and the regularity, the necessary delays and the impartial distribution of justice to rich and poor in our courts, are to them proofs of our barbarity and meanness."

Writing in the spring of 1814, Windship remarked that the French and Spanish were hanging on the news from Europe. Many hoped for an end to their American exile. "If Bonaparte has regained the empire," Windship said, summarizing the views of the most ardent irredentists, "he will have the power, seconded by the wishes of his faithful provincials, to re-annex this country to France. If Bonaparte is dethroned, the Bourbons will consider the sale of Louisiana as invalid and will repossess the country." Speaking in his own voice, Windship articulated a common concern among Americans in Louisiana. "If Bonaparte is conquered, and an attempt is made"—by the British—"to sever this state, I fear that . . . Louisiana will fall to the dominion of either France or England. Those who know the situation of this country, who see neither spirit in the people nor any means of resistance, fear this event."

Windship had been in Louisiana only a short while. Yet the country had changed him. "Indolence is common with us all. . . . The mind with the body is weakened. We suffer a relaxation which, to you Northerners, would be a subject of astonishment. The cool of the morning admits of some exertion. At noon we yield to a burning sun"—Windship was writing now in June—"and the evening is spent in repairing the exhausted system or in the indulgence of ease and tranquility. The nerve of the soul is wasted, and the strong passions of glory and ambition are faintly visible only in the moments of intemperance." Windship's time at Harvard seemed ages ago. There would be nothing like Harvard here. "It will be a phenomenon indeed if this state ever produces a man of genius or learning." Not only New England but the rest of America receded. Louisiana was a world unto itself. "The truth is, we are not Americans."

*Y*et among the non-Americans of Louisiana was one group that wanted to become American, if conditions were right. In a letter in which he railed against the ineffectiveness of the Louisiana government, Windship described the corruption to which this gave rise. "So weak is the Executive that the execution of the revenue laws is almost impossible. Smuggling is carried on to a great degree. . . . A force of 500 armed pirates are settled near the mouth of the Mississippi, and the Gulf of Mexico is tributary to them. It is said to be almost impracticable to disposses them. Too many of the merchants of New Orleans are interested in this trade. The Captain of the band is a French general. Governor Claiborne offered $500 for his head while he was in the city; the next day this buccaneer offered a reward of $1000 for the head of the governor, and his hand bill was distributed through the city."

Windship's "French general" was Jean Laffite, who had indeed placed a bounty on Claiborne's head, although whether in jest or earnest no one could say for sure. Laffite's sense of humor was as unpredictable as his nationality. He had been born in France or the West Indies, depending on who was asking. He was French or Spanish or Jewish. He was pleased to cultivate a reputation as a pirate, although his mastery of the nautical arts was suspect, and there were persons in New Orleans who said they had known him as a blacksmith with a shop at the corner of St. Philip and Bourbon streets.

Whatever his antecedents, in 1814 Laffite was best described as an entrepreneur, a businessman who specialized in the arbitrage of prices across borders. A principal item of his commerce was African slaves. Laffite purchased slaves in the West Indies, where they were cheap, and smuggled them into Louisiana, where they were expensive on account of the federal ban on slave imports. As with other black markets, that in black slaves corrupted otherwise law-abiding persons, who in turn corrupted government by causing it to avert its gaze from the illicit traffic. Purchasers got what they wanted: cheap slaves. Sellers got what *they* wanted: profits. No one got hurt except perhaps the slaves, who had no voice in the matter. If they *had* been asked, most probably would have said that conditions on the American Gulf Coast, grim as they were, were better than those of the Caribbean and South America, where the life expectancy of slaves was often measured in months, and not many of those.

Laffite and his business associates also arbitraged in the transition of Spanish America to independence. Much as the fledgling United States government had done in its revolution against Britain, the aspiring republics of Central and South America enlisted privateers—maritime mercenaries—to harass the commerce of imperial Spain. Laffite and his brothers—Alexander, who was known about Louisiana by his nom de guerre, Dominique, and Pierre—obtained privateer commissions from Cartagena (the parent of modern Colombia). Under the laws of Cartagena, the Laffites were entitled to all the Spanish commerce they could capture. Needless to say, Spanish law took a different view. Perhaps less obviously, so did American law, which prevented the Laffites from legally landing and selling their prizes in America. This hardly stopped them from the landing and selling, and in fact the booty from the sea nicely complemented—and sometimes included—the slaves they were already selling illegally.

The Laffites weren't the only privateers in the Caribbean, nor were they the only importers of illegal slaves. But in smuggling, as in many other businesses, location can be critical to success, and no one had a better location than Laffite and company. The bayous, swamps, and islands south of New Orleans were ideal for smuggling. The waterways, besides defying the best efforts of mapmakers to reduce them to charts, were deep enough to admit the coastal craft the Laffites launched into the Caribbean but shallow enough to bar the big warships of the Spanish navy (or any other fleet) that might chase them home. The West Indies, including Cuba, the richest of the Spanish colonies and, partly for that reason, the most loyal ("the ever faithful isle," it would be called), were not far to the south. New Orleans, the market for the goods seized from the Indies, was not far to the north. The Laffites and the community of seamen, soldiers, artisans, and accountants they gathered on the shores of Barataria Bay couldn't well have asked for more. "The quantity of goods brought in by the banditti is immense," remarked an American official who tracked Laffite's activities, in early 1814. "I have no doubt but they have entered and secured far more than a million of dollars within this last six months."

But into this entrepreneurial idyll sailed, one day in the late summer of 1814, an ominous vessel flying the ensign of the king of England. The British warship anchored outside the entrance to Barataria Bay and lowered a boat, which crossed the bar and approached the Laffites' headquarters. The boat bore a British officer who carried greetings and messages from Colonel Edward Nichols, the commander of the same squadron that was worrying Andrew Jackson at Mobile at just this time. The longest message was addressed not to the Baratarians alone but to the residents of Louisiana at large. "Natives of Louisiana! On you the first call is made to assist in liberating from a faithless, imbecile government your paternal soil. Spaniards, Frenchmen, Italians, and British, whether settled or residing for a time in Louisiana: on you also I call to aid me in this just cause. The American usurpation in this country must be abolished, and the lawful owners of the soil put in possession." Nichols said he headed a powerful fleet with accurate artillery and had at his disposal "a large body of Indians, well armed, disciplined, and commanded by British officers." He mentioned the Indians, of course, to strike terror into the hearts of the Louisianians—but not too much terror. "Rest assured that these brave red men only burn with an ardent desire of satisfaction for the wrongs they have suffered from the Americans, to join you in liberating these southern provinces from their yoke, and drive them into those limits formerly prescribed by my sovereign. The Indians have pledged themselves in the most solemn manner not to injure in the slightest degree the persons or properties of any but enemies to their Spanish or English fathers. A flag over any door, whether Spanish, French, or British, will be a certain protection."

Nichols wished this proclamation to reach all Louisianians. But he could hardly expect the state government to circulate it for him, which was why he delivered it to Jean Laffite, whose informal network was known to be incomparable. "You may be a useful assistant to me in forwarding them," he said of the "honorable intentions" his message conveyed.

Nichols had a second message, for Laffite alone. He hoped they could become friends and allies. "I call on you, with your brave followers, to enter into the service of Great Britain, in which you shall have the rank of a captain; lands will be given to you all, in proportion to your respective ranks." Laffite could keep the property he had gathered to Barataria; the

British government asked no questions. But neither would it show mercy in the event Laffite declined this generous offer. The captain of the warship at the mouth of Barataria Bay had orders to destroy the smugglers' camp and everything in it if they failed to cooperate. The choice was theirs: "war instantly destructive" or "the security of their property" and "the blessings of the British constitution."

*T*he British offer—and threat—placed Laffite in a delicate position. Although Nichols didn't put it quite so, Laffite was being asked to bet on the outcome of the war. If he bet on the British and the British won, he'd be a captain in the British navy—an intriguing notion for one who scarcely knew a topgallant from a staysail—and his men would be landholders. If he bet on the British and the British lost, he could certainly expect retribution from the Americans. Laffite didn't know Andrew Jackson by more than reputation at this point. But he'd heard about the Creek war and the Creek peace, and he had little cause to think Jackson would be kinder to him than to the Indians.

Laffite had another reason to lean toward the British. Of late the government of Louisiana had shown an intention to crack down on Barataria. Laffite couldn't tell quite why this was so, but he had to guess that it reflected a desire on the part of his commercial rivals in New Orleans to seize some of his market share. The bounty on his head—the five-hundred-dollar reward John Windship described—was an opening shot in the campaign. Laffite didn't know how serious Governor Claiborne and the legislature were. The bounty he responded with for Claiborne's head was, in part, an attempt to gauge their seriousness. But at best the campaign would be troublesome and certainly bad for business.

Laffite asked the British for two weeks to think the matter over. They agreed, even while sweetening their offer by thirty thousand dollars, payable in cash to Laffite personally at a location of his choice. This wasn't a huge amount for one who drank the finest bootleg wine from the best stolen goblets. But hard currency was a problem even for pirates.

Laffite employed the two weeks to explore his options on the other side.

To Governor Claiborne he intimated a desire to serve Louisiana and the United States. "I offer to you to restore to this State several citizens"—several hundred, he meant, but he preferred not to enumerate—"who perhaps in your eyes have lost that sacred title. I offer them, however, such as you could wish to find them, ready to exert their utmost efforts in defense of the country. This point of Louisiana which I occupy is of great importance in the present crisis. I tender my services to defend it. And the only reward I ask is that a stop be put to the proscription against me and my adherents, by an act of oblivion for all that has been done hitherto." The governor would agree that amnesty was apt, if he could see into Laffite's heart. "I am the stray sheep wishing to return to the sheepfold. If you were thoroughly acquainted with the nature of my offenses I should appear to you much less guilty, and still worthy to discharge the duties of a good citizen." The applicant was simply an honest privateer trying to make a living. "I have never sailed under any flag but that of the republic of Carthagena, and my vessels are perfectly regular in that respect. If I could have brought my lawful prizes into the ports of this State I should not have employed the illicit means that have caused me to be proscribed."

Claiborne was inclined to accept Laffite's offer and grant the amnesty he asked. But the Louisiana legislature, which included some of those most interested in scuttling the Baratarians' business, refused. Moreover, the government in Washington, worried that Laffite was going to draw the United States into war with Spain, and anyway annoyed at Laffite's cavalier attitude toward federal import and revenue laws, had determined to disperse the ruffians. The American naval commander at New Orleans, Daniel Patterson, received orders to move against Barataria. With the Louisiana legislature urging Patterson on, Claiborne declined to hold him back.

By the time Laffite learned that the American navy was coming, his two weeks with the British had expired, which meant that they'd be descending on Barataria, too. He decided that discretion was the better part of survival, took what could be moved from Barataria, and sailed away west. Patterson seized the leftovers, arrested some stragglers, and declared victory. The British weren't sure whether they were better off without Laffite than they would have been with him. Claiborne, who had taken the precaution of forwarding to Andrew Jackson a copy of Laffite's offer to defend New Orleans, hoped the general had more sense than the American navy and the Louisiana legislature.

*J*ackson had been to the Mississippi at Natchez and to the Gulf at Pensacola, but before the autumn of 1814 he had never approached the place where the river meets the Gulf. This connection, of course, was New Orleans's raison d'être, and it was the key to British strategy in the closing stages of the war. The negotiators chattered in Ghent. They might even reach an agreement. But no treaty would be final till approved by the respective governments, and the British government wouldn't approve any treaty till it learned the outcome of its final offensive. The aim of the offensive was simple: to sever Louisiana—the whole territory, not merely the state—from the rest of the United States. Britain had never accepted the transfer of Louisiana from France to the United States (or from Spain to France, for that matter). It preferred and intended to keep the Americans bottled up east of the Mississippi. The United States had grown alarmingly since 1783. Better for Britain that it be cut down to size. And so, even as the British quietly applauded the secessionists of New England, they prepared to peel the western half of American territory away from the East.

The offensive would start at New Orleans. The city controlled the lower Mississippi, which provided ready access to the interior of the continent and thereby allowed a link to British forces in Canada. New Orleans, moreover, had psychological value that transcended geography. The United States was a novelty in world affairs, a country founded not on kinship or shared history or language but on an idea: that people could govern themselves. The English didn't reject the notion entirely. Their Parliament was premised on just such thinking. But British self-government was restricted to the responsible classes, unlike the American version, which was rapidly evolving from republicanism to democracy. And democracy was dangerous, whether practiced in North America, where pushy democrats would perennially grasp for more land, or imported to England, where the lower classes would get unsettling ideas. New Orleans was a test case for the American mode of political organization. Its polyglot population shared nothing of history or language or culture. If the American idea of self-government could work in New Orleans and the state of Louisiana, it could work anywhere. The thought was appalling.

Approaching New Orleans was easy enough during peacetime. That, of course, was why the city was located where it was, on the left bank a bit more than one hundred miles above the main channel's entrance to the Gulf. But if the approach was easy, it was almost always slow. The river made several turns below the city, and these typically required sailing ships to stop and wait for a change of wind or at least a change of tide. After a voyage of weeks or months, a few hours or even days meant little to a merchant vessel. But to a hostile warship, such a delay would probably be fatal, as the French and then the Spanish and now the Americans had identified the bottlenecks and located gun batteries accordingly. Reducing an enemy squadron to kindling would be little more than target practice.

Yet if a direct approach upstream was impossible, other approaches to the city were not simply feasible but inviting. Indeed, an enemy commander had a choice of routes. He could land troops on the shore of Lake Borgne, east of the city, and march in from there. He could penetrate Lake Pontchartrain, west of Borgne, and send a force south to the city. He could move north from Barataria Bay or from some point west. This required crossing the Mississippi, which entailed difficulty but commensurate chance of surprise. A fourth route to New Orleans was the longest. An enemy might land at Pensacola or Mobile Bay and skirt north of Lake Pontchartrain to Baton Rouge. Once captured, this lightly defended town would allow the enemy to close the Mississippi above New Orleans, isolating the city. A march downriver would complete the job.

This fourth route was the one Jackson had hoped to preclude by taking Pensacola and chasing the British off. He couldn't be sure they wouldn't return, but he had the other approaches to worry about as he headed toward New Orleans in late November. The prospect should have discouraged him. The British owned the sea, which gave them mobility he lacked. The army they were bringing—from the Chesapeake, with reinforcements from the Caribbean—substantially outnumbered his. They possessed the advantage of the offensive, being able to choose their approach to the city. And given the restiveness of the population of New Orleans and Louisiana, they had reason to expect support or at least acquiescence from the locals.

Jackson couldn't change the balance of power in the Gulf or the geography of the Mississippi delta. But he could hope to alter the mood of the people he was charged to defend. He reached New Orleans on December 1 and discovered that John Windship was right about the irredentist and seditionist tendencies of the French and Spanish inhabitants. (He didn't have a chance to meet Windship, who had just died of one of the endemic diseases to which he thought he had become inured.) A few of the foreign-born openly hoped for defeat, circulating stories that a British victory would restore Louisiana to Spanish control. Others disguised their desires in defeatism, contending that Jackson's pitiful force of militia and volunteers could never defeat Britain's battle-hardened troops. The negative feelings of those who hoped for the worst spread, provoking fear among those who wished for better.

Jackson confronted the issue, and the populace, with characteristic boldness. "The Major General commanding has with astonishment and regret learned that great consternation and alarm pervade your city," he proclaimed to the citizens. He didn't deny that there were grounds for concern. "It is true the enemy is on our coast and threatens an invasion of our territory." But proximity and threat were hardly the sum of the story. "It is equally true, with union, energy, and the approbation of heaven, we will beat him at every point his temerity may induce him to set foot upon our soil." Jackson said he had heard the rumors that a victorious Britain would restore Louisiana to Spain. "Believe not such incredible tales. Your government is at peace with Spain." Jackson couldn't say how long the United States would be at peace with Spain; news of his raid on Pensacola was still crossing the Atlantic. But for now the danger came from Britain—"the vital enemy of your country, the common enemy of mankind, the highway robber of the world." Jackson hoped good sense would prevail against the seditious rumors. But he was prepared to supplement sense where its effects fell shy. "The rules and articles of war annex the punishment of death to any person holding secret correspondence with the enemy, creating false alarm, or supplying him with provision. . . . The general announces his unalterable determination rigidly to execute the martial law in all cases. . . . He will separate our enemies from our friends. Those who are not with us are against us, and will be dealt with accordingly."

Jackson might have waited for exhortation to have its effect, but on the very day the papers of New Orleans published his proclamation, word arrived that British vessels had captured American gunboats on Lake Borgne. As the lake was less than a day's march from the outskirts of New Orleans, this severely compressed Jackson's schedule for sorting the sheep from the goats.

He responded, as decisively as ever, by seizing complete control over the city and all within it. "Major General Andrew Jackson, commanding the Seventh United States Military District, declares the city and environs of New Orleans under strict martial law," a new proclamation read. It specified what martial law meant. "Every individual entering the city will report at the Adjutant General's office, and on failure, to be arrested and held for examination. No person shall be permitted to leave the city without a permission in writing signed by the General or one of his staff. No vessel, boat, or other craft will be permitted to leave New Orleans or Bayou St. John without a passport in writing." A strict curfew took effect. "The street lamps shall be extinguished at the hour of nine at night, after which period persons of every description found in the streets, or not at their respective homes, without permission in writing as aforesaid and not having the countersign shall be apprehended as spies and held for examination."

Jackson complemented martial law by taking charge of the Louisiana militia. His experience with the Tennessee militia had taught him the difficulty of making soldiers out of ordinary young men. But the Louisiana militia presented a challenge of a different order. He reviewed the militia companies in the Place des Armes on December 18, and as he gazed out across the square he must have wondered how he was going to defend the city with such a motley bunch. The ranks included Americans and Frenchmen and Spanish, whites and blacks and persons of mixed race, poor and middling and rich. Some mustered willingly, others with great reluctance. Some hoped for success, others for failure. Most simply hoped to survive whatever Jackson had in store for them. All knew they'd be fighting British regulars, the best battlefield soldiers in the world.

The sight of his new troops hardly inspired Jackson's confidence—which simply meant that *he* had to inspire confidence in *them*. The Creek campaign had already shown Jackson to be a capable tactician; the defense of New Orleans would prove him a master, and a brilliant organizer as well. But what truly set him apart from other generals was his ability to motivate his men. Many of them loved him, starting with those who named him Old Hickory on the march home from Natchez. Nearly all of them feared him, including the would-be mutineers he threatened with cannon fire and everyone who heard the sad story of John Wood.

Jackson had already threatened the Louisianians; now he appealed to them. To the native-born Americans, he described the enemy in terms of the American Revolution. "They are the oppressors of your infant political existence with whom you have to contend," he said. "They are the men your fathers conquered whom you are to oppose." To the Frenchmen he cast the challenge differently. "They are the English, the hereditary, eternal enemies of your ancient country, the invaders of that you have adopted, who are your foes." To the Spanish: "Remember the conduct of your allies at St. Sebastian's, and recently at Pensacola, and rejoice that you have an opportunity of avenging the brutal injuries inflicted by men who dishonour the human race." He appealed to them collectively, as free citizens of a republic. "Remember for what and against whom you contend: for all that can render life desirable, for a country blessed with every gift of nature, for property, for life, for those dearer than either, your wives and children, and for liberty, dearer than all."

Jackson took special note of the black militia. The planters and other whites who initially resisted his call to arm free men of color had changed their collective mind, fearing the approach of the British, or perhaps the wrath of Jackson, more than they feared the idea of black troops. "*Soldiers!*" he addressed the black militia. "From the shores of the Mobile I called you to arms. I invited you to share in the perils and to divide the glory of your white countrymen. . . . I knew that you could endure hunger and thirst, and all the hardships of war. I knew that you loved the land of your nativity and that, like ourselves, you had to defend all that is most dear to man. But you surpassed my hopes. I have found in you, united to those qualities, that noble enthusiasm which impels to great deeds."

$\mathcal{J}$ackson's authority to declare martial law and seize control of the militia was debatable at best. But he hadn't possessed authority to invade Spanish Florida, and to the extent he worried about reprimand or other sanction from Washington, he could assume that his sin against civil liberties in New Orleans would probably appear less grave than his waging war on a country the administration wished to keep neutral. In any event, Jackson rarely respected authority per se. If the end was worthy—and he knew no end more worthy than the preservation of American liberty—most means were, too.

He let the lawyers argue while he prepared the defenses of the city. "The lakes in complete possession of the enemy will give me a large coast to watch and defend, and the difficulty of finding out their point of attack is perplexing," he wrote on December 16. "But I trust with the smiles of heaven to be able to meet and defeat him at every point he may put his foot on land."

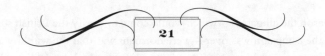

21

DAY OF DELIVERANCE

The British victory over the American gunboats on Lake Borgne placed the initiative in the invaders' hands, and they moved quickly to exploit their opportunity. It wasn't easy. British ships deposited thousands of troops on an island at the entrance to the lake, where they prepared to shift to shallow-draft boats for transport toward the city. Conditions at the rendezvous point were disheartening. "It is scarcely possible to imagine any place more completely wretched," recalled George Gleig, the redcoat who had admired the sublimity of Washington's burning. "It was a swamp, containing a small space of firm ground at one end, and almost wholly unadorned with trees of any sort or description. . . . The interior was the resort of wild ducks and other water-fowl; and the pools and creeks with which it was intercepted abounded in dormant alligators."

The reason the alligators—which would come to terrify the British soldiers before the campaign was over—were dormant was that the winter weather was as nasty as Louisiana gets. A driving rain drenched the soldiers all day. As night fell the rain stopped and a heavy frost set in. The Britons in the battle force, used to the cold and wet, suffered but survived. The West Indians who had lately been added to the army fared worse. "Many of the wretched negroes, to whom frost and cold were altogether new, fell fast asleep and perished before morning," Gleig wrote.

Crossing the lake required good luck, lest stormy weather swamp the boats; audacity, since the first arrivals on the opposite shore would be unable to defend themselves against American attack; and extraordinary effort, in the form of sixty miles of hard rowing. "Yet in spite of all this," Gleig remembered, "not a murmur nor a whisper of complaint could be heard throughout the whole expedition. . . . From the General down to the youngest drum-boy, a confident anticipation of success seemed to pervade all ranks." There was reason for the confidence, beyond the victories the troops had won in Europe and then at Washington. Defectors from the American side in New Orleans brought word of fear and disarray among the populace. Jackson commanded fewer than five thousand troops, they said, which made his force less than half that of the British. The defectors went on to describe the wealth of the city and the booty that awaited its capture—"subjects well calculated to tickle the fancy of invaders," Gleig said, "and to make them unmindful of immediate afflictions, in the expectation of so great a recompense to come."

Gleig's regiment and two others—totaling sixteen hundred men, with two small cannons—landed on the southern shore of Lake Borgne after a very long day at the oars. The landing place was a reed-covered marsh where humans rarely ventured. With disaffected locals acting as guides, the invaders followed a canal south toward the Mississippi. The going was slow. The path by the canal was slippery, and numerous intersecting waterways had to be bridged. For the first few hours the country appeared as wild as the marsh where they landed, but eventually they reached the edge of the plantation country, where the stubble of harvested sugar cane replaced the tall river cane that covered much of the rest of the region. They passed orange groves and then some farmhouses. Moving as quickly as they could, they captured the inhabitants of the houses to prevent their giving the alarm that the enemy had landed. "But becoming rather careless in watching their prisoners," Gleig recorded of the British troops guarding the captives, "one man contrived to effect his escape."

*T*his man was Gabriel Villeré, the son of Jacques Villeré, who had commanded the Louisiana militia before Jackson took over and who owned the plantation on which the British invaders now stood. The younger Villeré had been given responsibility for monitoring the approaches from Lake Borgne. His personal embarrassment at having been caught unawares now intensified his patriotism and spurred him to New Orleans to spread the alarm. He reached Jackson's headquarters in the early afternoon of December 23.

Unwelcome though it was, Villeré's report partly solved Jackson's most pressing problem: learning where the enemy was. He expected to be outnumbered by the British, but as the defender he could stand a modest deficit in the balance of troop strength. What he *couldn't* stand was being outflanked. Once that happened he'd lose the advantage of defense and probably lose the city. And the only way he could avoid being outflanked was to discover—or guess—where the enemy was.

With the report from Villeré's plantation, he knew where at least part of the enemy was. But he couldn't tell whether these troops were the spearhead of a larger landing force or a diversion designed to draw him away from the real invasion. And he wouldn't know for days—until it was too late to correct a wrong guess.

He didn't propose to wait. He would strike the invaders that very day—or night, by the time he got there. If they were the tip of the spear, he would blunt it and perhaps turn aside or at least slow the larger force to follow. If they were a diversion, a lightning strike would allow him to return to the city in time to meet the main blow.

"Perfectly convinced of the importance of impressing an invading enemy in the first moment of his approach with an idea of spirited resistance, I lost no time in making preparations to attack him that night," Jackson explained to James Monroe afterward. "I was not ignorant of the inferiority of my force, nor of the hazard of night attacks with inexperienced troops. But the fears to be entertained from these sources were overbalanced by the greater evils to be apprehended from delay. . . . If the attack were postponed till the next day, the fate of New Orleans must depend on the result of a general engagement in which the chances of success would be greatly against us, while by bringing it on at night, the enemy not being able to ascertain our numbers would of course magnify them, and be thrown into perplexity at any rate, if not into consternation." A night attack would also favor Jackson's side in case retreat was necessary. He and his men knew the ground. The British didn't.

Jackson cobbled together a force of some fifteen hundred troops drawn from his three army regiments, the Tennessee militia, and the New Orleans militia, and including two hundred black volunteers from Haiti (who feared anything that enhanced European power in the Caribbean and thereby threatened their country's hard-won independence). His own troops were eager for the chance to fight the British. "It may not be altogether a Christian spirit, but I really would like to see some redcoats in front of us, just once if no more," John Coffee had written his wife as the Creek campaign wound down. "Like all the rest of the boys, I am tired of thrashing redskins. . . . My men are so used to killing Indians that they are almost sorry for them. But they have no pity for the redcoats, who, they declare, are to be held responsible for all the devilment the Indians have done. Every one of my boys wants to get within fair buckrange of a redcoat."

From the bustle at headquarters and the mustering of the troops, the inhabitants of New Orleans soon discovered that the British had landed and were within six miles of the city. Alarm approaching panic convulsed many households, where lurid stories of a redcoat penchant for ravishing helpless women had been whispered for weeks and now were spoken in voices cracking from fear. Fathers readied their wives and daughters for flight upstream, while they buried the family cash and jewels in their gardens and oiled their rifles. Jackson, at the head of the column marching toward Villeré's plantation, told Edward Livingston, a local who became his aide-de-camp, to try to calm the people. "Say to them not to be alarmed," Jackson ordered. "The enemy shall never reach the city."

Jackson's implacable will could be terrifying—to enemies, to mutineers—but at times like this it was tremendously reassuring. When Jackson said the British would never reach the city, it was hard not to believe him.

His vow alone didn't dissipate the fear, but it did prevent a full-blown panic. New Orleans would give the general a chance to prove his mettle.

The march from the city took two hours, bringing Jackson within sight of the British just before dark. They weren't surprised to see him, but they didn't expect action before the next day. And they assumed they would be the ones initiating it. "As the Americans had never yet dared to attack," Gleig wrote, "there was no great probability of their doing so on the present occasion."

The British were hungry and cold and so kindled fires for cooking and warmth. Some of them observed the approach of a sailing vessel, which dropped anchor and furled its sails opposite the British camp. In the dark it was hard to identify the craft. Several supposed it was a British ship that had managed to elude the American forts downstream and would assist in the attack on New Orleans. Some of Gleig's comrades hailed the ship, but they received no answer—till an American voice called out, in words that carried distinctly across the water, "Give them this for the honour of America!" The roar of cannons followed instantly, and antipersonnel grapeshot screamed through the night air, raking the groups gathered around the campfires. Scattering for their lives, the British returned the American cannon fire with muskets, which had no effect, and rockets, which "made a beautiful appearance in the air," Gleig recalled, but which missed their target.

Jackson followed the artillery barrage with assaults at several points of the British lines. In the dark the British had no idea how many the Americans were or even where they were coming from. "Now began a battle of which no language were competent to convey any distinct idea," Gleig wrote, "because it was one to which the annals of modern warfare furnish no parallel. All order, all discipline were lost. Each officer, as he succeeded in collecting twenty or thirty men about him, plunged into the midst of the enemy's ranks, where it was fought hand to hand, bayonet to bayonet, and sabre to sabre."

The fighting lasted most of the night, and such was the confusion that both sides thought they had won. "The victory was ours," Gleig asserted. "True, it was the reverse of a bloodless one, not fewer than two hundred and fifty of our best men having fallen in the struggle. But even at the expense of such a loss, we could not but account ourselves fortunate in escaping from the snare in which we had confessedly been taken."

Jackson interpreted things differently. The enemy had been beaten back, the threat to New Orleans blunted. "The result equaled my expectations," he wrote. "From every point on which we assailed him, he was repulsed." Jackson thought he could have captured the entire British force if a heavy fog hadn't set in, impeding operations even more than the dark alone had. "The main object, however, had been effected. The enemy, taken at surprise and thrown into confusion, was unable to penetrate our designs and feared to prosecute his own."

In war, ties go to the defender. Jackson had the better of this argument, since the British failed in their effort to take New Orleans by surprise. And the strong showing of the Americans in the night battle of December 23–24 did wonders for the morale of the city. Jackson had said the British wouldn't enter the city, and they hadn't. Maybe he could keep them out after all.

$\mathcal{D}$uring the very hours when Jackson was repelling Britian's initial thrust toward New Orleans, the American diplomats at Ghent concluded a peace treaty with their British counterparts. Adams, Clay, and the others were still expecting a slow winter when, in early December, they started to detect a softening in the British position. The Americans gradually inferred that the simultaneous Congress of Vienna wasn't going the way the British had hoped. As it had for generations, Europe mattered more to Britain than America did, and the British government felt increasing pressure to terminate the hostilities across the Atlantic. Wellington himself weighed in with a damp blanket. "I feel no objection to going to America," the Iron Duke declared, "though I don't promise to myself much success there." Meanwhile he sent an encouraging note to American peacemaker Gallatin: "In you I have the greatest confidence. I hear on all sides that your moderation and sense of justice, places you above all the other delegates, not excepting ours."

Gallatin was grateful for the encouragement but even more appreciative of the abandonment by the British negotiators of the most onerous of their early demands. They accepted the prewar status quo as the territorial basis for peace, they dropped the idea of an Indian state, and they fell silent on navigation of the Mississippi.

Gallatin persuaded his colleagues to reciprocate. Adams and Clay continued to quarrel, but neither they nor the others could disguise their relief at the prospect of escaping the war with nothing lost save Washington's public buildings, some private property, and considerable American pride. They exceeded instructions by no longer insisting on a British renunciation of impressment, but they rationalized that the end of the European war had made the issue moot. They relinquished their indemnity claims, which had been a daydream all along. And they forgot about forswearing alliances with Indians, on the assumption that the peace would last and neither side would have occasion to employ Indians against the other.

The reciprocal concessions led to a treaty. On December 24 the delegates exchanged signatures and handshakes. "The terms of this instrument are undoubtedly not such as our country expected at the commencement of the war," Clay wrote Monroe, in one of the rare understatements of Clay's political life. "Judged of, however, by the actual condition of things, so far as it is known to us, they cannot be pronounced very unfavorable. We lose no territory, I think no honor." Adams received the copies of the treaty from his British counterpart. "I told him I hoped it would be the last treaty of peace between Great Britain and the United States," Adams recorded. That night he thanked God for the peace and offered "a fervent prayer that its result may be propitious to the welfare, the best interests, and the union of my country."

Like the others, including the British, young James Gallatin was simply glad the war was over. "The British delegates very civilly asked us to dinner," he wrote on Christmas Day. "The roast beef and plum pudding was from England, and everybody drank everybody else's health. The band played first 'God Save the King,' to the toast of the King, and 'Yankee Doodle,' to the toast of the President. Congratulations on all sides and a general atmosphere of serenity; it was a scene to be remembered." Gallatin added, after the excitement of the signing and dining wore off, "Although I am only seventeen years of age, I feel much older."

𝒩ew Orleans celebrated Christmas in more subdued fashion. Though the city sighed with relief at Jackson's repulse of the first British landing, everyone knew the real battle was yet to come. Many prepared for the worst, notwithstanding Jackson's strong showing at the Villeré plantation. The British army was now known to be much larger than Jackson's force, and in a full-scale battle this generation of redcoats had never been beaten. A rumor began circulating that Jackson had a plan for retreat in the event the British proved too strong and that on leaving the city he would set it afire. The inhabitants whose attachment to the city was deeper than their attachment to the United States wondered whether Jackson might be more dangerous to their interests than the British were. The speaker of the Louisiana senate made so bold as to ask Jackson's adjutant, Robert Butler, whether Jackson did indeed intend to burn the city if it couldn't be held. When Butler inquired why he asked, the speaker said frankly that the legislature wanted to know whether to consider surrendering the city to the British. It was fortunate for the speaker and the leaders of the legislature that Jackson at this time couldn't spare a minute from his preparations against the next British attack, or he might have had the lawmakers arrested for treason. As it was he ordered Governor Claiborne to keep an eye on them and seize the first ones who made a move toward surrender.

Yet he acceded to the lawmakers' concerns on another count. As the British drew near, the New Orleans committee of safety reconsidered the earlier decision to shun Jean Laffite and the pirates of Barataria. No one in the city had more experience at arms than these soldiers of fortune. At the moment of crisis, prudence required overlooking past indiscretions.

Jackson had to be convinced. He doubted the Baratarians' loyalty, which had never been to anything beyond their own self-interest. And he doubted even more their willingness to take orders. For Jackson, discipline remained the sine qua non of successful military operations. What pirate ever submitted to discipline?

The committee of safety pressed the issue. They visited Jackson's headquarters and personally made the case for employing the pirates. Jackson had two ships in the river—the *Louisiana* and the *Caroline*—but these were undermanned and especially lacked trained gunners. Laffite's men were the best gunners in the Caribbean. Surely Jackson could put them to use against the British.

Jackson took the committee's point but still resisted. The Baratarians, he said, were under federal indictment. Some were already in custody. In what must have seemed a patent rationalization—coming from the one who had imposed martial law on the city—Jackson said he didn't like to interfere in criminal prosecutions.

The committee thereupon sought out the local federal judge, Dominick Hall. They explained their case and Jackson's last objection. Judge Hall devised a scheme for suspending prosecution for four months and releasing the pirates already in custody.

Jackson acceded, by now perhaps thankful for the excuse. The Baratarians manned the ships and applied their expertise to the terrestrial batteries as well.

Jean Laffite, too, was thankful, in a different way. "This was the turning point of my career and the best moment of my life," he remembered, "when I decided once and for all to drive the English beasts from American soil."

(Laffite had a rather fanciful recollection of the events leading to Jackson's decision to accept the services of him and his men. "I could not waste any more time waiting for a chance that would put me face to face with General Jackson," he wrote many years later. "With a few officers of my staff, I came across the General at the northeast corner of Saint Philippe and Royal Streets. I explained to him that my conduct had been marked with a loyalty and a patriotism unequaled during the thirty-eight years that had passed since the declaration of American independence. I challenged the General to a duel, in reply to the unfounded and punishable insults directed upon us. In spite of the respect I had for his uniform, I must say that the general's intelligence seemed much inferior to mine. He refused to accept my challenge. I threatened to slap his face, but my eldest brother, Dominique Youx, intervened as a conciliator. Later the General received us in his office at 106 Royal Street." At this point in Laffite's story, Jackson saw the light and brought him aboard.)

*B*y the last week of December the nature of the battle for New Orleans was coming clearly into view, even if the armies that would wage the battle were not. The clash at Villeré's plantation ended with the British and American forces still in the field, still facing each other. Both sides pulled back a bit yet remained on the level, open plain that ran from Villeré's to the city.

Although the plain provided few places to hide, its very levelness inhibited observation. "Of the American army nothing whatever could be perceived, except a corps of observation, composed of five or six hundred mounted riflemen, which hovered along our front and watched our motions," George Gleig wrote. "The town itself was completely hid; nor was it possible to see beyond the distance of a very few miles either in front or rear, so flat and unbroken was the face of the country." Yet the British had other methods of gaining intelligence, namely spies and deserters, who apprised them of nearly everything that happened behind the American lines. "Nothing was kept a secret from us, except your numbers," a British officer captured in the battle told his captors.

Under the gaze of Jackson's riflemen, the British brought up the rest of the invasion force and built batteries for their field guns. "By the 25th, the whole of the troops were got on shore," recalled Charles Forrest, a major of British infantry. "From the 28th to the 31st December all exertions were made to get up from the ships ten eighteen-pounders and four twenty-four pound carronades, with the necessary ammunition and stores." British boats carried the guns as far along the canals from Lake Borgne as they could. From there they were "dragged by seamen with incredible labour," Forrest explained.

Arriving with the troops and guns was the man who would lead the British attack. Sir Edward Pakenham was a brother-in-law of Wellington and had served with the famous duke in Spain. Pakenham's division broke the center of the French line at Salamanca, causing Wellington to comment, "Pakenham might not be the brightest genius, but my partiality for him does not lead me astray when I tell you he is one of the best we have." Even with this endorsement Pakenham wouldn't have received the command at New Orleans if not for the death of General Ross at Baltimore. But the metaphorical winds of wars blew him to the van of the southern operation, and his arrival on Christmas Day—after his journey had been slowed by the actual winds of the Caribbean—raised the already buoyant hopes of his troops, who greeted him with a rousing artillery salute. Pakenham himself had every reason for confidence. His men had beaten Napoleon's finest, and they could certainly beat the gaggle of Indian fighters, frontiersmen, Frenchmen, Spaniards, blacks, pirates, and other outlaws that faced them. He carried in his kit bag a commission as governor of Louisiana, to be made public upon the victory. An earldom in England was hardly out of the question for one who would bring a third of North America under British rule.

*J*ackson's preparations mirrored those of the British during this period. He constructed earthworks for his cannon and dug ditches and threw up parapets across the mile-wide plain that stretched from the Mississippi on his right to the woods and swamp on his left. The cannons would fire grape and canister shot at the British troops once the battle began in earnest, but till then the gunners contented themselves lobbing occasional rounds behind the British lines. The potshots were distracting but no more than that. "The distance rendered her fire uncertain and harmless," British Major Forrest said of the American effort.

By the first day of the new year the guns on both sides were in position. Pakenham decided to raise the stakes. Arsène Latour, a French-born engineer in Jackson's army, described the commencement of the artillery duel: "The enemy opened a very brisk fire from his three batteries, of which the left, established on the road, mounted two twelve-pounders; the center, eight eighteen-pounders and twenty-four-pound carronades; and that on the right towards the wood opposite our lines mounted eight pieces of cannon and carronades. A cloud of Congreve rockets accompanied the balls, and for fifteen minutes the fire was kept up with unexampled celerity." The initial target of the British bombardment was the house where Jackson had his headquarters. The British gunners knew their business, as Latour recounted. "In less than ten minutes, upwards of one hundred balls, rockets, and shells struck the house and rendered it impossible to remain there. The general-in-chief and all his staff were in the apartments when the firing began, but though bricks, splinters of wood and furniture, rockets and balls were flying in all directions, not a single person was wounded."

Pakenham might or might not have appreciated how close he came to decapitating the American command, but he soon knew he had got Jackson's attention. Jackson ordered his own gunners to return fire, and a thunderous artillery battle commenced. The British objective was to blow holes in the American breastworks so that British foot soldiers might exploit their advantage in numbers and overwhelm Jackson's defenses. The American objective was to silence the British guns and keep the breastworks intact. The British had reason to think they'd prevail. "Every advantage was on the side of the enemy," Latour explained. "His batteries presented but a narrow front, and very little elevation, on a spacious plain, the soil of which was from four to six feet below the level of our platforms. His gunners had for a target a line about one thousand yards long, the top of whose parapet was eight or nine feet higher than his platforms; whilst our batteries might be said to have only points to aim at, and our balls could not rebound on so soft a soil."

Pakenham's gunners, moreover, were battlefield-tested artillerists, while Jackson's were an unlikely combination of Baratarian pirates and U.S. naval officers. The British were the better marksmen. "The cheeks of the embrasures of our batteries were formed of bales of cotton," Latour wrote, "which the enemy's balls struck and made fly in all directions. The rockets blew up two artillery caissons, in one of which were a hundred rounds." The spectacular explosion delighted even the hardened veterans among the British, who stopped shooting long enough to give three cheers for His Majesty's firepower. But the Americans refused to be dismayed. The British celebration was answered, Latour said, "by a general discharge of all the artillery of our lines."

Despite their advantages, the British failed to dislodge the Americans, and after absorbing hundreds of rounds of incoming fire, Jackson's men noted a lessening in the intensity of the British barrage. Pakenham was changing tactics. "At about ten o'clock the enemy ordered some platoons of sharp-shooters to penetrate into the woods on the left of our line, with a view to ascertain whether it could be turned," Latour recalled. Several volleys from American muskets suggested it couldn't and drove the British riflemen deeper into the woods. On this ground the Americans had the advantage. "Wellington's heroes discovered that they were ill qualified to contend with us in woods, where they must fight knee deep in water and mud, and that the various kinds of laurel which abound in Louisiana, in the cypress swamps and prairies, were not intended to grace their brows."

By noon the British attack was measurably weakening, and by three o'clock their guns had fallen silent. The British infantry retreated to their camps to await another opportunity. Jackson proudly summarized the engagement to Monroe: "Yesterday the enemy opened upon us a tremendous cannonade from several batteries which they had erected in the nights preceding. It was sustained by every corps under my command with a firmness which would have done honor to veterans. Too much praise cannot be bestowed on those who managed my artillery. . . . Our loss was inconsiderable, and certainly much inferior to that which the enemy must have sustained." Jackson added, "The enemy still occupy their former position; and whether they will renew their attempt today or ever, I am not able to judge."

*B*ut he could guess. Pakenham knew more about Jackson's plans than Jackson knew about Pakenham's, for the simple reason that refugees were sneaking *out* of New Orleans rather than in. But common sense indicated that once Pakenham had all his troops and guns in place, he would have little reason to delay and much reason not to, starting with the fact that Jackson could hope for reinforcements from upstream if the battle were postponed.

Jackson tried to keep the British off balance. "For two whole nights and days not a man had closed an eye, except such as were cool enough to sleep amidst showers of cannon-ball," George Gleig wrote after the New Year's artillery duel, adding that conditions behind the British lines didn't improve during the next few days. The Americans continued to lob cannonballs and mortar shells onto the British positions, not only from the American front but from batteries across the river. Beyond this harassing bombardment, a practice peculiar to the Americans imposed a constant and unexpected burden on the British. Gleig had learned the military profession in Europe, where civilized nations practiced war as an art. Except when actually engaged in battle, he explained, opposing sides treated each other with respect. "Thus, whilst two European armies remain inactively facing each other, the outposts of neither are molested. . . . Nay, so far is this tacit good understanding carried, that I have myself seen French and English sentinels not more than twenty yards apart." Military life was different west of the Atlantic. "The Americans entertained no such chivalric notions. An enemy was to them an enemy, whether alone or in the midst of five thousand companions, and they therefore counted the death of every individual as so much taken from the strength of the whole. In point of fact they no doubt reasoned correctly, but to us at least it appeared an ungenerous return to barbarity." It also represented a ceaseless strain on British bodies and minds. "Whenever they could approach unperceived within proper distance of our watchfires, six or eight riflemen would fire amongst the party that sat round them, while one or two, stealing as close to each sentinel as a regard to their own safety would permit, acted the part of assassins rather than that of soldiers, and attempted to murder him in cold blood. For the officers likewise, when going their rounds, they constantly lay in wait, and thus, by a continued dropping fire, they not only wounded some of those against whom their aim was directed, but occasioned considerable anxiety and uneasiness throughout the line."

Pakenham noticed the strain on his men and recognized that he must move forward soon. To stay in place risked the unraveling of his army. He conceived a plan to send a body of troops to the far side of the river, where the American defenses were far thinner. These troops would capture the American guns there and turn them on the American batteries on the near side, giving the signal for another frontal assault by artillery and infantry, which this time must succeed.

But crossing the river required transporting boats from Lake Borgne to the Mississippi. Luckily for Pakenham, he wasn't the first to have had such an idea. The planters who owned the farms along the river had dug—that is, had their slaves dig—canals in various places across their properties. To extend one such waterway so that it connected the lake to the river was not a complicated task. Backbreaking, yes; but a soldier's back in time of war—like a slave's at all times—was made to be broken. Pakenham set his engineers and their troops to work. "Being divided into four companies, they laboured by turns, day and night, one party relieving another after a stated number of hours, in such order as that the work should never be entirely deserted," Gleig explained. "The fatigue undergone during the prosecution of this attempt no words can sufficiently describe. Yet it was pursued without repining, and at length, by unremitting exertions, they succeeded in effecting their purpose by the 6th of January."

At once the boats were readied, and the troops—a mix of infantry and marines, totaling some fourteen hundred—were chosen for the crossing. But ill luck plagued the endeavor. The same softness of soil that permitted the rapid excavation now inhibited the movement of the boats, as the just-moved dirt slumped back into the ditches whence it had come. The larger boats bottomed on the mud, blocking passage of the other vessels. Only enough boats to carry a quarter of the crossing force reached the riverbank, and these were hours behind schedule. They were supposed to cross during the night of January 7, that they might storm the American batteries on the far bank before dawn the next day. But midnight came and went, and the boats were nowhere near their goal.

*J*ackson discovered the British strategy about the time the canal diggers broke through to the Mississippi. A half mile separated the American and British lines, and though Jackson and his scouts had observed general activity on the British side, they couldn't tell what that activity signified until some British prisoners revealed just enough to allow Jackson to piece the puzzle together. He acknowledged being impressed at the undertaking and the "infinite labor" it entailed. He considered trying to interdict the digging but concluded that an offensive operation against it was too risky.

This left him to decide how to reinforce the right bank against the British sortie. The prisoners didn't know, or wouldn't say, how strong the thrust across the river would be. Jackson had to parry the thrust, but to send more troops over than were absolutely necessary would weaken his main defenses on the left bank. He assigned the right bank to a combination of militia from Louisiana and Kentucky and hoped for the best.

The prisoners similarly did not reveal *when* the British attack would occur. Jackson certainly would have liked to know, to make the final preparations for defense. For two weeks his men and the supporting slaves had worked feverishly, and they continued to labor around the clock. Jackson examined the results of their efforts several times daily. The ditches they had dug would slow an infantry advance. The wall—or berm, really—that they had built with the dirt from the ditches and with anything else that looked solid, including more cotton bales, afforded protection for his riflemen and musketeers. Jackson could think of little he'd left undone. When the British attacked, most of the redcoats would have to march straight up the plain toward the American entrenchments. At that point the question would come down to the nerve of the men. With enemy cannon fire raining down upon them, would they hold their ground against the famously relentless approach of the British infantry?

ℐn the afternoon of the 7th it became evident that the enemy's design was to attack," Arsène Latour wrote. "Though at so great a distance we could not distinctly see what was passing in the enemy's camp, we perceived that a great number of soldiers and sailors were at work, endeavouring to move something very unwieldy, which we concluded to be artillery. With the assistance of a telescope in the upper apartment of headquarters, we perceived the soldiers on Laronde's plantations busy in making fascines, while others were working on pieces of wood, which we concluded must be scaling ladders. The picket guards near the wood had moreover been increased and stationed nearer each other." The British activity intensified as the daylight diminished. "Shortly after night-fall we distinctly heard men at work in the enemy's different batteries. The strokes of hammers gave 'note of preparation' and resounded even within our lines; and our outposts informed us that the enemy was re-establishing his batteries."

The Americans got little rest that night. Jackson ordered the ramparts manned continuously. Troops slept on their arms, if at all. They knew that they were outnumbered and that the enemy had beaten the greatest general of Europe. They didn't know how their own general compared with Napoleon or how they would perform under the hottest fire they could ever expect to see. Live or die, it would be the battle of a generation.

𝒲hat Wellington liked most about his brother-in-law was his boldness. Pakenham might be no genius, but he understood that fortune favored the bold and believed that courage could fill in where genius failed.

As the British troops formed up in the predawn dark of January 8, every soldier listened intently for firing on the far side of the river. The sound would indicate that the regiment that had gone over was attacking the American guns there and that the main assault, by these waiting, listening troops, could begin. But the fog that had enveloped the plain and the river in the dark started to whiten with the dawn, and still no sound was heard from across the water, leaving the troops to wonder whether the attack would commence after all.

A second problem surfaced when Pakenham discovered that many of his troops lacked the ladders they'd need to cross the ditches and scale the American walls. Such mundane tools could be fully as vital as the muskets and bayonets the soldiers carried. The men might drown in the ditches or be pinned at the base of the walls.

Pakenham had been through enough battles to understand that things never happened as planned. The troops sent over the river were late; they would simply have to fight harder and make up for lost time. The infantry didn't have enough ladders; they'd have to cross the ditches and scale the walls on one another's backs. This was the hour. The assault must go forward.

The dawn of day discovered to us the enemy occupying two-thirds of the space between the wood and the Mississippi," Arsène Latour remembered. It was a daunting sight: thousands of redcoats filling the plain, sixty or seventy men deep in a broad front, moving inexorably toward the American lines. Most of those on the American side had never seen a regular army in battle formation, certainly not one as large and impressive as this.

If Jackson was daunted he didn't let on. As soon as it was light enough for his gunners to see their targets, he gave the order to fire. Battery Six got off the first salvo, followed by Batteries Seven and Eight. Before long all three batteries were firing without pause, ignoring the return fire from the British guns, shaking the soft earth of the riverside plain, and mixing plumes of powder smoke with the rising fog.

The destructive effect of the American fire on the British soldiers in the open field was appalling. The American gunners aimed low, and each round cut a bloody, gaping hole in the redcoat ranks. No army, it seemed, could endure such carnage. But the British did, to the amazement of the Americans.

"Every discharge opened the column and mowed down whole files," Latour recalled, "which were almost instantly replaced by new troops coming up close after the first."

The British left made the swiftest progress. One especially intrepid company reached a redoubt where they engaged the Americans in hand-to-hand, bayonet-to-gunstock fighting. After a few furious minutes they drove the Americans away. Their success encouraged their comrades, who hoped it presaged a larger break in the American line.

Jackson feared what the British hoped, and he immediately determined that the redoubt must be retaken at whatever cost. Summoning fresh troops, he threw them against the redoubt. For a long moment the whole battle centered on this single hillock of mud. The earlier roles were reversed: the British now defended and the Americans attacked. The numbers, too, were switched; the Americans outnumbered the British at this critical spot on the field. And it was the American numbers that finally told. The British were forced to yield the position they had won so courageously. "Being opposed by overwhelming numbers," George Gleig wrote of his comrades, "they were repulsed; and the Americans, in turn, forcing their way into the battery, at length succeeded in recapturing it with immense slaughter."

Elsewhere on the field the lack of ladders among the British became a matter of life and mostly death. Members of two British regiments braved the American fire and reached the base of the American wall. "To scale the parapet without ladders was a work of no slight difficulty," Gleig observed. "Some few, indeed, by mounting one upon another's shoulders, succeeded in entering the works, but these were speedily overpowered, most of them killed, and the rest taken; whilst as many as stood without were exposed to a sweeping fire which cut them down by whole companies. It was in vain that the most obstinate courage was displayed. They fell by the hands of men whom they absolutely did not see, for the Americans, without so much as lifting their faces above the rampart, swung their firelocks by one arm over the wall, and discharged them directly upon their heads." At this point, the failure of the British force across the river to capture the guns there became dismayingly evident. "The whole of the guns, likewise, from the opposite bank, kept up a well-directed and deadly cannonade upon their flank; and thus were they destroyed without an opportunity being given of displaying their valour or obtaining so much as revenge."

Unable to move forward, the British ranks held for a few more minutes under the murderous fire of the Americans, but finally they broke. Some of the men sought refuge in a ditch. Others simply ran for their lives. British officers rode to the ditch and ordered the troops there to re-form. They did so, reluctantly. "And now, for the second time, the column, recruited with the troops that formed the rear, advanced," Arsène Latour wrote. "Again it was received with the same rolling fire of musketry and artillery, till, having advanced without much order very near our lines, it at last broke again, and retired in the utmost confusion. In vain did the officers now endeavour, as before, to revive the courage of their men; to no purpose did they strike them with the flat of their swords, to force them to advance. They were insensible to every thing but danger, and saw nothing but death, which had struck so many of their comrades."

Not even Pakenham, audacious as ever, could stem the retreat. "Sir Edward saw how things were going," George Gleig wrote, "and did all that a general could do to rally his troops. Riding toward the 44th, which had returned to the ground but in great disorder, he called out for Colonel Mullens to advance. But that officer had disappeared and was not to be found. He therefore prepared to lead them on himself, and had put himself at their head for that purpose, when he received a slight wound in the knee from a musket-ball, which killed his horse. Mounting another, he again headed the 44th, when a second ball took effect more fatally, and he dropped lifeless into the arms of his aide-de-camp."

Pakenham's charge to the front had inspired his men, and now his death disheartened them—and cheered the Americans, who could see him fall. The Americans were additionally encouraged—and the British further disheartened—when two other British generals, Samuel Gibbs and John Keane, went down. "A great number of officers of rank had fallen," Arsène Latour remembered. "The ground over which the column had marched was strewed with the dead and the wounded. Such slaughter on their side, with no loss on ours, spread consternation through their ranks, as they were now convinced of the impossibility of carrying our lines, and saw that even to advance was certain death. In a word, notwithstanding the repeated efforts of some officers to make their troops form a third time, they would not advance, and all that could be obtained from them was to draw them up in the ditch, where they passed the rest of the day."

In George Gleig's view, the critical event was the fall of Gibbs and Keane. "Riding through the ranks," Gleig said of the two generals' final effort to regather the troops, "they strove by all means to encourage the assailants and recall the fugitives, till at length both were wounded and borne off the field. All was now confusion and dismay. Without leaders, ignorant of what was to be done, the troops first halted and then began to retire, till finally the retreat was changed into a flight, and they quitted the ground in utmost disorder." Yet the British spirit wasn't entirely broken. "The retreat was covered in gallant style by the reserve. Making a forward motion, the 7th and 43rd presented the appearance of a renewed attack, by which the enemy were so much awed that they did not venture beyond their lines in pursuit of the fugitives."

*J*ackson was hardly awed by the British, and certainly not at this point in the battle, which had gone better than he had had any reason to hope. His untested troops had stood the shock of the vaunted British charge and repelled it gloriously. In the moment of victory he was tempted to pursue the retreating British and try to annihilate the whole army. But he quickly thought better of it. To pursue the redcoats onto the open plain, with untested troops that knew nothing of maneuver, would be reckless in the extreme. Better to remain behind the defenses that had served the Americans so well.

Just *how* well those defenses served the Americans—and how cruelly the British—became apparent in the aftermath. The serious fighting ended by eight in the morning. A short while later Jackson and the ranking active British officer, John Lambert, agreed to a ceasefire to allow each side to collect its wounded and bury its dead. George Gleig wasn't part of the British hospital detail, but he wanted to assess the damage his comrades had suffered. "Prompted by curiosity, I mounted my horse and rode to the front," he explained. What he observed burned an image in his brain. "Of all the sights I ever witnessed, that which met me there was beyond comparison the most shocking and the most humiliating. Within the narrow compass of a few hundred yards were gathered together nearly a thousand bodies, all of them arrayed in British uniforms. Not a single American was among them;

all were English, and they were thrown by dozens into shallow holes, scarcely deep enough to furnish them with a slight covering of earth. An American officer stood by smoking a cigar, and apparently counting the slain with a look of savage exultation, and repeating over and over to each individual that approached him, that their loss amounted only to eight men killed and fourteen men wounded."

Arsène Latour visited the same killing fields. He may have passed Gleig, though neither had any reason to remark the meeting. "The whole plain on the left, as also the side of the river, from the road to the edge of the water, was covered with the British soldiers who had fallen," Latour wrote. "What might perhaps appear incredible, were there not many thousands ready to attest the fact, is that a space of ground extending from the ditch of our lines to that on which the enemy drew up his troops, two hundred and fifty yards in length, by about two hundred in breadth, was literally covered with men, either dead or severely wounded." Latour couldn't count the bodies, but the British losses were obviously immense. "It cannot have amounted to less than three thousand men in killed, wounded, and prisoners. . . . Our loss was comparatively inconsiderable, amounting to no more than thirteen in killed and wounded."

22

THE SECOND WASHINGTON

*T*he winter of 1814–15 had been the darkest for America since the

grim season of Valley Forge. As during that earlier crisis, the very

existence of the republic was in danger. Federalists in Hartford plotted

against the administration and perhaps against the Union, while a powerful

British land and sea force prepared to invade the American South and slice

the nation from bottom to top. Easterners and especially visitors to

Washington, where the blackened ruins of the Capitol and the White

House stood starkly amid a heavy December snowfall, couldn't imagine

that the British might fail to defeat the motley regiments of a general who

had bested Indians but never confronted a real army. The only news from

Ghent, three thousand miles of stormy ocean away, was that the British

demands were extortionately unrealistic, designed to humiliate and dismember the country most Britons had never considered legitimate. One didn't have to be an alarmist to imagine that spring would find the United States *dis*united, with New England seceded and the trans-Mississippi territories apportioned among the Europeans and Indians. The Boston *Gazette* made no secret where its seditious hopes lay. "Is there a Federalist, a patriot in America, who conceives it his duty to shed his blood for Bonaparte, for Madison and Jefferson and that host of ruffians in Congress who have set their faces against us for years, and spirited up the brutal part of the populace to destroy us? Not one. Shall we, then, any longer be held in slavery and driven to desperate poverty by such a graceless faction?" The Madison administration struggled to convey an optimism it didn't feel. Its mouthpiece, the *National Intelligencer*, mustered no more than a double negative as it looked toward the Mississippi: "Appearances justify the expectation of the British expedition not being ineffectually resisted." Thirty-six years after George Washington had kept the American Revolution alive on a bleak hillside near Philadelphia, the experiment in republicanism seemed on the verge of dissolution.

And then, across the frozen fields and barren hopes of February, a blessed zephyr blew in from the South. Andrew Jackson had stood before New Orleans and defeated Wellington's invincibles. The South was secure, and with it the West. And New England also, for the defeatism that fed the secessionist dreams of the radical Federalists evaporated in the sudden glow of Jackson's triumph. Never had the mood of the nation changed so quickly, from despair to confidence. The republic survived. The Union was saved.

*L*ouisiana is still American," Mrs. Edward Livingston wrote her sister on the Thursday after the Sunday battle. "God has granted us a brilliant victory, and has spared the lives of those dear to us." Louise Moreau de Lassy Livingston was the widow of a French officer who had been stationed in New Orleans, and was now the wife of Jackson's attaché, Edward Livingston. With the rest of New Orleans she had endured the weeks of preparation for the battle, the heart-stopping rumors of what British soldiers did to innocent women, and the fearsome thunder of the artillery exchanges. "Such feelings cannot be described," she told her sister. "The battle-ground is only a league from the city, and I could not only hear the booming of the cannon, as the house shook each time, but every musket could be heard also." Yet she, with the others, had put faith in General Jackson. And they had been amply rewarded. "There never was a more glorious victory, nor one that cost less blood. Not a single father of a family was killed, and the joy of the people, thanks be to God, is unalloyed by private sorrow. Everybody thinks this battle will end the war, and that the enemy will at once re-embark. Should this prove the case, it is impossible to conceive a more brilliant success for American arms or one more full of disaster for the English."

Jackson didn't underestimate what he and his men had accomplished, but he wasn't quite ready to call the war over. On the day of the battle itself, even as his soldiers on the left bank were slaughtering and capturing redcoats by the thousand, the American militia on the right bank gave him a fright by collapsing in the face of the belated British attack there. The next day he still couldn't figure out exactly what happened. It was "strange and difficult to account for," he told James Monroe. But the gist of the sorry tale seemed to be that at the moment of truth "the Kentucky reinforcements ingloriously fled, drawing after them, by their example, the remainder of the forces." The defenders managed to spike the guns before leaving, thereby preventing the use of the weapons against their comrades across the river. But the defeat was galling and potentially dangerous. "This unfortunate rout had totally changed the aspect of affairs," Jackson told Monroe. "The enemy now occupied a position from which they might annoy us without hazard, and by means of which they might have been enabled to defeat, in a great measure, the effects of our success on this side the river." But then the complexion of things changed again, almost equally unaccountably. British general Lambert, clearly shaken by the disaster to the army he inherited, ordered the troops on the right bank to recross the river and join such of their fellows as had survived the bloody morning. "I need not tell you with how much eagerness I immediately regained possession of the position he had thus hastily quitted," Jackson said.

The recapture of the left bank allowed Jackson to judge the battle of January 8 a complete success, but it gave him little cause to conclude that the single victory would end the war. Lambert's army still sat a few miles outside New Orleans, and though it was in no shape to mount another assault, neither were the Americans in much condition to chase it away. The British fleet was anchored on the coast, with no American warships anywhere in sight. New Orleans might be safe, but the British could easily board their ships and harass some other part of the South. In fact the British did revisit Fort Bowyer, on Mobile Bay, and force its surrender. This incident merely strengthened Jackson's refusal to consider the war over till he saw a treaty declaring it so.

His stern attitude sat poorly with the people of New Orleans. Like Mrs. Livingston, most of them wanted to celebrate. And many did. A parade was held to honor the victorious general. Children threw garlands, and the city's odist proclaimed:

> *Hail to the chief! who hied at war's alarms,*
> *To save our threatened land from hostile arms. . . .*
> *Jackson, all hail! our country's pride and boast,*
> *Whose mind's a council, and who's arm an host. . . .*
> *Remembrance long shall keep alive thy fame,*
> *And future infants learn to lisp thy name.*

Honest joy and relief informed the hosannas, but so did a desire to have done with martial law. The residents of New Orleans had never liked it, but with the British at the door they couldn't object inordinately. Now that the British had been beaten back, the residents called for a return to civil law, including normal business and access to the courts.

Jackson refused. Even after Lambert loaded his troops on boats and withdrew to the ships that had brought them to the coast, Jackson held to the opinion that war was war till peace was declared. As yet no word of the settlement at Ghent had penetrated the Gulf. Jackson assumed, with most other Americans, that the negotiators in the Flemish city were waiting on the outcome of the battle for New Orleans. "As soon as their defeat reaches Ghent, we will have peace, in my opinion," he predicted. But not till then.

*V*incent Nolte was one of those who wanted Jackson to release the city from martial law. Nolte was an Italian-born German who had survived

Napoleon, the plague, the fires of Mt. Etna, the New Madrid earthquake, and an epidemic of yellow fever before establishing himself as a commodities broker in New Orleans. His warehouse bulged with cotton and wool as the British approached the city in the autumn of 1814. Shortly after Jackson arrived, the American quartermaster commandeered Nolte's inventory for uniforms and barricades. Nolte didn't begrudge the taking, as he supported Jackson, to the point of joining him in the field. But he expected compensation for his loss. Jackson at first seemed agreeable. He appointed a commission to examine claims and recommend payment. The commission set a figure for Nolte's loss in wool, but Jackson added a condition. The wool, he explained, had been used to make clothing for Tennessee militiamen. For this reason Nolte must be paid in Tennessee bank notes. Nolte felt cheated, as the Tennessee notes traded at sharp discount in New Orleans. But he held his tongue awaiting judgment on his 250 bales of cotton, which were worth far more than the wool.

"I produced my books," he explained afterward, referring to the records on the cotton bales. "Two years before, they had been purchased from the richest cotton planter, Poydras, at 10 cents [per pound]. The price, meanwhile, had never been less than 10 to 11 cents, and the day before we received the news of their seizure, I had bought two small lots at 11½ and 12 cents." Nolte cited this figure in support of his claim for compensation at that level. Jackson rejected the price. Nolte must take the lower price prevailing after the first British landing, when it seemed as though the city might fall. "I made a written protest," Nolte said, "but the general would not notice it. Then I determined to call on him in the hopes of awakening a sense of justice in him. He heard me, but that was all. 'Are you not lucky,' he asked, 'to have saved the rest of your cotton by my defence?' 'Certainly, General,' I said, 'as lucky as any body else in the city whose cotton has thus been saved. But the difference between me and the rest is that all the others have nothing to pay and that I have to bear all the loss.' 'Loss,' the general said, getting excited, 'why, you have saved *all*!' "

Nolte tried a different tack. "I saw that argument was useless with so stiff-necked a man, and remarked to him that I only wanted compensation for my cotton, and that the best compensation would be to give me precisely the quantity that had been taken from me, and of the same quality." Nolte suggested arbitration. Jackson rejected this as too complicated. "You must take 6 cents for your cotton. I have nothing more to say." But Nolte wasn't finished talking, and he continued to expostulate. Jackson brushed him off. "Come, sir, come," he said. "Take a glass of whiskey and water. You must be damned dry after all your arguing."

Nolte refused the drink. "General," he said. "I did not expect such injustice at your hands. Good morning, sir." And he walked out.

Jackson could hardly be asked to sympathize with speculators, even those who had fought on his side. Nolte and the other New Orleans merchants seemed to treat the troubles with Britain as a business expense. Jackson had no doubt that had the British won, Nolte and his ilk would have accommodated themselves to the new regime and carried on as before. Perhaps they had lost money in the defense of the city. If so, that was a cost they'd have to swallow. Jackson's soldiers had lost far more in the previous two years, including many lives.

Yet given that he still had to govern the city, he might have handled its leading citizens with greater tact. The first report of the Ghent treaty arrived in mid-February, seven weeks after its signing. But the report was only a newspaper column carried from the East Coast, saying that a treaty had reached Washington. Jackson insisted on notification from the War Department, from his superiors. The distinction seemed arbitrary to many of those under arms in New Orleans, who began seeking escape from military discipline. Some French nationals devised a scheme by which they appealed to the French consul in the city, who furnished documents declaring their freedom. French-speaking American citizens caught on to the game and, claiming French citizenship, were similarly rewarded.

Conceivably Jackson considered the safety of the city still at risk. After all, the war wasn't over till the treaty had been signed and *ratified*. And the British could be expected to learn about this latest unrest, as they had learned about everything else, and might be tempted to test the city's defenses again. But there was more involved. As in the instance of Nolte and the speculators, Jackson resented the narrow self-interest that lay at the heart of the subterfuge. Good men had died to defend the city, and these malcontents couldn't wait the few days for the war to end definitively. Jackson probably considered himself magnanimous in merely ordering the consul and the duty-dodging Frenchmen out of the city.

By now the Louisiana legislature was back in session, and most of its leaders thought they, rather than a general from Tennessee, ought to be making law for Louisiana. One of its members, Louis Louaillier, published an article complaining of Jackson's "abuse of authority." Jackson thereupon had Louaillier arrested. The prisoner appealed to the civil court system, which likewise sought to reassert its authority. Federal judge Dominick Hall upheld Louaillier's appeal and sent Jackson a writ of habeas corpus regarding Louaillier. Jackson seized the judge for abetting mutiny and exiled him from the city. "I have thought proper to send you beyond the limits of my encampment," he explained, "to prevent you from a repetition of the improper conduct for which you have been arrested and confined." The judge would remain outside the city until peace between the United States and Britain was ratified or until the British left the coast.

Hall's exile was brief. The treaty had indeed arrived in Washington, as the earlier report had stated. And it was quickly ratified by the Senate. A special courier dispatched to New Orleans reached the city on March 13, barely twenty-four hours after Hall was deposited at the city limits. Jackson wasted no time in relaying the news to the inhabitants. "The commanding general, with the most lively emotions of joy and of gratitude to heaven, announces to the troops under his command that a treaty of peace between the United States and Great Britain was ratified and exchanged at Washington on the 17th of February. . . . In consequence whereof, he loses not an instant in revoking and annulling the general order issued on the 15th"—actually the 16th—"day of December last, proclaiming martial law. . . . And in order that the general joy attending this event may extend to all manner of persons, the commanding general proclaims and orders a pardon for all military offenses heretofore committed in this district, and orders that all persons in confinement under such charges be immediately discharged."

Judge Hall could have contributed to the general joy by letting his past differences with Jackson go, but he followed a different course. He no sooner resumed his seat on the bench than he ordered Jackson to appear and explain why he should not be held in contempt of court for ignoring the habeas writ in the case of Louaillier.

Jackson knew perfectly well why he shouldn't. "Whenever the invaluable rights which we enjoy under our own happy constitution are threatened by invasion, privileges the most dear, and which, in ordinary times, ought to be regarded as the most sacred, may be required to be infringed for their security," he declared. "At such a crisis we have only to determine whether we will suspend, for a time, the exercise of the latter, that we may secure the permanent enjoyment of the former." Suppose an election had been scheduled for January 8, Jackson said. Should he have neglected the defense of the city in order that his men might go to the polls? Only a fool would think so. Habeas corpus was similar. "How can the civil enjoyment of this privilege be made to consist with the order, subordination and discipline of a camp? Let the sentinel be removed by subpoena from his post, let writs of habeas corpus carry away the officers from the lines, and the enemy may conquer your country by only employing lawyers to defend your constitution." Jackson acknowledged that his actions weren't universally popular. But he refused to apologize, regardless of the cost to his reputation. "I am not insensible to the good opinion of my fellow citizens. I would do much to obtain it. But I cannot, for this purpose, sacrifice my own conscience or what I conceive to be the interests of my country."

Jackson addressed these words, significantly, not to Judge Hall but to his "fellow soldiers," whose approbation he valued far more than that of the court. Jackson consented to appear in Hall's court, yet he refused to answer a series of questions put to him by the prosecuting attorney. He had drafted a defense of his actions and previously submitted it to the court, only to have the court reject it. "Under these circumstances," he told Hall, "I appear before you to receive the sentence of the court, and have nothing further to add."

Hall pronounced the expected verdict of guilty and imposed a fine of one thousand dollars. Jackson quietly left the courtroom and stepped outside—to be greeted by a large crowd shouting its own verdict, of delirious support for the hero. All dignity was lost in the surge of enthusiasm. Jackson had walked to the courthouse, but now he was made to ride in a carriage commandeered for the purpose. The horses were released from the traces that the people might have the honor of pulling him back to his quarters. Everyone shouted for Jackson, and more than a few muttered against Hall. Jackson calmed them long enough to caution against violence. Upon reaching his house he wrote a bank draft for one thousand dollars and sent it to the court, secure as ever in his own rectitude and a bit surprised at his popularity.

The war had been hard on Rachel Jackson. During its early phase, when her husband was fighting the Red Sticks, the news from the front alternately emphasized privation and danger, and though Jackson tried to calm her fears, she rightly guessed he was telling her less than the whole story. She couldn't decide which was worse: knowing or not knowing all he faced. "I received your letter by express," she wrote of a message that told of an engagement a few weeks before Horseshoe Bend. "Never shall I forget it. I have not slept one night since. . . . I cried aloud and praised my God for your safety." She hoped he would be able to come home at least briefly before completing the campaign. "My dear, pray let me conjure you by every tie of love, of friendship, to let me see you before you go again." Like most people of her time, including her husband, Rachel suffered from various maladies doctors could only vaguely diagnose and couldn't effectively treat. The strain of Jackson's absence—her worries for his safety, her responsibility for the Hermitage—aggravated her condition. "I have borne it until now it has thrown me into fevers. I am very unwell. . . . How long, oh Lord, will I remain so unhappy? No rest, no ease. I cannot sleep. . . . I never wanted to see you so much in my life."

Jackson replied as soon as Rachel's letter arrived. "I have this moment received your letter . . . and am grieved to think of the pain my absence occasions." But duty required that they remain apart awhile longer, as she must realize. "When you reflect that I am in the field and cannot retire when I please . . . I am in hopes that your good sense will yield to it yet a little while with resolution and firmness." He wanted to be with her as much as she wanted to be with him; their reunion would come the more quickly the harder he applied himself to the current task.

As he always did in writing Rachel, Jackson told her to give his love to their son. "Say to my little darling Andrew that his sweet papa will be home shortly, and that he sends him three sweet kisses." After the Battle of Horseshoe Bend, he instructed Rachel once more to kiss Andrew, adding, "Tell him I have a warrior's bow and quiver for him."

Jackson and Rachel were reunited in Nashville that spring following the surrender of William Weatherford. But their time together was short, as he soon turned south again, as commander of the Seventh District. From July 1814, when he went to Fort Jackson to make peace with the Creeks, till after the Battle of New Orleans, the war kept them apart. But as soon as word of the great victory of January 8 reached Nashville, Rachel set out south with some other wives of Tennessee officers. "May God preserve them from accident," Jackson wrote on learning of their winter departure down the Cumberland.

Rachel arrived in late February. The joy of the lovers' reunion certainly repaid some of the pain of separation, although like most intimate moments in history its details went unrecorded. And like most reunions, this one was both more and less than the partners had anticipated. Rachel hadn't realized what a hero her husband was to the Americans in the city or how he annoyed the French and other Europeans. While the former embraced her in their enthusiasm for Jackson, the latter poked fun at her homespun appearance. Vincent Nolte described one of several dinners held in their honor, before adding snidely (and in part inaccurately): "After supper we were treated to a most delicious *pas de deux* by the conqueror and his spouse, an emigrant of the lower classes, whom he had from a Georgia planter, and who explained by her enormous corpulence that French saying, 'She shows how far the skin can be stretched.' To see these two figures, the general a long, haggard man, with limbs like a skeleton, and Madame la Generale, a short, fat dumpling, bobbing opposite each other like half-drunken Indians, to the wild melody of *Possum up de Gum Tree*, and endeavoring to make a spring into the air, was very remarkable, and far more edifying a spectacle than any European ballet could possibly have furnished."

*I*t was a mark of Jackson's devotion to Rachel that he never uttered a negative word about the figure she cut or intimated in the slightest manner that she didn't fit perfectly into any setting in which she found herself. Nolte and others might mock her frontier ways, but Jackson closed his ears to the criticism and opened his eyes only to her.

Meanwhile he couldn't help realizing that in the eyes of most of America, he was the greatest hero since Washington. A Philadelphia printmaker wrote him with an urgent request: "My friends and many citizens of this City have called upon me to cause a painting of the Battle of New Orleans to be engraved in the best manner. . . . I beg you, sir, to have the goodness to furnish me with a ground plan of the fortifications, a sketch of the appearance of the country taken from within our lines looking down the road towards the British as they were advancing, a description of the times of the battle that will be the most favourable and interesting to make the picture from, and situations you were in at those times—what officers stood near you, their rank, etc." A painter and an engraver had already been commissioned to execute the work. They required only the raw materials for their art. "Be pleased, sir, to inform me whether there is a portrait of yourself, by whom painted, and whether I can be permitted at the time it will be wanted to have it here for the use of the engraver. Have the goodness, sir, also to inform me whether it is your intention of visiting our City, and if so, at what probable time. I have engaged our first rate portrait painter to paint your portrait for me on your arrival, by your permission."

Jackson's reply to this request has been lost. But he did sit for portraits, and he cooperated with artists and authors attempting to provide the American people with pictures—actual and literary—of what their army had accomplished at New Orleans. He spoke to journalists and endorsed the plan of aide John Reid to publish an account of the southern campaign. "I think it very proper that the public should be made acquainted with the opportunities he has had of acquiring full and correct information on the subject," Jackson said. "He had and now has charge of my public papers and has ever possessed my unlimited confidence."

*Y*et none of the paintings, prints, or literary renderings captured Jackson as he really looked during most of the two years in which he won his military reputation. At the beginning of the Creek campaign his left arm and shoulder had been unusable, still mending from his fracas with the Bentons. He had to be helped onto his horse and could consult maps and books only awkwardly. He needed help to write and couldn't even feed himself properly.

This last handicap would have been more of a problem if his stomach had been able to tolerate regular food. From childhood Jackson had been painfully thin. To some extent his slimness probably reflected a high metabolic rate, sometimes manifested in the intense, almost electric energy that seemed to radiate from his person. But it may well have indicated, too, the presence of parasites. As common as malaria was in the Carolinas and the river valleys of the interior, if Jackson avoided the disease he would have been luckier than very many of his neighbors. Intestinal parasites were equally prevalent but more diverse. The most virulent pathogens—for cholera and typhoid fever, for instance—often killed their hosts. But many others, typically unnamed, merely caused chronic diarrhea and other discomforts that people in preindustrial countries—then and later—simply learned to live with.

Jackson lived with intestinal troubles, though they caused him more discomfort than most of his contemporaries suffered. The difficult conditions of the Creek campaign—the lack of food and shelter, the exposure to the elements—aggravated his distress to the point where he often could barely sit up. If the army was in camp, he would prop himself in a chair or dictate correspondence from his cot. On the march he would lean forward in his saddle as though hugging his horse. Not even in New Orleans, as civilized a place as existed in the American West, could he find comfort. "I have had a serious attack of dysentery that reduced me very much," he wrote to a friend in February 1815. "I have not been clear of it for four months, except ten days after my first arrival at this place."

His soldiers might have taken alarm had the underlying complaint not been so unremarkable. No one needed to tell *them* about fractious bowels. Nor did the general have to apologize for a diet that often consisted of little more than gin and water, the only things his system could tolerate when his symptoms flared. Alcohol was the universal medicine. If it didn't cure the disease—and it never did—it diminished the pain.

Jackson's case differed from most of his contemporaries' in ways that made his symptoms worse. The bullets he carried—from the duel with Charles Dickinson and the affray with the Bentons—had created pockets of chronic infection. The infections were low-grade and not life threatening, but they put a constant strain on his immune system, leaving him susceptible to other, opportunistic infections. Jackson's official correspondence rarely mentioned his health, but his letters to Rachel and close friends revealed a succession of fevers, stomach and intestinal ailments, and joint pains.

The doctors were probably right to leave the bullets in place. The surgeon's nonsterile knife was certainly more threatening to Jackson's life than some small pieces of lead. But the lead wasn't innocuous. In fact it slowly poisoned him, leaching its heavy metal into his bloodstream. A study conducted in the late twentieth century, on locks of Jackson's hair, indicated levels of lead in Jackson's blood many times higher than is commonly considered safe. And many of the symptoms he recorded—abdominal cramping, nausea, headaches, constipation (which alternated with his diarrhea)—are consistent with lead poisoning.

Jackson didn't help himself by the medications he took. Calomel (mercurous chloride) and sugar of lead (lead acetate) were mainstays of nineteenth-century pharmacy, and for someone with Jackson's catalog of maladies they were medications of frequent choice. He drank calomel and sugar of lead for his intestinal troubles and applied sugar of lead to his wounded shoulder and arm, and to his eyes as an eyewash. The medications afforded symptomatic relief—and produced some recognized side effects, such as heavy salivation, in the case of calomel. They probably did less systemic harm than has sometimes been suggested, but they certainly didn't bolster his constitution.

Whatever the sources of his physical problems—gunshot wounds, parasites, heavy metals—Jackson was regularly but a step or two from physical collapse. Often the only thing that kept him upright—or bent over, rather than prostrate—was his remarkable will. Jackson could admit defeat to ill health no more readily than he could admit defeat to anything or anyone else.

Perhaps paradoxically, but in a way his men could appreciate, his chronic ill health made him seem the more heroic—even if it didn't sell lithographs of battle scenes. *They* knew what it took to stay in the saddle when one's intestines were about to explode, and how chronic pain can make cowards of the most courageous. In his unguarded moments, they could see the pain in his face and read, in his sallow skin and gaunt frame, the toll his ailments were taking on his constitution and spirit. And when they saw him rise above these, they believed they could rise above their own challenges.

Jackson's physical troubles partly explain one of the most singular aspects of his leadership style. Again and again, at crucial moments of his public life, Jackson carried the day because his opponents were terrified of his temper. Observers likened him to a volcano, and only the most intrepid or recklessly curious cared to see it erupt.

A man in chronic pain can't help being irritable, and irritation yields readily to anger. Jackson didn't suffer fools gladly, not least because he was suffering enough as it was. Few of Jackson's surviving letters are overtly introspective. He rarely spoke of his feelings per se. But one can't help thinking that in many cases, when enemies or bad luck sent him some new vexation, he wondered why heaven was testing him so. The pressure inside the volcano grew and grew, till it erupted with awesome force.

Yet even then the Jackson will remained in charge. Like many other great men, Jackson employed his temper to effect. His anger, when he let it show, was honest enough. Feigned anger is never so terrifying as the genuine article. But he almost always used his anger, rather than letting his anger use him. His close associates all had stories of his blood-curdling oaths, his summoning of the Almighty to loose His wrath upon some miscreant, typically followed by his own vow to hang the villain or blow him to perdition. Given his record—in duels, brawls, mutiny trials, and summary hearings—listeners had to take his vows seriously.

But when anger didn't serve, his temper could flash cold as well as hot. He never despised anything or anyone as much as he despised Britain, but he didn't waste his energy hurling imprecations at King George III or his successors. Revenge—for Britain's abuse of America in two wars and the oft-broken peace between, for the death of his brothers and mother, and for the scar that still etched his scalp—was a dish he was happy to take cold, that it might be taken better.

On March 21 Jackson bade farewell to the troops at New Orleans. The scene lacked the solemnity of George Washington's famous leave-taking at the end of the Revolutionary War, if only because Jackson, as befit a demo-crat, addressed the rank and file together with the officers. But it captured the same patriotic poignancy. "Go, full of honour and wreathed with laurels whose leaves shall never wither," he told them. "The man who slumbered ingloriously at home during your painful marches, your nights of watchful-ness and your days of toil, will envy you the happiness which these recollec-tions will afford." He praised them for their loyalty and devotion, and he assured them of "the gratitude of a nation of free men" and "the approba-tion of an admiring world."

Jackson and Rachel and a small entourage left New Orleans in early April. They proceeded slowly north to Natchez, taking two weeks to get there on account of spring rains that softened the roads, but also because everyone on the Mississippi wanted to see the man who had saved them from the British and the Indians. "He is every where hailed as the saviour of this country," John Reid remarked. "He has been feasted, caressed, and I may say idolized. They look upon him as a strange prodigy; and women, chil-dren, and old men line the road to look at him as they would at the Ele-phant." Jackson himself explained how he and the others had dined their way up the river. "In New Orleans there was two public dinners given to me and suit; one up the coast at which a number of the most respectable citizens of Orleans attended with Colonel Fortier's band; and every place dinners were prepared. . . . At Natchez a ball and supper was given to Mrs. Jackson, and the next day a dining to myself and suit at Washington, and on yester-day a dinner at Greenville."

The celebrating increased as the party neared Nashville. Militiamen who had preceded him home made an escort for the final miles. Politicians past, present, and prospective crowded to share his aura. Senator Grundy conveyed the gratitude of the state and the republic. Governor Blount hosted the finest dinner Tennessee had ever laid on. The procession didn't end till his supporters deposited him at the Hermitage and heard him explain the meaning of the recent events:

> The sons of America, during a most eventful and perilous conflict, have approved themselves worthy of the precious inheritance be-queathed to them by their fathers. They have given a new proof how impossible it is to conquer free men fighting in defense of all

that is dear to them. Henceforward we shall be respected by nations who, mistaking our character, had treated us with the utmost contumely and outrage. Years will continue to develop our inherent qualities until, from the youngest and the weakest, we shall become the most powerful nation in the universe.

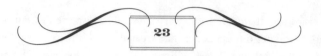

23

EAST BY SOUTHWEST

Some revolutions start quietly, with a change of minds. John Adams

contended that the American Revolution began this way. "The Revolution

was effected before the war commenced," he said. "The Revolution was

in the minds and hearts of the people, a change in their religious

sentiments of their duties and obligations."

Other revolutions begin with a bang, but few so literally as the

revolution Robert Fulton set in motion in 1807 when he nosed his

steamboat *Clermont* into the Hudson current at New York and headed

upstream toward Albany. The Pennsylvanian had apprenticed to a jeweler

in Philadelphia before falling for the visual arts and traveling to England

to study painting. But British art in the 1790s held less fascination for

Fulton (and most other objective observers) than British science and technology, and Fulton found himself hobnobbing with James Watt and other pioneers of steam power. Separately he studied navigation, especially the craft of canals, and won a patent for a better mechanism for lifting boats through locks. He crossed the English Channel to Paris, reflecting en route on the vagaries of wind and tide. In the calmer waters of the Seine he married his interest in steam to his navigational affinity and built a prototype steamboat. It worked but elicited insufficient approbation from the French government or French investors to make Fulton think he could become rich cruising the watercourses of Napoleon's empire. He returned to America, with higher hopes. And on the morning of August 17, 1807, with his Boulton & Watt (of Birmingham) engine belching and clattering, he launched a revolution that changed American lives, American politics, and the American economy as much as anything that ever happened between the Atlantic and the Pacific.

Andrew Jackson's victories in the War of 1812—over the Creeks in Mississippi, the Spanish in Florida, and the British at New Orleans—fairly annihilated the political will to separatism that had infected the American West since the birth of the republic. Robert Fulton's victory—over gravity on the Hudson and prospectively on the rivers of the American interior—eliminated the economic complaints that had kept separatism alive. Jackson never met Fulton (who died suddenly in 1815, before winning the wealth he had come home to attain), nor did his particular cast of mind and temperament attune him to technology as a shaper of human destiny. But between them, the soldier and the inventor cemented East and West together in the Union, securing the nation's future as Americans spread across the continental heartland.

𝒯hough Jackson didn't meet Fulton, there was a personal connection nonetheless. To commercialize his invention, Fulton formed a partnership with Robert Livingston, who outlived him and helped spread the new technology. Livingston was the brother of Jackson's attaché at New Orleans. Besides assisting in the great victory of January 8, Edward Livingston seems to have been the first to articulate the thought that would drive American politics—almost like a steam engine—during the next two decades. "General, you are the man," Livingston told Jackson not long after the battle. "You must be President of the United States."

James Madison wouldn't have gone that far, but he certainly believed that the victorious general ought to be associated with the Madison administration as closely as possible. Jackson had hardly reached Nashville on his return from New Orleans when he received a request that he visit Washington. The public motive for the invitation was to pick Jackson's brain regarding a reorganization of the American army. Madison was still fending off criticism for allowing the British to burn Washington and otherwise rampage about the country. The president needed to show that he was doing something to guarantee that such disaster not recur. And who better to advise the administration than the hero of New Orleans? Madison's private motive was to keep Jackson happy and supportive of the administration, lest he develop political ambitions of his own. James Monroe was in line to receive the Republican nomination, which, particularly after the Federalists' flirtation with secession, was tantamount to election. Neither Madison nor Monroe wished to jeopardize the anointing.

Jackson accepted the invitation, although he left open just when he would head east. After nearly two years away from home, he wasn't eager to depart. Rachel deserved better than that, as did Andrew Jr. and Lyncoya (the Creek child he rescued from the ruins of Tallushatchee). Various decisions about the operation of the Hermitage had to be made. Perhaps most important, his constitution required mending. "My health is not restored; I have frequent returns of the old complaint," he wrote Edward Livingston in July, referring to the dysentery.

He would have stayed home longer had he not received a puzzling letter from Washington. The War Department had naturally followed Jackson's trial on the contempt charges arising from the martial law question in New Orleans. Neither Madison nor Alexander Dallas, who had succeeded Monroe as war secretary, wanted to upset Jackson, but at the same time they couldn't well be caught on the wrong side of the Constitution. Dallas told Madison he would seek a formula whereby he could "manifest a just respect for the Constitution and laws without wounding the pride or feelings of General Jackson." It wasn't easy, and the letter Dallas sent Jackson simply confused the issue. The secretary said that military necessity could create situations in which the defense of the Constitution demanded suspension of certain of its parts. And the president was inclined to defer to the judgment of the commander on the spot. "Where no difference of opinion can occur as to the purity or the sincerity of the motive to action, where the exigency was great, and where the triumph has been complete, the judgment of a responsible and distinguished officer merits implicit confidence."

Had Dallas stopped there, Jackson would have felt vindicated. But the secretary wanted to cover his other flank and so switched to the opposite side of the issue. "The case of military necessity which creates its own law must not be confounded with the ordinary case of military service, prescribed and governed by the law of the land. In the United States there exists no authority to declare and impose martial law, beyond the positive sanction of the acts of Congress." Admittedly, a field commander must be able to ensure the safety of his forces. "But all his powers are compatible with the rights of the citizens and the independence of the judicial authority. If, therefore, he undertake to suspend the writ of habeas corpus, to restrain the liberty of the press, to inflict military punishments upon citizens who are not military men, and generally to supercede the functions of the civil magistrate, he may be justified by the law of necessity, while he has the merit of saving the country, but he cannot resort to the established law of the land for the means of vindication."

So what *was* Dallas—with the endorsement, Jackson accurately assumed, of the president—saying? Apparently that Jackson was right to have done what he did but that Judge Hall was, too. Jackson couldn't tell what the administration's game was, but he could guess that the president and his men wanted to have things both ways.

Jackson received this letter in early September. He penned a cursory rebuttal, deciding to save the rest for a personal meeting with Dallas and the president in Washington. "I expect to set out thither in a few weeks and hope, after my arrival there, to be able to give such explanation of my conduct as may be satisfactory," he told Dallas.

*J*ackson's journey east was another triumphal progress. The citizens of eastern Tennessee turned out to hail the greatest man the state had ever produced. In the Shenandoah Valley of Virginia he was likened to that commonwealth's first citizen, General Washington. A dinner at Lynchburg in Jackson's honor included among the guests the aging Thomas Jefferson, who perhaps marveled that war brought out the best in certain people, including this one who had always seemed so rash during Jefferson's presidency. The master of Monticello toasted the hero of New Orleans: "Honor and gratitude to those who have filled the measure of their country's honor." Jackson replied: "James Monroe, late secretary of war," which was interpreted as at once personally gracious, Monroe being a Virginia protégé of Jefferson's, and politically significant, in that Monroe was the leading contender for the succession to Madison.

Jackson and his party reached Washington on the evening of November 16, "having traveled all day in a cold rain," as John Reid explained to his wife. Reid went on to describe the peculiar protocol of the capital, at least as it applied to Jackson.

Yesterday we visited the President and his lady, the secretary of state and his lady, the secretary of the treasury and his lady, and the secretary of war and his lady. . . . Now from your country education, you may suppose we visited, respectively, these husbands and wives in the same apartment. By no means. First we enter the *Lord's* apartment, making a bow as we enter, and another, as you may guess, as we leave the room. The Lord follows us to the door and makes another low bow (all in the awkwardest style) just about the time our backs are turning upon him. We, of course, turn about two quarters round, which occasions in turn a very awkward position both of the body and mouth, while we are making our second bow and taking our second adieu. Then we enter a passage which leads directly to the door that opens upon the street, with hearts brim full of joy at our deliverance. All of a sudden this pleasing sensation is chilled by a great big footman who comes hurrying after us, enquiring, "Will you not see the lady? She expects and desires your presence in her parlour." So we turn immediately back and are conducted up stairs to the lady's parlour, where we either find her gently reclining on a couch, or the apartment empty, until she makes her appearance, full-rigged from the dressing room. A few very

Rachel Jackson
[UNIVERSITY OF TENNESSEE
SPECIAL COLLECTIONS]

John Coffee
[TENNESSEE STATE
LIBRARY AND ARCHIVES]

Henry Clay
[LIBRARY OF CONGRESS]

James Monroe
[LIBRARY OF CONGRESS]

John Calhoun
[LIBRARY OF CONGRESS]

Daniel Webster

[LIBRARY OF CONGRESS]

John Marshall

[LIBRARY OF CONGRESS]

John Quincy Adams

[LIBRARY OF CONGRESS]

Thomas Hart Benton

[TENNESSEE STATE
LIBRARY AND ARCHIVES]

Andrew Donelson

[TENNESSEE STATE
LIBRARY AND ARCHIVES]

Sam Houston

[TENNESSEE STATE
LIBRARY AND ARCHIVES]

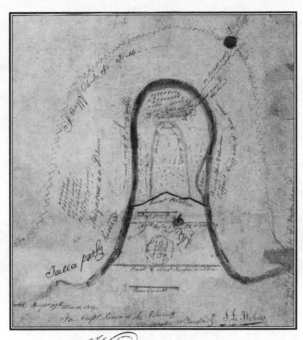

William Carroll's map of Horseshoe Bend

Jackson and William Weatherford

The Battle of New Orleans

Securing the Southeast
[LIBRARY OF CONGRESS]

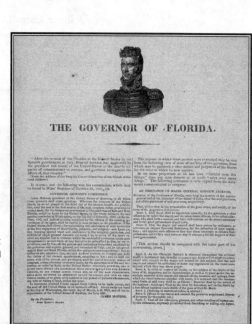

The Hermitage (Jackson in foreground)
[TENNESSEE STATE LIBRARY AND ARCHIVES]

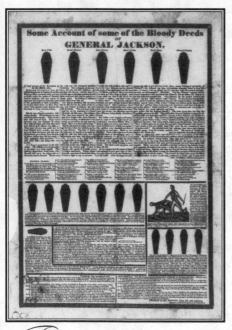

The "coffin handbill"
[LIBRARY OF CONGRESS]

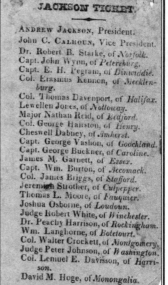

What the people actually voted for: 1828 Virginia ticket of Jackson electors
[LIBRARY OF CONGRESS]

FIRST CAPITOL INAUGURATION · 1829

*T*aking the oath (Marshall administering)

*T*he People's Day

Peggy Eaton (many years after the scandal)
[LIBRARY OF CONGRESS]

The Bank Veto
[LIBRARY OF CONGRESS]

VETO MESSAGE

From the President of the United States, returning the Bank Bill, with his objections, &c.

Jackson vs. Biddle
[LIBRARY OF CONGRESS]

GENERAL JACKSON SLAYING THE MANY HEADED MONSTER.

*H*ero
[TENNESSEE STATE
LIBRARY AND ARCHIVES]

*P*lanter
[TENNESSEE STATE
LIBRARY AND ARCHIVES]

*S*tatesman
[LIBRARY OF CONGRESS]

*P*atriarch
[LIBRARY OF CONGRESS]

civil things are said by her and the General, and then we retire again with our double bows. This is the routine of "high life."

Now this, undoubtedly, is the kindest, the most polite, and the best natured circle in the world. I'll give you a proof. While we were at the President's he turned to me and observed with the most smiling countenance, "I hope Mrs. Reid is with you in the city. I have a great desire to see her." I replied, "She is left on the way, but would undoubtedly have come had she known how warm a side you had for her." This was said (although said good humouredly) in such a way that methought he immediately became two inches lower—his hair became curly, and red both of his nostrils and eyelids appeared. The truth is, he was perplexed by the appearance of General Jackson, who, whenever the conversation flagged, was looking with a melancholy air out at the window, on the ruins of our public buildings.

To his surprise at the social customs of the capital, Reid appended his shock at the cost of living there. "Have our horses attended to and fattened; my expenses can't be less than forty dollars a week! Most monstrous!! What must the General's be? Our stay can't be long."

It really wasn't long, compared with the month in transit either way. Jackson enjoyed—or, increasingly, endured—more dinners. He visited Mount Vernon. "Judge Washington was not at home," Reid wrote of the nephew of the general. "But from Mr. Custis and the rest of the family we received the utmost hospitality and kindness." Jackson consulted with the new secretary of war, William Crawford, about a plan to divide the nation into two military divisions, one for the North and the other for the South, and confirmed to the administration that he would accept command of the southern division. In doing so he put the minds of Madison and Monroe at ease that he wouldn't upset the succession so carefully arranged. They, in turn, made clear that they sided with him against anyone tempted to reopen his dispute with Judge Hall and the federal courts.

By late December he was ready to leave. "I had the pleasure of seeing all the great men at the city, was friendly greeted by all, and was obliged to flee the proffered hospitality of the surrounding cities to restore my health and preserve life," he wrote from the safety of Lynchburg on the last day of the year. "I therefore am retracing my steps to avoid the various pressing invitations." Snow had fallen and was complicating travel west. "Tomorrow we move on for Nashville, where we will arrive as early as our horses and the season will permit. Our horses are thin and the depth of snow is very fatiguing to them."

The war was over and Jackson was the nation's hero, but the struggle continued. For Jackson the struggle always continued. Since his father died—which was to say, since before he was born—Jackson's life had been a struggle. He knew nothing else, and never would. In private life he found, or made, enemies; in public life as well. As he matured in office, from judge to militia general to major general of the army, his enemies increasingly became the enemies of his country. The British were an abiding foe, from the Revolution to the recent war and beyond. His anglophobia grew reflexive. On learning a few months after New Orleans that Napoleon had broken his exile and again challenged the British in Europe, Jackson applauded the Corsican. "The *wonderful revolution* in France fills every body and *nation* with astonishment, and the tricoloured cockade being found in the bottom of each soldier's knapsack tells to all Europe that Napoleon reigns in the affections of the soldiers." Bad news for Britain was good news for America. "What will be the effect of this sudden revolution on the relations with America? Will it not give us an advantageous commercial treaty with Great Britain?"

When the wonderful revolution ran out at Waterloo and Napoleon was cast into final exile on St. Helena, Jackson had to look elsewhere to discomfit England. Spain was a likely target. Despotic, Catholic, proximate (in Florida), and in obvious trouble (from the continuing revolts around the Americas), the Spanish provided an outlet for the aggressiveness that never let Jackson rest. Not that he lacked cause to complain against them. As before his departure from Mobile to New Orleans, the Spanish failed to keep Florida clear of enemies of America's peace. British warships and British troops no longer prowled the harbors and shore of the region, although British traders and agents did. But various Indians who refused to reconcile to American authority in the South made Florida their base for actions inimical to the peace of mind and hearth of Americans in Mississippi Territory.

The Seminoles were the worst offenders in this regard. In the early nineteenth century the Seminoles weren't a tribe in the traditional sense but rather a recent agglomeration of refugees from the American South, including a substantial portion of Africans and their descendants, some held as slaves by the Indians, some held by other Africans, and some simply runaways from the plantations in Georgia and Mississippi. In both a technical and a practical sense they were outlaws, living by geography outside the law of the United States and by Spain's weakness outside the law of Spanish Florida. For this reason a man like Jackson, charged with defending the southern borders of the United States, could easily conceive them a threat. Their mere existence provided a magnet for further runaways from the plantations and farms of whites and friendly Indians. Their camps and villages afforded a haven for those Creeks and other Indians who still resisted American control of Mississippi. Worst of all, in Jackson's view, they tempted the British to continue meddling in American affairs. Behind the Seminoles, behind the Spanish, Jackson saw the specter of Britain in Florida. So long as Florida remained beyond American control, it was a potential base for British adventurism. The law of life—the law of constant struggle—kept it from being otherwise.

Had the Seminoles been model neighbors, Jackson would have distrusted them; that they weren't models made his animus easier to justify. And it won him allies in the government at Washington. Before long Jackson would despise William Crawford, but for now, on the subject of Florida and the Seminoles, the Tennessee general and the Georgia politician found themselves in agreement. During the war some escaped slaves and unfriendly Indians had constructed a makeshift fort on the Apalachicola River in Florida, where they defied the authority of both Spain and the United States. By the spring of 1816 they numbered perhaps three hundred and were, in Crawford's description to Jackson, "well armed, clothed, and disciplined." More fugitives arrived regularly. "This is a state of things which cannot fail to produce much injury to the neighbouring settlements and excite irritations which may ultimately endanger the peace of the nation." Crawford directed Jackson to warn the Spanish governor or commandant at Pensacola to clean out the "Negro Fort" or let the United States do so itself.

Jackson was happy to oblige. Before approaching the Spanish authorities in Florida, he directed General Edmund Gaines, to whom he had delivered command of the garrison at New Orleans upon leaving that city, to prepare for a Florida campaign. By now the killing of two Americans near Fort Claiborne in southern Mississippi provided an additional complaint against the denizens of the Negro Fort. "The growing hostile dispositions of the Indians must be checked by prompt and energetic movements," Jackson told Gaines. "Half peace, half war is a state of things which must not exist. The murderers of Johnston and McGlaskey must be had and punished. No retreat must provide an asylum for them." Referring specifically to the Negro Fort and its occupants, Jackson said, "If the conduct of these people is such as to encourage the Indian war, if the fort harbours the Negroes of our citizens or friendly Indians living within our territory, or holds out inducements to the slaves of our citizens to desert from their owners' service, this fort must be destroyed." Jackson realized that destruction of the fort would violate Spanish territory. But he had violated Spanish territory before, and he was prepared to do so again. "This fort has been established by some villains for the purpose of murder, rapine and plunder. . . . It ought to be blown up regardless of the ground it stands on."

Jackson proceeded to pressure the Spanish governor at Pensacola in much the same way he had pressured the governor's predecessor in 1814. "The conduct of this banditti," Jackson informed Mauricio de Zuñiga, "is such as will not be tolerated by our government, and if not put down by Spanish authority will compel us in self-defence to destroy them."

Zuñiga had no desire to tangle with Jackson, or any particular reason to. The Negro Fort was utterly beyond the control of his undermanned garrison, and he decried the activities of its inhabitants, who also preyed on the Spanish settlements in Florida, hardly less than Jackson did. The governor was so far from resisting Jackson's demand to see the fort reduced as to offer the American general his support in the endeavor. Jackson's courier paraphrased Zuñiga: "If the object was sufficiently important to require the presence of General Jackson, he would be proud to be commanded by you."

ᑰ ᑰ ᑰ

*J*ackson had nothing personal against Zuñiga, who seemed an honorable enough character. But he couldn't help interpreting the governor's cooperativeness as further sign of Spain's pitiful weakness on the southern coast. Jackson might have moved at once against the Negro Fort had another issue not distracted him, one that changed his views of William Crawford. As the federal government had done for years, it sought to preserve Indian lands against illegal white encroachment. A desire to see justice done to the Indians, however belatedly, motivated the administration, but so also a concern for its own credibility. In addition, the Treasury in Washington was empty. Friction between whites and Indians might produce another war, which the federal revenues simply couldn't sustain. In all of this, the position of the government at Washington in the late 1810s was analogous to that of the British government in the 1760s, when, after another costly war (against France), London tried to keep the Americans from settling west of the mountains. And the reaction of westerners in the 1810s was similar to that of the Americans fifty years earlier: cries of tyranny and vows of resistance.

Jackson found himself in the middle of things when Crawford ordered him to remove illegal settlers in southern Tennessee and northern Mississippi. Jackson was directed to post a proclamation—very much like the British Proclamation of 1763—giving squatters a brief period of grace to remove themselves. But once the grace period ended, Jackson must take action. "You will, upon the application of the marshal of any state or territory, cause to be removed by military force all persons who shall be found upon the public lands within your command, and destroy their habitations and improvements." The order applied specifically to Indian lands. "Intrusion upon the lands of the friendly Indian tribes is not only a violation of the laws but in direct opposition to the policy of the government toward its savage neighbors. Upon application of any Indian agent stating that intrusions of this nature have been committed and are continued, the President requires that they shall be equally removed, and their houses and improvements destroyed by military force."

Jackson was no apologist for lawbreakers, but he couldn't escape the irony of being asked to play the role of Britain against Americans. And though he applauded fair-mindedness in principle, he thought the administration overlooked a fundamental difference between whites and Indians on the frontier: the former were citizens of the United States and almost certainly would fight for the Union against any foreign foe, while the latter were noncitizens and might well take the part of Britain or Spain, as they had in the past. Unlike many of his white contemporaries, who asserted a higher claim to the land on grounds that they were civilized Christians, Jackson rarely addressed the cosmic morality of the land question. Instead he asked whether a particular arrangement would make the Union more secure or less. And in nearly every case he concluded that white control served national safety.

Crawford's order caused another problem. The treaty Jackson had negotiated at Fort Jackson called for a continuous line of white settlement across the former territory of the Creeks. The war against Britain, not surprisingly, had hindered the demarcation of the line that would establish the limits of Indian territory. The survey commenced anew after the war, only to be blocked by legal action initiated by the Creeks, Cherokees, and others. Jackson deemed the survey essential to the original goal of uniting the various white settlements on the Gulf plain, and he sent John Coffee, his cavalry stalwart, to conduct it. "The line must be run," Jackson told Coffee. He instructed Coffee not to expect any help from the Indians in determining the location of the line. "Every person acquainted with the disposition of an Indian knows they will claim every thing and any thing. You will therefore proceed on the best information you have and can obtain from the chiefs of the Cherokees and Creeks and any other sources on which you can rely and finish the line as early as possible."

The pro-Indian policy of the government at Washington hindered the survey and thereby, in Jackson's view, undermined American security. He told Crawford how stupid he thought the policy was. "Why the government should feel a wish to aggrandize the [Cherokee] nation at the expense of the other tribes, or against the interest of their own citizens, is unknown. In this matter the Indians—I mean the real Indians, the natives of the forest—are little concerned. It is a stratagem only acted upon by the designing halfbreeds and renegade white men who have taken refuge in their country. If the course now adopted by the government is to be pursued, it is difficult to say at what remote period we may calculate on our uniting settlements and giving security to our frontiers."

Jackson had another reason for adopting a stern attitude toward the Indians. He believed that the only real alternative to sternness by the government was not something better for the Indians but something worse. Articulating a view that would inform his Indian policies as president, Jackson argued that separation between whites and Indians offered the only chance for Indian survival. "Tennessee, I hope, will never disgrace herself by opposing the Government, but when it is recollected that, in open violation of the orders of the United States in 1794, a campaign was set on foot that broke the hostile spirit of the Cherokees and secured peace, judging of human nature it may be believed that when these people are ordered from the old Creek villages burnt by General Coffee and which they aided to conquer, they will feel disposed to wreak their vengeance on this tribe." Jackson knew his neighbors, and he knew that abstract justice counted less with them than eighty acres for growing corn, especially when they thought those acres had been fairly won in war. And how, precisely, did Crawford propose to remove the settlers? The militia wouldn't do it. "Their feelings are the same with the settlers." Regular troops might be employed, but as soon as they left, the settlers would return. Anyway, did the administration really wish to send the army against its own citizens? Jackson didn't say he wouldn't follow such an order, but he made plain he didn't want to—which might amount to the same thing, given his stature and popular support.

The government at Washington needed to know how deep the feelings ran on this subject. "Candour to the Government and to that administration I have admired," he told Crawford, "compels me to be frank and state to you that the people of the West will never suffer any Indian to inhabit this country again that has been for thirty years the den of the murderers of their wives and helpless infants, and on the conquest of which, and for their security hereafter, they shed their blood and suffered every privation. I tell you frankly they never will unless coerced by Government, and when this is attempted I fear it will lead to scenes that will make human nature shudder. I might not be mistaken if I was to say it may lead to the destruction of the whole Cherokee nation, and of course civil war."

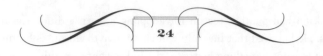

24

PARTY AND POLITICS

*M*adison didn't need the reminder, but Jackson's refusal to follow

orders against the settlers made plain that the Tennessean wasn't an

ordinary general. He had his own moral compass, and his popular prestige

gave him freedom to chart his own course. Madison could have fired

Jackson, but he didn't want to alienate Jackson's many followers and

perhaps tempt the general into entering the political arena. And he had to

acknowledge that much of what Jackson said was true: to uproot the

settlers would require sending federal troops against them. Whether or not

this would provoke the civil war Jackson predicted, it would certainly be

controversial. So Madison backed off. Rather than give Jackson an

ultimatum, the president appointed Jackson to a commission to settle the

Cherokee claims. If Jackson became responsible for the problem, Madison reasoned, he would have to accept responsibility for the solution. The other advantage of the commission was that it would postpone any difficult decisions till after the 1816 election.

Madison's strategy did buy him time, and the apparatus of American politics prepared to make James Monroe president. Almost three decades after the constitutional convention of 1787 the system of selecting presidents continued to evolve. Political parties, unrecognized by the framers of the Constitution, had become an accepted feature of the American landscape, except that the Federalist party had essentially self-destructed, leaving the Republicans in control of national politics, with the consequence that whoever won the party's nomination waltzed to election. That nomination lay in the hands of the party caucus, which was to say the Republican members of Congress gathered in unofficial and secret session. This hardly comported with the increasingly democratic spirit of the age, besides tilting the field in the direction of Washington insiders. Virginia, abutting the federal district and claiming the largest Republican delegation, had an apparent lock on the presidency. Of seven presidential terms thus far, six had gone to Virginians, with Monroe positioned to claim two more.

The situation prompted criticism. Aaron Burr wasn't unbiased in viewing Virginians, but he articulated the opinions of many when he analyzed the approaching election season. "A congressional caucus will, in the course of the ensuing month, nominate James Monroe for President of the United States, and will call on all good republicans to support the nomination," Burr told his son-in-law, Joseph Alston, who happened to be governor of South Carolina. "Whether we consider the measure itself, the character and talents of the man, or the state whence he comes, this nomination is equally exceptional and odious. I have often heard your opinion of these congressional nominations. They are hostile to all freedom and independence of suffrage. A certain junto of actual and factitious Virginians, having had possession of the government for twenty-four years, consider the United States as their property, and, by bawling 'Support the Administration,' have so long succeeded in duping the republican public." Burr urged Alston to defy the party leadership. "The moment is extremely auspicious for breaking down this degrading system. The best citizens of our country acknowledge the feebleness of our administration. They acknowledge that offices are bestowed merely to preserve power, and without the smallest regard to fitness."

Burr had just the man for the moment. It certainly wasn't Monroe, who, besides being the beneficiary of the system, was "naturally dull and stupid, extremely illiterate, indecisive to a degree that would be incredible to one who did not know him, pusillanimous, and, of course, hypocritical." Burr instead proposed someone who was everything Monroe wasn't. "If, then, there be a man in the United States of firmness and decision, and having standing enough to afford even a hope of success, it is your duty to hold him up to public view. That man is *Andrew Jackson*. Nothing is wanting but a respectable nomination, made before the proclamation of the Virginia caucus, and *Jackson's* success is inevitable."

For obvious reasons of history, Burr couldn't effectively forward Jackson's candidacy himself, which was why he urged Alston to do so. But Burr's letter arrived at just the wrong time. Alston's wife, Burr's daughter, Theodosia, had recently died, and the governor was prostrate from grief and kindred maladies. "I fully coincide with you in sentiment," he told Burr, "but the spirit, the energy, the health necessary to give practical effect to sentiment, are all gone. I feel too much alone, too entirely unconnected with the world, to take much interest in any thing."

Alston never recovered from his broken heart, and he died a short while later, leaving Jackson and the rest of the country to watch the election of 1816 unfold as Madison and the Republican leadership desired. But the many people who were hardly more enthusiastic than Burr about Monroe and the Virginians asked whether America's manner of choosing presidents might someday be different.

*E*arly September of that election year found Jackson at the Chickasaw council house in northern Mississippi hammering out a treaty with the Cherokees over the lands in dispute with the Tennesseans, and in dispute between the Tennesseans and the federal government. Jackson was still angry at William Crawford. "If all influence but the native Indian was out of the way," he told Robert Butler, his aide, "we would have but little trouble. But a letter from the Secretary of War to the [federal Indian] agent, which had been received and read to the nation in council before our arrival, has done much mischief."

With no little effort, Jackson and his fellow commissioners, Jesse Franklin and David Meriwether, managed to undo the mischief and reach an agreement. The Cherokees and Chickasaws surrendered title to the lands in dispute in exchange for a series of monetary payments. "We experienced some difficulty with the Chickasaws," Jackson told Monroe, by now president in all but name. The Chickasaws referred to a treaty negotiated with President Washington, which bound the United States to prevent intrusions upon the land in question. Jackson rejected the treaty as invalid. "The fact was that both President Washington and the present secretary of war were imposed on by false representation, as neither the Chickasaws or Cherokees had any right to the territory, as the testimony will show it being in the possession of the Creeks at that time and continued to be possessed by them until we conquered the territory in the fall 1813 and spring 1814." For Jackson, conquest provided the clearest title, which since Horseshoe Bend belonged to the United States. Yet he was willing to pay the Cherokees and Chickasaws to end the confusion. "All these conflicting claims are happily accommodated by the late treaties with those tribes at the moderate premium of 180,000 dollars payable in ten years."

He judged the result well worth the expense. "This territory, added to the Creek cession, opens an avenue to the defence of the lower country, in a political point of view incalculable. We will now have good roads, well supplied by the industry of our own citizens, and our frontier defended by a strong population."

When Jackson learned, about this time, that Crawford was leaving the War Department, he took the opportunity to offer Monroe some advice regarding a successor. He had heard good things about William Drayton of South Carolina, he said. "He is a man of nice principles of honor and honesty, a man of military experience and pride." He was also a Federalist, but not one of those secessionists from New England. "The moment his country was threatened, he abandoned private ease and a lucrative practice for the tented fields. Such a man as this, it is not material by what name he is called; he will always act as a true American." For this reason Monroe ought to consider him seriously.

Jackson thought the principle of nonpartisanship in federal appointments so vital that he repeated it in subsequent letters to the president. "In every selection, party and party feeling ought to be laid out of view (for now is the time to put them down) by selecting those the most honest, possessing capacity, virtue and firmness. By this course you steer the national ship to honor and preferment, and yourself to the united plaudits of a happy country. . . . Consult no party or party feelings in your choice. Pursue that unerring judgment you possess, that for so many years has added so much to the benefit of our common country."

Monroe couldn't have been surprised to receive Jackson's advice regarding the new secretary of war. Jackson's feud with Crawford was no secret, and, as the general charged with defending half the country, he had a right to air his opinion on a prospective superior. Monroe might have found Jackson's broader counsel about eschewing party somewhat less likely. Jackson's national stature owed exclusively to his military accomplishments. What did he know about national politics?

Yet Monroe replied politely and, to all appearances, sincerely. Monroe may not have known that Burr had promoted Jackson for the presidency, but he knew other people had and likely would, and he was canny enough not to antagonize a formidable competitor needlessly. Beyond that, Jackson's views on party were shared by many in the United States, and Monroe thought they deserved a response.

Monroe concurred in principle with Jackson's preference for nonpartisanship. "The chief magistrate of the country ought not to be the head of a party but of the nation itself." Yet parties weren't without meaning. "We have heretofore been divided into two great parties. That some of the leaders of the Federal[ist] Party entertained principles unfriendly to our system of government, I have been thoroughly convinced. And that they meant to work a change in it by taking advantage of favorable circumstances, I am equally satisfied." The Federalists had thus far failed in their schemes to undermine free government, but only because honest republicans had resisted their nefarious designs. Monroe credited Jackson's victory at New Orleans for dealing a body blow to Federalist perfidy. Yet the Federalist danger persisted, which was why Federalists must not be treated like Republicans. "To give effect to free Government and secure it from future danger, ought not

its decided friends, who stood firm in the day of trial, to be principally relied on?" Monroe noted that certain theorists contended that any administration required a healthy opposition, that free government couldn't exist
without parties. He disagreed. Republicanism rested not on a balance of vices,
as in other systems, but on the encouragement of virtue. Parties played to
vice, not virtue, and therefore hindered good government. Monroe avowed
his intention to "exterminate all party divisions in our country, and give new
strength and stability to our Government." He conceded that this was a
large and difficult task. "I am nevertheless decidedly of opinion that it may
be done."

Monroe's vision—of a one-party system of Republican saints—struck
Jackson as naive and unworkable. Jackson's abiding sense that life was a
struggle caused him to believe that rascals would always exist and would
probably organize to effect their aims; parties were unavoidable in a free society. Moreover, his own experience in politics revealed that Republicans
were hardly all saints. Most of the rascals Jackson had known were Republicans, starting with John Sevier and continuing through William Crawford.
Firmer evidence that the Republicans didn't have a monopoly on virtue was
hard for him to imagine.

In time Jackson would become the most partisan of presidents. But he
never denied the right of the opposition to exist. And for now he reiterated
to Monroe that placing party above personal character could lead the nation
astray. "Names are but bubbles, and sometimes used for the most wicked
purpose." Jackson cited an instance he thought Monroe might appreciate.

> I have once upon a time been called a Federalist. You will smile
> when I name the cause. When your country put up your name in
> opposition to Mr. Madison, I was one of those who gave my opin-
> ion that on the event of war (which was then probable) you would
> be my choice. Every person I knew esteemed Mr. Madison as one of
> the best of men and a great civilian, but I always believed that the
> mind of a philosopher cannot dwell upon blood and carnage with
> any composure and is not well fitted for a stormy sea. I was for these
> ideas unhesitatingly denounced as a Federalist. . . . I trust that,
> judging the tree by its fruit, it was unjustly ascribed.

ᗡ ᗡ ᗡ

$\mathcal{D}$espite their fundamental difference on political philosophy, Monroe continued to confide in Jackson. He revealed that he had considered making Jackson secretary of war. "My mind was immediately fixed on you," he said. But second thought convinced him that the country couldn't afford to remove the general from command of the army in the South, "where in case of any emergency no one could supply your place."

Monroe proceeded to explain that he sought to use the cabinet to unite the various sections of the country. Isaac Shelby of Kentucky, the man to whom he did offer the War Department, would represent the West. Georgia's William Crawford, Monroe's designate for the Treasury, would give the South a voice. Monroe didn't say so to Jackson, but Crawford had a sufficient following that he had to be made part of the administration. Yet placing him in the Treasury, rather than back at the War Department, would keep him and Jackson apart. John Quincy Adams of Massachusetts, Monroe's choice for secretary of state, would encourage New England to reenter the fold. Richard Rush of Pennsylvania would stay on at the Justice Department for the time being and anchor the middle of the country. Monroe hoped the regional balancing would help make the Republicans a truly national party. "By this arrangement, there can be no cause to suspect unfair combination for improper purposes."

Jackson had mixed feelings about Monroe's appointments. Adams was an inspired choice—"the best selection to fill the Department of State that could have been made," he told Monroe. But he had doubts about Shelby. "My anxious solicitude for your public and private welfare compels me to be candid and say to you that the acquirements of this worthy man are not competent to a discharge of the multiplied duties of the Department of War." Jackson hoped Shelby, recognizing his own limitations, would thank the president for the honor of the offer and politely decline—which was exactly what happened. In his stead Monroe nominated John Calhoun of South Carolina, who accepted.

ᗡ ᗡ ᗡ

*J*ackson also counseled—or lectured—Monroe on Indian policy. He stressed the need to populate the lands acquired from the Creeks, as quickly as possible. He knew his view wasn't universally held. "Short–sighted politicians may urge that by bringing too much land into market at once, it will reduce the price and thereby injure the finances of the country. Others, still more blind, may contend that it will drain other states of their population." This was fatuous. "The lower country is of too great importance to the Union for its safety to be jeopardized by such short-sighted policy. All the lands to be sold are, in a national point of view, but as a drop in the bucket when brought in competition with the value of that country to the Union, or when compared with the amount which it would cost the United States to retake it should it once fall into the hands of an enemy."

The question of the Creek lands was part of a larger issue. Jackson believed that a similar settlement policy ought to be adopted toward Chickasaw lands between the Ohio and the Mississippi. Jackson anticipated objections here, as well. "It may be said that we have sufficient territory already, and that our settlements ought not to be extended too far." But the counter-arguments were stronger. "Everything should be done to lessen our frontier and consolidate our settlements. This would at once have that effect. It would not only cut off all intercourse between the Northern Indians and the Chickasaws and Choctaws but insure safety to our commerce on the Ohio and Mississippi and afford a strong defence within striking distance of the settlements on the Mississippi and Missouri Rivers."

Jackson conceded that his recommendation collided with the refusal of the Chickasaws to relinquish the land. Nor could he stretch any previous treaty to cover the case. Yet Jackson saw a solution to this problem—a radical solution, he conceded, but not an insupportable one.

> I have long viewed treaties with the Indians as an absurdity not to be reconciled to the principles of our Government. The Indians are the subjects of the United States, inhabiting its territory and acknowledging its sovereignty. Then is it not absurd for the sovereign to negotiate by treaty with the subject? I have always thought that Congress had as much right to regulate by acts of legislation all Indian concerns as they had of Territories. There is only this differ-

ence: that the inhabitants of Territories are citizens of the United States and entitled to the rights thereof; the Indians are subjects and entitled to their protection and fostering care. The proper guardian of this protection and fostering care is the legislature of the Union. I would therefore contend that the Legislature of the Union have the right to prescribe their bounds at pleasure and provide for their wants; and whenever the safety, interest or defence of the country should render it necessary for the Government of the United States to occupy and possess any part of the territory used by them for hunting, that they have the right to take it and dispose of it.

Jackson questioned the plausibility of a situation that allowed the government to dispossess citizens of their property, under the public's right of eminent domain, but prevented the government from doing the same to Indians. "Can it be contended with any propriety that their rights are better secured than our citizens'?" He thought not.

Jackson believed the treaty system served the Indians as poorly as it served the whites. Their old world had vanished. "The game being destroyed, they can no longer exist by their bows and arrows and guns." Some Indians had adapted to the new world on their own; others needed to be compelled. "As long as they are permitted to roam over vast limits in pursuit of game, so long will they retain their savage manners and customs. . . . Circumscribe their bounds, put into their hands the utensils of husbandry, yield them protection, and enforce obedience to those just laws provided for their benefit, and in a short time they will be civilized. . . . There can be no doubt but that in this way more justice will be extended to the nations than by the farce which has been introduced of holding treaties with them."

*J*ackson was sometimes mistaken, but he was never less than sincere. And he was utterly sincere in contending that the policy he prescribed—of treating the Indians as subjects rather than sovereign nations—would, among the alternatives realistically available, yield the best results for the Indians. Yet from start to finish his foremost concern was the safety of the United States. The single goal of Jackson's public life—his career obsession—was to secure the Union from all dangers: internal and external, political and military. Some during his day, and many later, thought that he carried his obsession too far, that the warrior never knew when to stop fighting. But Jackson had reason for thinking as he did. In his lifetime to this point, the United States had never known true peace. Hardly a year had passed since the start of the American Revolution that Britain or France or Spain hadn't threatened or preyed on or actually attacked the United States. Jackson didn't underestimate what he had accomplished at New Orleans, but he had no reason to think that that victory would change the attitudes of the great European powers toward the American republic. The struggle continued.

Nor would it end until Americans demonstrated that they would—and could—demand respect from all who might be tempted to challenge republicanism. In several letters to Monroe, Jackson sketched a program of military preparedness. The program started with securing the Indian lands along the borders, but it went much further. The federal government should build forts at strategic places along America's frontiers. It ought to underwrite foundries and armories for the domestic production of weapons. The militia should be reorganized, the army upgraded.

"Then we will have peace," Jackson predicted, "for then we will be prepared for war. Every man with a gun in his hand, all Europe combined cannot hurt us. And all the world will be anxious to be on friendly terms with us, because all the world will see we wish peace with all but are prepared for defence against those who would wantonly infringe our national rights."

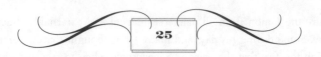

25

JUDGE AND EXECUTIONER

In January 1818 Jackson received a copy of orders from the War
Department to General Gaines to chase Seminole raiders across the border
into Florida. The order authorized Gaines to use force against the raiders
but forbade him from taking hostile action against Spanish troops or
fortifications in the area. Jackson heartily endorsed the first part of the
directive. "Your order . . . to enter the territory of Spain and chastise the
ruthless savages who have been depredating on the property and lives of
our citizens will meet not only the approbation of your country but the
approbation of Heaven," he told Monroe. But he thought the last part of
the order could lead to catastrophe. He sketched a likely scenario.
"Suppose the case that the Indians are beaten; they take refuge either in
Pensacola or St. Augustine, which open their gates to them. To profit by

his victory General Gaines pursues the fugitives and has to halt before the garrison until he can communicate with his Government. In the mean time the militia grow restless, and he is left to defend himself by the regulars. The enemy, with the aid of their Spanish friends and Woodbine's British partisans, or, if you please, with Aury's force, attacks him. What may not be the result? Defeat and massacre."

George Woodbine was a British officer who had led Indian troops against American forces during the War of 1812 and was still in Florida; Louis-Michel Aury was a French soldier of fortune employing Florida as a base for attacks on Spain in the name of an independent Mexico. Jackson's point was that Spanish Florida was a refuge for just such troublemakers, who stirred up the Indians as the British had done for years in the West and the French before them. To declare Spanish towns and forts off limits to American punitive expeditions would simply encourage the miscreants to take refuge there, to the disadvantage and danger of American soldiers and the loss of American honor. Jackson knew that the administration was engaged in diplomacy with Spain and that the president therefore was reluctant to sign an order for action that might upset the talks. Jackson thought that the danger from Florida precluded such delicacy and, in any case, that a bold stroke might move the diplomacy forward. "The whole of East Florida," he told Monroe, should be "seized and held as an indemnity for the outrages of Spain upon the property of our citizens. This done, it puts all opposition down . . . and saves us from a war with Great Britain or some of the Continental powers combined with Spain."

Jackson offered to take the responsibility upon himself, sparing the president potential embarrassment.

> Let it be signified to me through any channel . . . that the possession
> of the Floridas would be desirable to the United States, and in sixty
> days it will be accomplished.

At a much later date, the concept of executive deniability would become a standard feature of American foreign policy. Jackson didn't invent the idea, which certainly originated with some Stone Age Machiavelli. But Jackson's offer to Monroe is one of the earliest surviving instances of the strategy in American policy. And it threw American politics into a tizzy from which it hadn't emerged even a decade later when, like so much else involving Jackson's history, it became an issue in a campaign for president.

Monroe at that later time denied that he had understood Jackson's offer. "I well remember that when I received the letter from General Jackson . . . I was sick in bed, and could not read it," Monroe wrote John Calhoun. "You were either present, or came in immediately afterwards, and I handed it to you for perusal. After reading it, you replaced it, with a remark that it required my attention, or would require an answer, but without any notice of its contents. Mr. Crawford came in soon afterwards, and I handed it also to him for perusal. He read it, and returned it in like manner, without making any comment on its contents, further than that it related to the Seminole war, or something to that effect. I never shewed it to any other person."

Jackson's memory contradicted Monroe's. "In accordance with the advice of Mr. Calhoun, and availing himself of the suggestion contained in the letter," Jackson asserted, "Mr. Monroe sent for Mr. John Rhea (then a member of Congress), showed him the confidential letter, and requested him to answer it. . . . Mr. Rhea did answer the letter, and informed General Jackson"—Jackson was writing in the third person—"that the President had shown him the confidential letter, and requested him to state that he approved of its suggestions." Jackson obviously wasn't in Washington to observe Monroe consulting Calhoun or Rhea. His information on this point apparently was contained in the letter from Rhea. Unfortunately for Jackson after the matter became controversial, he burned the letter before he could use it to verify his version of the tale. "General Jackson and Mr. Rhea were both in the city of Washington," he explained. "Mr. Rhea called on General Jackson, as he said, at the request of Mr. Monroe, and begged him on his return home to burn his reply. He said the President feared that by the death of General Jackson, or some other accident, it might fall into the hands of those who would make an improper use of it." Jackson gave Rhea the promise he wanted. "Accordingly, after his return to Nashville he burnt Mr. Rhea's letter, and on his letter-book opposite the copy of his confidential letter to Mr. Monroe made this entry: 'Mr. Rhea's letter in answer is burnt this 12th April 1819.' " And in fact Jackson's letter book did (and does) read that way, except that he inadvertently wrote "1818" for "1819." On April 12, 1818, Jackson wasn't in Nashville but in Florida, implementing the strategy that started all the ruckus.

❧ ❧ ❧

The Seminole War began after an American attack on the Negro Fort. General Gaines had just established himself upstream from the fort, on American soil, when a supply convoy passing the fort en route to his camp came under fire. At least three Americans were killed and one was taken prisoner. An American expedition sent against the fort fell in with some friendly Seminoles who were hunting blacks to enslave. The Americans and the Seminoles made common cause against the Negro Fort, to which they laid siege. For several days nothing much happened. The blacks inside the fort fired their cannons at the Americans and Seminoles, who ducked behind the trees that surrounded the fort. But in late July 1816 an American gunboat reached the fort from the Gulf. It attracted the fire of the fort's cannon and returned fire of its own. At first the small rounds from the boat simply bounced off the walls of the fort. But then the artillerists increased the elevation of their guns and loaded them with balls heated to glowing. Lobbed over the parapets, one of these balls landed in the large stockpile of powder in the fort. An enormous explosion rocked the entire river valley. Everything inside the fort was flattened, and nearly all the more than three hundred persons there were killed. The Americans and Seminoles who entered the fort as the smoke cleared found it a welter of blood, gore, and body parts. One of the few survivors was the commander of the fort, who explained, apparently under duress, that the American captive had been executed after torture. The commander was given by the Americans to the Seminoles, who killed him.

The success of their joint venture might have disposed the Americans and Seminoles to continue cooperating, and in fact for several months an uneasy peace settled over the border. But Florida remained an outlaw zone, with the Spanish too weak to control what happened there and most of the residents happy to be out of control. The Seminoles resumed their raids on American territory, and American slaves continued their escapes south. Assorted filibusters—would-be revolutionists—launched anti-Spanish operations from Florida across the Caribbean. Smugglers, pirates, and garden-variety criminals made their home among the forests, swamps, and islands of the area.

Jackson determined to clean things up, starting with the Seminoles. He sent Gaines to lecture the Seminole chief King Hatchy on the failings of his tribe. "You have murdered many of my people, and stolen many good horses," Gaines said. "Many good houses that cost me money you have burned." Gaines demanded that Hatchy let him pursue the criminals and escaped slaves who had taken refuge in the Seminole lands in Florida. "If you give me leave to go by you against them, I shall not hurt any thing belonging to you." Gaines said he knew that British agents were fomenting trouble among the Seminoles; these must be cast out. If they weren't, Hatchy would have only himself to blame. "I have got good strong warriors with scalping knives and tomahawks."

Hatchy resented Gaines's arrogant attitude. "It is I who have cause to complain," he said. For every American killed, several Seminoles had died. What did Gaines propose to do about that? Hatchy denied that he harbored escaped slaves. And as for the Americans' trouble with the British, that wasn't the Seminoles' problem. "It is for you white people to settle those things among yourselves." Hatchy warned Gaines against getting pushy. "I shall use force to stop any armed Americans from passing my towns or my lands."

Gaines answered Hatchy indirectly. The head man of a Seminole village on the American side of the border, a place known as Fowltown, had been consorting with undesirables—in Jackson and Gaines's view—for some time. In November 1817 Gaines dispatched a mounted column to bring him in for questioning. The Seminoles fired on the approaching soldiers, who outnumbered them five to one. The soldiers returned the fire, killing a few of the Seminoles, including one woman, and scattering the rest. The soldiers entered the village and discovered a British military uniform of the kind given by British commanders to their Indian allies, and a letter from British Colonel Nichols to the local chief, describing him as a loyal friend of the Crown. The American soldiers took the letter and uniform as evidence and burned the village.

This angered the Seminoles, including Hatchy. A week later a boat on the Apalachicola River carrying American troops and several women and children was ambushed by Seminoles. Nearly all the Americans were killed and most were scalped. Other attacks followed, on soldiers and civilians alike. During the final weeks of 1817 the border region appeared utterly out of control.

$\mathcal{I}$t was at this juncture that Jackson, in Nashville, made his offer to Monroe to settle the Florida question definitively, without implicating the president. Whether or not he received Monroe's approval, he acted as though he had. He called his West Tennessee volunteers back into service. "With this force, in conjunction with the regular troops," he explained to War Secretary John Calhoun, "I can act promptly and, with the smiles of heaven successfully, against any force that can be concentrated by the Seminoles and their auxiliaries." He marched his men south from Nashville, gathering recruits along the way.

The size of his army—which eventually included almost two thousand friendly Creeks, led by William McIntosh, a mixed-race brigadier general in the U.S. Army—strained the supply network in the South. The winter weather didn't help. "The excessive rains have rendered the roads so bad that I ordered the troops, on their march here, to take their baggage on the wagon horses, and abandon their wagons," Jackson wrote from Fort Early, on the Flint River in Georgia. "This facilitated their march to this place, which they reached today; and eleven hundred men are now here without a barrel of flour or bushel of corn."

In March, Jackson reached Fort Scott, a post erected by Gaines in southern Georgia, above the place where the Flint and Chattahoochie rivers come together to form the Apalachicola. Supplies remained short, almost paralyzingly so, leaving Jackson to decide whether to turn back, wait for provisions, or press ahead. Naturally he pressed on. His initiative was rewarded when he met a boat coming up the Apalachicola laden with flour. He continued south to the ruins of the Negro Fort, which he ordered his engineers to rebuild—and rename, as Fort Gadsden, after chief engineer James Gadsden. He was joined by Gaines, who staggered into camp looking quite unlike a general. Gaines's boat had wrecked upriver; several men had drowned and all the food and extra clothing had been lost. The survivors wandered through the woods for nearly a week before finding Jackson.

While Gaines recovered, Jackson sent McIntosh and the friendly Creeks into East Florida. They encountered some of the Red Stick refugees from the war in Mississippi and resumed that conflict. Conditions were wretched. "The creek swamp was so bad we could not pass it for the high waters," McIntosh explained to Jackson, regarding his approach to the camp of an enemy chief. "My men had to leave their clothes and provisions and swim better than one half of the swamp, about six miles wide." McIntosh and his men surrounded the camp and carefully closed in. But the chief and most of the warriors somehow slipped the cordon and escaped. McIntosh rounded up those left behind: "fifty-three men and one hundred and eighty women and children."

McIntosh and others sent Jackson reports on the men presumed to be leading the Seminole resistance. One, a prophet named Francis, was a fugitive from the Creek War who had never accepted defeat and was determined to continue the struggle against Jackson and the Americans. Another, Alexander Arbuthnot, was a British national—Scot, to be precise—who had traded among the Seminoles for some while and was thought to be encouraging them to fight American encroachment. Jackson learned that these and other resisters, including runaway slaves from the United States, were headed for St. Marks, a Spanish fort east of the Apalachicola and above Apalachee Bay. "It is all important that these men should be captured and made examples of," he declared.

Jackson left Fort Gadsden in late March and linked up with McIntosh's Creek regiment on April 1. Later that day the combined force encountered a small party of hostile Indians occupying a point of land amid a swamp. "They maintained for a short period a spirited attack from my advanced spy companies, but fled and dispersed in every direction upon coming in contact with my flank columns," Jackson wrote Calhoun. Jackson's column occupied a Seminole village whose inhabitants had dispersed in advance of the invaders; he ordered the houses burned and the village's corn stores seized. If Jackson had wanted evidence to warrant the destruction, he soon found it. "In the council houses . . . more than fifty fresh scalps were found, and in the center of the public square, the old Red Sticks' standard, *a red pole*, was erected, crowned with scalps."

The grisly sight drove Jackson toward St. Marks. Though the fort was nominally Spanish, its garrison was too weak to keep foreigners and Indians out—and even less able to fend off Jackson. He ordered his troops to surround the fort while he delivered an ultimatum to the Spanish commander chastising Spain for failure to keep order in Florida and asserting an American right of self-defense in doing what Spain couldn't do or wouldn't. He unpersuasively asserted that he came "not as the enemy, but as the friend of Spain," and added, a bit more credibly, that Spanish property would be protected. Then he gave the order to occupy the place and packed the Spanish commandant off to Pensacola.

"I may fairly say that the modern Sodom and Gomorrah are destroyed," Jackson wrote Rachel, referring to the Seminole village and St. Marks. "These two places were the hot bed of the war." In St. Marks Jackson's men captured Arbuthnot. "I hold him for trial." The prophet Francis and another chief were lured onto an American vessel in the harbor, thinking it was British. The captain delivered the two to Jackson, who heard testimony of their involvement in the torture, murder, and mutilation of Americans. "These were hung this morning," he told Rachel.

The capture of St. Marks, while satisfying, didn't end the war. Too many hostiles had escaped east. "Tomorrow I shall march for the Suwanee River," Jackson wrote Calhoun on the second day in control of St. Marks. His objective was the stronghold of Bowlegs, a Seminole chief who harbored warriors, fugitive slaves, and sundry others with neither respect for nor fear of Americans or their laws. Between St. Marks and Bowlegs's village lay a hundred miles of waterlogged forest and plain.

McIntosh and his Creeks were the first to encounter resistance, in the form of a large group of enemy Creeks. "They were in a bad swamp, and fought us there for about an hour," McIntosh reported. "They ran and we followed them three miles. They fought us in all about three hours. We killed thirty-seven of them, and took ninety-eight women and children and six men prisoners, and about seven hundred head of cattle." McIntosh's company lost only three men killed and five wounded.

On the seventh day from St. Marks, Jackson's column neared the Suwanee, where he hoped to capture or kill Bowlegs and end the conflict. He pressed his men forward, only to find the route blocked by a lake still several miles short of Bowlegs's town. "Here I should have halted for the night had not six mounted Indians (supposed to be spies) who were discovered, effected their escape," he explained to Calhoun. Knowing the riders would report the approach of the invaders, Jackson ordered his men back on the march. The combined force of Americans and friendly Creeks struck Bowlegs's town at sunset. They killed a handful of Indians and blacks and took a few prisoners, including a British national named Robert Ambrister. But the main body of the enemy crossed the river and vanished even farther east.

The next day Jackson sent Gaines after the escapees with two days' provisions. Gaines didn't catch them, but he did seize more of their supplies, and he concluded that though they were free they would soon be very hungry. Jackson burned Bowlegs's village and prepared to call the war a success. "I believe I may say that the destruction of this place, with the possession of St. Marks, . . . will end the Indian War for the present," he told Calhoun.

*J*ackson turned out to be right. Although Seminole resistance to American power would revive and, during Jackson's presidency, erupt again, for the time being the insurgents were destitute and demoralized. The soggy earth of Florida was harder to scorch than that of the Red Sticks' Mississippi homeland, but Jackson went far toward making it uninhabitable for enemies of the United States.

As Jackson headed back west and north he tied up some loose ends of the conflict. He convened a special court at St. Marks to determine the fate of the captured Britons, Ambrister and Arbuthnot. Gaines headed the court, and other officers drawn from the regular army and the militia filled out the tribunal. The prisoners were charged with various crimes of which the common theme was incitement to war against the United States and giving aid and comfort to America's enemies. Though the court lacked any authority besides an order from Jackson, it observed certain legal forms. Witnesses were sworn and heard. The accused were permitted to defend themselves and their actions. The proceeding lasted three days, at the end of which the court delivered its verdict and its sentence recommendation to Jackson. Both men were found guilty. Arbuthnot was sentenced to death by hanging. Ambrister was initially sentenced to death by firing squad, but the court reconsidered and changed the sentence to fifty lashes and twelve months at hard labor.

Jackson could approve the sentences, modify them, or set them aside. He asked himself, in the case of Ambrister, whether a prison sentence was practical where no prisons existed and whether a whipping accorded with the gravity of waging war against the United States. Early the day after he received the court's findings, he left St. Marks for Mississippi and home. From the road outside the town he sent back a message conveying his decision.

> The Commanding General orders that Brevet Major A. C. W. Fanning, of the corps of artillery, will have, between the hours of eight and nine o'clock, A.M., A. Arbuthnot suspended by the neck, with a rope, until he is *dead*, and Robert C. Ambrister to be shot to *death*, agreeably to the sentence of the court.

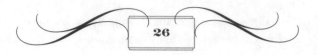

26

THE EYE OF THE STORM

*D*uring the half decade after the War of 1812, the money problem so long a source of vexation to westerners became a crisis of national proportions. Gold fled the country for foreign bourses, driven out by cheap banknotes. Silver was almost as scarce. The federal government had issued Treasury notes to fund the war, but because these weren't convertible into specie and because the government couldn't resist printing more of them, they depreciated rapidly. Sound banks suffered for the sins of the flimsy, leaving sellers reluctant to accept notes from any issuer. Merchants fell back on barter. Potential lenders were demoralized by the ruinous rates of inflation.

*S*o dire was the financial anarchy that the Republicans were driven to a measure the founders of the party had long considered Federalist anathema. In 1816 the Republican Congress resurrected the Bank of the United States. The original bank had been the brainchild of Alexander Hamilton, who hoped to marry wealth to power by granting the bank—a privately owned institution dominated by some of the richest men in the country—control over the financial business of the federal government. Republicans condemned Hamilton's bank as unconstitutional and as prima facie evidence of the Federalist plot to sacrifice liberty to profit. They lacked the votes in 1791 to prevent its charter but swore they would have if they could have. And when the bank's charter expired in 1811, with the Republicans firmly in control of Congress, the bank's opponents gleefully watched it die. The Federalists could do nothing to save it. But those Federalists who survived the War of 1812 had the satisfaction of seeing the worm turn and James Madison, one of the harshest critics of the first Bank of the United States, compelled by the financial crisis of the postwar period to call for its resurrection. In April 1816 the Republican Congress approved a bill chartering a second Bank of the United States for twenty years, and Madison signed it into law.

Two weeks later Congress approved another measure similarly fraught with significance. The Constitution had always allowed Congress to regulate commerce, by means including the levying of tariffs on imports. Until the troubles that produced the war, tariffs were treated as tools for raising revenue, and in fact import duties were the primary source of revenue for the federal government. With revenue as the object, rates were kept low, lest customers turn away and collections fall. Things changed during the war. The trans-Atlantic dislocations caused by the conflict allowed domestic industries—iron, arms, tools, and others—to emerge. As they did so, they developed political constituencies: owners, employees, distributors, suppliers. The constituents found friends in Washington who sponsored tariff legislation based on the novel principle of protection rather than revenue. The point was to maximize not the government's income but the incomes of the interested parties. The friends of industry, forming crucial alliances with cotton and woolen producers, persuaded Congress to pass the first explicitly protective tariff in American history.

ॐ ॐ ॐ

*A*ndrew Jackson contributed nothing toward the charter of the new bank or the passage of the protective tariff, though both the bank and the tariff would figure centrally in his career as president. By contrast, actions he had already taken made him the foremost author of a development that would transform American politics and the American economy no less than the bank and the tariff did.

Since the late sixteenth century, when hostile Indians had destroyed the first English colony planted in North America (at Roanoke Island on the Carolina coast), the indigenous peoples had been the principal barrier to the westward expansion of the American colonies and the states that became their successors. By crushing the Creeks and intimidating the other tribes of the Southwest, Jackson opened large swaths of land to settlement. Almost before the British sailed away from Louisiana after the Battle of New Orleans, the migration to the Southwest began, and during the next few decades what had been Indian-controlled wilderness when Jackson and his Tennessee volunteers first marched through became the center of a burgeoning American cotton industry. The deep black soil of the Gulf coastal plain grew long-staple cotton better than almost anywhere else on earth. With the help of Eli Whitney's cotton gin, which separated cotton seeds from fiber; Robert Fulton's steamboat, which transported the cotton to market; and tens of thousands of black slaves, who planted, hoed, and harvested the cotton, the cotton farmers who followed in Jackson's footsteps became wealthy and powerful. Slavery had been an institution with a doubtful future in the late eighteenth century, as the eastern lands on which the slaves worked grew tired and unproductive. Now slavery, or rather the slaveholders, ruled a cotton kingdom with a future limited only by the slaveholders' ambitions.

*S*ome people seek danger as a way of making themselves feel alive. They scale mountains or explore jungles when they feel existence becoming mundane, as they often do. Others seek confrontation, for similar reasons. Jackson wouldn't have admitted to *seeking* confrontation. He would have said he simply stood on principle, which was where confrontation found *him*. But the number and gravity of his duels and shooting affrays, and the frequency of his ignoring and exceeding orders suggest that confrontation wasn't some side effect of a boisterous personality but the raison d'être of Jackson's spirit—at least that portion of his spirit he showed the world at large. The private Jackson—the gentle husband to Rachel, the doting father to Andrew Jr. and his foster brothers, the solicitous uncle to Rachel's kin, the patron to the junior officers who served beneath him—was another character entirely. Within the circle he defined as family—and he defined it generously—he displayed all the tenderness he had been storing up since the early demise of his childhood family. But to the rest of the world—the world of hostile Indians just beyond the fringe of settlement, of partisan Tories burning and looting his home village, of imperious British officers demanding their boots blackened or invading American soil, of feckless Spanish commandants endangering the American South by their dereliction—he was always the embattled warrior.

More than a few of his battles he brought upon himself. In early 1817 the War Department reassigned one of his engineers without sending the reassignment order through Jackson's Nashville headquarters. Jackson protested the lack of courtesy, and when Washington failed to assure him it wouldn't happen again, he commanded the officers in his division to ignore any future directives from the War Department. They must listen only to him. "There is a chain of communication that binds the military compact, which, if broken, opens the door to disobedience and disrespect and gives loose to the turbulent spirits who are ever ready to excite mutiny."

Mutiny was exactly what some of Jackson's critics saw in the headstrong general's order. Hadn't Caesar and every other military dictator come to power by tying their men more closely to themselves than to the government all had pledged to serve?

Jackson heard the criticism, at first indirectly. In August 1817 an anonymous correspondent in New York warned him against enemies in the Northeast, including Winfield Scott, who headed the First and Third military departments, based in New York. "The War Office gentry and their adherents, pensioners, and expectants have all been busy," the nameless writer asserted, "but no one (of sufficient mark for your notice) more than Major General Scott, who, I am credibly informed, goes so far as to call the order in question an act of mutiny. In this district he is the organ of Government insinuations and the supposed author of the paper enclosed"—an unsigned newspaper article critical of Jackson and his order. "Be on your guard."

Jackson confronted Scott and demanded an explanation. "I have not permitted myself for a moment to believe that the conduct ascribed to you is correct," he said, unpersuasively. "Candor, however, induces me to lay them"—the anonymous letter and the article—"before you that you may have it in your power to say how far they may be incorrectly stated."

Scott didn't appreciate being haled into Jackson's court, especially on the testimony of someone who lacked the courage or decency to give his name. He denied being the author of the critical article, but he refused to disavow the sentiments ascribed to him. He pointed out the impossible position in which Jackson's order placed his subordinates. Suppose the president ordered one of Jackson's captains to take a certain action. "If the Captain obeys, you arrest him; but if in compliance with your prohibition he sets the commands of the President at naught, he would find himself in direct conflict with the highest military authority under the Constitution." Scott hoped Jackson would reconsider his order. But in any event, he wanted nothing more to do with the affair.

Perhaps Jackson's intestinal problems were particularly severe when he received Scott's answer and responded. Had Jackson been a heavy drinker, Scott must have thought him drunk. For whatever reason, Jackson wrote Scott a letter as intemperate and abusive as anything he ever composed. Scott, Jackson said, had approached the issue "with the designs of an assassin lurking under a fair exterior. . . . Is conduct like this congenial with that high sense of dignity which should be seated in a soldier's bosom? Is it due from a brother officer to assail in the dark the reputation of another and stab him at a moment when he cannot expect it? . . . I shall not stoop, sir, to a justification of my order before you, or to notice the weakness and absurdity of your tinsel rhetoric. . . . To the intermeddling pimps and spies of the War Department, who are in the garb of gentlemen, I hold myself responsible for any grievance they may labor under on my account, with which you have my permission to number yourself."

The outbreak of the Seminole War spared Americans the absurd and unseemly prospect of a duel between two of its ranking officers. Monroe calmed Jackson, who threatened to resign over the affair, by appealing to his sense of duty. "It is my earnest desire that you remain in the service of your country," the president said. "Our affairs are not settled. . . . The Spanish government has injured us and shews no disposition to repair the injury. . . . Should we be involved in another war, I have no doubt that it will decide the fate of our free government."

Monroe's contemporaries (and historians after them) often found the Virginian unimpressive. Yet he was shrewd enough to discover Jackson's vulnerability: the incapacity of the soldier-patriot to resist a call to the service of his country. Besides, even Jackson recognized that there was more glory in thrashing Spaniards than in quarreling with Winfield Scott. But the rift between the two men persisted, and Scott joined the growing ranks of Jackson's enemies.

$\mathcal{T}$here are serious difficulties in this business, on which ever side we view it," Monroe declared in July 1818. The business the president referred to was the diplomatic furor that followed Jackson's latest Florida venture. The British were protesting the execution of Arbuthnot and Ambrister, the Spanish Jackson's entire Florida campaign. To emphasize his point that Spanish power in Florida was a dangerous sham, Jackson had recaptured Pensacola on his way back from the Suwanee River. "This is justifiable on the immutable principles of self-defence," he wrote the Spanish governor, José Masot, as he approached the town. "The Government of the United States is bound to protect her citizens, but weak would be her efforts and ineffectual the best advised measures if the Floridas are to be free to every enemy." As it happened, the governor had fled to the Barrancas, the fort that commanded the bay below the town. Receiving no answer, Jackson sent a sterner note to the acting commander at Pensacola. "I am informed that you have orders to fire on my troops entering the city. . . . I wish you to understand distinctly that if such orders are carried into effect, I will put to death every man found in arms." The commander, a mere lieutenant colonel, chose not to test Jackson's sincerity, and Jackson took the town.

Proceeding to the Barrancas, he conveyed the same message to Masot in slightly more tactful fashion. "Resistance would be a wanton sacrifice of blood. . . . You cannot expect to defend yourself successfully, and the first shot from your fort must draw down upon you the vengeance of an irritated soldiery." The governor, who had more at stake than the lieutenant colonel, insisted on contesting the American takeover, but mostly for form's sake. The battle was brief and casualties were light.

Had Jackson taken the town and marched away, as he did in 1814, the difficulties he created for Monroe would have been modest. But Jackson's earlier experience convinced him that Spain couldn't be trusted with Florida, and so he garrisoned Pensacola with American troops who, from all appearances, would remain there permanently. The Spanish were predictably outraged. Their minister at Washington, Luis de Onís, filed a protest with the State Department as soon as he heard the news. President Monroe, he insisted, must return Pensacola to Spanish control at once and punish General Jackson.

Less predictably, certain Americans agreed with the Spanish minister. Though the American people, by and large, loved Jackson, many American politicians distrusted him deeply. Some honestly worried that he had the makings of a military dictator. Others feared for the Constitution if the executive branch—whether in the person of a general or of the president— could wage war without asking Congress. Still others saw in Jackson an impediment to their own political ambitions.

This last group was well represented in Monroe's own administration. The demise of the Federalists—who put up only token resistance to Monroe's election in 1816 and wouldn't nominate anyone in 1820—didn't end national politics in America. It simply shifted politics to within the Republican party, where those men who wished to succeed Monroe were already maneuvering for advantage. William Crawford scarcely bothered to hide his ambitions, which made for tense cabinet meetings with John Quincy Adams, who *did* try to hide his ambitions but didn't succeed. John Calhoun had hopes, besides an unrecognized capacity for intrigue.

"Mr. Calhoun is extremely dissatisfied with General Jackson's proceedings in Florida," Adams remarked after a series of meetings in which Jackson and Florida provided the consistent theme. "Thinks Jackson's object was to produce a war for the sake of commanding an expedition against Mexico, and that we shall certainly have a Spanish war." The South Carolinian's sniping persisted. "Calhoun says he has heard that the court-martial at first acquitted the two Englishmen, but that Jackson sent the case back to them. . . . He says, also, that last winter there was a company formed in Tennessee, who sent Jackson's nephew to Pensacola and purchased Florida lands, and that Jackson himself is reported to be interested in the speculation."

Less from love of Jackson than from enmity toward Crawford and Calhoun, Adams became Jackson's strongest, and then only, defender in the cabinet. "The opinion is unanimously against Jackson excepting mine," Adams wrote. Calhoun continued to attack Jackson for exceeding orders. Crawford joined in, predicting dire consequences from the general's rash action. If the president didn't restore Pensacola to Spain and reprimand Jackson, Crawford said, war would result, the economy would crash, and the administration would be punished by the American electorate.

Jackson's enemies within the administration had help from without. Henry Clay had been happy for a time to bask in Jackson's triumphs. "The Eighth of January shall be remembered, and the glory of that day shall stimulate future patriots!" the House Speaker told his colleagues. But he was quick to criticize when he sensed a negative reaction to Jackson's Florida impetuousness. Clay condemned the executions of Arbuthnot and Ambrister as illegal and reprehensible, and he asserted that Jackson's Florida campaign had usurped the exclusive authority of Congress to declare war. The general's disregard for the Constitution endangered everything America stood for. "We are fighting a great moral battle for the benefit not only of our country but of all mankind. The eyes of the whole world are in fixed attention upon us." The enemies of liberty had foretold the emergence of a military despot; for Jackson to escape censure would prove them right. And it would presage the end of the American republic. "Remember that Greece had her Alexander, Rome her Caesar, England her Cromwell, France her Bonaparte. . . . If we would escape the rock on which they split, we must avoid their errors."

Leaning into the wind, Adams continued to defend Jackson. Adams may have seen Crawford and Clay as greater threats than Jackson to his succeeding Monroe. Or he may simply have believed what he said about Jackson's being right. But whatever his motives, he argued on the general's behalf with the determination Jackson later would come to dread. To the Spanish minister, Onís, the secretary of state justified Jackson's intrusion as the necessary consequence of Spain's failure to police Florida. To Albert Gallatin, his partner from the Ghent negotiations, Adams explained that

Jackson had no alternative to executing Arbuthnot and Ambrister. He couldn't hold the two men as prisoners without provoking Britain. Yet "to dismiss them with impunity would have been not only to let them loose to renew the same intrigues and machinations, but to leave their example a pernicious temptation to others to offend in like manner." A sentence short of death would have had "little or no effect upon men to whom infamy was scarcely equivalent to any punishment at all." Jackson was right: "The necessity of a signal example was urgent and indispensable."

Had Jackson been even a little repentant, he would have made Monroe's task much easier. But he saw no reason to repent. "I have destroyed the Babylon of the South, the hot bed of the Indian war and depredations on our frontier, by taking St. Marks and Pensacola," he wrote Rachel a few days after occupying the latter (and a few weeks after likening St. Marks to either Sodom or Gomorrah). He had delivered "the just vengeance of heaven, having visited and punished with death the exciters of the Indian war and horrid massacre of our innocent women and children." To Monroe he defended his course as "absolutely necessary to put down the Indian war and give peace and security to our southern frontier." His occupation of Florida sprang from the highest ideals. "In all things I have consulted public good and the safety and security of our southern frontier. I have established peace and safety, and hope the government will never yield it."

Monroe could only shake his head at his impetuous general. The Spanish minister was demanding to know whether the president had ordered Jackson's invasion of Florida; Monroe couldn't decide how to respond. He couldn't claim, in truth or politics, that he had. But to disavow and censure Jackson would make the administration look inept, besides angering the general and his many supporters. "Had General Jackson been ordered to trial," Monroe told James Madison after the fact, "I have no doubt that the interior of the country would have been much agitated, if not convulsed."

Monroe split the difference by ordering the return of the Florida forts to Spain but refusing to censure Jackson. That the president feared Jackson as much as he did the Spanish became clear from the effort Monroe made to mollify the general. "If the executive refused to evacuate the posts, especially Pensacola, it would amount to a declaration of war, to which it is incompetent," Monroe told Jackson. "It would be accused with usurping the authority of Congress and giving a deep and fatal wound to the Constitution." Publicly Monroe defended Jackson by blaming the Spanish for the anarchy they had allowed to develop in Florida. Jackson may have exceeded orders—Monroe made no secret of that—but he did little more than any conscientious field commander would have done under like circumstances. Florida had become "the theatre of every lawless adventure," the president informed Congress. "With little population of its own, the Spanish authority almost extinct and the colonial governments in a state of revolution . . . it was in a great measure derelict."

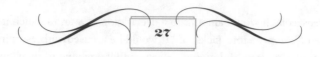

CONQUISTADOR

Spain got its forts back, but it couldn't hold the land on which they
stood. Jackson's seizure of St. Marks and Pensacola forced the Spanish
to acknowledge what had been implicit for some time: that with the
American population of Georgia and Mississippi growing rapidly and the
Spanish population of Florida growing not at all, Spain's days in Florida
were dwindling. John Quincy Adams made this point repeatedly in
discussions with Luis de Onís regarding Florida and other boundary
issues between the United States and the Spanish territory to the south
and west. Adams's strong support of Jackson signified not merely the
secretary of state's desire to frustrate his rivals for the presidency but
his appreciation of how Jackson's audacity strengthened his—
Adams's—bargaining position with Onís. What Spain couldn't defend
on the ground it couldn't well claim at the negotiating table.

Yet Adams was diplomatic enough not to leave Onís bereft. While insisting, with Jackson's aid, on having Florida, Adams gave up Texas. At the time of the Louisiana Purchase, the southwestern frontier of Louisiana remained vague. Thomas Jefferson claimed the Rio Grande, making Texas American. Spain said the border was the Sabine, making Texas Spanish. For ten years no one much bothered about Texas, as it was far from the settled regions of both Mexico and the United States and not on the way to anything important. But the war with Britain, and especially the attack on New Orleans, drew the American gaze southwestward, and after Adams assumed responsibility for the State Department, he set about reducing the uncertainty as to what was American and what wasn't. Texas remained distant and largely unpopulated (even by Indians, who had been ravaged by smallpox and other diseases), and Adams felt little compunction about swapping the American claim to Texas for Florida and Spain's claim to Oregon. Florida would pay off in the short term, rounding out the southeast. Oregon was a bet on the distant future, when the United States would require an outlet to the Pacific. Texas got lost in the middle.

*B*ut it didn't remain lost for long. The good times of the postwar period turned breathtakingly bad almost overnight just as Adams and Onís wrapped up their 1819 boundary treaty. The soaring price of cotton, which had been driving the settlement of the Gulf coastal plain, hit thirty-two cents a pound in Liverpool in 1818, but at year's end it skidded and didn't stop sliding till it broke fifteen cents going down. The American markets were granted a month's grace by the same delay that had kept Jackson fighting weeks after Ghent, yet when the first reports of the collapse hit New York and New Orleans they sent brokers and sellers into a swoon. The turmoil in commodities spread to the financial markets, which were already shaky from efforts by the new Bank of the United States to restore solidity to the currency by favoring specie—gold and silver—over paper. When the accidental deflation from the commodity dive met the deliberate deflation of the money men, American finances went into free fall.

"The years of 1819 and '20 were a period of gloom and agony," remembered Thomas Hart Benton, whose long career in the Senate featured an obsession with American finance.

> No money, either gold or silver. No paper convertible into specie. No measure, or standard of value, left remaining. . . . No price for property or produce. No sales but those of the sheriff and the marshal. No purchasers at execution sales but the creditor. . . . No employment for industry. No demand for labor. No sale for the product of the farm. . . . DISTRESS, the universal cry of the people. RELIEF, the universal demand thundered at the doors of all legislatures, state and federal.

Amid the panic, Americans did what they had always done when times got hard. They looked to the West, where land was cheap and past failure the common experience. The panic set in motion a human wave, carrying thousands of men, women, and children west. Much of the migration followed previous patterns, to the Gulf Coast territories (soon states) of Mississippi and Alabama. Another stream crossed the Mississippi into the lands of the Louisiana Purchase. Arkansas filled with settlers, then Missouri. The most adventurous—or most desperate—forsook American territory entirely. Following the lead of Moses Austin, a debt-burdened Missourian, and, after his untimely death, his son Stephen, a hardy band ventured into Texas. They weren't exactly ignoring the line John Quincy Adams had drawn between American territory and Spanish (which became Mexican territory upon Mexican independence in 1821). They knew they were leaving the United States and did so with the blessing of the Mexican government, which granted them land on which to settle. But their presence in Mexico threatened to blur the Adams line and eventually erase it.

*O*f those whom the panic didn't drive west, another group did what Americans have also habitually done when things turned bad: they went to court. The Bank of the United States was never without enemies, who included the partisans of state banks, unreconstructed Jeffersonians, and individuals damaged by the bank's contractionist policies. Legislatures of various states, including Maryland, passed laws imposing taxes on the bank's operations. The cashier of the Baltimore branch of the bank, James McCulloch, refused to pay the Maryland tax and was summoned to county court, which affirmed the state law. McCulloch appealed, and the Supreme Court agreed to hear the case.

The oral arguments took place in February 1819, just as the pillars of American finance were crashing to earth. The high court sat beneath the Capitol, not having achieved architectural independence of the legislative branch. Into its cramped hearing room crowded many who hoped to see the Bank of the United States dismembered, a separate phalanx who wished to see it vindicated, and some simply eager for the rhetorical display that could be expected whenever Daniel Webster spoke. Webster had been a Federalist in New Hampshire and a congressman from that state for two terms, but the dim future of Federalism after the War of 1812 prompted his retirement from politics. He moved from the Granite State to Boston, which afforded greater scope for a man of ability and ambition, especially in the practice of law. He made his money defending well-heeled clients and his reputation defending the poorly shod, including his alma mater, Dartmouth College. "It is, sir . . . a small college, and yet there are those who love it," he avowed in arguing that Dartmouth's charter was covered by the contract clause of the Constitution and therefore stood beyond the power of states to revise. Chief Justice John Marshall agreed, as did a majority of the court. The ruling delivered a blow against state power and a boost to the career of Webster, who turned to the McCulloch case almost before the damp handkerchiefs went back in the pockets of his listeners.

The Bank of the United States was a considerably less sympathetic client than plucky Dartmouth. Fortunately for Webster, Marshall was far beyond caring about popularity. Since defeating Jefferson in the Burr case, the chief justice had continued to bolster the judicial branch against the executive and the legislature, the federal government against the states, and property against the people. Federalists who relied on election for their paychecks had nearly all changed their tune and their stripes, but Marshall, ensconced in the court, beyond the reach of voters or competing government officials, continued to chart the course of the republic by Federalist stars.

The questions in the McCulloch case were two: whether Congress had the authority to charter the bank in the first place and whether the states had the authority to tax it. Marshall swept aside the strict constructionism of the old Republicans in answering the first question affirmatively. "Let the end be legitimate, let it be within the scope of the constitution, and all means which are appropriate, which are plainly adapted to that end, which are not prohibited but consist with the letter and spirit of the constitution, are constitutional." On the question of whether the states could tax the bank, Marshall was equally unequivocal. "The power to tax involves the power to destroy." If the states could tax the bank, they could tax—that is, destroy—any action or agency of the federal government. "This was not intended by the American people. They did not design to make their government dependent on the states."

In fact, what the American people had intended and designed in 1787 would vex the American political system for the next forty years (and, less acutely, for the century and a half after that). Marshall's saying something didn't make it so, even when the other six justices joined him, as they did in the McCulloch case. As for the bank, it lived for now, but its opponents plotted other ways to kill it.

*T*imes are dreadful here," Jackson wrote from Nashville in the summer of 1819. "Confidence entirely destroyed, specie payments suspended." Debt suits clogged the courts; barter replaced money transactions; interregional trade had almost stopped. "Eastern paper is not to be obtained here, and there is no such thing as obtaining a draft on Philadelphia or New York."

Yet Jackson could speak with relative equanimity of the effects of the panic. The postwar boom had been good to him. The rising cotton prices had allowed him to expand operations at the Hermitage and speculate in additional properties in the newly opened districts to the south. The details of the partnerships formed for the speculations were unclear to outsiders then and have remained so to historians since. Equally unclear were the profits the speculations produced. Jackson certainly made money on the boom and lost money on the bust. Whether he wound up ahead or behind on the deals is impossible to say.

But his standard of living didn't suffer. His salary as a major general in the regular army was secure, and in fact appreciated in value as prices fell.

He was sufficiently confident regarding his financial future to embark on a major construction project at the Hermitage. He had been intending for some years to replace the wooden house that came with the property when he had purchased it fifteen years before, but only got around to seeking bids about the time of the panic. The nation's bad luck, in this instance, became his good luck, for with work hard to find, contractors in the Cumberland didn't haggle on price. During the next several months the new house took shape: four rooms downstairs, four rooms up, with central hallways and high ceilings. Papered walls and carved balustrades ornamented the interior, while white columns adorned the facade. By the standards of southern gentry, the house was modest, even plain. But it stood comparison with the best in the neighborhood, as befit America's most distinguished soldier.

*H*ousing aside, Jackson adapted less well to the end of the Seminole War than he might have expected. The old physical afflictions annoyed him, as they often did when he stopped campaigning. "I reached Nashville . . . in a bad state of health, much emaciated," he wrote his nephew Andrew Jackson Donelson in July 1818. "I am still much pestered with a bad cough and pain in my left side and breast." A few weeks later he told Isaac Shelby, "My health is bad. I am much debilitated." The subsequent months brought little relief. "I was taken very ill and confined to my bed for ten days," he wrote in September 1819. Even after he managed to get up and about, he felt the effects of this and previous ailments. "My hand shakes from debility, and I cannot write with facility." Some days he didn't think he'd ever recover. "My health is gone," he told Andrew Donelson. "My constitution, I fear, will never bear up under another campaign."

On better days, though, he dreamed of fighting again. The American Senate had ratified the Adams-Onís treaty at once, but the Spanish government, beset by revolution throughout the Western Hemisphere and facing the loss of far more than Florida, balked. Jackson wasn't surprised. "I have never believed that Spain would ratify the treaty," he declared in the late summer of 1819. "I do not believe she will now." Florida might have to be conquered a third time—and the thought alone made Jackson feel better. "Were you to see how much I am emaciated," he wrote a friend, "you would scarcely believe I could ever again take the field. However, excitement has kept me alive, and it might raise me quickly to the necessary strength. I am beginning to eat with a good appetite." The prospect of war persisted for several months, restoring Jackson to a semblance of health. He couldn't understand why Congress didn't simply declare war and force Spain's hand. "Does Congress believe that it is consulting the feelings of the American nation when it is bearing with the perfidy and insults of Spain? . . . Are we thus to be humbled?" Jackson couldn't speak for the people of the East, but he knew his neighbors, and he knew they wouldn't suffer Spain to endanger, by incompetence or design, America's southern border. "Believe me, sir, the people in the West are prepared to live free or die in the last ditch. They are prepared to surrender the last cent before they will surrender their independence." For himself, he vowed to lead the army south again, this time taking more than Florida. Congress merely had to give the word. "If it will authorize the measure, Florida shall be in possession of the United States in three months . . . and if Congress should will it, with the regulars alone and the necessary equipment and naval aid, Cuba in six months."

Monroe had no desire to see Jackson loose again, and the war scare—war hope, in Jackson's case—passed when Spain ratified the treaty. Jackson was left to find his therapeutic violence vicariously. Andrew Donelson was attending the national military academy at West Point, with his uncle's partial approval. Jackson endorsed the soldier's calling but distrusted the War Department types who ran the academy. Donelson, a soul after his uncle's independent spirit, had defended a fellow cadet unfairly treated—in Donelson's view—by the academy's administration. Jackson applauded his nephew's stand for the right. "My dear nephew, I rejoice in the interest you have taken in aiding to procure redress for innocence unjustly injured. Such acts are the buds of virtue." Jackson told Donelson to watch out for himself as well. "If ever a superior forgets what he owes to you and to his station, and attempts to insult or maltreat you as has been the case with others, you have my permission to resign." Should Donelson suffer physical abuse, he had his uncle's permission—and encouragement—to retaliate in the most vigorous manner. "If the superior attempts either to strike or kick you, put him to instant death."

Donelson didn't have to kill anyone, and in fact went on to graduate from the academy second in his class. But Jackson continued to offer his protégés advice that, while honorable in spirit, was potentially lethal. John Eaton was a college man, a lawyer, a soldier under Jackson, the coauthor (with the deceased John Reid) of a Jackson biography published in 1817, and most recently senator from Tennessee. As a Jackson man he ran afoul of Andrew Erwin, another Tennessean, who had hitched his star to William Crawford. Erwin and Eaton quarreled over something minor, then something larger, till a duel seemed the only way to settle the affair. Eaton's second, Richard Call, asked Jackson for advice. Jackson didn't like Erwin, either, and provided a primer on how to kill him with honor.

> In prosecuting the business you have taken charge of for your friend Major Eaton, you must steadily keep in mind that the *man* you have to deal with is unprincipled. You will be guarded in your acts. Have every thing in writing, and hold no conversation with him unless in the presence of some confidential person of good character. He is mean and artful. It is possible, from what I think of the man, that he will propose rifles or muskets. These are not weapons of gentlemen, and cannot and ought not to be yielded to. Pistols are the universal weapons (with one solitary exception) of firearms gentlemen use. These, or swords, ought to be selected, and as neither of those concerned are in the habit of using swords, the offending party will make choice of this weapon.
>
> The next choice in the opponent is distance. Ten paces is the longest, and although the defendant may choose as far as ten paces, still if the offended is not as good a shot as the defendant, custom and justice will bring them to a distance that will put them on a perfect equality.
>
> Position: To prevent accident, let them keep their pistols suspended until after the word "fire" is given. The first rule is to let each man fire when he pleases, so that he fires one minute or two after the word. Charge your friend to preserve his fire, keeping his teeth *firmly* clenched, and his fingers in a position that if fired on and hit, his fire may not be extorted. Some times when the distance is long it is agreed that both or either may advance and fire. If this

arrangement is made, charge your friend to preserve his fire until he shoots his antagonist through the *brain*, for if he fires and does not kill his antagonist, he leaves himself fully in his power.

Jackson suspected that Erwin's animus was actually against him rather than against Eaton. He also believed that Erwin was a coward who might try to evade the duel with Eaton by declaring that he really wanted to challenge Jackson. "He may think that I will have nothing to do with him, and in this way get off." Jackson advised calling Erwin's bluff. "I charge you agree on my part without hesitation. He is a man I cannot challenge, but if a villain will run from one danger and hold out ideas of bravery, they ought always to be taken in." Jackson went so far as to specify terms of combat. "At seven feet, placed back to back, pistols suspended until after the word 'fire.' . . . I will soon put an end to this troublesome scoundrel. . . . If my pistol fires, I kill him."

*N*othing came of this, either. Erwin, Eaton, and their seconds found a formula that spared both body and spirit. Jackson was disappointed, partly for missing the thrill of another duel but mostly that Erwin remained alive to act as cat's paw for William Crawford. The bad blood between Jackson and Crawford antedated the Florida war, of course, but that conflict provided the Georgian a fresh opportunity to attack the general. Crawford likely believed most of the vicious things he said about Jackson, but he also aimed to keep Jackson from becoming the successor to Monroe. Conceivably Crawford hoped to undermine Monroe himself, to put the presidency into play as early as 1820. This was a trickier maneuver, at least as long as Crawford remained in the administration. How could he bring the administration down without being caught in the rubble? It was hard to say, but those who knew him didn't put the effort past him.

Jackson prepared to defend himself, in part by defending Monroe. "I am not insensible of the implacable hostility of Mr. Crawford towards me," he wrote Monroe in November 1818. "Nor have I any doubt of his hostility to you." Jackson suggested that Crawford had deliberately scrambled communications regarding the operations in Florida. "In this he would have the double object of injuring both you and myself in the estimation of our country. . . . To accomplish an object so desirable to himself and his colleagues, the injury, nay the *ruin*, of his country would interpose no barrier."

In January 1819 Jackson traveled to Washington to report on the Florida campaign and confront his accusers. Henry Clay had just given a long, critical speech to the House. "The combination formed was more extensive than I calculated on," Jackson observed, citing "Mr. Clay's anxiety to crush the executive through me." But Jackson was pleased to note that Clay's efforts were failing. "The whole Kentucky delegation except Clay, I am told, goes with me, and Clay is politically damned." A week later he wrote Rachel, "The insidious Mr. Clay will sink into that insignificance that all those who abandon principle and justice and would sacrifice their country for self-aggrandizement ought and will experience."

After Clay's attempt to sanction Jackson came to nothing in the House, criticism of the general shifted to the Senate. A committee stacked with Crawford allies conducted an investigation and filed a report condemning the invasion of Florida in general and Jackson's execution of Arbuthnot and Ambrister in particular. The report intimated that Jackson had speculative interests in Pensacola—despite explicit contradictions by other participants in the alleged scheme—and that these, not a concern for national defense, motivated his seizure of that town.

Jackson naturally bridled at the report. He grew angrier on hearing rumors—exaggerated but not wholly without basis—that Crawford was its actual author. As the battle lines were drawn, each side arranged its forces. Crawford and Clay brought Thomas Cobb, a congressman from Georgia, and others annoyed, affronted, or threatened by Jackson into open and covert alliance against the Tennessee general. Jackson's friends rallied around him. Willie Blount thought anyone who couldn't see the merits of the Florida campaign didn't warrant notice. "What poor minded bitches are Messrs. Cobb and Clay," Blount wrote Jackson. "You have the people and the Government on your side. . . . The Floridas are at last ours." John Clark was a Georgian who liked Crawford as little as Jackson did. Clark said he had intelligence linking some of Crawford's associates—including Andrew Erwin—to a slave-smuggling scheme, and he offered to share that intelligence with the world. Jackson was delighted. "I am happy to be informed that you are preparing a publication that will give to the world a full portrait of Mr. Wm. H. Crawford. If the painting is well drawn, from my own knowledge of the man, it will portray hypocrisy surrounded with all its horrid deformity, depravity, and baseness of human character."

Lacking military enemies for the first time in nearly a decade, Jackson took comfort in his political foes. For months he spoke of Crawford, Clay, and Cobb as an unholy cabal. "Having laboured from my youth to establish a character founded upon uprightness of conduct . . . ," he told a supporter, "the only solicitude I had upon the subject was that I should not be deprived of that character by the falsehood of a conspiracy formed by designing demagogues, of which I found William H. Crawford the chief, surrounded by his minions, Clay, Cobb, and company, who he wielded with the dexterity that a shewman does his puppets, to exalt himself by prostrating the executive through me and thereby raise himself to the Presidential chair."

As of early 1820 their efforts had failed. Monroe seemed to have secured his renomination. Jackson reveled in his enemies' discomfiture. *"Like Lucifer they have politically fallen, never to rise again,"* he said.

*H*e spoke too soon—much too soon. Jackson's grasp of national politics didn't yet match his grasp of military strategy, and his indirect acquaintance with his principal rivals left him unable to appreciate the full extent of their gifts and their guile.

The gifts and guile of Henry Clay became apparent to the world in the months that followed Jackson's forecast of his Luciferian fall. By 1820 Missouri had passed the sixty-thousand-person threshold for statehood, and its inhabitants clamored for the recognition and self-government statehood conveyed. But larger issues intruded. By now the population of the North exceeded that of the South, and the disparity seemed certain to grow. This meant that the preservation of southern interests depended on the Senate, where the southern states still balanced the northern. Foremost of the southern interests—or the one, at any rate, that most clearly distinguished the South from the North—was slavery. The Ordinance of 1787 still barred slavery from the Northwest, leaving the trans-Mississippi region—the Louisiana Purchase—as the hope for slavery's future. The state of Louisiana had been admitted to the Union with slavery inherited from its French and Spanish days. But not till after the War of 1812 did any other district beyond the Mississippi possess the population to qualify for statehood. Missouri seemed a harbinger of the fate of the West.

It also seemed a harbinger of the fate of the Union. Till now the North had acquiesced in the adoption of slavery by new states Kentucky, Tennessee, Mississippi, and Alabama. But each of those states had been created in territory that belonged to the Union at the end of the Revolutionary War, territory that seemed a natural extension of the southern states to their east. That Kentucky had been part of Virginia and Tennessee part of North Carolina simply reinforced the idea that the Southwest belonged to the South and slavery, just as the Northwest belonged to the North and freedom. The Louisiana Purchase was different, having been acquired after independence by the nation as a whole. Little could be done about the neighborhood of New Orleans and the exotics who lived there, but the rest of the purchase was virgin country, a tabula rasa upon which republican values might be inscribed at the dawn of the region's political life.

So thought James Tallmadge, at least. The New York congressman proposed to admit Missouri, which as a territory allowed slavery, on condition that she gradually free her slaves. The Tallmadge amendment produced applause among northerners, who wished to see the new West free and perceived this as a comparatively painless step in that direction.

The reaction in the South was quite different. A generation earlier, many in the South had perceived slavery as dying, and by no means did all of these expect to mourn its demise. But the cotton boom made slavery a much bigger issue economically than it had been. Whole states were settled on the premise that slaves would be available to tend the cotton. Their masters weren't the aristocracy of the Chesapeake or the Carolina coast, who owned their land clear and might have absorbed the shock of shifting from bound labor to free. The new planters were often speculators juggling debts that would crush them should anything shake the system they had inherited. These were the hard men of the frontier, men in the mold of Andrew Jackson. Even if they had suffered pangs of conscience for their slaves—and few seem to have suffered any more than Jackson did—they couldn't have afforded the remedy.

Southerners read the Tallmadge amendment as foretelling the future not of Missouri alone but of the South. And it was a future—of creeping manumission, of the destruction of the southern way of life—they could not accept. Thomas Cobb of Georgia glared at Tallmadge and vowed, "If you persist, the Union will be dissolved. . . . You have kindled a fire which all the waters of the ocean cannot put out, which seas of blood can only extinguish."

Till now Tallmadge had denied wanting to extend his Missouri principle to the South. "I would in no manner intermeddle with the slaveholding States, nor attempt manumission in any of the original States in the Union," he avowed. But under Cobb's cross-examination he abandoned his diffidence. "Sir, if a dissolution of the Union must take place, let it be so! If civil war, which gentlemen so much threaten, must come, I can only say, let it come!"

Into the arena strode Henry Clay. The House Speaker had been hinting at retirement. He owed more money than he could ever repay on a congressman's salary—which placed him in much the same predicament as many of those new planters who couldn't afford to free their slaves. "No man is more sensible of the evils of slavery than I am, nor regrets them more," he wrote a friend. "Were I the citizen of a State in which it was not tolerated, I would certainly oppose its introduction with all the force and energy in my power." But Kentucky was a slave state, and Clay a slave owner—besides being a politician. And the fact of his owning slaves gave him standing among other slave owners that northern politicians lacked. When the Missouri question grew virulent, Clay put off his return to the private practice of law in order to shape a statute that might hold the Union together in the face of threats like those of Cobb and Tallmadge.

There was no stopping the Tallmadge amendment in the House, where it passed on a sectional vote. The fight then moved to the Senate—as every fight on slavery during the next forty years eventually would. The South stood firm, blocking the amendment and keeping Missouri in limbo. It would have remained in limbo had Senate moderates not linked Missouri's admission to that of Maine, which had voted to secede from Massachusetts and form a—free—state of its own. House hardliners rejected the Senate package, leading Clay to propose a joint committee to resolve the differences. After his proposal was accepted, he packed the committee with compromisers like himself. The committee's report wrapped endorsement of the Senate bill in a promise of separate votes on each part of the package, which by now included a ban on slavery in the rest of the Louisiana Purchase north of the line of latitude at 36 degrees 30 minutes. Legislative amateurs wondered what Clay was doing. The enemies of compromise, they said, would divide and conquer. But the professional politicians understood: Clay's maneuver allowed his colleagues to vote their consciences on parts of the package and conciliation on the rest. By finagling the majorities, he'd get the compromise through, and they'd preserve their bona fides for constituents back home.

The result was a triumph of the legislative art. The Missouri Compromise averted the civil war of which Cobb, Tallmadge, and the hotheads spoke. It extended the line between North and South across the Mississippi. And it made Clay's reputation as a man who could transcend section in the interest of the Union.

It would be years before Jackson appreciated that he and Clay were on the same side of the great political issue of their era. This was Jackson's fault, for misjudging Clay, but also the fault of the times. Nationalism and sectionalism had long struggled for supremacy in American politics, but in the 1820s the orientation of the two ideas was shifting. For most of Jackson's political life, the primary sectional division had been East versus West, and the principal chore of American nationalists was to keep the West from drifting away down the Mississippi. Jackson's victory at New Orleans secured the West for the Union but in doing so let the divisions between North and South take precedence. The Missouri question wouldn't have arisen without the security afforded by the defeat of the British and the Indians, which allowed Americans to cross the Mississippi in large numbers. Yet, having arisen, it signaled that the differences between North and South might be even deeper than those between East and West had been. Thomas Jefferson heard the Missouri debate as a "firebell in the night." But Jefferson, who had promised equality to America and the world, suffered from a peculiarly bad conscience on slavery and therefore from particularly acute hearing. Less sensitive souls—like Andrew Jackson—were slower to recognize the new axis of danger to the Union for what it turned out to be.

𝒫ensacola is a perfect plain," Rachel Jackson wrote from the Florida capital to a friend back home in Nashville. "The land nearly as white as flour, yet productive of fine peach trees, oranges in abundance, grapes, figs, pomegranates, etc., etc. Fine flowers growing spontaneously. . . . The town is immediately on the bay. The most beautiful water prospect I ever saw; and from ten o'clock in the morning until ten at night we have the finest sea breeze. There is something in it so exhilarating, so pure, so wholesome, it enlivens the whole system."

Rachel had come south with her husband for the transfer of authority in Florida from Spain to the United States. Monroe—who had been reelected in 1820 in the only uncontested presidential race in American history—needed someone of stature to supervise the transfer, and Jackson was a natural, for one obvious reason and one not so obvious. The obvious reason was that the conqueror of Florida should accept the surrender. Jackson's many supporters expected as much. Monroe had gone to great lengths to keep the general happy, and this was an inexpensive way to continue doing so.

The less obvious reason was that Jackson had to be retired from the army. Congress had mandated the army's shrinking. Some of the shrinkers were avowed anti-Jacksonians who calculated that a smaller army would have no place, or perhaps merely no appeal, for Jackson. Others were simply acting in the American tradition of disbanding the army between wars, lest it eat out the people's means. Whatever the motives of the legislators, the new army would have room for one major general only, and Jacob Brown enjoyed seniority over Jackson. Monroe didn't relish having to force Jackson out, but he had no choice.

Florida enabled both men to save face. The territory required a governor, and Jackson knew it well. If his administrative temperament left something to be desired—the general's handling of martial law in New Orleans still roiled memories in the Crescent City—Monroe comforted himself that

Jackson probably wouldn't remain in Florida long. Careful soundings indicated that Jackson was willing to treat the Florida assignment as a victory tour. He would haul down the Spanish flag, raise the American flag, and go quietly into private life.

Jackson and Rachel traveled from Nashville to New Orleans in the latest style, aboard a river steamboat. From New Orleans they sailed to Pensacola, arriving at their destination in the early summer of 1821. The Spanish obviously hadn't been keeping the place up. "All the houses look in ruins, old as time," Rachel wrote her friend. "Many squares of the town appear grown over with the thickest shrubs, weeping willows, and the Pride of China. All look neglected." The people were a remarkable assortment. "The inhabitants all speak Spanish and French. Some speak four or five languages. Such a mixed multitude you, nor any of us, ever had an idea of. There are fewer white people far than any other, mixed with all nations under the canopy of heaven."

At Pensacola, Rachel and the locals witnessed the last days of Spanish rule in Florida. "Three weeks the transports were bringing the troops from St. Marks in order that they should all sail to Cuba at the same time," she recounted. Jackson remained outside the city during this period, communicating with the Spanish governor, José Maria Callava, by note. Rachel and some of the American officers tried to talk him into town, but he refused to enter till the transfer became official. "He said that when he came in, it should be under his own standard, and that would be the third time he had planted that flag on that wall." So he waited, with his small entourage. "At length, last Tuesday was the day. At seven o'clock, at the precise moment, they hove in view under the American flag and a full band of music. The whole town was in motion. . . . They marched by to the government house, where the two Generals met in the manner prescribed. Then his Catholic majesty's flag was lowered, and the American hoisted high in air, not less than one hundred feet."

It was with great satisfaction that Jackson accepted the surrender from Colonel Callava. "Yesterday I received possession of this place with the whole of West Florida and its dependencies," he wrote John Coffee. "I will have the pleasure to be enabled to lay the foundation of permanent happiness to the people and lasting prosperity to the city." And then, for himself, sweet freedom from public life. "I am contented that this will terminate my political career, and that I will have the pleasure to see you at your house in all the month of October next, fully satisfied with the Hermitage to spend the rest of my days."

*Y*et Jackson's hair-trigger sense of propriety kept him from leaving Florida quietly. Even after the formal transfer of authority, closing the Spanish accounts required considerable back-and-forth between Jackson and Callava, neither of whom was suited to the task. Jackson distrusted the Spanish and despised bureaucratic detail; Callava scorned Americans and resented their disregard for international law. It didn't help that Jackson spoke no Spanish and Callava no English. They depended on others to translate and interpret, and this dependence injected a note of uncertainty into their communications. From uncertainty to suspicion was a short step.

The origins of the explosion between the two were innocuous, almost ludicrously so. A woman resident of Pensacola filed a lawsuit involving an inheritance of land near the town. To make her case she required access to papers in the possession of Callava's subordinate, Domingo Sousa. She applied to Henry Brackenridge, whom Jackson had just appointed alcalde, or mayor. The request seemed reasonable to Brackenridge, and he carried it to Jackson, who agreed. Jackson sent Brackenridge and two helpers to Sousa to fetch the papers. Sousa declined to surrender them, saying he worked for Callava and couldn't turn anything over without an order from the colonel.

Brackenridge and the others returned to Jackson's office. Jackson's anger began to rise as he heard their story. The Spanish, he judged, were playing their games once more. Spanish authority—including Callava's over Sousa—had terminated with the transfer of authority. The only one who gave orders in Florida now was American governor Jackson. He ordered Sousa arrested and the papers seized. Jackson's men attempted to carry out the order, but by the time they got back to Sousa's, he had given the papers to Callava's steward, Antoine Fullarat. Upon his arrest and interrogation, Sousa told Jackson what he had done. Jackson became convinced that he was being played for a fool.

He sent Sousa under guard to Callava's to retrieve the papers. En route the group discovered Callava having dinner with several Spanish officers, some Americans, and their wives. Sousa and his guards entered the dining room, where Sousa explained his predicament. Callava said he'd handle it, and dispatched an aide to Jackson, requesting a written application for the papers. Callava seems at this point to have been inclined to surrender the papers. He just needed the paperwork to show his own superiors.

Jackson's day had been a long one, his bowels had been griping, and he was looking forward to bed. But Callava's insistence on a written request banished thoughts of sleep even as they twisted his guts the more. Would there be no end to Spanish procrastination? Now he ordered Callava to turn over the papers. "It is further ordered," he continued, "that if the said late Governor Don José Callava or his steward Fullarat, when the above described papers are demanded of them, should fail or refuse to deliver the same, that the said Don José Callava and his steward Fullarat be forthwith brought before me at my office, then and there to answer such interrogatories as may be put to them."

Callava had digestive trouble of his own, which the confrontation with Jackson wasn't improving. He left the dinner party early. He was at home when a company of American soldiers arrived to carry out Jackson's order. Accounts of the confrontation that ensued differed, reflecting the prejudices, allegiances, and native languages of those involved. An American colonel described Callava as belligerent in words, albeit less so in deed. "Colonel Callava repeatedly asserted that he would not be taken out of his house alive, but he seemed to act without much difficulty when the guard was ordered to prime and load." Callava considered the Americans abusive. "A party of troops, with the commissioners, assaulted the house, breaking the fence (notwithstanding the door was open), and the commissioners entered my apartment," he testified. "They surrounded my bed with soldiers with drawn bayonets in their hands. They removed the mosquito net; they made me sit up, and demanded *the papers, or they would use the arms against my person.*"

Callava was taken to Jackson's office. The American general's temper had burned to the nub. The Spanish colonel's wasn't much longer. The two shouted at each other, Jackson in English, Callava in Spanish, with the interpreters vainly trying to keep up and pondering, on the fly, how literally to render the insults. A Spanish officer present described Jackson as beside himself. "The Governor, Don Andrew Jackson, with turbulent and violent actions, with disjointed reasonings, blows on the table, his mouth foaming, and possessed of the furies, told the Spanish commissary to deliver the papers." Callava refused, according to Jackson out of "pompous arrogance and ignorance." Jackson ordered Callava imprisoned. Callava, hearing the translation, called the order unjust and dishonorable. "Rising to his feet," recalled the Spanish officer present, "he addressed himself to the secretary, whom the Governor kept on his right hand, and said, in a loud voice, that he protested solemnly, before the government of the United States, against the author of the violations of justice against his person and public character. The Governor, Don Andrew Jackson, answered to the protest that for his actions he was responsible to no other than to his government, and that it was of little importance to him whatever might be the result, and that he might even protest before God himself."

Callava was still in detention the next day when Jackson's men seized the papers from his house. The matter might have ended there had not an American judge, recently appointed to the territory, been found to serve Jackson a writ of habeas corpus regarding Callava. Jackson ignored the writ, telling the judge, Eligius Fromentin, that it deserved nothing but "indignation and contempt."

The whole affair made Jackson more enemies. Callava sailed away, mooting Fromentin's habeas writ, but the judge remained behind to spread lurid stories of Jackson's uncontrollable ambition. "The first time the authority of General Jackson is contested," Fromentin predicted, "I should not be surprised if, to all the pompous titles by him enumerated in his order to me, he should superadd that of grand inquisitor, and if, finding in my library many books formerly prohibited in Spain, and among others the Constitution of the United States, he should send me to the stake."

Jackson brushed the carping aside. He had worked too long securing America's southern border to let the scruples of a foolish judge diminish the satisfaction he felt on finally achieving his goal. He had fought Indians on the frontier, the British at New Orleans, and the Spanish in Florida, all to preserve the American way of life—in his part of the country, at least. At last his work was done. If personal enemies were the price of American liberty, he was happy to strike the bargain.

The

People's

President

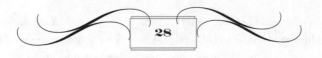

28

CINCINNATUS

"Our place looks like it had been deserted for a season, but we have a cheerful fire for our friends and a prospect of living at it for the balance of our lives," Jackson wrote upon his and Rachel's return to Nashville. Jackson was fifty-four, and Rachel the same age. His health was neither good nor improving, and he was already considerably older than his parents had been at the times of their deaths. He had little reason to expect many more years of life, and every reason to hope to spend those in the bosom of his home and family. His conscience had chronically nagged him regarding Rachel, who suffered, not always in silence, during his long departures. When his country called—when the Indians or British or Spanish threatened—he could justify placing duty to country above his duty to Rachel. But lesser chores—the administration of Florida, for example—he could leave to others. "I am truly wearied of public life," he wrote Monroe in tendering his resignation from the governorship. "I want rest, and my private concerns imperiously demand my attention. . . . My duties have been laborious and my situation exposed me to heavy expense, which makes it more necessary that I should retire to resuscitate my declining fortune to enable it to support me in my declining years."

Domestic life didn't improve his health. As before, the richer food of home aggravated his digestive troubles, and the absence of pressing responsibilities allowed him to focus on how bad he was feeling. "For four months I have been oppressed with a violent cough and costiveness," he wrote James Gadsden in the spring of 1822. Gadsden had suggested a tour of the North and East, to keep the general's name before the public and to allow his cordial presence to allay concerns about his martial past. Jackson said his health wouldn't allow it. "I have been recently visited by my old bowel complaint, which has weakened me very much, having a constant flow, in the last twelve hours, upwards of twenty passages." Of late his lungs had improved but were far from clear. "I continue to throw up great quantities of phlegm." He wrote to Monroe, "My health is not good, nor have I much hope of regaining it. Retirement and ease may prolong my life, but I fear never can restore my broken constitution."

Jackson's finances were healthier than his body, but not by much. A second reason compelling him to decline Gadsden's offer of a northern tour was a kink in his finances. Especially after the panic of 1819, the western states were like a separate country from the East with respect to the money supply. In the summer of 1822 the exchange rate between West and East— that is, the discount demanded for notes drawn on western banks—distinctly disadvantaged the former. "The state of our paper money would preclude the possibility of procuring Eastern funds"—which he would require to travel in the East—"without a great sacrifice," Jackson told Gadsden. In regular letters to Andrew Donelson, he warned his nephew to mind expenses. He had sent the young man some money but might not be able to send much more. "I remitted you two hundred dollars, one hundred in each letter, Nashville paper, which I hope has reached you and which will cover your present wants. It will at all times afford me pleasure to remit to you such sums as will be necessary to finish your education. But, my young friend, you must now reflect that I have no means by which I can be in the

receipt of money but from the product of my farm or the sale of my negroes. I name this to you that you may adopt economy . . . that your expences may be within my means."

The product of the Hermitage was chiefly cotton and corn. The corn
fed the slaves and the livestock; the cotton went to market. Like every other
commercial farmer, Jackson watched the price of his market crop as closely
as he watched the weather. It fluctuated wildly, sometimes doubling or halv-
ing within months. He was better off in this respect than producers of such
perishable crops as wheat, for if the cotton price fell too far he could store
his bales and hope for better. But storage cost money, and he couldn't pay
his bills with warehoused cotton. The coming of the steamboat improved
transportation and communication in the West, but distance from markets
remained a problem. During the autumn of 1822 Jackson asked his agents in
New Orleans about the market there. "The very best selections from choice
prime Louisiana cotton will not command over 14 or 14½ cents," they said.
Tennessee cotton couldn't expect to do that well. "The prime and best put
of the new crop would not now (if in market) command over 10 cents . . .
and common crops not more than from 6 to 8 cents."

Jackson's operation was modest as cotton farms went. The acreage he
had in cotton varied from year to year, as did the yield. But in 1825, a fairly
typical year, he planted 131 acres and harvested 71 bales of about five hundred pounds of cleaned, deseeded cotton each. Which was to say, of course,
that Jackson's slaves planted those acres and harvested those bales. An inventory at the beginning of 1825 counted eighty slaves at the Hermitage. All
lived with their families: some large ("Tom, wife, and nine children," "Old
Sampson, wife, and nine children"), some small ("Polydore, wife, and two
children," "Big Sampson, wife, and child"). Seven were over fifty years of
age (and hence not taxable, which was why their ages were recorded), and
thirty-two were under thirteen (same reason).

Most of Jackson's slaves accepted their lot without complaint that rose
to the level of his notice. Successful resistance to the will of a master was
next to impossible in Jackson's part of the country. A slave might escape supervision momentarily but, so far from foreign or free territory, couldn't expect to elude capture for long. Gilbert was a slave brought to Tennessee
from the East in 1820 or 1821. Jackson purchased him at about that time and
installed him on a plantation he had purchased in Alabama, which he called

the Big Spring farm. Gilbert married a woman from the area but in April 1822 ran away. "If he has left the neighborhood of his wife," Jackson conjectured to Egbert Harris, who had just been given responsibility for managing the Big Spring place, "he has attempted to go back to Carolina or Virginia, from whence he was brought." Jackson told Harris to print notices of the escape in the surrounding papers. "I still hope he is lurking about his wife's house." Jackson assumed Gilbert would be captured, and he told Harris what to do when he was. "If he can be got, I wish him well secured with irons until an opportunity may offer to send him down the river, as I will not keep a negro in the habit of running away." Jackson went on to explain his philosophy of disciplining slaves. "My dear sir, although you will find some of my negroes at first hard to manage, still I hope you will be able to govern them without much difficulty. I have only to say, you know my disposition, and as far as lenity can be extended to these unfortunate creatures, I wish you to do so." But lenity supposed obedience. "Subordination must be obtained first, and then good treatment."

(As it happened, Jackson didn't sell Gilbert down the river, despite at least two more escapes. But after the third flight and apprehension, in 1827, the desperate bondsman resisted the whipping Jackson's overseer, Ira Walton, attempted to administer, and was killed. Jackson's political rivals argued that Gilbert's death revealed Jackson's cruelty as a master. Most of that majority which voted for Jackson in 1828 apparently judged it no worse than a regrettable incident in an imperfect world.)

Like every other farmer, Jackson complained about the weather. It was either too dry or too wet. "I regret the drought with you," he wrote one summer to John Coffee, his old comrade in arms and currently fellow farmer. But in the same sentence he declared, "It has rained constantly here since my return. Cumberland up, and also Stone's River, and the fodder much injured by the continued rains."

Bad weather made the crops vulnerable to pests. Sometimes the damage occurred almost overnight. "I had sat down to write you about two weeks ago," Jackson told Coffee in May 1823. "I commenced my letter with the information of my fine prospect of my cotton crop. This was on Saturday. Whilst writing I was interrupted by company who remained with me until Tuesday, which days were cool and cloudy. I resumed my letter on Tuesday, but thought before I would conclude my flattering prospects of a cotton crop I would view it. . . . I never saw such ravages committed as had been on my cotton for those three days." The culprit was a worm that feasted on the new leaves. Fortunately the pests hadn't killed the crop, which was recovering slowly. Jackson added that his corn was knee high but was attracting pests of its own. "The crows, squirrels, and pigeons has been very bad."

Yet for all the troubles, Jackson got the Hermitage in a condition that caught the attention of the neighbors. Willie Blount visited Jackson and described to a friend what he saw.

Although I have ever considered him to be among the most industrious men of my acquaintance, both in public and private life, I was really surprised to find his farm in such excellent order, and so very productive, under all circumstances relating to his absence from home, attending the public relations during the late war and since. His farming land is, as you know, very fertile, very beautiful, and eligibly situated for comfort. It is largely improved, handsomely arranged with gratifying appearance to the visitors at his most hospitable house, open to all who have the pleasure of his acquaintance, and who travel through his neighborhood, none of whom pass that way without calling on him for social intercourse, viewing him to be the polite gentleman at home and abroad and the friend of man everywhere. His every arrangement for farming on an extensive scale delights the man of observation; his fields are extensive and nicely cultivated as a garden; his meadows and pastures are extensive and neatly kept; his stock of horses, cattle, sheep, and hogs are of the best kind, and all in excellent order.

*B*ut Jackson's supporters wouldn't let him tend his farm in peace. "The subject of the next President has, as you will perceive, been agitated in our papers," James Gadsden wrote from Washington. "Crawford's friends are intriguing deeply and in some quarters with success." Gadsden shared Jackson's opinion of Crawford. "To elevate him to the Presidential chair will produce a chain of evils and entail a series of misfortunes on our country that will require a century to remedy." The current alternative to the secretary of the Treasury, at least in the thinking of most Washington observers, was the secretary of state. Gadsden wasn't hopeful. "Mr. Adams' friends are not so active, and even the quarter from whence he should expect support appear lukewarm." New Yorkers were touting their governor, De Witt Clinton—vainly, Gadsden judged. "Mr. Clinton stands no chance; excepting his immediate party, he is execrated by a large majority of the community."

Gadsden was reporting in this letter, yet he was also inquiring. "I know not your opinions as to who should be the next President, but believe you agree with me as to the total unfitness as to a certain aspiring personage"— that is, Crawford. "If in this case you deem me worthy of your confidence, you will give me your views on the subject. You will appreciate my motives on this request: The good of our country requires that all honest men, who are in favour of a settled policy for the administration of our government, characterised by honest independence and a freedom from intrigue, should unite in elevating to the Presidency the man who will be governed accordingly." Gadsden suggested no candidate for Jackson's endorsement, but he reiterated that the man with the current advantage was definitely *not* what America needed. "Mr. Crawford is and has even been a most dangerous and unsettled politician."

Gadsden knew Jackson well enough to understand his former commander's psychology. Jackson could be formidable in support of a person or cause, but he was absolutely ferocious in opposition to something or especially someone. As subsequent letters and actions showed, Gadsden wanted Jackson to enter the race. Like many—probably most—others who had served under Jackson, he thought Jackson would make a better president than the scamps, scoundrels, and incompetents who currently held the seats of power in Washington. He admired Jackson's integrity and devotion to the public good. And he realized that the way to get Jackson into the race was to suggest that if he stayed out, Crawford would win.

At this point—November 1821—few people took a Jackson candidacy seriously. Loyalists like Edward Livingston had been praising him since the Battle of New Orleans. And opponents like Crawford and Clay were worried enough to set backfires against him. But no one like Jackson had ever been elected, or even nominated for the presidency. George Washington was the model Jackson's supporters cited: the hero soldier who led his country through war to the promised land of peace and independence. But Washington was far more than a soldier. He was the most eminent citizen of the most populous state and had been at the forefront of national politics since before the Revolution. As president of the constitutional convention of 1787, Washington oversaw the creation of the federal government under which he was then elected. The other presidents had all been insiders, groomed by their years of service to their predecessors. Since Jefferson, they had all been secretaries of state.

There were reasons for this political habit. In an age when news traveled slowly, and people still more so, a national reputation generally took years to cultivate. And it was most easily cultivated through the existing institutions of government. The men who came to the national capital from the several states got to know one another and to know those who held executive office. They formed impressions of one another and took those impressions home to their states, where their acquaintances in the state legislatures chose the electors who actually chose the president.

In part because of this personalized form of politics, political parties had come to play a very large role in the filtering of candidates. Indeed, since the self-destruction of the Federalists, the Republican party had essentially dictated the choice of president. Did James Monroe command support among the people at large? No one knew or much cared. He had the support of leading Republicans, which was all that mattered for twice becoming president.

Moreover, the Republican leadership was construed in a specific way: as the Republican caucus in Congress. Republicans in the states might be consulted, but they had no formal role in the winnowing process. To gain the nomination required the support of the Republicans in Washington.

Yet in the early 1820s there were signs of change. Westerners had never liked the clubbiness of the caucus system, which had the effect—and the intent—of keeping an eastern hold on the federal government. As the population moved west, more western states entered the Union, with the result that western views had to be taken into account. And the western states typically entered with fewer restrictions on voting than the eastern states imposed. Several endorsed the idea that voters—rather than the state legislatures—should choose the electors who chose the president. The result was that for the first time a westerner, and a man popular with the people even if not beloved of the party, might become president.

If Jackson dreamed of the presidency at this time, he kept his dreams to himself. He didn't tell Rachel, who liked having her husband home and certainly would have objected. He didn't tell Gadsden or various other correspondents, who would have spread the word quickly. Quite possibly he had no such dreams. He had little reason to think he was especially qualified for the presidency. His brief career in elective politics—as representative and senator from Tennessee—had convinced him that most of what Congress did was a waste of time. He might have fancied himself a capable commander in chief, but there was no war and none threatened, effectively eliminating most of that part of the president's job. For the rest of what presidents did—the distribution of patronage, dealing with Congress, administering the government—he had neither patience nor expertise.

In fact, by all evidence he did *not* want to be president. For habitual politicians, the presidency was a natural goal, the top rung on the ladder of ambition. But for a soldier, a general used to giving orders and having them obeyed—or seeing the disobedient imprisoned or executed—the presidency wasn't such an obvious prize. Presidents couldn't order Congress around, and they couldn't have recalcitrant civil servants shot. The pay was good, but the expenses of the office ate up the salary and more. Jackson had just got the Hermitage into shape; to leave it for four years or eight would require redoing all the work he had done—except that he would be that much older.

The age question raised the health issue. Jackson didn't expect to live a great deal longer. His family history argued against it, as did his personal medical history. He didn't know what made him sick; no one did. But people with such varied and serious ailments as afflicted him rarely lived to an old age. He counted himself lucky to have reached fifty-four. If he were still a gambling man, he wouldn't have bet on reaching sixty. Could he justify devoting his last years to public life, instead of to Rachel and the boys?

Could he risk running down the Hermitage, which was the only inheritance he would leave her or them?

These weren't easy questions. But there was one answer that fit them all, if only he could be persuaded to see things from a particular perspective. If the presidency could be cast as a duty rather than chiefly an honor, then it became, paradoxically, more attractive to him. The old soldier in Jackson couldn't help answering a call to duty. He had risked his life and broken his health defending America and the ideas of liberty and self-government on which it rested. If he could be persuaded that American liberty and self-government were under threat from ignoble and scheming politicians—as they had been under threat from the British and Spanish and Indians—then he would have no choice but to make himself available.

*M*aybe Gadsden and Jackson's other supporters calculatingly employed the duty argument against him. More likely they simply believed it themselves. In politics perhaps more than in most other arenas of human endeavor, interests and convictions tend to coincide. Whether convictions produce interests, or interests convictions, differs from person to person. But whatever their genesis, convictions and interests almost invariably end up pointing in the same direction. Those who can't master the coincidence don't succeed in politics, and they leave the game to those who can.

During most of the three years from the autumn of 1821 to the autumn of 1824, Jackson's supporters strove to convince him that the fate of the nation hung on his foiling the schemes of Crawford and Clay. Jackson didn't require much convincing that Crawford, especially, had to be stopped. "As to William Crawford," Jackson told Gadsden in December 1821, "I would support the Devil first." The following May he told James Bronaugh, another strong supporter at Washington, "I believe the welfare of our country in a great measure depends on thwarting the views of those who wish to bring William H. Crawford into the Presidential chair."

But from this belief to the conclusion that *he* had to do the thwarting was a larger step and required more time. Jackson initially hoped that Adams or Calhoun would block Crawford. "You know my private opinion of Mr. Adams' talents, virtue, and integrity," he told Gadsden. "I think him a man of the first rate mind of any in America as a civilian and a scholar, and I have never doubted of his attachment to our republican Government." The only potential candidate who impressed Jackson as much as Adams did was Calhoun. "I have always believed Mr. Calhoun to be a highminded and honourable man, possessing independence and virtue," Jackson told a correspondent who had detected a trend toward the South Carolinian. "It affords me great pleasure to hear that Mr. Calhoun's popularity is growing." Jackson preferred Calhoun but would be happy with Adams. "The nation will be well governed either by Mr. Calhoun or Mr. Adams," Jackson said.

Jackson's partisans in Washington didn't contradict his judgment of Adams and Calhoun, but they did question the electability of either man. "It appears to be the general opinion here," James Bronaugh said, "that Mr. Adams cannot succeed in opposition to a Southern man"—such as Crawford of Georgia. "He can not get the vote of Virginia, North Carolina, South Carolina, or Kentucky." Calhoun seemed the better bet to stop Crawford. "It has therefore been determined by those anxious to prevent the election of Crawford to bring forward Mr. Calhoun, who, it is believed, will unite not only the Southern and Western interest, but likewise the North." Yet the attention Calhoun received caused Crawford's allies to direct their sapping operations against the South Carolinian, and Calhoun began sliding back down the hill of viability.

The problem the anti-Crawfordites confronted was that the Treasury secretary had mastered the art of Washington politics. As keeper of the nation's purse, he was rumored to be channeling federal funds to favored members of Congress. The rumor may or may not have been true, but no one doubted that Crawford understood how to reward friends and punish enemies. If the presidential nomination came from the Republican caucus in Congress, Crawford was almost guaranteed to win.

His opponents felt compelled to discover, or create, an alternate path to the presidency. Restive Republicans in the states, seeking a larger role for themselves, suggested that if state legislators could choose presidential electors, they ought to be able to propose candidates. And if politicians in the states could propose candidates, there was no reason to restrict themselves to Washington insiders.

In the summer of 1822 a group of Tennessee lawmakers told Jackson they intended to nominate him for the presidency. The announcement didn't come as a surprise, as hints of the move had preceded it. Yet Jackson understood that his response to this first feeler could have large implications for what followed, and he drafted his answer with care. He noted that he hadn't brought this question upon himself. "I am silent, but the papers are not," he told Richard Call, who would relate his message to the Tennessee legislators. "The voice of the people, I am told, would bring me to the Presidential chair, and it is probable some of the legislatures may bring my name before the public. . . . I have long since determined to be perfectly silent. I never have been a candidate for office; I never will. The people have a right to call for any man's services in a republican government, and when they do, it is the duty of the individual to yield his services to that call."

The pro-Jackson forces required no more encouragement. Tennessee's Republicans met in caucus in late July and early August and unanimously endorsed Jackson for president. Among the state senators who supported Jackson was Sam Houston, recovered—albeit not completely—from the wounds he suffered at Horseshoe Bend and now a rising force in Tennessee politics. Houston remembered Jackson fondly and more than ever as a second father. Jackson's resolve struck Houston as the quintessence of character, perhaps because Houston's own resolve was sometimes lacking. He observed Jackson's rise from afar, but by the early 1820s he had determined that Jackson was the model for everything he wanted to be.

And he made himself Jackson's champion. "On this day a resolution has passed the Senate (unanimously) recommending you as a person the most worthy and suitable to be the next President of our Union," Houston wrote Jackson from Murfreesboro, where the Tennessee lawmakers were meeting. "The expression cannot be esteemed by you anything less than a gratified and honorable expression of the feelings of your fellow citizens." There was no time to waste. "The crisis requires that something should be done! The canker worms have been (already too long) gnawing at the very core and vitals of our Government." The people called their hero to service once more.

You are now before the eyes of the nation. . . . You have been your country's Great Sentinel, at a time when her watchmen had been caught slumbering on post, her capital had been reduced to ashes. You have been her faithful guardian, her well tried servant! . . . Will not the nation look to you again? Will it not regard your interests, when they are connected with your country's welfare? There will be no *caucus* at the next Congress. The next President will be the "People's choice." . . . You have friends throughout America; each has his sphere, and each will feel and act.

Jackson praised Houston as "a noble minded fellow," which he was, after his own fashion. He possessed substantial political gifts, including a charisma that, though utterly different from Jackson's austere, even frightening version, approached Old Hickory's for effect on the people Houston met. And Houston was devoted to the public interest, as he understood it. But he was also ambitious for higher office, and it didn't hurt his chances to associate himself with the hero of New Orleans and with what was becoming a popular insurgency against the professionals who controlled the Republican party in Washington.

Jackson watched from Nashville as the insurgency took shape, yet did little to encourage it. "I have received many letters from every quarter of the United States on this subject," he wrote Andrew Donelson in August 1822. "I have answered none, nor do I intend to answer any. I shall leave the people to adopt such course as they may think proper, and elect whom they choose to fill the Presidential chair, without any influence of mine exercised by me." As always, Jackson placed his faith in the people. "If left free to decide for themselves, uninfluenced by congressional caucuses, I have no doubt but they will make a happy choice." But if not, the choice could be disastrous. "If they should permit themselves to be dictated to by a congressional caucus, then as great a scoundrel as William H. Crawford might be elevated to the executive chair."

Andrew Donelson was a member of Jackson's family, a foster son; to him Jackson spoke more candidly and confidentially than to his political associates. Accordingly he was as sincere as he could be when he said, regarding the presidency, "Believe me, dear Andrew, that I never had a wish to be elevated to that station. . . . My sole ambition is to pass to my grave in retirement. . . . I am perfectly at ease, regardless of how the people may decide, having but one wish, that that decision may prove beneficial to their own happiness. I am fast going out of life, but my fervent prayers are that our republican government may be perpetual. And the people alone, by their virtue and independent exercise of their free suffrage, can make it perpetual."

Jackson stuck to this position as the groundswell in his favor grew. A Pennsylvania supporter wrote him in February 1823 with news that a meeting at Harrisburg had unanimously nominated him for president. This group had no legal or political standing except that it consisted of ordinary voters—which to Jackson was reason enough to answer the letter with respect and gratitude. The writer inquired whether Jackson would allow his name to be put forward for president. Jackson's answer was polished by now. "My undeviating rule of conduct through life, and which I have and shall ever deem as congenial with the true Republican principles of our government, has been neither to seek or decline public invitations to office." Supporters spoke of the presidency as Jackson's reward for accomplishments in the military; Jackson modestly demurred. "For the services which I may have rendered and which I have, it is hoped, proved in a degree beneficial to my country, I have nothing to ask. They are richly repaid with the confidence and good opinion of the virtuous and well deserving part of the community. I have only essayed to discharge a debt which every man owes his country when his rights are invaded; and if twelve years exposure to fatigue and numerous privations can warrant the expression, I may venture to assert that my portion of public service has been performed." Yet the loyal soldier could never ignore the call of duty. "The office of Chief Magistrate of the Union is one of great responsibility. As it should not be sought by any individual of the Republic, so it cannot with propriety be declined when offered by those who have the power of selection."

Jackson expected this letter to be published. It was, in several papers. The publication effectively announced his candidacy while making clear that the campaign wasn't his idea. He hadn't sought nomination, nor would he seek the presidency. But if the American people summoned him, he would serve.

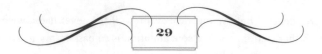

29

THE DEATH RATTLE OF
THE OLD REGIME

*U*nfortunately for his credibility, Jackson was soon forced into a step that belied his protestations of personal indifference as to his political fate. In the autumn of 1823 he let himself be elected to the Senate. As popular as Jackson was with most Tennesseans, he had some bitter enemies, including Senate incumbent John Williams. The Jacksonians hoped to make support for their hero a litmus test for Tennessee politicians, but Williams refused to nod to the general, and he had sufficient pull with the state legislature for his reelection to appear likely. This would have embarrassed the Jacksonians by undercutting their claims of overwhelming home-state enthusiasm for their man. They considered one candidate after another to oppose Williams, but none possessed the stature to defeat the incumbent. At wits' end, someone suggested Jackson himself for the Senate.

Jackson had to be convinced. He recalled his brief and unsatisfying experience in the Senate twenty-six years before and had no desire to repeat it. Yet he found himself caught on his own assertion that "office should be neither sought for nor declined," as one of the sudden Jackson-for-Senate advocates quoted back to him. Still he resisted. "There are many better qualified to meet the fatigues of journey than myself, and on whose services a reliance . . . might be safely reposed," he said. "I have therefore earnestly to request of my friends, and beg of you, not to press me to an acceptance of the appointment." But he was compelled to add, "If appointed, I could not decline."

Jackson honestly didn't want the job. He was certain the Senate hadn't improved since he resigned his seat in 1798. Washington was still a long, tedious journey from Nashville, and he didn't travel as well as he once had. Besides, election to the Senate would undermine his claim that he wasn't a politician. He would look like all the other politicians in Washington.

The worst of it, from a tactical standpoint, was that he would be required to take positions on issues of national concern. Jackson's supporters seem not to have thought through this consequence of their action, for in their haste to defeat Williams they made Jackson's presidential candidacy suddenly vulnerable. The beauty of their previous approach was that, not being a candidate, he didn't have to answer questions regarding troublesome issues. As a non-candidate he could remain above the fray. But as a member of the Senate, he would enjoy no such luxury. He might not have to speak, but he would have to vote. And his votes would be used against him.

Precisely because they failed to think things through, Jackson's supporters went ahead with the nomination, and the Tennessee legislature elected him. And he was compelled to accept. "Thus you see me a Senator, contrary to my wishes, my feelings, and my interests," he wrote John Calhoun.

𝒯he overland journey to Washington was cold and wearing, its one recompense being that it showed that Jackson was more popular among ordinary citizens than ever. He was mobbed at every stop, till he switched from horseback to stagecoach, which was less comfortable and slower but allowed a semblance of anonymity. He knew he shouldn't complain. "Although tiresome and troublesome," he wrote Rachel, "still it is gratifying to find that I have triumphed over the machinations of my enemies and still possess the confidence of the people." Yet this first long separation from Rachel since the Seminole War reminded him how much he missed her. "Should providence once more permit us to meet, I am solemnly resolved, with the permission of heaven, never to separate or be separated from you in this world."

Jackson reached Washington a day too late to hear the president's annual message (read by the Senate clerk). The one part he commented on, when he read it himself, was the one that would have the greatest impact in generations to come. Jackson didn't know, although he probably guessed, that this passage was really the work of John Quincy Adams, who asserted that the Americas must be free of future colonization or military intervention by the European powers. The "Holy Alliance" of continental monarchies was rumored to be plotting the restoration of Spain's control of her lost American colonies, and Adams and Monroe now warned them off. Not for decades would anyone call this warning the "Monroe Doctrine," but Jackson fully endorsed the idea. "The President takes a proper ground as it respects South America," he wrote John Overton. "If the Holy Alliance will maintain their neutrality as it regards South America, we will also. If they aid Spain, we will interpose in behalf of the colonies." (Jackson here went further than Monroe, who hadn't specified what the United States would do in the event of European meddling. Jackson was thinking what *he* would do in such event.)

He found life as a senator almost as tedious as he had when he was younger. "There is nothing done here but visiting and carding each other," he reported to Rachel, referring to the habit of leaving calling cards at other people's homes. "You know how much I was disgusted with those scenes when you and I were here. It has increased instead of diminishing." He avoided the social circuit whenever possible, preferring to spend evenings in the quarters John Eaton had procured for them. "We are in the family of Mr. O'Neal," Jackson told Rachel, "whose amiable pious wife and two daughters, one married, the other single, take every pains in their power to make us comfortable. . . . I can with truth say I never was in a more agreeable and worthy family. When we have a leisure hour in the evening, we spend it with the family. Mrs. Timberlake, the married daughter whose husband belongs to our navy, plays on the piano delightfully, and every Sunday evening entertains her pious mother with sacred music, to which we are invited, and the single daughter, who is also pious, and sings well, unites in the music."

That majority of Washington inhabitants who knew Jackson only by reputation must have been surprised at the modest, quiet figure he cut. To some extent, of course, he appreciated that he was on display and therefore put himself on best behavior. But with age and infirmity, the old fires of bellicosity were burning down. And as one of the most celebrated men in America, he had nothing to prove—except perhaps that he could make peace with old enemies, which he did. He reestablished a rapport with Thomas Hart Benton, last seen leaving Nashville after the shooting spree from which Jackson still carried a leaden souvenir. Benton had even better reason than Jackson to mend the rift: the first-term senator from Missouri wished to bask in the Jackson glow. Jackson made up with Winfield Scott, who half expected to fight a duel with his former antagonist. "General Scott and myself met before he left the city, and parted friendly," Jackson explained to one who knew their history. He continued, "I have become friendly with all here. . . . This has destroyed the stronghold of my enemies who denounced me as a man of revengeful temper and of great rashness. I am told the opinion of these whose minds were prepared to see me with a tomahawk in one hand and a scalping knife in the other has greatly changed."

Jackson's peace offensive extended to the Senate floor, where he took pains to avoid confrontation. This wasn't difficult at first, since the Senate conducted little business. "All things here appear to bend to the approaching election," he observed in February. Crawford's partisans were fully engaged lining up votes for their favorite. Jackson's supporters didn't intend to dispute the caucus, leaving them—and him—with nothing to do but watch disapprovingly. "It is now a contest between a few demagogues and the people," Jackson told John Coffee, "and it is to be seen whether a minority, less than one fourth of the whole members of Congress, can coerce the people to follow them."

In another matter, though, Jackson couldn't avoid attention. Since the tariff had become a political issue in the wake of the War of 1812, every session of Congress was tempted or pressured to revise the rates up or down, depending on the interests of those doing the tempting and pressuring. Jackson hoped the current Congress might skirt the issue, since any vote on any tariff bill was certain to antagonize someone. And it would further diminish the distance separating Jackson from ordinary politicians.

But the issue wouldn't be evaded, and Jackson was forced to take a stand. "You ask my opinion on the tariff," he replied to a person who identified himself as a Jackson man but said his enthusiasm would diminish if Jackson voted for a measure then before Congress. "I answer that I am in favor of a judicious examination and revision of it, and so far as the tariff before us embraces the design of fostering, protecting, and preserving within ourselves the means of national defense and independence, particularly in a state of war, I would advocate and support it. The experience of the late war ought to teach us a lesson, and one never to be forgotten. If our liberty and republican form of government, procured for us by our revolutionary fathers, are worth the blood and treasure at which they were obtained, it is surely our duty to protect and defend them." It was entirely like Jackson to test any measure by its effect on American security and independence. It was also a politically astute thing to do. "Can there be an American patriot who saw the privations, danger, and difficulties experienced for the want of a proper means of defense during the last war, who would be willing again to hazard the safety of our country if embroiled? . . . I hope there is not."

But there was more to the tariff than national defense. "Beyond this, I look at the tariff with an eye to the proper distribution of labor and revenue, and with a view to the discharge of the national debt. I am one of those who do not believe that a national debt is a national blessing, but rather a curse to a republic." No one reading Jackson's letter—which he expected to be published, as indeed it was—required a reminder that Alexander Hamilton and the Federalists had treated the national debt as a blessing, for tying the interests of the wealthy to the success of the government. Jackson agreed that a debt would bind the wealthy to the government, but for all the wrong reasons. "It is calculated to raise around the administration a moneyed aristocracy dangerous to the liberties of the country." The tariff could pay down the debt and meanwhile provide work for American laborers and markets for American farmers. Workers would be drawn into the manufacturing encouraged by the tariff, and would require food from American farms. America would become stronger, especially compared with Britain, which presumed to rule the world's commerce. "We have been too long subject to the policy of the British merchants. It is time we should become a little more *Americanized*."

In just a few years the tariff would emerge as the most explosive issue in American politics. But the bill Congress approved in 1824 only modestly adjusted previous schedules, and Jackson's vote in favor didn't noticeably diminish his popularity.

*L*ong before the session closed, Jackson had had his fill of congressional politics. The speeches bored him, and the socializing left him cold. The one event he valued was a party commemorating his victory at New Orleans, held on January 8. The date had become a second Independence Day in many circles, and in Washington that year John Quincy Adams and his wife hosted a very large reception. "There must have been a thousand people there," recorded a Senate colleague of Jackson's. "It is the universal opinion that nothing has ever equalled this party here either in brilliancy of preparation or elegance of the company." The hero of New Orleans naturally was the center of attention, gawked at by all, personally congratulated by many, who shook his hand till his arm grew weary. Jackson appreciated the honor and thanked the guests for their felicitations but wasn't unhappy when the evening ended.

The longer he was in Washington, the more he wished he was home. "The family we live in are truly kind and attentive," he wrote Rachel. "Still, my love, there has been a gloom unusual over my spirits this winter that I cannot well account for. I still try to arouse my former energy and fortitude to banish it, but it will obtrude itself on me at times. I suppose it arises from being placed in a situation in which I take no delight, and being forced from you when I least expected that separation." His thoughts were constantly of home. "Give my love to the Andrews. . . . Tell Lyncoya I expect him to be a good boy . . . and believe me to be your affectionate husband."

By May he could stand no more. "I declare to you I am worn out with the fatigue of legislating," he told a friend. "Nature never intended me for any such pursuit, I am sure. Day after day talking and arguing about things that might be decided in a few hours requires a Job-like patience to bear; it does not suit me. . . . Never have I been more solicitous to return to my own cottage." He requested and obtained a leave of absence from the Senate and headed home. By mid-June he was back at the Hermitage with Rachel and the children. "I have fine prospects of cotton, better than I have ever had, and my corn promising," he wrote neighbor Coffee with satisfaction.

*W*hile Jackson watched from Nashville, the campaign of 1824 entered its final, frantic stage. Crawford's prospects were slipping after the candidate suffered a minor stroke and recovered more slowly than expected. He still carried the congressional caucus almost unanimously, but chiefly because the backers of Jackson, Adams, and Clay boycotted the proceedings.

Jackson's campaign cast its man as the outsider, above the petty intrigues adopted by those who feared the people's judgment. Jackson himself described the caucus as "the last hope of the friends of Mr. Crawford. . . . It appears to me that such is the feelings of the nation that a recommendation by a congressional caucus would politically damn any name put forward by it." Six weeks later the strategy appeared to be working. "I am happy to see the good people of America are putting their faces against these congressional caucuses, and I do hope the one last held will put this unconstitutional proceeding to sleep forever."

Jackson's hope came true: the caucus died in 1824. But presidential politics grew livelier than ever. Crawford's supporters attacked Jackson, as now did those of Adams and Clay. Jackson still refused to campaign, but he answered letters from supporters, and though he declined to respond to the attacks, he wasn't above suggesting themes to those who did so on his behalf. George Wilson edited the *Nashville Gazette* and sent Jackson a piece by Thomas Ritchie of Virginia charging Jackson with collusion with Adams and Calhoun against Crawford. "Was I to notice the falsehoods and false insinuations of Ritchie and such unprincipled editors, I could have time for nothing else," Jackson told Wilson. But he added: "Should you, upon reference to the piece alluded to, think it deserves any notice, such a one as the following might be proper: That General Jackson's course requires neither falsehood nor intrigue to support it. He has been brought before the nation by the people, without his knowledge, wishes, or consent. His support is the people."

*J*ackson's support indeed *was* the people. When the votes were tallied, he had 154,000 to Adams's 109,000. Clay and Crawford were nearly tied for third, with about 47,000 apiece. These totals were a minority of voters in the states, as most states still chose electors by legislative decision. But they nonetheless showed clearly that the people preferred Jackson over any other candidate.

Regardless of the popular vote, however, the decision that counted lay with the electoral college. No one knew what the electors would do. Those from states where the people chose the electors felt bound, politically or morally, to follow the wishes of the voters. But what did this mean? Did the majority winner in a state get all the votes of that state or merely a proportion commensurate with the proportion of his majority? And what about the states where the legislators still chose the electors? Were those electors bound, or could they vote their consciences?

Until the electors met in December, no one could answer these questions with confidence. And even after they met, confusion persisted. The credentials of some electors were disputed, leading the president of the Senate, Vice President Daniel Tompkins, to refuse to accept their votes. For two weeks the capital scintillated with reports, rumors, and speculation regarding the outcome of the electoral contest. Papers printed incomplete results, throwing one side or the other into panic. Corrections sent the pendulum careening the opposite way.

Jackson arrived amid the uproar. He came for the new session of the Senate rather than the electoral vote, and this time brought Rachel, who was astonished at the bustle of the capital. "To tell you of this city, I would not do justice to the subject," she wrote a friend. "The extravagance is in dressing and running to parties. . . . There are no less than fifty to one hundred persons calling in a day." Some of it was the holiday season, and some the presence of the Marquis de Lafayette, returned to America after all these years. The famous Frenchman was staying at the same hotel as the Jacksons, which afforded Rachel a close view. "He is an extraordinary man. He has a happy talent of knowing those he has once seen. For instance, when we first came to this house, the General said he would go and pay the Marquis the first visit. Both having the same desire, and at the same time, they met on the entry of the stairs. . . . The emotion of revolutionary feeling was aroused in them both. At Charleston, General Jackson saw him on the field of battle; the one a boy of twelve, the Marquis, twenty-three." That someone scrambled the memory—Jackson never saw Lafayette in battle, though conceivably he saw him passing through Carolina, when Jackson was nine rather than twelve—mattered less than that fate had brought together these two icons of American liberty: Lafayette, a hero of the first war of independence, and Jackson, a veteran of the first war of independence and the hero of the second.

By the middle of December the shape of the electoral vote was finally coming clear. Jackson led, with Adams second. Uncertainty still surrounded the third-place finisher. This was no small matter, in that the Constitution decreed that in the event of failure of any candidate to receive a majority of the electoral votes, the House of Representatives would choose the president from the top three finishers. Everyone assumed that if Clay made it to the House, his long tenure and close alliances there could boost him past Adams and Jackson. But if Crawford nosed out Clay, Jackson would have the edge.

Jackson maintained his composure amid the confusion. "To say I have nothing of concern about the office would be doing injustice to the kind feelings of those who have sustained me, and would wear the appearance of affectation," he wrote Samuel Swartout, a friend and strong supporter. Yet Jackson was willing to accept any verdict that reflected the honest wishes of the people. "Who shall rule is of less importance than how he may claim to rule. . . . I would rather remain a plain cultivator of the soil, as I am, than to occupy that which is truly the first office in the world, if the voice of the nation was against it."

This was the politic thing for Jackson to say. It was also easy. By now he wanted to be president; in the contest his combative energies had become engaged. And the popular vote confirmed that he was the choice of the people. For him to lose would be for the people's will to be ignored, for democracy to be denied.

He had every reason to hope otherwise. The politicians wouldn't dare overturn the people's decision. He grew still more confident when the final electoral tally gave him 99 votes, Adams 84, Crawford 41, and Clay 37. The lion of the House would not be among those considered by the House for president. In the western states that Clay had carried, most voters seemed to rank Jackson second. It was natural to assume that their House delegations would swing to the Jackson column. "The Lord's will be done," Jackson said as the year ended, at a moment when the Lord appeared to agree with the American people that Andrew Jackson should be the next president of the United States.

On the first day of the new year, John Quincy Adams attended a dinner hosted by members of both houses of Congress, in honor of Lafayette. James Monroe was there, with several other officials of the executive branch and a number of military officers. A cold rain had been falling all day, and with evening it turned to snow. Adams and his wife wished to get home before the roads became dangerously slick, but they had to stay for the toasts. "The President's Administration was toasted, to which he answered by a brief address of thanks," Adams recorded in his diary. "General La Fayette answered also very briefly the toast to himself. Mr. Clay made a speech about Bolivar and the cause of South America, and seemed very desirous of eliciting speeches from me and Mr. Calhoun." Adams resisted, with one eye on the weather and one foot toward the door. But before he could make his escape, Clay approached him. "He told me that he should be glad to have with me soon some confidential conversation upon public affairs." Clay said nothing more about the subject of the conversation, but Adams was intrigued. "I said I should be happy to have it whenever it might suit his convenience." And when he got home that night, as he warmed himself by his fire, he wrote, "At the beginning of this year there is in my prospects and anticipations a solemnity and moment never before experienced."

Clay had commenced the new year in a mood as foul as the weather. Not until the vote from Louisiana had been recorded did he learn that he wasn't among the trio to be considered by the House. And he had lost in the Louisiana legislature by bad, dumb luck. "Two of my friends in the Legislature were overset in a gig the day before and thereby prevented from attending; two others who were expected did not arrive," he wrote an associate. That had made all the difference. "*Accident* alone prevented my return to the House of Representatives and, as is generally now believed, my election."

But if he couldn't be president, he might yet determine who would be. "You are a looker-on," he told a friend, "whilst I am compelled to be an actor in the public concerns here. And an actor in such a scene! An alternative made up of Andrew Jackson and John Quincy Adams!" Clay saw little to choose between the two. Clay's friend had suggested that the speaker might find a place in a new administration. Clay rejected the very thought. "I would not cross Pennsylvania Avenue to be in any office under any Administration which lies before us."

Yet soon he was crossing more than Pennsylvania Avenue. "Mr. Clay came at six, and spent the evening with me in a long conversation explanatory of the past and prospective of the future," Adams recorded in his diary on January 9. "He said that the time was drawing near when the choice must be made in the House of Representatives of a President from the three candidates presented by the electoral college; that he had been much urged and solicited with regard to the part in that transaction that he should take, and had not been five minutes landed at his lodgings before he had been applied to by a friend of Mr. Crawford's, in a manner so gross that it had disgusted him." Nor were Crawford's partisans the only ones seeking his favor. "Some of my friends also, disclaiming indeed to have any authority from me, had repeatedly applied to him, directly or indirectly, urging considerations personal to himself as motives to his cause." Clay had rebuffed the approaches, wishing to let public passions cool. Unfortunately, they had not, and currently remained as hot as ever. But the hour had come to address Adams directly. "He wished me, as far as I might think proper, to satisfy him with regard to some principles of great public importance, but without any personal considerations for himself. In the question to come before the House between General Jackson, Mr. Crawford, and myself, he had no hesitation in saying that his preference would be for me."

There is no reason to doubt that Clay told Adams just what Adams recorded. Yet only the day before, Clay had written to Francis Blair, a Kentucky editor (who, ironically, would become one of Jackson's closest advisers), in a rather different tone. "I consider whatever choice we may make will be only a choice of evils," Clay told Blair. "To both those gentlemen there are strong personal objections." Clay's objections to Adams, however, were less than those to Jackson. "The principal difference between them is that in the election of Mr. Adams we shall not by the example inflict any wound upon the character of our institutions; but I should much fear hereafter, if not during the present generation, that the election of the General would give to the military spirit a stimulus and a confidence that might lead to the most pernicious results. I shall therefore with great regret, on account of the dilemma in which the people have placed us, support Mr. Adams."

In his meeting the next day with Adams, Clay apparently elided his regret and his belief that the secretary of state was simply the lesser of evils. And after that meeting he changed his story about not wanting an office in the new administration. "I can tell you nothing of the formation of the new Cabinet," he informed a friend, before adding, "I believe that, if I choose to go into it, I can enter in *any* situation that I may please." Clay didn't want his friend to get the wrong idea. "This opinion is formed from circumstances, not from assurances to which I would not listen, but which I should instantly check if attempted to be made."

Whether or not Clay's friend got the wrong idea, others did. Or perhaps they got the right idea. Rumors swept through the halls of the Capitol and along the streets of Washington; by the end of the month Clay's preference for Adams was public knowledge. In a letter to Blair, Clay explained his thinking. "Mr. Adams, you know well, I should never have selected if at liberty to draw from the whole mass of citizens for our President. But there is no danger in his elevation now or in time to come. Not so of his competitor, of whom I cannot believe that killing 2500 Englishmen at New Orleans qualifies for the various, difficult and complicated duties of the Chief Magistrate." To another associate, Clay articulated more graphically what he saw as the danger from Jackson. "As a friend of liberty, and to the permanence of our institutions, I cannot consent, in the early stage of their existence, by contributing to the election of a military chieftain, to give the strongest guaranty that this republic will march in the fatal road which has conducted every other republic to ruin."

In the letter to Blair, Clay followed his explanation of preference for Adams by saying, "I perceive that I am unconsciously writing a sort of defence, which you may possibly think implies guilt." Clay had reason to feel defensive, for Jackson's supporters were already alleging a deal between Clay and Adams, with Adams to receive the presidency and Clay a high cabinet office, probably the secretaryship of state. Clay felt obliged to respond. After a Philadelphia paper carried a letter from an unnamed "member of the House of Representatives from Pennsylvania" likening Clay to Aaron Burr and describing the alleged Clay-Adams bargain as "one of the most disgraceful transactions that ever covered with infamy the Republican ranks," Clay called the author out. "I pronounce the member, whoever he may be, a base and infamous calumniator, a dastard and a liar; and if he ever dare unveil himself and avow his name I will hold him responsible . . . to all the laws which govern and regulate the conduct of men of honor."

The complaints of the Jacksonians failed to prevent Adams and Clay from getting what they wanted. The House of Representatives, voting by state delegations, selected Adams to be president over Jackson and Crawford, by a margin of thirteen to seven to four. "May the blessing of God rest upon the event of this day!" Adams inscribed in his diary.

Jackson accepted the decision with outward calm. He attended a reception hosted by President Monroe for the president-elect. "It was crowded to overflowing," Adams wrote. "General Jackson was there, and we shook hands. He was altogether placid and courteous." John Eaton observed the same equanimity in Jackson. "The old man goes quietly on, undisturbed and unmoved by the agitation around. Even enemies speak highly of his course."

Appearance, in this case, deceived. Privately Jackson was livid. Days after Adams's victory in the House, the president-elect openly offered the State Department to Clay, who duly accepted. Jackson spat his disgust. "The *Judas* of the West has closed the contract and will receive the thirty pieces of silver," he said. "His end will be the same."

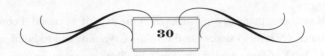

30

DEMOCRACY TRIUMPHANT

$\mathcal{A}$nd so began the longest, bitterest, ugliest campaign in American

political history. Adams wasn't even inaugurated before Jackson's

hometown paper, the *Nashville Gazette*, declared him a candidate for

president in 1828. The paper hadn't consulted Jackson but relied on the

general's assertion that a man called by the people to democratic office

couldn't refuse. Jackson himself fueled the enthusiasm by taking vigorous

and sarcastic exception to Clay's charge that he was a dangerous "military

chieftain." "It is for an ingenuity stronger than mine to conceive what

idea was intended to be conveyed by that term," Jackson said.

It is very true that early in life, even in the days of boyhood, I contributed my mite to shake off the yoke of tyranny, and to build up
the fabrick of free government; and when lately our country was involved in war, having the commission of Major General of militia
in Tennessee, I made an appeal to the patriotism of the western citizens, when 3000 of them went with me to the field, to support her
Eagles. If this can constitute me a "military chieftain," I am one.

Aided by the patriotism of the western people, and an indul-
gent providence, it was my good fortune to protect our frontier border from savages, and successfully to defend an important and
vulnerable point of our Union. Our lives were risked, privations
endured, sacrifices made, if Mr. Clay pleases, martial law declared,
not with any view of personal aggrandisement, but for the preservation of all and everything that was valuable, the honor, safety,
and glory of our country. Does this constitute a "military chieftain"? And are all our brave men in war, who go forth to defend
their rights, and the rights of their country, to be termed "military
chieftains," and therefore denounced?

Jackson couldn't resist noting that Clay had never risked life, limb, or treasure for his country. And now he seemed to be saying that those who had
done so should be disqualified from political office. Such demagogues were
the ones to be feared, not honest soldiers.

I became a soldier for the good of my country. Difficulties met me
at every step. I thank God it was my good fortune to surmount
them. The war over and peace restored, I sought to retire again to
my farm and to private life, where but for the call made by my
country to the Senate I should have contentedly remained. . . . If
this makes me so, I am a "military chieftain."

*J*ackson returned to his farm, although not exactly to private life. He was
one of the most famous men in America, and certainly the most popular, and
his supporters were determined to make him president. John Eaton and

some allies purchased a recently Crawfordist newspaper in Washington and transformed it into an organ of Jacksonism. Jacksonians in other cities followed suit, aiming to get out the good word on Jackson and the bad word on Adams and Clay. Eaton was joined in Congress by Sam Houston, who had emulated his surrogate father by becoming major general of the Tennessee militia and then fighting a duel (but only badly wounding his foe). In Washington, Houston and Eaton became Jackson's ardent advocates. They wrote letters to editors, and editorials, and kept Jackson apprised of the mood of Congress. "I have not in my life seen a cause rising so fast as *that of the people is*," Houston told Jackson, "nor one sinking faster than the cause of a *wicked and corrupt coalition!* . . . You lose no friends, but gain daily. It will be so until the great day of deliverance to our country arrives."

Jackson could have taken the temperature of Congress himself had he not resigned his Senate seat. He dreaded the thought of another season of windy rhetoric and barren posturing, but at first he couldn't figure out how to avoid it. His stated philosophy of neither seeking nor shunning office seemed to rule out resignation. But deliverance came in the form of an apparent conflict of interest. Congressional Jacksonians angered by the outcome of the 1824 election proposed a constitutional amendment forbidding the appointment of members of Congress to posts in the executive branch during the term of their election and for two years thereafter. If adopted, the amendment would have prevented appointments like that of Clay by Adams. The amendment went nowhere, but it gave Jackson an— apparently unintended—excuse to leave the Senate. For him to vote on a measure so clearly inspired by his defeat in the House would be improper, he told the Tennessee legislature. Therefore "I must entreat to be excused from any further service in the Senate."

If Jackson was relieved upon ending his senatorial career, Rachel was ecstatic. She had been disappointed for her husband at the result of the election but pleased for herself. The thought of life in the White House made her shudder. Washington's excitements were nothing next to what she called "the variety of dear little interests" of home. The journey west from Washington had been slow, but she didn't begrudge the delay, as each mile carried her closer to her heart's content. "Our time was delightfully occupied on the road," she wrote a friend. "From Baltimore to our farm we were honored by the most friendly and hospitable attentions."

The more Rachel pondered the matter, the more she concluded that she now enjoyed the best of all worlds. She had the honor of being married to the man the American people most wanted to lead them, yet she didn't bear the burden of being a president's wife. "To me," she told her friend, "the *Presidential charms* by the side of a *happy retirement from public life* are as the tale of the candle and the substantial fire, the first of which it is said is soon blown out by the wind but the latter is only increased by it."

$\mathcal{R}$achel's joy at returning home doubtless distracted her from the improvements in the route she and her husband traveled to get there. The slowness of their journey owed far more to the popular demands on her husband than to the condition of the road itself, which had changed dramatically during the three decades since Jackson had first ridden east. Private funds had built a pike from Baltimore to Cumberland, Maryland; from there the federal government picked up construction of what was called the National Road. By 1818 the road had reached the Ohio River at Wheeling, in the panhandle of western Virginia. Travel on the road was as convenient and pleasant as land travel could be in those days. Its crushed-stone surface shed rain, banishing the mud that had bogged wagons in rainy weather and most of the dust that had choked travelers in dry. Arched stone bridges eliminated dependence on ferrymen and susceptibility to the flooding of low-water crossings. Taverns lined the route, averaging more than one per mile in stretches. These establishments varied in quality, from stagecoach inns offering meals and beds to the well-heeled travelers aboard the scheduled coaches to wagon stands providing minimal services for those transporting themselves.

At Wheeling travelers to Nashville could board steamboats, which carried them down the Ohio and up the Cumberland. Steamboat passage was more expensive than travel by stage, but it was far more comfortable. First-class travelers—like the Jacksons—had private rooms, and they could stroll about the decks during the day. The earliest steamboats had a disturbing habit of blowing up, but by the mid-1820s explosions were infrequent enough to occasion surprise when they did occur. More common, though less spectacular, were groundings on sandbars, collisions with other craft, and minor fires from smokestack sparks.

Yet the really exciting development in water travel in the 1820s relied not on steam power but on mules. In 1825, after eight years of construction, the Erie Canal was completed. Governor De Witt Clinton, the driving force behind the construction, signaled the importance of the event by pouring two kegs of Lake Erie water into the harbor at New York City. The water link between the Atlantic and the Lakes transformed the economies of both the Northeast and the Northwest—in fact, made them part of a single economy for the first time. Transport costs from Ohio to New York fell by as much as 90 percent; now farm products from the interior, carried east on the mule-drawn canal barges, could compete with those grown on the seaboard.

The effect on both regions was revolutionary. Agriculture in Ohio and Indiana boomed, while agriculture in New England languished. New York City, lately a laggard behind Philadelphia, became America's foremost commercial center. Eastern producers of textiles and other manufactured goods shifted from handicraft methods to factories as displaced eastern farmers scrambled for work and as the canal opened new markets for manufactures in the interior. Standards of living rose on the fall in transport costs and the emergence of regional specialization. Easterners ate better; westerners went better clothed and shod. The change was as obvious as the shirts on people's backs; within a decade "homespun" almost vanished, replaced by factory-woven cloth even on the distant frontier.

Other effects of the revolution in transport were less visible but no less profound. As farmers and manufacturers shipped their goods over longer distances, they increasingly depended on a stable, predictable money supply, one that spanned not merely cities or states but the nation as a whole. The panic of 1819 had demonstrated what happened when money vanished; the next panic would spread more rapidly along the improved avenues of commerce. In Jackson's early days as a merchant, David Allison's failure to honor a note had left Jackson and a few others in the lurch; in the age of expanding markets, a critical bankruptcy in one part of the country could bring down hundreds of businesses all across America. The nation had never been so prosperous, but never had its economy been so sensitive to disruption.

$\mathcal{H}$enry Clay had hoped his appointment as secretary of state would be a personal blessing, the springboard to the presidency it had been for his four immediate predecessors. But the circumstances of his elevation and the unceasing attacks on his integrity by the partisans of Jackson made his tenure an unceasing agony.

John Randolph wasn't a Jacksonian so much as an anti-Adamsite. The most infuriatingly brilliant and exasperatingly eccentric politician of his day, Randolph had entered Congress in time to help fellow Virginian Jefferson defeat New Yorker Burr in the second round of the election of 1800. But Jefferson's devotion to Republican principles slipped below Randolph's high standard, and during Jefferson's second term Randolph excoriated the president with a vicious humor that evoked smiles among Jefferson's enemies— but not laughs, lest Randolph turn his rapier on them. Randolph crossed swords with Henry Clay when Clay led the war hawks of 1812 and Randolph aligned himself with the Federalist opponents of the war. He lost his seat as a result but returned to the House in time to tangle with Clay, again unsuccessfully, over the Missouri Compromise. When Clay became secretary of state in 1825, Randolph assaulted him from the Senate, to which he was elevated by Jacksonians in the Virginia legislature who wished to send the Adams-Clay administration a message of their outrage. Randolph savaged Adams and especially Clay for one failing and another and closed his most venomous diatribe with a description of Adams and Clay as "the combination, unheard of till then, of the puritan with the blackleg."

"The House was a perfect scene of confusion for half an hour, no one addressing the Chair, the Chairman crying out Order, Order, Order, hurley burley, helter skelter, Negro states and Yankees," John Marable wrote Jackson, regarding the Randolph speech. Marable was a Tennessee congressman who, like many others, had slipped into the Senate to hear Randolph slash Clay. "Yes, says he—Mr. R.—with uplifted hands, I swear to my God and

Country that I will war with this administration made up of the union of Puritans and Blacklegs."

Adams didn't mind being called a Puritan, but Clay couldn't let "blackleg" pass. He challenged Randolph to a duel. By this time dueling had lost favor even with many of its former practitioners; Thomas Hart Benton accepted Randolph's request to serve as second chiefly to talk Randolph out of going ahead. He succeeded too well; Randolph explained that he must answer Clay's challenge but wouldn't fire back. Yet just before the signal, Randolph's pistol accidentally went off. This disrupted his concentration, so that on the signal he did fire. But he missed. Clay missed also, his bullet disappearing in the billows of the thin Randolph's overcoat. Benton expected that the affair would end there. But Clay demanded a second round, and Randolph wouldn't refuse. Clay missed again. Randolph now fired deliberately in the air. "I do not fire at you, Mr. Clay," he said redundantly. Whether Clay was embarrassed more from twice missing Randolph or from not having his latest fire returned was hard to tell. Yet his relief outweighed his embarrassment, and he strode forward and offered his hand to his antagonist. Randolph wouldn't let him off quite so easily. "You owe me a coat, Mr. Clay," he said. Clay merely smiled and said, "I am glad the debt is no greater."

But neither the coat nor the brush with death cured Randolph of his scorn for Clay. "Randolph loses no opportunity to abuse him," John Eaton reported to Jackson a month later. "He gives it to him and Adams in great style whenever he takes the floor. Yesterday he made a speech of 4 or 5 hours." Eaton added that Randolph's windiness included high praise for Jackson. "He spoke of the abuse you had received from various sources heretofore, then said that you would live and last with posterity when your detractors should have sunk to forgetfulness, that like the great father of rivers, the Mississippi, your fame and splendid efforts for your country would roll its mighty volume on."

*J*ackson appreciated the support from Randolph, but he was more interested in the opinion of that other Virginian, Jefferson. As the fiftieth anniversary—the jubilee—of American independence approached in the summer of 1826, the eyes of the country turned to Monticello, where the author of the Declaration of Independence clung to life, but with weakening grip. They also turned to Quincy, Massachusetts, where John Adams was failing similarly. Jackson expected no good word from Adams, a founder of Federalism and the father of his chief rival, but he did hope for the benediction of Jefferson.

He didn't exactly get it, although he got something similar. Henry Lee, the son of Revolutionary War general Lighthorse Harry Lee (and the brother of Confederate general Robert E. Lee) and a strong Jacksonian, visited Jefferson on July 1. "As soon as I arrived, he sent for me," Lee told Jackson. "And though he seemed to look upon his end as approaching, he spoke of it as an event rather unpleasant than terrible—like a traveler expressing his apprehension of being caught in a rain. I was surprised at the energy of his grasp and the alacrity of his conversation, and could not but admire the general predominance of mind over matter in all his words and actions in so trying a moment." Jefferson didn't speak directly of politics to Lee, but he did to his daughter and other members of the household. "I learn from his family that he holds in contempt and abhorrence the men and measures of our present administration, and that his opinion as to the necessity of change at the next presidential election concurs with mine and that of the great mass of our countrymen."

With the rest of the nation, Jackson was astonished to discover two weeks later that Jefferson and Adams had lived till the fiftieth Fourth, then died that very day. "What a wonderful coincidence that the author and two signers of the Declaration of Independence, two of the ex-Presidents, should on the same day expire, a half a century after that that gave birth to a nation of freemen, and that Thomas Jefferson should have died the very hour of the day that the Declaration of Independence was presented and read in the Congress of 1776," Jackson wrote. "Is this an omen that Divinity approbated the whole course of Mr. Jefferson and sent an angel down to take him from the earthly tabernacle on this national Jubilee, at the same moment he had presented it to Congress? And is the death of Mr. Adams a confirmation of the approbation of Divinity also? Or is it an omen that his political example as President, and adopted by his son, shall destroy this holy fabric created by the virtuous Jefferson?"

❧   ❧   ❧

Jackson's enemies soon mobilized to deny him any claim on Jefferson's mantle. Administration allies began circulating stories that Jefferson had registered concern at Jackson's strong showing in the 1824 election. By one version Jefferson said that Jackson's popularity was "an evidence that the Republic would not last long." By another he declared, "There are one hundred men in Albemarle County better qualified for the Presidency."

Jackson couldn't convincingly dispute that Jefferson had said such things, as he hadn't been present at the purported utterance. But he did counter them by circulating a letter from Jefferson complimenting him on matters relating to the Seminole War. And he relayed the message from Henry Lee regarding Jefferson's hope that the current administration be removed.

Yet the reported Jefferson thrust was only a small part of what became a broad-front campaign of slander, slight, and innuendo. Jackson's rivals searched every part of his biography for openings. Owning slaves was no disqualification for high office and in southern states was nearly a prerequisite, but slave trading was considered low and disreputable; consequently Jackson was charged with "negro *speculation*." Though dueling still had its advocates and practitioners (including Clay), the ranks of its opponents continued to grow; for these, Jackson's dueling past was resurrected and related in bloody detail, and embellished to show that he took liberties with the code of honor and therefore with the lives of his antagonists. An old affidavit from Thomas Benton was published to cast the shooting affair at the Nashville City Hotel in the most unflattering light for Jackson. Copies of his old letters were obtained and published (and in some cases forged) to show that he couldn't spell. The Burr conspiracy was recounted to question Jackson's loyalty to the Union or at least his judgment of men. His military record, which his supporters portrayed as his strength, came under assault for his unmerciful treatment of subordinates. The John Wood execution was recapitulated, emphasizing the youth and innocence of the unfortunate soldier.

The most notorious, and widely reprinted, piece of literature from the 1828 election season was the "coffin handbill," a broadside topped by the silhouettes of six coffins in heavy black ink, representing six soldiers executed by Jackson's order near the end of the southern campaign of the War of 1812. The soldiers had been among some two hundred militiamen charged with mutiny, desertion, and other offenses related to abandonment of their posts at Fort Jackson in September 1814. The two hundred claimed that their term of service was three months, that it was over, and that they had the right to go home. Their commanding officers replied that the term was six months, that it was but half over, and that they must stay. Jackson was at Mobile at this time, preparing for the British invasion of the coast, and he naturally backed the officers. When the mutineers were arrested he ordered a court martial. Nearly all the prisoners were simply fined and ordered to be dishonorably discharged at the end of their terms of service. Six, however, the apparent leaders of the insurgency, were found guilty of the most serious charges and sentenced to death.

Jackson received the court's verdict at New Orleans in early January 1815, under the very cannons of the British. Not till after the great battle of January 8 did he have a chance to examine it. He didn't know that the peace treaty had been signed at Ghent or that the British would soon sail away. As far as he could tell, the war was still on and discipline was as crucial as ever. With no reason to question the verdict of the court, he signed it and ordered the sentences carried out.

The executions evoked little notice at the time. If any persons in the East even knew of the incident they kept their secret from the newspapers. But as the election of 1828 approached, the anti-Jacksonians resurrected the story and replayed it in detail, down to the last words of the condemned men. Jackson was portrayed as a vindictive monster, a despot who crushed the innocent beneath his boot heel. The "coffin handbill" summarized the case for the prosecution (that is, the posthumous defense). "The act was as cruel as uncalled for," the text said of Jackson's acceptance of the court's verdict, "and appeals to every man's best affections, and sympathies, for the meting out of retributive justice at the ensuing election, against the man who had no pity for his fellow man." A poet was pressed into service to provide a heart-wringing elegy for the condemned.

> See six black coffins ranged along,
>   Six graves before them made;

Webb, Lindsey, Harris, Lewis, Hunt,
And Morrow kneeled and prayed. . . .

Sure he will spare! Sure JACKSON yet
Will all reprieve but one—
O hark! Those shrieks! That cry of death!
The deadly deed is done!

*H*ad more of substance separated Jackson from Adams, the contest between the two might not have become so personal. In foreign affairs the two saw eye to nationalist eye, each deeming American security, assertively defined, the sine qua non of American diplomacy. Domestically, Adams backed federal spending on such internal improvements as the National Road, which Jackson didn't; but the country's depression-induced caution left the administration without traction on the issue. The most controversial matter of Adams's tenure was the tariff, but the controversy was so convoluted as to give voters little to choose between the candidates. Jackson had sufficiently waffled on the tariff while in the Senate that no one knew just where he stood; Adams was hardly more consistent. The only sizable group that took a straightforward stand on the tariff was the bloc of southern planters, who depended on exports and wanted a low tariff to prevent other countries' being tempted to erect barriers to American cotton. Yet even this position failed to translate cleanly into election-year politics. The chief spokesman for the South was John Calhoun, who had run for vice president in 1824 with support from both the Adams and the Jackson camps and naturally won. He currently served under Adams, but he favored Jackson for 1828.

Lacking issues, the Jacksonians ran on symbols. One symbol—a negative one—was the "corrupt bargain" between Adams and Clay. Like any other symbol, this suggested far more than it denoted. In the Jacksonian view, the theft of the 1824 election was emblematic of a deeper corruption that undermined American liberty and prevented the ordinary people of America from controlling their government and their lives. The anointing of successors by several presidents was one aspect of the corruption; the attempt by the Republican caucus in Congress to monopolize nominations was another; the trading of offices for political support—most notoriously in the Adams-Clay deal but practiced for years throughout the executive branch—was a third. For the people to take power, they must pierce this ring of corruption; for the people to maintain power, they must shatter the ring of corruption forever.

A second symbol, the antithesis of the first, was Jackson himself. Jackson didn't have to say a word to represent everything the incumbents were not. His biography spoke for itself: victor of New Orleans, savior of the nation, man of the people. Votes for Jackson were votes against corruption, votes for the principle of democracy, votes for the people by the people themselves.

The theme of democracy against corruption was hammered home again and again by the Jacksonians. In nearly every city, town, and county seat in America, Jackson committees held rallies for their hero, hosting speakers who waxed long and florid for the people's right to choose one of their own for president. Jackson papers reprinted the speeches, amplifying the praise and adding rebuttals of attacks from the Adams side. An inner circle of Jacksonians, consisting of Sam Houston, William Lewis, and a few other Tennesseans, formed a "whitewashing committee" devoted to neutralizing the Adamsite libels. They enlisted witnesses, took depositions, and drafted editorials. Occasionally they pleaded guilty: Jackson papers ran a squib, "COOL AND DELIBERATE MURDER: Jackson coolly and deliberately put to death upward of fifteen hundred British troops on the 8th of January 1815, on the plains below New Orleans, for no other offense than that they wished to sup in the city that night."

*J*ackson remained above the fray. He resented the attacks on his character, especially those that touched his wartime conduct. Where had the critics been at the hour of peril? Who had then made it possible for them now to enjoy the constitutional freedom to assassinate his character? But while the attacks were sharper and more concentrated than they had ever been, they didn't differ materially from what he had endured over the years, and he refused to dignify them with public answers. "Truth is mighty, and will prevail," he promised Felix Grundy.

Yet there was one class of slanders he couldn't ignore. Public-opinion polls didn't exist in the 1820s (and wouldn't for another century), but Jacksonians around the country reported confidently that the general had never been more popular with the ordinary people of America, who wouldn't tolerate another stolen election like that of 1824. Adams's partisans must have agreed, about Jackson's popularity if not about the legitimacy of the 1824 election, for they resorted to a risky tactic designed to shake the equanimity of the people's favorite. Stealthily at first, then more openly, they resurrected the tales of the irregularity in Jackson's early relationship with Rachel. The insatiable Jackson, as they portrayed things, had violated the sanctity of marriage by stealing another man's wife. Rachel was cast as an adulteress, in the milder accounts, and a whore, in others. More than a few papers crossed the color line in their treatment of Rachel. The *Commentator* of Frankfort, Kentucky, likened her to a "*dirty, black wench!*" Other editors reprinted the remark, giving it wide circulation.

It was a maneuver fraught with peril for Adams. Voters might well recoil from the dragging of Rachel through the mud. But the Adams men could think of nothing else so likely to provoke the general into doing something that would make him appear unpresidential.

Jackson was certainly provoked. To William Lewis he confessed "such feelings of indignation that I can scarcely control." To another associate he said, "When the midnight assassin strikes you to the heart, murders your family, and robs your dwelling, the heart sickens at the relation of the deed; but this scene loses all its horrors when compared with the recent slander of a virtuous female propagated by the minions of power for political effect." Jackson understood his enemies' aim. "It is evident that it is the last effort of the combined coalition to save themselves and destroy me," he told Richard Call. "They calculated that it would arouse me to some desperate act by which I would fall prostrate before the people." Jackson realized he could do nothing at once that wouldn't simply expose Rachel to additional insult. "For the present my hands are pinioned." But he vowed that the evildoers would be punished. "The day of retribution and vengeance must come, when the guilty will meet with their just reward."

❧ ❧ ❧

𝒫olitically speaking, the day of retribution came in the autumn of 1828. Not till decades later would Americans agree on the first Tuesday of November as the time to cast ballots for president. In 1828 they were still getting used to the idea that the people—as opposed to the state legislatures—should vote for the highest office in the land. Technically, of course, they still voted for electors, and substantial variation persisted regarding the manner in which the popular vote in a state bound its electors. Some states applied a rule of winner take all, with a popular majority for one candidate producing a unanimous vote for that candidate among the state's electors. Other states allowed split decisions.

Had the contest been close, these differences might have mattered. But by mid-October it was shaping up to be a runaway. "The political news from all quarters is of the most flattering kind," Jackson wrote Richard Call. "New York, it is constantly believed, will give against the administration 30, if not 33, votes. Ohio and Kentucky is believed to be safe for the people's cause, but both sides are sanguine. Pennsylvania and Virginia, immoveable. New Jersey and Delaware against the administration, and Maryland a majority. A few days more will test the result."

The result turned out to be overwhelmingly favorable. New England went for Adams, along with New Jersey and Delaware. New York and Maryland split between Adams and Jackson. But the rest of the country—all the West and nearly the whole South—voted for Jackson. The popular vote was 647,000 for Jackson against 508,000 for Adams. (The much larger totals than in 1824 reflected the continuing shift toward popular voting for electors in the states.) Jackson's victory in the electoral college—178 to 83—was even more decisive. In the congressional elections, the Jacksonians, who were beginning to call themselves Democrats, handily defeated their opponents, gaining a large majority in the House and a small majority in the Senate.

Jackson accepted the judgment with satisfaction. "The suffrages of a virtuous people have pronounced a verdict of condemnation against them and their slanders, whilst it has justified my character and course," he told John Coffee.

∽ ∽ ∽

And then he said something that must have surprised Coffee: "Still, my mind is depressed." He didn't specify what weighed upon him in the hour of triumph, saying only, "I will write you more fully shortly."

Not for two weeks did he write Coffee again. Congratulations from around the country poured into the Hermitage, and the obvious emotion of the letters pushed back whatever dark feelings haunted him. "Providence has procured for us a verdict of the people, which has condemned these wicked proceedings," he told Coffee when he had a moment, "and has pronounced to an admiring world that the people are virtuous and capable of self-government. . . . The liberty of our beloved country will be perpetual." On a more personal note, he commented that he was thankful that he and Rachel had survived the stresses of the campaign, against the wicked slanders of his enemies. "Providence has snatched us from the snares of the fowler," he said.

Jackson didn't return to the subject of his depression. But it almost certainly related to Rachel. A visitor to the Hermitage about this time—the daughter of an army officer—later remembered the master and mistress.

> Picture to yourself a military-looking man, above the ordinary height, dressed plainly but with great neatness, dignified and grave— I had almost said stern—but always courteous and affable, with keen, searching eyes, iron-gray hair, standing stiffly up from an expansive forehead, a face somewhat furrowed by care and time, and expressive of deep thought and active intellect. . . .
>
> Side by side with him stands a coarse-looking, stout, little old woman, whom you might easily mistake for his washerwoman, were it not for the marked attention he pays her, and the love and admiration she manifests for him. Her eyes are bright, and express great kindness of heart; her face is rather broad, her features plain; her complexion so dark as almost to suggest a mingling of races in that climate where such things sometimes occur. But, withal, her face is so good-natured and motherly that you immediately feel at ease with her, however shy you may be of the stately person by her side. Her figure is rather full but loosely and carelessly dressed, so that when she is seated she seems to settle into herself in a manner

that is neither graceful nor elegant. . . . I have heard my mother say that she could imagine that in her early youth, at the time the General yielded to her fascinations, she may have been a bright, sparkling brunette, perhaps may even have passed for a beauty. But being without any culture, and out of the way of refining influences, she was, at the time we knew her, such as I have described. . . .

I remember my father's telling an anecdote characteristic of Mrs. Jackson, which impressed my young mind forcibly. After the evening meal at the Hermitage, he and some other officers were seated with the worthy couple by their ample fire-place. Mrs. Jackson, as was her favorite custom, lighted her pipe, and having taken a whiff or two, handed it to my father, saying: "Honey, won't you take a smoke?"

Mismatched physically, in manners, and in exposure to the world, the Jacksons were nonetheless soul mates. "Their affection for each other was of the tenderest kind," the officer's daughter said. "The General always treated her as if she were his pride and glory, and words can faintly describe her devotion to him."

This was Rachel in her element. Jackson knew how she loved the Hermitage and how she hated Washington. And the beating she had taken in the Adams press during the campaign made her dread the capital more than ever. His victory vindicated him, but it sentenced her to a life she could hardly bear to ponder. Jackson knew that no one—no soldier, no political ally—had ever served him more faithfully than Rachel had. None had suffered such public abuse on his behalf. And now he would repay her loyalty and love by dragging her to the epicenter of the abuse, which would hardly end just because the election was over. The thought would have depressed any feeling man, and it cast a deep shadow over Jackson's victory.

Rachel didn't complain. "I could have spent at the Hermitage the remnant of my days in peace, and were it not that I should be unhappy by being so far from the General, no consideration could induce me again to abandon this delightful spot," she wrote a friend on December 1. "But since it has pleased a grateful people once more to call him to their service, and since by the permission of Providence he will obey that call, I have resolved—

indeed, it is a duty I owe to myself and my husband—to try to forget, at least for a time, all the endearments of home and prepare to live where it has pleased heaven to fix our destiny." To another friend she spoke in a more somber tone. "Hitherto my Saviour has been my guide and support through all my afflictions (which I must confess for the last four years have been many and unprovoked), and now I have no doubt but he will still aid and instruct me in my duties which I fear will be many and arduous."

Her fear didn't diminish as she and her husband prepared for the move to Washington. It preyed on her till, on December 18, it apparently contributed to a heart attack. Jackson was writing a letter; Rachel was sitting across the room. Suddenly she felt an "excruciating pain in the left shoulder, arm, and breast," as Jackson described it. He carried her to bed and called the doctor.

For three days, she held her own. The doctor bled her, at a loss as to any other treatment. On the fourth day she flagged. Jackson didn't know what to do. Washington awaited his inauguration, and the journey would be long. But he couldn't go. "I cannot leave her," he told Richard Call.

And then she died. Her heart, wounded on her husband's behalf, burdened by the strains of the election and the prospect of more, gave up its struggle.

Still he couldn't leave her. A friend recalled that he held her so tightly after death that the body had to be pried from his arms to prepare it for burial. Another remembered that he looked "twenty years older in a night."

He buried her in a corner of the Hermitage garden, in a gentle rain. For many months afterward his mind reverted to the moment when the ground closed over her. "Could I but withdraw from the scenes around me," he wrote from the White House the following summer, "to the private walks of the Hermitage, how soon would I be found in the solitary shades of my garden, at the tomb of my wife, there to spend my days in silent sorrow and in peace from the toils and strife of this world. . . . O, how fluctuating are all earthly things. At the time I least expected it, and could least spare her, she was snatched from me, and I left here a solitary monument of grief, without the least hope of happiness here below."

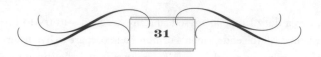

31

DEMOCRACY RAMPANT

In his grief, the only thing that enabled Jackson to carry on was the same thing that had allowed him to let his name be forwarded for the presidency in the first place: his sense of duty. The people had spoken; he must answer their call. But he wondered if this time duty didn't ask too much. As a soldier he had never put Rachel in danger. As a soldier he had *defended* her, and all the other innocents at their homes and firesides. In politics, though, apparently not even women were safe from enemy fire.

The cost of his latest victory was the life of the woman he loved. His various infirmities had long stolen sleep from his nights, but now they had a new ally in insomnia: the inescapable suspicion that this wouldn't have happened, that she would be living yet, if he had heeded her wishes and kept clear of politics. He had killed a man with his own hand, had ordered the execution of several others, had been responsible for thousands of deaths in battle, and never lost a minute of sleep to guilt. But this was different, and it was agonizing. His victory hadn't merely turned to ashes in his mouth. It turned to an ache in his heart that wouldn't cease.

He had all he could do to make himself go to Washington for his inauguration. He delayed his departure, lingering by Rachel's grave. Finally he set off, but with nothing like the joy he had felt at previous victories. And whatever victories might lie ahead, he was sure he would never experience happiness again.

General Jackson will be here about the 15th of February," Daniel Webster remarked in Washington. "Nobody knows what he will do. . . . Many letters are sent to him; he answers none of them." John Calhoun thought the silence eerie. "We have a dead calm in politics," he wrote.

The city that awaited Jackson's arrival was a work in progress. Residents of America's few real cities laughed at Washington's pretensions. "Our inimitable capital is a parody upon all other capitals that were ever actually built up and inhabited since the beginning of the world," remarked the architecture critic for the *Philadelphia Monthly*. A visitor, he said, could wander for hours through the federal district before stumbling on the city itself. "Unless he should be told, . . . he would hardly know whether the few straggling blocks of bricks and mortar that he beheld at intervals few and far between constituted *urbs in rure*, or the vast surface of vacant sand and marsh that stretched around them was *rus in urbe*." The most imposing structure was the Capitol. "It is a spacious edifice and a stately one, when seen out of doors, but strangers who are not *au fait* in the topography of the interior are often lost in the intricate passages and sudden sinuosities that have been contrived, probably as emblems of the crooked and narrow paths by which those for whose accommodation the house was built find their way to it."

The plan of the city specified several grand avenues, named for the states. But only one—Pennsylvania—came anywhere near matching the ambitions of the designer. "This is *the* avenue *par excellence*," the anonymous (in those un-bylined days) Philadelphia critic continued. "It conducts you from the capitol to the President's House, which is an immense pile without any extraordinary pretensions to the sublime or beautiful. Along this flat and uninteresting highway, fashionable ladies and gentlemen who cannot sport their carriages promenade, and the brilliant equipages of ambassadors, ministers, and opulent gentry are in perpetual whirl."

The ambitions of the gentry appeared in the manners they imposed on social life. "Every look, word and gesture in this aspiring city is regulated by the most fastidious etiquette. It is as much as your reputation is worth to transgress the rules provided for the defence of fashionable life." Even the innkeepers enforced the code. "One of them, who holds a high rank among the *aubergistes* of fashion, is reported to have established at his table the most rigid code of polite discipline. All who can afford to sit at his board are expected, out of pure politeness, to partake of a few spoon-fulls of soup, whether they relish it or not." The code extended no grace to the uninitiated. "Woe to the simple, unsophisticated visitor of Washington, who, in obedience to the promptings of nature and observance of the uncourtly manners which he had practiced in his native village or woods, ventures to speak, dress, look, eat, or perform any ordinary office of life without deference to fashion!"

*Y*et precisely such unsophisticates, an entire army of them, were descending on Washington. Jackson's election inspired many thousands of his supporters to visit the capital. Having rescued the republic, as they saw it, by electing their hero, they came to install him, just to make sure. Their arrival astonished the residents of the city. "No one who was at Washington at the time of General Jackson's inauguration is likely to forget that period to the day of his death," one resident declared. "To us, who had witnessed the quiet and orderly period of the Adams administration, it seemed as if half the nation had rushed at once into the capital. It was like the inundation of the northern barbarians into Rome, save that the tumultuous tide came in from a different point of the compass. The West and the South seemed to have precipitated themselves upon the North and overwhelmed it. . . . Strange faces filled every public place, and every face seemed to bear defiance on its brow." Other observers drew different historical analogies. The Philadelphia critic likened the arrival of the Jacksonians to the time when "the mighty Xerxes ferried or marched his mob of an army over the Hellespont, or Peter the Hermit led on his rabble of Christian vagabonds to drive the Musselmans from the Holy Sepulchre."

Late February was quite cold, but March brought a break in the weather. March 4 dawned warm and springlike. The city awakened early when Jackson enthusiasts spontaneously fired cannons to herald democracy's day. Spectators began streaming toward the Capitol grounds to claim seats and standing places for the inauguration ceremony. Jackson had spent the night at Gadsby's House; at ten-thirty he reviewed a company of fifteen aging veterans of the Revolutionary War who had traveled to Washington to pay their respects. Now they insisted on escorting him to the Capitol.

Jackson and his white-haired guard drew a crowd along the way. The Marine Band struck up "Jackson's March"—an air commemorating the Battle of New Orleans—as the general's carriage entered the south gate of the Capitol grounds. Ten thousand people roared their approval when they caught sight of Jackson stepping out of the carriage; the roar faded only after he disappeared into the building.

The clock showed half past eleven as Jackson entered the Senate chamber, accompanied by the Committee of Arrangements and the marshal of the District of Columbia. He sat down directly before the desk of the secretary of the Senate. In the chair of the Senate was Vice President Calhoun, who had been reelected to that post as part of the Jackson triumph. Calhoun proceeded to administer the oath of office to the fourteen new members of the upper house.

Chief Justice John Marshall entered the chamber and sat to Jackson's right. The associate justices followed Marshall and took their seats. The diplomatic corps—envoys from foreign countries—sat on Jackson's left. Members of the House of Representatives filed in and filled the gallery on the west side of the Senate.

Promptly at noon Calhoun gaveled adjournment of the Senate and a procession to the east portico commenced. The crowd on the grounds, numbering perhaps fifteen thousand by now, had gathered below the portico, waiting intently to see their hero again. When Jackson emerged between the columns of the portico, the crowd erupted, louder than before. Their cheers rumbled across the grounds, joined shortly by twenty-four cannons booming the official salute.

Jackson remained standing before the crowd. He wore two pairs of eyeglasses: one currently on his eyes, the other—his reading lenses—thrown on top of his head. While the tumult lasted he conversed with Calhoun, on his left.

The crowd composed itself somewhat when John Marshall stepped forward to administer Jackson's oath. Marshall's voice was strong, Jackson's almost inaudible. Only those standing very close could hear him pronounce the words specified by the Constitution. When he finished he took up the Bible on which he had sworn, raised it to his lips, and kissed it. Then he turned to the people and bowed, as a minister in a monarchy might bow to his sovereign.

The crowd strained to hear the president's inaugural address. It lasted but a few minutes. He emphasized the popular nature of his victory, crediting the "free choice of the people" for his elevation. He promised to interpret the Constitution strictly. "I shall keep steadily in view the limitations as well as the extent of the executive power." He would respect the rights of the states, "taking care not to confound the powers they have reserved to themselves with those they have granted to the confederacy." In foreign affairs he would seek "to preserve peace and to cultivate friendship on fair and honorable terms." He would strengthen the army, but he looked to the people for the ultimate safety of the republic. "The bulwark of our defence is the national militia, which in the present state of our intelligence and population must render us invincible as long as our government is administered for the good of the people and is regulated by their will. . . . A million of armed freemen possessed of the means of war can never be conquered by a foreign foe."

𝓗ad the spectacle closed here," Margaret Bayard Smith wrote, "even Europeans must have acknowledged that a free people, collected in their might, silent and tranquil, restrained solely by a moral power, without a shadow around of military force, was majesty, rising to sublimity, and far surpassing the majesty of Kings and Princes, surrounded with armies and glittering in gold."

Margaret Bayard's forebears were Federalist, but she had married a Republican just weeks before the first election of Thomas Jefferson. She moved with her husband, Samuel Smith, to Washington and for the next forty years observed the evolution of American politics. Till Jefferson died, the philosopher of Monticello was her favorite among American political figures, which disposed her to favor the people in theory but not always in practice. She socialized with Henry Clay and others of the Adams administration and shared their reservations about Jackson. She attended the inauguration out of curiosity, to see how the new president and his horde of followers would behave.

She was pleasantly surprised. "It was grand—it was sublime!" she wrote a friend regarding the ceremony at the Capitol. "Thousands and thousands of people, without distinction of rank, collected in an immense mass round the Capitol, silent, orderly and tranquil."

But the tranquility and sublimity couldn't be sustained in the face of the people's enthusiasm for their hero. "When the speech was over, and the president made his parting bow, the barrier that had separated the people from him was broken down and they rushed up the steps all eager to shake hands with him." Jackson obliged for a time, but the crush became too great. Only with difficulty was a path forced through the Capitol yard and down the hill to the gate that opened onto Pennsylvania Avenue. He couldn't get through the gate. "The living mass was impenetrable," Margaret Smith said. Eventually another path was opened and the president's horse brought forward. He mounted the white stallion and commenced the slow march to the executive mansion. "Such a cortege as followed him! Country men, farmers, gentlemen, mounted and dismounted, boys, women and children, black and white. Carriages, wagons and carts all pursuing him to the President's house."

Public receptions at the mansion had been a feature of inaugurations since Jefferson's day. Distinguished Washingtonians paid their respects to the new president and reconfirmed their solidarity as the governing class. Margaret Smith and most other veterans of the capital had expected a similar soiree this afternoon. But the crowd at the inauguration and in the procession behind the president on Pennsylvania Avenue suggested that something different was afoot, quite literally. Mrs. Smith refused to throw herself into the surging sea of democrats. She repaired to a friend's nearby home, to let the crowd diminish. Yet the torrent persisted. "Streams of people on foot and carriages of all kinds, still pouring toward the President's house," she noted more than an hour later.

Not till three o'clock did she manage to work her way through the crowd into the mansion. She thought she had stumbled on the aftermath of a battle.

> What a scene did we witness! The *Majesty of the People* had disappeared, and a rabble, a mob, of boys, negros, women, children, scrambling, fighting, romping. What a pity, what a pity! No arrangements had been made, no police officers placed on duty, and the whole house had been inundated by the rabble mob. . . . Cut glass and china to the amount of several thousand dollars had been broken in the struggle to get to the refreshments, punch and other articles had been carried out in tubs and buckets. . . . Ladies fainted, men were seen with bloody noses, and such a scene of confusion as is impossible to describe. Those who got in could not get out by the door again, but had to scramble out of windows.

After all her effort, Margaret Smith was disappointed at not meeting the president, who, having shaken some ten thousand hands, had escaped to his hotel.

The mob scene at the White House was what most people remembered about the inauguration. Even some Jacksonians were taken aback. "It was a glorious day yesterday for the *sovereigns*," James Hamilton wrote wryly. "The mob broke in, in thousands. Spirits black, yellow, and grey, poured in in one uninterrupted stream of mud and filth, among the throng many subjects for the penitentiary."

Those less favorably inclined toward the new president and the new democracy took a more skeptical view. Joseph Story, an associate justice of the Supreme Court, winced at what he called the "noise and tumult and hollow parade" of democracy's hour, and he shook his head at the spectacle at the White House. "I never saw such a mixture," he said. "The reign of King

'Mob' seemed triumphant. I was glad to escape from the scene as soon as possible."

Yet even the skeptics couldn't help perceiving that something remarkable had happened. Margaret Smith observed, "It was the People's day, and the People's President, and the People would rule."

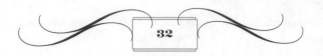

32

SPOILS OF VICTORY

The first order of business for the Jackson administration was repairing the damage done to the White House by the overly enthusiastic friends of democracy. The second order of business, commenced almost simultaneously, was repairing the damage done to American liberty by the foes of democracy.

Such, at any rate, was how Jackson viewed his mission. His election, though not unexpected by the time it happened, turned the American political world on its head. Not since Jefferson's victory in 1800 had there been a hostile takeover of the presidency, and no one expected Jackson to offer an olive branch like that put forward by Jefferson in his "we are all republicans; we are all federalists" inaugural address. A theme of the first Jackson administration would certainly be reform, after everything the

Jacksonians had said about corruption in government. In time reform would mean all things to all people, and consequently nothing much to many, but to the Jacksonians it meant something specific. They were republicans before they were democrats, and a fundamental feature of republican thought in America, from the days of the Revolution, was an insistence on civic virtue. The revolutionaries of 1776 decried the corruption they saw in British politics: the perversion of government to the illegitimate pursuit of private gain. The rebels demanded independence lest the corruption cross the Atlantic and infect America. When the Jacksonians raised the cry of corruption against the Adams administration, they spoke against this background of revolutionary rhetoric and were so understood. The reform they demanded would stop short of a violent revolution—although after the sack of the White House some skeptics weren't so sure—but it could hardly be less sweeping in its assault on entrenched power. The people had commenced the process by turning out Adams. The new president would continue the work by displacing the minions of the old regime.

*H*e began with the State Department, the first of the executive agencies. For secretary of state Jackson chose Martin Van Buren of New York. Van Buren had helped deliver the New York vote to Jackson and in the process had confirmed a reputation for political sorcery. His enemies intended to insult him by calling him a "magician," but his friends—some of them, anyway—took up the epithet and made it a mark of honor. His reputation as a climber didn't diminish when he resigned the New York governorship after less than three months in office to become the senior member of Jackson's cabinet.

Pennsylvania contributed the head of the Treasury. The state's support had been crucial in Jackson's election, but beyond this the new president wanted to brace himself for trouble with the Bank of the United States, headquartered in Philadelphia and a hotbed of holdover Federalism. Samuel Ingham couldn't expect to bring the bankers around, but he might keep their animus from infecting the entire Keystone State.

Jackson turned to Tennessee, to his friend and protégé John Eaton, for secretary of war. Eaton's qualifications mattered less than his loyalty, in that

Jackson intended to act as his own secretary of war should hostilities—with Britain, Spain, or the Indians—resume.

John Branch of North Carolina became secretary of the navy, an office of government Jackson knew little and cared less about. The navy should grow, but slowly, and any honest person ought to be able to handle that. John Berrien of Georgia was named attorney general, and William Barry of Kentucky postmaster general.

Beyond his official cabinet, Jackson gathered a council of informal advisers. Unlike every previous president except Washington, Jackson had almost no intimates in the national capital upon his inauguration. (Washington had almost no intimates anywhere, being famously above mere mortals.) Jackson knew his cabinet secretaries, other than Eaton, by reputation alone. For this reason he turned for advice to men whose judgment and loyalty he had learned to trust during the long campaign. William Lewis of Tennessee stood first among the equals. Amos Kendall, an ardently pro-Jackson editor from Kentucky, came next. Duff Green, a Missouri transplant who now edited the fiercely Jacksonian *United States Telegraph* at Washington, and Isaac Hill, for years a lonely Jacksonian in New Hampshire, rounded out the clique. Andrew Donelson, the president's nephew, surrogate son, and now personal secretary, was an ex officio member of the group.

Jackson's informal council served him as a sounding board for policy, but it also provided emotional sustenance, especially now that Rachel was gone. The group took shape after William Lewis, having helped install Jackson in the White House, prepared to return to Tennessee to his farm. "Why, Major," Jackson said, "you are not going to leave me here *alone*, after doing more than any other man to bring me here?" Lewis reconsidered and, when Jackson found him a minor post at the Treasury, stayed on. Kendall and Hill likewise received positions with the Treasury, while Green landed government printing contracts.

The cabinet appointments evoked little enthusiasm among outside observers but not much criticism either. John Eaton was charged with being merely a Tennessee favorite of the president—which prompted Jackson to embrace him all the tighter. "Great exertions have been made by Clay's friends to raise a clamour about my taking Major Eaton into my cabinet, and some of my friends from Tennessee, weak enough to be duped by the artifice, were made instruments," he told John Coffee. "The object was to intimidate me from the selection, and thereby destroy Major Eaton. I had to assume sufficient energy to meet the crisis. I did meet it, and Major Eaton will become one of the most popular men in the departments, be a great comfort to me, and will manage the department of war well."

Critics concentrated their fire against the "kitchen cabinet," as they derisively called Jackson's informal circle. William Lewis was assailed as the president's personal propagandist, while Amos Kendall, Duff Green, and Isaac Hill were branded hack writers remarkable only for their singular prejudice for all things Jacksonian. Even some of Jackson's friends acknowledged that appearances weren't good. "We lament to see so many of the editorial corps favored with the patronage of the Administration," Thomas Ritchie wrote to Martin Van Buren. Ritchie edited the Richmond *Enquirer* and had backed Jackson strongly, although not so strongly as Kendall, Green, and Hill. "A single case would not have excited so much observation, but it really looks as if there were a systematic effort to reward editorial partizans, which will have the effect of bringing the vaunted liberty of the press into contempt." Ritchie didn't question the ability of Kendall and the others, and he positively admired their courage. All the same, their personal standing with Jackson made him uneasy. "Invade the freedom of the press and the freedom of election, by showering patronage too much on editors of newspapers . . . and the rights of the people themselves are exposed to imminent danger."

Ritchie, who knew he was writing for the president's eyes as much as for Van Buren's, thought Jackson's choice of advisers reflected on the broader issue of reform. "What is reform?" he asked Van Buren. "Is it to turn out of office all those who voted against him, or who decently preferred Mr. Adams? Or is it not rather those who are incapable of discharging their duties: the drunken, the ignorant, the embezzler? . . . It is surely not to put out a good and experienced officer because he was a decent friend of J. Q. Adams, *in order* to put in a heated partizan of the election of General Jackson."

Ritchie had a point, and Jackson knew it. But the president responded defensively, as he often did to criticism, however well intended. "You may assure Mr. Ritchie . . . that the President has not, nor will he ever, make an appointment but with a view to the public good," he told Van Buren. "He never has, nor will he, appoint a personal friend to office unless by such appointment the public will be faithfully served." Having got that out of his system and on the record, Jackson continued in a more philosophical vein. "I cannot suppose Mr. Ritchie would have me proscribe my friends merely because they are so. If my personal friends are qualified and patriotic, why should I not be permitted to bestow a *few* offices on them?" Presidents Washington and Jefferson had rewarded friends, to the benefit of the public, as Ritchie certainly knew. "Before he condemns the tree, he ought to wait and see its fruit. The people expect reform. They shall not be disappointed. But it must be *judiciously* done, and upon *principle*."

*T*he principle Jackson decided on was that rotation in office, rather than permanent tenure, should be the norm in a democracy. As this was a departure from previous practice, and liable to misinterpretation, he took care to explain the reasoning behind it. "There are, perhaps, few men who can for any great length of time enjoy office and power without being more or less under the influence of feelings unfavorable to the faithful discharge of their public duties," he said. "They are apt to acquire a habit of looking with indifference upon the public interests and of tolerating conduct from which an unpracticed man would revolt. Office is considered as a species of property." Such thinking was wrong, and it was what Jackson intended to root out. "In a country where offices are created solely for the benefit of the people, no one man has any more intrinsic right to official station than another. Offices were not established to give support to particular men at the public expense. No individual wrong is, therefore, done by removal, since neither appointment to nor continuance in office is a matter of right."

This was why rotation *should* be practiced. That it *could* be practiced without damage to the common welfare followed from the nature of the work. "The duties of all public officers are, or at least admit of being made, so plain and simple that men of intelligence may readily qualify themselves for their performance." Far from damaging performance, rotation would actually improve it. "I can not but believe that more is lost by the long continuance of men in office than is generally to be gained by their experience."

Yet applying the principle of rotation wasn't painless. The replacement of federal officials worked real hardship in some cases. "My husband, sir, never was your enemy," the wife of one ousted official wrote Jackson. Her man had simply voted his conscience, and for this he had lost his job. "You were apprised of our poverty; you knew the dependence of eight little children for food and raiment upon my husband's salary. You knew that, advanced in years as he was, without the means to prosecute any regular business, and without friends able to assist him, the world would be to him a barren heath, an inhospitable wild."

Jackson couldn't ignore the protests, but he recognized that, however heartfelt, they were usually one-sided. A woman correspondent berated him for firing a man named Hawkins, the husband of a friend. "You can have no idea of the integrity, honesty and good principles of the man you have prostrated, and literally taken the bread out of the mouths of a helpless wife and two small children," she said. Jackson inquired after Hawkins and discovered that he habitually got drunk on the job. Yet he answered the woman tactfully. "It is a painful duty to be the instrument of lessening the resources of a family so amiable as that of Mr. Hawkins, but when the public good calls for it, it must be performed," he wrote. "As a private individual, it would give me the greatest happiness to alleviate their distresses, but as a public officer, I cannot devote to this object the interests of the country."

Jackson knew, and didn't mind, that the fear of being fired would affect many more persons than those actually dismissed. A little fear would have a sobering effect on the tipsy, a vivifying effect on the lazy, a straightening effect on the wayward.

But the fear got out of hand. After four administrations of indulgence, the merest hint of accountability pushed some to paranoia. "The gloom of suspicion pervaded the face of society," one officeholder asserted. "No man deemed it safe and prudent to trust his neighbor. . . . A casual remark, dropped in the street, would within an hour be repeated at headquarters; and many a man received unceremonious dismission who could not, for his life, conceive or conjecture wherein he had offended." Another critic contended that whatever good the replacements had done was overshadowed by the harm. "I question whether the ferreting out treasury rats, and the correction of abuses, are sufficient to compensate for the reign of terror which appears to have commenced. It would be well enough if it were confined to evildoers, but it spreads abroad like a contagion: spies, informers, denunciations—the fecula of despotism."

Jackson had never let criticism turn him from the course his conscience dictated, and he didn't let criticism turn him now. He hefted his shovel to "cleanse the Augean stables," as he put it to Coffee. But an inevitable side effect almost caused him to wish he'd left the matter alone. Once word got out that the new administration considered most federal appointments subject to review, Jackson was besieged by applicants for the places made vacant. Battalions of hopefuls wrote reciting their qualifications. Regiments appeared in person. "I have been crowded with thousands of applicants for office," Jackson lamented to Coffee, "and if I had a tit for every applicant to suck the Treasury pap, all would go away well satisfied; but as there are not offices for more than one out of five hundred who applies, many must go away dissatisfied."

How clean Jackson got the Augean stables is hard to say. His enemies had reason to exaggerate the carnage among the officeholders and to emphasize the virtue of those let go, while his friends had incentive to understate the number of political replacements and cast most removals as dismissals for cause. The best estimate is that between one-tenth and one-fifth of federal officeholders were replaced during Jackson's tenure other than by ordinary attrition. For obvious reasons, this figure was higher than under Jackson's immediate predecessors, but it appears to be comparable with the turnover after Jefferson defeated John Adams.

Yet Jackson's opponents had the last word, even if they stole it from a friend of the president. Governor William Marcy of New York applied the Jacksonian rule to his own state, without apology. "It may be, sir, that the politicians of New York are not so fastidious as some gentlemen are as to disclosing the principles on which they act. They boldly preach what they practice. When they are contending for victory, they avow their intention of enjoying the fruits of it. If they are defeated, they expect to retire from office. . . . They see nothing wrong in the rule that to the victor belongs the spoils."

Jackson insisted on calling his approach "rotation in office." But "spoils system" was what stuck.

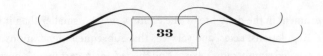

33

TOOLS OF WICKEDNESS

In the nineteenth century a new president had a long time to adjust

to his surroundings before having to deal with Congress in a meaningful

way. Each legislative session consisted of two terms: one beginning in

December and running till the following summer, the other commencing

in December again and lasting only till the end of winter. Jackson, like

other presidents, was inaugurated at the tail end of the short session,

which meant that he had till the following December—more than

a year after he learned that he would be the next president—to

prepare to do business with the legislators.

The long interval reflected the leisurely pace of life in those earlier

days (compared, of course, with what would come), but it also manifested

the limited expectations Americans had of government. The footprint of government in the daily life of the country was far smaller than it would be later. Regulations, taxes, and services that subsequent generations would take for granted simply didn't exist. And the *federal* government's portion of that smaller footprint was especially petite. The great majority of laws that touched the lives of citizens were written by their state legislatures. Politicians in Washington flattered themselves as being at the top of the food chain of government, and in certain respects they were. The great issues of war and peace were reserved to the federal government, as were relations among the states. But the smaller fish in the states collectively consumed far more of the attention—and resources—of the people than the whales in Washington.

With little substantive to consider during its first several months, a new administration could easily be distracted by matters of little substance. In Jackson's case the distraction came from a direction he could never have expected. Just weeks before the inauguration, John Eaton married Margaret O'Neal Timberlake. Eaton had known Peg O'Neal for a decade, having stayed in the Washington house of her father, along with numerous other paying guests, including at times Jackson. Peg was just a girl during those early years, but she blossomed into a beauty noticed and desired by the boarders and many besides. She appreciated the attention, as did her father, who observed its positive effect on the guest traffic and did little to curtail her naturally flirtatious ways. In time she paired off with John Timberlake, a young naval officer, and the two were wed. But Timberlake's duties took him from Washington for many months at a time, leaving Peg at her father's house with the other guests, who found her more attractive than ever. And she was just as friendly as ever, which inevitably set tongues wagging with respect to her faithfulness to her far-off spouse.

In 1828 came news that Timberlake had died, apparently by his own hand. Peg weathered the blow remarkably well, and in fact soon engaged to marry Eaton, himself the loser of a spouse. The proposed union provoked a new round of whispers, with the undercurrent of innuendo being that the lovers had conspired most intimately against Timberlake while he was still alive and that perhaps their conspiracy had pushed him over the edge of self-destruction. Eaton heard the whispers and traveled to the Hermitage to ask Jackson for counsel.

Jackson could demonize male rivals in a moment, but he could never bring himself to think ill of a woman. His female models were his sainted mother, who had died in the service of himself, his brothers, and his cousins, and Rachel, whose virtue had been impugned far longer than Peg O'Neal's and for no reason beyond the fame of her husband. Eaton arrived at the Hermitage before Rachel's heart attack but after the stress of the campaign had inflicted its emotional toll, and as he spoke of Peg, Jackson could look across the parlor to where Rachel rocked by the fire, puffing her pipe, and wish for Eaton such happiness as she had brought him. In most definite terms he told Eaton to take Peg to his heart and let their enemies be damned. Eaton valued the encouragement and esteemed the old man more than ever on its account. "It was a matter of infinite satisfaction to me," he wrote Jackson afterward, "to find that your advice and opinions accorded with my own. From that moment I was inspired with new and fresh decision as to the course to be pursued."

The wedding took place in Washington on the first day of the new year, giving the capital gossips something to twitter about pending Jackson's arrival. Their attention gradually strayed to such other topics as who would receive the plum appointments in the incoming administration, till the newlyweds hoped that the worst was over. But then Eaton himself landed the War Department, throwing him right back into the cauldron of political attack. His appointment reeked of favoritism, the critics said aloud, while behind their hands they murmured that a man who would steal another's wife, driving the cuckold to kill himself, couldn't be trusted with public money, the lives of America's soldiers, or anything else important. Even some of Jackson's allies, alarmed at the damage that might be done his presidency, gently encouraged him to reconsider Eaton's nomination.

By now Rachel was dead, and Jackson deeply despondent. He had difficulty rousing himself for anything, including battle with his enemies. But the attacks on Peg Eaton, which appeared of a piece with those that had just killed his own beloved, stirred the old spirit. He rose to the defense of Peg. "Mrs. Eaton is as chaste as those who slander her," he proclaimed. Of the tale that Timberlake had killed himself on account of Eaton, he thundered, "There never was a *baser lie told*." He vowed never to listen to these "most unblushing and unfounded slanders" or to waver in his support for Eaton and Peg. "I would sink with honor to my grave before I would abandon my friend."

Jackson succeeded in silencing some of the criticism. But for each rumor suppressed, another appeared. The most lurid asserted that Peg had become pregnant by Eaton and that the two, to hide their secret and their guilt, arranged an abortion. The rumors inspired a social boycott of the Eatons. Cabinet secretaries, being fewer in those days than they would become, were great men in Washington, and their wives were accustomed to visits by the wives of the influential and aspiring. But few women visited Peg Eaton. The wife of John Calhoun led the boycott, and the wives of several of Eaton's cabinet colleagues joined it. Even Emily Donelson, the wife of Jackson's nephew and personal secretary, refused to greet Peg Eaton.

Their behavior sorely tested Jackson's faith in female virtue. He railed at the "ridiculous attitude" of those women who shunned Peg and called them "a group of gossips . . . whose principal business it is to run about the country and point to the mote in their brother or sister's eye without being conscious of the beam that lurks in their own." To a Nashville friend he declared in frustration, "I did not come here to make a cabinet for the ladies of this place, but for the nation." He had never been in a more maddening predicament. There wasn't a thing he could do about Floride Calhoun or most of the other women who were persecuting Peg Eaton. But he did send the Donelsons back to Tennessee till they reassessed Emily's priorities. And he longed more than ever for Rachel, who would have taken Peg's part and, as White House hostess, shamed the rest of the capital into following suit.

*J*ealousy of Peg, who was still one of the most beautiful women in Washington, inspired much of the campaign against her, but political rivalries sustained the boycott far longer than it would have lasted on personal grounds. John Calhoun still wanted to be president, especially after having been elected vice president twice. But the vice presidency wasn't a promising springboard in those days, and Calhoun wasn't close to Jackson either politically or personally. His best hope, he apparently thought, was to undermine those who were, starting with Eaton. Floride Calhoun's honest dislike for Peg Eaton became his instrument for attacking John Eaton and the larger principle of Jacksonian favoritism.

Yet in attacking the Eatons, Calhoun opened the door for Martin Van

Buren. The secretary of state's sympathies lay with Peg Eaton. As a be-reaved widower and a thorough gentleman—like Jackson in both regards—he closed his ears to the vile things said against any woman. But Peg Eaton wasn't just *any* woman. She had become the president's cause, and the pres-ident her champion. It didn't take Van Buren long to realize he could cement his standing with Jackson by standing firm for Peg. He visited her at her house, and he invited her to his own house and, most conspicuously, to the dinners and receptions at the State Department. He let it be known to the ministers of other countries that Mrs. Eaton was to be treated with all the re-spect due any gentlewoman. The British minister cooperated, as did the Russian minister. The Dutch minister—or rather, the Dutch minister's wife—proved more troublesome. At a dinner hosted by the Russian minis-ter, the Dutch matron approached the table only to discover that her as-signed chair was next to Peg Eaton's. Having heard and apparently credited the stories about Peg, she refused to take the seat, instead gathering her hus-band and departing in horror. Van Buren bid them good riddance.

The secretary of state's strategy worked. "I have found the President affectionate, confidential, and kind to the last degree," Van Buren wrote a friend. "I am entirely satisfied that there is no degree of good feeling or con-fidence which he does not entertain for me." Jackson said as much himself. "I have found him every thing that I could desire him to be," the president told John Overton of Van Buren, "and believe him not only deserving *my* confidence, but the confidence of the nation. Instead of his being selfish and intriguing, as has been represented by some of his opponents, I have ever found him frank, open, candid, and manly. As a counsellor he is able and prudent, republican in his principles and one of the most pleasant men to do business with I ever saw."

With each new story that surfaced about Peg, and with each new vari-ant on the old stories, Van Buren's solicitude for her made Jackson more ap-preciative of him. Whether this caused Van Buren himself to contribute covertly to the pot's continued boiling is impossible to say. The stories came from everywhere and nowhere.

The Eaton affair consumed far more of Jackson's time than he should have let it. For months he collected evidence attesting to Peg Eaton's virtue and to the vice of those who traduced her. His obsession was demonstrably unhealthy for his administration, as would become apparent before long. It was also hurtful in a distinctly personal way. Jackson forced his nephew Andrew Donelson to make a choice: between his wife, Emily, and his uncle, the president. Jackson refused to allow Emily to return to the White House so long as she shunned Peg Eaton, which meant that Andrew could either live with his wife or work for his uncle, but not both. Not surprisingly, Andrew chose Emily, which pained and angered Jackson. "That my nephew and niece should permit themselves to be held up as the instruments and *tools* of such wickedness is truly mortifying to me," he wrote William Lewis.

The anger and mortification were public; the pain was private. Donelson was a second son to Jackson, and by blood as close to him as his adopted son, Andrew Jr. For Jackson to banish Donelson was to deprive himself of one of the dwindling number of things in life that gave him any hope of personal happiness. As long as the Eaton affair continued, Jackson pleaded with Donelson to come back to the White House, even as he refused to let Emily return. "I never knew any thing but disgrace to a family, where it united with strangers to disgrace its own kindred," he wrote accusingly to Donelson.

Some of Jackson's closest friends realized the old man had lost his perspective on this point. "He is wholly wrong," John McLemore told Donelson, by way of sympathy. But he went on to urge the young man to show understanding. "Let me *implore you to be mild in your correspondence with the General*. His feelings are not in a situation to bear irritation."

*M*arital problems of another sort intruded on Jackson amid the Eaton affair. "I have this moment heard a rumor of poor Houston's disgrace," the president wrote in April 1829. "My God, is the man *mad*?"

In fact Sam Houston *was* mad, from love gone wrong. By the second half of the 1820s Houston was being spoken of around Tennessee as the heir apparent to Jackson. Houston's two terms in Congress had been devoted to making Jackson president, and Jackson reciprocated by helping Houston become Tennessee governor. When Jackson entered the White House, Tennesseans began talking of a dynasty for the state akin to that once enjoyed by Virginia, with Houston following Jackson into the presidency. The one thing lacking from the Houston résumé was a wife. Houston had played the field of love with storied success for some years but at thirty-five was beginning to be considered rather old for such carefree behavior. With Jackson's encouragement he started courting seriously and found a likely partner in Eliza Allen, the daughter of a distinguished family of Gallatin, near Nashville. The wedding was the event of the social season in Tennessee. Every paper reported the nuptials of the towering, handsome Houston, with military valor in his past and perhaps the presidency in his future, and the beautiful, vivacious Eliza, the belle of the Cumberland.

Attention turned discreetly away from the newlyweds on their honeymoon, only to be riveted back when reports began circulating that Eliza had retired to her parents' house just weeks after the wedding. Shortly thereafter Houston submitted a letter of resignation of the governorship to the Tennessee legislature. He offered nothing by way of explanation beyond a vague reference to being "overwhelmed by sudden calamities." And then, while Nashville was absorbing these stunning developments, he disappeared down the Cumberland, heading west for parts unknown.

Nor did Houston ever explain what had caused the rupture in his marriage and the consequent implosion of his political dreams. The first thought that occurred to many in such circumstances—that Houston had discovered on his wedding night that Eliza wasn't a virgin—was contradicted by his own assertion that the break reflected nothing ill on Eliza's virtue and by his vow to write any libel against Eliza in the heart's blood of the libeler. A less lurid explanation is more likely: that Houston discovered that Eliza hadn't really wanted to marry him but had done so to please her ambitious parents. Houston was a romantic to the core, and the knowledge that she loved another crushed his spirit. Humiliated before the world, he threw over his career and fled the scene of his mortification.

For months Jackson heard only rumors about Houston. They weren't reassuring. One had Houston raving drunkenly about going to Texas and conquering that Mexican territory with the help of Cherokee Indians. Jackson certainly wasn't opposed to expanding the American domain, as his actions in Florida amply demonstrated. And he had had his eye on Texas for decades. But he was currently planning negotiations with Mexico to *purchase* Texas, which would be less controversial and, in the long run, probably cheaper than conquest. A Houston filibuster would spoil things.

In June 1829 Jackson finally received a letter from his wayward protégé.

The letter, posted at Little Rock, Arkansas Territory, made clear by itself that the reports of heavy drinking weren't unfounded, for none but a sot could have rambled as incoherently as Houston did. "Tho' an unfortunate, and doubtless, the most unhappy man now living, whose honor, so far as depends on himself, is not lost," he declared, "I can not brook the idea of your supposing me capable of an act that would not adorn, but rather blot the escutcheon of human nature." Houston seemed to be referring to the Texas boast, and he denied contemplating anything that would embarrass the president. He wallowed some more in self-pity. "What am I! An exile from my home and my country, a houseless, unsheltered wanderer among the Indians! Who has met, or who has sustained, such sad and unexpected reverses?" Yet he refused to admit defeat. "I am myself, and will remain, the proud and honest man! I will love my country and my friends"—including Jackson. "You, General, will ever possess my warmest love and most profound veneration!"

Jackson could only shake his head at such a performance. None of his protégés had shown more promise than Houston; none seemed a likelier political heir. And now Houston had thrown it all away. Jackson didn't know what caused the break with Eliza, but he did know that no challenge ever yielded to flight. The honest man, the brave man, stood his ground and fought for what he believed in. Houston instead took refuge in distance and drink. It was disgraceful and horribly disappointing.

𝒟isappointments came in multiples that year. Andrew Hutchings was the son of a friend and business partner who had died, leaving to Jackson the boy's care. Hutchings should have been old enough by now to start taking responsibility for himself, but he stubbornly refused. He wouldn't go to school or learn a trade. "His conduct has filled me with sincere regret," Jackson told John Coffee, who managed the boy's inheritance at Nashville. "I know not what to do with him." Jackson thought of bringing Hutchings to Washington, to the college at Georgetown the Jesuits had founded. "Perhaps under my own eye I might be able to control him and convince him of the impropriety of his ways." Yet he wondered if Hutchings would come if summoned. At times he was tempted to wash his hands of the boy. But he couldn't get himself to do it. "I cannot think of letting him be lost. . . . When I reflect on the charge given me by his father on his dying bed, and the great anxiety he had about him, I am truly distressed."

Andrew Jackson Jr. was better behaved than Hutchings, but he too required direction. The young man was twenty now and was managing the Hermitage in his father's absence. Jackson was upset to learn from a Nashville neighbor of the death of one of the Hermitage slaves, a man named Jim. "I pray you, my son," Jackson wrote Andrew, "to examine minutely into this matter, and if the death was produced by the cruelty of Mr. Steel"—the overseer—"have him forthwith discharged." Andrew was new to the business of running a plantation, and Jackson urged him to seek the advice of family friends. But by whatever means, he must learn to manage slaves and especially overseers. "My negroes shall be treated humanely. When I employed Mr. Steel, I charged him upon this subject, and had expressed in our agreement that he was to treat them with great humanity, feed and clothe them well, and work them in moderation. If he has deviated from this rule, he must be discharged." Jim's was the latest in a disturbing string of deaths. "Since I left home I have lost three of my family. Old Ned I expected to die, but I am fearful the death of Jack, and Jim, has been produced by exposure and bad treatment. Your Uncle John Donelson writes that *Steel has ruled with a rod of iron*. This is so inconsistent to what I expected that I cannot bear the inhumanity that he has exercised towards my poor negroes. . . . Unless he changes his conduct, dismiss him."

Other advice to Andrew was more personal. Jackson's neighbors reported that Andrew was courting a young woman. From eagerness or ignorance, he had initiated the suit without gaining permission from the girl's father. Jackson wrote to the father to apologize for Andrew's mistake and to testify to his son's good faith. "He has been reared in the paths of virtue and morality by his pious and amiable mother, and I believe has walked steadily in them." To Andrew himself he offered the advice of a loving father. "My son, having your happiness at heart more than my own . . . you can judge of the anxiety I have that you should marry a lady that will make you happy. . . . You are very young, but having placed your affections upon Miss Flora, I have no desire to control your affections or interfere with your choice. Early attachments are the most durable. . . . I have only to remark that no good can flow from a long courtship. Therefore I would recommend to you to be frank with her, say to her at once the object of your visit, and receive her answer at once."

Yet the young man must protect himself—and his heart. If Flora said yes, they should marry at once, and the two could come to the White House to live. If she said no, or if she vacillated, he should break off the suit. And in that case he should be in no hurry to form other attachments. "You have many years yet for the improvement of your mind, and to make a selection of a companion." Jackson was thinking of Andrew, but he admitted he was thinking of himself as well. "Remember, my son, that you are now the only solace of my mind and prospect of my happiness here below, and were you to make an unhappy choice, it would bring me to my grave in sorrow."

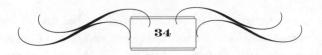

34

JACKSONIAN THEORY

𝒜fter a year consumed with the housekeeping of his
administration—and the airing of more dirty linen than almost anyone
outside Washington cared to see—Jackson turned his attention to the
issues that faced the nation. Presidents' annual messages were great events
in those days, at a time before national politics became a year-round
endeavor. First messages by new presidents were even more anticipated, as
potentially setting the agenda for an entire administration. In the case of
Jackson, who hadn't actively campaigned for office and had said next to
nothing on many important issues, the anticipation was doubled again.
He didn't disappoint, although he did provoke. The message he delivered
to Congress on December 8, 1829, was a landmark document, the
manifesto of democracy as defined by the man who embodied popular

government in America. Since Alexander Hamilton had drafted speeches and papers for George Washington, presidents' messages to Congress had always been collaborative affairs (and always would be). Jackson wrote out a sketch of what he intended to say and circulated it to his advisers; Martin Van Buren added thoughts and language, as did others. But the final draft was fully Jackson's, summarizing his considered views on the appropriate role of the federal government in the life of the nation, and in particular in the lives of the ordinary people.

He began with foreign affairs. Those members of Congress who knew Jackson's history—and they all knew *something* of it—must have been surprised at the mildness of his tone toward Britain, his lifelong bête noire. "With Great Britain, alike distinguished in peace and war, we may look forward to years of peaceful, honorable, and elevated competition. Everything in the condition and history of the two nations is calculated to inspire sentiments of mutual respect and to carry conviction to the minds of both that it is their policy to preserve the most cordial relations." Was this the voice of *Jackson*, the hammer of Albion, the slayer of two British generals and a host of redcoat soldiers? In fact, this part of the message owed much to Van Buren, who as secretary of state would have to conduct diplomacy with Britain. But it also revealed that Jackson understood the difference between being a general and being president. Two issues pended between the United States and Britain: the rectification of the border between Maine and Canada, and the opening of the British West Indies to American trade. On each point Jackson recognized that a velvet glove and soothing words might accomplish more than a flung gauntlet and an aggressive challenge.

After touching on relations with several other foreign countries, Jackson turned to his domestic agenda. The first item was a constitutional amendment to abolish the electoral college. In Jackson's time the Constitution had yet to acquire the patina of semidivine revelation subsequent generations would accord it. "Our system of government was by its framers deemed an experiment, and they therefore consistently provided a mode of remedying its defects," he said. Those in his audience who, like him, had *known* some of the framers, nodded in agreement as to principle if not detail. The primary defect was obvious to anyone who had observed the election of 1824. "To the people belongs the right of electing their Chief Magistrate; it was never designed that their choice should in any case be defeated." Jackson was on tenuous historical ground here. The point of the electoral college had been to temper and interpret the will of the people, if not actually to defeat it. But in the age of democracy, his political argument was increasingly persuasive. "Experience proves that in proportion as agents to execute the will of the people are multiplied, there is danger of their wishes being frustrated." Conversely, the danger would be diminished by reducing the number of agents, starting with the electors, who should be eliminated. Jackson proposed to leave alone the relative weight of the states in choosing presidents (he didn't say precisely how), but the power of election must rest more directly upon the people. As an adjunct to such an amendment, he recommended limiting presidents to a single term, of perhaps six years.

Of matters legislative rather than constitutional, the tariff was the most controversial. The biennial temptation to fiddle with the rate schedules had proved irresistible in 1828, when Congress raised rates to new heights. No genuine principles, besides political self-interest, informed the 1828 tariff, which reflected instead the ability of various manufacturers, shippers, and growers to shield themselves from foreign competition and pass the burden of supporting the federal government to others. But one result was clear: southerners detested the tariff, as it taxed much of what they consumed while protecting next to nothing of what they produced. Southern planters were already hurting after a British financial panic caused the price of cotton to plunge, and the 1828 tariff—shortly labeled the "tariff of abominations" by southerners—added domestic insult to foreign injury.

Jackson, as a southerner and a cotton producer, sympathized with the abomination school of thought on the tariff. But as president he had to acknowledge political realities. He broached the tariff topic cautiously, identifying the dominant economic interests of the country as agriculture, commerce, and manufacturing, and declaring, "To regulate its conduct so as to promote equally the prosperity of these three cardinal interests is one of the most difficult tasks of Government." His sympathies surfaced when he declared that the three interests, though all important, weren't equal. "The agricultural interest of our country is so essentially connected with every other, and so superior in importance to them, that it is scarcely necessary to invite to it your particular attention. It is principally as manufactures and commerce tend to increase the value of agricultural productions and to extend their application to the wants and comforts of society that they deserve the fostering care of Government." This pleased the anti-tariff party, as did some subsequent comments supporting the principle of free trade. But Jackson didn't propose tearing down the tariff entirely. "The general rule to be applied in graduating the duties upon articles of foreign growth or manufacture is that which will place our own in fair competition with those of other countries." Implicitly acknowledging a complaint of the southerners, he added, regarding the tariff, "Local feelings and prejudices should be merged in the patriotic determination to promote the great interests as a whole. . . . Discarding all calculations of political ascendancy, the North, the South, the East, and the West should unite in diminishing any burthen of which either may justly complain."

Though the protectionists might protest, Jackson linked the tariff to the broader question of government revenues. (The protectionists wanted a tariff for protection, not for revenue.) The president reported that the federal debt—mostly from the War of 1812—stood at $49 million. Government revenues currently exceeded expenditures by several million dollars per year, creating the prospect, "in a very short time," of paying off the debt. The American people would then face an important decision. Jackson didn't think the tariff could be responsibly reduced so far as to eliminate the surplus entirely, nor did he think surpluses should be allowed to pile up in the federal treasury. Advocates of internal improvements wanted the federal government to spend the excess on roads and other public works. Jackson acknowledged the value of such projects, but he feared that federal control of spending would encourage corruption in the way the projects were approved and funded. Congressmen would be tempted to approve one another's favorite projects regardless of the general good, while contractors would be tempted to bribe the lawmakers to land sweet deals. And the president had doubts regarding the constitutionality of many such projects. "To avoid these evils, it appears to me that the most safe, just, and federal disposition which could be made of the surplus revenue would be its apportionment among the several States according to their ratio of representation." What a much later generation would call revenue sharing appealed to Jackson as a means of reconciling the national interest in roads and waterways serving the country as a whole with the greatest degree of state autonomy in determining which projects would receive funding.

Jackson was a Unionist first and last, as those who challenged him would discover. But the umbrella of his Unionism sheltered a healthy respect for the wisdom of the states in treating issues important to ordinary lives. "The great mass of legislation relating to our internal affairs was intended to be left where the Federal convention found it—in the State governments. Nothing is clearer, in my view, than that we are chiefly indebted for the success of the Constitution under which we are now acting to the watchful and auxiliary operation of the State authorities. This is not the reflection of a day, but belongs to the most deeply rooted convictions of my mind. I can not, therefore, too strongly or too earnestly, for my own sense of its importance, warn you against all encroachments upon the legitimate sphere of State sovereignty."

The question of legitimate sovereignty extended to relations with the Indian tribes. No president before Jackson (and none after) had such intimate experience of Indian relations. For this reason the members of Congress listened carefully as Jackson explained the philosophy that would guide his approach to the Indians. A controversy had arisen of late between the states of Georgia and Alabama, on one hand, and certain Cherokees and Creeks, on the other. The Indians asserted tribal autonomy and therefore exemption from state laws, which exemption the states refused to grant. The Indians appealed to the president for protection. Jackson denied the appeal, citing the constitutional prohibition against creating new states within existing states. Autonomy for the Indians, he said, was tantamount to creating such new states. Many of those supporting the Indians lived in the northern states. "Would the people of Maine permit the Penobscot tribe to erect an independent government within their State?" he asked. "Would the people of New York permit each remnant of the Six Nations within her borders to declare itself an independent republic under the protection of the United States? Could the Indians establish a separate republic on each of their reservations in Ohio?"

Jackson believed there would be no peace for the Indians east of the Mississippi. This was a harsh prediction, but history allowed no other.

Our ancestors found them the uncontrolled possessors of these vast regions. By persuasion and force they have been made to retire from river to river and from mountain to mountain, until some of the tribes have become extinct and others have left but remnants to preserve for a while their once terrible names. Surrounded by the whites with their arts of civilization, which by destroying the resources of the savage doom him to weakness and decay, the fate of the Mohegan, the Narragansett, and the Delaware is fast overtaking the Choctaw, the Cherokee, and the Creek. That this fate surely awaits them if they remain within the limits of the States does not admit of a doubt.

Humanity and national honor demand that every effort should be made to avert so great a calamity. It is too late to inquire whether it was just in the United States to include them and their territory within the bounds of new States. . . . That step can not be retraced. A State can not be dismembered by Congress or restricted in the exercise of her constitutional power. But the people of those States, and of every State, actuated by feelings of justice and a regard for our national honor, submit to you the interesting question whether something can not be done, consistently with the rights of the States, to preserve this much-injured race.

What Jackson proposed was the legal transfer of land west of the Mississippi to the eastern tribes and the physical transfer of those tribes to the western land. This policy would circumvent the constitutional problem of states within states, as the transferred land would lie within no state but within federal territory. There the Indians could exist as autonomous tribes, "subject to no other control from the United States than such as may be necessary to preserve peace on the frontier and between the several tribes." Jackson stressed that the emigration across the Mississippi must be voluntary. "It would be as cruel as unjust to compel the aborigines to abandon the graves of their fathers and seek a home in a distant land." But the Indians must know the alternative. "If they remain within the limits of the States, they must be subject to their laws."

It was a long message, and Jackson was almost done. But he had to say a word about an issue that would arise soon. "The charter of the Bank of the United States expires in 1836, and its stockholders will most probably apply for a renewal of their privileges." Jackson warned that he didn't like the bank as it currently existed. "Both the constitutionality and the expediency of the law creating this bank are well questioned by a large portion of our fellow citizens, and it must be admitted by all that it has failed in the great end of establishing a uniform and sound currency." Jackson didn't rule out a substitute agency "which would avoid all constitutional difficulties and at the same time secure all the advantages to the Government and country that were expected to result from the present bank." But he offered no details.

Having provided Congress, and through Congress the American people, an outline of the work that would fill his tenure as president, Jackson commended Congress "to the guidance of Almighty God, with a full reliance on His merciful providence for the maintenance of our free institutions."

*T*he message appealed to the American people, who hadn't expected such depth from their hero. But Congress proved a tougher audience—or, rather, the anti-Jacksonian minority in Congress did. And the Democratic majority proved less coherent in the halls of the legislature than it had been on the hustings. It was one thing to shout for Old Hickory and reform, and quite another to agree on the nature of reform.

Trouble initially arose with Jackson's nominations to federal office. The Senate rejected Isaac Hill, the New Hampshireman who had been made part of the Kitchen Cabinet and offered a job at the Treasury. Certain senators claimed offense at Hill's criticism of President and Mrs. Adams. Others, including some favorably disposed toward Jackson, protested the use of public pay to reward friendly editors. Like Thomas Ritchie, they thought this practice undermined freedom of the press. Finally, and perhaps most to the point, advocates of the Bank of the United States, alarmed at Hill's editorial opposition to the bank and wishing to serve Jackson notice that they wouldn't yield without a fight, wanted to make an example of his nomination. The sum of the complaints was sufficient to block the appointment. Yet Hill—and Jackson—had the last laugh when, a short while later, the legislature of New Hampshire named Hill that state's new senator, and the man who might only have editorialized against the bank could now vote against it. Hill's allies reveled in his foes' discomfiture. "Were we in the place of Isaac Hill," said a friendly fourth-estater, "we would reject the presidency of the United States, if attainable, to enjoy the supreme triumph, the pure, the unalloyed, the legitimate victory of stalking into that very Senate and taking our seat—of looking our enemies in the very eye—of saying to the men who violated their oaths by attempting to disfranchise citizens, 'Give me room stand back do you know me? I am that Isaac Hill, of New Hampshire, who, in this very spot, you slandered, vilified, and stripped of his rights. The people, your *masters*, have sent me here to take my seat in this very chamber, as your equal and your peer.' "

The Hill case required months to play out, but the lesson wasn't lost on the anti-Jacksonians. Daniel Webster, who had predicted New Hampshire's reaction to the Hill rejection, recognized that though the Constitution specified a separation of powers, democracy could override it. "Were it not for the fear of the outdoor popularity of General Jackson," the Massachusetts senator wrote, "the Senate would have negatived more than half his nominations."

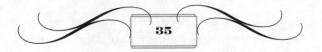

FALSE COLORS

$\mathscr{A}$mid the struggle over Jackson's nominations, another controversy developed, one that overshadowed the nominations and threatened to overwhelm the country as a whole. The South still simmered with discontent over the 1828 tariff, which grew more abominable in southern minds the more they pondered it. Whether the damage to South Carolina was greater than the damage to the other southern states, or whether South Carolinians were simply quicker to take offense, was hard to say. But one thing was certain: Jackson's birth state possessed the region's sharpest legal mind, which happened to be joined to an acute sense of propriety regarding the prerogatives of the states vis à vis the central government. Both the mind and the sense—the arguments and the emotion—belonged to John Calhoun, Jackson's vice president, who had drafted a formal protest against the tariff, one based on first principles of constitutional philosophy and calling into question the meaning of American republicanism.

For a vice president to protest a federal law wasn't unheard of; Jefferson had done just that in 1798. But such protest was a delicate business. Vice presidents lack both power and standing in matters of legislation: the executive power to veto an obnoxious bill and the political standing to challenge its authors. Moreover, if a vice president's actions contradict those of the president, he risks career suicide. For this reason Jefferson hadn't acknowledged his authorship in 1798, and even in 1829 it wasn't widely known.

From similar causes, Calhoun disguised *his* authorship of what came to be called the "South Carolina Exposition." Calhoun denied the authority of Congress to pass tariffs for protection. "It is true that the third section of the first article of the Constitution of the United States authorizes Congress to lay and collect an impost duty," he said, "but it is granted as a tax power, for the sole purpose of revenue; a power in its nature essentially different from that of imposing protective or prohibitory duties. The two are incompatible." Calhoun's exposition went on to delineate the unequal effect of the tariff on South and North. "We cultivate certain staples for the supply of the general market of the world; and they manufacture almost exclusively for the home market. Their object in the tariff is to keep down foreign competition, in order to obtain a monopoly of the domestic market. The effect on us is to compel us to purchase at a higher price, both what we purchase from them and from others, without receiving a correspondent increase of price for what we sell."

Yet the differential economics of the tariff was merely a symptom of a larger problem. Democracy was a fine thing, Calhoun asserted, but it wasn't the last word in politics, or at any rate shouldn't be. "No government based on the naked principle that the majority ought to govern, however true the maxim in its proper sense and under proper restrictions, ever preserved its liberty, even for a single generation. The history of all has been the same: injustice, violence and anarchy, succeeded by government of one or a few. . . . An unchecked majority is a despotism—and government is free, and will be permanent, in proportion to the number, complexity and efficiency of the checks by which its powers are controlled."

The most important of these checks limited the central government to those powers specifically delegated by the Constitution. "All others are expressly reserved to the States and the people." As no man could be a judge in his own case, so the central government could not judge the extent of its powers. But if not the central government, then who? "The right of judging in such cases is an essential attribute of the sovereignty of which the States cannot be divested without losing their sovereignty itself." This state sovereignty, Calhoun concluded, "clearly implies a veto . . . on the action of the General Government."

To this last assertion Calhoun's long document ultimately reduced. The vice president claimed for South Carolina a veto on the actions of the federal government: a right to nullify federal laws as they pertained to the state. Whether the federal government would honor the claim was the question that hung over Washington in the months after Calhoun penned his exposition. "The next two or three years will be of the deepest interest to us and the whole Union," he predicted.

*I*f the delicacy of Calhoun's position prevented his open espousal of the nullification cause, Robert Hayne had no such compunctions. Hayne was another South Carolinian, a senator whose constituents expected nothing less than a vigorous defense of the rights of the states. He determined to give it to them. He stalked the tariff issue, intending to leap on it and do it in at first opportunity. But when the tariff failed to appear during the early weeks of the congressional session, he adopted another approach. Daniel Webster, in a discussion of revenues from the sale of federal lands (including those brought to market by Jackson's treaties with the Creeks and Cherokees), asserted that reliance on federal revenues helped bind the nation together. Hayne responded indignantly. "Sir, let me tell that gentleman that the South repudiates the idea that a pecuniary dependence on the Federal Government is one of the legitimate means of holding the States together. A money interest in the Government is essentially a base interest, and just so far as it operates to bind the feelings of those who are subjected to it to the Government, just so far as it operates in creating sympathies and interests that would not otherwise exist, is it opposed to all the principles of free government, and at war with virtue and patriotism." But since Webster had raised the issue of money, Hayne pointed out that the South sent far more money to Washington than it received in return.

He turned to the larger question of the nature of the Union. The South, or at least South Carolina, had been charged with innovation in asserting a right to nullify, he said. He rejected the charge, claiming a long lineage for himself, his state, and its doctrines. "The party to which I am proud of having belonged from the very commencement of my political life to the present day, were the democrats of '98. Anarchists, anti-federalists, revolutionists, I think they were sometimes called. They assumed the name of democratic republicans in 1812, and have retained their name and their principles up to the present hour. True to their political faith, they have always, as a party, been in favor of limitations of power; they have insisted that all powers not delegated to the Federal Government are reserved, and have been constantly struggling, as they are now struggling, to preserve the rights of the States, and prevent them from being drawn into the vortex, and swallowed up by one great consolidated Government." The South was said to esteem the Union insufficiently. Hayne replied that it was the North that did so, by pushing the South to the brink of destruction with the abominable tariff and then refusing to hear the South's pleas. He shuddered at the future. "Good God, has it come to this? . . . Do gentlemen value so lightly the peace and harmony of the country? . . . Do gentlemen estimate the value of the Union at so low a price that they will not even make one effort to bind the States together with cords of affection? . . . If so, let me tell gentlemen the seeds of dissolution are already sown, and our children will reap the bitter fruit."

𝒲ebster was the last man to shrink from rhetorical combat. If anything, Hayne's challenge made him swell with indignation and self-importance. He took a deep breath and launched into a speech that lasted three hours over two days. He assailed Hayne's person and his arguments, condemning the South Carolinian's politics, his reading of the Constitution and history, and especially his willingness to place the Union in jeopardy for a few pennies of an import tax. The Union, Webster said, was infinitely more important than any tariff. "It is to the Union that we owe our safety at home, and our consideration and dignity abroad. It is to the Union that we are chiefly indebted for whatever makes us most proud of our country." The Union hadn't come easily. It was born of war and the derangements that followed war. But it had proved a benediction to Americans of every section. "It has been to us all a copious fountain of national, social, and personal happiness." Webster said he couldn't bear to consider the consequences of nullification, of life beyond the Union.

> God grant that, in my day at least, that curtain may not rise. God grant that, on my vision, never may be opened what lies behind. When my eyes shall be turned to behold, for the last time, the sun in heaven, may I not see him shining on the broken and dishonored fragments of a once glorious Union; on States dissevered, discordant, belligerent; on a land rent with civil feuds, or drenched, it may be, in fraternal blood. Let their last feeble and lingering glance, rather, behold the gorgeous ensign of the republic, now known and honored throughout the earth, still full high advanced, its arms and trophies streaming in their original lustre, not a stripe erased or polluted, nor a single star obscured, bearing for its motto no such miserable interrogatory as, What is all this worth? Nor those other words of delusion and folly: Liberty first, and Union afterwards; but every where, spread all over in characters of living light, blazing on all its ample folds, as they float over the sea and over the land, and in every wind under the whole heavens, that other sentiment, dear to every true American heart: Liberty *and* Union, now and forever, one and inseparable!

*I*n due course Webster's reply to Hayne would become the stuff of patriotic legend, and his peroration would be committed to memory by generations of students of public speaking. Its immediate impact was less, but it did set the stage for the most dramatic words ever uttered by Andrew Jackson as president. For years the followers of Jefferson had celebrated his April 13 birthday with toasts and other affirmations of the founding principles of republicanism. Only the most unreconstructed Federalists—John Marshall and a few others still clinging to life—did not feel obliged to render obeisance to the sage of Monticello. Everyone with political hopes or pretensions made a point of attending his birthday fete.

Jackson planned to attend in the spring of 1830, as did Calhoun. The rift between the president and the vice president had continued to grow, partly from Calhoun's unwillingness or inability to make his wife act civilly toward Peg Eaton, but increasingly from rumors that he was in league with the nullifiers of South Carolina. Jackson and Calhoun had avoided each other through most of 1829 by the simple expedient of Calhoun's staying away from Washington, at his plantation in South Carolina. With the Senate in recess the vice president's single constitutional chore stood in abeyance, giving him ample excuse for absenting himself. But in his absence the Van Burenites worked on Jackson, and their whispers caused the president to doubt Calhoun's good faith even more.

The whispering worked both ways. Calhoun's allies hoped to ride his coattails into office and so furnished a constant stream of information and innuendo against Van Buren, against John Eaton, and against Jackson himself. Virgil Maxcy, an old friend of Calhoun's and an inveterate capital gossip, provided the vice president a detailed description of the quarrels among the Jacksonians as they maneuvered for influence. Duff Green was dissatisfied at not receiving sufficient government contracts, Maxcy said. Green scorned Eaton for making the administration a hostage to his wife, who in Green's view (and Maxcy's) didn't merit such gallantry. William Lewis defended Peg to the president, who refused to listen to reason on the subject. "It is come to this," Maxcy said, for himself and Green: "that all our glowing anticipations for our country from the integrity, sagacity, and firmness of General Jackson must be extinguished, and we must submit to the melancholy conviction that the United States are governed by the President, the President by the Secretary of War, and the latter by his wife."

Calhoun eventually returned to Washington, but not before the strain between himself and Jackson was palpable. And as the day of the Jefferson dinner approached, all Washington wondered where it would lead. Calhoun was scheduled to give one of the many toasts that night. In the nineteenth century the art of the toast was highly refined and its able practitioners most admired. To convey a sentiment, summarize a philosophy, impale an opponent—in a dozen words or less—required skill, imagination, and sometimes courage. After the debate between Webster and Hayne, amid the tension afflicting the Jackson administration, the capital thrummed with the possibilities of the evening.

"There was a full assemblage when I arrived," Thomas Benton recalled, "and I observed gentlemen standing about in clusters in the ante-rooms, and talking with animation on something apparently serious, and which seemed to engross their thoughts. I soon discovered what it was: that it came from the promulgation of the twenty-four regular toasts, which savored of the new doctrine of nullification; and which, acting on some previous misgivings, began to spread the feeling that the dinner was got up to inaugurate that doctrine and to make Mr. Jefferson its father."

Jackson had learned of the project the day before, from a printed program of the dinner. He read the list of toasters and immediately concluded, as William Lewis remembered, "that the celebration was to be a nullification affair altogether." Jackson pondered the matter overnight and, the next day, wrote three rejoinders to the nullifiers. He tried them out on Lewis. "He handed them to me and asked me to read them, and tell him which I preferred," Lewis said. "I ran my eye over them and then handed him the one I liked best. . . . He said he preferred that one himself for the reason that it was shorter and more expressive. He then put that one into his pocket and threw the others into the fire."

Forewarned and forearmed, the president attended the dinner. He arrived late. Several guests had left in protest of the nullifying sentiments of the organizers of the toasting schedule. "But the company was still numerous, and ardent," Thomas Benton wrote. Persons not on the program clamored to add their impromptu remarks to those of the chosen two dozen.

The president, however, received the first opportunity to respond. Every eye in the hall turned to the haggard face of the old man; every ear strained to catch the words that might tell his willingness to compromise with the South Carolinians, or his determination to defeat them. Jackson's voice wasn't what it had been in younger days. One by one his teeth had fallen out or been pulled, leaving him too few to be able to articulate clearly when he spoke to a large audience. On this occasion his words weren't loud, but they didn't have to be. They thrust through the expectant silence and by the force of their determination sent involuntary shudders through all in the room. "Our Federal Union," he said. "It *must* be preserved."

*C*alhoun was next to speak. How would he answer? Would he embrace the nullifiers and risk an irreversible rupture with the president? Or would he temper his views in the interest of concord in the administration and of his own political future? The vice president was younger than Jackson by fifteen years, and far more presentable. In earlier days he had been one of the handsomest men in South Carolina, and some thought he still was. He prided himself on his facility with words, though he had to agree with friends who told him he occasionally ran on.

The format of the toast constrained him this night, but even so he rambled by comparison with the president. He knew he was in a tight corner, and he needed every word he could get. "The Union," he said, "next to our liberty the most dear. May we all remember that it can only be preserved by respecting the rights of the States, and distributing equally the benefit and burden of the Union."

Other speakers added their wisdom and temerity, and the event ran hours longer. But the toasts of the president and vice president were the only ones most in attendance remembered. They all knew how Jackson had dealt with mutiny during the War of 1812 and how he had executed Arbuthnot and Ambrister for endangering the Union. Some had wondered whether the volcano still smoldered in Jackson's breast after Rachel's death. As they walked and rode home that night, nearly all were convinced that it did indeed and that the country might soon witness its effects.

*C*alhoun's answer to Jackson sealed his fate with the president. Calhoun was no novice at the game of politics; the simple fact of his holding the vice presidency through the upheaval of Jackson's election demonstrated a certain virtuosity at political survival. Other things being equal, he might have undermined Van Buren as Van Buren was undermining him. He might have explained away his wife's actions as the kind of thing women did. But he could never explain away—not to Jackson's satisfaction—a failure to place the Union above all. Liberty was vital, to be sure. Yet Jackson's half century of struggle against the British, the Spanish, the Indians, and everyone else who threatened the safety and integrity of the United States had taught him one overriding lesson: that the Union was the only guarantor of American liberty. It was a cliché, but no less true for its triteness, that in union lay strength. Had the Union not held together, it would have fallen victim to Europeans or aboriginal marauders. If it did not hold together now, it still might. The nullifiers dreamed of a world at peace; Jackson lived in a world of struggle. And the struggle never ended.

A few weeks after the memorable dinner, Jackson wrote Calhoun a letter on an entirely different subject. The occasion for the letter was a message to Jackson from William Crawford, of all people, raising questions about Calhoun's behavior during the Seminole War. Jackson hadn't forgiven Crawford for what he considered Crawford's past sins, but at this point he considered him harmless, and potentially useful in building a case against Calhoun. "The submission, you will perceive, is authorised by the writer," Jackson explained in forwarding to Calhoun the Crawford letter. "The statements and facts it presents, being so different from what I had heretofore understood to be correct, require that it should be brought to your consideration." He invited Calhoun to explain the discrepancies.

The vice president responded curtly. "I cannot repress the expression of my indignation," he told Jackson, while adding snidely, "I must express my gratification that the secret and mysterious attempts which have been made by false insinuations for political purpose for years to injure my character, are at length brought to light." He said he would answer Jackson's request for explanation "as soon as my leisure may permit."

Calhoun was still angry two weeks later. "However high my respect is for your personal character and the exalted station which you occupy," he wrote Jackson, "I cannot recognize the right on your part to call in question my conduct. . . . I acted on that occasion in the discharge of a high official duty, and under responsibility to my conscience and my country only." All the same, he devoted a long letter to justifying his actions during the Seminole War and impugning the integrity of his critics.

He was wasting his breath. Jackson didn't want the truth in the Seminole affair. He knew what *he* had done, and could live with that. What *Calhoun* had done mattered, at this point, only to the degree it gave Jackson plausible grounds for rendering the vice president a pariah, for reasons that transcended the Seminole War. Calhoun's past position on Florida was nothing next to his current position on the Union. *This* was the danger, and why he had to be cast into the outer darkness.

*N*or was Calhoun the only one who had to go. Certain members of the cabinet, while not exactly nullifiers, were wobbly on issues Jackson considered vital to reforming the government. Treasury Secretary Ingham urged the president to move slowly against the Bank of the United States. "It must be admitted to be a field of experiment, in which no certain results can be calculated upon," Ingham explained. Attorney General Berrien was no bolder. "Whenever that subject shall be presented to the legislative body," Berrien said, "it will without doubt create a strong sensation." Ingham and Berrien, with Navy Secretary Branch, were generally accounted allies of Calhoun, and Jackson didn't want them around while he isolated the vice president. Anyway, he bridled at stories in the opposition press—which these days included Duff Green's *Telegraph*—that he dare not offend Ingham and the others, who had backing among groups whose support Jackson was thought to require. "The combination and coalition believed they had got me in the trap set for me, and that I could not extricate myself," Jackson wrote to Andrew Donelson. "My cabinet was divided, and I could not, nay durst not, remove those who had become the favorites of the Virginia senators, because they were also the favorites of Pennsylvania, and covered by the wand of Calhoun, who with Duff Green thought they could raise up and destroy empires, or make and unmake presidents at will." To John Coffee he commented, "How little do they know me."

As much to prove the smug reckoners wrong as to jettison the dead weight of his useless advisers, Jackson did something no president had ever done (and none would ever do more dramatically): he overthrew the whole cabinet. He didn't *fire* Ingham and the others, partly because there was some question regarding a president's authority to remove cabinet officers without the consent of the same body that had to approve their appointment—

the Senate—but also because he didn't wish to bruise political feelings any more than necessary. (Andrew Johnson would be impeached over the removal issue.) Instead he accomplished his purpose by an artfulness few suspected in the old soldier. He asked John Eaton and Martin Van Buren to resign, the former on suggestions that he might return to the Senate, the latter to take a post as minister to England, with the vice presidency awaiting his return from London. With Eaton and Van Buren, the most ardent loyalists in the cabinet, setting the example, Ingham and the others required only modest nudges to be persuaded to submit their resignations as well. Jackson accomplished his palace coup near the end of the legislative session, a timing that provided the finishing touch. The Senate wouldn't be ready to receive nominations for replacements till the following year, allowing tempers to cool before Jackson had to put new names forward. "I have changed my cabinet, and strengthened my administration thereby," he told Coffee in the denouement. "What a contrast!!"

*A*mid the coup, Jackson received a letter on a topic he almost never discussed in public and seldom in private. His religious views were orthodox for his time and place. Raised in the Presbyterian church of his Scots ancestors, he believed in a providential plan for humanity, though he doubted that humans could discover its details. He believed that religion supported personal and public morals and that morality conduced to personal and public prosperity and the general welfare. He thanked heaven for his victories and blamed himself—or other humans, but not God—for his defeats. He had supported Rachel's devotion, to the point of building her a chapel at the Hermitage so she would never miss a service, even if he missed more than a few himself. As president he alternated attendance between the First Presbyterian Church and St. John's Episcopal, reserving seats in both places by paying pew rent. He promoted efforts to Christianize the Indians of the West, along with the many frontier whites whose behavior suggested they could stand a dose of the gospel themselves.

This last matter was what elicited an exchange of correspondence regarding religion. A society promoting the establishment of Sunday schools in the West had scheduled a meeting in Washington. Its organizers requested Jackson's endorsement, and he casually complied. A few weeks later an alarmed constituent wrote inquiring why he was taking sides among sects. Jackson pleaded honest ignorance. "The first intimation I have received that the meeting . . . was sectarian is from your letter now before me," he answered. "I was induced to believe that it was a plan for disseminating the Gospel by a *union of all Christians* in the valley of the Mississippi, where it was considered from the late settlement of the country the circulation of the Bible, the education of the poor, and an observance of the Sabbath by children might be beneficial to their morals, and in the end prove essentially serviceable to the indigent." A federal unionist in politics, Jackson was an ecumenical unionist in religion, at least among Christians.

> I am no *sectarian*, though a lover of the Christian religion. I do not believe that any who shall be so fortunate as to be received to heaven, through the atonement of our blessed Saviour, will be asked whether they belonged to the Presbyterian, the Methodist, the Episcopalian Baptist, or Roman Catholic [church]. All Christians are brethren, and all true Christians know they are such *because they love one another*. A true Christian *loves all*, immaterial to what sect or church he may belong.

The president reiterated that he had understood the Sunday school project to be nonsectarian. "As such it had my best wishes, and as such will ever have them. But should it appear that the object is to give ascendancy and preference to any sect or denomination over others, then my constitutional notions will compel me to frown down such an attempt because in my opinion freedom and an established religion are incompatible."

Jackson subsequently revealed a bit more about his religious convictions. The early summer of 1832 produced an epidemic of cholera in the eastern part of North America. It apparently started in Quebec, where an infected ship dropped anchor in June and unleashed its cargo of pathogens on the inhabitants. Spreading through water supplies tainted by the waste of its victims, it invaded upper New York state, then traveled down the Hudson to New York City. Many thousands sickened, and eventually thousands died.

No one knew what caused the disease or understood how it spread. The only prophylactic that appeared to offer hope was religion. Henry Clay, returned to the Senate from Kentucky, sponsored a resolution asking the president to declare a national day of fasting and prayer. The Senate approved the measure but the House couldn't agree on language, and the bill died. Many churches, however, believing that politics shouldn't stand between Christian citizens and their God, called on the president directly, begging him to show moral guidance in this time of distress.

Jackson refused. "Whilst I concur with the synod in the efficacy of prayer and in the hope that our country may be preserved from the attack of pestilence . . . ," he told the ruling body of the Reformed Church, "I am constrained to decline the appointment of any period or mode as proper for the public manifestation of this reliance. I could not do otherwise without transcending those limits which are prescribed by the Constitution for the President, and without feeling that I might in some degree disturb the security which religion now enjoys in this country in its complete separation from the political concerns of the General Government." Jackson told the ministers to look to the states, and to themselves. "It is the province of the pulpits and the State Governments to recommend the mode by which the people may best attest their reliance on the protecting arm of the Almighty in times of great public distress. Whether the apprehension that cholera will visit our land furnishes a proper occasion for their solemn notice, I must therefore leave to their own consideration."

The pulpits and some of the states prayed, to no obvious avail. The disease ran its course in one city after another, till lack of victims and then cold weather stopped the pathogen from reproducing.

Jackson escaped the disease, although neither he nor anyone else could have said why. Perhaps he didn't drink water that summer, from his longstanding preference for alcoholic beverages and coffee. Perhaps he was just lucky.

His overall health was better than it had been in some time. During his first year in Washington his friends noted an alarming decline. "His whole physical system seemed to be totally deranged," William Lewis recalled. "His feet and legs, particularly, had been very much swollen for several months and continued to get worse every day, until his extreme debility appeared to be rapidly assuming the character of a confirmed dropsy." Jackson's worrisome condition was one thing that made the Calhoun question so important. No president had died in office or seriously threatened to. But Jackson looked as though he might. If he did, Calhoun would become president. If Jackson survived to be reelected, he might die during his second term, making Calhoun's successor president. Till now the State Department had been the springboard to the presidency, but Van Buren wasn't alone in reckoning that the advantage could be shifting to the vice presidency.

Jackson had sought relief for his ailments on the Virginia shore, at a spa called the Rip Raps. The cure consisted of daily swims in the Atlantic. "I cannot yet determine whether I will be benefitted by the salt water bath," he wrote after a few days. "It is very cold, though the day is clear and fine." In fact, to the extent the regimen had any positive effect, it was probably the clear air rather than the cold water that did it. Whatever took city residents out of their neighborhoods in warm weather, when infectious agents multiplied most prolifically, and exposed them to fresh air and sun was good for their health.

In subsequent summers Jackson traveled farther, usually home to Nashville. The vacations afforded him rest; they also allowed him to keep watch on the affairs of the Hermitage. His oversight wasn't simply the indulgence of the planter but a matter of economic necessity. As he had guessed, the expenses of the presidency outran his salary. He received fifty thousand dollars per year, but from this he had to entertain on a scale appropriate to the head of state of an aspiring nation. The dinners and receptions he held weren't sumptuous, but they were respectable and many. He couldn't cut back without insulting the office and the people who had placed him there.

His expenses went beyond entertainment. He insisted on dressing well. The firm of Tucker & Thompson was his tailor, and its monthly statements showed regular additions to his wardrobe, including a "white Valencia vest," a "fancy silk vest," a "velvet vest," "blue cloth pants," "black nankeen crape pants," "Canton crape pants," "broad summer cloth pants," a "black bombazine coat," a "fancy invisible frock"—whatever that might have been—"caster gloves," "linen drawers," and "Virginia drawers."

To support himself, Jackson depended on his income from the Hermitage to complement his salary. He monitored the price of cotton—at New

Orleans, Liverpool, and other markets—as carefully as he ever had, and when it was low he fretted almost as much as he had in the days when his farming was his primary occupation. "This year, with the bad season, I will not clear from my farm what its culture has cost me," he told neighbor Robert Chester at the end of 1830. Jackson might have covered some of his loss by selling slaves, but he disliked doing so, as it disrupted families. In at least one case, though, he made an exception—at the request of the slaves involved. He explained the unusual circumstance to Chester: "I received a letter from Mr. Steel, my overseer, informing me that Charlotte had applied to you to purchase her, being discontented where she is now. I bought her, being the wife of Charles, at his request. He now appears desirous that she with her children be sold. I have therefore come to the resolution to part with her."

Cotton was Jackson's staple, but a Tennessee farmer had to watch other crops, and livestock as well. "Have your hogs put up early," he wrote Andrew Jr. in the autumn of 1832, "so that they may be fatted before the cold weather, fattening none that will not weight 120 lbs., keeping all under as stock hogs by which next year you will have enough of large hogs for the family." Jackson told Andrew that he had contracted to sell a Nashville packer ten thousand pounds of pork on the hoof at $2.25 per hundred. The rest would remain at the Hermitage. "This will give you a stock of good hogs that next year, with attention, will average 200 round."

Cotton and hogs paid the rent, but horses remained Jackson's passion. His favorite was now a gray stud colt he called Bolivar, for the South American liberator. Jackson had sold the animal upon leaving for Washington at the beginning of 1829, but he bought him back a year later after suffering seller's remorse. Bolivar's bloodlines were noble; he descended from Truxton, Jackson's first prize horse. From the distance of the capital Jackson supervised Bolivar's management. He wanted him trained as a runner but not pushed too hard. "Knowing the merit of his blood, you see I am determined to keep its credit up until I can get it tested, by his offspring from a thoroughbred mare," he wrote Hardy Cryer, his horse man. "I shall direct the Virginian"—a recently acquired filly—"to be put to him, as the best blood I have except those that are too nigh kin to him. . . . Her colt will test his merit as a foal getter and turf horse."

Nothing angered Jackson more than mismanagement of the horses. He discovered in the spring of 1832 that overseer Steel had been running the animals too soon and hard. "I was truly mortified," he wrote Andrew Jr., "on being informed by Steel that he had turned them into training to run at the spring races in Tennessee." They should have been resting and growing. "Your filly would, I have no doubt, have won the sweepstake in the fall. If she does, she is worth to you $8000." To bar similar foolishness, Jackson ordered Andrew to take drastic measures at the Hermitage. "Have the turf closed, plowed up, and permit not a horse to gallop on it."

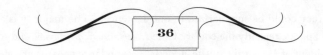

36

ATTACK AND

COUNTERATTACK

$\mathscr{A}$lexis de Tocqueville arrived in America midway through Jackson's first term as president. Like other students of politics, the French aristocrat was familiar with the concept of democracy, which history and reason informed him was the intermediate stage between republicanism and either despotism or civil war. Tocqueville was too young to have witnessed the degenerative process in France, having been born after Napoleon seized power. But he assumed that the same influences—self-interest, demagoguery, ignorance—that had subverted popular government in his own country would tend to do so in America. The question was whether they would be offset by other factors, perhaps peculiar to the New World.

Tocqueville traveled about America trying to answer this question.

At Boston, Jared Sparks explained that the philosophy of American democracy could be summarized in one sentence: "The majority is always right." Sparks, recently the editor of the *North American Review* and soon to be president of Harvard College, added, "By and large we are very well satisfied to have adopted it, but one cannot deny that experience often gives the lie to the principle." At Baltimore, Tocqueville dined with a man named Finley, who explained that democratic politics could get rather rough. Finley was an anti-Jacksonian, and he had spoken at a town meeting against the president. At least he had tried to speak; the boos of the Jacksonians drowned him out. "Several men came to fisticuffs. There were several broken limbs."

Tocqueville asked if Finley saw political danger in such tumult. Finley said he did not. "Our people is accustomed to that type of election. They know just how far they can go. . . . Besides, the very excess of democracy partly saves us from the dangers of democracy. All public appointments are annual. The party that loses this year hopes to succeed the next. So why should it resort to illegal means?"

Tocqueville knew that Americans had abandoned property qualifications for voting. Didn't their absence cause problems? Finley acknowledged that it did. "I have seen elections swayed by the paupers from the alms house, whom one of the candidates had had fetched," he said. This was a manifestation of what he considered the worst feature of American politics: that elections could be determined by "those who have no interest in stability, since they possess nothing and have but little understanding."

Tocqueville expressed puzzlement as to how democracy had ever taken hold. "It is yourselves, the members of the upper classes, who have made the existing laws," he said. "You were the masters of society fifty years ago." What had gone wrong? Finley answered succinctly: "Each party, to gain power, chose to flatter the people, and bid for its support by granting new privileges."

At Philadelphia, Tocqueville met Nicholas Biddle, the president of the Bank of the United States. Tocqueville had been struck by the lack of defining ideologies between parties in America, at least by comparison with the situation in France, where avowed monarchists denounced republicans and vice versa. In America everyone paid at least lip service to the sovereignty of the people.

"I can believe that you find it difficult to understand the nature and activity of parties in America," Biddle said, "for we get lost ourselves in just the same way. There has been a mix-up of all the old parties, and today it would be impossible to say what is the political belief of those who support the administration, or of those who attack it." Tocqueville inquired whether things had always been so. "No, certainly not," Biddle answered.

> For a long time we were divided between Federalists and Republicans. Those two parties were very like what you have in Europe; they had political doctrines to which interests and emotions were attached. They fought bitterly until the Federalist party, always short in numbers, was completely crushed by its adversary. Tired of their vanquished position, the Federalists ended up by giving up their own cause. They either merged in the successful party or rallied, under other names, about questions of detail. But the party standard has really been knocked down for good and all. This revolution finally worked itself out when General Jackson came on the scene. He claimed to make no distinction between the old parties in his choice. Since then there have been people who support the administration and people who attack it; people who extol a measure and people who abuse it. But there are no parties properly so called, opposed one to the other and adopting a contrary political faith. The fact is that there are not two practicable ways of governing this people now, and political emotions have scope only over the details of this administration and not over its principles.

Biddle convinced Tocqueville. When the Frenchman returned home and committed his reflections on America to a book—*Democracy in America*—he followed the Biddle line closely. "The Federalists, feeling themselves defeated, without resources and isolated within the nation, divided up," he wrote. "Some of them joined the victors; others lowered their flag and changed their name. For many years now they have ceased to exist as a party. . . . Thus today there is no sign of great political parties in the United States. . . . Lacking great parties, the United States is creeping with small ones, and public opinion is broken up ad infinitum about questions of detail."

Yet perhaps because his own experience of aristocracy was deeper than Biddle's, Tocqueville detected a continuing struggle between the few and the many in America, even if Americans couldn't see or wouldn't admit it. "I am certainly not saying that American parties always have as their open or even their concealed aim to make aristocracy or democracy prevail in the country," he disclaimed, only to declare: "I *am* saying that aristocratic or democratic passions can easily be found at the bottom of all parties, and that though they may slip out of sight there, they are, as it were, the nerve and soul of the matter." Tocqueville cited Biddle's bank as an example.

> The President attacks the Bank of the United States; the country gets excited and parties are formed; the educated classes in general line up behind the bank, while the people are for the President. Do you suppose that the people could understand the reason for their opinion amid the pitfalls of such a difficult question about which men of experience hesitate? Not at all? But the bank is a great establishment with an independent existence; the people, who destroy or elevate all authorities, could do nothing against it, and that was a surprise. With all the rest of society in motion, the sight of that stable point jars, and the people want to see if they can shake it, like everything else.

Nicholas Biddle agreed about the irrationality of the attack on the Bank of the United States. The Biddle family had been active in public life in Philadelphia since before he was born, and Biddles were expected to do their part in society. Yet the hurly-burly of the political arena put young Nicholas off. He decried "the violence of party" and said he felt "no disposition to become the follower of any sect, or to mingle political animosities with the intercourse of society." Friends talked him into running for the Pennsylvania legislature, but after two diffident sessions he retreated to the literary world, editing a journal of letters and respectable opinion. In 1819 James Monroe, whom Biddle had known for some years, offered him a spot on the board of directors of the second Bank of the United States, which had fallen into disrepute during its three years of existence. Biddle hesitated. "The Bank is of vital importance to the finances of the government and an object of great interest to the community," he conceded. "That it has been perverted to selfish purposes cannot be doubted. That it may—and must—be renovated is equally certain. But they who undertake to reform abuses, and particularly of that description, must encounter much hostility." Yet his public spirit, and Monroe's persuasiveness, eventually won out, and he took the job.

He impressed his fellow directors with his diligence and his devotion to the bank, and in 1822 they nominated him for their president. Again Biddle hesitated. To a fellow director he summarized the qualifications of an ideal president of the Bank of the United States: "talent for business, standing with the government, and residence in Philadelphia." Elaborating, he explained that *talent* for business differed from simply being a businessman. "The fact is that the misfortunes of the Bank . . . were actually occasioned by the men of business, and their errors were precisely the faults into which the men of business were most likely to fall." As for standing with the government: "He should be known to, and stand well with, the Government— not an active partizan—not even a party man—but a man in whom the government could confide." As for the president's residing in Philadelphia, the bank was headquartered there, and the city was rather clubby. "I fear that a stranger would not easily obtain the aid of such a board as ought to be collected." Reading back over his description, Biddle concluded that he himself approximated the ideal better than anyone else, and he accepted the nomination. His fellow directors apparently agreed, for they elected him their chief. He was thirty-six years old.

Biddle devoted his first years as president to putting the affairs of the bank in order: writing off bad loans, tightening credit requirements, straightening sloppy accounts, dismissing inefficient or corrupt officers. He shunned the limelight for himself and the institution. "I have been so anxious to keep the Bank out of view in the political world and bring it down to its true business character as a counting house that I have been reluctant to apply to Congress for anything," he wrote Daniel Webster in 1826.

Biddle strove to maintain this position as long as possible. He didn't wholly ignore politics. He cultivated John Calhoun and Henry Clay while Calhoun was John Quincy Adams's vice president and Clay his secretary of state. Clay was a special project, being a chronic debtor who received—and appreciated—Biddle's help in fending off creditors. Yet though Biddle preferred Adams over Jackson in 1828, he refused to divulge his preference. Not even his friends knew which way he was leaning. Some inferred that he mistook Jackson's public silence regarding the bank for support. More likely, he simply recognized that Jackson would win and saw no point in making a powerful enemy. For the record, Biddle asserted that the bank was above politics. "There is no one principle better understood by every officer in the Bank than that he must abstain from politics," he declared. "The course of the Bank is very clear and straight on that point. We believe that the prosperity of the Bank and its usefulness to the country depend on its being entirely free from the control of the officers of the Government, a control fatal to every bank which it ever influenced. In order to preserve that independence it must never connect itself with any administration—and never become a partizan of any set of politicians." Biddle told a friend that the officers of the bank, to a man, adhered to this view. "We have no concern with politics. Dean Swift said, you know, that money is neither Whig nor Tory, and we say with equal truth that the Bank is neither Jackson man nor an Adams man. It is only a bank."

$\mathcal{B}$ut it was a very powerful bank, as Jackson acknowledged in his first annual message. Biddle read Jackson's remarks with concern but not alarm. "They should be treated as the honest though erroneous notions of one who intends well," he said.

Biddle's patronizing attitude toward Jackson reflected the conventional wisdom of the East toward the warrior from the West, but it also followed from a rare personal meeting of the two men. Biddle had sent Jackson a plan to pay down the federal debt; in their meeting Jackson told Biddle he appreciated the advice. Biddle said it was the least he could do. Jackson explained his broader views on banking and the Bank of the United States. "I think it right to be perfectly frank with you," he said (in Biddle's rendering of the session). "I do not think that the power of Congress extends to charter a bank out of the ten mile square"—the federal district. The president added, "I do not dislike your bank any more than all banks. But ever since I read the history of the South Sea bubble I have been afraid of banks." Biddle found this explanation quaintly reassuring, for it suggested that Jackson's stance on the bank was his own idiosyncrasy and not the policy of the administration. "As such it is far less dangerous because if the people know that this is not an opinion which they must necessarily adopt as a portion of their party creed—but an opinion of the President alone, a very honest opinion though a very erroneous one—then the question will be decided on its own merits."

Biddle took comfort in this thought, but it wasn't even close to being true. Before long Biddle, not Jackson, proved to be the innocent on the bank question. In the autumn of 1830 Biddle received a letter from Henry Clay suggesting an early renewal of the bank's charter. Clay had done some vote counting and believed that a renewal bill would pass both houses of Congress. The measure would then go to the president. "What would he do with it?" the Kentuckian asked rhetorically. "If, as I suppose, he would reject it, the question would be immediately, in consequence, referred to the people, and would inevitably mix itself with all our elections. It would probably become, after the next session, and up to the time of the next Presidential election, the controlling question in American politics." This was precisely what Clay wanted, as he judged the bank a good issue on which to run against Jackson in 1832. Yet it was just the opposite of what Biddle wanted, as the bank president wished to keep his beloved institution out of the mud of a partisan campaign.

Clay was clever enough to realize that Biddle would require convincing. He acknowledged Biddle's reluctance to make an issue of renewal. What if he waited till after the 1832 election to apply? "Then every thing will be fresh; the succeeding Presidential election will be too remote to be shaping measures in reference to it; and there will be a disposition to afford the new administration the facilities in our fiscal affairs which the Bank of the United States perhaps alone can render." But there was a catch. "Suppose General Jackson should be again elected." What would his reelect mean for the bank? Would he be more likely, or less, to veto renewal? Clay initially argued for less. "He will have probably less disposition than he now has to avail himself of any prejudices against the Bank. He will then have also less influence, for it may be truly asserted, at least as a general rule, that the President will have less popularity in his second than his first term. And that, I believe, would emphatically be the fate of the present President." On this ground, Clay argued for caution. The worst thing Biddle could do would be to apply for renewal, for the renewal bill to be approved by Congress, for the bill to be vetoed by the president, and then for Jackson to be reelected. "Indeed, if there be an union of the President's negative of the Bank bill with the next Presidential election, and he should be reelected, would it not be regarded as decisive against any Bank of the United States hereafter?"

Maybe Clay *was* considering the best interests of the bank, or perhaps he was just easing Biddle into his net. When Biddle answered this letter by declaring that it was "inexpedient to apply at present for the renewal of the charter," Clay didn't disagree. Yet Biddle soon began to reconsider. Jackson's annual message of December 1830 reiterated his opposition to the bank as it existed, and called for modifications allowing the states larger participation in the banking system. Biddle had hoped the president would see the light and shed his prejudices against the bank. That Jackson apparently retained his full ignorance triggered a bellicosity in Biddle few observers had previously noticed. "In respect of General Jackson and Mr. Van Buren"—the latter alleged, as often, to be the malign mover of administration policies—"I have not the slightest fear of either of them, or both of them," he told an associate two weeks after the president's message. The American people would see through their machinations. "Our country-men are not naturally disposed to cut their own throats to please any body, and I have so perfect a reliance on the spirit and sense of the nation that I think we can defend the institution from much stronger enemies than they are."

The campaign for renewal began with preemptive propaganda. "It is obvious that a great effort will be made to array the influence of the Executive and all his party against the Bank," Biddle told one of his operatives. "It is not less evident that our most effectual resistance is the dissemination of useful knowledge among the people." Biddle had written a variety of articles outlining the benevolence and usefulness of the bank, and he now wished to distribute them to newspapers not irretrievably opposed to the bank. "For the insertion of these I will pay either as they appear or in advance. Thus for instance, if you will cause the articles I have indicated and others which I may prepare to be inserted in the newspaper in question, I will at once pay to you one thousand dollars." Biddle concluded his letter by saying that though he had nothing to conceal, he wished for the letter's return after it had been acted upon, "as it might be misconstrued."

While the campaign proceeded, Biddle tried to fathom Jackson's intentions. "The President is now perfectly confident of his reelection," he wrote in October 1831. "The only question is the greater or the less majority, but he is sure of success and wishes to succeed by a greater vote than at the first election. If, therefore, while he is so confident of reelection, this question is put to him as one affecting his reelection, he might on that account be disposed to put his veto on it, if he be, as it were, dared to do it."

Under the circumstances, Biddle was disinclined to dare the president. But Henry Clay had other plans. Like Biddle—and the rest of the country—Clay could see that Jackson remained overwhelmingly popular. Clay's only chance against him was to cause a political explosion. And for this he required Biddle's assistance. "Have you come to any decision about an application to Congress at this session for the renewal of your charter?" he inquired as the legislature convened for its last session before the election. "The friends of the Bank here, with whom I have conversed, seem to expect the application to be made." Congressional approval was all but guaranteed, Clay intimated. Only Jackson's response remained in doubt. "My own belief," he confided to Biddle, "is that if *now* called upon, he would not negative the bill; but that if he should be re-elected the event might and probably would be different."

Clay offered no evidence to support this belief, yet his words couldn't be dismissed. He had just been nominated for president by a convention of anti-Jacksonians whose platform characterized the bank as a "great and beneficent institution" worthy of the warm support of the American people.

Daniel Webster joined the chorus of support for the bank. Webster had long been friendly with Biddle, meeting with him at bank headquarters and the gathering places of the upper class. Lately he had been conducting intelligence operations on behalf of the bank, speaking with everyone in Washington who might know something worth hearing. "The result of all these conversations," he wrote Biddle, "has been a strong confirmation of the opinion which I expressed at Philadelphia that it *is* expedient for the Bank to apply for the renewal of its charter without delay. I do not meet a gentleman, hardly, of another opinion, and the little incidents and anecdotes that occur and circulate among us all tend to strengthen the impression. Indeed, I am now a good deal inclined to think that after General Jackson's re-election there would be a poor chance for the bank."

Persuaded, Biddle took the fateful step. "We have determined on applying to the present Congress for a renewal of the charter," he wrote at the beginning of 1832. "To this course I have made up my mind after great reflection and with the clearest convictions of its propriety." As earlier, Biddle professed to be above politics. "Neither I nor any of my associates have any thing whatever to do with the President or his election. I know nothing about it and care nothing about it. The Bank has never had any concern in elections. It will not have any now." Biddle refused to believe that the president would veto a worthy bill simply for politics' sake. "Even I, who do not feel the slightest interest in him, would be sorry to ascribe to a President of the United States a course much fitter for a humble demagogue than the Chief Magistrate of a great country."

The initial reactions were positive. "I cannot but think you have done exactly right," Webster said. "Whatever may be the result, it seems to me the path of duty is plain. In my opinion, a failure this session, if there should be one, will not at all diminish the chances of success next session." Biddle learned that if he hadn't put forward for renewal, the bank's backers in Congress would have. An associate met with John Quincy Adams, now a congressman from Massachusetts, and reported back to Biddle: "Mr. Adams told me that if you had not petitioned, as you did, that it had been his intention to have offered a resolution."

Biddle understood the stakes. "The present is a crisis for General Jackson and for the Bank," he said as the renewal bill hit the floor of the Senate. But the strength of his support caused him to expect that Jackson, rather than the bank, would be overthrown. Biddle's informational campaign appeared—to him—to have persuaded the country of the wrongheadedness of the bank's opponents. "We set to work to disenchant the country of their foolery, and we have so well succeeded that I will venture to say that there is no man, no woman, and no child in the United States who does not understand that the worthy President was in a great error." Biddle was confident the renewal bill would win congressional approval. What happened then would be up to Jackson. "If the bill passes and the President negatives it, I will not say that it will destroy him, but I certainly think it will, and moreover I think it ought to."

The debate began in the Senate, where it quickly assumed proportions that made clear that much more than a bank was at stake. As Biddle himself had admitted to Tocqueville, democracy had swept the field of American political philosophy; no one could credibly speak against it. But as Tocqueville countered (in his book), the old convictions died hard, and there were plenty of individuals in America who thought the ordinary people too ignorant to manage the affairs of the country, certainly on matters as technical as the operation of a national bank. For both sides, the bank became a proxy for popular rule.

Daniel Webster led off for the bank. His outspoken support surprised those many who recalled him as a staunch opponent of the bank's original charter in 1816, but not those fewer who knew him as an attorney who held to the philosophy that the rich deserved the best defense money could buy and who, not incidentally, had been on the bank's payroll for years. "I believe my retainer has not been renewed or refreshed as usual," he wrote to Biddle at a critical moment for the bank. "If it be wished that my relation to the Bank should be continued, it may be well to send me the usual retainers." Webster discovered the merits of sound money and of the bank in making it so. "A disordered currency is one of the greatest of political evils," he told the Senate. "It wars against industry, frugality, and economy; and it fosters the evil spirits of extravagance and speculation. Of all the contrivances for cheating the laboring classes of mankind, none has been more effectual than that which deludes them with paper money." Not for nothing had Webster become one of the best-paid lawyers in America; he now displayed his ingenuity by arguing the *democratic* case for Biddle's bank. Flimsy money, he said, hurt ordinary people more than anyone else. "This is the most effectual of inventions to fertilize the rich man's field by the sweat of the poor man's brow. Ordinary tyranny, oppression, excessive taxation: these bear lightly the happiness of the mass of the community, compared with fraudulent currencies and the robberies committed by depreciated paper." Webster deemed especially pernicious the wide use of paper notes in small denominations. The effect of such issues was to drive hard money—gold and silver coins—out of circulation. He told a story from English history. "When Mr. Pitt, in the year 1797, proposed in Parliament to authorize the Bank of England to issue one pound notes, Mr. Burke lay sick at Bath of an illness from which he never recovered. And he is said to have written to the late Mr. Canning, 'Tell Mr. Pitt that if he consents to the issuing of one pound notes, he must never expect to see a guinea again.' "

The odd thing about Webster's argument was that it might have been made, almost word for word, by the *opponents* of the bank. Webster's point was that the Bank of the United States was the surest bulwark against state banks, which issued notes that served as money and did so with no coordination—indeed, often in destructive, inflationary competition. This was true enough. And if paper money there must be, then the Bank of the United States could help keep inflation in check. Yet some Jacksonians took Webster's argument and pushed it further: toward the elimination of *all* banks, or at least those authorized to issue paper currency or its equivalent. Hard money was the only honest money, they contended. Everything else was, as Webster said, a plot against honesty, thrift, and personal industry.

The strongest opponent of the bank in Congress, or at any event the one who spoke the longest and loudest, was Thomas Benton. The senator from Missouri condemned the bank as the unconstitutional offspring of selfish private interest: wrong in law, wrong in policy, wrong in politics, wrong in morals. Where in the Constitution, he asked, was the article enabling Congress to create a national bank? *His* copy of the Constitution contained no such article. The policies of the bank were pernicious in favoring the East at the expense of the South and West. The bank was headquartered in Philadelphia; its lending policies drew hard currency from the rest of the country to the marble temple on Chestnut Street. "They lead to the *abduction of its gold and silver*," Benton declaimed. "Every body in the South and West knows that the hard money of the country is constantly disappearing; but those only who have observed the working of the machinery of the Bank of the United States can tell where all this hard money is gone." The directors of the bank and their minions were draining the very life from the West and South. "They gorge to repletion, then vomit their load into the vast receptacles of the Northeast, and gorge again." The West and South, deprived of money, were filled with farmers and merchants unable to pay even the interest on their debts. The day of reckoning for these honest folks was fast approaching. "When that dread day comes . . . the towns and cities of the South and West—the fairest farms and goodliest mansions—will be set up at auction, to be knocked down to the bank agent, at the mock prices fixed in the compting room of the bank itself." And from this would spring what had been implicit in the bank from the start.

> In these mock sales of towns and cities may be laid the foundation for the titles and estates of our future nobility—Duke of Cincinnati! Earl of Lexington! Marquis of Nashville! Count of St. Louis! Prince of New Orleans! Such may be the titles of the bank nobility to whom the next generation of American farmers must "crook the pregnant hinges of the knee." Yes, sir! When the renewed charter is brought in for us to vote upon, I shall consider myself as voting upon a bill for the establishment of *lords and commons* in this America, and for the eventual establishment of a *King*; for when the *lords and commons* are established, the *King* will come of himself!

It was demagoguery, of course, revealing little about the actual workings of the bank but much about the passions the bank provoked. If Webster wanted to have things both ways—hard currency but a bank that issued paper currency—so did Benton. Everyone knew that the chronic problem of the western economy—as it had been since the frontier days—was a shortage of money. There simply wasn't enough gold and silver to go around, and never had been. And everyone knew that the West and South suffered more from the discounting of banknotes for distance from the issuing bank than the North and East and therefore benefited more from the comparatively uniform currency the notes the Bank of the United States provided. Nor were Webster and the bank's backers the only ones who disguised their personal interest in the affair. Benton and the opponents of the bank found allies in the state banks that had seen the national bank steal their customers and suppress their profits; these state banks discovered ways of rewarding their often unacknowledged spokesmen in Congress.

Yet if economics cut both ways on the bank issue, emotion was all on the side of the opponents. No one warms to bankers. At best they gain a grudging respect for making money without seeming to work very hard. And the bigger the bank and the more powerful the bankers, the more grudging the respect. Biddle thought Jackson's suspicions of banks foolishly idiosyncratic. They may or may not have been foolish, but they certainly weren't idiosyncratic.

For all the suspicions of the populists and the thunderbolts of Benton, the renewal bill passed the Senate in a close vote, and the House by a somewhat larger margin. Opponents alleged bribery but couldn't prove it, most likely because it wasn't more blatant than the back scratching and palm greasing that passed for daily life in the legislature. Roger Taney, who had replaced John Berrien as attorney general and would become Jackson's strong right arm in the bank fight, made this point regarding one congressman who reconsidered his initial opposition after receiving a large loan on easy terms from Biddle. "Now I do not mean to say that he was directly bribed to give this vote. From the character he sustained and from what I knew of him, I think he would have resented any thing that he regarded as an attempt to corrupt him. But he wanted the money, and felt grateful for the favor. And perhaps he thought that an institution which was so useful to him, and had behaved with so much kindness, could not be injurious or dangerous to the public, and that it would be as well to continue it."

$\mathcal{J}$ackson hadn't intended to fight the 1832 election on the bank issue. In his annual message of December 1831 he had barely mentioned the subject. But when Clay, Webster, and Biddle insisted on making a contest over the bank, he couldn't resist such a tempting prospect. Better than any of them, Jackson understood the symbolism of the bank and what it meant for popular government in America. He received the renewal bill from Congress on July 4, which seemed fitting to those friends of capital who hoped the measure would secure their independence from ignorant democrats and provocatively ironic to those same democrats, who felt it fastened an aristocracy of finance upon the country. Jackson stood decisively with the democrats, returning the bill to Congress a week later, with a resounding message explaining his veto.

"A bank of the United States is in many respects convenient for the Government and useful to the people," he acknowledged. It managed government finances and expedited many transactions. For this reason he hadn't chosen to challenge the bank's existence in the declining years of its charter, despite his reservations about several aspects of its creation and continuance. The bill before him, however, would perpetuate the bank: both its conveniences and its much larger deficiencies. The latter were what required his veto.

The basic problem with the bank, Jackson said, was that it was unconstitutional. The bank's defenders cited political precedent and Supreme Court decisions as providing constitutional sanction. "To this conclusion I can not assent," he rejoined. "Mere precedent is a dangerous source of authority, and should not be regarded as deciding questions of constitutional power except where the acquiescence of the people and the States can be considered as well settled." If anything, the history of the Bank of the United States showed that the question was far from settled. Congress had approved a bank in 1791 and disapproved it in 1811. It had debated long before reapproving it in 1816. As for the states, Jackson reckoned that the sum of legislative, executive, and judicial opinions from the states ran against the bank by as much as four to one.

Regarding the Supreme Court, Jackson didn't think it had spoken in anything like a definitive tone on the bank. But more to the point, Jackson didn't believe the executive was bound by Supreme Court decisions. Nor, for that matter, was the legislature. To a later generation such a position might appear radical, even anarchic. But in the 1830s decisions of the Supreme Court had yet to acquire the finality they would eventually win, and Jackson saw no reason to defer to an unelected tribunal.

> The Congress, the Executive, and the Court must each for itself be guided by its own opinion of the Constitution. Each public officer who takes an oath to support the Constitution swears that he will support it as he understands it, and not as it is understood by others. It is as much the duty of the House of Representatives, of the Senate, and of the President to decide upon the constitutionality of any bill or resolution which may be presented to them for passage or approval as it is of the supreme judges when it may be brought before them for judicial decision. The opinion of the judges has no more authority over Congress than the opinion of Congress has over the judges, and on that point the President is independent of both.

Regardless, therefore, of what John Marshall had written in the McCulloch case or any other, it was for the president to render his own judgment on the constitutionality of the Bank of the United States. Like many other issues involving federal authority, the bank question turned on the "elastic" clause of the Constitution, the one endowing Congress with authority to enact measures "necessary and proper" to the accomplishment of the enumerated responsibilities. Jackson thought Congress had overstepped in establishing the bank. "It can not be *'necessary'* or *'proper'* for Congress to barter away or divest themselves of any of the powers vested in them by the Constitution to be exercised for the public good"—which it had done in giving the bank de facto control of the currency. The Constitution *did* give Congress the authority to legislate for the District of Columbia; within the federal square, Jackson acknowledged, a federally chartered bank could be constitutional. But in the states, no.

There was much more to Jackson's opposition than strict construction. Like Benton and other anti-bankers, the president feared the emergence of a monopoly of money. He didn't oppose monopolies per se. Patents and copyrights were monopolies that were both constitutional and conducive to the general welfare. But a monopoly of money was inherently dangerous. Of the bank's twenty-five directors, only five were chosen by the government, the rest by the stockholders of the bank. Thus the public interest was always outweighed by the interests of the bank's private owners, who must have been saints not to be tempted by the power they held over the nation's economy. "It is easy to conceive that great evils to our country and its institutions might flow from such a concentration of power in the hands of a few men irresponsible to the people," Jackson said. Nor was the economy the sum of what was at risk from the bank's excessive power. "Is there no danger to our liberty and independence? . . . Will there not be cause to tremble for the purity of our elections in peace and for the independence of our country in war?"

Jackson already feared for equality in America. "It is to be regretted that the rich and powerful too often bend the acts of government to their selfish purposes." Jackson was no leveler. "Distinctions in society will always exist under every just government. Equality of talents, of education, or of wealth can not be produced by human institutions." Yet those institutions should not magnify natural inequalities. "When the laws undertake to add to these natural and just advantages . . . to make the rich richer and the potent more powerful, the humble members of society—the farmers, mechanics, and laborers—who have neither the time nor the means of securing like favors to themselves, have a right to complain of the injustices of their Government." In a sweeping affirmation of the democratic promise, Jackson perorated:

> There are no necessary evils in government. Its evils exist only in its abuses. If it would confine itself to equal protection, and, as Heaven does its rains, shower its favors alike on the high and the low, the rich and the poor, it would be an unqualified blessing.

The bank renewal bill did just the opposite and therefore had to be rejected.

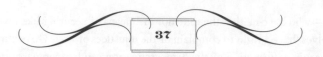

37

OR DIE WITH THE UNION

 $\mathcal{V}$ etoes were rare in the days before Jackson; his six predecessors had

turned back but ten bills total. Jackson exceeded that number by himself,

starting with a veto of a measure to build a road from Maysville,

Kentucky, to Lexington. His objection was precisely the one articulated

in his first annual message, that internal improvements were best and

most constitutionally left to the states. The many supporters of the

Maysville Road remarked the irony of Jackson, the self-proclaimed

champion of popular government, defying the will of the people

as expressed by their duly elected representatives.

 $\mathcal{B}$ ut the response to Jackson's bank veto made the earlier complaints

sound like quibbles. Henry Clay called the veto a vestige of royalty and

Jackson a would-be tyrant. Daniel Webster decried the "fearful and appalling aspect" of the power Jackson claimed for himself, and accused the president of trying to set "the poor against the rich." Pro-bank papers gnashed their type. "A more deranging, radical, law-upsetting document was never promulgated by the wildest Roman fanatic," one New England editor declared of the veto message. "The revolutionists of France went but little further." *Niles' Register* reported that the veto had brought business to a standstill around the country. In Philadelphia angry anti-Jacksonians gathered before the bank's headquarters to assert that Jackson had "wantonly trampled upon the interests of his fellow citizens and upon the constitution of his country." Should the veto stand, the result would be a "national calamity."

Jackson let his rivals rage. The veto cost him support in certain states, including Kentucky, where the Jacksonian candidate for governor won narrowly rather than by the comfortable margin he had enjoyed before the veto. But on the whole the veto served to consolidate Jackson's reputation as the defender of the common man against the moneyed interests. "It diffuses universal joy among your friends and dismay among your enemies," John Randolph wrote from Virginia. Jackson himself was pleased. "The veto works well everywhere," he wrote William Lewis. "It has put down the Bank instead of prostrating me."

And so it appeared as Americans moved toward the polls in the autumn of 1832. The threat and reality of the cholera epidemic that summer diminished the excitement that often surrounded politics in the age of democracy, yet enough remained to astonish certain foreign observers. Though Tocqueville had gone home by now, another French visitor, intrigued by the same phenomena, produced an account of the campaign. A pro-Jackson parade, held at night in New York, convinced him that democracy wasn't simply the reigning political philosophy but the American civic religion.

It was nearly a mile long. The democrats marched in good order, to the glare of torches. The banners were more numerous than I had ever seen them in any religious festival; all were in transparency, on account of the darkness. On some were inscribed the names of the democratic societies or sections: *Democratic young men of the ninth or eleventh ward*; others bore imprecations against the Bank of the United States; *Nick Biddle* and *Old Nick* here figured largely. Then came portraits of General Jackson afoot and on horseback; there was one in the uniform of a general, and another in the person of the Tennessee farmer, with the famous hickory cane in his hand. Those of Washington and Jefferson, surrounded with democratic mottoes, were mingled with emblems in all tastes and of all colors. Among these figured an eagle—not a painting, but a real, live eagle, tied by the legs, surrounded by a wreath of leaves, and hoisted upon a pole, after the manner of the Roman standards. The imperial bird was carried by a stout sailor, more pleased than ever was a sergeant permitted to hold one of the strings of the canopy in a Catholic ceremony. From further than the eye could reach, came marching on the democrats. I was struck with the resemblance of their air to the train that escorts the *viaticum* in Mexico or Puebla. . . . The democratic procession, also like the Catholic procession, had its halting-places; it stopped before the houses of the Jackson men to fill the air with cheers, and halted at the doors of the leaders of the Opposition, to give three, six, or nine groans.

Henry Clay, nominated by the anti-Jackson National Republican party, marshaled the support of the business classes, most newspapers and their editors, a majority of the well-educated elements of society, and assorted additional individuals and groups offended by Jackson on one topic or another. A separate wing of anti-Jacksonians mustered under the banner of the Anti-Masonic party, which nominated William Wirt of Maryland. (Jackson was a Mason, but that wasn't the only thing for which the Anti-Masons faulted him.)

Against these Jackson claimed the support of a broad array of farmers, mechanics, casual laborers, small merchants, and others for whom the dream of democracy—that ordinary people might control their own destiny—seem inextricably tied to all that he stood for. Van Buren joined Jackson on the ticket, the two having been formally nominated by a convention at Baltimore whose delegates had no difficulty choosing a presidential candidate (Jackson, by wild acclamation), a bit more selecting a vice presidential candidate (Van Buren, by ballot), and still more settling on a name for themselves (Democrats, by exhausting the alternatives and themselves). Van Buren elicited nothing like the adulation felt for Old Hickory—no one in

America did—but he helped secure New York and certain political figures who admired his cleverness and were willing to bet on his future.

The result was a resounding endorsement of Jackson and Jacksonism. The president received 219 electoral votes to Clay's 49. He carried sixteen of the twenty-four states, including the entire West except Clay's Kentucky home, nearly all the South except Calhoun's South Carolina (which voted for an obscure protest candidate), and several states of the Northeast, including parts of New England. The popular vote was 688,000 for Jackson and 530,000 for Clay.

*J*ackson had little time to savor his victory. The very papers that brought the news of the election returns also brought reports of alarming developments in South Carolina. State elections there had produced a strong majority for nullification, whose sponsors proceeded to call a convention. The convention denounced the tariff of 1828 and an 1832 revision that had reduced rates without abandoning the principle of protection. The convention proceeded to adopt an ordinance formally nullifying the tariffs—that is, forbidding the collection of the duties within the boundaries of the state, effective February 1, 1833. Finally, the convention asserted that any act by Congress to authorize the use of force against South Carolina would be considered "inconsistent with the longer continuance of South Carolina in the Union."

Secession had always been the implicit corollary of nullification, but by making the threat of secession explicit the South Carolinians brought the dispute to a head. Jackson had no choice but to act. He started by gathering intelligence from behind the enemy lines. Joel Poinsett had been minister to Mexico and was now back in his home at Charleston. A Unionist and a Jacksonian, Poinsett informed the president that the nullifiers had the bit in their teeth and were determined to run. "The impression on the minds of the Nullifiers undoubtedly is that no measures will be taken against them," he wrote. Poinsett assured Jackson that the Union had friends in South Carolina, but they were outnumbered and required encouragement. Weapons would help—"two or three hundred muskets and some hand grenades"—

but the central thing was a strong stand by the federal government. Much more was at stake than the future of South Carolina, Poinsett asserted. "On the issue of this contest between the federal government and a faction in this state depends the permanency of the Union."

Jackson appreciated the intelligence but hardly needed the advice. As soon as he read the state election results in South Carolina he directed the secretary of war, Lewis Cass, to prepare for trouble. Jackson told Cass to send orders to the commanders of the forts at Charleston, with a simple message. "They are to defend them to the last extremity." The president simultaneously dispatched his own secret agent to Charleston. George Breathitt's cover story was that he was a postal inspector coming to ensure prompt service to the citizens of South Carolina. His confidential instructions from Jackson were to gather all the information he could regarding the loyalty or disloyalty of federal officers in South Carolina and to assess the military situation in the harbor at Charleston. "You will observe the real situation of Sullivan's Island, and see whether it could be assailed and carried in its rear. You will also observe the situation of the armaments of Castle Pinckney, and what space of dry land surrounds the forts."

During the following weeks Jackson monitored the situation in South Carolina. Poinsett grew more and more nervous. The federal customs house at Charleston, he said, contained "many violent Nullifiers." Several officers of the army had been "seduced." Things were spinning out of the control of even those who had started the trouble. "The principal object of these unprincipled men has always appeared to me to be to embarrass your administration and defeat your election, but they have led the people on so far under other pretexts that they must proceed." Poinsett saw a slight difference between radical nullifiers, for whom secession was the goal, and tactical nullifiers, who chiefly wanted to gain political ground. On one point, however, the two groups agreed. "Both parties are anxious and indulge the hope that the general government will commit some act of violence, which will enlist the sympathies of the bordering states. Provided it be not their own, they care not how soon blood is shed."

The rising emotions in South Carolina simply solidified Jackson's determination to meet defiance with force. He ordered five thousand stand of muskets to Castle Pinckney and dispatched two warships to patrol the coast. He told Poinsett to let the South Carolina Unionists know that he would never allow secession. "In forty days I can have within the limits of South Carolina fifty thousand men, and in forty days more another fifty thousand. . . . The wickedness, madness, and folly of the leaders and the delusion of their followers in the attempt to destroy themselves and our Union has not its parallel in the history of the world. The Union will be preserved."

The president ordered Lewis Cass to gird for war against the secession movement. "We must be prepared to act with promptness and crush the monster in its cradle," he declared. He specified what he wanted for the outset of the campaign: "three divisions of artillery, each composed of nine, twelve, and eighteen pounders." He had Cass make arrangements to enlist volunteers for service against South Carolina and to transport the volunteers to Charleston.

To Cass, Jackson wrote as president and commander in chief. To John Coffee he wrote as an old friend and fellow soldier from the early days of the republic. Coffee was a westerner, a Tennessean, a person inclined by temperament and experience to favor states' rights over federal authority. On all these points he was Jackson's alter ego. For this reason, when Jackson explained his actions to Coffee, he was explaining them to himself as well. "Can any one of common sense believe the absurdity that a faction of any state, or a state, has a right to secede and destroy this Union, and the liberty of our country with it?" Jackson asked Coffee rhetorically. For Jackson, the linking of liberty and Union was crucial. Calhoun and the nullifiers contended that liberty allowed secession; Jackson believed that liberty *forbade* secession. Liberty didn't preserve itself; it had to be defended against a world bent on its destruction. And liberty's only sure protection was the Union. The Union had won American freedom from Britain; the Union had secured American liberty against numerous subsequent attacks. To damage the Union was to endanger liberty.

Jackson conceded that under the Articles of Confederation, the states had been sovereign and independent. But that first republican form had failed and had been deliberately replaced. "A constitution was proposed to the people," he told Coffee, "and in the language of the instrument, 'We the people, to make a more perfect union, do ordain and establish the following etc. etc.' This more perfect union made by the whole of the people of the United States granted the general government certain powers and retained others. But nowhere can it be found where the right to nullify a law, or to se-cede from the Union, has been retained by the states." The single way to amend the Constitution was by the method specified therein. "Every mode else is revolution or rebellion." States had a right to peaceful protest against what they judged to be usurpation. But they had no right to destroy the Union. "Therefore when a faction in a state attempts to nullify a constitu-tional law of Congress, or to destroy the Union, the balance of the people composing this Union have a perfect right to coerce them to obedience. This is my creed." It was also his mission. "The Union must be preserved. . . . I will die with the Union."

*W*hile preparing for war, Jackson took his case for the Union to the American people. He issued a proclamation blistering the nullifiers and warning South Carolina to rescind its illegal ordinance. The nullifiers had driven South Carolina—"my native State," he noted—to the "brink of in-surrection and treason." For what? For a tariff that they didn't like and that they had magnified into a cause for sundering the Union. The people of South Carolina must pull back. "You are deluded by men who are either de-ceived themselves or wish to deceive you. . . . They are not champions of liberty, emulating the fame of our Revolutionary fathers, nor are you an op-pressed people. . . . You are free members of a flourishing and happy Union." South Carolinians would remain members of the Union, despite anything the nullifiers said or tried to do. "Their object is disunion. But be not deceived by names. Disunion by armed force is *treason*." To resist trea-son was Jackson's sworn duty. "The laws of the United States must be exe-cuted."

The president followed his proclamation to South Carolina with a spe-cial message to Congress. South Carolina, he said, was engaged in "extraor-dinary defiance" of federal authority. If this defiance were not overcome, the Constitution would lose its meaning. A half century of American his-tory—of struggle, of sacrifice, of devotion to the ideals of human liberty—would go for naught. The work of two generations was at stake. "They bequeathed to us a Government of laws and a Federal Union founded upon the great principle of popular representation. . . . We are called to decide whether these laws possess any force, and that Union the means of self-preservation." Jackson knew how he would answer the call. "I have determined to spare no effort to discharge the duty which in this conjuncture is devolved upon me." That no one would think he acted alone, he requested Congress to reaffirm his authority to use force to ensure that the laws of the United States be executed.

John Calhoun answered Jackson on behalf of the nullifiers. Calhoun had resigned the vice presidency after the 1832 election to accept a Senate seat from South Carolina. For eight years he had presided over the upper chamber but been constitutionally mute; now he spoke with all the vigor that had made him famous and all the frustration that had been building while Jackson and Van Buren pushed him aside. There was not a state in the Union, he said, less predisposed to belligerence than South Carolina. The federal government, not the government of South Carolina, was the provocateur of the present crisis. Jackson had neglected to inform Congress of the measures he had already taken to prepare for war; these were what had alarmed South Carolina and driven it to resistance. The president had pleaded the longevity of the Union as reason for it to remain intact; Calhoun asserted, to the contrary, that longevity brought decay. "The only cause of wonder is that our Union has continued so long—that at the end of forty-four years our Government should still retain its original form." It could not retain that form much longer. "The time has at length come when we are required to decide whether this shall be a confederacy any longer, or whether it shall give way to a consolidated Government." The latter, which Jackson obviously intended, could not emerge without irreversible damage to American freedom. "It must inevitably lead to a military despotism." The president spoke of a government in which the central authority had the right to coerce the states. "South Carolina sanctioned no such government," Calhoun said. "She entered the Confederacy with the understanding that a state, in the last resort, has a right to judge of the expediency of resistance to oppression or secession from the Union. And for so doing it is we that are threatened to have our throats cut, and those of our wives and children." The president had asserted that the Union was in danger. So it was—but from the actions of the president himself in laying the foundation for a military despotism. "This is the greatest danger with which it is menaced, a danger the greatest which any country has to apprehend."

*M*r. Calhoun let off a little of his ire against me today in the Senate, but was so agitated and confused that he made quite a failure," Jackson wrote Poinsett. Jackson was repeating what he had heard from friends in the upper house. Calhoun's partisans naturally disagreed. But however well or poorly Calhoun had done at words, the president prepared to ensure that the federal government would win the battle at arms, if matters came to that. "Write me often and give me the earliest intelligence of the first armed force that appears in the field to sustain the ordinance," he directed Poinsett. "The first act of treason committed unites all to it, all those who have aided and abetted in the incitement to the act. We will strike at the head and demolish the monster."

Not surprisingly, the South Carolinians hoped for support from their southern neighbors. Virginia displayed a certain sympathy, reviving the Virginia resolutions of 1798 and sending a delegation to Charleston to commiserate with the nullifiers. Georgia spoke vaguely on behalf of states' rights. But the other southern states were silent, doubtless sobered by Jackson's threats, as he intended them to be. "They know that I will execute the laws, and that the whole people will support me in it and preserve the Union," he told Poinsett in late January, several days before the nullification ordinance was to take effect. Those few who hadn't got the message would get it soon. Jackson now said he could have two hundred thousand troops in South Carolina within forty days. And no one could stop him. "If the governor of Virginia"—the warmest of the outside sympathizers—"should have the folly to attempt to prevent the militia from marching through his state to put the faction in South Carolina down, and place himself at the head of an armed force for such a wicked purpose, I would arrest him at the head of his troops."

It was at about this time that Jackson gave voice to a stronger warning against the nullifiers. A congressman from South Carolina called at the White House before returning home to his constituents. He asked if the president had a message for them. "Yes, I have," Jackson replied. "Please give my compliments to my friends in your state, and say to them, that if a single drop of blood shall be shed there in opposition to the laws of the United States, I will hang the first man I can lay my hand on engaged in such treasonable conduct, upon the first tree I can reach."

*J*ackson's ferocious posture was perfectly sincere. He was as ready to arrest governors and hang nullifiers as he had been to arrest and execute Arbuthnot and Ambrister in Florida. Yet he rattled his saber for effect as well. He didn't want a civil war. He wanted the nullifiers to back down and any potential emulators to take the lesson to heart. And so, even while he conspicuously prepared to send the troops south, he quietly endeavored to provide the South Carolinians an avenue of retreat. He informed Poinsett that he would employ force only after South Carolina had done so. "Until some act of force is committed or there is an assemblage of an armed force by the orders of your Governor . . . the Executive of the United States has no legal and constitutional power to order the militia into the field to suppress it." When South Carolina deferred the date the nullification ordinance was to take effect, he discreetly supported efforts by Henry Clay to modify the tariff that had triggered all the trouble.

The strategy succeeded. Congress approved Jackson's force bill and the tariff revision almost in the same breath. The South Carolinians responded to the latter by rescinding their nullification ordinance. They responded to the former by nullifying *it*, but then they went home and the crisis passed.

Most of those involved claimed victory. Calhoun and the nullifiers pointed to the tariff revision. Henry Clay acknowledged his own genius for legislative compromise.

But the real victors were Jackson and the idea of the Union. Two days after he signed the tariff and force bills, Jackson was inaugurated for the second time. In his inaugural address he cited the twin pillars of American liberty: "the preservation of the rights of the several states and the integrity of the Union." Jackson didn't wave olive branches lightly, but having proved his point that the Union was indissoluble—at least while he was president— he assured his listeners that he wouldn't trample the rights of the states.

"The annihilation of their control over the local concerns of the people would lead directly to revolution and anarchy, and finally to despotism and military domination." This must not happen, and in a Jackson administration it would not. Yet states' rights presupposed a strong and vibrant Union. They always had and always would. "Without union, our independence and liberty would never have been achieved; without union they never can be maintained."

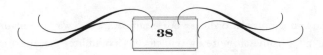

38

JUSTICE MARSHALL FOR

THE DEFENSE

Having vanquished the nullifiers of South Carolina, Jackson turned

his attention to that other enemy stronghold, New England. The

Federalists were long forgotten, and with them the secessionist tendencies

that had inspired the Hartford convention, but their collateral descendants,

calling themselves Whigs, included persons who were almost as distrustful

of democracy as the high Hamiltonians had been, and they enjoyed a

majority east of the Hudson River. New England Democrats, desperate

for help, called to the White House. They suggested that a visit from

Jackson would hearten their friends, discourage their enemies, and perhaps

win a seat or two for the party in the next congressional elections. Jackson

accepted the reasoning and the invitation, and headed north.

The first leg was by ordinary horse but soon gave way to one of iron. Twelve miles from Baltimore a proud citizens' committee met the presidential party in a spanking new train of the Baltimore & Ohio Railroad and insisted that Jackson join them for the journey back to their city. He had never ridden "the steam cars" (neither had any other president), and he enjoyed the ride, though it intensified the headache he often experienced these days. Large crowds turned out in Baltimore and followed him to the theater that evening. Also in the audience that night was the Sauk chief Black Hawk. Sour Whigs, unable or unwilling to fathom why anyone would want to see Jackson, contended that the crowds were for the Indian.

The next city on the itinerary, Philadelphia, sent a delegation and a steamboat to fetch the president. Thirty thousand men, women, and children lined the pier at the Philadelphia navy yard, where a coach drawn by four white horses waited patiently till he arrived, at which moment all patience vanished. The crowd surged into the street, clamoring to be close to the great man. The coach was pinned in place, and the horses grew frantic, till armed cavalry rode to the rescue and forced a passage for the president's vehicle. Jackson spent the Sabbath in the city of Friends, though he attended services with the Presbyterians. Afterward he shook the hand of a young boy. "And then—what a scene!" exclaimed a reporter covering the event. "One upon another's head, they all extended their hands." Jackson paused to consider, then declined to repeat his gesture. "The General, using his powers of foresight, soon perceived what would be the consequence, immediately sounded a retreat. . . . He wisely slipped out by a private door and eluded the mob." The next day the city turned out for a presidential parade to the shrines of American independence. The crush stalled the progress of the participants, leaving Jackson sitting on his horse for five hours under a broiling sun. When he finally reached Independence Hall, his head sunburned and splitting, the building was packed so full the guests could hardly breathe. Someone managed to raise a window. "A ludicrous scene ensued," said the same reporter. "Man, woman, and child came tumbling out from a height of six feet, some jumping, some diving, and some rolling." Jackson gamely tried to greet his supporters, shaking the hands of all who offered till he could barely move his arm.

Before he left Philadelphia he consulted the famous Dr. Physick, a practitioner of what later generations would call alternative medicine and what many in Physick's own day called quackery. The president apparently decided that since real doctors hadn't been able to cure what ailed him, he might as well go faux. "Now, Doctor," he said as the examination began, "I can do any thing you think proper to order, and bear as much as most men. There are only two things I can't give up: one is coffee, and the other is tobacco." Perhaps the medicine man decided that if Jackson wouldn't abandon those vices, there was nothing to be done. Maybe he reasoned he'd better not tamper with the presidential health. Whatever the cause, Physick left Jackson to his own nostrums.

The crowds in New York were even larger than in Philadelphia. "From the moment of landing, all was confusion," recorded Philip Hone, former New York mayor, leading Whig, and noted diarist. The confusion became bedlam when a bridge connecting the Battery to Castle Garden collapsed under the weight of thousands of onlookers who fell to the water and rocks below amid a tangle of wood and metal. Many were soaked and bruised, but miraculously no one drowned and none were seriously hurt. Not so lucky was a sailor aboard a customs cutter who touched off a cannon saluting the president but lost his hands and eyesight when the charge misfired. Jackson, who himself just missed being scorched by the wadding of another cannon and who was nearly thrown from his bucking horse after the roar of the discharge spooked it, found the experience as gratifying as it was unnerving. "I have witnessed enthusiasms before," he wrote Andrew Jr., "but never before have I witnessed such a scene of personal regard as I have today. . . . I have bowed to upwards of two hundred thousand people today. Never has there been such affection of the people before, I am sure."

The enthusiasm eased as the president entered New England. Connecticut appreciated his stand against the nullifiers, with a Norwich women's group waving banners recalling his Jefferson dinner toast in favor of the Union. But the heat of democracy diminished the closer he got to the cool heart of New England. Harvard had awarded honorary degrees to previous presidents visiting Boston, including James Monroe. Harvard's president, Josiah Quincy, feared that failing to honor Jackson similarly would be taken for partisanship, which he shunned for himself and the college. But the earlier recipients had been well educated, while Jackson's lack of schooling was famous. This lack, of course, was part of his appeal to ordinary folks, but it simply reminded Quincy and the board of Harvard's overseers that their college wasn't for ordinary folks. In Jackson's favor, as Quincy reasoned, he had practical experience. The degree in question was a doctorate of laws, and Jackson had been an attorney and a judge, besides being the current chief executive of the laws of the nation. Yet Quincy had to ask himself, what if Jackson insisted on speaking at the ceremony? In the man's ignorance he might make a fool of Harvard. Quincy couldn't bear the thought.

Neither could John Quincy Adams, observing cousin Quincy's dilemma from the distance of the village of Quincy (formerly Braintree, but renamed for all the Quincys about). Adams muttered to his diary as Jackson came north, complaining of the attention his old rival received. "The President must hasten back to Washington, or he will be glorified to his grave," Adams said. "They so fagged him by their reception on Friday, and their presentations and addresses on Saturday, that he failed going to the Brattle Street Church with Governor Lincoln on Sunday morning." Adams disbelieved that Jackson was as tired as he let on. "He is one of our tribe of great men who turn disease to commodity. . . . He is so ravenous of notoriety that he craves the sympathy for sickness as a portion of his glory. . . . Four fifths of the sickness is trickery, and the other fifth mere fatigue."

Adams's envy sharpened to outrage when Josiah Quincy decided to go ahead and give the president a degree. Adams was invited as a matter of course, but on principle he refused. "I *could not* be present to see my darling Harvard disgrace herself by conferring a Doctor's degree upon a barbarian and savage who could scarcely spell his own name," he told Quincy.

Jackson surprised Quincy and the other guests who likewise expected a barbarian. Or so Adams heard from a physician friend who attended the ceremonies honoring the president and confessed to having been "much captivated by the ease and gracefulness of his manners." (This doctor took Jackson's illness seriously. "He says Jackson is so excessively debilitated that he should not be surprised if he should never reach Washington again," Adams wrote.) The proceedings were as windy as academic convocations often are. Several eminent persons held forth at length before Jackson received his degree and spoke with much-appreciated brevity. The guests adjourned to a reception at Quincy's official residence, where Jackson shook hands with hundreds more and charmed the skeptics.

Yet those who weren't there weren't prevented by their absence from circulating stories about the event. One that drew smiles from both sides had

Jackson, after enduring the speeches in academic Latin, being urged to respond in kind, now that he was a doctor of laws. The president rose to the occasion with splendid succinctness. "E pluribus unum, my friends," he said. "Sine qua non."

An unrelated incident of Jackson's summer travels wasn't funny at all. On a brief trip to Alexandria, Virginia, the president was assaulted by a young man recently dismissed from the navy. Murder seems not to have been the motive, for the assailant simply struck Jackson in the face with his hand. He was instantly overpowered and hauled away, leaving the president lightly bloodied. A local stalwart, embarrassed at this breach of etiquette, offered to kill the attacker if Jackson would pardon him should he be convicted of the murder. Jackson declined the offer. "I can not do that," he said. "I want no man to stand between me and my assailants, and none to take revenge on my account." He wished only that he had been quicker to respond to the attack. He had been seated and unable to bring his cane to bear. "Had I been prepared for this cowardly villain's approach, I can assure you all that he would never have the temerity to undertake such a thing again."

In 1832 John Marshall celebrated his thirty-first year as chief justice of the United States. But Marshall didn't feel much like celebrating. At the end of the previous year, on Christmas Day, his wife of forty-eight years had died. No less than Jackson had Marshall devoted himself to his spouse; no less than Jackson was he prostrated emotionally at her passing. To his associates he never seemed the same after Mary's death. He suddenly showed his seventy-six years; the joy of life that had carried him through the controversies of his tenure on the court abandoned him. He found solace in neither Washington, his place of work, nor Richmond, his home.

Yet, like Jackson, he carried on. He lacked the energy of younger days, when he had made the court coequal with Congress and the presidency by the power of his will and intellect. Fortunately the big cases seemed fewer these days—but of course that wasn't just luck. The great battles—over the role of the court, the nature of contracts, the scope of federal power—had been fought and won. It was a measure of the respect in which the court was held that the nullifiers of South Carolina hadn't bothered appealing to the court for redress. They knew that with Marshall, the father of judicial nationalism, in charge they didn't stand a chance.

But if the battles weren't as central to American life as those earlier ones, this didn't make them any less bitter. In 1831 the court heard a case from Georgia involving the Cherokees and the jurisdiction of state law. During the previous three decades various bands of the Cherokees had adopted different strategies for dealing with the whites. Some fought, others relocated, still others assumed white ways. The Cherokees of Georgia followed the third path. Taking their cue from Sequoyah, who had served with Jackson's Cherokee allies in the Creek War and had later devised a written version of the Cherokee language, they produced a newspaper, books, and other accoutrements of what the whites called civilization. They prospered alongside their white neighbors, engaging in agriculture and commerce. In fact they prospered too well for the tastes of those neighbors, who conspired to dispossess them of the lands they retained under various treaties. The Georgia legislature passed laws transparently intended to make life miserable for the Cherokees, in order that they abandon their lands and follow their cousins west across the Mississippi. The Georgia Cherokees, showing again how much they had learned from the whites, sued to block the laws. They hired William Wirt, by now the most famous trial lawyer in America, to argue their case, which the Supreme Court agreed to hear. But the hearing went badly for the Cherokees. Marshall and the court's majority ruled in favor of Georgia, declaring that the Cherokees weren't a foreign nation, as they had contended, but a "domestic dependent nation." Foreign nations might sue state governments; domestic dependent nations could not.

This disappointing decision nonetheless guided Wirt and the Cherokees down a more promising path. The next year they brought suit under the 1789 Judiciary Act, which assigned to the Supreme Court jurisdiction over disputes involving treaties and the validity of state laws. The court agreed that the Cherokees had standing, and it listened to Wirt contend that the Georgia laws were invalid because they conflicted with federal treaties governing relations with the Cherokees. The court found for the Cherokees. "The acts of Georgia are repugnant to the constitution, laws and treaties of the United States," Marshall declared. They were therefore null and void. The Cherokees could stay put, unmolested.

$\mathscr{J}$ackson yielded nothing to Marshall on the issue of nationalism. But he remained unconvinced—despite Marshall's three decades of effort to the contrary—that the decisions of the courts bound the executive branch. And he remained convinced that the only long-term answer to the Indian question was for the tribes to move beyond the reach of the whites. In his annual message of December 1830 he had congratulated the Chickasaw and Choctaw tribes for accepting a swap of eastern lands for western. "Their example will induce the remaining tribes also to seek the same obvious advantages," he declared, with perhaps more hope than conviction. He specified the advantages of relocation. "It puts an end to all possible danger of collision between the authorities of the general and state governments on account of the Indians. . . . It will separate the Indians from immediate contact with settlements of whites, free them from the power of the states, enable them to pursue happiness in their own way and under their own rude institutions; will retard the progress of decay, which is lessening their numbers; and perhaps cause them gradually, under the protection of the government and through the influence of good counsels, to cast off their savage habits and become an interesting, civilized, and Christian community." Jackson avowed benign motives regarding the Indians. "Toward the aborigines of the country, no one can indulge a more friendly feeling than myself, or would go further in attempting to reclaim them from their wandering habits and make them a happy, prosperous people." Yet one must look facts in the eye.

> Humanity has often wept over the fate of the aborigines of this country, and philanthropy has long been busily employed in devising means to avert it, but its progress has never for a moment been arrested, and one by one have many powerful tribes disappeared from the earth. To follow to the tomb the last of this race and to tread on the graves of extinct nations excite melancholy reflections. But true philanthropy reconciles the mind to these vicissitudes as it does to the extinction of one generation to make room for an-

other. . . . Philanthropy could not wish to see this continent restored to the condition in which it was found by our forefathers.
What good man would prefer a country covered with forests and
ranged by a few thousand savages to our extensive Republic, stud-
ded with cities, towns, and prosperous farms, embellished with all
the improvements which art can devise or industry execute, occupied by more than 12,000,000 happy people, and filled with all the
blessings of liberty, civilization, and religion?

The policy of the administration was nothing but an extension of the
process that had been under way for two centuries. Jackson didn't deny that
relocation would be wrenching. But hadn't relocation been the story of
America from the first settlements? And wasn't it the story of America even
now? "Our children by thousands yearly leave the land of their birth to seek
new homes in distant regions." The Indians were being asked to do no more.

The Indians must either adopt the ways of the whites, including the
laws of the states in which they lived, or move. To stay where they were, under their old customs, was not an option. Jackson knew the Indians' neighbors, having dwelt among such people most of his life. They wouldn't leave
the Indians alone or let them keep large tracts of land lightly occupied. The
status quo was untenable; for the Indians it risked "utter annihilation."

Jackson's policy was self-serving but consistent. In matters not touching the integrity of the Union, he generally deferred to the states. Here he
refused to stand between the states and the tribes. The Indians must make
their peace with the states or relocate.

Moreover, Jackson's policy reflected a deep understanding of the life on
the frontier. Georgia wasn't as wild as it had been, but wherever whites
encountered Indians living apart, in tribes, the old frontier dynamics reemerged. The whites resented the Indians' immunity from state laws, and
they coveted the land the Indians owned. Congress might legislate, and the
courts might rule, but the struggle that had begun the moment the first Europeans set foot in North America wouldn't end until the descendants of
those Europeans claimed the whole continent, or as much as they chose to
take. Jackson was sincere—paternalistic, but no less sincere for that—in
saying he had the best interests of the Indians at heart. His adoption of Lyncoya and the other Indian boys he and Rachel took in attested to his good in-

tentions toward Indians as individuals. Perhaps moving the Indians across the Mississippi would merely buy them time. But the alternative was as grim as the future had always been for losers in the long struggle for North America—"utter annihilation," as he bluntly put it.

Jackson hadn't liked John Marshall before becoming president. The old Federalist bowed to property and stole authority from the states, besides having frustrated Jefferson's prosecution of Aaron Burr. Jackson's opinion didn't change after he became president, despite the fact that Marshall's long record of nationalism made Jackson's defense of the Union against the nullifiers easier than it would have been otherwise—easier, for example, than a similar defense by John Adams against the nullifiers of 1798 would have been.

Jackson didn't like the august airs the chief justice put on, and he didn't like the undemocratic nature of the court's decisions—which was why he refused in principle to defer to the court's decisions. And he didn't like Marshall's judgment in the Cherokee case of 1832. "Being more and more convinced that the destiny of the Indians within the settled portion of the United States depends upon their entire and speedy migration to the country west of the Mississippi set apart for their permanent residence," he wrote to Congress in February 1832, while the case was before the court, "I am anxious that all the arrangements necessary to the complete execution of the plan of removal and to the ultimate security and improvement of the Indians should be made without further delay." Marshall's ruling represented one such delay, one that encouraged foolish thinking on the part of reluctant Indians and their self-proclaimed supporters. Jackson reiterated that he simply proposed to treat the Indians as he treated the other inhabitants of Georgia and the several states—in fact, better, in that he was offering to pay their way west. "Should any of them, however, repel the offer of removal, they are free to remain, but they must remain with such privileges and disabilities as the respective states within whose jurisdiction they live may prescribe."

In his 1832 annual message, several months after the Supreme Court's decision, Jackson didn't deign to acknowledge the decision or even notice that the issue had come before the court. "I am happy to inform you," he told Congress, "that the wise and humane policy of transferring from the eastern to the western side of the Mississippi the remnants of our aboriginal tribes, with their own consent and upon just terms, has been steadily pursued, and is approaching, I trust, its consummation." Jackson's single reference to the recent court case was oblique to the point of being willfully obscure. "With one exception every subject involving any question of conflicting jurisdiction or of peculiar difficulty has been happily disposed of. . . . With that portion of the Cherokees, however, living within the State of Georgia it has been found impracticable as yet to make a satisfactory adjustment." Defending as generous his offers to the Georgia Cherokees, Jackson went so far as to say, "Whatever difference of opinion may have prevailed respecting the just claims of these people, there will probably be none respecting the liberality of the propositions, and very little respecting the expediency of their immediate acceptance."

In fact there was considerable difference of opinion regarding the liberality of the president's propositions. Indian advocates decried Jackson's defiance of the Supreme Court and his insistence on Indian removal, claiming he was playing agent for grasping Georgia speculators and rewarding his party allies in that state. Politicians and editors who opposed him for other reasons became sudden allies of the Cherokees.

Jackson might claim his policy was liberal, but the claim didn't make it so. He held out the alternative that the Cherokees might remain in Georgia by submitting to the authority of the state and living like whites. But considering how far the Cherokees had adopted white ways and how little their efforts had won them of respect from their neighbors, such a response would have required a daunting leap of faith. The harsh fact of the matter was that Georgia was determined to expel the Cherokees and take their land. Jackson knew this, and he refused to prevent it.

He was on firmer ground in declaring his policy inescapable. The defenders of the Cherokees were few and mostly far away from Georgia; their persecutors were many and near at hand. Given the racist realities of the time, Jackson was almost certainly correct in contending that for the Cherokees to remain in Georgia risked their extinction. To preserve the Cherokees as a tribe—to enforce Marshall's decision—would have required raising and sending federal troops to Georgia, stationing them there indefinitely, and ordering them to shoot white Georgians who threatened the Indians. Jackson realized that American democracy simply wouldn't sustain such a policy. It was one thing to threaten to use force to preserve the Union; in such an endeavor he could expect broad support from the people who would actually do the fighting. It was another thing to ask white citizens to risk death protecting Indians. They wouldn't do it. Horace Greeley put words in Jackson's mouth when the New York editor quoted the president as saying, "John Marshall has made his decision; now let him enforce it." Yet the words captured Jackson's attitude. The chief justice would have to enforce the decision, because nobody else would.

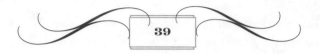

39

WEALTH VERSUS

COMMONWEALTH

*N*icholas Biddle was a more resourceful foe than John Marshall, in a very literal sense. The resources at the command of the Bank of the United States included a large portion of the country's money supply. If Biddle employed those resources against the administration, he could bring the American economy to its knees.

*H*e hoped this wouldn't be necessary. Even after Jackson's veto of the bank renewal bill, and after Jackson's reelection, Biddle believed the bank's position was impregnable. The critical issue for the bank—and for Jackson—was control of the deposits of the federal government. They constituted the bank's primary source of financial strength, providing the assets against which the bank made loans. They were under the control of the Treasury, which was to say, under the control of Jackson, and if the president were to remove the deposits, the bank would be crippled. But to do so would disrupt financial channels developed over the sixteen years of the bank's existence, would seriously inconvenience the government and the public, and would destabilize the economy.

Biddle felt secure, even smug. "They will not *dare* to remove them," he told Daniel Webster. "If the deposits are withdrawn, it will be a declaration of war which cannot be recalled."

*W*ar was precisely what Jackson intended, although he would have said that Biddle brought the conflict on himself. In February 1833 the president received an alarming report of what he considered the bank's continuing designs against democracy. "I am informed by a gentleman whose knowledge of the U.S. Bank is second only to that of its president . . . that the Bank counts upon being rechartered," James Hamilton wrote.

> Its purpose is for the next two years to fortify itself beyond all hazard by calling in its responsibilities gradually. . . . This operation will be performed under the avowed idea that it is necessary and preliminary to winding up its concerns. . . . At a proper time, about the expiration of the period referred to, it will by withholding bills and by other means within its power cause exchange to advance so as to cause the exportation of specie and thus occasion a run upon all the monied institutions. This *it* will be prepared for. And the affairs of the state banks will consequently be so deranged as to compel them to stop specie payments. The immense injury to the whole nation resulting from that event, it is believed, and not without foundation, will induce a strong public feeling in favor of recharter of the Bank as the only means of restoring a sound currency.

Jackson couldn't be sure that this was what Biddle intended, but it was just what he expected of banks and bankers. Jackson as president didn't know much more about currency questions than he had as a struggling businessman in Nashville, but what he did know disposed him to think the worst of those with their hands on the money supply. The fact that a few men in eastern cities could determine the fate of the nation outraged his democratic sensibilities. Who had elected Nicholas Biddle? None but his cronies on the bank board, whose interests were equally at odds with those of ordinary men and women. Jackson would have opposed the money power even had its intentions been benign. That they were so patently malignant—that the bank had become a "hydra of corruption," as he put it in a private letter—made his opposition that much easier.

During the spring of 1833 the president prepared his anti-bank offensive carefully. He dangled the possibility of creating a new national bank, confined to the District of Columbia, even as he polled his cabinet secretaries on the feasibility of relying on state banks to handle the fiscal affairs of the federal government. Jackson's survey had a dual purpose: to test his ideas and to test the loyalty of his secretaries. No less than Biddle did he know that removing the deposits would mean war, and he wanted to be sure that his lieutenants were as devoted to the cause as he was.

The one who displayed the greatest verve was Roger Taney, the attorney general. Like a seasoned prosecutor, Taney presented evidence that Biddle and the bank had consciously manipulated the money supply before the last congressional session. "Can any impartial and unprejudiced mind doubt the motive?" he asked rhetorically. "Was it not to compel the people to continue its monopoly and privileges, not on account of the benefits conferred by it, but to escape from the suffering which the corporation had the power to inflict?" Taney demonstrated that Biddle had bought favorable press coverage for the bank during the fight for renewal of the charter; this practice, of employing the people's money to manipulate the democratic process, was "pregnant with so much evil," Taney told Jackson, that it alone was cause for the severest censure. As for alternatives to Biddle's bank, Taney contended that state banks, "judiciously selected and arranged," would be able to perform the fiscal tasks of the federal government and supply "a general currency as wholesome and stable as that of the United States Bank." Taney acknowledged that taking on the bank was fraught with peril. Biddle would wage a "fierce and desperate struggle" to preserve the bank and its prerogatives. But the risk was worth taking. "The purity of our institutions and the best interests of the country call for prompt, firm and decisive measures."

Taney wasn't a close friend of Jackson's, but he knew him well enough to realize that nothing roused the old warrior like the promise of a bloody fight. Jackson indeed rose to the challenge, and by the end of June had fairly decided to remove the deposits and place them in state banks. But the man who would have to implement the policy, Treasury Secretary William Duane, was balking. Jackson sent him a paper defending the action. Duane and others worried that removal of the deposits would provoke Biddle to retaliate against the state banks that received the deposits, provoking financial panic. "If this apprehension be well founded, it proves two things of fearful import," Jackson's message to Duane asserted. "First, that the Bank of the United States has the power to accomplish the ruin of the state banks and cause general bankruptcy and distress among the people; and secondly, that there is a disposition to exercise that power, unless its forbearance be purchased by the Government." Jackson wasn't sure Biddle could bring down the economy, but if he could, that was all the more reason to bring down Biddle's bank. "If this despotism be now partially fixed upon the country, a struggle must be made to cast it off, or our people will be forever enslaved."

Duane, who had been one of the government-appointed directors of the Bank of the United States, wasn't convinced, and he continued to argue against removal. But Jackson pressed forward. He sent Amos Kendall about the country to determine which state banks were willing and able to support the president against Biddle. In Baltimore, perhaps because it was so close to Philadelphia, the bankers were very hesitant. "Most of the banks there will answer precisely as the Bank of the United States desires," Kendall reported. Boston was braver. "Some of the banks are not only willing to undertake the government business on the same terms that the Bank of the United States does it, but to give the personal responsibility of their directors and all they possess, for the security of the government." Boston's confidence was infectious. "The Maine bank at Portland has made the same tender. I expect to receive a similar offer from Portsmouth." Yet all the state bankers said that if the deed were to be done, it must be done quickly. Biddle's bank could crush any state bank that sided with the government but was left short of cash. "The only question, therefore, seems to me to be *an immediate removal* or *no removal*."

Three weeks later Jackson announced the decision to his cabinet. He reiterated the constitutional arguments against the bank from his veto message but now emphasized the political and especially the moral elements of the case. The fight against the bank was the current battleground in the long struggle for liberty, he said. "The divine right of kings and the prerogative authority of rulers have fallen before the intelligence of the age. Standing armies and military chieftains can no longer uphold tyranny against the resistance of public opinion. The mass of the people have more to fear from combinations of the wealthy and professional classes—from an aristocracy which through the influence of riches and talents, insidiously employed, sometimes succeeds in preventing political institutions, however well adjusted, from securing the freedom of the citizen." The moneyed aristocracy had attained a stranglehold over the nation's economy. "The Bank has by degrees obtained almost entire dominion over the circulating medium, and with it, power to increase or diminish the price of property and to levy taxes on the people in the shape of premiums and interest to an amount only limited by the quantity of paper currency it is enabled to issue." The Founding Fathers had revolted against England when such power was wielded against them. The current generation—in particular, the current administration—could do no less. Nor would it. By October 1, 1833, Jackson declared, the federal deposits would be transferred from the Bank of the United States to the state banks.

The decision, when it came, didn't surprise Biddle. His spies had informed him of the debates within the administration and of the soundings of the state banks by Amos Kendall. He considered a preemptive strike by buying off vulnerable members of the administration and Congress. "In half an hour," he boasted to an intimate, "I can remove all the constitutional scruples in the District of Columbia. Half a dozen presidencies"—of bank branches—"a dozen cashierships, fifty clerkships, a hundred directorships, to worthy friends who have no character and no money." But he held back, not quite believing that Jackson would really go through with removal.

When Jackson did, Biddle launched a counterattack. He called in loans, tightened credit, and otherwise reduced the bank's financial exposure. His publicly stated purpose was to strengthen the bank against the uncertainty that must follow the president's hasty action, but his deeper aim was to demonstrate the economy's need for a central bank beyond the reach of what he privately called the "nest of gamblers" in the administration. To complement his fiscal tightening, Biddle went ahead with his bribery, offering lucrative positions to Jackson loyalists if they would abandon the president and join the bank.

The attack on the money supply had an immediate effect, starting in the nation's financial capital. Samuel Swartout, Jackson's customs collector at New York, was one of those to whom Biddle offered a bank directorship. Swartout declined the offer but pleaded with Biddle to have mercy on the nation's finances, which were beginning to scream. "It is dreadful here, and no hope of relief except through your institution," Swartout said. "You must be *liberal*." Swartout was no radical bank hater, which was why Biddle had thought he might be seduced. Speaking as one businessman to another, Swartout appealed to the better angels of Biddle's nature, and to his political self-interest. "Now that the effect of the late measure has been made manifest, you can relieve the whole community. . . . Rely upon it, you would receive due credit and consideration for it." Biddle must act before it was too late. "Nothing but extensive discounts by your institution can save your friends and the public in general. . . . The old friends and dependents of the Bank are perishing."

Biddle refused to relent. The financial panic spread from New York across the country. Banks collapsed in Washington and Philadelphia while a Boston paper described conditions there as "absolutely frightful." But Biddle maintained his choke hold on the money supply. "My own view of the matter is simply this," he explained to the president of the Boston branch of his bank. "The projectives of this last assault on the Bank regret and are alarmed by it. But the ties of party allegiance can only be broken by the actual conviction of existing distress in the community. Nothing but the evidence of suffering abroad"—that is, in the country as a whole—"will produce any effect in Congress." The president and the administration had started this fight. They would have to see it to the end. "If the Bank remains strong and quiet, the course of events will save the Bank and save all the institutions of the country which are now in great peril. But if from too great a sensitiveness, from the fear of offending or the desire of conciliating, the Bank permits itself to be frightened or coaxed into any relaxation of its present measures, the relief will be cited as evidence that the measures of the government are not injurious or oppressive, and the Bank will inevitably be prostrated."

The louder the economy shrieked, the more determined Biddle grew. "The whole future is full of gloom and confusion," he wrote in February 1834. "My own course is decided. All the other banks and the merchants may break, but the Bank of the United States shall not break." Pleas for relief were in vain. "You may rely on it," he told one pleader, "that the Bank has taken its final course, and that it will be neither frightened nor cajoled from its duty by any small driveling about relief to the country." Jackson had chosen the wrong man to tangle with. "This worthy President thinks that because he has scalped Indians and imprisoned judges, he is to have his way with the Bank. He is mistaken. . . . He may as well send at once and engage lodgings in Arabia."

𝒯his was what it came down to: the will of Jackson versus the will of Biddle. Banks might crumble, markets collapse, crops go unplanted, but one man would win. Jackson had no doubt who that would be. "The Bank, Mr. Van Buren, is trying to kill me," he told the vice president. "*But I will kill it!*"

Yet victory was no sure thing. The initial requirement was to secure his own ranks. Jackson realized that Biddle was encouraging defections, but, given that jobs with Biddle's bank paid much better than government jobs, there was little Jackson could do besides exhort the tempted to keep the democratic faith. Certain other individuals he threw overboard himself. Treasury Secretary Duane continued to oppose the removal of the deposits even after Jackson made his decision. Jackson didn't relish replacing Duane after having replaced his entire cabinet already, but he needed a stalwart in that crucial position. He fired Duane and moved Roger Taney from the Justice Department to the Treasury.

The removal process itself seemed to be going well. "We have got the Bank in Baltimore, Philadelphia, New York and Boston perfectly under *check mate*," Jackson wrote Van Buren. The state banks that were receiving the federal deposits—"pet banks," their critics called them—had laid in financial stores. And Jackson prepared to send reinforcements and apply whatever pressure was needed to bring Biddle down. "I am ready with the screws to draw every tooth and then the stumps. . . . We will, if I mistake not, have Mr. Biddle as quiet and harmless as a *lamb* in six weeks."

Jackson rarely underestimated his opponents, but he underestimated Biddle. The bank president proved as politically astute as he was financially ruthless. Having starved large parts of the economy of cash, he encouraged the sufferers to take their case to Congress and the White House. Jackson found himself bombarded with memorials and petitions crying distress and demanding restoration of the deposits and a return to the status quo ante. Meanwhile Henry Clay, with Biddle's support, introduced resolutions in the Senate condemning Jackson for overstepping his constitutional authority by removing the deposits without leave of Congress.

Jackson was unmoved. "Were all the worshippers of the golden calf to memorialise me and request a restoration of the deposits," he told Van Buren, "I would cut my right hand from my body before I would do such an act." Jackson had rarely felt so confident of his rectitude. "My conscience told me it was right to stop the career of this destroying monster," he wrote Andrew Jr. "I took the step fearlessly, believing it a duty I owed to my God and my country."

Jackson's conviction allowed him to ignore much of the havoc the panic played on the economy. "There is no real general distress," he declared privately in February 1834. "It is only with those who live by borrowing, trade on loans, and the gamblers in stocks." Perhaps Jackson forgot that he himself had once lived on borrowing and that millions of farmers and businessmen still did. In any event, he declared that it would be a "god send to society if all such were put down."

He spoke somewhat more openly to a delegation of New York merchants who came to the White House bearing a petition signed by six thousand of their fellow sufferers. Jackson had reason to believe Biddle had put the merchants up to the mission and helped them gather the signatures. So he made them wait in an outer office before he examined their petition, and when he did let them in, he answered their spokesman's plea for relief with a vehemence that scorched their ears. "Relief, sir!" he thundered. "Come not to me! . . . Go to the monster! . . . Go to Nicholas Biddle. We have no money here. . . . Biddle has all the money. He has millions of specie in his vaults at this moment, lying idle, and yet you come to *me* to save you from breaking." By one version of this meeting, Jackson's anger at Biddle grew so uncontrollable that he couldn't continue speaking. By another, more believable version, the president didn't lose control for a second. "Didn't I manage them well?" he asked an aide as the merchants filed out.

As Clay's censure resolutions moved toward passage in the Senate, Jackson accounted them simply more of what he had long expected of Clay. "The storm in Congress is still raging, Clay reckless and as full of fury as a drunken man in a brothel," he told Andrew. But the furor would have no effect. "This mammoth of power and corruption must die. . . . The *monster must perish.*" When the Senate approved the censure, Jackson blamed Biddle's greedy reach. "Nicholas Biddle now rules the Senate, as a showman does his puppets."

Yet the worst was already over. The liquidity crisis eased as the federal deposits flowed into the state banks, and from the state banks into the economy. Biddle might own Clay and the Senate, but the people were retaking the economy. "The clamour of pressure in the money market is vanishing," Jackson observed in March 1834. "All things will end well here."

*A*nd so it seemed for several months. The bank war broke Biddle's power. The Democrats trounced the Whigs in the congressional elections of 1834, successfully blaming Biddle and the bank for the financial panic that followed the removal of the deposits. Whig leaders thereupon abandoned Biddle as quickly as they could. Thurlow Weed, the voice of New York Whiggism, told Biddle and the bank good riddance. "After staggering along from year to year with a doomed bank upon our shoulders," Weed declared, "both the bank and our party are finally overwhelmed. The burden, however, is now removed."

The beginning of the new year brought further glad tidings. When the federal accounts were tallied on January 1, 1835, the United States government was no longer in debt. Jackson had been paying down the debt since his first day in office, in the Jeffersonian belief that the debt was a Federalist plot to fatten bankers and subvert the republic. After six years, his administrative reforms and spending vetoes paid off in this proud accomplishment, which gave the lie to charges that a democracy could never control its fiscal appetites.

But if the fiscal problem had been solved, the monetary problem remained. In fact it got worse, primarily as a result of Jackson's war against the Bank of the United States. Freed from the restraints Biddle's bank had imposed, the state banks issued notes by the basketful. These fueled a rampant speculation in every kind of commodity. Jackson couldn't do much about the speculation overall, except worry that it jeopardized the stability of the economy and threatened the welfare of millions of ordinary people. But he could curb the speculation in land, which had particularly painful effects on folks trying to get started in farming. In July 1836 he approved the "specie circular," which required that purchasers of federal lands pay gold or silver for their acreage.

Jackson's move burst the land bubble at once, and as the air blew out it chilled the broader economy. Not till 1837, after Jackson had left office, would the full effects be felt, but the lesson was clear, or should have been: that in matters monetary, there were no easy answers, and perhaps never would be.

Politics in the age of Jackson wasn't for the faint of heart and especially not for the weak of mind. The rhetoric was extravagant, sometimes violently so, and those persons who couldn't mind the difference between metaphor and reality could become a danger to themselves and others. In January 1835 Jackson attended a memorial service at the Capitol for a departed congressman. He was exiting the building when a man quietly emerged from the crowd of onlookers and from a distance of less than ten feet leveled a pistol at the president's heart and fired. The percussion cap exploded but failed to ignite the powder in the barrel. "The explosion of the cap was so loud that many persons thought the pistol had fired," Thomas Benton remembered. "I heard it at the foot of the steps, far from the place, and a great crowd between." The sound startled all present and froze them in their steps. The assailant took advantage of the collective pause to raise a second pistol, aim, and squeeze the trigger. Again the cap fired, but again it failed to ignite the powder.

Jackson by this time realized he was under mortal attack, and he charged the man with his cane. Yet others moved more quickly, and a knot of angry cabinet secretaries, military officers, and bystanders collapsed upon the man. He was roughly carried away to police custody.

Interrogation revealed that his name was Richard Lawrence and that he had been born in England. He was a painter of houses by trade, but the panic of the previous year had thrown him out of work. No American president had ever been assassinated, and the attempt alone suggested to police that Lawrence was insane. They summoned doctors to assist with the examination. The doctors inquired as to the assailant's health. "He replied that it had been uniformly good, and that he had never labored under any mental derangement," the doctors reported. "Nor did he admit the existence of any of those symptoms of physical derangement which usually attend mental alienation." The doctors inquired into motive. "He replied that he had been told that the president had caused his loss of occupation, and the consequent want of money. . . . He believed that to put him out of the way was the only remedy for this evil." The doctors asked who told him this. He couldn't identify anyone in particular, but he did say he had often attended the debates in Congress.

The doctors pressed him on why he wanted Jackson dead. "He answered, because he was a tyrant." The doctors asked who told him that. "He answered, it was a common talk with the people, and that he had read it in all the papers." He was asked whether he thought he personally would benefit from the president's death. "He answered, he could not rise unless the president fell, and that he expected thereby to recover his liberty, and that the mechanics would all be benefited; that the mechanics would have plenty of work; and that money would be more plenty." He was asked why money would be more plenty. "He replied, it would be more easily obtained from the bank." What bank? "The Bank of the United States."

To this point in the interrogation, Lawrence's comments made him seem simply an extreme Whig. But when he asserted that he was in regular correspondence with the governments of Europe and that he was the rightful heir to the throne of England, the doctors decided he was indeed insane.

As a result he was never tried for the attempted assassination. Some observers hoped the incident would cause the participants in the political debates to reconsider their rhetoric, to ask whether allegations of despotism might drive others to similar acts of deluded tyrannicide. But if any of the debaters did reconsider, the effect wasn't noticeable.

Indeed, a contrary conclusion was drawn by some of Jackson's partisans, though apparently not by Jackson himself. Restraint was unnecessary, they said, because God protected democrats. In the course of the investigation the police tested the pistols Lawrence had aimed at the president. Each time now, the weapons fired perfectly. "The circumstance made a deep impression upon the public feeling," Thomas Benton explained, "and irresistibly carried many minds to the belief in a superintending Providence, manifested in the extraordinary case of two pistols in succession—so well loaded, so coolly handled, and which afterwards fired with such readiness, force, and precision—missing fire, each in its turn, when levelled from eight feet at the President's heart."

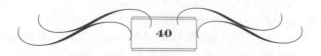

40

AN OLD FRIEND AND

A NEW FRONTIER

$\mathscr{A}$mid the battle over the bank, Jackson received some welcome news

of a personal sort. Sam Houston had made a remarkable comeback from

the depths of his drunken self-pity. He still drank, but not more than many

in America in those sodden days when liquor was safer than water and

most meals began and ended with a crook of the elbow and a nod to the

vine or the cornstalk. He looked almost as good as he had before he threw

his career away over a broken heart: tall, with broad shoulders and a

leonine head framed in flowing black hair and bushy side-whiskers.

Business of an undisclosed sort brought him east to New York and then

Washington. In the capital he happened to tangle with a congressman who,

remembering Houston's support for Jackson, lashed the younger man as a

way of hitting the older. The congressman, William Stanberry, spoke on the floor of the House and on that account thought himself immune from retaliation. Houston recalled enough from his own service in the House to interpret its rules of order otherwise and, when he caught Stanberry on Pennsylvania Avenue, caned him vigorously. Stanberry thereupon filed charges in the House against him.

Jackson didn't like Stanberry, who opposed him on the bank, and thought he deserved the thrashing. The president was particularly touched that Houston had employed a hickory cane to apply the strokes. He brought Houston to the White House and offered encouragement. "It's not you they are after, Sam," he said. "Those thieves, those infernal bank thieves, they wish to injure your old commander." Jackson gave Houston money for a new suit for the trial and told him, "When you make your defense, tell those infernal bank thieves, who talk about privileges, that when an American citizen is insulted by one of them, he also has some privileges."

Houston defended himself floridly in the trial. He couldn't deny he had beaten Stanberry, but he pleaded extenuating circumstances. The congressman had insulted him beyond endurance, he said, and then had refused to meet him in an honorable duel. What was a gentleman to do? He closed his defense with a flight of oratory that impressed even gallery denizens used to Daniel Webster. "So long as that flag shall bear aloft its glittering stars," he declaimed, pointing at the flag behind the Speaker's chair, "so long, I trust, shall the rights of American citizens be preserved safe and unimpaired, and transmitted as a sacred legacy from one generation to another, till discord shall wreck the spheres, the grand march of time shall cease, and not one fragment of all creation be left to chafe on the bosom of eternity's waves."

Houston won the galleries but lost the case. The House voted him guilty and ordered the Speaker to reprimand him. Stanberry then filed a suit in criminal court against Houston, who lost again, incurring a five-hundred-dollar fine. Yet Houston won something five hundred dollars couldn't have purchased: vindication in the eyes of Jackson and the Jacksonian public. "I was dying out, and had they taken me before a justice of the peace and fined me ten dollars, it would have killed me," he recollected. "But they gave me a national tribunal for a theatre, and that set me up again."

Jackson agreed. Houston's impassioned defense of himself—and implicitly of Jackson—rehabilitated the prodigal son in the eyes of his surrogate father. Jackson blasted the House trial of Houston as "the greatest act of tyranny and usurpation ever attempted under our government," and he predicted, "The people will inquire into this act of usurpation and make these little tyrants who have thus voted feel the power of the people." The Constitution prevented the president from doing anything about the House's chastisement of Houston, yet he was able to remit the fine imposed by the Washington district court.

Jackson would have been happy for Houston to return to Tennessee politics, but as in the case of the Bible's prodigal son, the siblings of the wayward child were less delighted than the father at his sudden reappearance. Tennessee wouldn't have Houston, who himself experienced mixed emotions about returning to the scene of his humiliation at love. So he set his eye farther west.

$\mathcal{J}$ackson had been thinking about Texas since Aaron Burr had plotted to free that province from Spanish control and add it to the American empire or his own. Burr's disgrace and Jackson's own efforts to distance himself from the fiasco made forgetfulness about Texas a virtue for a time. In any case, with his hands full in Mississippi, Louisiana, and Florida, he had little attention to spare for the region across the Sabine. Yet he wasn't entirely oblivious. Like Jefferson, Jackson believed that the Louisiana Purchase had included Texas, and so with most southwesterners he objected when John Quincy Adams as secretary of state consigned Texas to Spanish control in 1819. But he couldn't object too loudly, given that the same Spanish treaty delivered Florida to the United States and that Adams was Jackson's staunchest defender against charges of high-handedness in the Seminole War. Mexican independence in 1821 complicated the Texas question for Jackson and other defenders of democracy. So long as Texas—and Mexico—had labored under Spanish rule, taking Texas could be cast as spreading liberty and self-rule. The Mexicans, after flirting with a domestic version of empire, in 1824 embraced republicanism, with a federal constitution modeled on that of the United States. Americans began emigrating to Texas at the invitation of the Mexican government and under the supervision of Stephen Austin and other *empresarios*. Republican respect and simple good-neighborliness suggested a patient approach to Texas, which Jackson initially adopted.

Yet he couldn't help thinking that Texas ought to be American. The settled parts of Texas were much closer to Louisiana than to any comparably populated portion of Mexico, and by the time Jackson took office, the Americans in Texas outnumbered the native Mexicans. (Jackson knew that Austin and most of the early settlers were naturalized citizens of Mexico, but he—and many of the settlers themselves—considered them still Americans at heart.) Most to the point, Jackson's attitude toward Texas mirrored his earlier attitude toward Florida. Mexican authority in Texas was nearly as nonexistent as Spanish authority in Florida had been. Everything in Jackson's experience suggested that political power abhorred a vacuum, and what wasn't filled by the United States, in the regions along America's borders, would be filled by some other nation or people, potentially hostile to the United States. Spain's 1829 attempt to reconquer Mexico had failed on account of the heroics of a brilliant young general named Santa Anna. But the Spanish might try again. Or the British might exploit Mexico's weakness as they had exploited Spain's weakness in Florida. Or the French, fast recovering from their post-Napoleonic malaise, might try to recapture some of the New World glory Bonaparte had bargained away. Indians, including some who had taken refuge in Texas from American pressure, would be tempted to raid back across the border into the United States. And American slaves, inspired by the knowledge that Mexico had abolished slavery, would try to escape to Texas as other slaves had escaped to Florida. Borders were always trouble, which was why Jackson continually tried to push them back.

For these several reasons Jackson, during his first term as president, sought to purchase Texas from Mexico. To conduct the negotiations he chose Anthony Butler, an army colonel who "in addition to his many merits has that of frankness and honesty which are so well taught in the school of war," Jackson explained in commending Butler to Mexican vice president (and former general) Anastasio Bustamante. Butler's frankness was joined to an impulsiveness that required Jackson on occasion to calm him down. After the envoy reported political turmoil in Mexico City and hinted at helping those he considered most devoted to republicanism, Jackson told him to keep hands off. "No contingency can authorise your interference with her concerns," the president said. "Let them take what form they may in setting up and pulling down rulers, friendly or unfriendly to free government. Yours is the part of neutrality. . . . This is the course of duty as well as prudence."

It was also the most direct route to the acquisition of Texas. For reasons of diplomacy, Jackson typically spoke not of buying Texas but of adjusting the border between the United States and Mexico, a technical-sounding process that might be more acceptable to nationalistic Mexicans than the alienation of an entire province. But his intention became clear when he described what he considered the appropriate location of the border: amid "the desert or grand prairie" southwest of the American settlements in Texas. Jackson's grasp of Texas geography was uncertain; he didn't know where this barren zone started or where it ended. But he probably intended a line between the Rio Grande and the Nueces, a zone that was indeed deserted— and, as far as he could tell, always would be. That was the point: Jackson wanted space between the American settlements and the Mexican settlements, a buffer guaranteed by geography. "The grand prairie . . . ," he told Butler, "would be a boundary that would give permanent peace to the two republics." Jackson worried less about Mexico encroaching across a border farther north and east than about Americans doing so. He knew his countrymen and how pushy they were. "The citizens of the United States will never be contented until this boundary is acquired," he said. And he enjoined Butler to use his "best exertions" to secure it.

When Butler's initial efforts produced nothing, Jackson's concerns increased. "I feel great anxiety with regard to the boundary between us and Mexico," he told Butler in August 1831. Jackson had just heard that a company of Americans was intending to settle ten thousand new colonists in Texas. Added to the Americans already there, they would create tremendous pressure on the status quo. "When these get possession and become permanently fixed, they will soon avail themselves of some pretext to throw off the Mexican authority and form an independent government of their own. This would beget great disquietude, and might eventually endanger the peace and tranquility of both countries."

The prospect of an independent Texas initially alarmed Jackson even more than the idea of a Texas attached to Mexico. At a moment when South Carolina, a state within the Union, was causing him migraines, the last thing he needed was an independent country of Americans who wouldn't have to pay even lip service to the Union. Constitutional questions—and his oath of office—aside, his objection to an independent Texas was of a piece with his refusal to let South Carolina secede. In each case he believed that the multiplication of autonomous political systems multiplied the chances of war and lesser troubles. Self-government *within* the American Union was well and good; self-government *outside* the Union was a potential danger.

Jackson hoped to make the Mexican government see things his way. After all, trouble in Texas would harm Mexico more than it harmed the United States. "I cannot but think that a thorough examination of the whole subject will satisfy Mexico that her true policy recommends a cession of the province," he told Butler, who was instructed to conduct such an examination with Mexican officials. Promptness was crucial. "A revolt in Texas may close the door forever to its advantageous settlement, and may eventuate not merely in the loss of that province to Mexico with much blood and treasure, but break up the friendly understanding which is now established between this government and hers, and lead to a train of events that may obscure for a long period the sun of liberty in that quarter."

*M*exican officials resisted Jackson's logic, not least since few stayed in office long enough for Butler's lessons to sink in. Since independence, Mexico had been plagued with insurrections in various parts of the country and revolving-door governments in Mexico City. Even if Jackson had been able to convince a Mexican administration that Mexican national interests dictated divesting the country of Texas, such an administration couldn't bargain away a piece of the national patrimony without signing its own political death warrant. As death warrants in Mexican politics came soon enough anyway, no foreign minister or president saw need to hasten the process.

Butler, as frustrated as Jackson, suggested monetary inducements. A six-hundred-thousand-dollar loan from Mexican capitalists currently sustained the government. "This is but a drop, and will very soon be exhausted," Butler wrote. "And as I am confident that the experiment cannot be successfully repeated, I shall be ready to offer a supply to their necessities the moment they are found to be pressing." He had already broached the subject with relevant officials. "I intimated a few days since to the Secretary for Foreign Affairs that if he became much pressed for money I thought ways and means could be devised for obtaining through the United States a few millions." The secretary, Lucas Alamán, hadn't thrown Butler out of his office, which the American took as a positive sign. "My suggestion will not be forgotten, and the first serious difficulty will no doubt send him to me for an explanation of my remark."

Jackson liked the idea. "The intimations you so appropriately gave to the secretary of foreign affairs, of devising 'ways and means' should their pecuniary distresses become pressing, were happy and opportune," he told Butler. Jackson said he had begun to seek the money. "Your private letter was submitted, *confidentially*, to the chairman of our committee on foreign relations."

Butler had in mind more than a loan or grant to the Mexican government. The millions he spoke of would include something personal for those Mexican officials who helped move the Texas question along. In the summer of 1832 he thought he was making progress with Alamán, who had resigned from the cabinet but retained influence over foreign affairs. "He still directs the Department of Foreign Affairs *sub rosa*, and is in fact as much the minister as at any period before," Butler explained to Jackson. The fact that he wasn't formally in charge apparently made it easier for him to negotiate, and Butler thought they were close to a deal. The purchase price for Texas remained undetermined, but Butler suggested that any payment from the United States would "very probably be in part applied to *facilitate the negotiation*." That part of the arrangement should be provided for "by a secret article." Butler added that he would bring the treaty home himself "for the purpose of making explanations in regard to the contemplated secret article"—in other words, to explain the bribe to Congress.

Unfortunately for Jackson and Butler, the revolving door of Mexican politics kept turning. In the autumn of 1832 Alamán fled the capital with the rest of the regime. The new man of the hour was Santa Anna, who after repulsing the Spanish reconquest could immediately have made himself president of the country but preferred to let the other aspirants beat themselves senseless till he could ride in and save the day. He did so in October 1832 at Puebla, where his followers routed government troops and opened the path to Mexico City. Santa Anna entered the capital in triumph at the beginning of 1833, commencing his rule in Mexico about the time Jackson was starting his second term in the United States. Perhaps not surprisingly, given their common backgrounds as soldiers, Jackson initially thought Santa Anna's accession would mark a turn for Mexico's better. Soldiers were natural patriots, he assumed. As things happened, change came slower than Jackson anticipated, but he didn't give up. "I still hope that General Santa Anna's patriotism and good fortune may succeed in tranquilising that unhappy country," Jackson told Butler, "giving it peace, a true republican government, not executed by the bayonet but by the wholesome administration of just and equal laws."

Butler, on the ground in Mexico City, was less sanguine. The new regime might have restored order to Mexico, but it evidently hadn't ended the corruption of Mexican politics. Yet this might work to America's advantage regarding Texas, he conjectured. Butler reported "a very singular conversation" with an official he declined to name—lest his letter fall into the wrong hands—but who "is one of the most shrewd and intelligent men in the country, holds at the present time a high official station, and has much influence with the President General Santa Anna." This individual told Butler that the Texas question might be reopened under the right conditions. "There is one man who must be brought over to us in this affair, without whom we can do nothing; with him on our side, every thing." The official didn't identify Santa Anna by name, and neither did Butler, but he was the only one in Mexico City who fit the description. The official went on: "Have you command of money?" Butler said he had. "There will be a large sum necessary," the official said. "Half a million or upwards. This man, so important for us to gain, must have himself two hundred or three hundred thousand dollars. There are others among whom it may become necessary to distribute three or four hundred thousand more. Can you command that sum?" Butler nodded. "Assure me of the object," he said, "and the money shall not fail."

Jackson read Butler's letter with what he described as "astonishment." Till now much of the correspondence between Jackson and Butler had been sent in cipher, but Butler, for reasons known only to himself, had sent this letter unciphered. Jackson could hardly believe that Butler had been so foolish as to relate such sensitive information in a form any postal clerk or security official could read. The president also feared that Butler was being set up. "My dear sir," he replied, "be careful lest these 'shrewd fellows' may draw you into imputations of attempting to bribe these officers." But Jackson was even more upset that Butler's letter intimated that he—the president of the United States—was willing to bribe the Mexican government. "Nothing could be farther from my intention," Jackson wrote, in deliberately unciphered text.

Perhaps Jackson was sincere. Perhaps he really hadn't intended to corrupt the Mexican government. Maybe Butler read too much into the president's approval of his suggestions for easing the burdens of Mexico's debt. On the other hand, just before receiving Butler's latest from Mexico City, Jackson had written the envoy, "Provided you keep within your instructions and obtain the cession, it is not for your consideration whether the government of Mexico applies the money to the *purchase of men or to pay their public debt.*"

Obviously Jackson didn't want to be compromised by any public allegation of bribery, which would tarnish his reputation and perhaps spoil a Texas deal. "I admonish you to give *these shrewd fellows* no room to charge you with tampering with their officers to obtain the cession through corruption," he sternly instructed Butler. By now Jackson had settled on five million dollars as his ceiling price for Texas. Butler was authorized to offer that. Jackson repeated that what the Mexicans did with the money was their own business. "We are not interested in her distribution of the consideration." But he added a crucial proviso. "We are deeply interested that this treaty of cession should be obtained without any just imputation of corruption on our part."

Butler thought Jackson was naive in rejecting bribery. "What you advise of being cautious . . . proves how little you know of Mexican character," he wrote, with the bluntness Jackson had professed to admire. "I can assure you, sir, that *bribery* is not only common and familiar in all ranks and classes, but familiarly and freely spoken of." If Jackson wanted Texas peacefully, there was only one way. "Resort must be had to bribery—or by *presents*, if the term is more appropriate."

Still Jackson refused. He didn't want to be associated with bribery in any fashion. It would make him and the United States government look bad, and it would complicate various other diplomatic dealings. During the same period Jackson was seeking to acquire Texas, he was trying to settle a longstanding dispute with France regarding debts left over from the Napoleonic wars. France had agreed to pay but was maddeningly tardy in doing so.

Jackson was casting the issue as a matter of American honor. "Ask nothing but what is right and permit nothing that is wrong," he instructed Edward Livingston, who handled the negotiation in Paris. The squabble ended amicably but not before Jackson threatened to seize French ships and asked Congress for money to expand the navy. Being caught bribing Mexican officials would, needless to say, undermine the honor Jackson made such a show of upholding.

Besides, he wasn't sure bribery would work. What would keep the Mexicans from taking the money and refusing to turn over Texas? What recourse would the American government have? Or if the United States bribed one Mexican administration into relinquishing Texas, what was to prevent that regime from being overthrown—perhaps on account of the bribery—and its successor from disavowing the deal? The United States would be out the money, embarrassed, and required to start all over again.

*B*ut if bribery wouldn't work, other methods might. According to the 1819 treaty between the United States and Spain, the eastern boundary of Texas was the Sabine River. Jackson couldn't get Mexico to redefine the treaty, so he sought to redefine the river. Two streams empty into Sabine Lake, which in turn feeds the Gulf of Mexico. Ordinary usage called the eastern river the Sabine and the western river the Neches. Yet there was some confusion on the subject, not least since *sabinas* (cypress trees) were more common along the Neches than along the Sabine. This gave Jackson a pretext for calling the Neches the western branch of the Sabine and declaring it the true boundary between the United States and Mexico. The claim was flimsy in the extreme. Had the question been submitted to a neutral arbiter, Jackson's interpretation would have been dismissed with derision. But Jackson didn't intend to submit the question to an arbiter. Rather he intended to use the Neches claim as a device for intimidating Mexico and loosening its grip on Texas as a whole. "Begin at the Gulf of Mexico, run up the west branch of the Sabine, and continue up the west side of its west fork," he wrote Butler by way of summarizing his negotiating stance. From this first step, others would follow.

But it would be a delicate business, and after the way Butler had mishandled the bribery business, Jackson wondered if he had the right man in Mexico City. Butler responded to the new approach with a worrisome enthusiasm. "I will succeed in uniting Texas to our country before I am done with the subject or I will forfeit my head," Butler vowed. Jackson couldn't tell whether Butler was indulging in hyperbole or accurately conveying his designs and determination. If the latter, the president recognized that though it might be Butler's head, it would be America's reputation that would be forfeited. "Keep within your instructions," he warned Butler. "What a scamp," he wrote to himself.

Yet the scamp understood how Jackson's new approach might lead to the acquisition of Texas. "Should the present incumbents continue in office . . . ," Butler said of Santa Anna's regime, "no other mode is left us but to occupy that part of the territory lying west of the Sabine and east of the Neches (so called by the Mexicans) and to garrison Nacogdoches by the troops from Cantonment Jessup." Nacogdoches was the most important town between the rivers, and Cantonment Jessup was the American fort just east of the Sabine. Butler pointed out that there were no Mexican troops between the rivers, as they all had been deployed farther west to deal with troubles with the American colonists. The occupation would therefore be unopposed. And with troops on the ground, the United States government would be in position to enforce a favorable settlement of the whole Texas question.

*W*hile Jackson was trying to decide whether Butler was doing more harm than good as America's acknowledged representative in Mexico, the president worked quietly with an unacknowledged agent in Texas. Three years earlier Jackson had responded harshly to Sam Houston's drunken boast of going to conquer Texas. "I must really have thought you deranged to have believed you had so wild a scheme in contemplation," he lectured Houston. And while the purchase of Texas remained a possibility, Jackson didn't want any American filibusters making the Mexican government angry. But as his hopes for the peaceful acquisition of Texas diminished, he reconsidered the Houston option.

Houston still wanted to conquer Texas, although in his newfound sobriety he was more discreet about broadcasting his plans. He maintained his discretion during and after a meeting with Jackson at the Hermitage in the summer of 1832. Jackson was vacationing at home, and Houston was heading west following his latest Washington trial. Neither man recorded the conversation that took place in Jackson's study, which suggests that it wasn't intended for public knowledge. And indeed the denouement indicates that it was meant to be secret. Jackson apparently gave Houston five hundred dollars for the road. More valuable than the money was the cover Jackson provided. From Tennessee, Houston traveled to Arkansas, where he obtained a federal passport requesting "all the tribes of Indians, whether in amity with the United States or as yet not allied to them by treaties, to permit safely and freely to pass through their respective territories, General Sam Houston, a citizen of the United States, thirty-eight years of age, six feet, two inches in stature, brown hair and light complexion; and in case of need to give him all lawful aid and protection." As Jackson's Indian agent, Houston proceeded to Texas, nominally to investigate the affairs of the tribes there. "It has been my first and most important object to obtain all the information possible relative to the Pawnee and Comanche Indians," Houston reported en route. "To reach the wild Indians at this season will be difficult, and only practicable by way of St. Antone."

Yet Houston—and Jackson—had much more in mind than cultivating Indians. This might be a first step, but the longer project was the acquisition of Texas. The Americans in Texas had grown restive under Mexican rule following an 1830 law that prohibited legal immigration from the United States and specifically banned the introduction of slaves. On account of the political upheavals in Mexico City, the law went unenforced, stopping neither immigration nor the import of slaves. But it made outlaws of people who considered themselves blameless, made comparative respectables of people who *did* deserve blame, and weakened the political grip of Mexico on its northeasternmost province.

Jackson wanted to know how serious the disaffection of the Americans had grown. Houston told him. "Nineteen twentieths of the population," he said, wanted the United States to acquire Texas. "They are now without laws to govern or protect them. Mexico is involved in civil war. The Federal Constitution has never been in operation. The Government is essentially despotic and must be so for years to come. The rulers have not honesty, and the people have not intelligence." Texas was halfway to independence from Mexico, Houston said. "She has already beaten and expelled all the troops of Mexico from her soil, nor will she permit them to return. She can defend herself against the whole power of Mexico, for really Mexico is powerless and penniless." Mexico would lose Texas, to one country or another. "If the United States does not press for it, England will most assuredly obtain it by some means." Houston knew that the mere mention of a British interest in Texas would arrest Jackson's attention. But allowing for the unlikely possibility that that didn't suffice, Houston expatiated on the charms of the province. "I have travelled near five hundred miles across Texas . . . and I have no hesitancy in pronouncing it the finest country to its extent upon the globe. . . . The greater portion of it is richer and more healthy, in my opinion, than West Tennessee. There can be no doubt but the country east of the River Grand of the North"—the Rio Grande—"would sustain a population of ten millions of souls."

If Houston believed everything he told Jackson about Texas, he was deluding himself. There was indeed unrest among the Americans in Texas, but sentiment for transfer to the United States was not nearly as overwhelming as he suggested. A substantial number of Texans, including Stephen Austin and his early colonists, wanted merely a separate state government for Texas within the Mexican federation. Yet that wasn't what Houston wanted, so he left it unsaid. In any case, what he had learned about Mexican politics during his short time in the country caused him to conclude that the Mexican government would not accept statehood for Texas. Its refusal rendered full separation nearly inevitable.

Events made Houston appear a prophet. Santa Anna, for reasons having little to do with Texas, gathered more and more power to himself in Mexico City, alarming republicans throughout Mexico and especially advocates of states' rights. The latter objected, to the point of rebellion in such provinces as Zacatecas. Santa Anna responded by crushing the rebellion in Zacatecas with brutality sufficient to send shudders north to Texas, as it was intended to. But rather than intimidate the Texans it prompted a growing number of them to believe that their only security lay beyond the reach of Santa Anna, which was to say, beyond the authority of Mexico. By the autumn of 1835 Texans were forming into militias and drilling. As they drilled they talked more openly than ever of independence.

Amid the news of these developments Jackson received a curious letter from Houston and six other Texans. The seven identified themselves as a "committee of vigilance and safety for the department of Nacogdoches." Houston had told the others about Jackson's claim of American sovereignty to the Neches—in other words, that Nacogdoches was on what Jackson considered to be American soil—and the committee accordingly felt obliged to alert the American president to reports that a large band of Creek Indians ("not less than five thousand") were preparing to occupy the disputed zone. The Texans reminded Jackson that a treaty between the United States and Mexico allowed each country to prevent the unauthorized movement of Indians along the mutual border, and they implored the president to take action on behalf of themselves and their neighbors, "a sparse and comparatively defenceless population unprotected from the evils which were so tragically manifested on the frontiers of Georgia and Alabama, evils which can only be remedied by the skill and generalship of a Jackson." Houston and the committee went on to say, quite pointedly, that they expected no protection from the government of Mexico. "The unhappy distractions of this government have been such as to command the attention of the president"—Santa Anna—"to the interior condition of the country."

The odd thing about this letter was that there was little evidence that any Creek incursion was under way or even contemplated, and certainly not of the size Houston and the others alleged. Nor did any such incursion ever take place. The letter seems to have had a different purpose: to remind Jackson of the troubles in Texas, to inform him that Mexican troops were nowhere near, and to signal that the Americans in Texas looked eagerly to Washington for protection.

𝒯he Houston letter complemented intelligence Jackson was receiving from Anthony Butler in Mexico City. "You have heard of the revolt in Texas, where it is said there has been some skirmishing between the Mexican troops and the Texas riflemen, always resulting in favor of the latter,"

Butler wrote in November 1835. "The course pursued by the people of Texas has greatly exasperated General Santa Anna as we hear, and he vows to chastise the insolence of these borderers even if he goes in person to do so."

By the time Jackson received Butler's letter the revolt in Texas had escalated. The rebels captured San Antonio, the seat of Mexican authority in Texas, and drove Mexican military forces south across the Rio Grande. The news created a sensation in Mexico City. "This country is in a perfect tempest of passion in consequence of the revolt in Texas," Butler wrote in December. "General Santa Anna is perfectly furious." Santa Anna blamed the Texans, but he also blamed the United States, "who he has identified with the revolt, charging our Government and people with promoting and supporting that revolt with sinister views, with the view toward acquiring the territory." The general vowed armed resistance against this perceived American attack. "He has sworn that not an inch of the territory shall be separated from Mexico, that the United States shall never occupy one foot of the land west of the Sabine." In fact, he swore much more than that. "I understand that General Jackson sets up a claim to pass the Sabine, and that in running the division line hopes to acquire the country as far as the Neches," he said. "I mean to run that line at the mouth of my cannon, and after the line is established, if the nation will only give me the means, only afford me the necessary supply of money, I will march to the capital. I will lay Washington City in ashes."

Jackson's initial response to Santa Anna's threat went unrecorded, although it can well be imagined. Yet as his outrage subsided, he recognized something he hadn't till now: that the United States would be involved in the revolutionary events in Texas whether he wished it or not. Santa Anna was already blaming the United States, and there was no reason to expect him to change his mind, even if Jackson maintained strict neutrality.

In fact Jackson did maintain strict neutrality, in the formal sense. During the first months of 1836 the Texans sent agents to the United States to recruit money and volunteers in support of their cause. The Mexican minister in Washington complained that this represented illegal interference in the internal affairs of Mexico. Jackson's State Department answered that it did no such thing. The American government carefully avoided taking sides in the Texas troubles. What American citizens did on their own was another matter. Federal law prohibited the launching of war from American soil, and this law was being conscientiously enforced. But if Americans wanted to travel to Texas, that was their business. What they did in Texas was Mexico's business.

Yet the administration prepared to intervene. In March 1836 the Texans lost one large force at San Antonio when Santa Anna's army overran the Alamo, and another at Goliad when nearly four hundred Texan prisoners were executed. The twin debacles triggered a flood of refugees ahead of Santa Anna, who had determined to solve his Texas problem by driving all the Americans across the Sabine. Sam Houston by now had been named commanding general of the Texas army—largely on the strength of his service under Jackson—but that army was greatly outnumbered by the Mexicans, and it and Houston were retreating almost as fast as the refugees.

At the Sabine, observing the approach of the refugees and Houston's army, was General Edmund Gaines, Jackson's old comrade from the Seminole War and currently commander of American military forces in the southwestern district. Gaines recalled the lesson he had learned from Jackson in Florida, that borders are best defended on their far side, in the territory of the enemy, and as the fighting in Texas approached the American border he prepared to mount a forward defense. Noting the "sanguinary manner in which the Mexican forces seem disposed to carry on the war," Gaines told Lewis Cass, the secretary of war, "I take leave to suggest whether it may or may not become necessary, *in our own defence*, to speak to the contending belligerents in a language not to be misunderstood—a language requiring *force*." Gaines proposed raising an army of eight to twelve thousand men from among the citizens of Louisiana and neighboring states. With this he would repulse the Mexicans and likely settle the Texas question definitively.

Cass consulted with Jackson before responding. "It is not the wish of the President to take advantage of present circumstances, and thereby obtain possession of any portion of the Mexican territory," the war secretary wrote. "Still, however, the neutral duties, as well as the neutral rights, of the United States will justify the Government in taking all necessary measures to prevent a violation of their territory." Cass, speaking for Jackson, authorized Gaines to assume "such position, on either side of the imaginary boundary line, as may be best for your defensive operations." Gaines was explicitly authorized to advance to Nacogdoches, "which is within the limits of the United States, as claimed by this Government."

Houston and the Texans knew of Gaines's movements and disposition. Texas agents met with the American general and discussed how he might help their cause. Gaines committed himself—and the United States—to nothing specific on behalf of the Texans, but he conveyed the strong impression of readiness to fight. "He will maintain the honor of his country and punish the aggressor, be him whom he may," wrote Sam Carson, the secretary of state of the recently declared Texas republic, after a meeting with Gaines.

Houston kept his own counsel during the retreat across Texas, but his prior history and his contemporary actions suggest that he hoped to lure Santa Anna into a trap. Santa Anna claimed Texas to the Sabine, Jackson claimed Louisiana to the Neches, and Gaines was prepared to defend the region in between. If Houston could lure Santa Anna across the Neches, Gaines and his American army would pounce on the Mexicans. Jackson's hands would be clean, as American forces would be defending American soil, or what Jackson was pleased to call American soil. And it was impossible to imagine that any such conflict would end without Jackson and Houston getting what they both had wanted for years: the transfer of Texas to the United States.

Things didn't work out that way. Houston's men, who weren't in on his plans, refused to continue retreating. They demanded to avenge their fallen comrades and, at a critical junction of a road east turned *toward* Santa Anna rather than away. Houston had never managed to instill the kind of discipline that made Jackson famous (and infamous), and he had no choice but to accept that in the Texan army decisions flowed not from the top down but from the bottom up. Days later the Texans met Santa Anna and a small advance contingent of the Mexican army and won a stunning victory at San Jacinto. Santa Anna, captured after the battle, agreed to give the Texans their freedom, and Houston became a hero sooner than he expected.

*J*ohn Quincy Adams didn't quite accuse Jackson of fomenting the revolution in Texas, but he came close. By the end of Jackson's second term there was almost nothing Adams thought Jackson incapable of. The president had ruined republicanism by pandering to the mobs. He had ravaged the economy by destroying the Bank of the United States. He had sullied Harvard by accepting an honorary degree. And now he was threatening personal liberty and affronting the American conscience by acting as the agent of the slave conspiracy that was subverting the American government.

This last charge against Jackson was something novel. And it signaled not that Jackson had changed but that America had changed. Views on slavery continued to evolve. With the triumph of democracy came a growing intolerance for those forms of inequality that remained from former days, of which the most obvious was slavery. By now the North was essentially free of slaves (the exceptions being a few elderly survivors in states that had emancipated gradually, by outlawing the acquisition of *new* slaves). This made it easy for northerners to indulge their consciences. Abolitionism, once the province of cranks and Quakers, became almost unremarkable.

Predictably, the South grew defensive. Spokesmen emerged to describe slavery not as a necessary evil—the standard interpretation of eighteenth-century slaveholders—but as a positive good, the bedrock of southern society. John Calhoun told the Senate that "a mysterious Providence" had brought the white and black races together in the American South, with the former to be masters and the latter slaves. "The very existence of the South," Calhoun continued, "depends upon the existing relations being kept up, and every scheme which might be introduced, having for its object an alteration in the condition of the negro, is pregnant with danger and ruin." In the House slaveholders and their allies, claiming a constitutional right to property in persons, led a movement to keep antislavery petitions from even being heard.

Adams resented the "gag rule," as it was called, and battled against it. He resented everything about the hardening of the southern position on slavery. Like his father—and most of the generation of the Founders—he had long assumed that slavery would fade and eventually disappear. That it didn't, but instead fastened itself on the American republic more tightly than ever, and had the gall to claim the Constitution as its guarantee of perpetual life, simply struck Adams as another sordid aspect of the country's descent into democracy.

The war in Texas was the latest crime of the slaveholding conspiracy,

Adams believed. And Jackson was the arch-conspirator. "It is said that one of the earliest acts of this administration was a proposal, made at a time when there was already much ill humor in Mexico against the United States, that she should cede to the United States a very large portion of her territory," Adams told the House. "A device better calculated to produce jealousy, suspicion, ill will, and hatred could not have been contrived. . . . This overture, offensive in itself, was made precisely at the time when a swarm of colonists from these United States were covering the Mexican border with land-jobbing, and with slaves, introduced in defiance of Mexican laws, by which slavery had been abolished throughout that republic." The war in Texas was not a war for independence but "a war for the re-establishment of slavery where it was abolished, . . . a war between slavery and emancipation." Adams knew of the movements of Gaines along the Texas border, and he suspected that Jackson had put the general up to the kind of things Jackson himself had done in Florida. Speaking to the president and his partners in crime, Adams warned, "You are now rushing into war—into a war of conquest, commenced by aggression on your part, and for the re-establishment of slavery where it has been abolished. . . . In that war, sir, the banners of freedom will be the banners of Mexico; and your banners, I blush to speak the word, will be the banners of slavery." Nor would that contest culminate the evil. The "inevitable consequence" of the war with Mexico would be a civil war in America, "the last great conflict . . . between slavery and emancipation."

*H*ouston's victory at San Jacinto spared Jackson the decision of whether to intervene in the Texas revolution. Jackson was just as happy not to get involved directly in the war, although he couldn't resist offering Houston advice. "I have seen a report that General Santa Anna was to be brought before a military court, to be tried and shot," he wrote his old lieutenant.

> Nothing now could tarnish the character of Texas more than such an act at this late period. It was good policy as well as humanity that spared him. It has given you possession of Goliad and the Alamo without blood or loss of the strength of your army. His person is

still of much consequence to you. He is the pride of the Mexican soldiers and the favorite of the priesthood, and whilst he is in your power the priests will not furnish the supplies necessary for another campaign, nor will the regular soldiers *voluntarily* march when their reentering Texas may endanger or cost their favorite general his life. Therefore preserve his life and the character you have won, and let not his blood be shed unless it becomes necessary by an imperative act of just retaliation for Mexican massacres hereafter. This is what I think true wisdom and humanity dictates.

Houston must have wondered at the striking difference between this Jackson and the general who had executed Arbuthnot and Ambrister for far less than Santa Anna had done to the Texans. Maybe he reflected that the difference was the difference between a theater commander and the commander in chief. Maybe he concluded that his old leader had simply mellowed after all these years. In any event, Houston himself had decided within moments of his capture that Santa Anna was worth more to Texas alive than dead.

Houston intended to employ Santa Anna in a diplomatic effort to end the Texas war. The Mexican government remained unreconciled to Texas independence, having deposed Santa Anna in absentia and rejected the promises he had given the Texans in exchange for his life. Houston by this time was the elected president of the Texas republic, and his first task was to terminate the war on the basis of Texas independence. He and Stephen Austin, now the Texas secretary of state, drafted a letter to Jackson, ostensibly written by Santa Anna. The letter proposed that Santa Anna and Jackson work out a deal to guarantee the future of Texas. "Let us establish mutual relations, to the end that your nation and the Mexican may strengthen their friendly ties, and both engage amicably in giving existence and stability to a people that wish to figure in the political world, in which they will succeed, within a few years, with the protection of the two nations."

Jackson was skeptical. Whether or not he recognized the words as Houston's and Austin's, Jackson had to doubt Santa Anna's sincerity, as the man remained a prisoner of the Texans and rightly feared for his life. More to the point, Santa Anna no longer represented anyone besides himself. Maybe Mexico's soldiers still loved him, but the men in charge of Mexico's government wanted nothing to do with him. And it was these men with whom Jackson as American president had to deal. "Until the existing Government of Mexico ask our friendly offices between the contending parties, Mexico and Texas," Jackson replied, "we cannot interfere."

If Houston was surprised at Jackson's coolness, he shouldn't have been. Jackson had been prepared to fight if Santa Anna brought the Texas war to the American border, but he saw no reason to get tangled in a conflict the Texans had already won, at least for the present. Jackson could tell that a final resolution of the Texas question would require a settlement between the United States and Mexico. Mexico wasn't Spain, which could be ejected from Florida (and North America) once and for all. Mexico would always be the neighbor of the United States, regardless of where the border between the two countries eventually fell. And there was one other thing: Jackson was beginning to look farther than Texas for America's western boundary. He was eyeing California, which together with Texas would round out the American Southwest nicely. Forcing the Texas issue would make acquiring California more difficult.

Yet Houston was persistent. He sent Santa Anna to Washington, hoping that what he and Santa Anna hadn't been able to accomplish by mail Santa Anna might manage in person. Jackson consented to an interview, which turned out to be one of the oddest diplomatic sessions of the era. In Jackson's White House bedroom, the embodiment of American democracy discussed the fate of rebel Texas with the erstwhile Mexican caudillo. Jackson still insisted that any arrangement regarding Texas be made through official channels. Yet, realizing that official channels had a way of changing course in Mexico and that Santa Anna, currently deposed, might find his way back to power upon his return to Mexico City, the American president suggested that the Mexican government might wish to settle the Texas affair as part of a package including California. Jackson mentioned $3.5 million as an appropriate price.

Santa Anna seemed receptive, the more so when Jackson offered him transport home. An American frigate carried the defeated general to Veracruz, where he disappeared, for the time being, into the swirl of Mexican politics.

1837–1845

Patriarch

of

Democracy

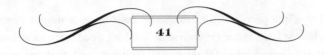

41

THE HOME FRONT

*J*ackson had been an old man when he entered the White House, and he was a very old man as he prepared to leave it almost eight years later. At the dying end of his seventh decade, his body bore the tracks of all those years: the smallpox scars and the crease in his skull from the Revolutionary War, the bullet wounds from his duels and shooting scrapes, the gaunt frame and hollow cheeks from a lifetime battling intestinal parasites, the sallow complexion from an equally protracted contest with malaria. His heart no longer ached as badly as it had during the first year after Rachel's death, but his spirit still sagged under the conviction that he'd never know joy till they met again, in his own death. He was relieved to relinquish power, especially to one he trusted as much as he did Martin Van Buren. It didn't strike him as odd that he, the champion of the people's right to choose their leaders, should essentially appoint his own successor. Of course he had long since come to believe that he spoke for the people, and there was no denying that Van Buren was popular, at least among the Jackson loyalists. They nominated Van Buren unanimously at their Baltimore convention, partly because he was as charming as ever but mostly because he promised to carry on in the tradition of Old Hickory—"to tread generally in the footsteps of President Jackson, happy if I shall be able to perfect the work he has so gloriously begun."

Yet while Van Buren inherited Jackson's mantle, he also inherited Jackson's enemies. The Whigs, of course, wanted nothing to do with Jackson or Van Buren. They nominated William Henry Harrison, the other hero from the War of 1812. More hurtful to Jackson was the defection of one-time allies. South Carolina's hostility wasn't surprising, after the nullification crisis, but the animus of much of Tennessee was. Jackson's old rivals from the days when he tangled with John Sevier found new friends, including David Crockett, who had parlayed a reputation as a bear hunter, Indian fighter, and raconteur into election from western Tennessee to Congress. At first he identified with Jackson, but as his persona grew, so did his attractiveness to Jackson's foes, who whispered in his ear that he might one day be president himself. They sent him on an eastern tour, which made him a national celebrity, the subject of popular plays and multiple biographies. He was touted as the anti-Jackson, living evidence that Jackson didn't speak for all the common people, even of his home state. But Jackson spoke for enough of the common people, at least in Crockett's congressional district, that Crockett lost his race for reelection in 1835, whereupon he told his constituents that "they might go to hell and I would go to Texas." In Texas he became even more famous by dying at the Alamo.

Despite the rifts in the Democratic coalition, Van Buren managed to hold off Harrison and two lesser candidates (one being Daniel Webster) in the 1836 election. The result gratified Jackson, who prepared to usher Van Buren into the White House even as he was showing Santa Anna the door. The old man wished he could have tied up such loose ends as Texas before leaving office, but he had confidence that Van Buren's views matched his on this issue and others. "They are, like my own, always based upon the just grounds of the prosperity for our country and the general good," he assured himself in a letter to Van Buren.

⌒ ⌒ ⌒

A Van Buren presidency was one of Jackson's parting gifts to the American people; a farewell address was another. Some of Jackson's advisers cautioned him against emulating George Washington in this regard, saying he would be considered presumptuous or undemocratic or both. But he went ahead, in the belief that his decades of public life had taught him lessons worth passing on. Jackson had named Roger Taney to replace John Marshall as chief justice when the old Federalist finally died in 1835, and though Taney now headed the judicial branch of the government, he ignored the separation of powers long enough to help his friend and sponsor craft the farewell message.

"We have now lived almost fifty years under the Constitution framed by the sages and patriots of the Revolution," Jackson said. "We have had our seasons of peace and of war, with all the evils which precede or follow a state of hostility with powerful nations." The cost had been great but the accomplishment still greater. "Our Constitution is no longer a doubtful experiment. . . . We find that it has preserved unimpaired the liberties of the people, secured the rights of property, and that our country has improved and is flourishing beyond any former example in the history of nations." Taney was always too wordy, and Jackson didn't sufficiently rein him in. The message refought the battles of the past eight years till even the most devoted Jacksonian started to nod.

But the heart of the message was pure Jackson, and straight to the point of everything to which his years in public service had been devoted. Though the Union flourished, its permanence wasn't assured. "The signs of evil are sufficiently apparent to awaken the deepest anxiety in the bosom of the patriot. We behold systematic efforts publicly made to sow the seeds of discord between different parts of the United States, and to place party divisions directly upon geographical distinctions, to excite the *South* against the *North* and the *North* against the *South*." Jackson didn't blame any party or section exclusively. Aggrandizers of the federal government, by encroaching on states' rights, could be as threatening to national life as the nullifiers. But disagreement must never cross into disunion. "Delude not yourselves with the belief that a breach once made may be afterwards repaired. If the Union is once severed, the line of separation will grow wider and wider, and the controversies which are now debated and settled in the halls of legislation will then be tried in the fields of battle and determined by the sword."

*H*e left the White House after a harder winter of illness than usual. "I was confined to my bed by a severe hemorrhage from the lungs, which threatened a speedy end to my existence," he wrote as the electoral votes were being counted. The cause was a mystery that remained so as the symptoms eased. "My strength is slowly recovering, but much impeded by the onerous weight of official business now pressing upon me," he declared as the weeks in office ran out. In fact the burden of business was less than earlier, but the closer he got to the end, the more each task seemed to weigh. Yet the end drew him on. "A few days more and I am again a free man."

The journey home was a triumphal progress. "From the time I left you, I have been literally in a crowd," he wrote Van Buren from Kentucky. "Such assemblages of my fellow citizens I have never before seen on my passage to or from Washington." For a generation Jackson had embodied the dreams of ordinary Americans—dreams of valor at arms, of a voice in their own governance—and now he was departing. Men who remembered the wars against Britain and women who wanted their children to see the hero of the age turned out by the thousands along the roads he traveled and at the towns where his steamboat called. Even his enemies came to see him. "I have been every where cheered by my numerous Democratic Republican friends, and many of the repenting Whigs," he said, doubtless conflating curiosity and repentance. "This is truly the patriot's reward, and a source of great gratification to me, and will be my solace to the grave."

*T*he Hermitage had missed its master. The horses in particular wanted care. "I find my blooded stock in bad order and too numerous for empty corn cribs and hay lofts," he wrote Andrew Hutchings. "I have determined to sell out part to enable me to feed the balance better."

The horses proved to be the easy part of his reconstruction efforts. Jackson's problems with overseers continued. They were alternately too lax and then too severe, in the former phase allowing behavior they felt obliged to punish harshly in the latter. By now Jackson owned some 150 slaves, whose management required skills he couldn't find at the price he was willing to pay. But what he saved on overseers he expended on legal costs after a large gathering of slaves, including some of his own, turned into a riot in which one slave was killed. Especially since the Nat Turner rebellion of 1831, which claimed the lives of nearly sixty whites in Virginia, southern authorities had been acutely sensitive to anything hinting at a servile revolt, and the local sheriff indicted four of Jackson's slaves for murder. Jackson became convinced of the men's innocence, and he hired legal counsel to defend them. The defense succeeded but cost Jackson over a thousand dollars, which he didn't have. He borrowed the cash, then sold some of his land to pay the debt.

His money problems persisted. As the twenty-fifth anniversary of the Battle of New Orleans approached, he was invited to return to the scene of his triumph. He at first declined. "I am out of funds," he explained to Andrew Donelson. "And I cannot bear to borrow or travel as a pauper." Besides, it still rankled that after he had saved the city from destruction, the court there had found him guilty of contempt. "I have sacrificed both property and health in the salvation of New Orleans . . . and the Legislature thereof has never attempted to have that unjust sentence removed." In the event, common sense prevailed. New Orleans couldn't celebrate without its hero, and Jackson couldn't stay away. He borrowed against his cotton crop, friends paid some of his travel expense, and an initiative was put in motion to overturn his conviction.

Yet he never got out from under the shadow of debt. Andrew Jr. was demonstrating his incompetence at business; though well-intentioned, he managed to lose thousands to feckless partners and outright frauds. "No man has been more completely swindled than he has been," his father remarked in sorrow. Jackson felt obliged to rescue his son, to the eventual extent of some fifteen thousand dollars. He sold land, unfortunately on a buyer's market, to cover Andrew's debt. A friend pointed out that he'd realize more if he waited. "This I well know," Jackson answered. "But a little imprudence has caused this necessity, and I would always rather sacrifice property than the credit of my adopted son or myself." To Andrew, who had married by now and started a family, he preached frugality and future care. "If I live to realise it, I will die contented in the hope that you will never again encumber yourself with debt that may result in the poverty of yourself and little family of so much promise, and whom I so much love."

𝒫erhaps to his surprise, Jackson discovered that politics afforded a respite from the vexations of farm and family. Or maybe he wasn't surprised. Maybe he finally knew himself well enough to understand that struggle was the essence of his life. On several occasions the struggle had come close to killing him, but now he could see—or perhaps only feel—that the struggle was what kept him alive. He wished to be reunited to Rachel, but he wasn't ready to join her just yet. Dangers to the Union remained and evildoers to be vanquished.

Nicholas Biddle never rested, or so it seemed to Jackson. The financial troubles that followed Jackson's decision of the summer of 1836 to require specie payments for federal land only worsened, producing the most severe contraction in decades. Fingers of blame pointed to Jackson for bursting the bubble, to the speculators for inflating it in the first place, to the banking system for extending excessive credit on the bubble's expansion and insufficient credit on the collapse. Jackson was sure Biddle was behind the new panic. The Bank of the United States, upon the expiration of its federal charter, had been reincorporated in Pennsylvania, and Biddle reinstalled as its president. He had as much incentive as ever to throttle the economy, in order to restore the primacy of banks, and nearly as much power as ever to do so. Van Buren must continue the struggle Jackson had started. "I have done my duty," Jackson wrote Francis Blair. "My only anxiety now is for the success of the present administration. But if it listens to Biddle and his satellites . . . it will fall." Jackson worried that Van Buren wouldn't stay the course. He would feel pressure from the bankers and merchants and would be tempted to compromise to please them. Jackson urged the president to hold steady, citing his own experience during the bank war. "Remember the panic I passed through. The present will pass away as soon as all the overtraders, gamblers in stocks and lands, are broke." Steadfastness was needed above all. "No temporising with the opposition, or it is lost."

From the distance of Nashville, Jackson waged the fight against Biddle and the bankers with all the devotion he had exhibited as president. If Jackson believed that Van Buren ought to establish his own identity as chief executive, he gave no clue of it. He wrote Van Buren at least twice a month on matters of current interest, mostly held over from his own administration. "Biddle is in the field," he warned Van Buren in the summer of 1837. "All the state banks have combined with him to resist the resumption of specie payments as long as possible, for now they are reaping great gains. Bank paper is depreciating daily, and Biddle expects to profit by it and to obtain a recharter of his Bank. You must meet this with firmness." The struggle against the bankers never ended. "Nothing can be more dangerous to a republican government than their corrupting influence."

The financial crisis eventually eased, but not before eroding Van Buren's political base. An 1837 New York election, in which the Whigs trounced the Democrats, seemed an evil omen. Jackson never had trouble detecting the authority in the voice of the people when they agreed with him, but when they disagreed, as they did now, he concluded that they had been deceived by the "machinations and conspiracy" of the enemies of democracy. Yet he refused to be discouraged. "The recoil at the next elections in New York will be tremendous." Jackson urged Blair and other patriot editors to rally to the cause. "Lash those conservators and traitors with the pen of gall and wormwood."

Another crisis carried Jackson further into his past. Following Jackson's refusal to enforce John Marshall's decision in the 1832 Cherokee case, the state of Georgia had continued to make life miserable for that eastern remnant of the tribe. Jackson's Indian commissioners pressed the Cherokees to sign a treaty ceding their lands in exchange for money and for territory west of the Mississippi. To concentrate the minds of the tribe's leaders, those who resisted a deal were arrested and held until the others put their signatures to a pact. The treaty provoked protests from a majority of the tribe and from many people around the United States. But Jackson rammed the treaty through the Senate. "The national policy, founded alike in interest and in humanity, so long and so steadily pursued by this Government for the removal of the Indian tribes originally settled on this side of the Mississippi to the west of that river, may be said to have been consummated," he declared. The Cherokees had two years to depart for the West.

The exodus began in the autumn of 1838 and quickly became an appalling disaster. Traveling through rain and snow, lacking sufficient food, clothing, and shelter, the refugees succumbed to exposure, infectious disease, and simple exhaustion. Thousands died on the route that became known as the "trail of tears." The debacle seemed to summarize all that was wrong with American policy toward the Indians and made a mockery of Jackson's claim that his policy was founded in humanity. The least he could have done was express regret at the way the exodus was managed. But by this time he was no longer president and wasn't required to comment. His silence said enough.

He did comment on a related issue. The experience of the Cherokees redoubled the determination of the Seminoles to avoid a similar fate. A second Seminole war erupted in the mid-1830s. Larger than the one that had inspired Jackson's invasion of Spanish Florida, this conflict involved at least a thousand Indians and several times that number of American soldiers. The War Department at first sent Winfield Scott, Jackson's old rival, to Florida to deal with the uprising, but Scott accomplished nothing productive. "The whole Florida war from the first to the present time has been a succession of blunders and misfortune," Jackson fairly said in disgust after several months. Scott was fired and eventually replaced by Zachary Taylor. Jackson urged Taylor to apply the lessons he—Jackson—had learned fighting Indians, to hit them where they were weakest. "The commanding general ought to find where their women are, and with his combined forces by forced marches reach and capture them," he said. "This done, they will at once surrender."

Catching the women was harder than Jackson anticipated. Although the arrest of the Seminole chief Osceola, who was lured into American custody by a false flag of truce, broke the back of the armed resistance, fighting sputtered on till the early 1840s. At that point some of the Seminoles accepted that they had no choice but to move west of the Mississippi. They were joined during the following decade by nearly all their surviving cousins. But a stubborn few remained, determined to die in the land of their birth.

Jackson sometimes wished he could treat his white rivals as summarily as he had dealt with the Indians. Though the Whigs had lost to Van Buren in 1836, they sensed his vulnerability. Van Buren had won on the basis of his connection to Jackson; the next time around he'd have to win on his own merits. These weren't inconsiderable, but they were hardly on the order of Jackson's.

To ensure their triumph, the Whigs stole a page from the Democrats. They nominated Harrison again and touted his war record. Beyond this they cast him as the common man, the candidate who knew life as it was lived by ordinary men and women. The pose was a stretch, in that Harrison hailed from Virginia gentry and had a college education. But the formula had worked for Jackson, and the Whigs were determined to make it work for them.

Jackson couldn't decide which was worse: Harrison's politics or his hypocrisy. Jackson identified the Whigs with the defunct and now almost forgotten Federalists, the better to damn them for the sins of days past. In Harrison's case the connection was plausible, as he was old enough to have been a Federalist when that party still existed. "General Harrison, to shew his identity with the Federalists, pasted on his hat the black cockade," Jackson declared, referring to the symbol for arch-Federalism. Jackson had this only secondhand, but he convinced himself it was true, and he repeated it several times.

Jackson overstated the Federalist ancestry of the Whig party. It was true that most of those who would have been Federalists, had that party survived, now leaned Whig. But the Whigs also included many who for one reason or another had fallen out with Jackson and his interpretation of democracy. Jackson never appreciated, or at any rate never admitted, how the same passion that inspired his followers put off those who weren't so devoted. His campaign against the Bank of the United States had alienated nearly everyone who looked to business to get ahead, a portion of the electorate that continued to grow. By the time Jackson left office, city dwellers constituted 10 percent of the population, which itself had passed fifteen million. The factory system was maturing in New England and creeping west. Railroads complemented canals and were starting to supplant them in linking cities to towns and towns to the countryside. The economy had never been more tightly woven, and the weave grew tighter by the year. The business class remained small, but the number of people affected by business was increasing rapidly. Even farmers, those yeomen who had been the backbone of the party of Jefferson, found themselves drawn into the nexus of the market. Some resented the commercialization of their calling; others embraced it eagerly. But almost none could ignore it. And more than a few were susceptible to the claims of the Whigs that their new party offered them more of what they valued most—economic opportunity, the chance for material security—than Jackson's Democrats did.

The continuing change in attitudes toward slavery likewise made the politics of the 1840s more complicated than the politics of previous decades. When Jackson had first run for president, the slave question hardly came up, but now it surfaced all the time. The Whigs were by no means abolitionist on principle. Clay still owned his slaves, comfortably enough. But abolitionists fit more easily into the Whig coalition than they did into the Democratic party. It didn't help matters on this point that John Calhoun found his way back to the Jacksonian fold. Van Buren reported the moment of rapprochement to Jackson, and how Calhoun explained it. "Being sincerely with me in politics, and having out lived his personal prejudices against me, he took pleasure in thus putting an end to the non-intercourse which had so long prevailed between us." Calhoun increasingly identified himself and the South with slavery. Though his support bolstered the Democrats in the South, it alienated those northerners who asked whether slavery was what America ought to stand for.

Harrison wasn't an abolitionist. No national candidate with any hopes of election could be. But the Democrats were happy to condemn him by association. "I have a letter today from Vermont," Blair wrote Jackson in September 1840, "stating that the Abolition missionaries who have been busy in the election in that state applied the funds which they had collected for the emancipation of the Negroes, freely in promoting the election of Harrison's friends." Nor was it only domestic abolitionists who were said to be backing Harrison. Britain had abolished slavery in the early 1830s and since then had been sponsoring abolition abroad. Blair and other Democrats detected a new and especially insidious British influence in American life. "Having succeeded in effecting emancipation elsewhere, England now turns the whole force of the world, which she calls moral force, to accomplish her object in the South. She sends her missionaries and her money to our shores, and her old Federal allies are now found in strict alliance with the abolition proselytes whom she has so successfully encouraged in the North."

Jackson opposed abolition on several grounds. As a slaveholder, he had a large personal stake in the slave system. Abolition wouldn't necessarily have bankrupted him, especially if the British model of emancipation—in which the government compensated slaveowners for their loss—were adopted. But it would have required him, or his heirs, to learn a radically new method of cotton culture. As a constitutionalist, he considered slavery a matter for the states to decide, and he couldn't imagine the southern states giving it up voluntarily. As a student of human nature, he doubted the ability of white Americans to accept the presence of large numbers of black Americans on any basis approaching equality. Would the blacks have political rights? If not, what would that do to democracy? But most of all, as a Unionist, he recognized that holding the country together would be nearly impossible should the abolitionists seize control of a major political party. At the end of the nullification crisis with South Carolina, he had predicted privately that the next constitutional crisis would be over "the negro, or slavery, question." Now he saw it approaching, and he knew it would be far harder to resolve than a fight about tariffs.

Oddly, though, the thing that most provoked Jackson about the Harrison campaign was its plebian tone. Having learned from the Jacksonians how the common touch now ruled American politics, the Whigs applied the lesson with a vengeance, in what quickly came to be called the "log cabin and hard cider" campaign. Jackson had always bowed to the will of the people, at least in principle, but he had never thought this required him to demean himself—or, for that matter, to demean the people. The Whig campaign, he judged, demeaned Harrison and the people both. He could only hope the strategy would backfire. "The attempt by their mummeries to degrade the people to a level with the brute creation has opened the people's eyes," he asserted optimistically after an especially raucous Whig rally in Nashville. "It is saying to them in emphatic language that they are unfit for

540 Ｏ PATRIARCH OF DEMOCRACY

self government and can be led by hard cider, coons, log cabins and big balls. . . . I have a higher opinion of the intelligence of the American people than this."

When Van Buren lost, Jackson had to reconsider. But he did so just long enough to conclude—on the basis of suggestive but hardly overwhelming evidence—that the people hadn't been deceived so much as cheated again. "Corruption, bribery and fraud has been extended over the whole Union," he wrote Van Buren in commiseration. And he predicted that the people would rise again. "The democracy of the United States has been shamefully beaten, *but, I trust, not conquered*. I still hope there is sufficient virtue in the unbought people of this union to stay the perjury, bribery, fraud, and imposition upon the people by the vilest system of slander that ever before existed. . . . I do not yet despair of the Republic. . . . I trust still in the virtue of the great working class."

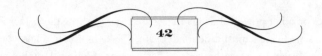

42

TO THE RAMPARTS

ONCE MORE

he defeat of Van Buren threatened to make Jackson irrelevant. The election of 1840 was the first test of Jacksonism separate from Jackson, of the Democratic party distinct from its hero, and it failed the test. Van Buren and the Democrats had looked to the Hermitage for counsel and legitimacy while they held the White House, but with the new men in charge, America looked elsewhere.

his was especially irksome to Jackson, who turned seventy-three in the month of Harrison's inauguration but felt better than in years. He credited the exertion of the campaign for his recovery, but he also acknowledged a medication he was taking. His current potion was something called the Matchless Sanative, a patent medicine whose secret recipe certainly included alcohol and may well have included opium,

cocaine, or other powerful drugs that were legal in those days. Jackson became the medicine's most ardent advocate. "Take as directed and you must
live more freely than you have done," he wrote Andrew Hutchings, who
had complained of sundry physical and mental distresses. "In two months
it will restore you to perfect health."

Jackson's health was far from perfect, but it enabled him to tend to the
affairs of his farm. He continued to liquidate his holdings to pay Andrew
Jr.'s debts. "Should you meet with a rich Virginian who wants to come
to our country and has money," he told Andrew Donelson, "sell him the
Hunter's Hill tract"—which Jackson had reacquired in the early 1830s. "If
an advance of $6,000 can be made, let it go for $14,000. It is now for sale to
the first purchaser who presents himself and has money." More painfully, he
had to sell some of his best horses, including descendants of his first favorite, Truxton. His descriptions of the animals—"a beautiful dark bay
or brown filly, fine size, form, and action . . . a beautiful rich sorrel stud
colt . . . a beautiful bay filly . . . a large and fine dark bay mare . . . a fine
bright sorrel mare"—were intended to entice the buyer into paying all they
were worth, but they also reflected his own feelings about them and suggested the difficulty he had in letting them go.

As word got out that Jackson was selling land and horses, his friends and
supporters grew alarmed. One, a Boston Jacksonian of ample means, offered to underwrite his retirement. Jackson politely refused. "You may assure him," he told William Lewis, the intermediary in the offer, "although I
have been greatly pestered, and have had to make sacrifices of property, as
well as has Andrew, that we are not broke." Cash was short at the moment,
as it had been so often, but Jackson's capital foundation was solid. He owned
the 980 acres of the Hermitage free and clear, and another 1,180 acres on the
Mississippi River in the state of Mississippi. The latter investment hadn't begun to pay but would before long. Most of it was covered with hardwood
forest, which could be cut and sold as fuel for the steamboats on the river.
And as the trees were removed, the land would be planted to cotton.

Jackson didn't want charity, but he did need a loan. "Six thousand dollars for six years, at six per cent, would be a great convenience to us, and
save us from some sacrifices of property to meet our accruing liabilities," he
wrote Lewis. Such a loan would allow the settlement of Andrew's debts and
"restore us once more to perfect freedom."

᧬ ᧬ ᧬

month to the day after Harrison's inauguration, Francis Blair wrote to Jackson with stunning news. "At 12 o'clock last night President Harrison died," Blair said. The shock was not so much that a president had died but that it had been Harrison. For most of Jackson's eight years in office Americans had braced themselves for a White House funeral; his age and general ill health made him a prime candidate to test the constitutionally prescribed order of succession. But he hadn't died, and Americans sighed with relief and assumed the danger of presidential death was past.

Harrison undeceived them. The cause of death was pneumonia, but ardent Democrats read deeper meaning into his demise. "His temperament could not stand the weighty honors and the weighty functions devolved upon him," Blair told Jackson. Harrison had campaigned as a man of the people but couldn't hold the pose. "His pampered vanity added to the tension of the other passions which strained all his faculties beyond their capabilities, and at last every thing gave way at once."

Harrison's death changed the political equation dramatically. There was some doubt as to what John Tyler, the vice president, inherited upon Harrison's death. Was Tyler now *president* or merely *acting* president? The Constitution said that the "powers and duties" of the presidency should "devolve on the Vice President," but not that the vice president should become president. It soon grew apparent, however, that the technical question was less important than the political one (which was why the technical question was allowed to linger till 1967, when the Twenty-fifth Amendment explicitly declared that upon the death of the president, "the Vice President shall become President"). Whether or not Tyler was actually president, he had almost no political legitimacy. He was the creature of the Whig leadership in Congress and evidently at their mercy.

But to the amazement of nearly everyone, especially the Whig leadership, Tyler soon began acting like a real president—and something like a Democrat. He vetoed a new bank bill that Henry Clay pushed through Congress. "It will do Old Hickory's heart good when he hears of the veto," a Jacksonian in Washington remarked. Another declared, speaking of Tyler's blunt veto message, "He has found one of old Jackson's pens."

Jackson was indeed pleased that Tyler had done the right thing regarding the bank, but it didn't change his view of the Whigs, whom he continued to consider a "clique who has got into power by deluding the people by the grossest slanders, corruptions, and vilest idolatry of coons and hard cider." And he continued to believe that the man most likely to deliver the country from Whiggism was Martin Van Buren. This was by no means a universal opinion among the Democrats at this juncture. Van Buren had lost once, and many in the party feared he would lose again. John Calhoun was making a quiet comeback, telling the Democrats that the South was their natural home. Jackson was skeptical—more of Calhoun than of his argument—but even he was willing to lower his guard in the interest of what he considered the greater good. "I am happy to learn that Mr. Calhoun is got right," he told Blair. "God send that he may continue so. . . . If Mr. Calhoun remains firm, I am sure I will not throw the least shade over him. To err is human, to forgive divine." But Jackson wasn't putting any faith in his old rival. "I have no confidence in Mr. Calhoun," he told Van Buren, in whom he *did* have confidence. Of Van Buren he said, looking toward the 1844 nomination, "He is the strongest man that can be presented. If brought out, he will be triumphantly elected, and that by a larger majority than any other president has attained."

*B*ut fate, with the help of Sam Houston, intervened. The Democrats condemned the Whigs for corruption in the 1840 election and sniped at Clay and the party's leadership on the bank, the tariff, and other issues dear to Whig hearts. But as the election of 1844 approached, the unresolved question of Texas crowded to the fore. That it did so revealed, among other things, an undiscovered aptitude for diplomacy in Jackson's prodigal son.

Houston had intended all along for Texas to become part of the United States. Most of his fellow Texans shared his desire and required only an invitation from the American government to join their political destinies to that of the country from which the great majority of them sprang. But the antislavery forces in the United States, led by John Quincy Adams, refused to countenance annexation, with the result that the most Jackson could offer, in the final days of his administration, was diplomatic recognition of the Texas republic.

Houston accepted the offer, on behalf of his fellow Texans, and during the next several years kept in touch with his now retired mentor. Writing as one soldier-president to another, he applauded Jackson's abiding faith in the people and expressed thanks for what he had learned at Jackson's knee. "To you, General, I find myself vastly indebted for many principles which I have never abandoned throughout life. One is a holy love of country, and a willingness to make every sacrifice to its honour and safety; next, a sacred regard for its Constitution and laws, with an eternal hostility and opposition to all banks."

What Houston left hanging was *which* country and constitution he loved: Texas and the Texan or the United States and the American? The ambiguity was deliberate, for Houston was engaged in a delicate double game. Some of his Texas compatriots had grown enamored of independence, to the point of envisioning a western empire for Texas that would have made Aaron Burr blush and would have blocked the westward expansion of the United States. As president of the Texas republic, and one who wanted the votes of its enfranchised inhabitants, Houston couldn't well bad-mouth its prospects. But precisely because he *was* the president of Texas he knew how tenuous those prospects were. The finances of the republic were a wreck, the butt of many bad jokes. Crime, both organized and opportunistic, made life and property insecure. The borders of Texas were impossible to defend. Indians threatened the northwest, while Mexico, unreconciled to Texas independence, sent armies across the Rio Grande that twice recaptured San Antonio. Houston knew Texas needed help. He preferred that such help come from the United States, but he would take it where he could find it.

This was what he told Jackson, in terms he knew would get the old man's attention. Houston said he still desired the annexation of Texas to the Union. A marriage of the two republics would benefit both. Unfortunately, certain persons and groups within the United States—Houston didn't mention Adams by name, but with Jackson he didn't have to—had caused many Texans to conclude that they weren't wanted by the Union. Necessity, therefore, required Texas to contemplate indefinite independence. The outlook wasn't wholly grim. With the West on its doorstep, Texas could expand the way the United States had expanded. And it could anticipate the support of European powers eager to cultivate an alternative supplier of cotton and a counterweight to American ambitions. Houston didn't specify Britain in this letter, but Jackson had no difficulty discerning what Houston meant when he said that should Texas be rejected by the United States again, "she would seek some other friend."

Jackson responded just as Houston guessed he would. Jackson was still bitter at Adams—"that arch enemy," he called him—for thwarting annexation eight years earlier. He was determined not to be thwarted again. "We must regain Texas, *peaceably if we can, forcibly if we must,*" he told William Lewis. It was intolerable that Britain might elbow her way in where America had declined to go, on account of the scruples of such as Adams. For Jackson, the threat from Texas was the same as the threat from Florida had been: that the British would use Texas, as they had used Florida, to mount attacks on American territory. The United States might have to fight the Battle of New Orleans all over again. "Great Britain, forming a treaty with Texas . . . could have an army of 40,000 men organised and fully equipped, declare war and take possession of Memphis and Baton Rouge before we could raise and organise an army to meet them, possess herself of New Orleans, and reduce all our fortifications, and having command of the ocean, could keep the country a long time. . . . It would cost oceans of blood and millions of money to regain it."

Houston's letter convinced Jackson to mobilize the Democratic party behind annexation. By the early 1840s the Texas question had become linked in the minds of many American expansionists to that of Oregon. Army expeditions led by such officers as John C. Frémont, the son-in-law of Thomas Benton, had carved a trail to Oregon, and thousands of emigrants were packing their lives and goods into covered wagons and streaming across the plains and mountains to the Willamette Valley. Title to Oregon remained in doubt, with Britain and the United States sharing a joint occupancy under a treaty originally negotiated by Adams. American expansionists demanded that the doubt be erased and Oregon made exclusively American.

Jackson was among these. And, even more than most expansionists, on account of his history with Britain, he linked Oregon and Texas in his vision of America's destiny. The twin questions of Oregon and Texas, he told Francis Blair after receiving Houston's letter, were "all important to the security and the future peace and prosperity of our Union." American patriots must do their duty. "I hope there are a sufficient number of pure American democrats to carry into effect the annexation of Texas and extending our laws over Oregon. No temporising policy, or all is lost." To William Lewis, his liaison to Democrats in Congress, Jackson said, "I hope this golden moment will be seized to regain Texas, or Texas may from necessity be compelled to throw herself into the arms of Great Britain, who will endeavour to unite Oregon with Texas, which would cost us more blood and treasure to relieve us from the dilemma than we have spent in gaining our independence and our last war with Great Britain."

Regarding Texas in particular, decisive action was crucial, as Houston's letter had made plain. Jackson acknowledged the risks to the United States from annexation. Mexico would deem it an act of war and might call on Britain for support. But the dangers wouldn't diminish from hesitation or delay. Texas offered a treaty. "I say, for one, ratify the treaty, and take all the consequences. . . . Houston and the people of Texas are now united in favour of annexation. The next President of Texas may not be so. British influence may reach him, and what can be now got from Texas, freely and peaceably, may evade our grasp."

*I*n a letter to William Lewis at this time, Jackson wrote, "I am now suffering much, and have been for several days. A severe and continued pain in my side, shortness of breath. . . . I have wrote this with great labour."

The recuperation of his first retirement years had given way to a broad decline. The old annoyances became debilities, and new ones added to his physical and emotional cost of living. "My eyesight has failed me much," he wrote at the end of a letter to Van Buren. "I am apt therefore to make repetitions. You will therefore please overlook them. I now write with great difficulty from that cause." To Amos Kendall he explained, "I have been brought low with a severe attack of chills and fevers, added to my other afflictions, which has left me with a painful shortness of breath, which disables me from taking necessary exercise." Yet he still experienced good days. "I am like a taper, which when nearly exhausted will have sometimes the appearance of going out, but will blaze up again for a time."

More than ever he thought about Rachel, and seeing her again. He knew to a moral certainty that she was in heaven, and though he had no such confidence that *he* merited heaven, he worried as little about his salvation as he worried about most else. His conscience was as clear as it had always been. He wouldn't have said this made him a saint; on the contrary, he knew he was as sinful as the next man. But he believed that God gave credit for trying, and by his own lights he had generally done what he thought was the honest and upright thing to do. He had trouble sleeping, but it was his body, not his soul, that kept him awake.

He resigned his fate to God and his estate to his family. As the candle burned short, he drafted his will. Andrew Jr. would get the Hermitage and most of its slaves. Andrew's wife, Sarah, would receive in her own name several house servants, "as a memento of her uniform attention to me and kindness on all occasions, and particularly when worn down with sickness, pain, and debility. She has been more than a daughter to me." Andrew and Sarah's sons, Andrew and Samuel, would each receive a slave boy for companion and life servant. Years earlier the state of Tennessee had awarded Jackson a ceremonial sword, which would go to Andrew Donelson, "with this injunction, that he fail not to use it when necessary in support and protection of our glorious Union, and for the protection of the constitutional rights of our beloved country should they be assailed by foreign enemies or domestic traitors." He wished he could have done more for Donelson and other relatives and friends. But he was prevented by "the great change in my worldly affairs of late." After his and Andrew's various debts were paid, little besides the Hermitage would remain.

The health of John Quincy Adams was better than that of Jackson, though they were the same age. The more challenging climate of New England probably had something to do with the difference. Parasites and pathogens found it as unattractive as many people did, and, lacking the provisions for protection against cold that humans could devise, and missing the determination that came with the Puritan faith, they ceded the region to such homo sapiens as insisted on making it their home. Of course, Adams's advantage over Jackson in health also had something to do with his avoidance of dueling and gun fights and his spending America's wars in the drawing rooms of diplomacy rather than the mountains, forests, and swamps of the frontier.

Yet if Adams's state of body was better than Jackson's, his state of mind was worse. With each passing year he grew more convinced that the republic had taken a grave wrong turn at the end of his presidency. Quality counted for nothing in this age of democracy; popularity counted for all. If popularity had reflected honest accomplishment in the realm of public affairs, it might not have been a terrible guide to the selection of public officials. But it rarely did. It rather reflected the fortunes of war and the ability to fool ordinary people into thinking that what they wanted was what they needed. Democracy begot demagoguery, and both begot bad government.

These past several years the badness of democratic government had manifested itself in the rise of the slave power of the South. Like many of his generation and most of his section, Adams had expected slavery to wither and die. But it hadn't, instead planting new roots in the territory opened by Jackson in the Southwest. And the slave power grew bolder as it broadened its base. Supporters of slavery stifled Adams and others in Congress who sought to debate it, leading Adams to ponder this new twist of democratic irony: that the very advocates of rule by the people refused to let the people speak. Yet he refused to abandon what he called "the life-and-death struggle for the right of petition," though his enemies ridiculed him in the House, slandered him on the stump, libeled him in the press, and threatened him through the mails. "My conscience presses me on," he told himself. "Let me but die upon the breach."

He was hardly surprised to encounter Jackson in that breach. The general had been retired these eight years, but his influence followed Adams everywhere. Jackson's supporters resurrected the old issues, in the old terms. They demanded that Congress rescind Jackson's fine from New Orleans, and they excoriated all who opposed them. "When Weller moved, yesterday, the committee on the Jackson fine to rise," Adams grumbled, "it was for the purpose of having a full, fresh morning hour to disgorge his bilious venom against the Whigs and his sycophancy to Jackson." After Adams objected to a Jacksonian subterfuge to silence him, the leader of the Jackson forces "exploded with a volley of insolent billingsgate upon me."

And when the Texas question reemerged, at the instance of Jackson and his followers, Adams felt the battle personally joined. The Democrats tried to make it a party issue by blaming Adams for giving away Texas in the 1819 treaty with Spain. They conspicuously called for the *re*annexation of Texas, the reclaiming of what had been America's and should never have been relinquished.

Adams answered that Jackson had supported the treaty at the time and that any statements to the contrary were "bold, dashing, and utterly baseless lies." Adams reiterated his charge that the attempt to attach Texas to the United States was part of the ever more audacious conspiracy of the slaveholders against American freedom. The opponents of slavery must awake to the danger. "Your trial is approaching. The spirit of freedom and the spirit of slavery are drawing together for the deadly conflict of arms. The annexation of Texas to this union is the blast of the trumpet for a foreign, civil, servile, and Indian war. . . . Burnish your armor, prepare for the conflict. . . . Think of your forefathers! Think of your posterity!"

Those were precisely the audiences Jackson was thinking of when, against all prior expectation, including his own, he ruined the political career of Martin Van Buren. As the 1844 election approached, the Texas question became even more pressing and more divisive. Henry Clay surprised no one by announcing against annexation and by becoming the leading candidate for the Whig nomination partly by virtue of that fact. Jackson judged that Clay's opposition gave Van Buren just the issue he needed to reclaim the presidency for the Democrats and democracy.

Van Buren himself wasn't so sure. As a New Yorker he was far more sensitive than Jackson to the complaints of the northern antislavery forces and far less attuned to the issues of border security that had never let Jackson rest. Beyond that, his political style was everything Jackson's wasn't. He was a conciliator, not a polarizer; he sought common ground, rather than to scorch the earth beneath his opponents' feet. To Van Buren it made perfect sense to issue a statement that artfully avoided committing himself on the Texas question.

If Jackson hadn't long since included him within his circle of friendship, he would have damned Van Buren's waffling for cowardice. As it was, he shook his head at his protégé's folly. "If Mr. Van Buren had come out in favour of annexation, he would have been elected almost by acclamation," Jackson told Blair. But Van Buren hadn't, thereby risking what Jackson considered double damage to the country: first by letting Texas get away and second by giving Clay and the Whigs a chance to win. Jackson had spoken in public only rarely since leaving the White House, and then chiefly on innocuous matters of uncontested patriotism. But Van Buren's failure to make the cause of Texas his and the party's own compelled Jackson to break his silence. In a letter to the *Nashville Union* he contended that Texas was vital to the future of democracy. "If Texas be not speedily admitted into our confederacy, she must and will be inevitably driven into alliances and commercial regulations with the European powers, of a character highly injurious and probably hostile to this country. What would then be our condition? New Orleans and the whole valley of the Mississippi would be endangered." Texas was now as vital as New Orleans had been thirty years earlier. "She is the key to our safety in the South and the West. She offers this key to us on fair and honorable terms. Let us take it and lock the door against future danger."

Jackson's letter proved devastating to Van Buren. The New Yorker's rivals in the Democratic party took advantage of his difference with Jackson on Texas to create opportunities for themselves. Most successful was James K. Polk, a former congressman and Tennessee governor, an ardent Jacksonian, and an equally ardent annexationist. Polk added "dark horse" to the lexicon of American politics by bolting from the pack of candidates and seizing the nomination at the Democratic convention in Baltimore. And he made the annexation of Texas—and of Oregon as well—the central theme of his campaign.

Jackson got the news of the nomination from Andrew Donelson. "The dark sky of yesterday has been succeeded by the brightest day democracy has witnessed since your election," Donelson told Jackson.

Jackson agreed, and looked forward to the general election with confidence. "The Texan question has destroyed Clay in the South and West," he said. "*Texas must and will be ours.*"

So it proved. Clay carried the Northeast and a handful of states elsewhere, but Polk dominated the South and West and won the election handily.

Jackson was relieved and gratified. "Polk and Dallas are elected and the republic is safe," he declared.

$\mathcal{J}$ackson and most other observers assumed that the annexation of Texas awaited the inauguration of Polk. But Tyler, with little else to claim for his presidency, decided to lay claim to Texas. The antislavery minority in the Senate still prevented annexation of Texas by treaty, so Polk sought the alternative of a joint resolution of the House and Senate.

His decision to do so gave Adams an unexpected last chance to prevent what he considered a political, diplomatic, and moral disaster. No one could gag him now, with the Texas question fairly before the House. Adams could read the election returns as well as anyone, and he could see that expansion was in the blood of the American people. On this account he pointed to his own record as secretary of state to show that he had nothing against expansion per se. He endorsed the acquisition of Oregon, even if it bruised British feelings. But Texas, he said, was different. To take Texas would be to make slavery the essence of American expansion, not merely a side effect. It would trigger a war with Mexico, and it might well lead to a war between the American North and the American South.

But so long had Adams been railing against slavery that the House hardly heard him, and the country still less. The Jackson forces had won the election, and Jackson now won this last battle. The Texas resolution carried both houses.

Adams hadn't been so discouraged since the day of Jackson's inauguration, and for much the same reason. "The Union is sinking into a military monarchy," he muttered. "The prospect is deathlike."

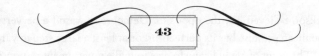

43

THE SOUL OF
THE REPUBLIC

For twenty years Jackson and Adams had bracketed American opinion

regarding the most important political development of their era, the

emergence of democracy. And at the end of that time they remained as

divided over its meaning as they had been at the start. Adams believed

that ordinary Americans weren't fit to govern themselves, that left to their

own ignorance they would choose military heroes and demagogues who

told them what they wanted to hear while leading them where they had

no business going. Their choice of Jackson for president was an early

sign of the collapse of the republic, their seizure of Texas the most

recent. More evidence doubtless would follow, culminating in a conflict

that set one section against the other and utterly undid the handiwork

of the Founders. Wherever George Washington's deistic soul

resided these days, it must be weeping for his country.

Jackson believed just the opposite. Democracy wasn't a perversion of the republican promise but its perfection, or at least a large step toward perfection. The point of republicanism was to make government responsible to the people who lived under its laws. Whatever diminished responsibility was monarchy or aristocracy, and if the American Revolution had been about anything, it was about throwing off those twin incubi of despotism. Democracy made mistakes; Jackson didn't deny that. But its mistakes were the honest and correctable mistakes of human misjudgment, not the interested, entrenched mistakes of selfish elites. Did the people know what was best for them? Not always. But they knew better than anyone else knew for them. God alone was perfect, and He ruled in heaven. Below, the people ruled, if imperfectly.

The question of Jackson's day—as of every day since—was, who was right? Adams or Jackson? In 1845 it was difficult to tell. Adams saw slavery as the acid test of American politics, and he perceived the acid eating through the Constitution, the Declaration of Independence, and everything Americans held, or ought to hold, dear. He saw section replacing nation in the affections of the people, and civil war the near-certain result. The prospect was deathlike indeed.

Jackson saw the same events but interpreted them differently. Slavery wasn't the issue; sectionalism was. Jackson defended slavery, in part because he couldn't envision the political economy of the South without it, but mostly because he perceived the attacks on slavery as threats to the Union. The abolitionists might not intend to shatter the Union, but that would be the consequence of their actions. South Carolina had almost seceded over a tariff; how much more dangerous must it consider attempts to abolish the institution on which its whole way of life rested? Nor would South Carolina be alone on this issue. Its southern neighbors would feel compelled to rally to its side. And who, in any case, were the abolitionists to dictate morality to the rest of the country? They were but a noisy minority. The northern states had abandoned slavery peacefully when a majority of voters there decided slavery no longer served their interests. When a majority of voters in the southern states decided the same thing, slavery would end in the South. To force the issue was to assert that the people couldn't be trusted with political power. Jackson could never accept that.

Jackson's devotion to democracy was unsurprising in one born of the people and bred in the school of hard experience. He trusted the people because he was one of them, in a way none of his predecessors in the White House had been. His attachment to the Union was more difficult to explain. On most subjects his politics aligned with the traditional states'-rights preferences of the party of Jefferson. His principal complaint against the Federalists—aside from their arrogance—was that they stole power from the states, which he considered almost always more reliable in determining the will of the people than the central government at Washington. And throughout his presidency, on such bellwether issues as the Bank of the United States and internal improvements, he checked those in Congress who would have exceeded what he considered the proper bounds of federal authority. But he drew the line—a bright, sharp line, defended by arms if necessary—at anything that even hinted at secession. He would die with the Union, he said at the time of greatest strain with South Carolina. And he would take many with him.

Jackson wouldn't have admitted it, and might not even have recognized it, but his devotion to the Union was at least as much emotional as it was political, at least as reflexive as considered. Sometime in his early life—perhaps when the blood from that British saber wound streaked his face, perhaps when his mother and brothers died and he found himself alone, perhaps when he crossed the mountains to the frontier West—he became peculiarly attached to the cause of his country. Lacking a family, he identified with the American people. Jackson's enemies weren't wrong to describe him as a military chieftain, but they misunderstood what this meant. His deepest loyalties were not to friends and relations, except for Rachel, or even to his Tennessee neighbors. The clan of Old Hickory, the tribe of Sharp Knife, was the American people. Whatever endangered them—the designs of the British, the weakness of the Spanish, the resistance of the Indians, the disloyalty of the Hartford Federalists, the machinations of the nullifiers, the corruption of the Whigs—elicited an immediate response, and sometimes an intemperate one. He could no more control his devotion to the Union than he could measure his attachment to Rachel. Had he been a different man—had he inherited a different temperament from his Ulster ancestors, had he experienced a warmer childhood, had he not been forced to struggle for everything he achieved—he might have turned out less belligerent, less likely to interpret question as affront and challenge as attack. But he was the man he was.

Yet there was more to his sensitivity to slight than his heredity and personal experience. His times contributed to the way he turned out. If he defined life as a struggle, it was largely because life for America in the late eighteenth and early nineteenth centuries *was* a struggle. Eventually, of course, the United States would turn out to be the great power of the Western Hemisphere and then of the world. But during Jackson's lifetime this outcome was neither obvious nor inevitable. In his youth America had to struggle for its very existence against the most powerful empire in the world. Till his middle age it was beset by Britain, France, and potentially Spain, not to mention the numerous Indian allies of the Europeans. His victory at New Orleans meant the United States wouldn't be torn in two, but the country might still be hedged about by enemies and weakened at the borders.

Nor was the danger only external. Divisions within could be as lethal as assault from without. John Calhoun might consider nullification a constitutional issue, but for Jackson it was an existential question—in the literal sense of whether the nation would continue to exist. American life was precarious enough with the country united; with the country broken apart, the pieces would fall prey to those greedy foreigners, and to one another. Jackson's willingness to wage war against the nullifiers signaled his conviction that in a dangerous world—the only world he knew—unity was the closest thing to a guarantee of security. Confronted by danger, the clan closed ranks. Anyone who obstructed the closing became an enemy.

Jackson's appeal to the American people was the appeal of the chieftain to the tribe. They loved him because he was their protector, their hero. But they also loved him because he embodied their hopes and fears, their passions and prejudices, their insight and their ignorance, better than anyone before him. By the standards of a later day, Jackson's democracy had far to go. The "people" he and his contemporaries spoke of were almost exclusively adult white males. But even this minority of the American population signified a tremendous expansion of political participation since Jackson's youth. Democracy, as he would have been the first to admit, was a work in progress. And the American people were happy to march forward behind him. They chose him for what he was, but equally for what *they* were. His strengths were their strengths, his weaknesses their weaknesses. Democracy was—and is—a leap of faith. They placed their faith in him because *he* placed *his* faith in them.

At the time that Jackson learned Congress had voted to annex Texas, he knew he was dying. "When I attempt to walk, I am at once suffocated for the want of breath," he wrote James Polk at the end of February. Merely writing was "a great oppression." In March he informed Francis Blair, "This may be the last letter I may be able to write you." Yet though his body was failing, his mind and will remained strong. "Strange as it may appear, my nerves are as steady as they were forty years gone by."

Slowly, one system after another shut down. His kidneys gave way, causing his body to retain fluids. "I am swollen from the toes to the top of the head," he wrote. The fluid collected around his stomach, triggering nausea that kept him from eating. The fluid pressed on his lungs, making breathing harder than ever, and on his heart, causing it to flutter and strain.

At the end of May he got word that the last chapter in the Texas story was being written, as the people of the republic overwhelmingly approved the annexation offer. "Texas comes into the Union with a united voice," he said. "I knew British gold could not buy Sam Houston."

Even as Jackson wrote, Houston was returning once more to the house of his second father. Houston had left Texas and was at New Orleans, awaiting a steamboat to take him upriver to Nashville. He wanted to be the one to tell Jackson that Texas was finally part of the Union. He also wanted his new wife and their year-old son to meet the greatest man he had ever known.

On the way he heard that Jackson was fading and couldn't be long for earth. Houston tried to make the captain push the steamboat faster, but the current in the river held them back. The small family arrived at Nashville on the evening of June 8. The city knew, and Houston now learned, that Jackson's condition was critical. Houston commandeered a carriage and ordered the driver to summon all the speed the horses could muster. Through the twilight they galloped toward the Hermitage.

On the road they discovered they were too late. Jackson's doctor, coming from the deathbed, informed them that the old general had died at six o'clock. He had retained his faculties to the end and, after bidding good-bye to his family and the members of his household, had slipped quietly away.

The Houstons proceeded, sadly and now slowly, to the house, where Jackson's body lay in the peace of death. Taking Sam Jr. in his arms, Houston raised the child to the edge of Jackson's high bed. "My son," he said, "try to remember that you have looked on the face of Andrew Jackson."

$\mathcal{J}$ackson had bested some rivals and outlasted others. John Marshall, of course, was gone, his place on the nation's highest court taken by one of the country's most ardent Jacksonians. Nicholas Biddle died in retirement under a cloud created, ironically, by the very properties of the banking system Jackson had assailed and he had defended. Biddle and his new bank speculated in cotton as the country recovered from the panic of 1837; when cotton plunged, the bank was left holding notes it couldn't redeem. Biddle escaped before the crash, but the experience did nothing for his once formidable reputation. The bank expired in 1841, Biddle in 1844.

John Quincy Adams was too stubborn to let go. And the more deathlike the prospect for the nation, the more tenaciously he clung to life. He had the grim satisfaction of witnessing the outbreak of the war against Mexico he had predicted as a result of taking Texas. He watched the war aggravate the tensions between North and South, as he had also predicted. He had prayed to die in the breach, and he was finally granted his prayer. In February 1848, just as the treaty ending the war and definitively confirming American possession of Texas (and California) reached Washington from Mexico City, he suffered a stroke in the well of the House. He was placed unconscious on a sofa. He died there two days later.

Henry Clay held on a few years more. At the very moment the negotiators in Mexico were concluding the peace treaty, James Marshall quite by accident discovered gold in California. The discovery touched off an astonishing migration to this newest American West, as hundreds of thousands of people rushed from all over the world to California to stake their claim to the golden bounty. By the summer of 1849 California contained enough people to qualify for statehood; by the end of that year those people had written a constitution and sent it to Washington for approval.

California's demand for admission touched off the most portentous debate in the Senate since the nullification crisis of 1833. As Jackson had predicted, the crisis this time was about slavery—in particular, about whether the territory acquired from Mexico would be slave or free. John Calhoun, also clinging to life but looking more like Jackson every year, as tuberculosis consumed him from within and gave him the haunted look of one living on will alone, insisted that it be slave. Anything else, he said, any abridgment of the right of slaveholding citizens to establish themselves in any part of the federal domain, was unconstitutional and grounds for secession.

Daniel Webster was no more willing to brook such inflammatory talk from Calhoun than he had been during Jackson's presidency. And he answered the South Carolinian in terms no less eloquent than before. The Union must survive, he said. The Union *would* survive.

As he had in 1833, although without the war-threatening help of Jackson, Clay arranged a compromise. California was admitted to the Union free, but the rest of the Mexican cession was opened to slavery. And the South received a second quid pro quo: a much harsher fugitive slave law.

Calhoun died amid the debate over the Compromise of 1850. Clay and Webster survived till 1852. By then the Compromise of 1850 was looking less like a formula for keeping the Union together than a recipe for blowing it apart. North and South each fixed on the parts of the package it didn't like. The Whigs, the party created in opposition to Jackson, disintegrated. Jackson's own party, the Democrats, divided more deeply along sectional lines than ever.

Sam Houston held out the longest. Elected to the Senate from the post-republic state of Texas, he carried the banner of Jackson and the Union back to Washington. He decried the extremism on both sides of the slavery issue, condemning in a single breath the abolitionists of the North and the fire-eaters of the South. The charisma that had marked him, a generation earlier, as the likely heir to Jackson grew manifest again, and he was spoken of for president, a southern Unionist in the Jackson tradition. But he wasn't Jackson, and the 1850s weren't the 1820s. His foes in the Texas legislature defeated his reelection to the Senate, and, though he was promptly chosen governor by the people of Texas, he couldn't stop his state from seceding after the election of 1860. He thereupon signed his own political death warrant by refusing to forsake the Union for the Confederacy. In announcing his refusal, he summoned the spirit of Jackson. "I have seen the patriots and statesmen of my youth, one by one, gathered to their fathers, and the government which they had created rent in twain," he said. "And none like them are left to unite it once again. I stand the last almost of a race, who learned from their lips the lessons of human freedom."

*B*ut even as Houston lamented the apparent demise of the Jacksonian dream—that the people could govern themselves and defend the government they created—another heir to the tradition stepped forward. Abraham Lincoln was an unlikely Jacksonian: an opponent of slavery, a corporate attorney, a defender of banks. But he was also a child of the frontier, a son of the West, an Indian fighter, a common man, and, most decisively, a devout believer in democracy and the Union. It was Lincoln who articulated the Jacksonian creed best—better than Jackson himself—when he declared that "government of the people, by the people, for the people" must not perish from the earth. And when it didn't, when the Union emerged intact from its severest trial, it stood as a monument to Andrew Jackson, who had devoted his life to making democracy possible and the Union indivisible.

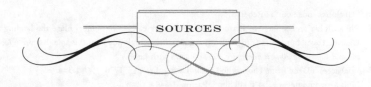

SOURCES

The principal sources for this book are the words of Andrew Jackson and his contemporaries: their letters, diaries, memoranda, and recollections. References to these constitute the great majority of the citations below. Two published collections of Jackson papers have been invaluable: the *Correspondence of Andrew Jackson (CAJ)*, edited by John Spencer Bassett, and *The Papers of Andrew Jackson (PAJ)*, edited by Sam B. Smith and Harriet Chappell Owsley. These collections together contain a very large portion of the most valuable materials from Jackson's hand. Of the unpublished Jackson collections, the most important is at the Library of Congress. When a manuscript letter of Jackson or someone else has been published, the published version has usually been cited in the notes below, for reasons of accessibility.

The citations cover all direct quotations and certain specific items of information. Sources of background information or context have not been cited but can be identified in the Annotated Bibliography.

In many of the quotations, spelling and punctuation have been corrected or brought to modern norms. One aim is to spare readers of this long book the fatigue of wrestling with unfamiliar orthography. The other aim is to do justice to the authors of the quotations, who lived before spelling became standardized. Poor spelling today is considered a mark of ignorance; most persons in Jackson's day harbored no such prejudice. Thomas Jefferson's orthography wasn't as imaginative as Jackson's, but it could be idiosyncratic in its own way, and no one thought the sage of Monticello the dimmer for it. Readers who feel they have been deprived of the flavor of the original spelling are invited to seek it out, in the sources cited.

CHILD OF THE REVOLUTION (1767–1805)

1. THE PRIZE

page
6   "Through an aperture": Parkman, 217. (Full bibliographic information on this title and others can be found in the bibliography.)
7   "It is amazing": Amherst, 310.
7   "Could it not be contrived . . . execrable race": Knollenberg, 492–93.
7   Bouquet distributed: Kent, 763.
7   "The smallpox . . . by the disorders": Knollenberg, 493–94.
8   "Every day . . . in the woods": Parkman, 279–81.
9   "When I do consider . . . forward that way": Ford, 93, 103.

10   "His looks spoke out": Fischer, 615.

12   Philadelphia seems likeliest: Parton (1:48) and other early biographers place the landing at Charles Town, but James (*Life*, 789–90) argues convincingly for Pennsylvania. Remini (*Jackson and Course of American Empire*, 427) concurs with James.

15   "200 acres": Deed from Thomas and Sarah Ewing, Dec. 17, 1770, *PAJ*, 1:3–4.

17   "But he would never . . . I'll kill him": Parton, 1:64.

2. I COULD HAVE SHOT HIM

22   "A picture of a man": Parton, 1:83.

22   "full of enterprise": Buchanan, *Road*, 60.

23   "mangled in the most shocking manner": Ibid., 63.

23   "If any persons": Bass, 79.

24   "Not a man was spared": Buchanan, *Road*, 84.

24   "I have cut": Bass, 81–82.

26   "I'll warrant Andy thought of it": Parton, 1:89.

27   "I frequently heard": Jackson recollections, undated, *PAJ*, 1:7.

28   "Tarleton passed . . . could have shot him": Ibid., *PAJ*, 1:5

3. ALONE

31   "Andrew, if I should not see you . . . made my way": Buell, 1:56–57.

32   "a very proud and haughty disposition": Jackson recollections, undated, *PAJ*, 1:7.

32   "He had a habit": Buell, 1:63–64.

32   "I immediately answered": Jackson recollections, undated, *PAJ*, 1:7.

33   "It was too foolish . . . avoided him after that": Buell, 1:63–64.

33   "three hundred or four hundred pounds sterling": Ibid., 1:57.

34   "I had new spirits": Parton, 1:98.

37   "None of them believed": Buell, 1:69.

37   "What? Jackson for president?": Parton, 1:109.

37   "is sufficiently recommended": S. Ashe and J. Williams to Justices of North Carolina, September 26, 1787, *PAJ*, 1:10.

38   "1. I will practice law because it affords me": Advertisement by William Tatham of Knoxville, reprinted as appendix 2 in Parton, 1:628–29.

39   "did with force and arms": Jackson for Randolph County, March 1788, *PAJ*, 1:11–12.

40   "Paid at the battle of New Orleans": Bassett, 1:13. Lister's daughter presented the bill to Jackson in the White House; he denied that he owed it (ibid.).

40   "I often met him . . . any other young man": Buell, 1:68–69.

4. AWAY WEST

43   "Took our departure from the fort . . . by Capt. Robertson and his company": Heiskell, 1:157–65.

48   "Extend the sphere": *Federalist*, 61.

49   "The people had a coffin . . . the fruits of it": Main, 122–34.

50   "A neighbor might as well ask": Franklin to John Jay, October 2, 1780, Franklin, *Writings*, 1029.

51   "The leading characters of Kentucky . . . in eternal oblivion": Wilkinson memorial to Miró and Navarro, September 5, 1787, quoted in Shepherd, 501.

51   "until the Kentuckians attain the independence . . . hope of remuneration": Summary of meeting of Spain's Supreme Council of State, November 20, 1788, Wilkinson, "Papers," 749–50.

52   "That section of the country . . . to great embarrassment": Wilkinson to Miró, September 18, 1789, ibid., 765–66.

53   "The cause was going": Parton, 1:161–62.

53   "When a man's feelings": Jackson to Avery, August 12, 1788, *PAJ*, 1:12.

53   "My father was no duelist . . . friendly ever after": Parton, 1:162.

54   "I had my saddlehorse": Buell, 1:71–72.

5. SHADOWED LOVE

57   "beautifully molded form": Heiskell, 3:279.

58   "The old lady told me . . . to restore harmony": Parton, 1:148–49.

58   "Not many months elapsed . . . reasonably be expected": Ibid., 1:149–50.

59   "I had the pleasure of seeing . . . peace with the savage": Jackson to Daniel Smith, February 13, 1789, *PAJ*, 1:16.

61   "June 2d, 1791": Parton, 1:139.

63   "that the defendant hath deserted": "An Act Concerning the Marriage of Lewis Robards," December 20, 1790, *PAJ*, 1:424.

63   Spanish and other records reveal: Remini, *Jackson and Course of American Empire*, 64–65; Burstein, 243–44; Toplovich. These three sources are the basis for the reconstruction of events that follow.

63   At that time he had sworn the oath of allegiance to Spain: Remini, "Andrew Jackson Takes an Oath."

65   "My Dearest Heart": Jackson to Rachel Jackson, May 9, 1796, *PAJ*, 1:91.

65   "To this suggestion": Parton, 1:152.

6. REPUBLICANS AND REVOLUTIONARIES

68   "to make a county": Buell, 1:93.

68   "If any one attacks you": Parton, 1:159–60.

69   "contingent expences": Account of freight expenses, May–August 1795, *PAJ*, 1:58.

69   Its inventory included butcher knives: Account book, 1795, *PAJ*, 1:455ff.

69   "to bear an equal proportion": Partnership agreement with Overton, May 12, 1794, *PAJ*, 1:46.

69   contracted to purchase 15,000 acres for 500 pounds (and subsequent details of transactions): Calendar of transactions and agreements, 1770–1803, *PAJ*, 1:429ff.

69   "candid and unreserved . . . as few difficulties": Overton to Jackson, March 8, 1795, *PAJ*, 1:54.

70   "To my sad experience . . . almost unto death": Jackson to Overton, June 9, 1795, *PAJ*, 1:59–60; agreement with David Allison, May 14, 1795, *PAJ*, 1:56–57.

70   "They have not the smallest expectation . . . forward the boat on": Donelson to Jackson, June 29, 1795, *PAJ*, 1:62–63.

71 "We are sorry so soon": Meeker, Cochran & Company to Jackson, August 11, 1795, *PAJ*, 1:64.

71 "His note therefore": John B. Evans & Company to Jackson, January 4, 1796, *PAJ*, 1:79.

72 He acquired what appears to have been his first slave (and subsequent slave transactions): Calendar of Jackson transactions, *PAJ*, 1:432–47.

73 In 1796 he purchased: Deed for Hunter's Hill, March 10, 1796 (summary), *PAJ*, 1:84.

73 "The convulsions in France": Franklin in Brands, *First American*, 705–06.

74 "liberty of the whole earth" and following description: Brands, *What America Owes the World*, 3–4.

76 "What an alarming situation . . . consented to it": Jackson to Macon, October 4, 1795, *PAJ*, 1:74.

76 A 1795 census: Heiskell, 1:294–95.

76 "counting the whole of the free persons": Ibid.

77 "Jackson, though exerting . . . he was driving at": Buell, 1:108–11.

78 "as sweet a flavor": Ibid., 1:111.

79 "the least imperfect and most republican": Jefferson quoted in Heiskell, 1:298.

80 " 'Tis our true policy": Washington's Farewell Address, September 19, 1796, *American Historical Documents*, 246.

80 "From the president's speech": Jackson to Robert Hays, December 16, 1796, *PAJ*, 1:103.

80 "In my mind, this address": Jackson quoted in Buell, 1:116.

80 "just and necessary . . . to take the field": Jackson to the House of Representatives, December 29 and 30, 1796, *PAJ*, 1:106–08.

81 Congress appropriated $22,816: Buell, 1:120.

82 "That an equal participation": 29th section of Tennessee bill of rights, Heiskell, 1:98.

82 In this letter Blount spoke vaguely . . . "decided opinion respecting it": Blount to Carey, April 21, 1797, and Senate Committee report, no date given; both ibid., 82–86.

7. FIGHTING WORDS

84 "War is their principal study . . . colours among us": William Fyffe in Woodward, 33.

84 "We cannot live without war": Unidentified Cherokees in Ramsey, 83.

84 "They are more serviceable": Washington in John Brown, 81.

85 "We proceeded": Marion in ibid., 111.

86 "In a few years the Shawnees . . . and destroy them": Cornstalk in ibid., 144–45.

87 "You have bought a fair land": Dragging Canoe in ibid., 12.

88 "You know you began . . . compensation for it": Heiskell, 1:316–17.

89 "At a crisis in the great struggle": Roosevelt, 3:121.

89 "Had the destroying angel": Ramsey, 428.

90 "Viewing, sir, with horror": Jackson to Sevier, May 8, 1797, *PAJ*, 1:136.

91 "the scurrilous expressions": Ibid.

91 "Why those private letters . . . feelings requires redress": Ibid.

92 "The voice of calumny . . . of mild philosophy": Sevier to Jackson, May 8, 1797, *PAJ*, 1:137–38.

92 "Facts may be misstated . . . any other person": Jackson to Sevier, May 10, 1797, *PAJ*, 1:141.

92 "It is painful to hear the cries . . . if not its existence": Sevier to Jackson, November 26, 1797, *PAJ*, 1:154–55.

93 "The prevention of a settlement": Ibid.

94 "Bonaparte with 150,000 troops": Jackson to Robertson, January 11, 1798, *PAJ*, 1:165.

95 "No news that can be relied on . . . the right of thinking": Jackson to Donelson, January 18, 1798, *PAJ*, 1:167–68.

95 "Sticks and spittle are substituted . . . of Eastern quarrels": Jackson to Blount, February 21, 1798, *PAJ*, 1:182–83.

8. RENDERING JUDGMENT

97 "His passions are terrible": Notes of 1824 conversation with Jefferson, Webster, *Papers of Webster*, 1:376.

97 "I feel much alarmed": Ibid.

98 "I mean to retire . . . your affectionate husband": Jackson to Rachel, May 9, 1796, *PAJ*, 1:91–92.

99 "I must now beg of you": Jackson to Hays, November 2, 1797, *PAJ*, 1:152.

99 "It is such a neglect": Jackson to Rachel, January 26, 1798, *PAJ*, 1:174.

99 "I hold myself much indebted": Ibid.

100 "I have come to a conclusion": Jackson to Ryerson, July 5, 1801, *PAJ*, 1:249.

100 "It has been communicated to me": Sevier to Jackson, August 29, 1798, *PAJ*, 1:209.

101 A story was told . . . "and so I did": Parton, 1:228–29.

102 "during good behavior": Commission as superior court judge, December 22, 1798, *PAJ*, 1:215.

102 "I am in possession . . . would be too great": Jackson to Hays, August 24, 1801, *PAJ*, 1:252–53.

102 "general wish and opinion . . . and humble servant": Robertson to Jackson, September 7, 1803, *PAJ*, 1:358.

102 "Talents like yours . . . struggle with the loss": Enclosure (1) in Jackson to George Roulstone, October 8, 1803, *PAJ*, 1:372–73.

102 "Retirement to private life . . . voice is obeyed": Enclosure (2), ibid.

103 "if health will permit me": Ibid.

103 "confined me for some days": Jackson to John Overton, February 23, 1798, *PAJ*, 1:184.

103 "During this distressing scene": Jackson to Rachel, March 22, 1803, *PAJ*, 1:326.

106 "To do this is not my wish . . . every good citizen in it": Jackson to Benjamin Bradford, July 19, 1803, *PAJ*, 1:337–46.

106 "Services? . . . young men at Knoxville": Isaac Avery in Parton, 1:165.

107 "The ungentlemanly expressions": Jackson to Sevier, October 2, 1803, *PAJ*, 1:367–68.

107 "Your ungentlemanly and gasconading conduct . . . me and my meaning": Sevier to Jackson, October 2, 1803, *PAJ*, 1:368.

108 "This, sir, I view . . . of one hour": Jackson to Sevier, October 3, 1803, *PAJ*, 1:368–69.

108 "I am happy to find you": Sevier to Jackson, October 3, 1803, *PAJ*, 1:369.

108 "To all who shall see": Jackson to the public, October 10, 1803, *PAJ*, 1:379.

108 "I am again perplexed . . . for the campaign": Sevier to Jackson, October 10, 1803, *PAJ*, 1:380–81.

109 "Sevier replied . . . protect Mr. Jackson": Statement by Vandyke, October 16, 1803, printed in *Tennessee Gazette and Mero District Advertiser*, December 21, 1803, *PAJ*, 1:505–06.

109 "Judge Jackson swore": Affidavit of Andrew Greer, October 23, 1803, *PAJ*, 1:489–90.

110 "Let us ask . . . retreat with credit": "A citizen of Knox county" to the *Knoxville Gazette*, November 10, 1803, *PAJ*, 1:493–94.

110 "vulgar and ungentlemanly expressions": "Veritas" to *Tennessee Gazette*, December 14, 1803, *PAJ*, 1:496–501.

SON OF THE WEST (1805–1814)

9. CONSPIRACY

113 "My own affections": Jefferson to William Short, January 3, 1793, *Selected Writings of Jefferson*, 522.

113 "If they see their interests": Jefferson quoted in Abernethy, 4.

114 "It is rare that the public sentiment": Jefferson in Malone, 4:100.

115 "There is on the globe": Jefferson to Robert Livingston, April 18, 1802, Jefferson papers.

117 "He is by far not so dangerous a man": Hamilton to Oliver Wolcott Jr., December 16, 1800, *Papers of Hamilton*, 25:257.

118 "He understands as well": Burr to Jackson, June 2, 1805, *PAJ*, 2:59.

119 "But notwithstanding . . . and your honor": Burr to Jackson, March 24, 1806, *PAJ*, 2:91–92.

119 Jackson compiled the list: *PAJ*, 2:93n3.

119 "The certain consequence . . . of acquiring fame": Jackson to James Winchester, October 4, 1806, *PAJ*, 2:110–11.

120 "This armed force . . . ready to march": Jackson to brigadier generals, October 4, 1806, *PAJ*, 2:111–12.

120 "The public sentiment": Jackson to Jefferson, c. November 5, 1806, *PAJ*, 2:114–15.

120 "Their intention was to divide . . . at the head": Jackson to George Washington Campbell, January 15, 1807, *PAJ*, 2:148–49.

122 "There is something rotten . . . the Union disunited": Jackson to Claiborne, November 12, 1806, *PAJ*, 2:116.

122 "A difference exists . . . to New Orleans": Jackson to Smith, November 12, 1806, *PAJ*, 2:117–19.

123 "He is meditating the overthrow": Anonymous letter to Jefferson, December 1, 1805, quoted in Abernethy, 38.

123 "Spanish intrigues": Daviess quoted in ibid., 90.

124 In August Jefferson . . . from Spanish control: Ibid., 63, 184–85.

124 "an express pledge of honor": Jackson to Claiborne, January 8, 1807, *PAJ*, 2:140–41.

125 "Should danger threaten you": Ibid.

125 "Burr's chief agent here . . . the national interests": Wilkinson to Jackson, December 19, 1806, *PAJ*, 2:126.

125 "a numerous and powerful association . . . an auxiliary step": Wilkinson to Jefferson, October 20, 1806, in Abernethy, 150–51.

126 "Everything internal and external . . . glory and fortune": Burr to Wilkinson, July 22–29, 1806, *Papers of Burr*, 2:986–87.

126 "Burr's enterprise is the most extraordinary": Jefferson to Charles Clay, January 11, 1807, Jefferson papers.

126 "He might be hid": Wilkinson to Jackson, December 19, 1806, *PAJ*, 2:126.

127 "Burr said surely": Jackson testimony to grand jury, June 25, 1807, *PAJ*, 2:168–69.

128 "I am more convinced . . . pass with impunity": Jackson to William Anderson, June 16, 1807, *PAJ*, 2:167–68.

10. Affair of Honor

129 "one bay horse": Appraisal of horse, December 12, 1783, *PAJ*, 1:9.

130 Jackson solved Verell's financial problem: Memorandum of agreement between Jackson and Verell, May 11, 1805, *PAJ*, 1:57.

132 "a damned liar": Swann to Jackson, January 3, 1806, *PAJ*, 2:78.

132 "The harshness of this expression": Ibid.

132 "Let me, sir . . . with an anodyne": Jackson to Swann, January 7, 1806, *PAJ*, 2:79–80.

133 "As to the word *coward*": Dickinson to Jackson, January 10, 1806, *PAJ*, 2:81–82.

133 "Think not . . . receive of another": Swann to Jackson, January 12, 1806, *PAJ*, 2:82.

133 "not suffer passion . . . avoiding a duel": Robertson to Jackson, February 1, 1806, *PAJ*, 2:83–84.

134 "On Thursday the 3rd": Clover Bottom race notice, March 1, 1806, *PAJ*, 2:90.

135 "the largest concourse . . . the fate of Ploughboy": Jackson to John Hutchings, April 6, 1806, *PAJ*, 2:94.

135 "I declare him": Dickinson to editor of *Impartial Review*, May 21, 1806, *PAJ*, 2:97.

135 "Your conduct and expressions . . . will point out": Jackson to Dickinson, May 23, 1806, *PAJ*, 2:98.

136 "If you can not obtain pistols": Overton to Catlet, May 23, 1806, *PAJ*, 2:99.

136 "For god's sake": Overton to Catlet, May 24, 1806, *PAJ*, 2:99–100.

136 "not now be convenient": Catlet to Overton, May 24, 1806, *PAJ*, 2:100.

136 "It is agreed": Statement by Overton and Catlet, May 24, 1806, *PAJ*, 2:100.

137 "I should have hit him": Jackson quoted in Parton, 1:297. The outlines of the duel as given here follow Parton, who got details from those close to the event.

11. All Must Feel the Injuries

139 "There is a few long faces": John Overton to Jackson, June 1, 1806, *PAJ*, 2:100–01.

140 "The thing is so novel": Jackson to Thomas Eastin, June 6, 1806, *PAJ*, 2:101, and headnote to same.

140 "To dupe the citizens": Jackson to Watkins, June 15, 1806, *PAJ*, 2:102.

140 "He observed that he was not": Caffery to Jackson, August 25, 1806, excerpted in *PAJ*, 2:103n.

140 "every circumstance in the affair": Statement by Catlet, June 25, 1806, *PAJ*, 2:104.

141 "A report arrived here . . . for better purposes": John Overton to Jackson, September 12, 1806, *PAJ*, 2:108–09.

143 "British Outrage . . . satisfaction is not given": Malone, 5:425.

144 "made up for war . . . old and the new": Jefferson to William Duane, July 20, 1807, Jefferson papers.

144 "The degradation offered . . . nation is inevitable": Jackson to Thomas Bayly, June 27, 1807, *PAJ*, 2:170.

145 he led a protest: *PAJ*, 2:170n. As a tactical measure, the rally endorsed Jefferson's actions, but the mood was clearly more belligerent than the administration's.

146 "Is it possible": Jackson to McNairy, January 20, 1808, *PAJ*, 2:183.

146 to pay him $999: Headnote to Jackson to McNairy, January 20, 1808, *PAJ*, 2:182.

146 "Our enemies have long calculated . . . liberty and independence": Jackson address, January 16, 1809, *PAJ*, 2:210–11.

12. MASTER AND SLAVES

149 "They are family Negroes": Wade Hampton to Jackson, June 3, 1810, *PAJ*, 2:248.

150 "Fifty Dollars Reward . . . of three hundred": Jackson advertisement in *Tennessee Gazette*, September 26, 1804, *PAJ*, 2:40–41.

150 "1 bottle castor oil": Jackson account with John Bedford, October 26, 1809, to September 29, 1812, *PAJ*, 2:223.

150 In 1810 he formed a partnership: This account is from the headnote to Jackson memorandum, May 18, 1811, *PAJ*, 2:261–62.

151 "It was well known": Jackson to Blount, January 25, 1812, *PAJ*, 2:277–79.

151 "the said Andrew Jackson": Jackson affidavit, February 29, 1812, *PAJ*, 2:286–89.

151 "A. Jackson amount of proportion": Entry from Bank of Nashville account book, *PAJ*, 2:262n1.

151 promissory notes: May 18, 1811, *PAJ*, 2:262–63n1; Jackson to arbitrator, February 29, 1812, *PAJ*, 2:286–89.

153 But no bill . . . appears in the state records: Headnote to account with Bedford, *PAJ*, 2:218.

153 "I arrived at his house . . . not do that": Benton, *Thirty Years' View*, 1:737.

13. NOR INFAMY UPON US

154 "I cannot make out a statement . . . accounts are mentioned": Jackson to Francis Preston, May 3, 1810, *PAJ*, 2:243–44.

155 "I find it impossible . . . tone of thought": Jackson to Jenkin Whiteside, February 10, 1810, *PAJ*, 2:233–34.

155 "There is no business . . . during his pleasure": Caffery to Jackson, May 20, 1810, *PAJ*, 2:246.

155 "The people in this country": Caffery to Jackson, June 10, 1810, *PAJ*, 2:249.

155 "If you have never visited": Walter Overton to Jackson, September 26, 1810, *PAJ*, 2:253.

156 "I am well aware": Jackson to Jenkin Whiteside, February 10, 1810, *PAJ*, 2:233–34.

156 "The only two converts": Sampson Williams to Jackson, April 25, 1808, *PAJ*, 2:195.

157 "The present Congress . . . amusement or business": Jackson to Jenkin Whiteside, February 10, 1810, *PAJ*, 2:233–34.

158 "No man in the nation . . . at your feet": Clay speech of February 22, 1810 (he was still in the Senate at this point), *Papers of Clay*, 1:449–50.

159 "Your Committee . . . appeal to arms": Calhoun report for Committee on Foreign Relations, June 3, 1812, *Papers of Calhoun*, 1:121–22.

160 "with anxious expectation . . . nobly in the cause": Jackson to brigadier generals, December 19, 1808, *PAJ*, 2:203.

160 "If he knows his duty": Jackson to Winchester, March 15, 1809, *PAJ*, 2:214.

160 "Our independence and liberty . . . an invading foe": Jackson to Blount, February 15, 1810, *PAJ*, 2:236–38.

SOURCES ᎧᎧ 569

161 "If the trumpet of hell": Anderson to Jackson, November 17, 1810, *PAJ*, 2:255.

161 "My friend, Patton Anderson": Parton, 1:344.

161 "He was then a remarkable man . . . our intimacy began": Benton, *Thirty Years' View*, 1:736.

162 "I have always been resolved . . . by your approbation": Benton to Jackson, January 30, 1812, *PAJ*, 2:280.

162 "The clouds of war": Jackson to William Eustis, May 10, 1811, *PAJ*, 2:261.

162 "The Rubicon is passed": Grundy to Jackson, November 28, 1811, *PAJ*, 2:271.

163 "Citizens! . . . a foreign tyrant": Jackson to the Second Division, March 7, 1812, *PAJ*, 2:290–92.

14. NATIVE GENIUS

164 "The implicit obedience . . . to war against us": Harrison to William Eustis, August 7, 1811, *Letters of Harrison*, 1:547–48.

165 "My children": Sugden, 118–19.

165 "I concluded that . . . he was a visionary": Jefferson to John Adams, April 20, 1812, Jefferson papers.

166 "One of the finest looking men": George Floyd to wife, August 14, 1810, Sugden, 198.

166 "You, Father, have nourished us": Tecumseh speech in Elliott to Claus, November 16–18, 1810, ibid., 213.

167 "Do not think that the red coats . . . on the Wabash": Harrison to the Prophet, July 19, 1810, *Letters of Harrison*, 1:447–48.

167 "the great man of the party": Harrison to William Eustis, August 22, 1810, ibid., 1:460.

167 "They gave us many presents . . . in killing them": Tecumseh speech of August 20, 1810, attached to Harrison to Eustis, August 22, 1810, ibid., 1:464–66.

169 "with great vehemence and anger" . . . called the governor a liar: Harrison to Eustis, August 22, 1810, ibid., 1:468.

169 "As the Great Chief": Sugden, 202.

169 "There can remain no doubt . . . we cannot fight": Jackson to Jefferson, April 20, 1808, *PAJ*, 2:191–92.

170 "In all probability . . . to court danger": Jackson to Jefferson, May 14, 1808, *PAJ*, 2:196–97.

171 "I am willing to act justly . . . ten-fold the expense": Blount to Jackson, December 28, 1809, *PAJ*, 2:226–27.

172 "My heart bleeds . . . for the balance": Jackson to Blount, June 4, 1812, *PAJ*, 2:300–02. This is a draft; the letter Jackson sent differs slightly. The draft includes material Jackson apparently communicated to Blount in other letters, which is why it is used here.

172 "I shall wait no longer . . . and the captors": Jackson to Blount, July 3, 1812, *PAJ*, 2:307–08.

173 "The Massacre at the Mouth . . . *the Creek nation?*": From the *Democratic Clarion*, July 8, 1812, reprinted in *PAJ*, 2:310–11. Jackson didn't sign this piece, but its peroration, combined with his known impatience with Washington, made a signature superfluous.

15. OLD HICKORY

174 "British cruisers have been . . . shocking to humanity": Madison message to Congress, June 1, 1812, *Papers of Madison* (Presidential Series), 4:432–36.

175 Yet the vote wasn't nearly unanimous: Roger Brown, 45.

175 "Before we march . . . *not my son*": Ibid.

176 "I have no reason to doubt": Harrison to William Eustis, October 6, 1811, *Letters of Harrison*, 1:595.

177 "Our killed and wounded": Harrison to Eustis, November 8, 1811, ibid., 1:615.

177 The Indian losses were considerably fewer: See, for example, Elliott to Brock, January 12, 1812, ibid., 1:616–18. Also Sugden, 235–36.

178 "Opened the northern hive of Indians . . . women and children?": Hickey, 83–84.

178 according to an eyewitness: Ibid., 84.

179 "The disaster of the northwestern army": Jackson to the Second Division, September 8, 1812, *PAJ*, 2:320.

179 "Every man of the western country . . . of the Republic": Jackson to Tennessee volunteers, November 14, 1812, *PAJ*, 2:341.

180 Jackson ordered the cavalry to report: Jackson to Tennessee volunteers, November 24, 1812, *PAJ*, 2:342.

180 "The success of military men": Jackson to Alpha Kingsley, December 23, 1812, *PAJ*, 2:345–46.

180 "I shall wear it near my bosom . . . for his papa": Jackson to Rachel, January 8, 1813, *PAJ*, 2:353–54.

181 "We had an extreme hard frost . . . we met with": Entries for January 11, 25, 29, and 30, and February 2, 3, and 16, 1813, "Journal of the Trip Down the Mississippi."

183 "If it is in my power": Wilkinson to Jackson, January 22, 1813, *PAJ*, 2:358–59.

183 "the substance of which . . . indolence creates disquiet": Jackson to Wilkinson, February 16, 1813, *PAJ*, 2:365.

183 "The causes for embodying . . . of the United States": John Armstrong to Jackson, February 6, 1813, *PAJ*, 2:361. This message mistakenly carried the date January 5, causing Jackson to believe it was even slower to arrive than it really was.

184 "Those that could escape . . . agents of Government": Jackson to Armstrong, March 15, 1813, *PAJ*, 2:383–85.

185 "must have been drunk . . . stick by them": Jackson to Grundy, March 15, 1813, *PAJ*, 2:385–86.

185 "He knows that if you had met . . . honors of war": Jackson to Tennessee volunteers, March 16, 1813, *PAJ*, 2:390–92.

186 "I dare not incur": Wilkinson to Jackson, March 20, 1813, *PAJ*, 2:393.

186 "provide the means for their support": Jackson to Wilkinson, March 22, 1813, *CAJ*, 1:299.

187 "Long will the General live . . . Jackson has them": *Nashville Whig*, no date given, Parton, 1:384.

16. SHARP KNIFE

189 "You conducted it . . . approve his course": Benton to Jackson, July 25, 1813, *PAJ*, 2:414.

190 At this point the story becomes confused: The account here of the Nashville fight comes primarily from Parton, 1:391–97, and Benton to the public, September 10, 1813, *PAJ*, 2:425–27.

191 "I am literally in hell here . . . is in danger": Benton quoted in Parton, 1:395.

192 "I have heard many great orators . . . earth shall shake": Sam Dale quoted in Griffith, 102–04.

194 "Every Indian was provided . . . every solitary one": Thomas Holmes quoted in ibid., 109–10.

195 "Indians, negroes, white men . . . with dead bodies": Major Kennedy quoted in Parton, 1:418.

196 "Brave Tennesseans! . . . command in person": Jackson to Tennessee Volunteers, September 24, 1813, *PAJ*, 2:428–29.

196 "My health is good": Jackson to Rachel Jackson, October 11, 1813, *PAJ*, 2:436.

196 "I wish you to receive . . . or deer's tails": Jackson to Coffee, October 7, 1813, *PAJ*, 2:435–36.

197 "I have spies out constantly": Pathkiller to Jackson, October 22, 1813, *PAJ*, 2:439–40.

197 "We are now within twenty miles": Jackson to Blount, October 28, 1813, *PAJ*, 2:442–43.

197 "I yesterday sent out . . . honor to the government": Ibid.

198 "What I dread": Jackson to Thomas Flournoy, October 24, 1813, *PAJ*, 2:441.

198 "He has executed this order . . . the age of Theodore": Jackson to Rachel Jackson, November 4, 1813, *PAJ*, 2:444.

199 "At sunrise we came . . . formed of them": Jackson to Willie Blount, November 11, 1813, Jackson papers, Library of Congress.

200 "We were out of provisions . . . of the men": Jackson to Rachel Jackson, November 12, 1813, *PAJ*, 2:448–49.

200 "It is with extreme pain . . . into the settlements": Jackson to Blount, November 14, 1813, *CAJ*, 1:345.

202 "Summer before last . . . bones upon them": Tecumseh speech of September 18, 1813, enclosed with Harrison to Meigs, October 11, 1813, *Letters of Harrison*, 2:541–43 (speech), 575–76 (letter).

203 "He was dressed . . . from our view": Richardson quoted in Sugden, 370.

203 "Father, tell your young men": Ibid.

203 "His inferior officers say . . . for a moment doubtful": Harrison to Meigs, October 11, 1813, *Letters of Harrison*, 2:575–76.

203 "The American backwoodsmen ride better": Harrison to John Armstrong, October 9, 1813, ibid., 2:562.

204 Harrison counted: Ibid., 2:565.

204 "I saw him with my own eyes": Rowland quoted in Sugden, 375.

17. THE RIVER OF BLOOD

206 "If they do not get home soon": Martin to Jackson, December 4, 1813, *CAJ*, 1:369.

206 "This was one of our strongest arguments . . . noble hearted soldiers": Ibid., 1:369–70.

207 "It is well known . . . do my duty": Jackson to Martin, December 4, 1813, *CAJ*, 1:370–73.

207 "If permitted to return . . . modify your order": Cannon et al. to Jackson, December 8, 1813, *CAJ*, 1:374–75.

208 "In the name of God . . . has ever arrived": Jackson to John Cocke, December 6, 1813, *CAJ*, 1:374.

208 "What may be attempted . . . they are subdued": Jackson to Coffee, December 9, 1813, *CAJ*, 1:378.

208 "The commanding general being informed": Jackson quoted in Reid and Eaton, 84.

209 "The general rode along the line": Ibid., 84–85.

210 "By the Creeks . . . and very poor": Crockett, 15, 71–75, 88–90.

212 "the wild liberty of the red man . . . in after years proved": Houston, *Life*, 1.

214 "Which is the damned rascal?": Parton, 1:508. Parton, who had a chance to interview many of those involved, is the source of the facts of the version of the Wood story recounted here.

214 "The offenses of which . . . be known also": Jackson to Wood, March 14, 1814, *PAJ*, 3:48–49.

215 "Painful as it was": Reid and Eaton, 143.

215 "It is impossible to conceive a situation": Jackson to Thomas Pinckney, March 28, 1814, *CAJ*, 1:488–89.

216 "An opportunity is at length offered . . . shall suffer death": Jackson general order, March 24, 1814, *CAJ*, 1:486–88.

217 "I had ordered the Indians . . . they were fighting you": Coffee to Jackson, April 11, 1814, Horseshoe Bend Accounts. Also Gideon Morgan to Willie Blount, April 1, 1814, ibid.

217 "I never had such emotions": Reid to Betsy Reid, April 1, 1814, Horseshoe Bend Accounts.

217 "A terrible conflict ensued . . . muzzles of our guns": Reid to father, April 5, 1814, Horseshoe Bend Accounts.

217 "At length we mounted the walls . . . shouts of the victors": Ibid.

218 "The event could no longer be doubtful": Jackson to Blount, March 31, 1814, *CAJ*, 1:491.

218 "The *carnage* was *dreadful*": Jackson to Rachel Jackson, April 1, 1814, *CAJ*, 1:492–93.

218 John Coffee estimated the dead . . . "the instant they landed": Coffee to Jackson, April 11, 1814, Horseshoe Bend Accounts.

219 "The river ran red with blood": Bradford to William Henry Harrison, April 5, 1814, Horseshoe Bend Accounts.

219 "The Tallapoosa might truly be called": Alexander McCulloch quoted in O'Brien, 151.

219 "I think it is the most complete victory": Carroll to unidentified friend in Nashville, April 1, 1814, printed in Nashville *Clarion and Tennessee State Gazette*, April 12, 1814, extract reproduced in Horseshoe Bend Accounts.

219 "What effect this will produce": Jackson to Rachel Jackson, April 1, 1814, *CAJ*, 1:493.

219 "The fiends of the Tallapoosa": Jackson to Tennessee troops, April 2, 1814, *PAJ*, 3:58.

219 "I will give them": Jackson to Rachel Jackson, April 1, 1814, *CAJ*, 1:493.

220 "High up on the central pole": James Campbell, as told to a correspondent for the Richmond *Daily Dispatch*, printed September 16, 1861, Horseshoe Bend Accounts. Campbell's remarks are paraphrased, so the precise wording may not be his. But the memory certainly is.

220 During one battle . . . soon was gone: Parton, 1:530.

221 "He was a little scant . . . it might be": Carroll quoted in Buell, 1:335–36.

221 "I had directed": Jackson quoted by Reid in Reid and Eaton, 165.

221 "I am in your power": Weatherford speech to Jackson, March 28, 1814, quoted in Griffith, 116–17. See also Owsley, 83–85, and Reid and Eaton, 165–67.

222 "General Jackson said to Weatherford . . . by their chiefs": Thomas Woodward, 92–93.

AMERICAN HERO (1814–1821)

18. PEACE GIVER

225 "The opposite parties live separate:" Clement Moore to his mother, May 30 and June 4, 1812, quoted in Roger Brown, 178.

226 "When war is declared": Baltimore *American*, July 16, 1812, quoted in Hickey, 55.

226 "We'll feather and tar": Ibid., 65.

226 "I have intended, my dear Rodney . . . in their places": Clay to Caesar Rodney, December 29, 1812, *Papers of Clay*, 1:750.

227 "You are sufficiently aware . . . to the United States": Gallatin to Clay, April 22, 1814, *Papers of Clay*, 1:883–84.

227 "Having advanced within sixteen miles . . . across the Potomac": Ross to Earl Bathurst, August 30, 1814, in Auchinleck, 359–60.

228 "It would be difficult to conceive": Gleig, 70.

228 "THE LEADER OF A HOST OF BARBARIANS": *Niles' Register*, October 27, 1814, in Hickey, 204.

228 "George Washington founded this city": Ibid., 202.

229 After three weeks they produced a report: Buckley, 22–24.

229 "No sensible man ought to expect": Boston *Gazette*, January 9, 1815, in Hickey, 278–79.

230 "These kind of men . . . have condemned them": Jackson to Monroe, January 6, 1817, *CAJ*, 2:272–73.

230 "Something ought to be done for General Jackson": Armstrong to Madison, May 14, 1814, Madison papers.

230 "All therefore that can be done": Armstrong to Jackson, May 22, 1814, *CAJ*, 2:4.

231 "Accept the expression of your general's thanks . . . not to be expressed": Jackson to Tennessee troops, April 28, 1814, *PAJ*, 3:65–67.

232 "grand policy of the government. . . . It must be done": Jackson to Williams, May 18, 1814, *PAJ*, 3:73–75.

233 "The truth is . . . to be killed": Jackson reply to Big Warrior, August 7, 1814, *PAJ*, 3:109.

233 "Had you listened to them": Jackson to Creek and Cherokee representatives, August 5, 1814, *PAJ*, 3:103.

234 "The spilling blood of white people . . . I hold fast": Speech of Big Warrior, August 6, 1814, *PAJ*, 3:106–08.

234 "The war is not over . . . be destroyed together": Jackson reply to Big Warrior, August 7, 1814, *PAJ*, 3:109–11.

235 "The whole Creek nation": Jackson to John Armstrong, August 10, 1814, *CAJ*, 2:25.

235 "Could you only see the misery": Jackson to Rachel Jackson, August 10, 1814, *PAJ*, 3:114.

235 "They *must* be *fed* and *clothed*": Jackson to Armstrong, August 10, 1814, *CAJ*, 2:25.

19. THE SPANISH FRONT

236 "The Creeks were depressed": Harry Toulmin to Jackson, June 22, 1814, *CAJ*, 2:9.

237 "Will the government say to me": Jackson to Armstrong, June 27, 1814, *CAJ*, 2:12–13.

237 He ordered Jackson: Armstrong to Jackson, July 18, 1814, *CAJ*, 2:13n2.

237 "I am informed that the enemies . . . with the United States": Jackson to González Manrique, July 12, 1814, *CAJ*, 2:15–16.

238 "impertinent . . . such a demand": Gordon to Jackson, July 20, 1814, *CAJ*, 2:17–18.

238 "Whatever may be the wishes": Jackson to Claiborne, August 22, 1814, *CAJ*, 2:27.

238 "Take no measures . . . of your duties": Monroe to Jackson, October 21, 1814, *CAJ*, 2:79.

238 "murderous, barbarous, rebellious banditti . . . scalp for scalp": Jackson to González Manrique, August 24, 1814, *CAJ*, 2:28–29.

239 "I received this evening . . . the surrounding country": Jackson to Butler, August 27, 1814, *CAJ*, 2:31–32.

239 "There will be bloody noses . . . a desperate struggle": Ibid.

240 "I shall arm my Indians . . . will take it up": Jackson to González Manrique, September 9, 1814, *CAJ*, 2:45.

240 "the gallant efforts": Jackson to Monroe, September 17, 1814, *CAJ*, 2:50.

241 "This country is strong by nature . . . we individually feel": New Orleans committee of safety to Jackson, September 18, 1814, *CAJ*, 2:51–54.

241 "Through a mistaken policy . . . of your countrymen": Jackson to the Free Coloured Inhabitants of Louisiana, September 21, 1814, *CAJ*, 2:58–59.

242 "They think that in putting arms . . . would prove dangerous": Claiborne to Jackson, October 17, 1814, *CAJ*, 2:76–77.

242 "It is in every sense an enemy's port": Jackson to Claiborne, October 17, 1814, *CAJ*, 2:75.

242 "I trust shortly . . . to our cause": Jackson to Rachel Jackson, October 21, 1814, *CAJ*, 2:78–79.

243 "As I act without the orders": Jackson to Monroe, October 26, 1814, *PAJ*, 3:173.

244 "I come not as the enemy of Spain . . . and Indian warriors": Jackson to González Manrique, November 6, 1814, *CAJ*, 2:92.

244 "I am at a loss, sir": Jackson to González Manrique, November 6, 1814, *CAJ*, 2:93.

244 "My duty does not permit me": González Manrique to Jackson, November 7, 1814, *CAJ*, 2:94. Also González Manrique to Jackson, November 6, 1814, *CAJ*, 2:93.

244 "begged for mercy": Jackson to Monroe, November 14, 1814, *CAJ*, 2:97.

245 "A tremendous explosion was heard": Ibid., 98.

245 "I had the satisfaction": Ibid., 99.

245 "He means well for his country": Franklin to Robert Livingston, July 22, 1785, in Franklin, 1065.

245 "dislike of all parties and all men": Jefferson to James Madison, quoted in McCullough, 318.

246 "eighty-eight one hundreds of an inch": Brookhiser, 66.

246 "pimping to the popular passions": Ibid., 67.

247 "Ghent looks clean and cheerful . . . by getting drunk": Entries for July 7 and 15 and August 21, 1814, Gallatin, 27.

247 "man of much irritation . . . better than yourself ": Adams to Louisa Adams, December 16, 1814, J. Q. Adams, *Writings of John Quincy Adams*, 5:237.

247 "They sit after dinner and drink bad wine": Diary entry for July 8, 1814, J. Q. Adams, *Memoirs*, 2:656.

247 "Mr. Adams is in a very bad temper . . . to keep peace": Entries for July 15, August 10, and October 29, 1814, Gallatin, 27–32.

248 "Our negotiations may be considered at an end": A. Gallatin to Monroe, August 20, 1814, quoted in entry for August 20, 1814, Gallatin, *Diary*, 29.

20. PIRATES AND PATRIOTS

249 "Louisiana is a delightful country": Windship to William Plumer, November 1, 1813, Windship, "Letters from Lousiana," 571.

249 "The War of the U.S. is very unpopular": Windship to Plumer, March 20, 1814, ibid., 574.

250 "Our political parties differ entirely": Windship to Plumer, November 1, 1813, ibid., 571.

250 "The most enlightened men of this country . . . 50 cents per head": Windship to Plumer, April 2, 1814, ibid., 575.

251 "They fondly recur to the despotism . . . fear this event": Windship to Plumer, July 7, 1814, ibid., 578–79.

251 "Indolence is common with us . . . we are not Americans": Windship to Plumer, June 15, 1814, ibid., 576–77.

252 "So weak is the Executive": Windship to Plumer, April 2, 1814, ibid., 575–76.

254 "The quantity of goods brought in by the banditti": Walker Gilbert to Thomas Freeman, February 18, 1814, in Arthur, 34.

254 "Natives of Louisiana! . . . a certain protection": Nichols to residents of Louisiana and Kentucky, in Parton, 1:578.

254 "You may be a useful assistant . . . honorable intentions": Nichols to Laffite, ibid., 584.

254 "I call on you . . . the British constitution": Nichols to Laffite, ibid., 584; William Percy to the inhabitants of Barataria, ibid., 585.

256 "I offer to you to restore . . . to be proscribed": Laffite to Claiborne, ibid., 588.

259 "The Major General commanding . . . dealt with accordingly": Jackson to New Orleans citizens and soldiers, December 15, 1814, *PAJ*, 3:204–05.

260 "Major General Andrew Jackson . . . held for examination": General order, December 16, 1814, *PAJ*, 3:206–07.

261 "They are the oppressors . . . dearer than all": Jackson address to troops, December 18, 1814, *CAJ*, 2:118–19.

261 "*Soldiers!* . . . to great deeds": Jackson to black troops, December 18, 1814, *CAJ*, 2:119.

262 "The lakes in complete possession of the enemy": Jackson to James Winchester, December 16, 1814, *PAJ*, 3:208.

21. Day of Deliverance

263 "It is scarcely possible . . . effect his escape": Gleig, 142–49.

265 "Perfectly convinced of the importance . . . if not into consternation": Jackson to Monroe, February 13, 1815, *CAJ*, 2:167–68.

266 "It may not be altogether": Coffee to wife, no date given, excerpted in Buell, 1:357–58.

266 "Say to them not to be alarmed": Jackson quoted in Reid and Eaton, 287.

267 "As the Americans had never yet dared . . . had confessedly been taken": Gleig, 159.

268 "The result equaled my expectations . . . prosecute his own": Jackson to Monroe, February 13, 1815, *CAJ*, 2:168.

268 "I feel no objection": Wellington quoted in Hickey, 295.

268 "In you I have the greatest confidence": Wellington to Gallatin, no date given, excerpted in entry for December 12, 1814, Gallatin, 35.

269 "The terms of this instrument . . . I think no honor": Clay to Monroe, December 25, 1814, *Papers of Clay*, 1:1007.

269 "I told him I hoped . . . of my country": Entry for December 24, 1814, J. Q. Adams, *Memoirs*, 3:126–27.

269 "The British delegates very civilly asked us . . . I feel much older": Entries for December 25 and 27, 1814, Gallatin, 35–36.

270 A rumor began circulating . . . move toward surrender: Reid and Eaton, 318–21.

271 "This was the turning point . . . 106 Royal Street": Laffite, 58–59.

272 "Of the American army nothing whatever": Gleig, 165.

272 "Nothing was kept a secret": Unidentified British officer quoted in Reid and Eaton, 319.

272 "By the 25th . . . with incredible labour": Forrest, 33–35.

272 "Pakenham might not be the brightest" . . . commission as governor of Louisiana: Introduction by Rankin to Forrest, 9.

273 "The distance rendered her fire": Ibid., 33.

273 "The enemy opened a very brisk fire . . . grace their brows": Latour, 96.

274 "Yesterday the enemy opened . . . able to judge": Jackson to Monroe, January 2, 1815, *CAJ*, 2:130.

275 "For two whole nights and days . . . the 6th of January": Gleig, 167–76.

277 "infinite labor": Jackson to Monroe, January 9, 1815, *CAJ*, 2:136.

278 "In the afternoon of the 7th . . . re-establishing his batteries": Latour, 107–08.

279 "The dawn of day . . . after the first": Ibid., 107–09.

280 "Being opposed by overwhelming numbers . . . so much as revenge": Gleig, 179.

281 "And now, for the second time . . . of their comrades": Latour, 108–09.

281 "Sir Edward saw how things were going . . . his aide-de-camp": Gleig, 179.

281 "A great number of officers . . . of the day": Latour, 109.

282 "Riding through the ranks . . . of the fugitives": Gleig, 179–80.

282 "Prompted by curiosity . . . fourteen men wounded": Ibid., 182.

283 "The whole plain on the left . . . killed and wounded": Latour, 111. British officers reported their losses as totaling a bit more than two thousand (Remini, *Battle of New Orleans*, 167).

22. THE SECOND WASHINGTON

285 "Is there a Federalist": Boston *Gazette*, no date given, quoted in Parton, 2:242.

285 "Appearances justify the expectation": *National Intelligencer*, no date given, ibid., 244.

285 "Louisiana is still American . . . for the English": Louise Livingston to her sister, January 12, 1815, Hunt, 59–61.

286 "strange and difficult to account for . . . thus hastily quitted": Jackson to Monroe, January 9, 1815, *CAJ*, 2:137–38.

287 "Hail to the chief!": Unidentified poet, in Reid and Eaton, 369.

287 "As soon as their defeat reaches Ghent": Jackson to Winchester, January 19, 1815, *PAJ*, 3:252.

288 "I produced my books . . . Good morning, sir": Nolte, 233–34.

290 "abuse of authority": *Louisiana Courier*, March 3, 1815, in Parton, 2:309.

290 "I have thought proper": Jackson to Hall, March 11, 1815, *CAJ*, 2:189.

290 "The commanding general . . . be immediately discharged": Jackson proclamation, March 13, 1815, *PAJ*, 3:310.

290 "Whenever the invaluable rights . . . of my country": Jackson to Jean Baptiste Plauché et al., March 16, 1815, *PAJ*, 3:312–14.

291 "Under these circumstances": Jackson quoted in Reid and Eaton, 387.

292 "I received your letter by express . . . so much in my life": Rachel Jackson to Jackson, February 10, 1814, *PAJ*, 3:28.

292 "I have this moment received . . . three sweet kisses": Jackson to Rachel Jackson, February 21, 1814, *PAJ*, 3:34.

292 "Tell him I have": Jackson to Rachel Jackson, April 1, 1814, *PAJ*, 3:55.

293 "May God preserve them from accident": Jackson to Robert Hays, February 4, 1815, *CAJ*, 2:157.

293 "After supper we were treated": Nolte, 238–39.

294 "My friends and many citizens . . . by your permission": Joseph Delaplaine to Jackson, March 25, 1815, *CAJ*, 2:196–97.

294 "I think it very proper": Jackson recommendation, date not given, Heiskell, 2:77.

295 "I have had a serious attack of dysentery": Jackson to Hays, February 17, 1815, *PAJ*, 3:281.

296 A study conducted in the late twentieth century: Deppisch, 569–71.

296 They probably did less systemic harm: Ibid. Remini (*Jackson and Course of American Freedom*, 1–3) is among the historians and biographers who seem to have overstated the damage done by Jackson's medications.

298 "Go, full of honour . . . an admiring world": Jackson to troops, March 21, 1815, *CAJ*, 2:195–96.

298 "He is every where hailed": Reid to Sophia Reid, April 20, 1815, Reid papers.

298 "In New Orleans there was two public dinners": Jackson to John Coffee, April 24, 1815, *PAJ*, 3:348.

298 "The sons of America": Jackson speech at the Hermitage, in Parton, 2:330–31.

23. EAST BY SOUTHWEST

300 "The Revolution was effected before the war commenced": Adams to H. Niles, February 13, 1818, John Adams, *Works of John Adams*, 10:282.

301 "General, you are the man": Livingston quoted in Hunt, 52.

302 "My health is not restored": Jackson to Livingston, July 5, 1815, *PAJ*, 3:370.

302 "manifest a just respect": Dallas to Madison, May 20, 1815, Madison papers.

303 "The case of military necessity": Dallas to Jackson, July 1, 1815, *CAJ*, 2:212–13.

303 "I expect to set out thither": Jackson to Dallas, September 5, 1815, *PAJ*, 3:384.

304 "Honor and gratitude . . . secretary of war": toasts quoted in Parton, 2:334.

304 "having traveled all day . . . can't be long": Reid to Elizabeth Reid, November 18, 1815, *PAJ*, 3:391–92.

305 "Judge Washington was not at home": Reid memorandum, November 1815 (no day given), *CAJ*, 2:219.

305 "I had the pleasure of seeing . . . fatiguing to them": Jackson to Robert Butler, December 31, 1815, *CAJ*, 2:223.

306 "The *wonderful revolution* in France . . . with Great Britain?": Jackson to Edward Livingston, May 17, 1815, *PAJ*, 3:357.

307 "well-armed, clothed, and disciplined . . . peace of the nation": Crawford to Jackson, March 15, 1816, *CAJ*, 2:236–37.

308 "The growing hostile dispositions . . . it stands on": Jackson to Gaines, April 8, 1816, *CAJ*, 2:238–39.

308 "The conduct of this banditti": Jackson to Zuñiga, April 23, 1816, *CAJ*, 2:241–42.

308 "If the object was sufficiently important": Ferdinand Amelung to Jackson, June 4, 1816, *CAJ*, 2:242–43.

309 "You will, upon the application . . . by military force": Crawford to Jackson, January 27, 1816, *CAJ*, 2:227–28.

310 "The line must be run . . . as early as possible": Jackson to Coffee, February 13, 1816, *CAJ*, 2:231–32.

310 "Why the government should feel . . . with the settlers": Jackson to Crawford, June 10, 1816, *CAJ*, 2:244–45.

311 "Candour to the Government": Jackson to Crawford, June 13, 1816, *CAJ*, 2:248.

24. PARTY AND POLITICS

313 "A congressional caucus will . . . success is inevitable": Burr to Alston, November 20, 1815, Burr, *Memoirs*, 2:433–35.

314 "I fully coincide with you": Alston to Burr, February 16, 1816, ibid., 2:437.

314 "If all influence but the native Indian": Jackson to Butler, September 5, 1816, *CAJ*, 2:259.

315 "We experienced some difficulty . . . a strong population": Jackson to Monroe, October 23, 1816, *CAJ*, 2:261–62.

315 "He is a man . . . a true American": Jackson to Monroe, October 23, 1816, *CAJ*, 2:261–62.

316 "In every selection . . . our common country": Jackson to Monroe, November 12, 1816, *CAJ*, 2:265.

316 "The chief magistrate . . . it may be done": Monroe to Jackson, December 14, 1816, *CAJ*, 2:266–68.

317 "Names are but bubbles . . . was unjustly ascribed": Jackson to Monroe, January 6, 1817, *CAJ*, 2:272–73.

318 "My mind was immediately fixed . . . for improper purposes": Monroe to Jackson, March 1, 1817, *CAJ*, 2:276–77.

318 "the best selection . . . Department of War": Jackson to Monroe, March 18, 1817, *CAJ*, 2:282–83.

319 "Short sighted politicians . . . holding treaties with them": Jackson to Monroe, March 4, 1817, *CAJ*, 2:277–81.

321 "*Then we will have peace*": Jackson to Monroe, March 18, 1817, *CAJ*, 2:282–83.

25. JUDGE AND EXECUTIONER

322 "Your order . . . will be accomplished": Jackson to Monroe, January 6, 1818, *CAJ*, 2:345–46.

324 "I well remember . . . any other person": Monroe to Calhoun, May 19, 1830, *Papers of Calhoun*, 11:165.

324 "In accordance with the advice . . . of its suggestions": Jackson "Exposition," unpublished pamphlet, 1831, in Benton, *Thirty Years' View*, 1:170.

324 "General Jackson and Mr. Rhea": Ibid., 178–79.

324 And in fact Jackson's letter book: *CAJ*, 2:346n4.

326 "You have murdered many . . . or my lands": Gaines-Hatchy colloquy quoted in Parton, 2:427–28.

327 "With this force": Jackson to Calhoun, January 12, 1818, *CAJ*, 2:347.

327 "The excessive rains": Jackson to Calhoun, February 26, 1818, *American State Papers: Military Affairs*, 1:698.

328 "The creek swamp was so bad . . . women and children": McIntosh to Jackson, March 16, 1818, Jackson papers, Library of Congress, and Parton, 2:446–47.

328 "It is all important": Jackson to Isaac McKeever, no date given, Parton, 2:447–48.

328 "They maintained for a short period . . . crowned with scalps": Jackson to Calhoun, April 8, 1818, *CAJ*, 2:358.

329 "not as the enemy": Jackson to Francisco Caso y Luengo, April 6, 1818, Parton, 2:451.

329 "I may fairly say . . . hung this morning": Jackson to Rachel Jackson, April 8, 1818, *CAJ*, 2:357–58.

329 "Tomorrow I shall march": Jackson to Calhoun, April 8, 1818, *CAJ*, 2:359.

329 "They were in a bad swamp . . . head of cattle": McIntosh to William Mitchell, no date given, quoted in Parton, 2:459.

330 "Here I should have halted . . . for the present": Jackson to Calhoun, April 20, 1818, *CAJ*, 2:361–62.

331 "The Commanding General orders": Jackson order, April 29, 1818, *American State Papers: Military Affairs*, 1:734. Parton has the fullest account of the trial of Arbuthnot and Ambrister (2:463ff.).

26. THE EYE OF THE STORM

335 "There is a chain of communication": Jackson division order, April 22, 1817, *PAJ*, 4:113–14.

335 "The War Office gentry . . . on your guard": Anonymous to Jackson, August 14, 1817, *PAJ*, 4:134.

336 "I have not permitted myself": Jackson to Scott, September 8, 1817, *CAJ*, 2:325.

336 "If the Captain obeys": Scott to Jackson, October 4, 1817, *PAJ*, 4:142–43.

336 "with the designs of an assassin . . . to number yourself": Jackson to Scott, December 3, 1817, *PAJ*, 4:157–58.

336 "It is my earnest desire . . . our free government": Monroe to Jackson, October 5, 1817, *PAJ*, 4:148.

337 "There are serious difficulties": Monroe to Madison, July 10, 1818, *Writings of Monroe*, 6:54.

337 "This is justifiable": Jackson to José Masot, May 23, 1818, *PAJ*, 4:208.

337 "I am informed that you have orders": Jackson to Luis Piernas, May 24, 1818, *PAJ*, 4:210.

337 "Resistance would be a wanton sacrifice": Jackson to Masot, May 25, 1818, *PAJ*, 4:211.

338 "Mr. Calhoun is extremely dissatisfied": Diary entry for July 13, 1818, J. Q. Adams, *Memoirs*, 4:107.

338 "Calhoun says he has heard . . . in the speculation": Diary entry for July 21, 1818, ibid., 113.

339 "The opinion is unanimously against Jackson": Entries for July 15 and 16, 1818, ibid., 108–09.

339 "The Eighth of January shall be remembered": Clay address to House, January 29, 1816, *Papers of Clay*, 2:148.

339 "We are fighting . . . avoid their errors": Clay address, January 20, 1819, ibid., 646, 650, 658–59.

340 "to dismiss them with impunity . . . urgent and indispensable": Adams to Gallatin, November 30, 1818, *Writings of John Quincy Adams*, 6:513.

340 "I have destroyed the Babylon . . . women and children": Jackson to Rachel Jackson, June 2, 1818, *PAJ*, 4:212.

340 "absolutely necessary to put down the Indian war . . . never yield it": Jackson to Monroe, June 2, 1818, *PAJ*, 4:213–15.

340 "Had General Jackson": Monroe to Madison, February 7, 1819, Madison Papers.

340 "If the executive refused to evacuate": Monroe to Jackson, July 19, 1818, *PAJ*, 4:225–26.

341 "the theatre of every lawless adventure . . . great measure derelict": Monroe annual message to Congress, November 16, 1818, *Annals of Congress*, 15th Congress, 2nd session, Senate, 12.

27. CONQUISTADOR

343 "The years of 1819 and '20 . . . state and federal": Benton, *Thirty Years' View*, 1:5–6.

345 "It is, sir . . . a small college": Curtis, 170.

346 "Let the end be legitimate . . . on the states": Marshall opinion for the majority in *McCulloch v. Maryland*, Hall, 537.

346 "Times are dreadful here": Jackson to James Gadsden, August 1, 1818, *PAJ*, 4:307.

346 "Eastern paper is not to be obtained": Jackson to Andrew Jackson Donelson, September 17, 1819, *PAJ*, 4:322.

347 "I reached Nashville . . . side and breast": Jackson to Donelson, July 14, 1818, *PAJ*, 4:222.

347 "My health is bad": Jackson to Shelby, August 11, 1818, *PAJ*, 4:235.

347 "I was taken very ill . . . under another campaign": Jackson to Donelson, September 17, 1819, *PAJ*, 4:322–23.

347 "I have never believed that Spain . . . a good appetite": Jackson to George Gibson, September 7, 1819, *PAJ*, 4:318.

348 "Does Congress believe . . . in six months": Jackson to George Gibson, February 1, 1820, *PAJ*, 4:356.

348 "My dear nephew . . . to instant death": Jackson to Donelson, December 28, 1818, *PAJ*, 4:262–63.

349 "In prosecuting the business . . . I kill him": Jackson to Call, September 9, 1819, *PAJ*, 4:319–20.

350 "I am not insensible . . . interpose no barrier": Jackson to Monroe, November 15, 1818, *PAJ*, 4:247.

351 "The combination formed . . . politically damned": Jackson to William Lewis, January 30, 1819, *PAJ*, 4:268–69.

351 "The insidious Mr. Clay": Jackson to Rachel Jackson, February 6, 1819, *PAJ*, 4:271.

351 "What poor minded bitches": Blount to Jackson, April 18, 1819, *PAJ*, 4:285.

351 "I am happy to be informed": Jackson to Clark, July 13, 1819, *CAJ*, 2:420.

352 "Having laboured from my youth": Jackson to John Clark, January 6, 1820, *PAJ*, 4:349.

352 "*Like Lucifer*": Ibid.

354 "If you persist . . . let it come!": Tallmadge and Cobb, February 16, 1819, in *Annals of Congress*, 15th Congress, 2nd session, House, 1203–04.

354 "No man is more sensible": Clay to J. Sloane, August 12, 1823, in Remini, *Clay*, 180.

355 "firebell in the night": Jefferson to John Holmes, April 22, 1820, *Selected Writings of Jefferson*, 698.

356 "Pensacola is a perfect plain . . . one hundred feet": Rachel Jackson to Eliza Kingsley, July 23, 1821, in Parton, 2:603–06.

357 "Yesterday I received possession . . . of my days": Jackson to Coffee, July 18, 1821, *CAJ*, 3:105.

359 "It is further ordered": Jackson to Robert Butler and James Bronaugh, August 22, 1821, *PAJ*, 5:95.

359 "Colonel Callava repeatedly asserted": From the official report by Butler and Bronaugh, no date given, in Parton, 2:624.

359 "A party of troops": Callava's account, ibid., 626.

359 "The Governor, Don Andrew Jackson": Unnamed Spanish officer, ibid., 630–31.

360 "pompous arrogance and ignorance": Jackson to John Quincy Adams, August 26, 1821, *CAJ*, 3:115.

360 "Rising to his feet . . . before God himself": Unnamed Spanish officer, Parton, 2:631–32.

360 "indignation and contempt": Jackson to Fromentin, September 3, 1821, *PAJ*, 5:100.

360 "The first time the authority . . . to the stake": Fromentin narrative, no date given, Parton, 2:636.

THE PEOPLE'S PRESIDENT (1821–1837)

28. CINCINNATUS

363 "Our place looks like it had been deserted": Jackson to Richard Call, November 15, 1821, *PAJ*, 5:116.

364 "I am truly wearied . . . my declining years": Jackson to Monroe, November 14, 1821, *CAJ*, 3:129.

364 "For four months . . . quantities of phlegm": Jackson to Gadsden, May 2, 1822, *CAJ*, 3:161.

364 "My health is not good": Jackson to Monroe, July 26, 1822, *CAJ*, 3:171–72.

364 "The state of our paper money": Jackson to Gadsden, May 2, 1822, *CAJ*, 3:161.

364 "I remitted you two hundred dollars . . . within my means": Jackson to Andrew Donelson, August 28, 1822, *CAJ*, 3:178.

365 "The very best selections . . . 6 to 8 cents": McCoy & Co. to Jackson, December 13, 1822, *CAJ*, 3:180–81.

365 But in 1825 . . . he planted 131 acres and harvested 71 bales: Arthur Hayne to Jackson, January 14, 1826, *PAJ*, 6:131n.

365 "Tom, wife, and nine children . . . Big Sampson, wife, and child": Inventory of slaves, January 1, 1825, *CAJ*, 3:271.

366 "If he has left the neighborhood . . . then good treatment": Jackson to Harris, April 13, 1822, *PAJ*, 5:170.

366 As it happened, Jackson didn't sell Gilbert: See Jackson's slave inventory, January 1, 1825, *CAJ*, 3:271; note 2 to Jackson to Harris, April 13, 1822, *PAJ*, 5:170–71.

366 "I regret the drought with you . . . the continued rains": Jackson to Coffee, August 22, 1823, *CAJ*, 3:204.

366 "I had sat down to write you . . . has been very bad": Jackson to Coffee, May 24, 1823, *CAJ*, 3:197.

367 "Although I have ever considered . . . in excellent order": Statement by Willie Blount, undated, *CAJ*, 3:226–27n.

367 "The subject of the next President . . . and unsettled politician": Gadsden to Jackson, November 20, 1821, *CAJ*, 3:132–33.

371 "As to William Crawford": Jackson to Gadsden, December 6, 1821, *CAJ*, 3:141.

371 "I believe the welfare of our country": Jackson to Bronaugh, May 29, 1822, *CAJ*, 3:163.

372 "I have always believed . . . or Mr. Adams": Jackson to Gibson, January 29, 1822, *PAJ*, 5:139.

372 "It appears to be the general opinion . . . likewise the North": Bronaugh to Jackson, December 30, 1821, *PAJ*, 5:125.

373 "I am silent . . . to that call": Jackson to Call, June 29, 1822, *PAJ*, 5:199.

373 "On this day a resolution . . . feel and act": Houston to Jackson, August 3, 1822, *Writings of Houston*, 1:13–14.

374 "a noble minded fellow": Jackson to Gadsden, May 2, 1822, *CAJ*, 3:162.

374 "I have received many letters . . . make it perpetual": Jackson to Andrew Donelson, August 6, 1822, *CAJ*, 3:173–74.

375 "My undeviating rule of conduct . . . power of selection": Jackson to H. W. Peterson, February 23, 1823, *PAJ*, 5:253.

29. THE DEATH RATTLE OF THE OLD REGIME

377 "office should be neither sought for nor declined": Abram Maury to Jackson, September 20, 1823, *PAJ*, 5:298.

377 "There are many better qualified . . . could not decline": Jackson to Maury, September 21, 1823, *PAJ*, 5:298–99.

377 "Thus you see me a Senator": Jackson to Calhoun (the letter actually has no addressee, but Calhoun seems the likeliest recipient), October 4, 1823, *PAJ*, 5:301.

377 "Although tiresome and troublesome . . . in this world": Jackson to Rachel Jackson, November 28, 1823, *PAJ*, 5:320.

378 "The President takes a proper ground": Jackson to Overton, December 5, 1823, *PAJ*, 5:321.

378 "There is nothing done here . . . instead of diminishing": Jackson to Rachel Jackson, December 7, 1823, *CAJ*, 3:216.

378 "We are in the family . . . in the music": Jackson to Rachel Jackson, December 21, 1823, *CAJ*, 3:218.

379 "General Scott and myself . . . has greatly changed": Jackson to George Martin, January 2, 1824, *CAJ*, 3:222.

379 "All things here appear . . . to follow them": Jackson to Coffee, February 15, 1824, *PAJ*, 5:357.

380 "You ask my opinion on the tariff . . . a little more *Americanized*": Jackson to L. H. Coleman, April 26, 1824, *CAJ*, 3:249–50.

381 "There must have been a thousand people there": Senator Mills quoted in *CAJ*, 3:220n3.

381 "The family we live in . . . your affectionate husband": Jackson to Rachel Jackson, March 27, 1824, *CAJ*, 3:240–41.

381 "I declare to you . . . my own cottage": Jackson to Henry Baldwin, May 20, 1824, *PAJ*, 5:411–12.

382 "I have fine prospects of cotton": Jackson to Coffee, June 18, 1824, *CAJ*, 3:257.

382 "the last hope of the friends . . . forward by it": Jackson to Andrew Donelson, January 21, 1824, *CAJ*, 3:225.

382 "I am happy to see the good people": Jackson to Coffee, March 28, 1824, *CAJ*, 3:242.

382 "Was I to notice the falsehoods . . . is the people": Jackson to Wilson, August 13, 1824, *PAJ*, 5:434.

383 "To tell you of this city . . . the Marquis, twenty-three": Rachel Jackson to Elizabeth Kingsley, December 23, 1824, *PAJ*, 5:456.

384 "To say I have nothing . . . was against it": Jackson to Swartout, December 14, 1824, *CAJ*, 3:269.

385 "The Lord's will be done": Jackson to John Coffee, December 27, 1824, *CAJ*, 3:270.

385 "The President's Administration was toasted . . . never before experienced": Entry for January 1, 1825, J. Q. Adams, *Memoirs*, 6:457–58.

385 "Two of my friends in the Legislature": Clay to Francis Brooke, December 22, 1824, *Papers of Clay*, 3:900.

386 "*Accident* alone prevented my return": Clay to James Brown, January 23, 1825, ibid., 4:38.

386 "You are a looker-on . . . lies before us": Clay to Benjamin Leigh, December 22, 1824, ibid., 3:901.

386 "Mr. Clay came at six . . . would be for me": Entry for January 9, 1825, J. Q. Adams, *Memoirs*, 6:464–65.

387 "I consider whatever choice . . . support Mr. Adams": Clay to Blair, January 8, 1825, *Papers of Clay*, 4:9–10.

387 "I can tell you nothing . . . to be made": Clay to James Brown, January 23, 1825, ibid., 39.

387 "Mr. Adams, you know well": Clay to Blair, January 29, 1825, ibid., 47.

387 "As a friend of liberty": Clay to Brooke, January 28, 1825, ibid., 45–46.

387 "I perceive that I am unconsciously writing": Clay to Blair, January 29, 1825, ibid., 47.

388 "member of the House of Representatives . . . the Republican ranks": Letter to the editor, Philadelphia *Columbian Observer*, January 28, 1825, excerpted in *PAJ*, 6:24.

388 "I pronounce the member": Clay notice in Washington *Daily National Intelligencer*, January 31, 1825, *Papers of Clay*, 4:48.

388 "May the blessing of God . . . placid and courteous": Entry for February 9, 1825, J. Q. Adams, *Memoirs*, 6:501–02.

388 "The old man goes quietly on": Eaton to John Overton, February 7, 1825, *PAJ*, 6:28.

388 "The *Judas* of the West": Jackson to William Lewis, February 14, 1825, *CAJ*, 3:276.

30. DEMOCRACY TRIUMPHANT

389 "It is for an ingenuity stronger than mine . . . a 'military chieftain' ": Jackson to Swartout, February 22, 1825, *CAJ*, 3:278–80. Published in *New York National Advocate*, March 4, 1825, and many other papers.

391 "I have not in my life . . . our country arrives": Houston to Jackson, January 1827 (no day given), *CAJ*, 3:329; Houston to Jackson, January 5, 1827, ibid., 331.

391 "I must entreat to be excused": Jackson to Tennessee legislature, October 12, 1825, *CAJ*, 3:295.

391 "the variety of dear little interests . . . increased by it": Rachel Jackson to Katherine Duane Morgan, May 18, 1825, *PAJ*, 6:72.

394 "the combination, unheard of till then": Randolph in Senate, March 30, 1826, *Register of Debates*, 19th Congress, 1st session, Senate, 401.

394 "The House was a perfect scene . . . Puritans and Blacklegs": Marable to Jackson, April 3, 1826, *PAJ*, 6:161.

395 "I do not fire at you . . . is no greater": Benton, *Thirty Years' View*, 1:76–77.

395 "Randolph loses no opportunity . . . mighty volume on": Eaton to Jackson, May 5, 1826, *PAJ*, 6:169–70.

396 "As soon as I arrived . . . of our countrymen": Lee to Jackson, July 1, 1826, *CAJ*, 3:305–06.

396 "What a wonderful coincidence . . . the virtuous Jefferson?": Jackson to Richard Call, July 26, 1826, *PAJ*, 6:191.

397 "an evidence that the Republic . . . for the Presidency": Jefferson quoted in *Niles' Register*, December 29, 1827, in *PAJ*, 6:341.

397 "negro *speculation*": *National Banner and Nashville Whig*, August 2, 1828, quoted in *PAJ*, 6:486.

398 "The act was as cruel as uncalled for . . . The deadly deed is done!": "Coffin Handbill," October 18, 1828, *CAJ*, 3:455–61. The most thorough account of the whole affair is Parton, 2:277–300. According to Parton, the court and Jackson were correct in asserting that the militiamen had agreed to serve for six months but the order from Governor Blount specifying the six-month term was invalid.

400 "COOL AND DELIBERATE MURDER": Parton, 3:144.

400 "Truth is mighty, and will prevail": Jackson to Grundy, August 15, 1828, *PAJ*, 6:495.

401 "*dirty, black wench!*": Frankfort *Argus*, April 18, 1827, quoting Frankfort *Commentator*, in *PAJ*, 6:344n2.

401 "such feelings of indignation": Jackson to Lewis, December 12, 1826, *CAJ*, 3:323.

401 "When the midnight assassin strikes you": Jackson to Keene, June 16, 1827, *PAJ*, 6:344.

401 "It is evident . . . their just reward": Jackson to Call, May 3, 1827, *CAJ*, 3:354.

402 "The political news from all quarters . . . test the result": Jackson to Call, October 18, 1828, *PAJ*, 6:515–16.

402 "The suffrages of a virtuous people": Jackson to Coffee, November 24, 1828, *CAJ*, 3:447.

403 "Still, my mind is depressed . . . more fully shortly": Ibid.

403 "Providence has procured for us . . . of the fowler": Jackson to Coffee, December 11, 1828, *CAJ*, 3:452.

403 "Picture to yourself a military-looking man . . . devotion to him": Unidentified correspondent of the author in Parton, 3:160–62.

404 "I could have spent . . . fix our destiny": Rachel Jackson to Louise Livingston, December 1, 1828, *PAJ*, 6:536.

405 "Hitherto my Saviour": Rachel Jackson to Mrs. L. A. W. Douglas, December 3, 1828, *PAJ*, 6:538.

405 "excruciating pain": Jackson to Francis Preston, December 18, 1828, *PAJ*, 6:546.

405 "I cannot leave her": Jackson to Richard Call, December 22, 1828, *PAJ*, 6:546.

405 A friend recalled . . . "twenty years older in a night": Parton, 3:163–64.

405 "Could I but withdraw . . . happiness here below": Jackson to John Donelson, June 7, 1829, *CAJ*, 4:42.

31. DEMOCRACY RAMPANT

407 "General Jackson will be here": Webster memorandum, February 1829 (no day indicated), *Letters of Webster*, 142.

407 "We have a dead calm": Calhoun to Patrick Noble, January 10, 1829, *Papers of Calhoun*, 10:550.

407 "Our inimitable capital . . . deference to fashion!": "A Few Days at Washington," *Philadelphia Monthly Magazine*, April 1829, 419–21.

408 "No one who was at Washington . . . defiance on its brow": Parton, 3:169.

409 "the mighty Xerxes ferried or marched": "A Few Days at Washington," *Philadelphia Monthly Magazine*, April 1829, 410–11.

409 He sat down directly: "The Inauguration," *National Intelligencer*, March 5, 1829, reprinted in *Saturday Evening Post*, March 14, 1829, 2.

410 "free choice of the people . . . a foreign foe": Inaugural address, *United States Telegraph*, March 4, 1829, reprinted in *Saturday Evening Post*, March 14, 1829, 2.

410 "Had the spectacle closed here": M. Smith to Mrs. Kirkpatrick, March 11, 1829, M. Smith, 291.

411 "It was grand . . . to the President's house": Ibid., 290–91, 294.

412 "Streams of people on foot . . . out of windows": Ibid., 294–96.

412 "It was a glorious day . . . for the penitentiary": Hamilton to Martin Van Buren, March 5, 1829, Van Buren papers, Library of Congress.

412 "noise and tumult . . . as soon as possible": Story to Mrs. Story, March 7, 1829, *Letters of Story*, 1:562–63.

413 "It was the People's day": M. Smith, 296.

32. SPOILS OF VICTORY

416 "Why, Major . . . bring me here?": Jackson quoted in Parton, 3:180.

416 "Great exertions have been made . . . department of war well": Jackson to Coffee, March 19, 1829, *CAJ*, 4:13–14.

417 "We lament to see so many . . . election of General Jackson": Ritchie to Martin Van Buren, March 27, 1829, *CAJ*, 4:17–18n1.

417 "You may assure Mr. Ritchie . . . and upon *principle*": Jackson to Van Buren, March 31, 1829, *CAJ*, 4:19.

418 "There are, perhaps, few men . . . by their experience": Jackson message to Congress, December 8, 1829, *Compilation of Messages and Papers*, 1011–12.

418 "My husband, sir . . . an inhospitable wild": Mary Barney to Jackson, June 13, 1829, *CAJ*, 4:46–47.

419 "You can have no idea": Mrs. F. Pope to Jackson, May 30, 1829, *CAJ*, 4:40.

419 "It is a painful duty": Jackson to Mrs. F. Pope, June 8, 1829, *CAJ*, 4:42–43.

419 "The gloom of suspicion . . . he had offended": Mr. Stansbury quoted in Parton, 3:212–13.

419 "I question whether the ferreting": unidentified correspondent in Parton, 3:213.

420 "cleanse the Augean stables": Jackson to Coffee, May 30, 1829, *CAJ*, 4:39.

420 "I have been crowded with thousands . . . go away dissatisfied": Jackson to Coffee, March 22, 1829, *CAJ*, 4:14.

420 The best estimate is that between one-tenth and one-fifth . . . Jefferson defeated John Adams: Eriksson, 529, 540.

420 "It may be, sir . . . belongs the spoils": Marcy quoted in Parton, 3:378.

33. TOOLS OF WICKEDNESS

423 "It was a matter of infinite satisfaction . . . to be pursued": Eaton to Jackson, December 7, 1828, *PAJ*, 6:541.

423 "Mrs. Eaton is as chaste . . . *baser lie told*": Jackson to John McLemore, April 1829 (no day given), *CAJ*, 4:20–21.

423 "most unblushing and unfounded slanders": Jackson to Coffee, May 30, 1829, *CAJ*, 4:38.

423 "I would sink with honor": Jackson to McLemore, May 3, 1829, *CAJ*, 4:31.

424 "ridiculous attitude . . . in their own": Jackson to Call, July 5, 1829, *CAJ*, 4:52–53.

424 "I did not come here to make a cabinet": Jackson to McLemore, April 1829 (no day given), *CAJ*, 4:21.

425 "I have found the President affectionate . . . entertain for me": Van Buren to Jesse Hoyt, c. April 1829, in Parton, 3:292.

425 "I have found him every thing . . . I ever saw": Jackson to Overton, December 31, 1829, *CAJ*, 4:108–09.

426 "That my nephew and niece . . . mortifying to me": Jackson to Lewis, July 28, 1830, *CAJ*, 4:167.

426 "I never knew any thing but disgrace": Jackson to Andrew Donelson, May 5, 1831, *CAJ*, 4:277.

426 "He is wholly wrong . . . to bear irritation": McLemore to Andrew Donelson, November 10, 1830, *CAJ*, 4:197n2.

426 "I have this moment heard": Ibid.

427 "overwhelmed by sudden calamities": Houston to William Hall, April 16, 1829, *Writings of Houston*, 1:131.

428 "Tho' an unfortunate . . . most profound veneration!": Houston to Jackson, May 11, 1829, ibid., 132–33.

428 "His conduct has filled me . . . am truly distressed": Jackson to Coffee, July 21, 1829, *CAJ*, 4:54–55.

429 "I pray you, my son . . . dismiss him": Jackson to Andrew Jackson Jr., July 4, 1829, *CAJ*, 4:49–50.

429 "He has been reared in the paths of virtue . . . steadily in them": Jackson to Francis Smith, May 19, 1829, *CAJ*, 4:36.

429 "My son, having your happiness . . . answer at once": Jackson to Andrew Jackson Jr., July 26, 1829, *CAJ*, 4:56–57.

430 "You have many years yet . . . my grave in sorrow": Jackson to Andrew Jackson Jr., August 20, 1829, *CAJ*, 4:63.

34. JACKSONIAN THEORY

432 "With Great Britain . . . our free institutions": Jackson's annual message to Congress, December 8, 1829, *Compilation of Messages and Papers*, 3:1005–25.

437 "Were we in the place of Isaac Hill . . . and your peer'": New York *Courier and Enquirer*, no date given, in Parton, 3:276.

438 "Were it not for the fear": Webster to Dutton, May 9, 1830, Parton, 3: 276–77.

35. FALSE COLORS

440 "It is true that the third . . . the General Government": South Carolina Exposition, December 19, 1828, *Papers of Calhoun*, 10:445, 457–59, 493, 497, 507.

441 "The next two or three years": Calhoun to Patrick Noble, January 10, 1829, ibid., 550.

441 "Sir, let me tell that gentleman . . . the bitter fruit": Hayne speech, January 25, 1830, *Register of Debates*, 21st Congress, 1st session, Senate, 46–50.

443 "It is to the Union that we owe . . . one and inseparable!": Webster's reply to Hayne, January 26–27, 1830, ibid., 80.

444 "It is come to this": Maxcy to Calhoun, April 6, 1829, *Papers of Calhoun*, 11:17.

445 "There was a full assemblage . . . Jefferson its father": Benton, *Thirty Years' View*, 1:148.

445 "that the celebration was to be . . . into the fire": Lewis quoted in Parton, 3:284.

445 "But the company was still numerous . . . burden of the Union": Benton, *Thirty Years' View*, 1:148.

447 "The submission, you will perceive . . . to your consideration": Jackson to Calhoun, May 13, 1830, *Papers of Calhoun*, 11:159–60.

447 "I cannot repress the expression . . . leisure may permit": Calhoun to Jackson, May 13, 1830, ibid., 162–63.

447 "However high my respect . . . my country only": Calhoun to Jackson, May 29, 1830, ibid., 173, 187, 189.

448 "It must be admitted to be": Ingham to Jackson, November 27, 1829, *CAJ*, 4:93–94.

448 "Whenever that subject": Berrien to Jackson, November 27, 1829, *CAJ*, 4:95.

448 "The combination and coalition believed . . . presidents at will": Jackson to Donelson, May 5, 1831, *CAJ*, 4:277.

448 "How little do they know me": Jackson to Coffee, April 24, 1831, *CAJ*, 4:269.

449 "I have changed my cabinet . . . What a contrast!!": Jackson to Coffee, May 13, 1831, *CAJ*, 4:281.

450 "The first intimation I have received . . . religion are incompatible": Jackson to William Conway, April 4, 1831, *CAJ*, 4:256.

451 "Whilst I concur with the synod . . . their own consideration": Jackson to the Synod of the Reformed Church, June 12, 1832, *CAJ*, 4:447.

451 "His whole physical system . . . a confirmed dropsy": Lewis attachment (from some indefinite later time) to Jackson to John Overton, December 31, 1829, *CAJ*, 4:109.

452 "I cannot yet determine . . . clear and fine": Jackson to Andrew Donelson, August 22, 1829, *CAJ*, 4:66.

452 "white Valencia vest . . . Virginia drawers": Statements from Tucker & Thompson, January 3 and December 22, 1831, *CAJ*, 4:221, 388.

453 "This year, with the bad season . . . part with her": Jackson to Chester, November 7, 1830, *CAJ*, 4:198–99.

453 "Have your hogs put up early . . . average 200 round": Jackson to Andrew Jackson Jr., October 21, 1832, *CAJ*, 4:482–83.

453 "Knowing the merit of his blood . . . and turf horse": Jackson to Cryer, January 10, 1830, *CAJ*, 4:117.

454 "I was truly mortified . . . gallop on it": Jackson to Andrew Jackson Jr., May 13, 1832, *CAJ*, 4:438.

36. ATTACK AND COUNTERATTACK

456 "The majority is always right": Undated entry, Tocqueville, *Journey*, 58–59.

456 "Several men came . . . new privileges": Entry for November 3, 1831, ibid., 82–84.

457 "I can believe that you find it difficult . . . not over its principles": Entry for November 18, 1831, ibid., 87–88.

457 "The Federalists, feeling themselves defeated . . . like everything else": Tocqueville, *Democracy*, 176–78.

458 "the violence of party . . . intercourse of society": Biddle to Monroe, July 6, 1807, *Correspondence of Biddle*, 3–4.

458 "The Bank is of vital importance . . . encounter much hostility": Biddle to Monroe, January 31, 1819, ibid., 12.

459 "talent for business . . . to be collected": Biddle to unidentified recipient (evidently another director), October 29, 1822, ibid., 26–28.

459 "I have been so anxious": Biddle to Webster, February 16, 1826, ibid., 39.

460 "There is no one principle . . . only a bank": Biddle to Samuel Smith, December 29, 1828, ibid., 62–63.

460 "They should be treated": Biddle to Alexander Hamilton, December 12, 1829, ibid., 91.

460 "I think it right . . . afraid of banks": Memorandum by Biddle, undated (between October 1829 and January 1830), ibid., 93.

460 "As such it is far less dangerous": Biddle to Smith, January 2, 1830, ibid., 94.

461 "What would he do with it? . . . United States hereafter?": Clay to Biddle, September 11, 1830, *Papers of Clay*, 8:263–64.

462 "inexpedient to apply at present": Biddle to Clay, November 3, 1830, *Correspondence of Biddle*, 115.

462 Jackson's annual message of December 1830: Second annual message, December 6, 1830, *Compilation of Messages and Papers*, 3:1091–92.

462 "In respect of General Jackson . . . than they are": Biddle to Mr. Robinson, December 20, 1830, *Correspondence of Biddle*, 122.

462 "It is obvious that a great effort . . . might be misconstrued": Biddle to William Lawrence, February 8, 1831, ibid., 123–24.

462 "The President is now perfectly confident . . . dared to do it": Biddle memorandum, October 19, 1831, ibid., 131.

463 "Have you come to any decision . . . would be different": Clay to Biddle, December 15, 1831, *Papers of Clay*, 8:432–33.

463 "great and beneficent institution": Statement by National Republican convention, no date given, Parton, 3:395.

463 "The result of all these conversations . . . for the bank": Webster to Biddle, December 18, 1831, *Correspondence of Biddle*, 145–46.

463 "We have determined on applying . . . of a great country": Biddle to Smith, January 4, 1832, ibid., 161–64.

464 "I cannot but think . . . success next session": Webster to Biddle, January 8, 1832, ibid., 169.

464 "Mr. Adams told me": John Connell to Biddle, January 10, 1832, ibid., 169–70.

464 "The present is a crisis": Biddle to Charles Ingersoll, February 6, 1832, ibid., 174.

464 "We set to work to disenchant the country": Biddle to Ingersoll, February 11, 1832, ibid., 179–80. Though Biddle was writing to a friend, he crossed out these remarks before sending the letter. They remained legible, though.

464 "If the bill passes": ibid., 181.

465 "I believe my retainer . . . the usual retainers": Webster to Biddle, December 21, 1833, ibid., 218.

465 "A disordered currency is one . . . a guinea again' ": Webster speech to Senate, no date given, excerpted in Benton, *Thirty Years' View*, 1:244.

466 "They lead to the *abduction* . . . come of himself!": Benton speech to Senate, January 20, 1832, *Register of Debates*, 22nd Congress, 1st session, Senate, 139–41.

468 "Now I do not mean to say": Taney quoted in Schlesinger, 87n.

468 "A bank of the United States . . . an unqualified blessing": Jackson veto message to Congress, July 10, 1832, *Compilation of Messages and Papers*, 3:1139, 1143–47, 1153.

37. OR DIE WITH THE UNION

472 Henry Clay called the veto a vestige: Clay speech to Senate, no date given, Benton, *Thirty Years' View*, 1:255.

472 "fearful and appalling aspect . . . poor against the rich": Webster speech to Senate, July 11, 1832, *Register of Debates*, 22nd Congress, 1st session, Senate, 1240.

473 "A more deranging, radical . . . but little further": Portland, Maine, *Daily Advertiser*, reprinted in Washington *National Intelligencer*, August 9, 1832, in Taylor, 33.

473 *Niles' Register* reported: *Niles' Register*, no date given, excerpted in Benton, 1:281.

473 "wantonly trampled upon . . . national calamity": Resolutions adopted by Philadelphia public meeting, July 16, 1832, *Niles' Register*, July 21, 1832, in Taylor, 30–32.

473 "It diffuses universal joy": Randolph to Jackson, July 15, 1832, *CAJ*, 4:462.

473 "The veto works well . . . of prostrating me": Jackson to Lewis, August 18, 1832, *CAJ*, 4:467.

473 "It was nearly a mile long . . . or nine groans": M. Chevalier in Parton, 3:424–25.

475 "inconsistent with the longer continuance": South Carolina ordinance of nullification, November 24, 1832, quoted in Freehling, 263.

475 "The impression on the minds . . . of the Union": Poinsett to Jackson, October 16, 1832, *CAJ*, 4:481–82.

476 "They are to defend them to the last extremity": Jackson to Cass, October 29, 1832, *CAJ*, 4:483.

476 "You will observe . . . surrounds the forts": Jackson to Breathitt, November 7, 1832, *CAJ*, 4:484–85.

476 "many violent Nullifiers . . . blood is shed": Poinsett to Jackson, November 16, 1832, *CAJ*, 4:486–87.

477 "In forty days . . . will be preserved": Jackson to Poinsett, December 9, 1832, *CAJ*, 4:498.

477 "We must be prepared to act . . . eighteen pounders": Jackson to Cass, December 17, 1832, *CAJ*, 4:502–03.

477 "Can any one of common sense . . . with the Union": Jackson to Coffee, December 14, 1832, *CAJ*, 4:499–500.

478 "my native State . . . must be executed": Jackson proclamation, December 10, 1832, *Compilation of Messages and Papers*, 3:1203–04, 1215–18.

478 "extraordinary defiance . . . devolved upon me": Jackson special message to Congress, January 16, 1833, ibid., 3:1174, 1180, 1183–84, 1194.

479 "The only cause of wonder . . . has to apprehend": Calhoun speech to Senate, January 16, 1833, *Papers of Calhoun*, 12:11–15. This speech was reported in the *Register of Debates* and in various newspapers. Different versions have slightly different wordings. Here some of Calhoun's remarks that were reported in the past tense (in the fashion of news accounts) but are otherwise verbatim have been restored to the present tense in which they were delivered.

480 "Mr. Calhoun let off a little of his ire . . . demolish the monster": Jackson to Poinsett, January 16, 1833, *CAJ*, 5:5–6.

480 "They know that I will execute . . . of his troops": Jackson to Poinsett, January 24, 1833, *CAJ*, 5:11–12.

481 "Yes, I have . . . I can reach": William Lewis quoting Jackson in Parton, 3:284–85.

481 "Until some act of force is committed . . . to suppress it": Jackson to Poinsett, February 7, 1833, *CAJ*, 5:14–15.

481 "the preservation of the rights . . . never can be maintained": Jackson's second inaugural address, March 4, 1833, *Compilation of Messages and Papers*, 3:1222–24.

38. JUSTICE MARSHALL FOR THE DEFENSE

484 "the steam cars": Jackson to Andrew Jackson Jr., June 6, 1833, *CAJ*, 5:107.

484 "And then—what a scene! . . . eluded the mob": Washington *National Intelligencer*, June 20, 1833, quoted in Green, 215.

484 "A ludicrous scene ensued": Ibid., 216.

485 "Now, Doctor . . . other is tobacco": Jackson quoted by Nicholas Trist, no date given, in Parton, 3:489.

485 "From the moment of landing": Hone, 1:96.

485 "I have witnessed enthusiasms before . . . I am sure": Jackson to Andrew Jackson Jr., June 14, 1833, *CAJ*, 5:109.

486 "The President must hasten back to Washington . . . other fifth mere fatigue": Entries for June 25 and 27, 1833, J. Q. Adams, *Memoirs*, 9:4–5.

486 "I *could not* be present": Adams to Quincy, no date given, in Nagel, 343.

486 "much captivated by the ease . . . reach Washington again": Entry for June 27, 1833, J. Q. Adams, *Memoirs*, 9:5.

487 "E pluribus unum": Moore, 433.

487 "I can not do that . . . a thing again": Jackson quoted without date in Parton, 3:488.

488 "domestic dependent nation": *Cherokee Nation v. State of Georgia*, 30 U.S. 1 (1831).

488 "The acts of Georgia are repugnant": *Worcester v. State of Georgia*, 31 U.S. 515 (1832).

489 "Their example will induce . . . utter annihilation": Jackson annual message, December 6, 1830, *Compilation of Messages and Papers*, 3:1082–86.

491 "Being more and more convinced . . . live may prescribe": Jackson to Senate and House of Representatives, February 15, 1832, ibid., 1128–29.

491 "I am happy to inform you . . . their immediate acceptance": Jackson annual message, December 4, 1832, ibid., 1167.

493 "John Marshall has made his decision": Greeley quoted in Garrison, 193.

39. WEALTH VERSUS COMMONWEALTH

495 "They will not *dare* to remove them . . . cannot be recalled": Biddle to Webster, April 8, 1833, *Correspondence of Biddle*, 202.

495 "I am informed by a gentleman . . . a sound currency": Hamilton to Jackson, February 28, 1833, *CAJ*, 5:22–23.

496 "hydra of corruption": Jackson to Hardy Cryer, April 7, 1833, *CAJ*, 5:53.

496 "Can any impartial and unprejudiced mind . . . and decisive measures": Taney to Jackson, March 1833 (no day given), *CAJ*, 5:37–41.

497 "If this apprehension . . . be forever enslaved": Jackson to Duane, June 26, 1833, *CAJ*, 5:122.

497 "Most of the banks there": Kendall to Jackson, August 2, 1833, *CAJ*, 5:146.

497 "Some of the banks . . . or *no removal*": Kendall to Jackson, August 25, 1833, *CAJ*, 5:169–70.

498 "The divine right of kings . . . enabled to issue": Jackson message to cabinet, September 18, 1833, *CAJ*, 5:192–203, and *Compilation of Messages and Papers*, 3:1224–38. The former version is Jackson's draft and captures more of his language; the latter is the revision by Taney, which was the version published.

498 "In half an hour": Biddle to J. S. Barbour, April 16, 1833, *Correspondence of Biddle*, 207–08.

499 "nest of gamblers": Biddle to Thomas Cooper, July 31, 1833, ibid., 214.

499 "It is dreadful here . . . Bank are perishing": Swartout to Biddle, November 23, 1833, ibid., 217–18.

499 "absolutely frightful": Boston *Courier*, January 20, 1834, in Catterall, 326.

499 "My own view of the matter . . . inevitably be prostrated": Biddle to William Appleton, January 27, 1834, *Correspondence of Biddle*, 219.

500 "The whole future is full of gloom . . . shall not break": Biddle to John Watmough, February 8, 1834, ibid., 221.

500 "You may rely on it . . . to the country": Biddle to Joseph Hopkinson, February 21, 1834, ibid., 222.

500 "This worthy President thinks . . . lodgings in Arabia": Ibid.

500 "The Bank, Mr. Van Buren": Van Buren, *Autobiography*, 625.

500 "We have got the Bank in Baltimore . . . in six weeks": Jackson to Van Buren, October 5, 1833, *CAJ*, 5:216.

501 "Were all the worshippers": Jackson to Van Buren, January 3, 1834, *CAJ*, 5:238.

501 "My conscience told me . . . and my country": Jackson to Andrew Jackson Jr., October 11, 1833, *CAJ*, 5:217.

501 "There is no real general distress . . . were put down": Jackson to James Hamilton, February 2, 1834, *CAJ*, 5:244.

501 "Relief, sir! . . . you from breaking": *Niles' Register*, March 1, 1834, in Catterall, 351–52; unidentified informant to Parton, no date given, Parton, 3:549–50.

502 "Didn't I manage them well?": Ibid.

502 "The storm in Congress is still raging . . . *monster must perish*": Jackson to Andrew Jackson Jr., February 16, 1834, *CAJ*, 5:249.

502 "Nicholas Biddle now rules the Senate": Jackson to Edward Livingston, June 27, 1834, *CAJ*, 5:272.

502 "The clamour of pressure in the money market . . . end well here": Jackson to Swartout, March 15, 1834, *CAJ*, 5:255.

502 "After staggering along": Weed in Albany *Evening Journal*, November 15, 1834, in Catterall, 357.

503 "The explosion of the cap . . . great crowd between": Benton, *Thirty Years' View*, 1:521.

504 "He replied that it had been . . . Bank of the United States": Report by Dr. Caussin and Dr. Thomas Sewell, no date given, quoted in Benton, *Thirty Years' View*, 1:522–23.

505 "The circumstance made a deep impression . . . the President's heart": Benton, *Thirty Years' View*, 1:524.

40. AN OLD FRIEND AND A NEW FRONTIER

507 "It's not you they are after . . . has some privileges": Jackson quoted in Terrell, 126.

507 "So long as that flag shall bear aloft . . . of eternity's waves": Houston speech to House, May 7, 1832, *Writings of Houston*, 1:224.

507 "I was dying out . . . set me up again": James, *Raven*, 172.

507 "the greatest act of tyranny": Jackson to Anthony Butler, April 19, 1832, *CAJ*, 4:436.

508 "The people will inquire": Jackson to Andrew Jackson Jr., May 13, 1832, *CAJ*, 4:438.

508 yet he was able to remit the fine: Attachment to Houston to Jackson, April 20, 1834, *Writings of Houston*, 1:289.

509 "in addition to his many merits": Jackson to Bustamante, October 7, 1830, *CAJ*, 4:185.

509 "No contingency can authorise . . . as well as prudence": Jackson to Butler, March 23, 1830, *CAJ*, 4:129.

510 "the desert or grand prairie": Jackson to Butler, October 6, 1830, *CAJ*, 4:183.

510 "The grand prairie . . . best exertions": Jackson to Butler, October 7, 1830, *CAJ*, 4:184.

510 "I feel great anxiety . . . of both countries": Jackson to Butler, August 24, 1831, *CAJ*, 4:335.

511 "I cannot but think . . . in that quarter": Jackson to Butler, February 15, 1831, *CAJ*, 4:244–45.

511 "This is but a drop . . . of my remark": Butler to Jackson, February 27, 1832, *CAJ*, 4:413.

512 "The intimations you so appropriately gave . . . on foreign relations": Jackson to Butler, April 19, 1832, *CAJ*, 4:435.

512 "He still directs the Department of Foreign Affairs . . . contemplated secret article": Butler to Jackson, July 18, 1832, *CAJ*, 4:463–64.

513 "I still hope that General Santa Anna's patriotism": Jackson to Butler, October 1, 1833, *CAJ*, 5:213.

513 "a very singular conversation . . . shall not fail": Butler to Jackson, October 28, 1833, *CAJ*, 5:219.

513 "astonishment . . . from my intention": Jackson to Butler, November 27, 1833, *CAJ*, 5:228–29.

514 "Provided you keep within your instructions . . . *their public debt*": Jackson to Butler, October 30, 1833, *CAJ*, 5:222.

514 "I admonish you . . . on our part": Jackson to Butler, November 27, 1833, *CAJ*, 5:228–29.

514 "What you advise of being cautious . . . is more appropriate": Butler to Jackson, February 6, 1834, *CAJ*, 5:244–46.

515 "Ask nothing but what is right": Jackson to Livingston, June 27, 1834, *CAJ*, 5:272. Remini's *Andrew Jackson and the Course of American Democracy* has the fullest account of the French spoliations dispute (3:201ff.).

515 "Begin at the Gulf of Mexico": Jackson to Butler, September 4, 1832, *CAJ*, 4:472.

516 "I will succeed in uniting Texas to our country": Butler to Jackson, January 2, 1833, *CAJ*, 5:2.

516 "Keep within your instructions": Jackson to Butler, February 14, 1833, *CAJ*, 5:17.

516 "What a scamp": Jackson note in margin of Butler to Jackson, March 7, 1834, *CAJ*, 5:252.

516 "Should the present incumbents continue": Butler to Jackson, September 26, 1833, *CAJ*, 5:210.

516 "I must really have thought you deranged": Jackson to Houston, June 21, 1829, Jackson papers, Library of Congress.

517 Jackson apparently gave Houston five hundred dollars: Haley, 89.

517 "all the tribes of Indians . . . aid and protection": Houston passport, no date given, ibid., 90.

517 "It has been my first . . . way of St. Antone": Houston to Henry Ellsworth, December 1, 1832, *Writings of Houston*, 1:267–70.

517 "Nineteen twentieths . . . ten millions of souls": Houston to Jackson, February 13, 1833, ibid., 1:274–76.

519 "committee of vigilance and safety . . . of the country": Houston et al. to Jackson, September 11, 1835, ibid., 1:299–300.

519 "You have heard of the revolt in Texas . . . to do so": Butler to Jackson, c. November 1835, *CAJ*, 5:375–76.

520 "This country is in a perfect tempest . . . in ashes": Butler to Jackson, December 19, 1835, *CAJ*, 5:381.

521 "sanguinary manner in which . . . language requiring *force*": Gaines to Cass, March 29, 1836, *Papers of the Texas Revolution*, 5:231–33.

521 "It is not the wish of the President . . . by this Government": Cass to Gaines, April 25, 1836, ibid., 6:53–54.

522 "He will maintain": Carson to David Burnet, April 14, 1836, ibid., 5:469.

522 Houston kept his own counsel during the retreat: Houston's strategy is discussed at some length in Brands, *Lone Star Nation*, 423ff.

523 "a mysterious Providence . . . danger and ruin": Calhoun speech to Senate, January 27, 1837, *Register of Debates*, 24th Congress, 2nd session, Senate, 566.

524 "It is said that one . . . slavery and emancipation": Adams speech to House, May 25, 1836, *Register of Debates*, 24th Congress, 1st session, House, 4041–47.

524 "I have seen a report . . . and humanity dictates": Jackson to Houston, September 4, 1836, *CAJ*, 5:425.

525 "Let us establish mutual relations": Santa Anna to Jackson, July 4, 1836, *CAJ*, 5:411–12.

526 "Until the existing Government": Jackson to Santa Anna, September 4, 1836, *CAJ*, 5:425–26.

526 Jackson mentioned $3.5 million: Remini, *Jackson and the Course of American Democracy*, 365.

PATRIARCH OF DEMOCRACY (1837–1845)

41. THE HOME FRONT

530 "to tread generally in the footsteps": Van Buren quoted in *Albany Argus*, June 1835, in Niven, 397.

530 "they might go to hell": Brands, *Lone Star Nation*, 331.

530 "They are, like my own": Jackson to Van Buren, September 29, 1833, *CAJ*, 5:212–13.

531 "We have now lived almost fifty years . . . by the sword": Jackson address to the nation, March 4, 1837, *Compilation of Messages and Papers*, 4:1511–15.

532 "I was confined to my bed": Jackson to Emily Donelson, November 27, 1836, *CAJ*, 5:439.

532 "My strength is slowly recovering . . . a free man": Jackson to Maunsel White, January 27, 1837, *CAJ*, 5:455.

532 "From the time I left you . . . or from Washington": Jackson to Van Buren, March 22, 1837, *CAJ*, 5:465.

532 "I have been every where cheered . . . to the grave": Jackson to Van Buren, March 30, 1837, *CAJ*, 5:466.

532 "I find my blooded stock in bad order . . . the balance better": Jackson to Hutchings, April 4, 1837, *CAJ*, 5:474.

533 "I am out of funds . . . unjust sentence removed": Jackson to Donelson, December 10, 1839, *CAJ*, 6:41–42.

533 "No man has been more completely swindled": Jackson to Hutchings, August 12, 1840, *CAJ*, 6:71.

533 "This I well know . . . son or myself": Jackson to Hardy Cryer, February 5, 1840, *CAJ*, 6:49.

534 "If I live to realise it . . . so much love": Jackson to Andrew Jackson Jr., December 31, 1839, *CAJ*, 6:48.

534 "I have done my duty . . . it is lost": Jackson to Blair, April 24, 1837, *CAJ*, 5:478.

535 "Biddle is in the field . . . their corrupting influence": Jackson to Van Buren, August 7, 1837, *CAJ*, 5:506, 505.

535 "machinations and conspiracy . . . gall and wormwood": Jackson to Blair, November 29, 1837, *CAJ*, 5:520–21.

536 "The national policy": Jackson annual message to Congress, December 5, 1836, *Compilation of Messages and Papers*, 4:1475.

536 "The whole Florida war from the first": Jackson to James Gadsden, c. November 1836, *CAJ*, 5:434.

536 "The commanding general ought to find . . . at once surrender": Jackson to Poinsett, October 1, 1837, *CAJ*, 5:512.

537 "General Harrison, to shew his identity": Jackson to Charles Dancy and Thomas Murphy, July 3, 1840, *CAJ*, 6:67.

538 "Being sincerely with me in politics": Van Buren to Jackson, February 2, 1840, *CAJ*, 6:48.

538 "I have a letter today from Vermont . . . in the North": Blair to Jackson, September 10, 1840, *CAJ*, 6:75–76.

539 "the negro, or slavery, question": Jackson to Andrew Crawford, May 1, 1833, *CAJ*, 5:72.

539 "The attempt by their mummeries . . . people than this": Jackson to Blair, September 26, 1840, *CAJ*, 6:78.

540 "Corruption, bribery and fraud": Jackson to Van Buren, November 12, 1840, *CAJ*, 6:82.

540 "The democracy of the United States . . . great working class": Jackson to Van Buren, November 24, 1840, *CAJ*, 6:83–84.

42. TO THE RAMPARTS ONCE MORE

542 "Take as directed . . . to perfect health": Jackson to Andrew Hutchings, December 30, 1840, *CAJ*, 6:87–88.

542 "Should you meet with a rich Virginian . . . and has money": Jackson to Andrew Donelson, February 19, 1840, *CAJ*, 6:53.

542 "a beautiful dark bay . . . bright sorrel mare": Description of horses sold to F. Davis, no date given, *CAJ*, 6:111–12n1.

542 "You may assure him . . . to perfect freedom": Jackson to Lewis, August 19, 1841, *CAJ*, 6:119–20.

543 "At 12 o'clock last night . . . gave way at once": Blair to Jackson, April 4, 1841, *CAJ*, 6:97–98.

543 "powers and duties . . . on the Vice President": Section 1, article 2, United States Constitution.

543 "It will do Old Hickory's heart good . . . old Jackson's pens": Dabney Carr to Jackson, August 18, 1841, *CAJ*, 6:119.

544 "clique who has got into power": Jackson to Blair, April 19, 1841, *CAJ*, 6:105.

544 "I am happy to learn . . . to forgive divine": Jackson to Blair, August 12, 1841, *CAJ*, 6:118–19.

544 "I have no confidence in Mr. Calhoun": Jackson to Van Buren, November 22, 1842, *CAJ*, 6:177.

544 "He is the strongest man . . . president has attained": Jackson to Blair, November 22, 1842, *CAJ*, 6:178.

545 "To you, General . . . to all banks": Houston to Jackson, January 31, 1843, *Writings of Houston*, 3:313–14.

546 "she would seek some other friend": Houston to Jackson, February 16, 1844, ibid., 4:261–65.

546 "that arch enemy . . . to regain it": Jackson to Lewis, September 18, 1843, *CAJ*, 6:229–30.

546 "all important to the security . . . or all is lost": Jackson to Blair, March 5, 1844, *CAJ*, 6:272.

547 "I hope this golden moment . . . with Great Britain": Jackson to Lewis, March 11, 1844, *CAJ*, 6:272.

547 "I say, for one": Jackson to Blair, May 7, 1844, *CAJ*, 6:284; Jackson to Lewis, April 8, 1844, *CAJ*, 6:278.

547 "I am now suffering much . . . with great labour": Jackson to Lewis, April 8, 1844, *CAJ*, 6:278.

547 "My eyesight has failed me much . . . from that cause": Jackson to Van Buren, March 4, 1841, *CAJ*, 6:92–93.

547 "I have been brought low . . . for a time": Jackson to Kendall, June 18, 1842, *CAJ*, 6:159.

548 "as a memento of her uniform attention . . . affairs of late": Jackson will, June 7, 1843, *CAJ*, 6:221–22.

549 "the life-and-death struggle": Entry for December 21, 1843, J. Q. Adams, *Memoirs*, 11:455.

549 "My conscience presses me on . . . upon the breach": Entry for March 29, 1841, Adams diary, Adams papers.

549 "When Weller moved, yesterday": Entry for January 2, 1844, J. Q. Adams, *Memoirs*, 11:468.

549 "exploded with a volley": Entry for January 5, 1844, ibid., 475.

550 "bold, dashing, and utterly baseless . . . Think of your posterity!": Adams in Bemis, 474.

551 "If Mr. Van Buren had come out": Jackson to Blair, May 11, 1844, *CAJ*, 6:286.

551 "If Texas be not speedily admitted . . . against future danger": Jackson to *Nashville Union*, May 13, 1844, *CAJ*, 6:290–91.

551 "The dark sky of yesterday": Donelson to Jackson, May 29, 1844, *CAJ*, 6:296.

551 "The Texan question": Jackson to Blair, June 7, 1844, *CAJ*, 6:297.

551 "*Texas must and will be ours*": Jackson to William Russell, June 8, 1844, Jackson papers, Center for American History.

552 "Polk and Dallas are elected": Jackson to Donelson, November 18, 1844, *CAJ*, 6:329.

552 "The Union is sinking . . . prospect is deathlike": Entries for December 20, 1844, and February 19, 1845, J. Q. Adams, *Memoirs*, 12:128, 171.

43. THE SOUL OF THE REPUBLIC

557 "When I attempt to walk": Jackson to Polk, February 28, 1845, *CAJ*, 6:373.

557 "a great oppression": Jackson to Lewis, March 22, 1845, Jackson papers supplement.

557 "This may be the last letter": Jackson to Blair, March 9, 1845, *CAJ*, 6:378.

557 "Strange as it may appear": Jackson to Jesse Elliott, March 27, 1845, *CAJ*, 6:391.

557 "I am swollen": Jackson to Samuel Hays, May 27, 1845, Jackson papers supplement.

557 "Texas comes into the Union . . . not buy Sam Houston": Jackson to Polk, May 26, 1845, *CAJ*, 6:412.

558 "My son": As related to Marquis James by the elder Houston's daughter, James, *Raven*, 786.

560 "I have seen the patriots and statesmen": Houston statement to the people of Texas, March 16, 1861, *Writings of Houston*, 8:277.

560 "government of the people": Gettysburg Address, November 19, 1863, *American Historical Documents*, 415.

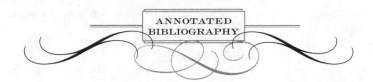

ANNOTATED
BIBLIOGRAPHY

The collections and works listed below include all those cited in the text and selected others the author has found especially useful.

MANUSCRIPTS

Adams Family. Papers. Massachusetts Historical Society, Boston. One of the great American historical collections, featuring (for the present purposes) the papers of John Quincy Adams.

Ayer, Edward E. Collection. Newberry Library, Chicago. Includes a small number of items dealing with Jackson's Indian affairs. Also correspondence between Jackson and William Blount.

Benton, Thomas Hart. Papers. Library of Congress. Writings of Jackson's aide, then foe, then ally.

Biddle, Nicholas. Papers. Library of Congress. Correspondence and other dispatches of the enemy commander in the bank war.

Butler, Anthony. Papers. Center for American History, University of Texas at Austin. The archconspirator regarding Texas.

Coffee, John. Papers. Tennessee State Library and Archives, Nashville. Jackson's trusted lieutenant and personal friend.

Donelson, Andrew Jackson. Papers. Library of Congress. Manuscripts of Jackson's nephew and personal secretary, showing Jackson at work and at home.

Horseshoe Bend Accounts. Alabama Department of Archives and History, Montgomery. Contemporary and recollected versions of the pivotal battle in the Creek War, drawn from various archives.

Houston, Sam. Papers. Center for American History, University of Texas at Austin. The protégé gone bad, then good.

Jackson, Andrew. Letters. Center for American History, University of Texas at Austin. A small collection.

———. Papers. Library of Congress. The foremost collection of Jackson manuscripts. Mainly on microfilm, but recent additions in manuscript and in some cases typescript.

———. Papers. Microform supplement edited by Harold D. Moser et al. Wilmington: Scholarly Resources, 1986. Compiled from many archives in the process of publishing *The Papers of Andrew Jackson* (see below).

———. Papers. Tennessee State Library and Archives, Nashville. Complements other collections.

Jefferson, Thomas. Papers. Library of Congress. The other patron saint, besides Jackson, of the Democratic party.

Madison, James. Papers. Library of Congress. The brilliant constitutionalist and problematic president.

Monroe, James. Papers. Library of Congress. Helpful but not definitive for determining what Jackson was and wasn't authorized to do in Florida.

Overton, John. Papers. Tennessee State Library and Archives, Nashville. Jackson's oldest Nashville friend.

Reid, John. Papers. Library of Congress. Includes letters to members of the family of Jackson's aide in the New Orleans campaign.

Sevier, John. Papers. Tennessee State Library and Archives, Nashville. Jackson's patron and then rival.

Van Buren, Martin. Papers. Library of Congress. The magician still at work: few secrets fully demystified.

———. Papers. Massachusetts Historical Society, Boston. A small collection but occasionally illuminating.

Whitcomb, Samuel. Papers. Massachusetts Historical Society, Boston. His diary describes an encounter with Jackson and Rachel at the Hermitage in 1818.

Published Papers, Letters, Memoirs, and Documents

Adams, Charles Francis. *The Diary of Charles Francis Adams*. Edited by Marc Friedlaender and L. H. Butterfield. Cambridge: Belknap Press of Harvard University Press, 1974. The son of John Quincy Adams reveals the father.

Adams, John. *The Works of John Adams*. Edited by Charles Francis Adams. 10 volumes. Boston: Little, Brown & Co., 1856.

Adams, John Quincy. *Memoirs of John Quincy Adams, Comprising Portions of His Diary from 1795 to 1848*. Edited by Charles Francis Adams. 12 volumes. Philadelphia: J. B. Lippincott, 1874–77. One of the great American diaries, mostly unexpurgated.

———. *Writings of John Quincy Adams*. Edited by Worthington Chauncey Ford. 7 volumes. New York: Macmillan, 1913–17.

American Historical Documents. Edited by Charles W. Eliot. New York: P. F. Collier & Son, 1938.

American State Papers: Documents, Legislative and Executive, of the Congress of the United States. Various series, years, and volumes.

Amherst, Jeffery. *The Journal of Jeffery Amherst: Recording the Military Career of General Amherst in America from 1758 to 1763*. Edited by J. Clarence Webster. Toronto: Ryerson Press, 1931. A soldier who mistakenly thought he deserved better.

Auchinleck, G. *A History of the War between Great Britain and the United States of America during the Years 1812, 1813, and 1814*. Toronto: Maclear & Co., 1855; reprinted London: Arms & Armour Press, 1972. Includes many contemporary documents among its Anglophilic opinions.

Benton, Thomas Hart. *Thirty Years' View: Or, A History of the Working of the American Government for Thirty Years, from 1820 to 1850*. 2 volumes. New York: D. Appleton & Co., 1854. Long-winded and partisan, but incomparably detailed.

Biddle, Nicholas. *The Correspondence of Nicholas Biddle*. Edited by Reginald C. McGrane. Boston: Houghton Mifflin, 1919. Edited for clarity and discretion yet still illuminating.

Blount, William. *The Blount Journal, 1790–1796*. Nashville: Tennessee Historical Commission, 1955. The elder Blount as governor of the Southwest Territory.

Burr, Aaron. *Memoirs of Aaron Burr, with Miscellaneous Selections from His Correspondence.* Edited by Matthew L. Davis. 2 volumes. 1837. New York: Da Capo, 1971. The memoirist is Davis, but the many letters are Burr's and his contemporaries'.

———. *Political Correspondence and Public Papers of Aaron Burr.* Edited by Mary-Jo Kline. 2 volumes. Princeton: Princeton University Press, 1983. The puzzle of the conspiracy remains.

Calhoun, John C. *The Papers of John C. Calhoun.* Edited by Robert L. Meriwether. 28 volumes to date. Columbia: University of South Carolina Press, 1959–. An acute mind that grew narrower as it grew sharper.

Claiborne, W. C. C. *Official Letter Books of W. C. C. Claiborne, 1801–1816.* Edited by Dunbar Rowland. 6 volumes. Jackson, Miss.: State Departments of Archives and History, 1917. Life in the old Southwest.

Clay, Henry. *The Papers of Henry Clay.* Edited by James F. Hopkins et al. 11 volumes. Lexington: University Press of Kentucky, 1959–92. The man who tried harder than any other to be president and still fell short.

Compilation of the Messages and Papers of the Presidents. Edited by James D. Richardson. 20 volumes. New York: Bureau of National Literature, 1897. The Old Testament of presidential pronouncements.

Crockett, David. *A Narrative of the Life of David Crockett of the State of Tennessee.* 1834. Facsimile edition edited by James A. Shackford and Stanley J. Folmsbee. Knoxville: University of Tennessee Press, 1973. The great storyteller's own story; to be treated like most of his stories.

Diplomatic Correspondence of the Republic of Texas. Edited by George P. Garrison. 3 volumes. Washington: Government Printing Office, 1908–11. How Jackson came to recognize Texas, and how Texas joined the Union.

Eaton, Margaret. *The Autobiography of Peggy Eaton.* New York: Charles Scribner's Sons, 1932. Told many years after the fact and published many years after the telling; it shows its age.

The Federalist: A Commentary on the Constitution of the United States. By Alexander Hamilton, John Jay, and James Madison. Edited by Edward Mead Earle. New York: Modern Library, no date given (based on the 1938 edition). The ur-text of American constitutional criticism.

Fisher, Sidney George. "The Diaries of Sidney George Fisher, 1841–1843." *Pennsylvania Magazine of History and Biography* 79 (1955): 217–36. Life in Nicholas Biddle's Philadelphia.

Forrest, C. R. *The Battle of New Orleans: A British View. The Journal of Major C. R. Forrest.* Edited by Hugh F. Rankin. New Orleans: Hauser Press, 1961. From across the lines on the plain of Chalmette.

Franklin, Benjamin. *Writings.* Edited by J. A. Leo Lemay. New York: Library of America, 1987. The best one-volume version of the works of the famous polymath.

Gallatin, James. *The Diary of James Gallatin.* Edited by Count Gallatin. 1914; New York: Charles Scribner's Sons, 1926. An inner history of the Treaty of Ghent.

[Gleig, George Robert.] *The Campaigns of the British Army at Washington and New Orleans in the Years 1814–1815.* London: John Murray, 1847. The most instructive and compelling British account of the Battle of New Orleans.

Hamilton, Alexander. *The Papers of Alexander Hamilton.* Edited by Harold C. Syrett. 27 volumes. New York: Columbia University Press, 1961–87.

Hamilton, Thomas. *Men and Manners in America.* 1833; New York: Augustus M. Kelley, 1968. An English traveler in Jacksonian America.

Harrison, William Henry. *Messages and Letters of William Henry Harrison.* Edited by Logan Esarey.

2 volumes. Indianapolis: Indiana Historical Commission, 1922. Reprinted New York: Arno Press, 1975. The hero of Ohio in his own eyes and words. An essential source on Tecumseh.

Hone, Philip. *The Diary of Philip Hone*. Edited by Allan Nevins. New York: Dodd, Mead & Co., 1936. One of the great diaries in American history.

Houston, Sam. *The Autobiography of Sam Houston*. Edited by Donald Day and Harry Herbert Ullom. Norman: University of Oklahoma Press, 1954. Houston's own words, but gathered from various sources by the editors.

———. *Life of General Sam Houston: A Short Autobiography*. 1855; Austin: Pemberton Press, 1964. Very short and reflective of its origins as campaign literature written while Houston was weighing a run for president (of the United States).

———. *The Writings of Sam Houston*. Edited by Amelia W. Williams and Eugene C. Barker. 8 volumes. Austin: University of Texas Press, 1938–43. The best published version of Houston.

Hunt, Louise Livingston. *Memoir of Mrs. Edward Livingston, with Letters Hitherto Unpublished*. New York: Harper & Brothers, 1886. Includes an account of the Battle of New Orleans from the perspective of a well-placed civilian.

Jackson, Andrew. *Correspondence of Andrew Jackson*. Edited by John Spencer Bassett. 7 volumes. Washington: Carnegie Institution, 1926–35. The first full-scale published collection of Jackson's papers. Still very valuable, especially for the last third of Jackson's life. Abbreviated in the notes as *CAJ*.

———. *The Papers of Andrew Jackson*. Edited by Sam B. Smith and Harriet Chappell Owsley. 6 volumes to date. Knoxville: University of Tennessee Press, 1980–. More scholarly than Bassett but still far from completion. The calendar of papers at the end of each volume is an invaluable guide to the archival collections from which this edition draws. Abbreviated in the notes as *PAJ*.

Jefferson, Thomas. *The Life and Selected Writings of Thomas Jefferson*. Edited by Adrienne Koch and William Peden. New York: Modern Library, 1944. An excellent one-volume version.

"Journal of the Trip Down the Mississippi." Author unidentified, but probably Robert Searcy. In *CAJ*, 1:256–71. The voyage of the Tennesseans from Nashville to Natchez in January and February 1813.

Kendall, Amos. *Autobiography of Amos Kendall*. Edited by William Stickney. Boston: Lee & Shepard, 1872. Not so much a traditional autobiography as a compilation of letters, journal entries, and other writings by Kendall.

Laffite, Jean. *The Journal of Jean Laffite*. New York: Vantage Press, 1958. Probably authentic, although the provenance is sketchy. Written from memory years after the fact.

Latour, Arsène Lacarrière. *Historical Memoir of the War in West Florida and Louisiana in 1814–15*. Edited by Gene A. Smith. 1816; Gainesville: Historic New Orleans Collection and University Press of Florida, 1999. The Battle of New Orleans as told by Jackson's French engineer.

Madison, James. *The Papers of James Madison*. Edited by William T. Hutchinson and William M. E. Rachal. 17 volumes. Chicago: University of Chicago Press, and Charlottesville: University Press of Virginia, 1962–91.

———. *Letters and Other Writings of James Madison*. 4 volumes. Philadelphia: J. B. Lippincott, 1865. An early edition, by order of Congress.

Mercer, William Newton. "From Louisville to New Orleans in 1816: Diary of William Newton Mercer." Edited by Edwin Adams Davis and John C. L. Andreassen. *Journal of Southern*

History 2 (1936): 390–402. A steamboat ride, with groundings, explosions, and other quotidian excitements.

Monroe, James. *The Writings of James Monroe.* Edited by Stanislaus Murray Hamilton. 7 volumes. New York: G. P. Putnam's Sons, 1898–1903. Hardly comprehensive but illuminating.

Nolte, Vincent. *The Memoirs of Vincent Nolte: Reminiscences in the Period of Anthony Adverse, or Fifty Years in Both Hemispheres.* 1854; New York: G. Howard Watt, 1934. The adventures of an adventurer.

The Papers of the Texas Revolution, 1835–1836. Edited by John H. Jenkins. 10 volumes. Austin: Presidial Press, 1973. Imperfect but invaluable for students of Texas history. Illuminating for others.

Quincy, Josiah. *Figures of the Past from the Leaves of Old Journals.* Boston: Roberts Brothers, 1892. The title page identifies the author as "Class of 1821, Harvard College." Enough said.

Santa Anna, Antonio López de. *The Eagle: The Autobiography of Santa Anna.* Edited by Ann Fears Crawford. Austin: Pemberton Press, 1967. Not very good but still irreplaceable.

Sargent, Nathan. *Public Men and Events from the Commencement of Mr. Monroe's Administration, in 1817, to the Close of Mr. Fillmore's Administration, in 1853.* 2 volumes. Philadelphia: J. B. Lippincott, 1875. "Oliver Oldschool" drops the nom and writes under his own.

[Shepherd, William R.] "Papers Bearing on James Wilkinson's Relations with Spain, 1787–1816. *American Historical Review* 9 (1904): 748–66. Helpful.

Smith, Margaret Bayard [Mrs. Samuel Harrison Smith]. *The First Forty Years of Washington Society.* Edited by Gaillard Hunt. New York: Charles Scribner's Sons, 1906. Gossip, yes, but shrewd and often insightful.

Story, Joseph. *Life and Letters of Joseph Story.* Edited by W. W. Story. 2 volumes. Boston: C. C. Little & J. Brown, 1851. Fascinating view of Washington and the Supreme Court during the first half of the nineteenth century.

Stuart, James. *Three Years in North America.* 2 volumes. Edinburgh: Robert Cadell, 1833. A Scotsman tours the former colonies.

Timberlake, Henry. *Memoirs, 1756–1765.* Edited by Samuel Cole Williams. Marietta, Ga.: Continental Book Co., 1948. Travels among the Cherokees in time of war.

Tocqueville, Alexis de. *Democracy in America.* Edited by J. P. Mayer. Translated by George Lawrence. New York: Harper & Row, 1966; New York: HarperPerennial, 1988. The most famous analysis of Jacksonian America.

———. *Journey to America.* Edited by J. P. Mayer. Translated by George Lawrence. London: Faber & Faber, 1959. The journal that provided the basis for the above.

United States Congress. *American State Papers.* Various series and years.

———. *Annals of Congress (The Debates and Proceedings in the Congress of the United States).* Washington: Gales & Seaton, various years. Far from a verbatim account but the best that exists for the period in question.

———. *Register of Debates.* Various series and years. Successor to the previous.

———. *Congressional Globe.* Ditto.

Van Buren, Martin. *The Autobiography of Martin Van Buren.* Edited by John C. Fitzpatrick. Washington: Government Printing Office, 1920. Incomplete and never printed during Van Buren's lifetime but revealing of the Jackson years.

Webster, Daniel. *The Letters of Daniel Webster.* Edited by C. H. Van Tyne. New York: McClure,

Phillips & Co., 1902. Mostly from the archives of the New Hampshire Historical Society. Shows the fully human side of the "godlike Daniel."

———. *The Papers of Daniel Webster*. Edited by Charles M. Wiltse. 5 volumes. Hanover, N.H.: University Press of New England for Dartmouth College, 1974–83.

———. *Reminiscences and Anecdotes of Daniel Webster*. Gathered and edited by Peter Harvey. Boston: Little, Brown, & Co., 1901. Mostly anecdotes.

Wikoff, Henry. *The Reminiscences of an Idler*. New York: Fords, Howard & Hulbert, 1880. One who observed Jackson and much else.

Wilkinson, James. "Papers Bearing on James Wilkinson's Relations with Spain, 1787–1816." *American Historical Review* 9 (1904): 748–66. Consisting mostly of Wilkinson's second memorial to the Spanish government, regarding his hopes for Kentucky and Louisiana.

Williams, John S. *History of the Invasion and Capture of Washington and of the Events Which Preceded and Followed*. New York: Harper & Brothers, 1857. By one of the defenders, who contends that they weren't as hapless as they seemed.

Windship, John. "Letters from Louisiana, 1813–1814." Edited by Everett S. Brown. *Mississippi Valley Historical Review* 11 (March 1925): 570–79. Life in New Orleans.

Woodward, Thomas S. *Reminiscences of the Creek, or Muscogee, Indians*. Tuscaloosa: Alabama Book Store, 1939.

SECONDARY WORKS

Abernethy, Thomas Perkins. *The Burr Conspiracy*. New York: Oxford University Press, 1954. Untangles the web of intrigue; only a small knot of uncertainty remains.

Adams, Henry. *History of the United States during the Administrations of Thomas Jefferson*. Edited by Earl N. Harbert. New York: Library of America, 1986. An abridgment of Adams's master historical work.

Anderson, Fred. *Crucible of War: The Seven Years' War and the Fate of Empire in British North America, 1754–1766*. New York: Alfred A. Knopf, 2000. A masterly account, at once detailed and sweeping.

Aptheker, Herbert. *Abolitionism: A Revolutionary Movement*. Boston: Twayne, 1989. An introduction to the movement that Jackson neither appreciated nor fully understood.

Arthur, Stanley Clisby. *Jean Laffite, Gentleman Rover*. New Orleans: Harmanson, 1952. The title conveys the tone, but the book includes useful letters and other primary documents.

Auchinleck, G[ilbert]. *A History of the War between Great Britain and the United States of America during the Years 1812, 1813 & 1814*. 1855; London: Arms & Armour Press, 1972. By a Briton who considered the war ended with the signing of the Treaty of Ghent in December 1814 and who thereby spared himself having to write about Jackson's victory at New Orleans.

Barber, James G. *Andrew Jackson: A Portrait Study*. Seattle: University of Washington Press, for National Portrait Gallery and Tennessee State Museum, 1991. The changing face of the hero.

Barker, Eugene C. "President Jackson and the Texas Revolution." *American Historical Review* 12 (1907): 788–809. Absolves Jackson of conniving in the illegitimate overthrow of Mexican authority.

Bartlett, Richard A. *The New Country: A Social History of the American Frontier, 1776–1890*. New York: Oxford University Press, 1974. Includes material on those unruly Scotch-Irish.

Bass, Robert D. *The Green Dragoon: The Lives of Banastre Tarleton and Mary Robinson.* New York: Henry Holt, 1957. The most hated man in America.

Bassett, John Spencer. *The Life of Andrew Jackson.* New York: Macmillan, 1931. This two-volumes-in-one version is a solid life by the editor of the most important completed edition of Jackson's papers.

Bemis, Samuel Flagg. *John Quincy Adams and the Union.* New York: Alfred A. Knopf, 1965. The best account of Adams's diplomacy, and very good on the rest of his career.

Boucher, Chauncey Samuel. *The Nullification Controversy in South Carolina.* Chicago: University of Chicago Press, 1916. Especially solid on Palmetto politics.

Brands, H. W. *The First American: The Life and Times of Benjamin Franklin.* New York: Doubleday, 2000. The worldly founder.

———. *Lone Star Nation: How a Ragged Army of Volunteers Won the Battle for Texas Independence and Changed America.* New York: Doubleday, 2003. What Houston—and many others—wrought.

———. *What America Owes the World: The Struggle for the Soul of Foreign Policy.* New York: Cambridge University Press, 1998. Varieties of exceptionalism.

Brookhiser, Richard. *America's First Dynasty: The Adamses, 1735–1918.* New York: Free Press, 2002. The family that fell as democracy rose.

Brown, John P. *Old Frontiers: The Story of the Cherokee Indians from Earliest Times to the Date of Their Removal to the West, 1838.* Kingsport, Tenn.: Southern Publishers, 1938. Contains a wealth of material not available elsewhere.

Brown, Roger H. *The Republic in Peril, 1812.* 1964; New York: W. W. Norton, 1971. Takes the rhetoric of the war hawks seriously.

Buchanan, John. *Jackson's Way: Andrew Jackson and the People of the Western Waters.* New York: John Wiley & Sons, 2001. The struggle for the old Southwest.

———. *The Road to Guilford Courthouse: The American Revolution in the Carolinas.* New York: John Wiley & Sons, 1997. The bitterest theater of the war.

Buckley, William Edward. *The Hartford Convention.* New Haven: Yale University Press, 1934.

Buell, Augustus C. *History of Andrew Jackson: Pioneer, Patriot, Soldier, Politician, President.* 2 volumes. New York: Charles Scribner's Sons, 1904. Especially useful on Jackson's early years.

Burstein, Andrew. *The Passions of Andrew Jackson.* Jackson as Lear. For those who think Remini is too forgiving. Includes a careful reconstruction of the events surrounding the Jackson-Rachel elopement.

Caffrey, Kate. *The Lion and the Unicorn: The Anglo-American War, 1812–1815.* London: Andre Deutsch, 1978. A British perspective.

Catterall, Ralph C. H. *The Second Bank of the United States.* 1902; Chicago: University of Chicago Press, 1960. Still the most thorough study of that star-crossed institution.

Chambers, William Nisbet. *Old Bullion Benton: Senator from the New West; Thomas Hart Benton, 1782–1858.* Boston: Atlantic Monthly/Little, Brown, 1956. The title, like the nickname, is a bit misleading, as Benton's devotion to specie was but one aspect of a long and eventful life, otherwise told well here.

Cox, Isaac Joslin. "General Wilkinson and His Later Intrigues with the Spaniards." *American Historical Review* 19 (1914): 794–812. Showing that Jackson was right about Wilkinson.

Curtis, George Ticknor. *Life of Daniel Webster.* 2 volumes. New York: D. Appleton & Co., 1870.

Dangerfield, George. *The Awakening of American Nationalism, 1815–1828*. New York: Harper & Row, 1965. Jackson and America, from the victory at New Orleans to his election as president.

———. *The Era of Good Feelings*. New York: Harcourt, Brace & World, 1963. How Jeffersonian democracy became Jacksonian democracy.

De Grummond, Jane Lucas. *The Baratarians and the Battle of New Orleans*. Baton Rouge: Louisiana State University Press, 1961. How the pirates turned patriots.

Deppisch, Ludwig M., Jose A. Centeno, David J. Gemmel, and Norca L. Torres. "Andrew Jackson's Exposure to Mercury and Lead." *Journal of the American Medical Association* 282 (1999): 569–71. The most recent work of Jacksonian toxicology.

Dickson, R. J. *Ulster Emigration to Colonial America, 1718–1775*. London: Routledge & Kegan Paul, 1966. Jackson's people.

Doherty, Herbert J. Jr. *Richard Keith Call: Southern Unionist*. Gainesville: University of Florida Press, 1961. A Jackson protégé who defected to the Whigs.

Drake, Benjamin. *Life of Tecumseh*. 1841; New York: Arno Press and the New York Times, 1969. By a near contemporary of the Shawnee chief.

Driver, Carl S. *John Sevier: Pioneer of the Old Southwest*. Chapel Hill: University of North Carolina Press, 1932. Tennessee's hero before Jackson.

Eaton, John Henry. *The Life of Andrew Jackson*. Philadelphia: Samuel F. Bradford, 1824. A campaign biography that focuses on Jackson's war record.

Eckert, Allan W. *A Sorrow in Our Heart: The Life of Tecumseh*. New York: Bantam Books, 1992. Surprisingly detailed.

Eriksson, Erik McKinley. "The Federal Civil Service under President Jackson." *Mississippi Valley Historical Review* 13 (1927): 517–40. The most thorough accounting of Jackson's personnel policy in action.

Fischer, David Hackett. *Albion's Seed: Four British Folkways in America*. New York: Oxford University Press, 1989. The cultural roots of the Anglo-American civil war—that is, the American Revolution.

Fleming, Thomas. *Duel: Alexander Hamilton, Aaron Burr and the Future of America*. New York: Basic Books, 1999. The fatal rivalry, recounted with flair.

Ford, Henry Jones. *The Scotch-Irish in America*. Princeton: Princeton University Press, 1915. The tribe from which Jackson sprang.

Freehling, William W. *Prelude to Civil War: The Nullification Controversy in South Carolina, 1816–1836*. New York: Harper & Row, 1966. How Jackson and the nullifiers nearly came to blows.

Garrison, Tim Alan. *The Legal Ideology of Removal: The Southern Judiciary and the Sovereignty of Native American Nations*. Athens: University of Georgia Press, 2002. The Cherokees and other tribes in the courtroom.

Gayerré, Charles. *History of Louisiana*. 4 volumes. New York: Redfield and William J. Widdleton, 1854–66. Deep background on the Battle of New Orleans, and much else.

[Gordon, T. F.] *The War on the Bank of the United States*. 1834; New York: Augustus M. Kelley, 1968. A contemporary view; includes many speeches and documents.

Govan, Thomas Payne. *Nicholas Biddle: Nationalist and Public Banker, 1786–1844*. Chicago: University of Chicago Press, 1959. Gives Biddle his due and then some.

Green, Fletcher M. "On Tour with President Andrew Jackson." *New England Quarterly* 36 (1963): 209–28. Democracy hits the road.

Griffith, Lucille. *Alabama: A Documentary History*. Revised and enlarged edition. Tuscaloosa: University of Alabama Press, 1972. Geographic context of the Creek War.

Haley, James L. *Sam Houston*. Norman: University of Oklahoma Press, 2002. The most thorough and judicious account of an almost unbelievable life.

Hall, Kermit L., ed. *The Oxford Companion to the Supreme Court of the United States*. New York: Oxford University Press, 1992.

Heiskell, S. G. *Andrew Jackson and Early Tennessee History*. Nashville: Ambrose Printing Co., 1918–21. 3 volumes. Like many other antiquarian chronicles, includes much of worth and much not.

Hickey, Donald R. *The War of 1812: A Forgotten Conflict*. Urbana: University of Illinois Press, 1989. Less forgotten after this able survey.

Jacobs, James Ripley. *Tarnished Warrior: Major-General James Wilkinson*. New York: Macmillan, 1938. Sober and scholarly, unlike the man.

James, Marquis. *The Life of Andrew Jackson*. Indianapolis: Bobbs-Merrill, 1938. This edition comprises the two volumes published separately as *The Border Captain* (1933) and *Portrait of a President* (1937). A great story, but when history and literature collide, literature wins.

———. *The Raven: A Biography of Sam Houston*. New York: Grosset & Dunlap, 1929. Ditto.

Jennings, Francis. *Empire of Fortune: Crowns, Colonies, and Tribes in the Seven Years War in America*. New York: W. W. Norton, 1988.

Kaplan, Edward S. *The Bank of the United States and the American Economy*. Westport, Conn.: Greenwood Press, 1999. The context of the bank war.

Kent, Donald H. "Communications." *Mississippi Valley Historical Review* 41 (March 1955): 762–63. Bacteriological warfare on the frontier.

Knollenberg, Bernhard. "General Amherst and Germ Warfare." *Mississippi Valley Historical Review* 41 (December 1954): 489–94. More on the previous.

Lamar, Howard R., ed. *The New Encyclopedia of the American West*. New Haven: Yale University Press, 1998. A landmark of American historical literature. Lamar's West starts at the Appalachians.

Madeleine, Sister M. Grace. *Monetary and Banking Theories of Jacksonian Democracy*. Philadelphia: no publisher given, 1943. Among the few works that take Jacksonian monetary theory seriously.

Main, Jackson Turner. *The Anti-Federalists: Critics of the Constitution, 1781–1788*. New York: W. W. Norton, 1974. The losers get their licks, including the Bill of Rights.

Malone, Dumas. *Jefferson and His Time*. 6 volumes. Boston: Little, Brown & Co., 1948–81. A Jefferson for the ages; enormously informed, sympathetic but well short of hagiographic.

Marszalek, John F. *The Petticoat Affair: Manners, Mutiny, and Sex in Andrew Jackson's White House*. New York: Free Press, 1997. The most thorough dissection of the Eaton affair.

McCullough, David. *John Adams*. New York: Simon & Schuster, 2001. Elevates the elder Adams perhaps above his merits.

Meier, Hugo A. "Technology and Democracy, 1800–1860." *Mississippi Valley Historical Review* 43 (1957); 618–40. Jacksonism and the Industrial Revolution.

Melton, Buckner F. Jr. *Aaron Burr: Conspiracy to Treason*. New York: John Wiley & Sons, 2002. A recent attempt to unravel the case.

Meyers, Marvin. *The Jacksonian Persuasion: Politics and Belief*. New York: Vintage, 1960. The minds of Jacksonians.

Moore, Maureen T. "Andrew Jackson: 'Pretty Near a Treason to Call *Him* Doctor!' " *New England Quarterly* 62 (September 1989): 424–35. The hero visits Harvard.

Nagel, Paul C. *John Quincy Adams: A Public Life, a Private Life*. New York: Alfred A. Knopf, 1997. The best single volume on Jackson's ally-turned-rival.

Newman, Richard S. *The Transformation of American Abolitionism: Fighting Slavery in the Early Republic*. Chapel Hill: University of North Carolina Press, 2002. The troubled—and troubling—conscience of democracy.

Niven, John. *Martin Van Buren: The Romantic Age of American Politics*. New York: Oxford University Press, 1983. The political journey of Jackson's heir.

O'Brien, Sean Michael. *In Bitterness and in Tears: Andrew Jackson's Destruction of the Creeks and the Seminoles*. Westport, Conn.: Praeger, 2003. A thorough and sometimes graphic account of Jackson's Indian wars.

Owsley, Frank Lawrence Jr. *Struggle for the Gulf Borderlands: The Creek War and the Battle of New Orleans, 1812–1815*. Gainesville: University Presses of Florida, 1981. How Jackson became famous, and much else.

Parkman, Francis. *History of the Conspiracy of Pontiac, and the War of the North American Tribes against the English Colonies after the Conquest of Canada*. 1851; New York: Book League of America, 1929. A great work by America's greatest historian.

Parton, James. *Life of Andrew Jackson*. 3 volumes. New York: Mason Brothers, 1860–61. The first serious Jackson biography, by an author close enough to his subject to interview many who knew him but distant enough to escape most of the emotional eddies Jackson set in motion. Contains many documents since lost.

Peterson, Merrill D. *Olive Branch and Sword: The Compromise of 1833*. Baton Rouge: Louisiana State University Press, 1982. How the nullification crisis stopped short of war.

———. *The Great Triumvirate: Webster, Clay, and Calhoun*. New York: Oxford University Press, 1987. In the shadow of Jackson.

Pierson, George Wilson. *Tocqueville and Beaumont in America*. New York: Oxford University Press, 1938. The journey that produced *Democracy in America*.

Pitch, Anthony S. *The Burning of Washington: The British Invasion of 1814*. Annapolis: Naval Institute Press, 1998. The most ignominious moment in American military history.

Putnam, A. W. *History of Middle Tennessee, or, Life and Times of Gen. James Robertson*. 1859; Knoxville: University of Tennessee Press, 1971. The making of the Cumberland Valley.

Ramsey, J. G. M. *The Annals of Tennessee to the End of the Eighteenth Century*. Charleston: Walker & James, 1853. Includes an account of the lost state of Franklin.

Reid, John, and John Henry Eaton. *The Life of Andrew Jackson*. 1817. Edited by Frank Lawrence Owsley Jr. University: University of Alabama Press, 1974. Authorized and corrected by the subject; as close to a Jackson memoir as exists.

Remini, Robert V. *Andrew Jackson and the Bank War: A Study in the Growth of Presidential Power*. New York: W. W. Norton, 1967. Much of this was subsumed in Remini's big biography, but still a good introduction to the subject.

———. *Andrew Jackson and the Course of American Empire: 1767–1821; Andrew Jackson and the Course of American Freedom, 1822–1832; Andrew Jackson and the Course of American Democracy, 1833–1845*. New York: Harper & Row, 1977–84. A monumental work of research and exposition by the dean of Jackson studies.

———. *Andrew Jackson and His Indian Wars*. New York: Viking, 2001. From the first skirmishes with the Cherokees to the second Seminole War; argues that Jackson's removal policy saved the southeastern Indians from extinction.

———. "Andrew Jackson Takes an Oath of Allegiance to Spain." *Tennessee Historical Quarterly* 54 (Spring 1995): 2–15. Which he later wished he hadn't.

———. *The Battle of New Orleans*. New York: Viking, 1999. Learned and succinct.

———. *Henry Clay: Statesman for the Union*. New York: W. W. Norton, 1991. Jackson's longtime rival.

Roosevelt, Theodore. *The Winning of the West*. 6 volumes. New York: Current Literature, 1905. The conquest of the old Southwest, written by one who would have loved to have been there.

Royall, William L. *Andrew Jackson and the Bank of the United States*. New York: G. P. Putnam's Sons, 1880. Hardly more than a pamphlet, but includes insights into the problem of the American money supply.

Satz, Ronald N. *American Indian Policy in the Jacksonian Era*. Norman: University of Oklahoma Press, 2002. Beyond removal, beyond Jackson.

Schlesinger, Arthur M. Jr. *The Age of Jackson*. Boston: Little, Brown, 1945. The classic study of Jacksonism; makes Old Hickory out to be the first New Dealer.

Sellers, Charles G. *The Market Revolution: Jacksonian America, 1815–1846*. New York: Oxford University Press, 1991. How the American economy shaped democracy, and vice versa.

Shackford, James Atkins. *David Crockett: The Man and the Legend*. Chapel Hill: University of North Carolina Press, 1956. Captures the spirit of the man while correcting the more egregious parts of the legend.

Shepherd, William R. "Wilkinson and the Beginnings of the Spanish Conspiracy." *American Historical Review* 9 (1904): 490–506. The opportunistic roots of contemplated treason.

Smith, Justin H. *The Annexation of Texas*. New York: Barnes & Noble, 1941. Jackson as one player among many in the final drama of his public life.

Sugden, John. *Tecumseh: A Life*. New York: Henry Holt, 1998. The best biography of the incomparable Indian leader.

Taylor, George Rogers, ed. *Jackson vs. Biddle's Bank: The Struggle over the Second Bank of the United States*. 2nd edition. Lexington, Mass.: D. C. Heath, 1972. Documents, speeches, editorials, and some historical interpretation.

Terrell, A. W. "Recollections of General Sam Houston." *Southwestern Historical Quarterly* 14 (1912): 113–36. What Houston remembered about Jackson and others.

Toplovich, Ann. "Marriage, Mayhem, and Presidential Politics: The Robards-Jackson Backcountry Scandal." Unpublished paper. Contains the latest on the origins of Jackson's marriage to Rachel.

Van West, Carroll, ed. *The Tennessee Encyclopedia of History and Culture*. Nashville: Tennessee Historical Society, 1998. Indispensable on matters Tennessean.

Walker, Alexander. *The Life of Andrew Jackson*. Philadelphia: John E. Potter, 1867. An utterly misleading title; the book is actually an extended account of the Battle of New Orleans.

Wilburn, Jean Alexander. *Biddle's Bank: The Crucial Years*. New York: Columbia University Press, 1967. Brief but insightful.

Williams, Samuel Cole. *History of the Lost State of Franklin*. New York: Press of the Pioneers, 1933. Many surviving states lack such a detailed history.

Wiltse, Charles M. *John C. Calhoun*. 3 volumes. Indianapolis: Bobbs-Merrill, 1944–51. A thoroughly researched, closely argued life of the great sectionalist.

Woodward, Grace Steele. *The Cherokees*. Norman: University of Oklahoma Press, 1963. A solid study, with many eyewitness observations.

The author would like to thank the many archivists and librarians who made this book possible. Particularly helpful have been the staffs of the Library of Congress, especially Bruce Kirby; the Tennessee State Library and Archives; the Tennessee Historical Society, especially Ann Toplovich; the Hermitage; the University of Tennessee Special Collections Library, particularly Aaron Scott Crawford; the Massachusetts Historical Society; the Newberry Library; the Alabama Department of Archives and History; the Center for American History and the Perry-Castañeda Library at the University of Texas at Austin; and the Sterling Evans Library at Texas A&M University, especially Joel Kitchens.

The author would also like to thank Roger Scholl of Doubleday and James D. Hornfischer of Hornfischer Literary Management. Finally, thanks to Roslyn Schloss for a virtuoso performance as copy editor.

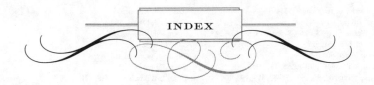

INDEX

abolitionist movement, 72, 523, 538–39, 554
Adams, Abigail, 245–46
Adams, John, vii–viii, 127, 245, 247, 300, 491
    death of, 396
    in election of 1796, 79
    in election of 1800, 114, 246, 420
    land policy of, 93–94
    presidency of, 82, 93–95
Adams, John Quincy, vii–ix, 97, 191, 381, 415, 437,
    486
    AJ's Florida campaign defended by, 338–40, 508
    AJ's New England trip and, 486
    AJ's opinion of, 371–72
    Bank of the U.S. and, 459, 464
    election of 1820 and, 338, 459
    election of 1824 and, viii, xi, 368, 371–72, 382–88
    election of 1828 and, 399, 402
    Ghent peace commission and, 246–48, 268–69
    Monroe Doctrine and, 378
    presidency of, viii–ix, 389, 391, 399
    Randolph's speeches against, 394–95
    as secretary of state, 318, 339–40, 342–43, 344, 508
    slavery issue and, 522–24, 549–50, 552
    Texas and, 508, 522–24, 544, 545, 546, 548–50,
        552, 553–54, 558
Adams-Onís treaty (1819), 342–43, 347–48
Alabama, 344, 353, 435
Alamán, Lucas, 511–12
Alamo, Battle of the, 521, 524, 530
Alien and Sedition Acts (1798), 114
Allen, Eliza, 427, 428
Allison, David, 70–71, 393
Alston, Joseph, 313–14
Alston, Willis, 225–26
Ambrister, Robert C., 330–31, 337, 339–40, 351, 446,
    481, 525
American Revolution, 86–89, 285
    AJ in, ix, 20–28
Amherst, Jeffrey, 6–8
Anderson, Patton, 160–61
Anderson, William, 160
antifederalists, 48, 49, 66

Anti-Masonic party, 474
Apperson, Richard, 150, 151, 152
Arbuthnot, Alexander, 328, 329, 330–31, 337,
    339–40, 351, 446, 481, 525
Arkansas, 344
Armstrong, John, 183–85, 230, 238
Articles of Confederation (1781), 45–46, 477
Aury, Louis-Michel, 323
Austin, Moses, 344
Austin, Stephen, 344, 508, 509, 518, 525
Avery, Isaac, 107
Avery, Waightstill, 53–54

Baltimore, Md., 226, 228, 484
Baltimore & Ohio Railroad, 484
Bank of the United States, 332–33, 343, 415, 455–71
    AJ and, 448, 455–73, 494–503, 507, 523, 534–35,
        555
    Clay and, 459, 461–63, 468, 472, 501, 502, 543, 544
    Jackson assassination attempt and, 504
    McCulloch case and, 344–46, 469
    Van Buren and, 462, 500, 501, 534–35
    Webster and, 459, 463, 464, 465–66, 467, 468,
        472–73, 495
Barbary pirates, 123, 124
Barron, James, 143
Barry, William, 416
Bayard, James, 246
Beasley, Daniel, 194
Benton, Jesse, 189–91, 295
Benton, Thomas Hart, 161–62, 546
    AJ's feud with, 188–91, 295, 397
    AJ's peacemaking with, 379
    Bank of the U.S. and, 466–67, 470
    on Jackson assassination attempt, 503–4, 505
    nullification issue and, 445
    on Panic of 1819, 343–44
    Randolph-Clay duel and, 395
Berrien, John, 416, 448–49, 468
Biddle, Nicholas, 456–65, 467, 468, 494–503, 534–35,
    558

Big Warrior (Creek leader), 234–35
Bill of Rights, 66
Blair, Francis, 77–78, 386–88, 534, 535, 538–39, 543, 544, 546, 551, 557
Blount, James, 90
Blount, William, 67, 81–82, 95, 151
Blount, Willie, 67, 95, 160, 171–72, 196, 197, 200, 239, 367
Bolivar (horse), 453
Bolívar, Simón, 385
Boston *Gazette*, 285
Bouquet, Henry, 7–8
Bowlegs (Seminole leader), 329–30
Brackenridge, Henry, 358
Bradford, William, 219
Branch, John, 416, 448–49
Breathitt, George, 476
Brock, Isaac, 178
Bronaugh, James, 371, 372
Brown, Jacob, 356
Buford, Abraham, 23
Burke, Edmund, 465–66
Burr, Aaron, 113–14, 116–28, 545
    Clay compared to, 388
    conspiracy of, 118–28, 183
    in election of 1796, 117
    in election of 1800, 117, 394
    election of 1816 and, 313–14, 316
    Hamilton's duel with, 117–18, 134
    treason trial of, 127–28, 158
Bustamante, Anastasio, 509
Butler, Anthony, 509–16, 519–20
Butler, Robert, 270, 314

Caffery, Donelson, 140, 145–46, 155
Calhoun, John C., 158–59, 338, 339, 377
    AJ's opinion of, 371–72
    as AJ's vice president, 439–49
    Bank of the U.S. and, 459
    Compromise of 1850 and, 559
    Eaton affair and, 424–25, 444
    election of 1824 and, 382, 385, 388
    election of 1828 and, 399
    election of 1844 and, 544
    Florida campaign and, 324, 327, 328, 329, 330, 447–48
    Ghent peace commission and, 246–48
    Jackson inauguration and, 407, 409
    nullification issue and, 439–41, 444, 446, 477, 479–80, 481, 556
    Van Buren as enemy of, 444, 446, 452, 479
    Van Buren's reconciliation with, 538
California, 558, 559
Call, Richard, 349, 373, 401, 402, 405
Callava, José Maria, 357–60

Campbell, Arthur, 88
Campbell, David, 102
Campbell, William, 89
Canada, x, 228
Canning, George, 466
Carey, James, 82
Carroll, William, 189, 219, 221
Carson, Sam, 522
Cartagena, Republic of, 253, 256
Cass, Lewis, 476, 477, 521–22
Catawbas, 12
Catlet, Hanson, 136–38, 140–41
caucus system, 313, 369, 372, 379, 382
census, U.S., 115
Charleston, S.C., 30, 33–34
Cherokees, 67, 82, 94, 171, 233
    AJ and, 233, 310, 311, 312, 314–15, 435, 436, 441, 535–36
    in American Revolution, 86–88
    background and history of, 83–84
    Creek War and, 196, 197, 216–17
    forced removal of, 488–93, 535–36
    in French and Indian War, 85–86
    Sam Houston and, 212–13
    Sevier expedition against, 80–81, 87–88
    Treaty of Holston with, 69
Chesapeake incident, 143–45, 156
Chester, Robert, 453
Chickasaws, 171, 172, 233, 314–15, 319, 489
Choctaws, 151, 192, 243–44, 319, 436, 489
cholera, 103, 450–51, 473
Chota alliance, 86–88
Churchill, Winston S., 142
Civil War, U.S., 560
Claiborne, William, 122, 125, 193–94, 242
    Battle of New Orleans and, 270
    Laffite and, 252, 255–57
Clark, John, 351
Clay, Henry, 158–59, 226, 227, 228, 391, 411
    AJ opposed by, 368
    AJ's Florida campaign condemned by, 339, 351–52
    AJ's rebuttal of attack by, 389–90
    Bank of the U.S. and, 459, 461–63, 468, 472, 501, 502, 543, 544
    Burr compared to, 388
    Burr conspiracy and, 124, 158
    cholera epidemic of 1832 and, 451
    Compromise of 1850 and, 558–59
    election of 1824 and, 371, 382–88
    election of 1832 and, 474, 475
    election of 1844 and, 550–51
    Ghent peace commission and, 246–48, 268–69
    Jackson censure and, 501, 502
    Missouri Compromise and, 352–55
    nullification issue and, 481

Randolph and, 394–95
as secretary of state, 388, 394
Clermont (steamboat), 300, 301
Clinton, De Witt, 368, 393
Clinton, Henry, 22–23
Cobb, Thomas, 351–52, 354, 355
Coffee, John, 310, 311, 366–67, 379, 402–3, 416–17, 448, 449, 477
Battle of New Orleans and, 266
Creek War and, 196, 197, 201, 208, 211, 216–19, 220
as Hutchings's executor, 428–29
Jackson-Benton feud and, 190
War of 1812 and, 242, 243
"coffin handbill," 397–99
Coleman, Joseph, 150
Comanches, 517
Compromise of 1850, 558–59
Confederation Congress, 67
Congress, U.S., 381
Bank of the U.S. and, 333, 543
French debt and, 515
legislative sessions of, 421–22
presidential elections and Republican caucus in, 313, 369, 372, 379, 382
slavery issue in, 147, 352–55, 523, 559
Texas annexation and, 557
"war hawks" faction in, 157–59, 162–63, 175, 394
War of 1812 and, 174–75
Constitution, U.S., 66
Bank of the U.S. and, 466, 469–70
contract clause of, 345
drafting and ratification of, 46–49
"elastic" clause of, 470
nullification and, 477–78
slavery and, 47, 554
tariffs and, 333
Twenty-fifth Amendment to, 543
Constitutional Convention (1787), viii, 46, 67
Continental Army, 20–21
Continental Congress, 20, 21, 46
Conway, George, 105
corn, 365
Cornstalk (Shawnee leader), 86
Cornwallis, George, 21, 33, 88
cotton, 334, 343, 353, 365, 452–53
Crawford, James (AJ's cousin), 30
Crawford, James (AJ's uncle), 12, 16, 17
Crawford, Jane, 12, 16, 17, 26
Crawford, Thomas (AJ's cousin), 26, 27
Crawford, Thomas (AJ's uncle), 32, 33
Crawford, William (AJ's cousin), 30
Crawford, William H., 316, 317, 318, 349
AJ's feud with, 309–10, 314, 316, 350–52
Calhoun and, 447–48
election of 1820 and, 338, 339

election of 1824 and, 368, 371, 372, 374, 379, 382–86
Florida campaign and, 324
as secretary of war, 305, 307, 309–10, 311, 314, 315
Creeks, 238, 307, 310, 315, 319, 435, 436, 441
Meadows massacre fraud and, 169–70
in Seminole War, 327, 328, 329
Texas and, 519
See also Creek War; Red Sticks (Creek faction)
Creek War, 193–200, 205–22, 328
beginning of, 172–73
peace settlement in, 231–35
westward expansion promoted by, 334
Crockett, David, 210–12, 530
Crowley, Martha, 172
Cryer, Hardy, 453
Cuba, 253

Dallas, Alexander, 302–3
Dallas, George Mifflin, 552
Dartmouth College, 345
Daveiss, Joseph Hamilton, 123, 124
Davidson Academy, 67
Declaration of Independence (1776), 71–72, 74, 396, 554
Delawares, 4–5, 83, 86, 176, 436
Democracy in America (Tocqueville), 457–58
Democratic Clarion, 173
Democrats, 402, 437, 474–75, 483, 502, 535
Compromise of 1850 and, 559
in election of 1836, 530
in election of 1840, 537–40, 541, 544
in election of 1844, 550–52
tariff and, 544
Texas annexation and, 546
See also Republicans, Jeffersonian
de Soto, Hernando, 83–84
Dickinson, Charles, 131–34, 135–38, 139, 140–41, 295
diseases, 4, 7–8, 27, 84, 103–4, 115, 343, 450–51, 473
Donelson, Alexander, 190
Donelson, Andrew Jackson, 347, 348–49, 364–65, 374–75, 416, 448, 533, 542, 551
AJ's will and, 548
Eaton affair and, 424, 426
Donelson, Elizabeth, 152
Donelson, Emily, 424, 426
Donelson, John (father), 42–45, 49, 55, 56, 57, 64
Donelson, John (son), 95
Donelson, Mrs., 56, 57, 58, 62, 63
Donelson, Samuel, 69, 70–71
Donelson, Severn, 152
Dragging Canoe (Cherokee leader), 86, 87
Drayton, William, 315

Duane, William, 497, 500
duels and dueling, x, 53–54, 107–10, 117–18, 134,
    139–40, 395, 397
    AJ's advice on, 349–50

Eaton, John, 349–50, 378, 388, 390–91, 395
    marriage scandal of, 422–26, 444
    as secretary of war, 415–17, 449
Eaton, Margaret O'Neal Timberlake, 422–26, 444
Edwards, Jonathan, 116
elections
    of 1796, 79, 117
    of 1800, 114, 117, 246, 394, 414, 420
    of 1804, 123
    of 1808, 156
    of 1810, 158
    of 1816, 313–14, 316, 338
    of 1820, 338, 339, 356, 459
    of 1824, viii, xi, 367–68, 371–72, 374, 379, 382–88,
        391–92, 399, 401
    of 1828, 366, 389–403
    of 1832, 473–75
    of 1834, 502
    of 1836, 530, 531
    of 1840, 537–40, 541, 544
    of 1844, 544, 550–52
    Republican congressional caucus and, 313, 369,
        372, 379, 382
electoral college, 47, 432–33
Erie Canal, 393
Erwin, Andrew, 349, 351
Erwin, Joseph, 131, 134
Ewing, Thomas, 15

Fagot, Anthony, 59–61
Fanning, A. C. W., 331
Federalist Papers, 48, 75
Federalists, 66, 75–76, 79, 93, 94–95, 117, 302, 313,
    316, 338, 368, 444, 555
    Bank of the U.S. and, 333, 415
    Burr trial and, 127–28
    J. Q. Adams and, 246
    tariff issue and, 380
    Tocqueville on, 457
    War of 1812 and, 225–30, 284–85
    Whigs as successors to, 483, 537
Ferguson, Patrick, 88–89
Finley, Mr., 456
Florida, Spanish, x, 35, 220, 234
    AJ's campaign in, 306–8, 322–31, 337–41, 342
    U.S. acquisition of, 342–43, 508
Florida Territory, 356–60, 364
Forrest, Charles, 272, 273
Fort, John, 120–21, 124

Fort Bowyer, 240, 287
Fort Dearborn massacre, 178
Fort Gadsden, 327, 328
Fort Jackson, 221, 398
Fort Jackson, Treaty of (1814), 233–35, 236, 293
Fort Mims massacre, 193–95, 206, 210, 220, 222
Fort Pitt, 6, 8
France
    in American Revolution, 33
    debts owed U.S. by, 514–15
    French and Indian War and; see French and Indian
        War
    Louisiana Purchase and, 115–16
    Native American policy of, 6
    Texas and, 509
    U.S. maritime friction with, x, 114, 141–42, 157
Francis (Seminole leader), 328, 329
Franklin, Benjamin, 18, 49–50, 73–74, 245, 246, 247
Franklin, Jesse, 315
Franklin, state of, 49–50, 52, 73, 89
free blacks, 241–42, 261–62
Fremon, Anne and Charles, 190
Frémont, Jessie Benton, 190
Frémont, John C., 190, 546
French and Indian War, 4–5, 19, 84–85
French Revolution, 73–74, 94
Fromentin, Eligius, 360
Fullarat, Antoine, 358, 359
Fulton, Robert, 300–301, 334

Gadsden, James, 327, 364, 372
    Jackson presidency supported by, 367–68, 370, 371
"gag rule," 523, 549, 552
Gaines, Edmund, 521–22
    Florida campaign and, 308, 322, 323, 325, 326,
        327–28, 330
Galbraith, Captain, 32–33
Gallatin, Albert, 81, 227, 246–48, 268–69, 339–40
Gallatin, James, 247, 269
Gates, Horatio, 25, 27, 67
Georgia, 342, 435
    Cherokee removal issue and, 488–93, 535–36
    secession issue and, 480
Ghent, Treaty of (1815), 245–48, 268–69, 284–85,
    287, 289, 290
Gibbs, Samuel, 281, 282
Gilbert (slave), 365–66
Gleig, George, 228, 263–65, 267, 272, 275, 276, 280,
    281, 282, 283
gold rush, 558–59
Goliad massacre, 521, 524
González Manrique, Mateo, 237–38, 239, 240, 244–45
Gordon, John, 238
Graves, Samuel, 39

Great Britain
    abolitionist movement and, 538–39
    AJ's Florida campaign and, 337
    AJ's policy toward, 432
    in American Revolution, 20–28, 29, 33–34
    Chesapeake incident and, 143–45
    in French and Indian War, 4–5, 84–85
    Ghent peace conference and, 247–48
    impressment issue and, 75–76, 142–43
    Indian policy of, 6, 84–86, 166–67, 175, 193, 254
    naval blockade by, 141–42
    Pontiac's War and, 5–9
    Texas and, 509, 518, 546, 547
    U.S. maritime friction with, 75–76, 141–46, 156,
        157–59
    in War of 1812, x, 174, 175, 177–78, 193, 201–4,
        227–29, 236–45, 254–56, 258–61, 263–83, 285,
        286–87
Greeley, Horace, 493
Green, Duff, 416–17, 448
Green, Horace, 150, 151, 154
Greene, Nathanael, 27–28
Grundy, Felix, 185, 400–401

Haiti, 115, 266
Hall, Dominick, 271, 290–92, 305
Hamilton, Alexander, 115, 117
    Adams's disdain for, 75, 94
    Bank of the U.S. and, 333
    Burr's duel with, 117–18, 134
    Constitution and, 46
    in election of 1800, 114
    Jay treaty and, 75–76
    tariff issue and, 380
    Washington's speeches drafted by, 432
Hamilton, James, 412, 495
Hanging Rock, Battle of, 24–25
Harris, Egbert, 366
Harrison, William, 136, 138
Harrison, William Henry, 543
    commission resigned by, 230–31
    in election of 1836, 530
    in election of 1840, 537, 538, 539
    Tecumseh and, 164–65, 166, 167–69, 203–4, 227
    Tippecanoe and, 176–77
Hartford Convention (1814–15), 229–30, 284, 483
Harvard University, 485–87
Hatchy, King (Seminole leader), 326
Hay, George, 127
Hayne, Robert, 441–43
Hays, Nathaniel, 148–49
Hays, Robert, 99
Hays, Stockley, 190
Henry, Alexander, 6
Hill, Isaac, 416–17, 437–38

Holmes, Thomas, 194, 195
Holston, Treaty of (1791), 69
horses, horse racing, 129–31, 134–35, 453–54, 532, 542
Horseshoe Bend, Battle of, 215–19, 227, 230, 248
House of Representatives, U.S.
    AJ in, 79–81
    Bank of the U.S. and, 468
    Constitution and, 46–47
    Florida campaign and, 351
    "gag rule" and, 523, 549, 552
    Houston-Stanberry affair and, 506–8
    Jay treaty in, 75–76
    slavery issue in, 353–54, 523
    Tallmadge amendment in, 354
    Tennessee's representation in, 79
    War of 1812 and, 175
Houston, Sam, 212–13, 218
    AJ and, 373–74, 391, 400, 426–28, 506–8, 516–19
    AJ's death and, 557–58
    marriage and political failure of, 426–28
    in Senate, 559–60
    Texas annexation and, 544–47, 557
    Texas independence and, 506–8, 516–19, 521–22,
        524–26
Houston, Sam, Jr., 558
Hull, William, 178
Hunter's Hill, 73, 148, 149, 542
Hutchings, Andrew, 428–29, 532, 542
Hutchings, John, 151, 154

Impartial Review, 134, 135, 139, 140
impressment issue, 75–76, 142–43, 248, 269
Indiana Territory, 165
Ingham, Samuel, 415, 448–49
Iroquois confederacy, 3–4, 12

Jackson, Andrew
    abolitionist movement and, 539, 554
    Adams and, 94–95, 338–40, 371–72, 486, 508, 552,
        553–54
    adultery issue and, 62–64, 401
    in American Revolution, ix, 20–28, 29–30
    antifederalism of, 114, 555
    appearance of, 40–41
    army career of, 230–35, 236–45, 254, 257–62
    assassination attempt against, 503–5
    assault upon, 487
    Bank of the U.S. and, 436–37, 448, 460, 467,
        468–71, 494–503, 507, 523, 534–35, 555
    Battle of New Orleans and, 265–68, 273–75,
        277–78, 279, 280, 282, 284–99
    Benton and, 161–62, 188–91
    Big Spring (Ala.) plantation of, 365–66
    birth of, 16

Jackson, Andrew (*cont.*)
British imprisonment of, 27–29
Burr conspiracy and, 118–23, 125, 127–28, 397
as businessman, 68–71, 99–100, 102, 154–56, 346–47, 364–67, 452–53
Chesapeake incident and, 143, 144
childhood and youth of, 17–18
Clay's attacks rebutted by, 389–90
as congressman, 79–81, 97
Constitution and, 47–48
in Creek War, 196–200, 215–22, 231–35
death of, 557–58
democracy's importance in life of, 553–57
Dickinson affair and, 131–34, 135–38, 139–40
domestic policy of, 432–34
dueling advice of, 349–50
duels of, x, 53–54, 107–10, 134, 135–38, 397
early political career of, ix–x
early support for candidacy of, 367–75
Eaton scandal and, 422–26
election of 1808 and, 156
election of 1816 and, 313–14
election of 1824 and, 382–88
election of 1828 and, 366, 389–403
election of 1832 and, 473–75
election of 1840 and, 537–40, 541
election of 1844 and, 544, 550–52
embargo and, 145–46
Fagot affair and, 59–61
farewell address of, 531–32
farewell to troops of, 297–98
financial problems of, 533–34
first inauguration of, ix, xi, 407–13, 415
Florida campaign of, 306–8, 322–31, 337–41, 342
as Florida territorial governor, 356–60, 364
foreign policy of, 432
Hartford Convention and, 229–30
Hermitage home of, 148–49, 302, 346–47, 363–67, 452–53, 517, 532–34, 542
horses and racing as love of, 129–31, 134–35, 453–54, 532, 542
Houston and, 373–74, 391, 400, 426–28, 506–8, 516–19
Hunter's Hill farm of, 73, 148, 149, 542
Hutchings as dependent of, 428–29
illnesses of, ix, 30, 103–4, 294–97, 302, 347–48, 364, 370, 451–52, 532, 541–42, 547
Indian policy of, x–xi, 169–71, 172–73, 196, 309–11, 314–15, 319–21, 435–36, 489–93, 535–36
inheritance lost by, 33–34
Jay treaty and, 76
in Jonesboro, 53–54
as judge, 100–103
Laffite and, 255, 256–57, 269–71
law practice of, 35–40

Madison and, 302–3, 312–13
marriage of, 64–65, 98–99
martial law issue and, 260, 262, 290–92, 302–3, 305, 356
as Mero District attorney, 67–68
as militia commander, 104, 105, 159–60, 179–87
militia mutiny put down by, 205–10
Monroe counseled by, 315–21
mother's influence on, 29, 31–32
Nashville journey of, 52–55
as national hero, 293–94, 298–99
New England trip of, 483–87
New Orleans habeas corpus case and fining of, 290–92, 549
Old Hickory nickname of, 186, 261
oratorical skills of, 77–78
Overton's partnership with, 69–71
as parent, 152–53
political views of, 316–17
postwar trip to Washington of, 303–6
presidency of; *see* Jackson, Andrew, first presidential administration of; Jackson, Andrew, second presidential administration of
Rachel Jackson's death and, 405, 406–7
religious views of, 449–51, 548
retirement years of, 529–52
Robards's confrontation with, 57–59
rotation in office principle of, 418–20
Scott's conflict with, 335–37
second inauguration of, 481–82
in Senate, 82, 92–96, 97, 376–82, 383, 391
Sevier's feud with, 90–92, 105–10, 159–60
slander campaign against, 397–99
as slaveholder, 71–73, 149–50, 365–66, 533, 539
tariff issue and, 380–81, 399, 433–34, 439–43, 475, 481
Tennessee statehood and, 76–79
Texas annexation and, 544–47
Tocqueville on, 457
Van Buren and, 529–30, 531, 532, 541
veto and, 468–71, 472, 494, 503
in War of 1812, x, 174–76, 179–87, 198–201, 205–22, 236–45, 254, 257–62, 265–68, 273–75, 277–78, 279, 280, 282, 285
wild behavior of, 36–37, 39
Wilkinson and, 52
will of, 548
Wood execution and, 213–15, 261, 397
Jackson, Andrew, first presidential administration of, 414–83
AJ's nominations in, 437–38
annual messages to Congress in, 431–37, 462, 468, 489, 491
Bank of the U.S. and, 436–37, 448, 455–73
cabinet of, 415–17
cabinet reshuffling in, 448–49

electoral college issue and, 432–33
force bill secured by, 481
as hostile takeover, 414
Indian removal issue and, 488–93
"kitchen cabinet" of, 416–17, 437
nullification issue and, 439–49, 475–82
spoils system in, 417–20, 437
tariff and, 433–34, 439–43, 475, 481
Texas and, 509–12
Jackson, Andrew, second presidential administration
of, 481–82, 494–526
AJ's censure in, 501, 502
Bank of the U.S. and, 494–503
federal debt eliminated in, 502–3
"specie circular" in, 503, 534
Texas independence and, 508–9, 512–26
Jackson, Andrew, Jr., 152–53, 154, 181, 292, 335, 426,
501
courtship advice from AJ to, 429–30
financial problems of, 533–34, 542
Hermitage bequeathed to, 548
Hermitage managed by, 453, 454
Jackson, Andrew, III, 548
Jackson, Andrew (father), 11–13, 15–16, 34
Jackson, Elizabeth (mother), 11–13, 15, 16–17, 18
AJ's personality shaped by, 29, 31–32
in American Revolution, 24, 25, 29–30
death of, 30
Jackson, Hugh (brother), 11, 15, 24, 30
Jackson, Hugh (grandfather), 11, 33
Jackson, Rachel Donelson (wife), x, 72, 302, 382, 548
AJ's courtship of and marriage to, 62–65
AJ's devotion to, 98–99, 335, 363, 423, 555
on AJ's election, 404–5
AJ's letters to, 98, 198, 200, 218, 219, 235, 242,
329, 351, 377–78, 381
AJ's political career and, 370
death of, xi, 405, 406–7
description of, 403–4
Dickinson affair and, 132, 133
election of 1824 and, 391–92
election of 1828 and, 401, 403
Hermitage purchase and, 148–49
illnesses of, 292
as parent, 152–53
in Pensacola, 356–57
Sevier's slander of, 106, 110
War of 1812 and, 180–81, 292–93
in Washington, D.C., 383–84
Jackson, Robert (brother), 11, 15, 25–30
Jackson, Samuel, 548
Jackson, Sarah, 548
James I, King of England, 9–10
Jamestown colony, 9
Jay, John, 50, 75, 246
Jay treaty, 75–76

Jefferson, Thomas, 113–17, 245, 285, 369, 397, 411,
440, 508, 555
on AJ's temper, 97
AJ toasted by, 304
annual birthday fete for, 443–46
Burr conspiracy and, 120, 123–27
Burr trial and, 127–28, 491
Chesapeake incident and, 143–45, 156
death of, 395–96
in election of 1796, 117
in election of 1800, 114, 246, 394, 414, 420
in election of 1804, 123
in election of 1808, 156
embargo instituted by, 145–46, 156, 157
Indian policy of, 165–66, 167
Jay treaty and, 75–76
Kentucky Resolves drafted by, 114
Louisiana border question and, 343
presidency of, viii, 80
as secretary of state, 74–75
slavery issue and, 355–56
on Tennessee constitution, 79
Johnson, Andrew, 449
Jonesboro, Tenn., 53–54
Judiciary Act (1789), 488

Keane, John, 281, 282
Kendall, Amos, 416–17, 497, 498, 547
Kentucky, 51, 353, 354, 473
Kentucky Resolves (1798), 114
Key, Francis Scott, 228
King's Mountain, Battle of, 88–89, 105
"kitchen cabinet," 416–17, 437

Lafayette, Marquis de, 383–84, 385
Laffite, Alexander (Dominique Youx), 253, 271
Laffite, Jean, 252–57, 269–71
Laffite, Pierre, 253
Lake Erie, Battle of, 202, 227
Lambert, John, 282, 286
Land Grab Act (1783), 69
land ownership, 13–15
Latour, Arsène, 273, 274, 278, 281, 283
Lawrence, Richard, 504–5
Lee, Henry, 396, 397
Leopard, H.M.S., 143, 144
Lewis, Joel, 90–91
Lewis, William, 400, 401, 416–17, 426, 444, 445,
451–52, 473, 542, 547
Lincoln, Abraham, 18, 560
Lister, John, 39–40
Livingston, Edward, 266, 285, 301–2, 368, 515
Livingston, Louise Moreau de Lassy, 285–86, 287
Livingston, Robert, 115, 301

Louaillier, Louis, 290
Louisiana, 35, 52, 59, 171
    political and cultural differences in, 249–52
    slavery in, 352–53
    state militia of, 260–61
    in War of 1812, 249–52, 258, 259, 260–61
Louisiana, U.S.S., 270
Louisiana Purchase, 113, 115–16, 237, 343, 344, 352, 353, 355, 508
Louis XVI, King of France, 73
Lyncoya (AJ adoptee), 198, 302, 381, 490

Macay, Spruce, 36, 37
McCamie, George and Margaret, 13
McCulloch, Alexander, 219
McCulloch, James, 345
McCulloch case, 344–46, 469
McIntosh, William, 327, 328, 329
Mackinac massacre, 5–6
McNairy, John, 26, 52–53, 54, 145–46
McNairy, Nathaniel, 134
Madison, James, 340
    AJ as political rival to, 302–3, 312–13
    Bank of the U.S. and, 333
    Constitution and, 46, 48–49
    in election of 1808, 156
    as *Federalist* coauthor, 48, 75
    presidency of, viii, 156–57
    Sevier expedition and, 81
    Virginia Resolutions drafted by, 114
    War of 1812 and, 163, 174, 175, 196, 226, 227–28, 230–31, 237, 238, 239, 243, 246–47, 285
Magna Carta, ix
Magness, David, 161
Maine, 354
malaria, 104
manufacturing, 393
Marable, John, 394–95
Marcy, William, 420
Marion, Francis, 85–86
Marshall, James, 558
Marshall, John, 444, 558
    AJ inauguration and, 409, 410
    Burr trial and, 127–28, 345, 491
    death of, 531
    Indian removal issue and, 487–93, 535
    McCulloch case and, 345–46, 469
Marshall, Mary, 487
Martin, William, 206–7
Masot, José, 337–38
Massachusetts, 72, 485–87
"Massacre at the Mouth of Duck River, The" (Jackson), 173
Matchless Sanative, 541–42
Maxcy, Virgil, 444

Meadows, William, 169, 170
Meriwether, David, 315
Mero District, 52–55, 59–60, 67–68, 69, 90
Mexican War, 558
Mexico, x, 52, 343
    Butler mission to gain Texas from, 509–16, 519–20
    independence of, 344, 508
    slavery and, 509, 517, 524
    Spanish attempt at reconquest of, 509, 512
    Texas annexation and, 545, 552
    Texas war for independence from, 519–21, 524
Miller (innkeeper), 136, 138
Mims, Samuel, 193
Miró, Estevan, 51, 60
Mississippi, 342, 344, 353
Mississippi River, 49–51, 59–60, 82, 237, 240, 248, 257
Missouri, 344, 352–53
Missouri Compromise (1820), 352–56, 394
Mobile, Ala., 237, 238, 239, 240, 242, 243, 254, 258, 287
Monck's Corner, Battle of, 23
money, currency, 364, 393–94, 437
Monroe, James, viii, 364, 369, 485
    AJ as adviser and counselor to, 315–21
    AJ's Florida campaign and, 322–24, 327, 337, 340, 341–42, 348
    AJ's toast to, 304
    Bank of the U.S. and, 458–59
    in election of 1820, 356
    election of 1824 and, 385, 388
    Jackson-Crawford feud and, 350–51, 352
    Jackson-Scott conflict and, 336–37
    Lafayette and, 385
    Louisiana Purchase and, 115
    as Madison's successor, 302–3, 312–13
    in War of 1812, 238, 240, 243, 245, 248, 265, 269, 274, 286
Monroe Doctrine, 378
Montgomery, Lemuel, 217
Morgan, George, 124
Mullens, Colonel, 281

Napoleon I, Emperor of France, 94, 113, 115–16, 141, 227, 251, 285, 509
Napoleonic Wars, 227, 228, 251
Nashville, Tenn., 42–45, 52–55
Nashville, University of, 67
Nashville Gazette, 382–83, 389
Natchez Trace, 188
National Intelligencer, 143, 285
National Republican party, 474
National Road, 392, 399
Native Americans
    disease and decimation of, 4, 7–8, 84, 343
    Donelson party and, 43–44

European settlers' conflicts with, 4–9, 13–14, 35, 54–55, 60, 61–62, 80–81, 83–88, 164–73
Florida as refuge for, 306–8
forced removal of, 488–93
land cessions by, 67, 69
land ownership and, 13–14
pre-Columbian culture of, 3–4
War of 1812 and, x, 175, 240, 243–44, 254
See also Creek War; Red Sticks (Creek faction); *specific tribes*
Navarro, Martín, 51
Neches River, 515, 522
"Negro Fort" (Florida refuge), 307, 308, 309, 325, 327
Netherlands, 227, 246
New England, 483–87
secessionist movement in, 229–30, 284, 285
New Hampshire, 437–38
New Madrid earthquake, 201, 288
New Orleans, Battle of, x, 40, 263–83, 556
aftermath of, 284–99
American preparations for main assault in, 273, 277–78
artillery duel in, 273–75
British Lake Borgne advance in, 263–65
British main assault in, 279–82
British river crossing attempt in, 275–77, 286–87
casualties in, 282–83
first engagement of, 265–68
Haitian volunteers in, 266
Laffite and, 269–71
West Indian troops in, 264
New Orleans, La., 51, 60, 115–16, 353
Burr conspiracy and, 118, 119, 121, 122
pirates and smuggling in, 252–57
in War of 1812, 240, 241, 242, 248, 257–62
New York City, 393, 485
Nichols, Edward, 254–55, 326
Niles' Register, 228, 573
Nolte, Vincent, 287–89, 293
Nonintercourse Act (1809), 157
North Carolina, 353
Sevier's arrest by, 89–90
western land claim of, 49, 52, 54, 90
Northwest Territory, 72
nullification doctrine, 439–49, 475–82, 488, 491, 510, 554, 555, 559
Calhoun and, 439–41, 444, 446, 477, 479–80, 481, 556
Webster-Hayne debate on, 441–43

Ojibwas, 5–6
Onís, Luis de, 338, 339, 342–43
Oolooteka (Cherokee leader), 212, 213
Ordinance of 1787, 352
Oregon, 343, 546, 547, 551, 552

Orleans Territory, 120, 122
Osceola (Seminole leader), 536
Ottawas, 5, 8, 86
Overton, John, 57–59, 63, 65, 69–71, 139–40, 141, 378, 425
Overton, Thomas, 136–38, 139, 140

Pakenham, Edward, 272, 273, 274, 275, 276, 278–79, 281
Panic of 1819, 343–44, 364, 393
Paris, Treaty of (1783), 34–35, 246, 247
Pathkiller (Cherokee leader), 197
Patterson, Daniel, 256
Pawnees, 517
Penn, William, 10
Pennsylvania, 10–11, 72
Penobscots, 435
Pensacola, Fla., 236, 237, 242, 243–45, 258
AJ's occupation of, 337, 340–41
as seat of Florida Territory, 356–60
Perry, Oliver Hazard, 202, 227
Philadelphia, Pa., 10–11, 103, 484–85
Philip, King (Native American leader), 4
Physick, Dr., 484–85
Pinckney, Charles, 156
Pitt, William, the Younger, 465–66
Pizarro, Francisco, 83
plantation economy, 72
Ploughboy (horse), 134–35
Poinsett, Joel, 475–77, 480, 481
Polk, James K., 551–52, 557
Pontiac (Ottawa leader), 5–8, 175
Pontiac's War, 5–9, 19, 175
Potawatomis, 178
Potter, Elisha, 225–26
Presbyterians, Presbyterianism, 10, 13, 17
Presque Isle massacre, 7
Proctor, Henry, 202–4
Prophet (Shawnee leader), 165, 167, 169, 176, 193
Prophetstown, 176, 177

Quincy, Josiah, 485–86

Randolph, John, 394–95, 473
Red Sticks (Creek faction), 193–95, 196–200, 202, 212, 215–22, 233, 234, 248, 328
See also Creek War; Weatherford, William
Reid, John, 208–9, 215, 217–18, 294, 304–5, 349
Republicans, Jeffersonian, 75–76, 114, 117, 313, 338, 368, 457
Bank of the U.S. and, 333
Burr trial and, 127–28
congressional caucus of, 313, 369, 372, 379, 382

Republicans, Jeffersonian (*cont.*)
  J. Q. Adams and, 246
  War of 1812 and, 225–26
  See also Democrats
Rhea, John, 324
Richardson, John, 203
riots, in Baltimore, 226
Ritchie, Thomas, 382–83, 417–18, 437
Roane, Archibald, 105, 106
Roanoke Island colony, 334
Robards, Lewis, 57–59, 62–64, 73, 152
Robards, Mrs. (widow), 57, 58
Robertson, Elijah, 71
Robertson, James, 43, 45, 71, 94
  on AJ's judgeship, 102
  Dickinson affair and, 133–34, 139, 141
  Tennessee statehood and, 77, 78
Roosevelt, Theodore, 89
Ross, Robert, 227, 228, 272
rotation in office principle, 418–20
Rowland, Thomas, 204
Rush, Richard, 318
Russell, George, 211
Russell, Jonathan, 246
Russia, 246
Rutherford, Anne Jarret, 40–41

Sabine River, 515, 522
St. Marks, Fla., 328–29, 330, 331, 340, 342
San Jacinto, Battle of, 522, 524
Santa Anna, Antonio López de, 509, 512–13, 516,
    518, 520, 522, 524–26, 530
Saratoga, Battle of, 21, 25
Scott, Winfield, 335–37, 379, 536
secession, 475–82
sectionalism, 49, 50–52, 54, 60, 301, 355, 439–41, 444,
    446, 475–82, 488, 510, 554, 555
Seminoles, 192, 307, 325, 330
Seminole War, First, 322–31, 397, 508
Seminole War, Second, 536
Senate, U.S.
  Adams-Onís treaty ratified by, 347
  AJ censured by, 501, 502
  AJ in, 82, 92–96, 97, 376–82, 383, 391
  AJ's nominations and, 438, 448–49
  Bank of the U.S. and, 465–68
  Calhoun's nullification speech in, 479–80
  cholera epidemic of 1832 and, 451
  Constitution and, 46–47
  Florida campaign and, 351
  Ghent treaty ratified by, 290
  Houston in, 559–60
  Indian removal and, 536
  Jay treaty in, 75
  slavery issue in, 352, 354–55, 523

  southern representation in, 352
  Tallmadge amendment in, 354–55
  "war hawks" faction in, 162–63, 175
  War of 1812 and, 175
  See also Congress, U.S.; House of Representa-
      tives, U.S.
Sequoyah, 488
Sevier, James, 109
Sevier, John, 87–94, 132, 171, 317, 530
  AJ's feud with, 90–92, 105–10, 159–60
  in American Revolution, 87–89
  Cherokee campaigns of, 80–81, 87–88
  as governor of Tennessee, 90–93, 105
  judgeship offered to AJ by, 100
  militia command sought by, 104–5
Shawnees, 4–5, 165
Shays, Daniel, 46
Shelby, Isaac, 89, 318
Short, Peyton, 57
slaves, slavery, 13, 147–52, 353
  Adams's opposition to, 522–24, 549–50, 552
  AJ and, 71–73, 149–50, 365–66, 533, 539
  Compromise of 1850 and, 559
  Congress and, 147, 352–55, 523, 559
  Constitution and, 47, 554
  election of 1840 and, 538–39
  Florida "Negro Fort" as refuge for, 307, 308, 309,
      325
  Laffite and, 252
  Mexican abolition of, 509, 517, 524
  Missouri Compromise and, 352–56
  in Northwest, 352
  population of, 115
  Texas and, 509, 517, 522–24, 549–50
  War of 1812 and, 241
  westward expansion and growth of, 334
smallpox, 7–8, 27, 84, 103, 343
Smith, Daniel, 59, 61, 96, 122–23
Smith, Margaret Bayard, 410–13
Smith, Samuel, 411
Sousa, Domingo, 358–59
South Carolina, nullification issue and, 439–41, 444,
    446, 475–82, 488, 510, 554, 555
"South Carolina Exposition" (Calhoun), 440
South Sea bubble, 460
Southwest Territory, 50, 66, 72, 90
Spain, x, 35, 59–60, 193, 227, 306
  Adams-Onís treaty and, 342–43, 347–48
  AJ's Florida campaign and, 337
  Florida ceded by, 342–43
  Louisiana and, 115
  Mexican reconquest attempted by, 509, 512
  War of 1812 and, 236–45, 253
  Western secession and, 50–52
Sparks, Jared, 455–56
"specie circular," 503, 534

speculators, 14–15, 56–57, 67
spoils system, 417–20, 437
squatters, 14–15
Stamp Act (1765), 20
Stanberry, William, 506–7
steamboats, 300–301, 334, 392–93
Steel, Mr. (AJ's overseer), 453, 454
Stokes, John, 37
Story, Joseph, 412–13
Supreme Court, U.S.
    Bank of the U.S. and, 469–70
    Indian removal issue and, 487–93
    McCulloch case and, 344–46, 469
Swann, Thomas, 131–34, 141
Swartout, Samuel, 384, 499

Talladega, Battle of, 199–200, 211
Tallmadge, James, 353, 354
Tallmadge amendment, 353–55
Tallushatchee, Battle of, 198, 211
Taney, Roger, 468, 496, 531
tariff, 333–34, 380–81, 399, 433–34, 439–43, 475, 481,
    544, 554
Tarleton, Banastre, 22–24, 28
Taylor, Zachary, 536
Tecumseh, 164–69, 219, 227, 232, 233, 234
    final battle and death of, 201–4
    War of 1812 and, 175, 176, 177–78, 179, 192–93,
    195, 201–4, 205
Tennessee
    formation of, 49–50
    horse racing in, 130–31
    nickname origin of, 179
    settlement of, 42–45
    slavery in, 353
    statehood of, 76–79
Tennessee Gazette, 106, 139
Texas, 344
    AJ's attempt to acquire, 509–12
    annexation of, 544–47, 552, 557
    eastern boundary of, 515, 522
    election of 1844 and, 550–52
    independence of, 506–26
    J. Q. Adams and, 508, 522–24, 544, 545, 546,
    548–50, 552, 553, 558
    Mexican War and, 558
    slavery issue and, 509, 517, 522–24, 549–50
Theodore (AJ adoptee), 198
Thompson, John, 61
Timberlake, John, 422
Timberlake, Mrs., 378–79
Tippecanoe, Battle of (1811), 176–77
Tocqueville, Alexis de, 455–58, 465, 473
Tompkins, Daniel, 383
Tories (Loyalists), 20–21, 35–36

Townshend duties (1767), 20
"trail of tears," 535–36
Treasury Department, U.S., 415, 416, 437
Truxton (horse), 130–31, 134–35, 453, 542
Truxton, Thomas, 124, 130
tuberculosis, 103
Turner, Nat, 533
Tuscaroras, 12, 84
Twenty-fifth Amendment, 543
Tyler, John, 543, 552
typhoid fever, 103

Ulster, 9–11
United States
    French naval conflict with, x, 114, 141–42, 157
    population of, 115
    sectionalism in, 49, 50–52, 54, 60, 301, 355,
        439–41, 444, 446, 475–82, 488, 510, 554, 555
    in War of 1812; see War of 1812
    westward expansion of, viii, 334, 344, 545; see also
        California; Louisiana Purchase; Oregon; Texas
United States Telegraph, 416, 448

Valley Forge encampment, 21
Van Buren, Martin, 417, 547
    AJ's speeches and, 432
    as AJ's successor, 529–30, 531
    Bank of the U.S. and, 462, 500, 501, 534–35
    Calhoun as enemy of, 444, 446, 452, 479
    Calhoun's reconciliation with, 538
    Eaton affair and, 425–26
    election of 1832 and, 474
    in election of 1836, 530, 531
    in election of 1840, 537, 540, 541
    election of 1844 and, 544, 550–51
    presidency of, 534–35
    as secretary of state, 415, 449
Vandyke, Thomas, 109
Vattel, Emmerich von, 76
Verell, John, 130
Vermont, 72
Vienna, Congress of, 268
Villaré, Gabriel, 265
Villaré, Jacques, 265
Vincennes peace council (1810), 167–69, 176
Virginia, 353, 480
Virginia Resolutions (1798), 114

Walton, Ira, 366
War Department, U.S., 80, 105, 315
    AJ's conflict with, 335–37
    Calhoun as head of, 318
    Florida campaign and, 322

War of 1812 and, 179, 183–84, 230–31, 235, 237, 238, 289
War of 1812, x
  AJ in, x, 174–76, 179–87, 198–201, 205–22, 236–45, 254, 257–62
  Battle of New Orleans in, x, 40, 263–83
  British provocations leading to, 75–76, 141–46, 156, 157–59
  Florida campaign of, 236–45
  free blacks in, 241–42, 261–62
  Ghent peace commission in, 245–48, 268–69
  Monroe and, 238, 240, 243, 245, 248, 265, 269, 274, 286
  political effects of, 225–30
  Tecumseh in, 175, 176, 177–78, 179, 192–93, 195, 201–4, 205
  U.S. mobilization for, 163
  War Department in, 179, 183–84, 230–31, 235, 237, 238, 289
  Washington, D.C., burned in, 227–29, 242–43, 248, 284
  Wilkinson in, 182–83, 189
  See also Creek War
Washington, D.C., 407–13
  British burning of, 227–29, 242–43, 248, 284
Washington, George
  AJ's opposition to, ix–x
  in American Revolution, 21, 33, 116, 285
  Creeks and, 234
  farewell address of, 79–80, 297–98, 531
  in French and Indian War, 84–85
  Hamilton as speechwriter for, 432
  as hero soldier ideal, 368–69
  Jay treaty and, 75–76
  lack of political intimates of, 416
  presidency of, 73, 74–76, 79, 90, 246
Watkins, Thomas, 140
Watt, James, 301
Waxhaw district, 12, 15, 20–28, 30
Weatherford, William, 193, 194, 197, 198, 215, 220–22, 227, 231, 248, 293
Webster, Daniel, 97, 345, 407, 438
  Bank of the U.S. and, 459, 463, 464, 465–66, 467, 468, 472–73, 495
  Compromise of 1850 and, 559

  in election of 1836, 530
  Hayne's nullification debate with, 441–43
  Houston compared to, 507
Weed, Thurlow, 502
Weller, John B., 549
Wellington, Arthur Wellesley, first Duke of, 239, 248, 268, 272, 274, 278, 285
West Indies, 252, 253
West Point, 348–49
westward expansion
  Creek War and, 334
  democracy as product of, viii
  Panic of 1819 and, 344
  Texas as potential block to, 545
Whigs, 502, 535
  abolitionist movement and, 538–39
  disintegration of, 559
  in election of 1836, 530
  in election of 1840, 537–40, 544
  in election of 1844, 550–52
  as Federalists' successor, 483, 537
  Tyler and, 543, 544
Whitney, Eli, 334
Wilkinson, James, 51–52, 60
  AJ and, 52, 127–28, 182–83
  Burr conspiracy and, 121, 122, 123, 125–26, 127–28
  War of 1812 and, 182–83, 189
Williams, John, 232, 376
Wilson, George, 382–83
Winchester, James, 119, 160
Windship, John, 249–52, 255, 259
Winning of the West, The (Roosevelt), 89
Wirt, William, 474, 488–89
Wood, John, 213–15, 261, 397
Woodbine, George, 323

yellow fever, 103, 115
York, Upper Canada, 228
Yorktown, Battle of, 33

Zacatecas rebellion, 518
Zuñiga, Mauricio de, 308, 309

ALSO BY H.W. BRANDS

THE FIRST AMERICAN
The Life and Times of Benjamin Franklin

He was the foremost American of his day, yet today he is little more than a mythic caricature in the public imagination. Benjamin Franklin, perhaps the pivotal figure in colonial and revolutionary America, comes vividly to life in this masterly biography. Wit, diplomat, scientist, philosopher, businessman, inventor, and bon vivant, Benjamin Franklin was in every respect America's first Renaissance man. From penniless runaway to highly successful printer, from ardently loyal subject of Britain to architect of an alliance with France that ensured America's independence, Franklin went from obscurity to become one of the world's most admired figures. Drawing on previously unpublished letters and a host of other sources, H. W. Brands has written a thoroughly engaging biography of the eighteenth-century genius. A much needed reminder of Franklin's greatness and humanity, *The First American* is a work of meticulous scholarship that provides a magnificent tour of a legendary historical figure, a vital era in American life, and the countless arenas in which the protean Franklin left his legacy.

Biography/0-385-49540-4

THE AGE OF GOLD
The California Gold Rush and the New American Dream

"I have found it." These words, uttered by the man who first discovered gold on the American River in 1848, triggered the most astonishing mass movement of peoples since the Crusades. California's gold drew fortune-seekers from the ends of the earth. It accelerated America's imperial expansion and exacerbated the tensions that exploded in the Civil War. And, as H. W. Brands makes clear in this spellbinding book, the Gold Rush inspired a new American dream—the "dream of instant wealth, won by audacity and good luck." Brands imparts a visceral sense of the distances they traveled, the suffering they endured, and the fortunes they made and lost. Impressive in its scholarship and overflowing with life, *The Age of Gold* is history in the grand traditions of Stephen Ambrose and David McCullough.

History/0-385-72088-2

LONE STAR NATION
The Epic Story of the Battle for Texas Independence

In *Lone Star Nation*, Pulitzer Prize finalist H. W. Brands demythologizes Texas's journey to statehood and restores the genuinely heroic spirit to a pivotal chapter in American history. From Stephen Austin, Texas's reluctant founder, to the alcoholic Sam Houston, who came to lead the Texas army in its hour of crisis and glory, to President Andrew Jackson, whose expansionist aspirations loomed large in the background, here is the story of Texas and the outsize figures who shaped its turbulent history. Beginning with its early colonization in the 1820s and taking in the shocking massacres of Texas loyalists at the Alamo and Goliad, its rough-and-tumble years as a land overrun by the Comanches, and its day of liberation as an upstart republic, Brands' lively history draws on contemporary accounts, diaries, and letters to animate a diverse cast of characters whose adventures, exploits, and ambitions live on in the very fabric of our nation.

History/1-4000-3070-6

ANCHOR BOOKS
Available from your local bookstore, or call toll-free to order:
1-800-793-2665 (credit cards only).